British Army mutineers
1914–1922

Julian Putkowski is a freelance military historian, researcher and broadcaster. Since graduating from Essex University in 1976 he has been researching military discipline and dissent. He is the co-author of *Shot at Dawn*, the standard reference work on military executions during the First World War. He lives in London.

Julian Putkowski

British Army mutineers 1914–1922

Francis Boutle Publishers

First published 1998 by
Francis Boutle Publishers
23 Arlington Way
London EC1R 1UY
0171 278 4497

Copyright © Julian Putkowski, 1998

All rights reserved.
No part of this book may be reproduced, stored
in a retrieval system, or transmitted, in any form
or by any means, electronic, mechanical photocopying
or otherwise without the prior permission of the
publishers.

ISBN 0 9532388 2 2

Printed in Great Britain by Redwood Books

Acknowledgements

This book has been a long term project which could not have been produced without the historical knowledge and encouragement – unwitting in some cases – of the following:
Dr Ian Beckett, Nicholas Boyack, Dr Michael Dockrill, Ashley Ekins, Douglas Gill, Dr Christoph Jahr, Dr Keith Jeffrey, Dave Lamb, Andrew Mackinlay MP, Professor Desmond Morton, Nicolas Offenstadt, Gerry Oram, Dr Alfred Peacock, Dr Jane Plotke, Paul Reed, Peter Scott, Dr Gary Sheffield, Anna Shanes, Dr Yigal Sheffy, Professor Steve Smith, Dr Rick Stanwood, Julian Sykes, Tony 'Sweet Patootee' T, Ray Westlake, Ken Weller and mutineers with whom I corresponded, including Roy Henley and Charles Kerrigan.

The assistance of the staff at the Public Record office, and in particular William Spencer, was invaluable in directing attention to the relevant War Office files. Nigel Steel and his colleagues in the Imperial War Museum's Department of Documents were consistently helpful, and patiently coped with often hasty requests for papers. Also gratefully acknowledged for their professionalism and cordiality are the staffs of the British Library at Bloomsbury, Euston and Colindale; the Liddell Hart Centre for Military Archives; Commonwealth War Graves Commission and the National Army Museum. The staffs of the National Library of Scotland; National Archives of Ireland; Radio Telefis Éireann were equally of great assistance in the early stages of research.

Overseas, Bob Cotton and Louise Coulter independently provided valuable material from the National Archives and the National Library of New Zealand. Mary Pollard from the Research Centre, Australian War Memorial, carried out a search to identify references to mutinies via the ANGRAM programme. Elyse Boutcher and her colleagues at the Australian Archives, Canberra decoded my references to ANZAC courts martial, accessed and promptly forwarded papers unobtainable from British sources. The staff of the National Archives of Canada, including Leslie K. Redman, traced and despatched invaluable material about the Canadian Expeditionary Force.

I would like to thank Celia Coram and the eponymous feline madame of Maison Hattie for their support and forebearance; Clive, Kate and Francis; the Reningelst, Ieper and Rabbit Companies, Belgian Hommel Corps, and the ribald British auxiliaries who served with distinction.

Extracts from Crown Copyright material held in the Public Record Office; Oriental and India Office Collections, British Library, appear by permission of the Controller of Her Majesty's Stationery Office. Canadian, Australian, New Zealand material is quoted with due acknowledgement of the Copyright Acts of those countries. Direct quotations are less than I would have desired but to Bill Turner (F. Sayer), Rose Hunt (Charles Miller) and Stephen Venom (M.I. Leared) who granted permission for me to quote from papers whose copyright they own, my thanks.

The author has made every effort to trace individuals for permission to reproduce copyright material quoted in this publication but some remain elusive. To anyone whose copyright this work unintentionally infringes, I extend apologies.

Contents

9 Introduction

19 Notes to the Introduction

20 Narratives

39 Notes to the Narratives

42 JAG Registers: contents

43 Abbreviations

45 Alphabetical list of men charged with mutiny

86 List by unit of men charged with mutiny

129 Chronological list of men charged with mutiny – Home

144 Notes

145 Chronological list of men charged with mutiny – Abroad

173 Notes

175 Bibliography

Introduction

Between 1914 and 1922 more than 2,000 men serving with the British Army and Dominion, Colonial and auxiliary forces were charged with mutiny and faced courts martial. Almost ninety per cent were found guilty. Their names and punishment were announced in Army Routine Orders, otherwise wartime secrecy and enduring official sensitivity about such matters have combined to restrict public knowledge of them. Detailed dossiers about the mutineers and the proceedings of their trials were locked up in military archives, but little of this, literally, inflammable material survived enemy bombing during the Second World War. However, the courts martial registers escaped destruction.

The registers were compiled by the staff of the Judge Advocate General (JAG), the Army's chief legal authority, and have been available for inspection at the Public Record Office, Kew, only recently. They consist of dozens of bound volumes, rather like those used by accountants in the pre-computer era. Their contents are systematically arranged: each case was allocated a single line; each double page contains details relating to approximately twenty-six men's courts martial. The majority of the seventy volumes covering the period between 1914 and 1922 are each crammed with more than two hundred pages of data relating to courts martial for a variety of crimes by officers and men.

Apart from the physical effort involved in handling the weighty volumes, they are frustratingly difficult to use for research purposes. Two or three weeks – or even longer – elapsed before entries relating to courts martial in France were recorded. Sometimes months went by before entries were made involving more distant theatres of operations (e.g. Mesopotamia). For example, register No.WO213/5, dated 1916, contains entries relating to the previous year. So, prior knowledge of the exact date on which a man was court martialled is little guarantee that the entry may be readily discovered in a particular register, nor is there any index of names to assist users with page references.

The registers are confined to details of courts martial that were conducted under the British Army Act, which also covered Dominion and Colonial soldiers, plus non-combatant military labourers from China and elsewhere. British forces raised in India were subject to the provisions of the Indian Army Act, and their details were recorded separately. A few – no more than two or three dozen cases – involving mutinies by Australian and other Imperial troops being shipped back to their homes, have been left out of the registers, probably because their offences were dealt with by their home commands. The registers also give details of Russian soldiers who were executed while serving under British command in North Russia but whose fates were omitted from the War Office compendium:

Statistics of the Military effort of the British Empire during the Great War 1914–1920.

The registers confirm that, in the decades before the First World War, although British soldiers were often insubordinate, insolent and ill-disciplined, they were rarely charged with mutiny. After 1914, indictments for mutiny became more common, mushrooming during 1919, then finally tailing off in September 1922.

The offence

According to the Manual of Military Law, the Army's reference book about disciplinary rules and regulations, mutiny had to involve more than one soldier. Individual soldiers, acting on their own behalf, could be charged with being disobedient, insubordinate or acting 'to the prejudice of good order and military discipline.' However, mutiny, 'a combination of two or more persons to resist or induce others to resist lawful military authority' was essentially collective insubordination and akin to criminal conspiracy.

The Manual declared a mutineer to be specifically 'every person subject to military law who…

1. causes, or conspires with any other persons to cause, any mutiny or sedition in any forces belonging to His Majesty's regular, reserve, or auxiliary forces, or Navy; or
2. endeavours to seduce any person in His Majesty's regular, reserve, or auxiliary forces, or Navy, from allegiance to His Majesty, or to persuade any person in His Majesty's regular, reserve, or auxiliary forces, or Navy, to join in any mutiny or sedition; or
3. joins in, or, being present, does not use his utmost endeavours to suppress, any mutiny or sedition in any forces belonging to His Majesty's regular, reserve, or auxiliary forces, or Navy; or
4. coming to the knowledge of any actual or intended mutiny or sedition in any forces belonging to His Majesty's regular, reserve, or auxiliary forces, or Navy, does not without delay inform his commanding officer of the same.'

It was also noted that soldiers could be found guilty of conspiring to mutiny if their efforts to start a revolt were unsuccessful and no outbreak actually occurred. Even if a soldier was accidentally present, or a passive onlooker, when an incident occurred he could be classed as a mutineer.[1]

The decision to charge disaffected soldiers with mutiny was the responsibility of a handful of officers, including not only those directly involved in the original incident, but also the brigade commanders and other officers who were authorised to convene courts martial. The latter officers, generally pre-war professionals, were strict disciplinarians when dealing with the rank and file. In deciding whether to prosecute soldiers for mutiny, the personal opinion of convening officers was no less crucial than the text of the Manual of Military Law, and the discretion the officers were allowed was generous.

Even in 1965, when taxed to explore the possibility of revising the established definition of mutiny, a memorandum from the office of the Judge Advocate-General candidly conceded: 'The definition of mutiny has always been and probably will have to remain, very wide, and one has to rely on the good sense of the convening officers not to allow trials on this charge to go forward unless the offence really merits it.'[2]

Convening officers' appreciation of what constituted a mutiny derived not only from their interpretation of the official definition of mutiny, but also from immediate reports and the findings of courts of inquiry.

Courts of inquiry were tribunals exclusively composed of officers who were assigned to investigate an incident. The three or so officers who staffed the courts assembled evidence, drew up an account based on evidence submitted by all concerned of what happened, apportioned responsibility and made recommendations.[3] The proceedings of courts of inquiry, with their wider remit than courts martial, would have included appraisal of mutiny as a failure of command, drawing attention to the officers' shortcomings as well as the men's misbehaviour.

Unfortunately, very few reports of courts of inquiry into mutinies have survived and there is insufficient data to test the extent to which mutiny by the rank and file was regarded as a failure of command by their officers. What is easier to substantiate is that officers were never tried for mutiny. When officers conspired to refuse to obey orders they disliked, most notably at the Curragh Camp in 1914, they were never court martialled for mutiny.[4] Only two junior officers, both identified in this book, were charged with the offence, but their cases proceeded no further. Mutiny was an offence that was wholly determined by officers but only the rank and file were ever prosecuted for it.

Courts martial
Men formally charged with mutiny were tried by courts martial. These were more like ad hoc judicial tribunals than civilian courts dealing with capital cases, because there was no jury and members and president of the court had to be commissioned officers, albeit experienced ones. Nor was there a system of appeal against the verdict or sentence.

The Manual of Military Law identified four kinds of court martial: regimental, district, general, and field general. The severity of punishments each could award, the numbers of officers involved in passing judgement and their authority to try commissioned officers varied.

Regimental courts martial dealt with minor offences. They could not try a commissioned officer, and the maximum punishment they could award was forty-two days' detention. No mutineers appear to have been tried by regimental courts martial during the period covered by this book.

A district court martial consisted of three officers, and it also was not permitted to try a commissioned officer, but it could award punishments of up to two years' imprisonment to soldiers found guilty of mutiny or other military offences.

A general court martial, composed of between five and nine officers, was allowed to try all ranks, and could award death sentences.

Field general courts martial were similarly empowered, but required only three officers and were generally convened to hear serious offences committed by personnel on active service overseas. The capital sentences passed by field general courts martial, including those in cases involving mutiny, have excited a good deal of controversy.[5]

It was not unusual for officers from the accused's unit to serve as members of a court martial, and the prosecution was conducted by the adjutant of the accused's unit. Consequently, the court may have had a more intimate understanding of the perspectives of those involved in the outbreak but it is most unlikely they would have been sympathetic to men who had usurped the authority of their brother officers.

For serious cases, including mutiny, the army assigned a courts martial officer to advise about procedure and points of law, rather similar to the role of a clerk advising a civilian magistrates court.[6] However, apart from the court martial officer, who customarily had legal training but not necessarily any great experience of military law, the course and outcome of the trial were determined by officers with minimal legal training.[7]

The vast majority of the 304,262 courts martial cases that took place at home and abroad between 4 August 1914 and 31 March 1920 involved soldiers and non-commissioned officers, of whom approximately ninety per cent were found guilty.[8] Two factors probably account for this comparatively high rate of convictions. The most obvious is that the courts martial were more preoccupied with enforcing discipline than granting defendants any benefit of the doubt. It was certainly true that most defendants would have been unskilled in self-advocacy and unsupported in presenting their defence.

Prior to 1918, even when facing a possible death penalty, the accused were very rarely assisted by a 'prisoner's friend', a junior officer who assisted the accused in preparing and presenting a case for the defence. Even this assistance was limited when the prisoner's friend lacked legal expertise or experience, and had only a few hours in which to prepare a defence and secure sympathetic witnesses. Most defendants, particularly the ill-educated and inarticulate, would have been easily over-awed when facing rigorous cross examination by either the court or the prosecuting officer.

Since there was no system of appeal, courts martial verdicts could not be effectively challenged. Official secrecy and censorship muffled protests during the war, and bitter complaints voiced by MPs and a few newspapers tended to focus on individual cases.[9] Since they had no access to the written proceedings, their criticisms concentrated on punishments awarded by courts martial and the hardship caused to the men's families. During the war, had the rank and file, let alone the general public, realised the measure of indulgence afforded officers who breached regulations compared with what was directed against the other ranks, there would have been uproar.

The relevant figures, covering all courts martials, including mutiny cases were finally published in 1922, covered the period from 4 August 1914 to 31 March

1920 but were linked to proceedings rather than individuals. Inevitably, some individuals were convicted more than once. Comparative analysis reveals that courts martial dealt more leniently with officers than other ranks. Much may be made of the point that officers were invariably assisted by a defending officer, even though the latter were not always as effective as their legal qualifications might suggest. More may be made of the common social values, wealth and privileged education that officer-defendants shared with those who staffed the courts martial.[10]

Confirmation and punishment
Defendants, including men accused of mutiny, were informed immediately if they had been found not guilty. Otherwise they had to await formal ratification of the verdict and sentence. The confirmatory process in Britain routinely involved proceedings being checked for legality by the JAG before the papers were despatched to the Director of Personal Services, a senior staff officer in the department of the Adjutant General (AG). Because sentences inflicted on mutineers in Britain tended to be comparatively light, the sanction of the Secretary of State for War was often a formality.

At first, overseas expeditionary forces followed similar procedures, but after a few months the system was overhauled, and a succession of ever more senior officers were systematically invited to attach their opinions to the verbatim proceedings of courts martial. This initially involved the affected unit's commanding officer, or perhaps a camp commandant, making observations about the accused's character and behaviour on and off the battlefield, the disciplinary record of his unit and whether the offence had been committed deliberately. Thereafter, comments were invited from the brigade commander, who had also been responsible for convening the court martial.

Then the report of the proceedings was forwarded to the commanders of the relevant division, corps and army for their observations. After the JAG attached to an expeditionary force had checked a case, the dossier was sent for final appraisal by the Deputy Assistant Adjutant General (DAAG), who was responsible for discipline and courts martial. The AG himself drew the attention of the Commander-in-Chief (C-in-C) to particularly serious cases, and had to secure his final confirmation of capital sentences.[11]

Discipline overseas was the responsibility of adjutants general attached to general headquarters of the various expeditionary forces, rather than C-in-Cs. Major General B.E.W. Childs maintained that Field Marshal Sir John French deliberated at length over the proceedings of all capital sentences, but the claim needs to be treated with reserve.[12] The sheer volume of death sentences plus the busy work schedules of French and his successor as commander of the British Expeditionary Force (BEF), Field Marshal Sir Douglas Haig, left little time for them to do more than scan a brief written summary accompanied by some remarks from the AG.[13] When the AG was otherwise engaged, Haig was briefed by a DAAG, Brigadier General J.B. Wroughton.[14]

This brigadier was an experienced staff officer, a bureaucrat whose tasks as the chief of the BEF's Personal Services embraced not only courts martial but also disciplinary matters, including disturbances involving troops. Though his name features quite commonly in connection with the administration of capital courts martial, it is impossible to assess accurately his influence in the confirmatory process. Nor did Wroughton appear on the scene of every mutiny that occurred on the Western Front. However, his arrival at an outbreak was a certain sign that the incident was regarded by the General Staff as a particularly grave affair, and it was Wroughton who appraised the punishment inflicted on convicted mutineers.

The situation was rather different in other expeditionary forces and the wartime garrison of India. Because the numbers of troops were much smaller than in France and also because of the comparative infrequency of serious mutinies, the C-in-Cs appear to have been more directly involved in dealing with outbreaks. However, the contribution of officers engaged in the confirmatory process was consultative. The JAG could veto verdicts or sentences on legal grounds and Wroughton and his fellow officers in Personal Services exercised a disproportionate influence in determining punishments.

Once confirmed, the sentences were communicated to the convicted man, and details of the man, his offence and punishment were promulgated via army routine orders. Mutineers sentenced to penal servitude were transported to prisons in Britain; those with lesser custodial sentences were sent to field punishment compounds and military prisons administered by the expeditionary force to which they belonged. Executions were not carried out by men from the mutineers' own unit, except in North Russia.

Punishment for the majority of mutineers involved a combination of confinement, physical pain and deprivation. Those sentenced to penal servitude became convicts, and were lashed into submission along with civilian criminals. The remainder were segregated in military prisons in the field, where they were employed as penal labourers, routinely bullied and brutalised. Military prisoners who continued to rebel while in custody were sometimes sentenced to death but more usually attracted some of the longest spells of penal servitude recorded in the JAG registers.

Few mutineers were sentenced to Field Punishment No.1. This was usually carried out in special wired-off compounds on the lines of communication, where prisoners were subjected to a harsh daily regime of heavy manual labour and exhausting pack drill. The distinctive feature was that for a couple of hours a day soldiers undergoing sentences were tethered to a wheel or post, or, with their hands tied behind their backs, were suspended by their wrists.[15] Aside from physical pain, most who underwent field punishment recall hunger, degradation and the brutality of the guards. Some prisoners were court martialled for mutiny while undergoing punishment, attracting extended sentences, penal servitude, or sentence of death, which on one occasion in France was carried out.

Non-commissioned officers were rarely charged with mutiny, but if found guilty were liable to be more heavily punished than private soldiers. Clearly, there was an expectation of good discipline associated with non-commissioned rank, and its betrayal was not to be tolerated. Commissioned officers, on the other hand generally escaped harsh punishment at the hands of courts martial.

Mutinies in Great Britain

Nearly 800 soldiers were arraigned as mutineers in Britain between 1914 and 1922. Just over 300 were prosecuted during the war, of whom the majority – 211 – were involved in just four of fifty-one mutinies in the Home Forces. Nor do these mutinies – involving 2/4 Bn. Sussex Regiment (Canterbury, July 1915); the Royal Defence Corps (Towcester, November 1916); 337 Bde. Royal Field Artillery (Canterbury, January 1917) and the Canadian Army Service Corps (Bramshott, November 1917) – appear to have been punished with the rigour advocated in the Manual of Military Law.

The authorities were possibly lenient because the pattern of charges also suggests that the wartime mutineers in Britain were generally non-violent and sober, whether directing their animus against officers or property.

Though the provisions of military law allowed for the death penalty in Britain during the First World War the firing squad was never deployed to execute convicted men. This may partly be explained by the convening of district courts martial, which could not pass death sentences, but more generally by official policy. As a rule, wartime mutineers in Britain were given more lenient sentences than their counterparts overseas. The heaviest sentences were those imposed on the mutineers arraigned at Towcester who were jailed for a year.

Apart from a handful of reservists, at the time of their offence most mutineers were serving with territorial or home service units originally raised in England. More generally, the dates and locations recorded in the JAG registers do not suggest a pattern of discontent that could be associated with civil unrest or any contemporary industrial action. For example, neither the Dublin uprising of 1916 nor the massive wartimes strikes in Britain's industrial heartlands prompted mutinies. The JAG registers also appear to call into question General Haig's negative views of the threat to military discipline posed by freebooting Australian soldiers. The ANZAC's legendary contempt for military authority attracted a solitary conviction for mutiny in Britain, a record much better than that of the Canadians with their reputation for strict discipline. As for the generation of men who were compelled to join the army after conscription was introduced, there is no quantifiable evidence that they ever mutinied.

However, three factors suggest that the JAG registers present only a partial view of the extent to which mutinies occurred in Britain. Firstly, commanding officers sometimes agreed to the men's demands, or they quelled the outbreak with threats or summary action.[16]

Unfortunately, official records about units stationed in Britain are scanty or non-existent, so there is no reliable method of assessing the full extent to which this occurred. Secondly, some officers simply omitted to report a mutiny, and nobody was charged with the offence. In either case, the incident would not have featured in the JAG registers. Lastly, senior military commanders, and possibly the AG, either maintained a policy of charging disaffected soldiers with insubordination rather than mutiny, or sometimes overlooked mutinies by the rank and file.

Prosecuting men on a lesser, non-capital charge such as insubordination certainly had several merits from the Army's point of view, mainly because there was no requirement to prove conspiracy. Clusters of simultaneous cases of soldiers accused of insubordination or indiscipline are easy enough to identify in the JAG registers. For example, in March 1918 two dozen soldiers enlisted in 39 Bn. Royal Fusiliers were simultaneously punished with two years imprisonment for insubordination.[17]

However, it is impossible to prove that such mass prosecutions were linked to what may have been substantive mutinies. No written directive exists to substantiate such a policy, and, because of collective action by groups of conscientious objectors, it is impossible to tease out data recorded after the introduction of conscription.

Insubordinate members of the Non-Combatant Corps are easy enough to identify separately, as are a few well-known anti-War 'absolutists', including Pte. Fenner Brockway, Rifleman Guy Aldred and Pte. Fred Crowsley.[18] However, the bulk of the 5,739 conscientious objectors, many of whom were charged with a variety of offences, including insubordination, remain virtually indistinguishable from less principled military offenders.[19]

That the Adjutant General and senior officers disregarded the odd protest by war-weary, disgruntled soldiers would be unsurprising. However, extending this indulgence to include tens of thousands of troops, especially in late 1914 and early 1919, strains credibility in the consistent application of military law to the rank and file. During 1914 there were numerous reports of refusals to parade and mass protests by reservists and new recruits alike. Protests by soldiers about inadequate rations, insufficient bedding and inadequate accommodation were commonly recorded. The trouble stemmed from having too few experienced staff, insufficient accommodation and equipment to cope with the massive influx of volunteers. What made matters worse was that many soldiers, including some newly arrived Canadian units, were still under canvas in vast improvised camps when the winter gales blew down tents and turned the sites into quagmires.[20]

Two incidents involving British army reservists who had been recalled to the colours ended with mutineers being punished.[21] Raw recruits should also have been punished when they engaged in mutinies, because there was nothing in the Manual of Military Law that excused dissent by inexperienced soldiers who may have been ignorant of their offence. However, they were often treated leniently, and it is easy to see why. The victualling, accommodation and other problems that provoked the men's action were a direct consequence of the ill-controlled voluntary recruiting campaign.[22]

To have prosecuted volunteers for mutiny would have caused problems for the army and politicians. Censorship was far from perfect, and news of any trials would certainly have leaked out. Allegations of military incompetence and maladministration, and punishing the guilty, would also have adversely affected recruitment. Instead of courts martial, the army responded by commandeering temporary accommodation in nearby towns, billeting men in seaside holiday resorts and sometimes even sending them back home until the supply and quartering crisis eased. These measures eased unrest until adequate provisioning, sufficient clothing and other supplies were eventually provided, and hutted camps were built.[23]

The opening months of the war also witnessed a more protracted dispute about soldiers' terms of service, involving Territorial Army volunteers who objected to being posted overseas. Whether what occurred could be characterised as mutiny is debatable, but only ten per cent of the pre-was force declared they were prepared to serve overseas. Thousands of territorials, classically composed of shopkeepers and clerks and officered by the squirearchy and professional classes, insisted quite correctly that they had originally enlisted for four years' service in a home defence force. Some were under nineteen and therefore too young to serve. Others had important family responsibilities, jobs and business commitments to maintain.[24] A couple of divisions agreed to serve in India, to free regular army units for combat, and were promised by the Minister of War, Lord Kitchener, that they would have priority for shipment home when the war ended.

Resistance by the remainder compelled the army to categorise territorials according to their readiness to serve abroad. First-line territorials were combat formations serving overseas; the second, initially totalling fourteen divisions, were reservists who agreed to serve overseas; the third line were composed of home service volunteers and men who were unfit or otherwise unsuited for overseas service. The introduction of conscription and eventually a prohibition on direct recruitment into territorial formations ended protests in Britain about the issue.[25] However, in 1919 the territorials who had sailed away to India were to organise one of the biggest mutinies in the history of the British army (see Narrative, 'India, 1919').

The fate of the British army's first soviet was also settled without courts martial for mutiny. On 3 June 1917, pacifists and socialists attending the national convention in Leeds to hail the overthrow of Tzarism, called for the establishment of British soldiers' and workers' councils, modelled on Russian revolutionary soviets. Their exhortation had little effect on the British army, but there was a positive response from the Home Counties and Training Reserve. On 24 June, representatives from half a dozen battalions from this formation inaugurated a workers' and soldiers' council at Tunbridge Wells and approved a manifesto drawing attention to a range of material grievances. They also called on the government to declare terms for negotiating with the enemy.

The author of the document, Lance-Corporal Dudley, was promptly posted to France, and within two days a brigadier disciplined or dispersed the remainder of those involved.[26] Thereafter, the army and the secret services successfully used wartime emergency legislation, spies and agents provocateurs to prevent revolutionary subversion or even any democratic political agenda being advanced by soldiers.[27]

A far graver crisis confronted the army in early 1919. In late January and early February there was hardly a major camp in Britain unaffected by strikes, mass demonstrations or protest marches. The trouble began at Dover and Folkestone on 3 January when 9–10,000 soldiers – estimates vary – returning to the continent after Christmas leave in Britain refused to embark on the ferries. The mutineers compelled the army to agree to grant summary demobilisation for men who could prove they had civilian contracts of employment.

In the weeks that followed, direct action was taken by not fewer than 50,000 more soldiers, all demanding accelerated demobilisation. Hundreds, if not thousands, of clearly identifiable protesters ought to have been charged with mutiny, yet the JAG registers record only three cases.[28]

The Army's failure to charge more than a trio of mutineers seems particularly surprising in the light of remarks made by the Metropolitan Police Assistant Commissioner in charge of Special Branch, Sir Basil Thomson. He declared that 'during the first three months of 1919 unrest touched its high-water mark. I do not think at any time in history since the Bristol Riots have we been so near revolution.'[29]

As in 1914, when confronted by a rash of mutinies, the Army made no move to court martial those involved. This time, the Government intervened and changed the established scheme of demobilisation that had involved the gradual release of men according to a priority based on their civilian employment or profession. Sir Winston Churchill, recently appointed Minister of War, immediately announced that men would be demobbed according to their length of service. Individuals who caused further trouble had their release quite illegally deferred.[30]

After this concession, the wartime Army rapidly began draining away. Attempts were made to stem the flow by delaying the release of certain categories of volunteer, maintaining conscription and increasing pay. These measures were simultaneously accompanied by redoubling covert measures to identify, and root out, Bolshevik agitators who the army was convinced, were intending to set up British soviets. This turned out to be a red mirage. However, mutinies provoked by a variety of grievances, but mostly arising from delays in releasing war-service volunteers whose demobilisation had been deferred, continued to develop.[31] To deal with outbreaks occurring after February 1919, GHQ Home Forces used force, rounding up mutineers and punishing them by courts martial.

The effect of this change in policy was amply demonstrated after April 1919 by proceedings held successively in Liverpool, Sutton, Aldershot, Ripon and Devizes.[32] As had occurred during the war, the majority of the accused men were found guilty as charged. However, there was a marked increase in the number of men who were acquitted. For example, the trials of the Kinmel Park rioters at Liverpool between April and June 1919 featured eighteen acquittals; all the thirty-nine Labour Corps men tried at Sutton in June escaped conviction; and a dozen of the Dragoons tried at the Curragh in September 1919 were also acquitted.[33] In all, twenty per cent of men charged as a consequence of the post-war mutinies in Britain were either found not guilty or acquitted, yet those convicted were given spells of imprisonment which were on a par with wartime punishments.[34] The high rates of acquittal may be explained by the ubiquity of defending officers in the post-war trials.

References in the JAG registers to the regimental affiliation of mutineers during the post-war period confirm that the majority of incidents involved units that had been recruited in England and were mostly composed of war-service volunteers. They included infantrymen serving with notionally regular army battalions, but dissident Labour Corps, artillery and cavalry also featured strongly. In almost every case, including the mass mutiny of men of 5 Dragoon Guards, the men's principal demand was linked with demobilisation – they were specifically dissatisfied at being retained beyond the duration of the war in which they had volunteered to fight. The fighting had ended in November 1918, and, although the Germans had signed the Versailles Peace Treaty and it had been ratified by the House of Commons in July 1919, the Naval, Military and Air Service Force Act, which maintained conscription, did not lapse until April 1920. Those whose release was deferred certainly did not wish to be sent overseas again to join either the post-war Army of Occupation, imperial garrisons, or engage in fighting the Bolsheviks in Russia.[35]

Most of the strikes and demonstrations in which soldiers engaged between 1914 and 1922 were directly associated with the terms and conditions of service, including their duration. In most cases, it was matter of soldiers collectively taking the initiative, reminding the army of its obligations to care for soldiers or at least recognise that the rank and file had valid grievances. There were several factors, including the scale of unrest, public opinion, the political climate and the military paternalism, that combined to restrict the use of courts martial in Britain. Still, the army's sensitivity on these issues should not be exaggerated, nor was senior officers' appreciation of the mutineers' political complexion particularly accurate.

During 1918 military commanders, particularly Field Marshal Sir William Robertson, were frankly alarmed about syndicalists and Bolsheviks influencing the rank and file. The views of Robertson and Haig, who succeeded him as Commander in Chief, Home Forces in 1919, generally reflected the contemporary fears of the British upper class and the paranoia of secret service chiefs such as Sir Basil Thomson.[36]

Their concern had little substance though their sentiments influenced press reports. For example, rioting by Canadian troops in early March 1919 was greeted with lurid press reports about revolutionary red flags being flaunted by the mutineers and two dozen men being killed. However, the court of inquiry and ensuing courts martial confirmed that the affair had been a protest about delays in the men's repatriation to Canada. The significance of the red flags had been exaggerated, and, while it was true five soldiers were killed in a melee, they had been shot by the camp authorities and not by the mutineers.[37]

Revolutionary intent was equally absent in the less bloody confrontations involving Canadians at Epsom, Witley and Ripon. The Canadians declared that they were not being treated fairly by profiteering local shopkeepers, the military or civil authorities, and they were furious about delays in their transportation back to Canada.[38]

Mutinies by British troops stationed in Britain have generally attracted the critical attention of historians interested in identifying links with domestic political radicalism. Direct links are hard to identify, and comparisons with the industrial activism of the Shop Stewards movement are difficult to sustain.[39] Yet both share a commitment to direct collective action as a means of securing improvements in their situation, and the recipe for success in either case was not so very different. However, while the achievement of striking workers' demands is universally recognised as a victorious strike; a victorious mutiny remains a conundrum.

Mutinies overseas

The manner in which the military authorities controlled soldiers serving overseas was relatively uniform. In general, it involved a system of rewards and punishments that applied to all the rank and file on active service. The rewards included regular wages, rations, health care, leave and leisure activities – ranging from concerts and organised games to access to alcohol and prostitutes – as well as the commendations and medals reserved for the obedient and the brave. However, soldiers whose bearing or behaviour failed to match the army's exacting requirements were punished.

On active service, the punishments were severe, and ranged from fatigues, through fines, stoppages of pay, loss of leave, field punishment, imprisonment with hard labour and penal servitude to execution by firing squad. Field Punishments No.1 or No.2, were most generally applied by unit commanders and courts martial. Field Punishment No.2 involved a soldier being billetted in the guard room or tent when out of the line, plus loss of pay, heavy labour, inspections and drill for hours in full kit, while being harassed by NCOs. In contrast to the enforced mobility which accompanied Field Punishment No.2, Field Punishment No.1, sometimes called crucifixion, consisted of being secured by the wrists and ankles to a fixed object (typically a wheel or fence) for two hours a day.[40]

The majority of soldiers obeyed orders well enough not to be punished; only a minority mutinied. Compared to the millions of men who served overseas, the number that figure in the JAG registers appear almost insignificant. Yet between the outbreak of war and September 1922, more than 1,500 men stationed overseas were charged with involvement in approximately 250 mutinous incidents. A minority escaped conviction, but half of those found guilty were jailed for more than three years, and almost 200 were sentenced to penal servitude for at least ten years. Official statistics confirm that fifty-six men were sentenced to death, and sentences were carried out in four cases. However, the JAG registers reveal that a further eleven men, all Russians serving with the Slavo-British Legion in North Russia, were executed in July 1919.[41]

Far more soldiers were executed for mutiny than those convicted by courts martial under the British Army Act. However, aside from summary annihilation and shootings of Indian soldiers under the provisions of the Indian Army Act, the British army was initially reluctant to execute mutineers sentenced to death by courts martial. The reluctance did not apply to those sentenced to be shot at dawn for other offences, including desertion, but, with the exception of a death sentence passed on a mutineer – but later commuted – in Gallipoli in September 1915, it was not until August 1916 in France that a second death sentence for mutiny was passed, and no mutineers were actually executed until the end of October 1916. Exactly why this was so remains open to speculation, for there were no obvious legal reasons why the sentences should not have been carried out.

Imprisonment of mutineers was the punishment

preferred by the Army overseas, yet the majority of sentences tended to be relatively brief. Prior to August 1917, only two mutineers were sentenced to more than five years' penal servitude.[42] Even a spectacular week-long mutiny by thousands of British troops at Etaples Base in September 1917 (see Narrative, Etaples Base, 1917), yielded only four prosecutions for mutiny, and the actual execution of a solitary mutineer. Moreover, although mutinous incidents, and prison sentences, increased during 1918, the most spectacular trials and harshest sentences occurred after hostilities ceased.[43]

The increased frequency of mutinies and severity of punishments after Germany's defeat suggest that post-war overseas mutinies were generally viewed as being far more serious than the wartime confrontations. The reasons why this was so cannot be wholly explained by the demands for demobilisation, a more relaxed disciplinary regime (including suspension of the death penalty for non-fatal military crimes by British personnel) or an eddy of political radicalism disturbing the troops.[44] Not all mutinies were solely concerned with demobilisation, and changes in the Army's execution policy remained secret. As with the mutinies that happened in Britain, assessment of mutineers' motives relied on convening officers' appreciation of the causes, the nature of the men's demands, their behaviour and the wider local context. To these must also be added the combat status of the men, their ethnic composition and terms of service of the mutineers. Otherwise, the dynamics of mutiny overseas were not very different from those in Britain, though more men committed the offence and the penalties inflicted on men convicted of mutiny were far heavier.

The majority of men arraigned for mutiny overseas were British, predominantly serving with units raised in England. Although most were infantrymen, they included a high proportion of physically low-grade garrison troops who were prosecuted for three mutinies that occurred in Egypt and India. Of the Welsh soldiers prosecuted for mutiny, most were involved in only two mutinies which took place in Northern France: 12 Bn. South Wales Borderers in January 1916 and the trench mortar men of 38 (Welsh) Division in September 1917. The majority also faced an additional charge, usually disobedience, and were jailed.[45]

Sentences meted out to the South Wales Borderers were almost all commuted to Field Punishment No.1, but death sentences (commuted) were passed on two mutineers serving with 2 Bn. Royal Welsh Fusiliers at Ranikhet, in North West India in July 1920. Scots mutineers, particularly those prosecuted in France during the war, were punished very harshly. Four attracted death sentences (subsequently commuted) and a dozen were awarded ten years' penal servitude (mostly later quashed or commuted).[46]

The mutiny cases involving units raised in Ireland reveal an extraordinary situation. All 121 cases, involving men from two infantry battalions that mutinied in France during the war, were tried on 15 April 1918.[47] Eight men were found not guilty, but all the others were sentenced to five or more years' Penal Servitude, subsequently suspended. Suspension of sentences for convicted mutineers was very rare and the authorities' clemency contrasts sharply with the sentences passed on Irish mutineers after 1918.

Thirty-three New Zealanders were charged with mutiny. Most were arraigned for offences committed before the war ended; one was prosecuted for being involved in a post-war outbreak. The former took part in nine mutinies, of which the biggest, by the 1 Employment Battalion, ended with thirteen men being punished. However, the most serious outbreak, led six New Zealanders of 2 Battalion, Otago Regiment, each being sentenced to ten years' penal servitude. The case of Pte. Braithwaite, the only New Zealand mutineer to be executed, was a direct consequence of his involvement in the Blargies prison (Rouen) protest of 1916 which involved mutineers from a variety of British and Imperial forces.[48]

More Australians than any other Imperial troops were prosecuted for mutiny. In all, there were 296 proceedings initiated against 283 men (some soldiers were prosecuted for mutiny on more than one occasion). Nearly all of the 191 wartime sentences were confirmed, and four Australians were sentenced to death, but not executed, for their part in the Blargies prison mutiny.[49]

Though they had acquired a reputation for indiscipline in Egypt before the transfer of ANZAC forces to France during 1916, very few Australians had been prosecuted for mutiny there. Even after they arrived in France, the bulk of Australian mutineers were tried for involvement in only three incidents: 1 Bn. AIF (October 1918), Rouen (January 1919) and the No.6 Military Prison (March 1919).[50] Aside from these incidents, the Australians were no more prone to charges of mutiny than any other Imperial formations, nor were they punished more heavily than any other BEF troops.

Only four of the forty-one Canadians tried for mutiny overseas committed their offence during wartime. As with the Australians, long sentences were passed on men involved in the No.6 Military Prison mutiny, an event that led to two Canadians being sentenced to death but not executed.[51] Otherwise the heaviest sentence, ten years' Penal Servitude, was meted out to Trooper Flint for his part in the Etaples Base mutiny in September 1917.

At the beginning of the war, many Afrikaners actively opposed the involvement of South African troops in Britain's war effort, and there is some evidence of protest by locally raised white troops before the outbreak of war. However, only two white South African soldiers were prosecuted for mutiny during the war, one of them serving overseas. The black South Africans who served with the Army Service Corps, Cape Auxiliary Horse Transport and Native Labour Contingent had a more troubled record. All separately featured in mutinies during their service in Northern France, on board a homeward bound transport ship or (as with the 1 Cape Corps) in Egypt. From the dates entered in the JAG registers, it appears that the black South Africans mutineers were tried collectively. Their sentences do not appear to have been demonstrably heavier than those meted out to white troops, even though one ASC man received a death sentence (later quashed) and three were jailed for life (commuted to five years' imprisonment). The Cape volunteers were the only South African troops who were prosecuted for mutiny after the armistice, and, in almost all cases, sentences of five years' Penal Servitude were subsequently reduced by one or two years.[52]

The only other non-combatants in France with whom comparisons could be made were the Egyptian Labour Corps, fifteen members of which were tried for mutiny and indiscipline at Boulogne in June 1917, and a trio of mutinous workers with the Chinese Labour Corps who were convicted of mutiny and associated offences in 1918 as a result of three separate incidents. None of the sentences appears to have been more than three years' Penal Servitude (commuted to two years' hard labour), and were comparatively unexceptional punishments. The execution of Mahmoud Mahomet Ahmed of the Egyptian Labour Corps for his part in an incident in Marseilles in 1917 (see Narrative, 'Labourers' revolt') was for striking an officer and conduct to the prejudice of military discipline, and not mutiny.

Ninety-one black infantrymen recruited from the Caribbean were also prosecuted for mutiny. The British West Indies Regiment (BWIR) and the West India Regiment (WIR) were designated as combat units, but most of the former were largely employed as military labourers during the war. Apart from four BWIR mutineers who were convicted in Mesopotamia in January 1918, the West Indians do not feature in the JAG registers until the mass trials of forty-six mutineers from 1, 4 and 9 Bns. BWIR in Italy during the winter of 1918–19.[53]

Those involved generally faced more than one charge, and all the trials were convened at Taranto in the aftermath of the 6–9 December 1918 mutiny by the West Indians. The sentences were comparatively heavier than those imposed on the South African labourers. One BWIR man was sentenced to death (commuted to twenty years' penal servitude); thirteen others were condemned to penal servitude for five or more years and proportionally fewer of the Taranto sentences were subsequently commuted. The thirty-two WIR mutineers who were tried en masse in Egypt during May 1919 and given stiff prison sentences of five or seven years' penal servitude (later commuted), have attracted less attention than the Taranto mutineers. Also their sentences were commuted to one or two years' hard labour.[54]

Only four Asian mutineers appear in the JAG registers, all from the Malay States Guides, who had been involved in a refusal to serve overseas after being compulsorily 'volunteered' by an over-enthusiastic NCO. Their action was a prelude to the bloody 5 Bn. Light Infantry mutiny. No other Asian troops appear in these registers because they were dealt with under the Indian Army Act, and were recorded separately.[55]

Thousands of locally raised troops and carriers were engaged in the campaigns in Africa. Two *askaris* with the 1/6 King's African Rifles were charged with mutiny in August 1917. Others would have been dealt with summarily, or under the provisions of an Imperial ordinance. In either event, their cases would not appear in the JAG registers.[56] The low incidence of mutinies by non-European troops in the BEF may also be accounted for by the fact that it was not until after 1916 that the Army was prepared to deploy any non-white troops (other than the Indian Army) in Northern France. From the JAG registers it is evident that, when black and non-European personnel were accused of mutiny, most were tried together in batches and invariably found guilty.

Black mutineers may have been treated harshly, but Russian mutineers of the 1 Bn. Slavo-British Legion (SBL) in July 1919 were executed on a scale unparalleled under the provisions of the British Army Act. Not only were these cases omitted from officially published statistics, but also General Ironside, the commander-in-chief at Archangel, had originally considered executing a further nine SBL mutineers.[57] Moreover, there is evidence to suggest that the number of Russian mutineers who were executed during the campaign far exceeded those noted in the JAG registers.[58]

The registers do not always make clear where mutinies took place. However, the historical consensus holds that British combat troops, particularly the infantry, never rebelled in the front line. Few dispute that the men had an abundance of reasons to feel aggrieved, but explaining why they did not rebel continues to exercise military historians. High morale, variously defined, and male bonding appear to be more commonly invoked than coercion.[59]

Interesting though the theoretical debate continues to be, the absence of mutinies in the front line may principally be accounted for by obstacles confronting the organisation of collective action. Unlike disgruntled trade unionists or soldiers stationed in Britain, men serving in the expeditionary forces could not find facilities and meeting places for rallies. The process of collective bargaining requires an arena or point of assembly, a place or situation in which mutineers could securely gather to exchange information, air grievances, plan a strategy and identify co-ordinators. It all sounds rather pedestrian, but lack of opportunity to initiate and organise, no less than punitive sanctions, was significant in preventing mass expressions of discontent.

For example, had the rank and file on the Western Front wished to organise collectively they would have been handicapped by the topography of the trenches. The arrangement of troops in cramped static positions on the edge of no-man's land did not grant opportunities for soldiers to develop a dialogue with more than their immediate neighbours. The deployment of infantry in companies occupying several traverses in narrow trenches made verbal communication with men in adjacent positions difficult and dangerous, especially if the enemy was alert.

For similar reasons, communication between troops in forward positions with those in support trenches was no less difficult. Soldiers in the forward area as elsewhere were systematically controlled by routine inspections and surveillance, and the area behind the front was particularly closely monitored to prevent troops straggling or deserting.[60] Ration parties and runners provided a possible conduit for unofficial exchanges of information, but this was an unreliable way of communicating.

Soldiers were also wholly dependent on the hierarchy of NCOs and officers who monopolised control over the organisation of communication, food supplies and detailed knowledge of a geographical locality. In the final analysis, brute coercion confronted the laggardly, let alone the disobedient.

For example, during an assault on Trones Wood in October 1916, a Lt. W. Kendall, Liverpool Regt, recalled that he needed to get his men out of the forward trenches as swiftly as possible. When he saw they were lagging behind, and one man claimed that he could not get over the parapet, Kendall brandished his revolver at the soldier and gave him a couple of seconds to crawl over the top.[61] Another officer, witnessing a similar episode during the battle of Festubert, recalled seeing a company sergeant major of the Irish Guards brandishing his revolver towards a few men who were apparently reluctant to go over the parapet, which was disintigrating under a hail of shrapnel and machine-gun fire.[62]

On other occasions soldiers were threatened by their officers because they did not remain in the line, typically as a consequence of a German assault. Thus, for example, Pte. Percy Tweed, 1 Grenadier Guards, witnessed the flight of British troops at Gouzeacourt. As his unit marched towards the front they came across hundreds of demoralised British troops, and he saw his officers shoot and kill the apparent ringleaders. When the dead mens' comrades were challenged about their flight, they explained that the Germans had captured part of the front line and killed the majority of their officers and NCOs. The survivors had simply bolted.[63]

When officers did not shoot at retreating troops, they were inhibited by utility rather than sentiment. Lt. W.B. St Leger, Coldstream Guards, noticed some men from another regiment running back from the trenches. He ordered them to halt, and when they carried on running, St Leger drew his revolver with the intention of shooting them. He decided not to pull the trigger because the fleeing men had their backs to him and they might have thought that the shooting was from the Germans. Nor could he give chase, as his own men might have concluded that he was also running away.[64]

Soldiers were, of course, capable of retaliating against trigger-happy superiors, and sometimes conspired to murder NCOs and officers.[65] Punishment for assaulting a superior was harsh, even when it was a minor affair or evidence to support the allegation was thin. For example, Pte. J. Fox, 2 Highland Light Infantry, was executed for kicking a lieutenant's shins following a reprimand for parading with a dirty rifle.[66]

Though the layout of the trenches made it physically impossible for soldiers to get together with their comrades, it also provided the circumstances and proximity for communication and sometimes fraternisation with the enemy. Cease-fires, trench truces and the phenomenon of the 'quiet front', as both Ashworth and Brown have demonstrated, were not restricted to Christmas 1914.[67] Some ceasefires lasted for weeks, and were repeated at different times later in the war. But it was officers who determined when a ceasefire ended. Thus the Christmas truce of 1914 was certainly disobedience on a grand scale, but much was sanctioned by NCOs and junior officers.

Men collectively leaving the trenches or refusing to go into action attracted charges of cowardice or desertion, rather than mutiny.[68] This is exemplified by the actions of one hundred men from 1 Bn. Australian Infantry Force serving with the BEF who refused to attack the Germans at Ruby Wood on 20 September 1918. The unit had been expecting to be relieved after a successful assault on the enemy and returned to the support lines rather than engage in a further attack when ordered to do so. Six Lance-Corporals and forty Other Ranks were subsequently court martialled for mutiny but because their refusal had been accompanied by walking away from the trenches they were convicted on an alternative charge of desertion.[69]

Even when in reserve or rest areas, troops were again subjected to a wearisome routine of roll calls, rigorous training, as well as organised leisure and sports and a limited measure of access to rigorously policed civilian establishments. These activities were intended to afford some respite, improve the men's combat worthiness and affirm cultural legitimation of the common struggle.[70] However, troops behaviour and communication were tightly controlled and open disobedience attracted heavy punishment.

Elsewhere, constant movement inhibited or masked mutinies along the lines of communication. Combat troops moving into and out of forward positions, casualties being evacuated to dressing stations, trains disgorging ammunition or supplies and endless files of reinforcements were all hustled along by military police and transport officers. At night, the communication trenches and supply tracks were traversed by the heavy traffic of vehicles, men and animals that sustained the front. Even when not engaged in an offensive, the agencies controlling the movement of units and men limited opportunities for autonomous activity by the rank and file.

Apart from formal control, it would have been difficult for mutinous conspiracies to be sustained in combat units much beyond a tour of duty in the line. In some infantry battalions, the casualty rates were so heavy that a company's personnel could be eliminated several times in a few months. If fact, total extinction was avoided only by retaining a small cadre in reserve, around whom a unit could be reconstituted with drafts of reinforcements. Less dramatically, units were scourged by sickness, physical injury and mental trauma sustained in the poisonous filth and detritus of the combat zone. In winter, cold and damp conditions, exacerbated by wind, made hypothermia a no-less deadly enemy than the Germans.[71]

Discipline remained strict, but less punitive, for British and white Imperial military personnel who staffed base camps – the so-called 'base wallahs'. Sometimes stigmatised by combat troops as 'lead swingers' or habitual malingerers, they included labourers, transport staff, specialist technical, medical and administrative staff in stationary hospitals, repair workshops and training camp troops. The conditions within the base camps afforded greater opportunities for such troops to engage in collective action. Within their perimeter, most large base camps and depots were open, and, once the day's duties had been discharged, staff were comparatively free to meet in canteens, YMCA institutes, cinemas and theatres.[72]

These predominantly non-combatant troops were relatively static, numerous and could communicate and organise themselves more easily than the men at the front. That they did not feature significantly as mutineers until after the end of the war invites speculation about the reasons. The two most obvious are that they knew they could be shot for mutiny and they were aware that their situation was a good deal more tolerable than that experienced by men at the front. The latter perspective was informed by direct experience, for many had been injured or wounded earlier in the fighting, and were given non-combatant duties because they were physically unfit to serve at the front. Others, witnessing the passage of tens of thousands of wounded through their midst, needed no reminder of the uncomfortable consequences of being exiled for indiscipline to a more hazardous situation, closer to the front.

A further, less easily quantifiable, deterrent would have related to the age and marital status of personnel allocated to permanent base duties. For combat, military commanders preferred to use fitter, younger men who were statistically less likely to have dependents. Older men back at base, even if they had included conscripted industrial militants, would have hesitated to mutiny, knowing their execution or imprisonment would cause great financial hardship for their families.

Between the vast base camps and the front there were thousands of small units, straddling the lines of communication. Their composition, size and function varied and the scope of their work and location sometimes shifted, influenced for example by preparations for a big offensive, enemy bombing or administrative developments. Such units included sanitary squads, POW guards, railway workers, engineers, salvage units, forestry troops, road construction companies, military police, signallers and the ubiquitous labour battalions. Generalising about mutinies in these units remains conjectural, not only because of their diversity, but also because they have been comparatively neglected in studies about rank and file dissent.

Interpretation

Socialist and left-wing commentaries about mutinies in the British Army during the First World War draw attention to the gulf that existed between officers and other ranks, and have elaborated alternative definitions of mutiny, generally drawing attention to the phenomena in the context of more general class conflict. For example, Wintringham, Rothstein, Lamb, Gill and Dallas all view the rank and file as the proletariat in uniform, and speculate about several contemporary developments that may have had an impact and stirred unrest, particularly in Northern France.[73] These include general war-weariness, recruitment of reluctant conscripts, Irish nationalism and the 1916 Easter Rising, the impact of the Russian Revolution, troubles in the French Army, contemporary industrial unrest and post-war demobilisation. They were certainly issues that worried senior commanders, but the JAG registers tend to confirm what was evident in censors' reports and surveys of army morale, namely that, with the important exception of demobilisation, none of these inspired soldiers to mutiny.[74]

However, these incidents challenged the authority of officers, and with some qualification, an analogy can be sustained between the action of workers going on strike and soldiers collectively refusing to obey orders. That is not to say that the action of mutineers was the same as that of factory workers going on strike, because, of course, the soldiers were not engaged in industrial production. However, it is possible to draw parallels between mutineers and the behaviour of public service sector workers engaging in an unofficial strike. Certainly, defining mutinies as a form of collective bargaining by armed public service sector workers represents a novel compromise between the criminality enshrined in the Manual of Military Law and the political left's proto-revolutionaries.

The extent to which the mutineers themselves subscribed to the notion that their activity was akin to direct action by service sector workers requires qualification. Mutineers sometimes legitimated their action by referring to their terms of enlistment, particularly during 1919 when demanding demobilisation.[75] However, in the majority of incidents, due to lack of opportunity or perhaps disinclination to advance more than a preremptory demand for redress, mutineers did not articulate their grievances by referring directly to any contractual relationship between themselves and the army.

Allowing for the genuinely deranged and a minority of drunks, only the most reckless mutineers would candidly concede that their activity was a military offence. Equally, for the same reasons that trade unionists did not generally feel impelled to declare industrial action a political act, soldiers on strike, in all except one or two cases (e.g. the Connaught Rangers, who demanded the withdrawal of British troops from Ireland) never advanced any radical political rationalisation for their action. Instead, mutineers commonly insisted that their action was prompted by a desire to secure 'fair treatment'.

Exactly what was meant by 'fair treatment' tended to vary, but it was associated with a recognition of two contractual issues. Firstly, that in return for the rank and file having surrendered their civil liberties on enlistment, the army had an almost feudal duty to care for their welfare. The latter obligation was also recognised in officers' training, albeit as a means of enabling officers 'to exact instant obedience to orders and to maintain the strictest discipline.'[76] Secondly, that it was also unfair to retain War Service volunteers in the army beyond a few months after the end of hostilities.[77] A claim for fair treatment might in itself have sparked off a mutiny but it was not enough to sustain one for very long. Indeed, the absence of a more developed critique seems to have limited the duration of a mutiny as much as the threat of the firing squad.

Why, therefore, did soldiers engage in radical action to achieve what sometimes appear to have been very limited objectives? After all, the lives, reputations and careers of the individuals involved, as well as the welfare of their families, dependents and communities, were at stake. Ultimately, the answer lies in the mutineers' estimate of the risks involved. At best, they could achieve their demands, and at worst they would be heavily punished. Even in failure, they might influence generals and politicians alike.

However, when officers drew the attention of mutinous troops to the penalties for continuing to disobey orders, martyrdom had little appeal, and the mere threat of retribution usually would have been enough to quell most outbreaks.[78]

Persistence very occasionally brought rewards but as in the case of the territorial soldiers who mutinied in India during 1919, it was the sheer number of mutineers that ultimately compelled the army to accede to the collective bargainers' demands. The men whose names figure in the JAG registers are those who sometimes fatally overestimated the strength of their bargaining power.

Notes

1. *Manual of Military Law* (WO,1914) Pt.1, sec.7, paras 1–4.
2. Memo: Judge Advocate General (JAG) to Director of Personal Services (DPS) in response to outside minute 110/Gen/7690/PS2,8.3.65: Definition of mutiny. Public Record Office, Kew (PRO) WO32/14081.
3. J Putkowski and J Sykes, *Shot at Dawn* (Pen and Sword, London, 1992), p.13.
4. In March 1914, opposition by the Ulster loyalists to the Asquith Government's Irish Home Rule Bill was so strong that the use of troops to maintain order in Northern Ireland was mooted. Over fifty officers of 3 Cavalry Brigade stationed at Curragh Camp near Dublin declared that they would rather be dismissed than engage in operations against Ulster loyalists. The officers successfully secured a written assurance from the Chief-of-Staff that they would not be compelled to enforce the Home Rule Bill in Ulster.
5. A Babington, *For the Sake of Example* (Leo Cooper, London, 1992), p.209
6. e.g. Routine Orders, Adjutant and Quartermaster General, 4 Division, 7.9.15. PRO WO95/1449
7. Babington, op.cit., p.119
8. *Statistics of the Military Effort of the British Empire during the Great War 1914–1920* (HMSO, 1922), pp. 644–5, 699
9. e.g. *The Dreadnought* 22.4.16; *John Bull* 2.3.18; Parliamentary Debates V series, LIV, 14.3.18, c.c. 562–72.
10. *Statistics*, op.cit., p.670; P E Razzell 'Social Origins of officers in the Indian and British Home Army', *British Journal of Sociology* 14 (Sept 1963), pp. 248–260.
11. B.E.W. Childs, *Episodes and Reflections* (Cassell, London, 1930), p. 141–2.
12. Ibid. p.135.
13. G. Oram, *Death sentences passed by military courts of the British Army 1914–1924* (Francis Boutle, London, 1998) pp. 52–56.
14. Haig Diary, 17.3.18. PRO WO 256/28.
15. *Gunfire* (Journal of the Northern Branch, Western Front Association), No.14, pp.2–10; Field Punishment No.1, PRO WO32/5460; A. Baxter, *We Will Not Cease* (Gollancz, London, 1939), pp.104–7; 'Warden', *His Majesty's Guests – Secrets of the Cells* (Jarrolds, London, n.d.), pp. 137–140.
16. e.g. Seaford Camp, November 1914. Letter: Sir Charles Wooley to J. Putkowski, 6.12.78; P Simkins, *Kitchener's Army* (M.U.P., 1988), pp. 243–244.
17. Pte A. Weinstock et al, WO86/81, p.92.
18. See: WO86/74: p.157 (Brockway); p.185 (Crowsley); WO86/76 (Aldred), p.35.
19. J. W. Graham, *Conscription and Conscience* (Allen and Unwin, London, 1922), p.348.
20. For grievances of soldiers during late 1914, see Correspondence, Nov–Dec 1914 in *War Emergency: Workers' National Committee Papers*, Labour Party Archives (WNC), 7/1/7/11–68.
21. 3 Leicesters, Portsmouth 27.8.14; 3 Dorsets, Dorchester, 29.12.14.
22. R. J. Q. Adams and P. Poirier, *The Conscription Controversy in Great Britain* (Macmillan, London, 1987), pp.90–91.
23. Simkins, op.cit, pp. 244–252.
24. Memo: Oughterson to Mansbridge re. London Territorials, 14.6.16, pp.1–2.
25. P. Dennis, *The Territorial Army 1906–1940* (Royal Historical Society, 1987), ch.2.
26. Soldiers' and Workmen's Councils, WO32/5455; Intelligence Circular No.15, December 1917, p.4, PRO AIR1/720/36/1.
27. J. J. Putkowsi, 'Those Nasty Crawling Things, A2 and the Labour Movement', *Lobster*, 29.8.95, 30.2.96.
28. G. Dallas & D. Gill, *The Unknown Army* (Verso, London 1985), pp. 104–6, 136–7; J.J. Putkowski, 'A2 and the Reds in Khaki', *Lobster*, 27, 1994, pp.18–26.
29. A. Rothstein, *The Soldiers' Strikes of 1919* (Macmillan, London, 1980), ch. 3; B. Thomson, *Queer People* (Hodder & Stoughton, London, 1922), pp. 424–5.
30. Havelock Wilson to WO, 14.3.19 et seq., WO 32/11337.
31. Putkowski, *Lobster*, op.cit., p.18.
32. See listing.
33. See listing.
34. In the United Kingdom 451 men were prosecuted for mutiny between 11.11.18 and the end of 1922. Of these 73 were acquitted and 15 were found not guilty.
35. ibid., *Daily Herald* 12.9.19; *Solidarity*, 14, Oct.–Nov. 1980, pp. 14–15.
36. B.H.Thomson, Bolshevism in England, 28.12.18, FO371/3300; Brigadier-General (Lucas?), DAG, Great Britain to General Officer Commanding-in-Chief, Aldershot Command, 4.3.19, British Intelligence papers in the Ralph Heyward Isham Collection, Yale University Library (Isham Papers), 1/1.
37. J. J.Putkowski, *The Kinmel Park Camp Riots 1919* (Flintshire Historical Society, Hawarden, 1989), pp. 37–8.
38. See D. Morton, 'Kicking and Complaining: Postwar Demobilisation Riots in the Canadian Expeditionary Force 1918-1919', *Canadian Historical Review*, 61, 1, Sept. 1980.
39. D. Englander and J. Osborne, 'Jack, Tommy, and Henry Dubb: The Armed Forces and the Working class', *Historical Journal,* 21, 3 (1978), pp. 593–606. D Englander, 'Troops & Trade Unions, 1919', *History Today,* March 1987, pp. 8–13.
40. For contrasting views of Field Punishment No.1 see WO 32/5460, Pt. 2 and A. Baxter, *We will not cease* (Victor Gollancz, London, 1939), pp. 105–6.
41. See listing.
42. See listing.
43. See listing.
44. WO to G.O.C. in C., France etc., 15.11.18, WO32/5479, op. cit.
45. See listing.
46. See listing.
47. See listing.
48. See listing.
49. See listing.
50. See listing.
51. See listing.
52. See listing.
53. See listing.
54. See listing.
55. ibid.; For a full account of the 5 Light Infantry mutiny, see R.W.E. Harper & H. Miller, *Singapore Mutiny* (O.U.P., Singapore ,1984).
56. ibid.; G. Hodges, *The Carrier Corps: Military Labour in the East African Campaign 1914–1918* (Greenwood, Connecticut, 1986), pp. 158–9.
57. Telegrams: 9689, Ironside to WO, 18.7.19; 2694 WO to Ironside, 19.7.19, WO 33/967A; G.R. Singleton-Gates, *Bolos & Barishnyas* (Gale & Polden, Aldershot, 1920), pp. 38–9.
58. O.C. Seletskoe Column to GHQ Archangel, 2.7.19 and enclosure, Imperial War Museum Department of Documents (IWM DOCS), A.E. Sturdy Papers, Box 73/9/2; *Nottingham Journal* 26.4.20; D. Gordon, *Quartered in Hell* (Doughboy Historical Society, Missoula, 1982), p. 235.
59. e.g. J. Baynes, *Morale* (Cassell, London, 1967), pp. 253–4; J.M. Bourne, *Britain and the Great War 1914-1918* (Edward Bond, London, 1989), pp. 214–224.
60. Stragglers Posts (unpub. Ms., circa 1919), FWW File, Royal Military Police Archives, Chichester; G.D. Sheffield, *The Redcaps* (Brassey's, London, 1994), pp. 63–5.
61. W.J. Kendall, Ms. diary, 28.10.16, IWM DOCS.
62. C.J. Lane, Ms. memoirs, p. 6, IWM DOCS.
63. P. Tweed, Ms. memoirs, November 1917,IWM DOCS. See also Haig Diary, op. cit., 23.11.17, 30.11.17. See also F.P. Crozier, *The Men I Killed* (Michael Joseph, London, 1937), pp. 83–6; W. Moore , *The Thin Yellow Line* (Leo Cooper, London, 1974), pp. 142–4.
64. W. B. St. Leger , Ms diary, 30.11.17, IWM DOCS.
65. Evidence of men shooting officers tends to be anecdotal, e.g. M. Bragg, *Speak for England* (Alfred Knopf, New York, 1977), pp. 73–4.
66. Fox, who had family problems, claimed to have been drunk when he committed the assault but he had previously been convicted of insolent behaviour. He was executed on 12.5.16. WO 71/466.
67. T. Ashworth, *Trench Warfare 1914–1918* (Macmillan, London, 1980); M. Brown & S. Seaton, *The Christmas Truce* (Leo Cooper, London, 1984); J. Putkowski, 'The 1914 Christmas Truce', *Gunfire*, 14, p. 56.
68. e.g. FGCM L/Cpls. P. Goggins and J. MacDonald, 19 Bn. DLI, WO71/534.
69. FGCM L/Cpl. T.J. Blackwood et al, 1 Bn. AIF, Australian War Memorial (AWM) File 51/122, pts. 1–7.
70. See J.G. Fuller, *Troop Morale and Popular Culture in the British and Dominion Armies 1914–1918* (Clarendon Press, Oxford,1990), ch. 9.
71. M. Brown, *Tommy Goes to War* (J.M. Dent, London, 1980 edn.), p. 191; T.J. Mitchell & G.M. Smith, *History of the Great War: Medical Services – Casualties and Medical Statistics* (HMSO, London, 1931), ch. 3.
72. D. Gill & J.J. Putkowski, *The British Base Camp at Etaples 1914–1918* (Musee Quentovic, Etaples-sur-Mer, 1997), chs. 3–8.
73. T. Wintringham, *Mutiny* (Latimer Trend, London, 1936); Rothstein, op. cit.; D. Lamb, *Mutinies 1917–1919* (Solidarity, London, 1975); G. Dallas & D. Gill, *The Unknown Army* (Verso, London, 1985). See also C.J. Lammers, 'Strikes and Mutinies: A Comparative Study of Organisational Conflicts between Rulers and Ruled', *Administrative Science Quarterly,*vol. 4, no. 4, December 1969.
74. For postal censorship reports, see for e.g. M. Hardie Papers, Box 84/46/1 IWM DOCS; Papers of Field Marshal Sir Douglas Haig , National Library of Scotland, Acc. 3155/H220 d–f.
75. For e.g., No.1 Loco Depot – Audricq to OC 'A' Company, 20/1/19. Papers of Field Marshal Sir Henry Wilson, Correspondence, Box 73/1/16, File 7C,IWM DOCS
76. B.C. Lake, *Knowledge for War* (Harrison & Sons, London, n.d.), p.7.
77. Until 20.5.20 conscription was used to retain men in the army. C. Braithwaite, *Conscientious Objections to compulsions under the Law* (William Sessions, York, 1995). p. 165.
78. For e.g., W.R. Bion, *The Long Weekend 1879–1919* (Free Association Books, London, 1986), pp. 284–6.

Narratives

In this section I have described a number of mutinous incidents involving men subject to the provisions of the British Army Act, though not all the incidents were defined as mutinies by the military authorities. More mutinies took place in the period 1914–1922 than may be concluded from studying the table of court martial prosecutions at the end of the book. Indeed, it is interesting to speculate why one event might have been considered a mutiny and another not. Take, for example, the incident at Upwey in 1914 – in reality nothing more than a drunken brawl, although it did involve a fatality – which led to prosecutions for mutiny, and the outbreak at Poona in 1919, which involved thousands of disaffected troops, where there were none. Some thoughts on the subject might be found in the introduction, but I hope the examples in this section in the book will at least highlight the contradictions.

All the narratives are based on contemporary accounts or reports from British and Commonwealth archives which make reference to the men's motives and actions, and scale and settlement of the outbreaks. The selection of material has also been guided by the need to illustrate the fact that mutinies involved a variety of troops at home and abroad. I have included a lengthy description of the events that took place in India in 1919, because no account has ever been published about the episode.

Excluded from this selection are a number of fascinating and important mutinies. Some have had to be omitted for reasons of space; for example, the mutinies at Dover, Folkestone and Calais in January 1919. Others, like the strike at Kantara Base, Egypt at Easter 1919, or the Connaught Rangers' mutiny in India during 1920 have been adequately dealt with elsewhere.[1] In other cases, further archival research is required before a substantial account can be presented – the Slavo-British Legion in Russia, for example. Lastly, the omission of incidents involving Australian troops is informed by the fact that exhaustive research in Australian archives by Ashley Ekins will prove far more definitive about ANZAC mutinies than anything likely to be gathered from British archives.

Upwey 1914

The massive increase in the size of the British Army during the closing months of 1914 caused major supply, accommodation and victualling problems. The onset of winter made life miserable. Recently constructed camps on Salisbury Plain and elsewhere became muddy quagmires, and soldiers shivered in tents. Many endured hardship without demur until they were relocated to seaside towns and billetted in municipal buildings and private houses. Others protested, voicing bitter complaints about inadequate accommodation and a range of other issues.[1] Some mutinied, but only five men, all reservists who had been recalled to serve with 3 Bn. Dorsetshires, were court martialled for the offence.

The incident involved a handful of the eighty officers and men who had been detailed to guard the Portland Waterworks at Portesham near Upwey, Dorsetshire. They had recently been transferred into spartan wooden huts after being under canvas at Gould's Bottom Camp when the site was lashed by a thunderstorm on Sunday 29 November.

At 8.40 p.m., following an altercation between Sgt. Richard Probert and Pte. Wallace 'Happy' Williams in the canteen hut, Pte. John Anscombe and L/Cpl. James Cattel had been ordered by Company Sergeant Major William Simpson to leave the canteen huts and escort an unwilling and drunken Sgt. Probert back to his quarters in the orderly tent. Struggling in the face of a howling gale, the trio encountered Williams, whom Probert, in a 'cantankerous mood' and without further ado, punched in the face. Cattel responded by striking Probert, while Williams went to the cook-house to get his injuries treated. Williams later re-appeared and was spotted throwing stones at the orderly tent.

Thereafter, Williams, his face covered in blood, entered the hut he shared with about thirty other men and found around twenty of them enjoying a singsong around the stove. Williams roared 'Mutiny, Mutiny!' and 'Fix bayonets and charge magazines!'. Most of the men did not obey, but L/Cpl. Alfred Wilson picked up a rifle and went outside with Williams. A few minutes later Wilson returned and ordered the men to load their weapons because Sgt. Probert had struck Williams. Williams then armed himself and was joined by Corporal Amey. Rather bizarrely, Amey, who had been outside the hut, was upset because he had been struck from behind with a 15lb. lump of cheese. It was never made clear who threw the cheese, but Amey told those in the hut that it been witheld from the unit's rations by Probert.

The fuss attracted Captain Harold Graham, a couple of lieutenants and Company Sergeant William Simpson to the scene. They immediately made for the men's quarters. The hut was poorly lit by a solitary candle, little could be seen in the gloom and the raging storm made communicating orders very difficult. On hearing scuffling at the far end of the hut, Graham shouted 'Order,' but was ignored. Then Wilson, standing a few paces away, levelled his rifle at the Captain. The captain drew, but did not fire his revolver. Instead, he wrested the rifle from Wilson. In the ensuing uproar, men shouted out 'Don't fire!' as Graham and his party escaped outside, pursued by Wilson complaining to Sergeant Simpson about Probert's unprovoked attack on Williams.

Graham deployed a cordon of armed men around the hut but ordered them to hold their fire while a fifteeen minute fusillade was discharged from within the hut by Amey, Cattel, Wilson and Williams. Fortunately, most of between fifty and a hundred rounds were shot through the roof, but one of the sentinels was wounded. A fatality occurred after Williams roamed outside and was killed after Wilson loosed off a promiscous shot through the side of the hut.

The episode ended about half an hour later when the battalion commander, Col. Castleman-Williams, arrived with reinforcements from Weymouth, and arrested everyone in the hut. Wilson, Anscombe, Amey, Cattell and Pte. A.E. Parsons (who had witnessed Probert assault Williams) were charged with mutiny and threatening Captain Graham with violence, forcing him to leave the hut and opening fire.[2]

Almost every other wartime mutiny that occurred in mainland Britain was heavily censored, but very full reports of what happened at Upwey featured in local newspapers, probably in order to reassure local residents who had been alarmed by the incident. Most details came from the coroner's inquest into 31-year-old Williams' death, which concluded that Wilson was guilty of manslaughter. However, the coroner's jury advocated that the very contrite Wilson be treated leniently, and they were critical of Sgt. Probert's behaviour and queried the spartan camp facilities, commenting particularly on the poor illumination in the men's hut.

In his own defence, Sgt. Probert said it was not he but Williams, who had been stealing his comrades' cheese. Probert insisted that Williams had started the fight outside the canteen by lashing the sergeant with a piece of wood, and that he had been knocked unconscious by a third party after punching Williams on the nose. Probert claimed he had remained insensible until the following morning and knew nothing about the shooting. Captain Graham excused the lack of facilities by explaining that the uncompleted hut and rudimentary illumination were a big improvement on tented accommodation, particularly during bad weather.[3]

There was general agreement that Williams had been an unstable, excitable alcoholic. Colonel Castleman-Smith was at pains to draw attention to an assessment of Williams' character. It had been written on 24 November by the colonel's predecessor as commanding officer Captain C.S. Jarvis. Of Williams, Jarvis wrote, 'In my opinion the man is mentally deficient. He has given a considerable amount of trouble, and his conduct is such as to undermine discipline. He was drafted to headquarters for a month or so, and the company sergeant major there would know all about him. It would be in the interest of the service if he were discharged as unfit for service.'

Perhaps conveniently for all concerned, Jarvis's reference to Williams volatile temperament ensured that the latter could partly be regarded as the author of his own demise. However, even had he survived to give evidence, many questions remain unanswered, not the least of which was the number of men who had actually been shooting and how many rounds were fired. In spite of Wilson's abject conviction that he had killed Williams, empty cartridge cases and at least one bullet hole in the hut revealed that someone had been firing at the hut from outside. Moreover, the post mortem revealed that the dead soldier had been killed by a firearm discharged at very close range, even though the fatal shot was supposed to have been fired by Wilson, who was about ten yards away inside the hut. It was never satisfactorily established how many rifles were fired, and Castleman-Smith explained away variations in the estimates by maintaining that noise of the storm may have confused witnesses.

Was the whole business simply a drunken brawl? Certainly Probert and Wilson admitted to having been drinking, and his character assessment suggests that it is quite likely that Williams had been drinking too. However, nobody else admitted having touched a drop of alcohol.

Of those charged with mutiny, Wilson was sentenced to six months and the others were jailed for four months' hard labour apiece. Anscombe and Sgt. Probert, charged separately with drunkeness and striking Pte. Williams, were found not guilty.[4]

Tidworth 1915
In May 1915 the men of 152 Field Company, Royal Engineers, part of the newly-formed 37 Division, were encamped in tents at South Tidworth in Hampshire.[1] Conditions in the camp were spartan and the combination of fresh air and energetic training gave everyone a healthy appetite.

The Army Service Corps usually delivered rations which were then prepared by volunteers from the unit, but at Tidworth, civilian contractors carried out the catering. At the end of a day's duties, the final meal of the day consisted of bread, margarine and jam, but the men felt that a more generous meal ought to have been served, and that their rations were being pilfered. Individually, soldiers could have complained to the duty officer at mess time, but they were deterred from doing so by the fear they might be regarded as troublemakers. Since army pay was insufficient to buy food to supplement the inadequate rations the men became annoyed.[2]

The majority of the rank and file men were war service volunteers, with a few old soldiers who had been returned to service after being wounded during the opening weeks of the war.

Matters came to a head very quickly, as one of a newly arrived draft from 68 Company, Royal Engineers, Pte. A.E. Henderson, was later to record. Henderson noted that the food began to deteriorate, and that the meat, particularly the sausages seemed to be 'off'. The men deliberated about how to draw attention to their grievance without openly nominating a leader. And so, when the sausages were next served up for breakfast, the men put their plates and the sausages, untouched, on top of their bedding and stood to attention. Officers inspected their ranks and a bugle then called the men to parade. The men dutifully responded, but they assembled at the edge of the parade ground and made no further moves to fall in.[3]

About 150 men were involved in the action, and although the company commander was very well aware of the protestors' grievances, it was left to senior NCOs to conduct 'confabulations'. Exactly with whom the NCOs confabulated remains unclear, but after a short while the protestors were told that their grievances would be looked into and that nobody would be detained or punished for mutiny.[4]

The men all resumed duties, rations improved and the

remaining month's training was conducted without further incident.

What happened at Tidworth was unsullied by drunkeness, violence or death, but it was unquestionably a mutiny. The reason why courts martial were not used at Tidworth invites speculation, but Pte. Henderson was of the opinion that the authorities had little choice but to parley and concede to the men's demands because the way in which the men had acted would have made any other response difficult – other than perhaps punishing every tenth man.[5]

Refusals to parade were a common form of protest by troops stationed in Britain during the First World War. As at Tidworth, most were settled without recourse to courts martial and consequently feature neither in official reports nor in the Judge Advocate General's registers. It seems likely that only when threats of violence were made, or actually broke out during the negotiating process, as with the Gloucesters at Malvern Wells in June 1915, men were court martialled.[6]

Blargies North Prison, 1916

To relieve the pressure on commanding officers and economise on labour, the army established several military prisons on the lines of communication.[1] Men undergoing substantial spells of field punishment were sent to them. They were really penal labour camps rather than secure institutions, and to a surprising extent their routine operation relied on a measure of co-operation on the part of inmates. Within their confines, and when neither tied up nor undergoing solitary confinement, the prisoners were able to communicate and organise collectively to agitate for an improvement in their conditions.

It was just such an initiative that led to the first executions for mutiny in the BEF. Gunner William Lewis, 124 Battery Royal Field Artillery and Pte. John Braithwaite, 2 Otago Regiment, New Zealand Expeditionary Force, were shot together on 29 October 1916 after being tried separately for their involvement in two nominally unconnected mutinies that occurred in No.1 Military Prison, Blargies North Camp, near Abancourt.

The prison was one of a pair that had been established near the small village of Blargies. Both consisted of a rectangular barbed wire perimeter fence enclosing a corrugated iron stockade, within which approximately three hundred prisoners were confined. The prisoners were herded into about two dozen bell tents or confined in a separate punishment block of some thirty cells. Facilities were spartan: thirty-six washing basins, three showers, a steam room and a small cookhouse. Discipline was enforced by a staff of twenty-six NCOs under the command of a captain.[2]

The prisoners had been convicted by courts martial, and sentenced to many months' hard labour. This consisted of being regularly detailed for arduous work in labouring gangs for the Royal Engineers in the vicinity of the prison. The rigidly enforced official range of punishments involved sustained sentences of Field Punishment No.1 – being tied up for a couple of hours a day to poles specially erected for the purpose. Staff also shackled prisoners with leg irons and handcuffs, isolated them in the punishment block or restricted their rations to No.1 diet. These punishments were supplemented by physical assaults by the staff.[3]

At 1.30 p.m. on 14 August 1916, the majority of prisoners were marched off as working parties, but sixty-seven refused to move, insisting they wanted to see the Deputy Governor of Military Prisons, Captain A. Barker. The latter recalled what next occurred: 'I went to the parade ground & called them to attention – they came to attention – I asked them what their grievances were. Several of them demanded that some of their party should be released from leg irons & taken off punishment diet. The spokesman [sic] of this party at this time were Ptes. McCorkindale & Gunner Lewis. I gave the command that all men willing to travel were to take one pace forward, not a man moved.'[4]

After declining to negotiate, the Deputy Governor ordered an armed escort to handcuff the prisoners. The prisoners started yelling as Acting Staff Sergeant Aves handcuffed one of their number and began handcuffing a second. He noted: 'On proceeding to start handcuffing three men came forward viz. Pte. McCorkindale, Gunner Lewis & Pte. Garden... they demanded in an insubordinate manner that I should take the handcuffs from the man I had put them on. I refused to do this until I got Captain Barker's orders. These three men said, practically together, "Fuck Captain Barker & his orders, he is fuck all now, you will take your orders from us or we will murder you you fucking bastard".'[5] The escort responded by levelling their revolvers at the prisoners.

In order to prevent bloodshed, Barker halted the process and ordered the protestors to occupy half a dozen tents which had been erected in another part of the prison compound. They did as ordered, but 'went independently not as a military party'.[6]

At the trial of seven men held responsible for the mutiny, defendants explained that the protest had been prompted by the lack of general cleanliness and brutality by the guards: 'There were about 300 prisoners in the camp & only from 12 to 14 seats in the latrine. We were only allowed from 1.15 p.m. to 1.30 p.m. to use the latrine. Supposing there were 100 men who wanted to use the latrines at a time, it would be impossible for them to do so without being late for parade. Our underclothing was in a filthy & lousy & we could not get soap to wash with, our blankets were lousy & the mess tins we took food from were filthy. The tents we slept in were also filthy. Our clothing came back from the wash in the same state as we took it off. If awarded punishment, we were tied up to a pole, very often men would faint. If they said anything they got a punch in the ribs or jaw from any of the staff NCOs near. If the men complained to Captain Barker he would turn round and say: "That is all right" & walk away.'[7]

However, Barker had previously demonstrated that he was prepared to discuss grievances with other groups of inmates. The defendants had witnessed him negotiating with thirty-five newly-arrived Australian prisoners who had refused to work: 'They stated that they wanted their own private razors & clean clothing & men to look after their tents. This request was granted them.'

To satisfy the Australians, who had also secured relief from dietary punishment, they had been given two of the six razors that had hitherto been shared between thirty-six British prisoners.[8]

Thereafter, Scots troops amongst the British prisoners

wanted parity of treatment and similar improvements in their compound, a development that Barker later had admitted was under consideration. The verbal abuse that broke out as the first two men were being handcuffed had been provoked by the sight of a third prisoner, Pte. Thom, being injured by guards' efforts to shackle him with unsuitably small handcuffs. The onlookers had been incensed when Thom was flung to the ground and kicked by a staff sergeant. The staff had responded to the outburst by levelling their revolvers at the prisoners until ordered by Captain Barker to desist and unshackle the handcuffed men.

Gunner Lewis was not going to admit to being part of a mutinous conspiracy at his trial. He therefore maintained that he and Pte. Daniel McCorkindale, 11 Royal Scots, had been arbitrarily selected by a Staff Sergeant to answer questions after Captain Barker had demanded to know the men's grievances. However, Lewis also claimed that after the protest he had been confidentially encouraged by the staff to persuade the men to escalate their action and demand full parity of treatment with the Australians. Had it been achieved, two hours would have been lopped off the afternoon's work for inmates and camp staff. Lewis declined to respond to encouragement by the staff, and refused to continue to represent the protestors in subsequent negotiations.[9]

On 15 August all three hundred prisoners had been paraded at 7.00 a.m. and ordered to march off. None moved except for the original sixty-seven protestors, who initially complied with the order but soon changed their minds. Giving evidence at the court martial, Colonel Umfreville, the Director, Military prisons in the Field, called to testify in support of his subordinates, said: 'The parade was perfectly orderly but I soon saw that there was an unanimous feeling against going out to work. Seeing this, I directed the Governor, Captain Barker to tell each section to appoint one man as representative & I would go into any grievances they had to bring forward. I saw the representatives at 9 a.m. After hearing them in the presence of the Camp Commandant ... I had the whole parade fallen in, explained to the men how trivial the complaints proved to be & how easily matters might have been righted had they taken the proper action.'[10]

Umfreville denied saying, as Thom had previously declared, that he had promised that if the protestors went to work on the 15 August 'bygones will be bygones', but conceded that subsequent negotiations lasted for two hours. Umfreville recalled that the men complained about general lack of cleanliness, inadequate rations, lack of latrines, poor clothes-washing arrangements, insufficient razors for shaving, that 'men with skin diseases were not segregated' and that an unidentified soldier had been tied up and beaten by prison staff.

Umfreville exonerated his staff of responsibility for the criticisms expressed by the defendants and directed blame for inciting mutiny on the arrival of unruly Australians: 'The general conduct of the camp, apart from some few offences of escaping was perfectly normal until the Australian prisoners arrived. The Australians had no grounds for complaint, they objected to being treated as the British prisoners were treated. No case of ill-treatment of prisoners was reported to me. It is a common thing for prisoners when tied to a pole fainting. We had cases of this. I know of no case of a man being taken to hospital on account of being tied up. There is nothing in regulations prohibiting prisoners when doing F.P.1 not being blindfolded. If it is done it is done for some particular reason, for instance if a man makes faces or played the fool generally he would probably be blindfolded by bringing his "stocking cap" over his eyes if his head could not be turned in another direction. The Camp was usually clean but on the 15th the men had not done their cleaning up work. There is no limit to the time prisoners may be kept in leg irons... the men had shorter hours than any other prisoners in France.'[11]

However, Umfreville's evidence to the court dealt only partly with the men's grievances. He declared complaints about cleanliness were due to a general water shortage problem that could not be rectified. He then insisted the remaining issues could have been dealt with as ordinary complaints, and dismissed the latrines issue as absurd. Umfreville's disingenuousness may partly be accounted for as a robust defence of his subordinates, but he must have known that at least one inmate had been suffering from amoebic dysentry. Further, on 29 August 1916, the Specialist Sanitary Officer investigating outbreaks of diarrhoea reported that the prisoners' compound was the worst affected area.[12]

Moreover, Driver Willam Peden testified that after the meeting, Umfreville had promised: 'As regards washing, I will see that you will have it clean & as regards to latrine accommodation I will see you have more seats, but tea is not allowed in prison but you can have lime juice at night provided you do not have vegetables during the day.'[13] The allegations by prisoners that they had been brutally treated were flatly denied by Captain Barker and the Blargies camp staff when they testified against the mutineers.

Thus, they affirmed, no prisoner was sent to hospital as a result of being tied up. Pte. Thom had not been assaulted. He had cut himself because he struggled and not because the handcuffs were too small. Cap comforters were pulled over the eyes of prisoners undergoing Field Punishment No.1 if they laughed or talked to others who had been similarly sentenced. In fact no member of staff had ever been seen to ill-treat a prisoner.[14] By inference, therefore, the mutineers had no reason to complain. Summing up the legal aspects of the trial, the Judge Advocate commented: 'Provocation by a superior, or the existence of a grievance, is no justification for mutiny though it would of course be allowed due weight in considering the punishment... anyone with the most rudimentary idea of discipline must see that such a method of obtaining redress is contrary to all ideas of discipline.'[15]

In spite of the earnest but ineffectual efforts of a legally unqualified Prisoners' Friend, all the defendants were found guilty. Trooper Thom was sentenced to six years' penal servitude, and the remaining six were to be executed. The Commander-in-Chief, Sir Douglas Haig, reduced the former and commuted the latter to heavy prison sentences, except in the case of Gunner Lewis.[16]

The mutiny which led to Pte. John Braithwaite, 2 Otago Regiment NZEF being shot alongside Gunner Lewis took place in the Australian and New Zealand soldiers' compound on 28 August 1916. The immediate cause of the incident involved an Australian soldier, Pte. Alexander Little. While Little was having a brief hot shower after a morning's work, the water had been cut off and Little had verbally abused an NCO.[17] Arriving back at the Camp, Staff Sgt. F.E. Shearing, MPSC, was ordered by Acting Sergeant Major Gill to confine Pte. Alexander Little in the nearby punishment compound. Shearing recalled: 'I marched Pte. Little to the Punishment Compound about 30 yards away. He came quietly. On marching him to the gate of the punishment compound before the gate was opened Pte. Little shouted out to the mess orderly, "Bring my dinner over, this fucking bag of slime is putting me inside". I opened the gate, and told Little to go in, he refused to do so and made a good deal of noise. The rest of the Section rushed over in a body... & took Pte. Little away from me."[18]

The thirty or so prisoners who snatched Little from Shearing then raucously dispersed to their tents, the prison staff unable to halt their departure without bloodshed.[19]

John 'Jack' Braithwaite (the mess orderly) and three Australians, Ptes. Mitchell, Le Guier and Sheffield, were identified as being in the crowd, and were charged with mutiny. Umfreville did not attend the brief hearing on 6 October 1916, but Barker and his staff gave evidence for the prosecution. The Prosecuting Officer, Judge Advocate, Prisoners' Friend and two of the five officers hearing the case had also been involved in the earlier trial.[20]

The defence unsuccessfully challenged witnesses' evidence of identification but Braithwaite admitted that he had taken a meal over to Little as the crowd surrounded him. He explained: 'My motive in getting Pte. Little away to the tent was really to prevent trouble, as I had been given permission to petition General Birdwood on behalf of the Australian and New Zealand prisoners for release to go back to the front. The petition had gone, and we were expecting an answer at any time.'[21]

The Commander-in-Chief commuted the death sentences against the three Australians to two years' imprisonment with hard labour, but confirmed Braithwaite's sentence. Braithwaite, an articulate 35-year old ex-journalist, had been repeatedly punished by courts martial for absence before being confined in Blargies Prison, and had circumstantially been involved in the negotiations that had earlier secured the razors for colonial prisoners.[22]

Although nominally separate incidents, these two Blargies' mutinies were linked by a number of factors that have been neglected in accounts by New Zealand historians, who have been primarily concerned with addressing the fairness of Braithwaite's 'judicial murder'.[23] The punishments in both Blargies Prison mutiny cases were reviewed almost simultaneously by Haig. Confirmation was relayed to the Inspector General of Communication (IGC) by Colonel J.B. Wroughton on 26 October. The IGC, Lt General F.T. Clayton, suggested that the capital sentences in both trials be commuted to penal servitude, but was overruled.[24] Though Haig attached his signature confirming the sentences, the draft decisions had already been processed by the AG's staff, and circumstantially, therefore, the decision to execute Lewis and Braithwaite was initially taken by Col. Wroughton.

At least notionally, Wroughton would have reviewed the sentences in the light of three criteria applied by all confirming officers. These consisted of the convicted man's character, performance in combat and the state of morale in his unit. However, Lewis and Braithwaite were the most articulate recidivists who were judged to have initiated two of three confrontations that had occurred in the space of a fortnight. Lewis, an old soldier who had originally enlisted in 1908, would have been considered as having no excuse for breaching regulations.[25] Apart from morbid equity, Braithwaite's death may also be taken as a move by the British to demonstrate that service in France demanded more rigorous levels of obedience from Australians than those which had prevailed during their previous service in Egypt.[26]

In November 1916 Umfreville approved the construction of a separate prison at Les Attaques, specifically for Australian prisoners, thereby eliminating grievances over parity of treatment.[27]

Etaples Base, 1917

The mutiny at the British Army camp complex at Etaples began at 3.00 p.m. on 9 September 1917 with the arrest of a New Zealand artilleryman, Pte. Healy, who had overstayed his leave to visit the adjacent town. He was arrested by the camp police as he re-entered the complex at Three Arch bridge, one of three access points that spanned the railway line separating the eastern end of the camp from Etaples.[1]

Healy was detained only temporarily, but within a few hours an angry crowd of 2,000 soldiers surrounded the police hut demanding his release. Then one of the camp policemen fired a pistol over the heads of the protesters, fatally injuring a Gordon Highlander, Corporal W.B. Wood, who had been standing on the edge of the crowd. A woman bystander was also wounded. The police ran for their lives, pursued into the town by an angry mob, many of whom, like Wood, were Scottish soldiers.[2]

The camp adjutant tried to restore order with a force of more than two hundred officers and men who carried weapons but without ammunition. The latter peacefully dispersed the crowd at Three Arch bridge and later persuaded New Zealanders and Scots troops with cajolery and promises of redress to stop hunting the police who had sought refuge in the town. A couple of policemen were badly battered, but there were no further casualties, and by 9.00 p.m. the town was cleared and the camp quietened down.[3]

On the following day, routine training and other activities continuing normally, although the police who normally patrolled the town had been replaced by soldiers from one of the infantry base depots (IBD) where reinforcements were billeted. Around 4.00 p.m., hundreds of soldiers assembled in the vicinity of the bridges, which granted access across the railway line separating the camp from the town. Efforts were made by the authorities to stop the generally good tempered crowds of men leaving the camp and crossing the bridges into Etaples. Lt. Charles Miller recalled that the mutineers, if so they might be termed, simply formed a compact mass and repeatedly charged through the picket. After a while, anyone who wanted to leave the camp and go to Etaples could do so without hindrance.[4]

Some wanted to enjoy a drink after a day's arduous training; others still wished to attack the police responsible for Wood's death. To prevent disturbances spreading beyond Etaples, the authorities deployed one hundred men from the Machine Gun School at Le Touquet to protect the nearby beach resort of Paris Plage, a few miles to the west of Etaples. However, their services were not required because the Etaples Camp Commandant, Brigadier-General Andrew Thomson and his staff successfully parleyed with roving bands of soldiers and persuaded them to return to camp. Again, by 9.00 p.m., all was quiet.[5]

The following day witnessed a similar pattern of activity. In the late afternoon, pickets guarding the railway bridges that gave access to Etaples were again bowled over by masses of soldiers. The latter rushed on through the town heading towards the picket guarding the River Canche bridge and the main road to Le Touquet on the western extremity of the town. One of the picket, Pte. Frank Edwards later recalled: 'We heard the sound of singing, and a mob of soldiers in various states of undress and all unarmed swarmed into view. They were led by a Canadian private, who, with his tunic unbuttoned and his cap on the back of his head, occasionally gave vent to his feelings by shouting, "Down with the Red Caps," "Lets release the prisoners," etc. which were loudly echoed by his companions. They seemed to be attracted by our little force, and came towards us laughing and jeering.[6]

'Our commander ordered us to load, but only one man near me did so. The Canadian advanced right up to our front rank, closely followed by the mob, and the whole crowd surged across the bridge. A tram car was following closely, and the leader with many of his followers, boarded it, singing and shouting in great humour. In fact it was a cheerful affair, the only man to suffer being he who had foolishly loaded his rifle, who had his hat thrown into the river by one of the crowd who had seen him do it.'[7]

The mob went on towards Paris Plage, but was persuaded to return to quarters. No disturbances occurred after 9.00 p.m., but five soldiers were arrested and reinforcements were confined to camp.[8]

On Wednesday, 12 September, orders were given to prevent soldiers crossing either of the two bridges that traversed the River Canche. Lt. S.J.C. Russell later recalled: 'The men picked for this duty grumbled quietly as we distributed ball ammunition, for there was much sympathy with the mutineers, though these now consisted of the riff-raff of the camp... The guard for the bridge that carried the main road to Le Touquet was put under the command of a major. The other guard, a small one for the railway bridge over the river, was put under... a young officer from the Border regiment. With fixed bayonets the two guards marched off... The bridge over the railway was unguarded, so Etaples was open to those who ignored the order that all leave was stopped, and a number of men left the camp.'[9]

At 3.00 p.m., a thousand-strong crowd stormed out of the camp and headed across the town towards the armed pickets. Russell saw what happened next: 'When this crowd of rioters... had pushed through Etaples they reached the main-road bridge in an impetuous mood, and swept along toward the guard. The major ordered his men into two ranks, with the front rank kneeling, with rifles loaded and bayonets at the ready and then walked out to remonstrate with the mob. The ringleaders pressed on arguing with him and pushing him back until his men had to put up their bayonets to avoid wounding him. The rioters pushed aside the rifles and went through the guard.'[10]

On reaching Paris Plage, the soldiers turned around and went back to their quarters. Except for a soldier who was knocked out in a confrontation with an officer commanding the picket on the railway bridge and some half-hearted attempts to interfere with motor vehicles, no other disturbances or damage were reported. However, since pickets recruited from the camp were ineffectual, four hundred troops and military police were drafted into the camp by the authorities.[11]

There was no further trouble until Thursday, 13 September, when one hundred troops broke out of the camp, and went into Etaples in the afternoon. Later, when roll calls were held to discover how many failed to return to the camp, twenty-three absentees were noted. There was a breakout by a couple of hundred men from the camp during the early evening but all returned to the base by mid-evening. Only two soldiers who had unsuccessfully tried to break out of camp were injured.[12]

Thereafter, a massive counterforce of more than 2,300 troops from outside the area were used to cordon off the camp complex. Troops from the Infantry Base Depots were then marched to the training area, or 'Bullring', and warned by the camp staff that the counterforce had been ordered to open fire if there was any further trouble. Except for a relatively small party of fifty or sixty men, who challenged the pickets and managed to reach Etaples before being arrested, no more confrontations occurred.[13]

On Saturday, 15 September, with order fully restored in the camp, men from the camp were permitted to visit Etaples, and the counter-force enjoyed a couple of days rest and recreation.[14]

Reviewing the tumultuous events of what has come to be known as the Etaples mutiny, it is clear that the initial confrontation between the New Zealanders and the police was over by Monday evening. The New Zealanders were not involved in any trouble subsequently and three days after Wood's death complained about the continuing disruption caused by the Scots.[15]

The motives of the Scots soldiers are easy to understand. They wanted revenge for the killing of their fellow Scot by the police. However, their prominence in the disturbances appears to decline after Tuesday, probably because they failed to find any of the camp police.

From Wednesday onwards, it seems that most soldiers who forced their way out of the camp were simply looking for alternatives to the entertainment or leisure that was provided inside the camp complex. They broke out in the afternoon, after having carried out their day's training, and returned when night fell.

Although there are numerous lurid accounts of fighting and suggestions that there was an organised conspiracy behind the affair, most were written years after the end of the war and exaggerated by imaginative journalists or creatively embroidered by playwrights.[16] It is certainly true that the confrontations at the bridges were extremely violent, but nobody was bludgeoned to death, and fighting was confined to the southern end of the camp complex. One rioter armed with a knife tried, wholly unsuccessfully, to hijack a car but trains continued to run according to schedule and reinforcements dutifully departed for the front.

Though alarmed, no women stationed in the camp were molested. Miss M.I. Leared, the VAD driver of the

Etaples Camp Assistant Provost Marshal, recalled that all the members of the Women's Auxiliary Army Corps (WAACS) were sent back to camp as quickly as possible. On 9 September a noisy mass of men collected around the wire perimeter of the camp and threatened to break in. They dispersed after a WAAC officer and a Red Cross nurse asked them to leave. The proceedings were conducted with a musical accompaniment provided by 500 women singing hymns in their camp recreation hut. Leared recalled that the singing was tongue in cheek, but conceded that they experienced a measure of fear in their hearts. Although disturbances continued for a week, the women were left alone by the rioters.[17]

Tales about an elusive devil-may-care ringleader, masquerading as an officer and master-minding the week-long disruption, are mythical. The leading contender, Pte. Percy Toplis, creatively dubbed the 'The Monocled Mutineer' by two British authors, William Allison and John Fairley, was given the sobriquet during the 1970s.[18] A thief, vagabond and rapist before the war, Pte. Toplis joined the Royal Army Medical Corps in London during August 1914. Of his war service, contemporary official records state: 'Toplis went to the Dardanelles in 1915 with a Field Ambulance Company, and it appears he was either invalided or wounded, and sent home to the Depot at Aldershot. From there he went on trooping duty to Salonika, Egypt, and back to the Depot, and then to India on the troopship *Orontes*. After a few months to Bombay, from there to Egypt, and it is supposed that in August or September, 1918, he was missing and the next that was heard of him was at Nottingham, where he was wanted for false pretences, and was later arrested in Clerkenwell as a suspected person. During this time he had been masquerading as an Army officer, and on the 22nd November, 1918 he was sentenced to six months for false pretences at Nottingham.'[19]

After being released, Toplis robbed and murdered a taxi driver and was subsequently shot dead by the British police.

However, what occurred at Etaples was mutiny, and fifty-four men were court martialled for various offences in the camp during the period 9–24 September. Of these, only four ringleaders were charged with, and found guilty of, mutiny; three were jailed and one was executed.[20] The ill-fated mutineer was a veteran who had served with 26 Bn. Northumberland Fusiliers, Corporal Jesse Short.[21]

Short had been arrested soon after 9.00 p.m. on 11 September by the picket guarding the main River Canche bridge. The following day he was informed of the charges and immediately brought before a field general court martial. The trial proceedings disclosed that, after being brushed aside by a crowd of boisterous soldiers a picket was being admonished by an officer for having given way. Short, who had been loitering nearby, had advised the picket not to listen to their 'bloody officer', adding: 'What you want to do with that bugger is to tie a rope round his neck and throw him in the river.' He was swiftly arrested and the following morning had been charged with mutiny.[21]

Defending himself, Short apologised, explaining that he had been drunk when insulting the officer. However, witnesses stated that men with whom he had earlier been seen associating were carrying red flags – hinting at political radicalism. The inference was considered enough evidence for the court to recommend that Short be executed.[22]

Short's fate was sealed a fortnight before his sentence was formally confirmed by Sir Douglas Haig. On 12 September, Lieutenant General G.H. Fowke, the Adjutant General, had told the commander in chief that the outbreak at Etaples had been fomented by some men with revolutionary ideas and red flags, who had stirred up trouble in the reinforcement camps. Fowke reported that the ringleaders had been arrested, and the remainder of the troublesome troops had been sent to the trenches.[23]

On 23 September, General J.J. Asser, Officer Commanding the Lines of Communication, though conceding that there had been insufficient officers to control fifty thousand new drafts billetted in the IBDs at Etaples, further endorsed Fowke's interpretation of revolutionaries and red flags having been instrumental in stirring up trouble. Asser told Haig that the disturbances had primarily involved Scots troops, 'the scum of the earth, from the slums of Glasgow', and that lax discipline by the camp commandant had allowed matters to get out of hand. Their remedy was to have Short executed and to uphold a sentence of ten years' penal servitude passed on fellow mutineer, seventeen-year-old Rifleman McIntosh. Possibly because very few Imperial troops were arrested, the two remaining ringleaders, a Canadian and an Australian, had their ten year sentences reduced to two years' hard labour.[24]

These exemplary measures confirmed that what had occurred at Etaples was viewed by the army hierarchy as a serious mutiny. But what made the outbreak so grave? Though crowds of soldiers chased military policemen and regularly broke out of the camp, guns were not deployed by the rioters, no general harrassment of officers was reported, routine training continued, trains continued to operate without interruption and absenteeism was minimal. On the other hand, Fowke, Asser and Haig all attached great significance to the testimony of a couple of junior officers, who claimed that amongst some flags being trailed along by rioters were some red ones and dignified Short's drunken abuse as socialist rhetoric.[25]

Yet their interpretation was unsubstantiated by more general military intelligence appraisals, and any political aspect of the Etaples mutiny was almost completely artificial, whether manufactured on the spot or embellished by staff officers anxious to demonstrate their zeal and efficiency. In fact revolutionaries were conspicuous by their absence in the BEF during the First World War. Even had the British rank and file at Etaples heard about the mutinies in the French Army or the bloody suppression of the Russian Brigade at La Courtine during 1917, there was little reason why they should have viewed the incidents as anything more than hampering the speedy conclusion of the war.[26]

The Labourers' revolt

During the First World War in Northern France, both the British and French armies employed black and non-European labourers. This policy was driven by the need to free white military labourers for redeployment as combat troops.[1]

By mid-1917, the ports, timber procurement, transport, salvage, repair and supply networks serviced by the Labour Directorate would have been disabled without the contribution of an ethnically diverse array of labourers, which included Fijians, Seychellois, Mauritians, the South African Native Labour Contingent and the Cape Coloured, Egyptian, Indian, Chinese Labour Corps.[2] Predominantly engaged in carrying out unskilled labouring work in companies commanded by white officers or NCOs, they also included literate, articulate men well capable of organising and representing others with little or no previous experience of collective bargaining. So it was not long before the rank and file of the Labour Corps gave vent to their dissatisfaction by going on strike.

Though authoritative accounts create the impression that mutinies involving non-European labourers began in September 1917, it is evident that the men had engaged in direct action many months previously. For example, in mid-March, South African Native Labour Contingent (SANLC) men were court martialled for having gone on strike at Dieppe. There was also bloodshed at Dannes, near Camiers, when an incident at a SANLC camp resulted in one man being accidentally shot. As for Egyptian labourers, collective protests had been reported in Northern France since at least the end of May.[3]

The men's confinement in prison-like camps provoked aggravation. The SANLC were segregated at the behest of the South African Government who wished to prevent black workers from becoming familiar or intimate with European civilians, especially white women.[4] However, it was a perspective readily shared by the British, and extended to embrace Chinese, Indian and Egyptian labourers. Labourers' camps were concealed from public view behind corrugated iron palisades and the accommodation was little different to Blargies North prison. Segregation from the outside world was enforced by guards and military police.[5]

The army ensured that the labourers were also controlled by fellow labourers who acted as gangers and police. Because efforts had been made to create companies of men from the same village, tribe or ethnic minority, the latter were frequently of a higher social status than their fellows, including, for example, tribal chiefs, members of influential families or clerics. While the level of co-operation of rank and file labourers may have depended on the circumstances which attended their recruitment, the gangers functioned organisationally and perhaps politically as an extension of the collaborating elites that supported imperial rule in overseas territories. Although evidence remains scanty, the gangers, police and probably many interpreters exercised informal authority that complemented the formal recognition and support they derived from the white NCOs and officers who commanded non-European labour companies.[6]

Because of strict censorship and rigid prohibition of access to the compounds and even hospitals, it was very difficult for labourers to develop contacts with others outside their camp. In any case, non-European Labour companies were differentiated on the basis of skin colour, language, village of origin, lengths of contract and the army's generally racist estimates of their particular skills and aptitudes. Even had they been able to overcome censorship or evade surveillance and contact other labour companies, there was little guarantee that labourers from different ethnic groups would have shared a common language.[7]

In some cases internicine or ethnic hostility would also have impeded collective action. For example, the Indian Labour Corps was made up of at least ten separate tribal groups from all over India; the Chinese and SANLC were cool towards one another; Basutos and Zulus of SANLC were mutually hostile.[8] Labourers were also zoned according to the type of work for which they had been recruited, for example Indians carried out salvage work on the lines of communication whereas Egyptians were used as stevedores in seaports.[9]

Though conditions for labourers in the camps were hard and poor rations prompted protests, the fact that they would lose earnings and come up against a hostile civilian population prevented labourers from breaking out of the camps for very long. Furthermore, mutinies provoked a summary response. For example, on 23 July, one of the five hundred or so men serving with No. 24 Company, SANLC, at No.7 Labour Camp, Dieppe was arrested for having defied an officer by doing his washing in a stream outside the compound. The man's comrades demanded an explanation for the action from the arresting officer, who refused to discuss his motives.

Others may have been detained as a consequence of the intervention as argument escalated into action when fellow labourers, bent on liberating the arrested man, pick-axed open the lock securing the compound gate. Their initiative collapsed when the crowd was fired on by a party of twenty-five white troops, who had been ordered to quell the disturbance. Four SANLC men were killed, eleven were wounded and sixteen of those who survived the shooting were later summarily sentenced to eighty-four days' Field Punishment No.1 for breaking out of camp. At some point three white personnel had also been wounded, though by whom is unclear. Details are sketchy, but it is apparent that the foray out of the compound was provoked by the labourers' anger over the arrest and the officer's refusal to develop a dialogue.[10]

The labourers' complaints did not always go unheeded, even though the extent to which a grievance could be pressed by strike action was very limited. Take, for example the experiences of labourers working at Dunkirk. On 22 May 1917, when 1,925 men of Nos. 75 and 76 companies, Egyptian Labour Corps (ELC), employed as stevedores in the docks, secured an increase in their bread rations after threatening to strike. Six days later, after more than two dozen were killed or wounded by an enemy air raid, they protested about the hazards of being billetted in an area that was an enemy target and demanded to be moved elsewhere. Again, their collective efforts enjoyed a measure of success, as sandbag walls were erected to protect their dormitory tents. However, instead of being re-located, they were surrounded by armed guards mounted over their camp to prevent 'panics' during air raids, such as occurred on 30 May after a siren warned about the approach of enemy bombers.[11]

Finally, after suffering two successive nights' bombing, the Egyptians refused to spend the night in camp. They armed themselves with sticks and stones, frightened away their officers and tried to seek sanctuary in Dunkirk, only to be driven off at bayonet point after a volley had been fired over their heads by a mixed force of British and French guards. Though none of the labourers was injured, their direct action over what was essentially a health and safety issue finally persuaded the Base Commandant to permit the labourers to spend the night outside the camp, huddled in sand dunes. In early June, the Egyptians were evacuated from Boulogne and sent to the relatively less dangerous ports of Le Havre and Rouen.[12]

Their work at Dunkirk was taken over by labourers from Nos. 17, 20 and 22 Chinese Labour Corps (CLC). Unlike the largely illiterate *fellahin* who had been drafted into the ELC, the Chinese included skilled artisans, factory workers, medical auxilaries (dressers) and interpreters, all well able to negotiate improvements in their rations. Their commanding officer was informed that there was no guarantee that the Chinese would work unless a recent cut in their supply of rice was revoked. The men gained a partial restoration of the ration but the immediate sequel revealed that their unanimity was fragile. A large scale brawl, the cause of which remains unknown, broke out between the men of No.11 and No. 20 companies, ending with a newly erected camp being demolished and armed guards being employed to halt the fighting.[13]

However, at the beginning of September their former solidarity was restored following two consecutive nights of enemy bombing which caused twenty-three Chinese casualties. The Deputy Assistant Director of Labour attempted to mollify the frightened and angry men by suggesting to the Base Commandant that dugouts be provided for their use as air raid shelters but it was too late. At least half of the 4,300 Chinese labourers left their camps and settled in dykes and ditches in the countryside west of St. Pol. Initially, they carried on working on the wharves and simply slept outside their camps at night but on 3 September, after heavy bombing killed or injured four Chinese and damaged the docks and part of the town, they escalated their action and refused either to work or return to camp.[14]

On 4 September, Major R.I. Purdon, the second-in-command of the CLC, arrived to confer with all the gangers. For a number of reasons, his negotiating position was weak, even though he could use force to compel the men to resume work. The legal status of the labourers was complicated because they had been hired by the British Emigration Bureau rather than the Government and were not soldiers, even though China had declared support for the Allies and entered the war on 14 August.

Customarily subjected to the disciplinary provisions of the British Army Act, the labourers, who were initially reported to be 'well behaved, except for refusing to work', were mutineers, but their contracts stipulated that they were not to be employed in dangerous zones such as Dunkirk had become.[15] Yet their labour was urgently needed to discharge cargoes from ships already at the dockside and others whose arrival was imminent. Nor was it likely, after the shooting episode involving the ELC during May, that Dunkirk's townsfolk would tolerate the Chinese being replaced black labourers, whether they originated from Egypt or South Africa.

By promising that the men's safety would be enhanced by the provision of secure air raid dugouts and that their camps would be moved to a safer location, Purdon managed to persuade four hundred labourers to resume work. A move away from Dunkirk on the grounds that it was in a dangerous zone was ruled out, for enemy air raids had similarly affected other docks and bases.[16]

Purdon appears to have been optimistic about the prospects of the remainder following the example of the four hundred. However, the latter were reported to be causing a public nuisance by damaging civilian property and housebreaking (presumably in search of food and shelter) in the Fourth Army area. Nevertheless, by dispersing the CLC into smaller groups in different locations and erecting air raid shelters in camps and docks, further CLC casualties from continued heavy bombing were avoided, and this encouraged all except six labourers to return to work by 22 September.[17]

The air raids that provoked the withdrawal of labour at Dunkirk also affected Nos. 73 and 78 companies, ELC, employed in Boulogne. After heavy bombing on 4 and 5 September, 1,300 Egyptians went on strike, asserting that they had served out the duration of their six-month contracts. Demanding to be sent back to Egypt, they also declared that had been upset by the air raid, and were disenchanted by the cold, wet weather.

Following earlier practice, the Assistant Director of Labour summoned the Egyptian Adviser, Lt.Col. Malcolm Coutts, to negotiate with the strikers. Coutts, formerly the Director of Stores, Prisons and Police in the Sudan, reported that the men adamantly refused to modify their sole demand. They had included in their calculation the time taken to travel and return to their home villages. Coutts, however, asserted that the six-months referred only to the time they spent in France.[18]

Colonel E.C. Wace, the Deputy Director of Labour, dealt brusquely with Coutts, insisting that the dispute was not a matter for negotiation but a disciplinary issue to be settled by force if the strike continued. Coutts relayed the ultimatum to the men on 6 September, and the camp was surrounded on three sides by a detachment of the garrison battalion. When the defiant strikers broke out of their camp, they were gunned down. The final casualty toll was twenty-three dead and twenty-four wounded. Thereafter, the Egyptians resumed work.[19]

The use of force at Boulogne and the accompanying death toll produced the bloodiest outcome of any mutiny that occurred in the BEF during the war. The order to employ force was issued by Wace but it was prompted chiefly by the necessity of supplying munitions and of the movement of men. Unlike Dunkirk, where construction materials and engineers' stores were imported, the tonnage discharged at Boulogne included fuel and roughly half the ordnance stores and a quarter of the ammunition required by the BEF. With the unprecedented artillery barrages then being discharged around Ypres, no interruption to the supply of shells would have been tolerated.[20]

More seriously from the authorities point of view, had news of the strike at Boulogne spread, then there was a possibility that other labourers who were being bombed, or whose contracts were ending, could copy the Egyptians' action. The Directorate of Labour would have had no alternative workforce immediately available that could be used to substitute for the strikers. All this might explain why the soldiers opened fire but does not readily account for the high number of casualties.

A clue about the latter may be gleaned from the personnel customarily included in a garrison battalion. They were composed of troops who were physically unsuitable for duty in combat units. Some were veteran combat troops but others were ill-versed in fire control, as may be deduced from a hospital report stating that the casualties of the Boulogne massacre included one soldier killed and three others who had been wounded by their own comrades' fire.

The use of force to break the strikes became an established routine. On 10 September, Egyptian Labourers at Rouen and Calais also went on strike, claiming that their contracts had ended. The base commandant suppressed the outbreak at Rouen without recourse to gunfire, but Coutts was harsher in dealing with the men of No. 74 Co. ELC at Calais. On 11 September, using a guard from the nearby reinforcement camp, he repeated the exercise he had supervised at Boulogne, ending the strike at Calais with a fusillade that killed four and wounded fifteen Egyptians.[21]

The manner in which these confrontations developed may be best appreciated from events that took place in Marseilles in mid-September. Although elements emerge that have much in common with other examples of labourers' collective bargaining, the ELC action at Camp Fournier in that city appears to be unusual in one key respect – the subsequent court martial and execution of No. 385 Mahmoud Mahomet Ahmed.

How 28-year old Ahmed came to join the Egyptian Labour Corps remains unknown. However the general means by which he and other Egyptian Labour Corps personnel were recruited, 'compulsory volunteering', was acknowledged to be 'shameful and corrupt' and akin to the hated *corvée*, a system of unpaid labour owed to their feudal lord by vassals.[22] On 31 March 1917, Ahmed's unit, No. 71 ELC was posted to Camp Fournier, where it was engaged in coaling ships. The closed camp system and use of the lash contained challenges from the labourers, but it was small wonder that the date at which their contract ended was of great importance to the labourers.

At 6 a.m. on Sunday, 16 September 1917, the five hundred men stockaded in Camp Fournier were seated on parade, awaiting orders to march off to carry out their allotted tasks outside the camp. Having heard a report on Wednesday 12 September that they were to be retained for the duration of the war, all the Egyptian labourers had persuaded their gangers to make representations to the commandant. The commandant had granted an interview with the gangers on the following Saturday. The commandant's response to the labourers' claim that they had fulfilled their contracts, and should therefore be transported back to Egypt, was brusquely communicated at 9 p.m. on Saturday evening. According to Ahmed, Acting Sergeant-Foreman Joseph A. Selek had told the labourers: 'You sons of dogs are to remain here as long as you are wanted.'[23]

The next morning, Lt. H.V. Diacono, the officer commanding No.71 Company, ordered No.5 gang to move off the work, when: 'Mahmoud Mahomed Ahmed started off a riot by shouting out in Arabic "Get up boys, make for the officers first", on which Lt. Turley tried to arrest him, but he and all the men on parade, except No.4 gang, rushed to their tents & armed themselves with sticks.'[24]

Diacono, Second Lieutenants S.B. Chapman and A.G. Turley, accompanied by Selek, pursued the exodus from the parade ground and managed to persuade six men to parade once more in front of their tents. However, Selek recalled: '[Ahmed] ran to his tent, took off his jacket, threw it at the door of the tent and then rushed in & got a stick & coming out struck me across the head. Lt. Diacono was with me then & the accused tried to strike him too, but I caught the blow on my arm. Lt. Chapman who was near pulled me away from the crowd.'[25]

Turley, Chapman and Selek then went away to get firearms as Ahmed and 100–150 labourers armed with sticks began to move out of their compound, going in the direction of Camp Fournier's officers' lines and a nearby French canteen. Acting Corporal Richard Obeid witnessed the men leave their compound within the camp, but he was intimidated by the labourers' threatening demeanour. He watched helplessly as Ahmed caught up with Turley: 'I saw 2nd Lieutenant Turley going towards his tent when Mahmoud Mahomed Ahmed came up from behind & struck him over the head a heavy two-handed blow with his stick which knocked him down saying at the same time "You dog of a Christian take that".'[26]

While Obeid helped to carry the unconscious Turley to hospital, Sergeant Selek was returning with a rifle and bayonet borrowed from the British rest camp. Selek later remembered: 'About half way to the depot office I met the accused who threatened me with his stick. I opened and shut the bolt of the rifle & seeing this he ran away. I then rushed through the crowd in order to get Lt. Diacono out of it but I couldn't find him. Then two men caught hold of my arms from behind & the accused managed to get the rifle from me. He then with others hit me several times with a stick.'[27]

Diacono had been hemmed in by the crowd, and witnessed the attack on Turley. The crowd then turned on Diacono and threatened to kill him but he was able to escape when the commandant, Captain Cairns, first arrived on the scene. Thereafter, Ahmed, armed with Selek's weapon, was witnessed 'exciting the men with violent language against officers and men & NCOs', 'challenging the officers to come out and fight' and inciting the men to destroy the surrounding fences and cut through the barbed wire.[28]

Around 6.30 a.m. British and Indian troops arrived, the labourers peacefully abandoned their protest and Ahmed handed over Selek's bayonet, rifle and a solitary round of ammunition to Captain Cairns. The labourers resumed work at Marseilles docks, supervised by five replacement NCOs and guarded by Indian troops. On 24 September, 121 of the labourers were shipped off to Taranto and the remainder were eventually shipped back to Egypt with the rebellious Nos. 76 and 78 companies on 17 November.[29]

The officers and NCOs identified Ahmed as the ringleader, and Ahmed was charged with striking a superior officer and conduct to the prejudice of military discipline, rather than mutiny. Defending himself at his Field General Court Martial on 28 September, Ahmed insisted the men would not have rebelled had they not heard from Selek and Yosri, a ganger, that they were to be retained beyond the time stipulated in their contracts.[30]

He was found guilty, and his sentence of execution was confirmed by Haig on 5 October. He was shot five days later at No.8 Rest Camp, Marseilles. While Ahmed had previously been lashed a couple of times for defying his superiors, it was recognised that he was not wholly to blame for the situation that had developed.[31] The contracts of employment, it was candidly admitted by Lt. Col. Coutts, had provoked unrest amongst the majority of

ELC companies in France. He complained that the contracts had been badly worded and never properly explained to the labourers and that: 'Not a single officer of the Egyptian Labour Corps who came to France was aware of the nature of the contract signed by their men. They had merely hazy notions about it.'[32]

Nor, in Coutts' opinion, did he have enough experienced officers, Arabic speaking or otherwise, to control the labourers. As for the NCOs: 'The majority… are utterly incapable of performing the duties expected of them. They have no military experience and are, for the most part, drawn from a class incapable of inspiring in, or commanding any respect from natives and others. They are mostly low class Europeans and refugee Jews with a sprinkling of Egyptians. Egyptians will not work for, or obey, this class of European; and Jews they utterly despise.'[33]

Unfortunately for Ahmed, the decision whether to confirm his sentence of death coincided with further acts of protest by labourers in Northern France. These involved separate actions by South African and Chinese labourers during October 1917. Discontent developed simultaneously in a number of separate SANLC companies. As with the Egyptian labourers, the immediate cause of unrest was to do with the expiry of the men's contracts.

The first contingent of SANLC men had left South Africa on 28 October, and arrived in France on 20 November 1916, having agreed to serve for a year from the date they left South Africa. By October 1917 many of the men considered their one-year contracts were close to expiry. Thus, on 12 October, men of Nos. 5, 6, 7 and 9 SANLC companies at Abancourt went on strike, insisting that it was time they were shipped home. Reference to the Foreign Office revealed that the protestors were correct, and the commandant conceded to No.7 Company that the SANLC men would not be expected to work after 18 October, the day their contracts ended. Simultaneously, brief strikes were reported by No.8 Company at Rouen and Basutos of No. 13 Company at No. 19 Labour Group, Saigneville (Abbeville).[34]

Given the endorsement of the men's claim by the Foreign Office, the fact that they were not soldiers and the likely increase in disruption if their prompt repatriation were not implemented, the army capitulated. Pending shipment home, contract-expired SANLC men were moved to a rest camp at Le Havre. GHQ also ordered that contract-expired SANLC men refusing to carry out work should not be forced to do so. However, the latter concession did not apply to more recent arrivals who still had time to serve.[35]

For the 8,000 SANLC labourers who remained in France, discipline remained harsh, particularly in relation to disputes over the labourers' length of service. For example, when SANLC men of No.8 Company went on strike at Rouen in November 1917, and sixteen were sentenced to two years' hard labour, the Staff Officer, SANLC, requested that 'the authority of the Adjutant General be sought for their retention in France to complete a fair portion of their sentences after their company had been repatriated. Considers this action necessary to put a stop to the increasing tendency to refuse to work evidenced by some coys. whose period of contract is nearing completion.'[36]

Unrest involving the Chinese labourers in Northern France persisted. In early 1917, the Director of Labour was informed of a serious shooting incident in the 4 Army area, in which five Chinese labourers were killed and fourteen wounded. Details are unclear, but an inquiry concluded that the disturbance, which had occurred on 10 October, was 'due to a lack of appreciation on the part of the Officer Commanding the Company of the standard of discipline to be maintained among his officers and British NCOs as regards the treatment of the Chinese labourers.'[37]

Again, on 16 December a 'serious disturbance', arising from bullying by British NCOs, was reported amongst No. 21 CLC at Fontinettes. The incident concluded with the armed guard opening fire, wounding nine and killing four Chinese and fatally wounding a Canadian soldier.

After a day's protest, a British infantry platoon forced the Chinese back to work but it was not until 23 December, after key protestors were jailed, that all further protest ceased. The affair coincided with a complaint from the Directorate of Labour to the Quartermaster General, about the desparate need for officers 'who have good experience and knowledge of the Chinese and their language' and problems arising from, 'undue familiarity between British NCOs and the Chinese.'[38]

However, officers' facility with spoken Chinese did not mean the camp regime was thereby liberalised. Corporal Fred Sayer, attached to No. 84 company CLC, recalled: 'We had three officers (Missionaries) who had no idea of the workings of the British Army or discipline. They were really tough, and had flogging as their one deterrent.'[39]

As for 'undue familiarity', Sayer added: 'The whole of the Chinese were treated as prisoners behind barbed wire and even when out on working parties were not allowed to visit shops or canteens. Some supplies were resold to Tommies working with them and this could spell trouble.'[40]

It was this form of 'undue familiarity' that caused labourers from No. 151 company to conspire to kill their Sergeant Major on Christmas Day, 1917. Captain J.C. Dunn reported that the NCO had been an extortioner and had flogged the men 'too heavily'. Dunn added that the sergeant, a 'half-caste', had been been thrashed until nearly dead and then shot. Efforts by their British officers to protect the NCO had been blocked by the labourers.[41]

Two hundred men from the Royal Welch Fusiliers turned out to round up some of the labourers, whom they found 'as quietly satisfied as men coming from a band of Hope Meeting' near Reninghelst. Others had fled, and were in the vicinity of 5 Corps HQ, Locre. Their fate was witnessed by Signaller David Doe, Royal Engineers, who had been looking forward to seeing a football match. Instead of enjoying the game, Doe saw the Chinese, who had broken out of their compound, armed with improvised cudgels, rush across the pitch, pursued by some artillerymen firing rifles. Doe and other spectators were ordered to grab their guns and shoot the Chinese. Doe recalled that eight were shot on the football ground and a further ninety-three were imprisoned after being hunted down.[42]

Even allowing for the murder of the NCOs and the more general exingencies of war, the officially sanctioned policy of annihilating protest by summary shootings had limits. These were pointed out to the Director of Labour by the

CLC organiser, Lt. Col. Fairfax, when the Locre shootings were taking place.[43] Much of what he had to say was not new, but now reports of the suffering of the labourers in the British press and Foreign Office demanded that reports be forwarded about the shooting of Egyptian and other coloured Labour units.[44] The response of the Director of Labour, Brig. General E Gibb, remains unknown, but within a few weeks he was replaced by Colonel E.G. Wace.

No policy directive was ever issued, but before Wace was appointed as the newly designated BEF Controller of Labour in early February 1918, the summary shooting of labourers ceased. Instead, troublesome individuals were charged with 'Conduct, disorder, or neglect to the prejudice of good order and military discipline', tried by field general courts martial and fined or imprisoned.[45] Chinese labourers were almost the last of the BEF to be repatriated after hostilities ended, but after March 1918 no more were sent from China to France.

India, 1919
Demobilising the forces after Germany was defeated was a lengthy and complex business. In India, the task began in November 1918 when five hundred soldiers 'capable of doing clerical work' were urgently requisitioned from Mesopotamia to assist the Indian Military Accounts Department at Poona. In order to curb delay and inconvenience for men being returned to Britain for demobilisation, the Indian authorities opted to process as much of the necessary paperwork before they embarked. The men drafted to carry out the clerical work were told that the work was not expected to take more than three to five months.[1]

However, the work of demobilisation of the Military Accounts Department at Poona did not even begin to accelerate until mid-December, when the War Office sanctioned the demobilisation of priority categories. This slow start in India and elsewhere was made worse by a transport crisis. The organisational aspect was partly solved by deferring the demobilisation of men from the Veterinary, Ordnance and Army Service Corps. The shortage of troopships to repatriate men from distant overseas garrisons was less easy to resolve. Worse still, there were simply not enough reinforcements immediately available to replace the troops who were being demobilised.[2]

The Army of India had substantial forces in the Middle East and East Africa but they could not be spared by those commands for return to India. Since white troops were not forthcoming from anywhere else, the Indian administration came to regard the war-weary troops in Mesopotamia as a reserve army.

These additional troops were also needed to combat seething discontent which had developed in India during the war. The population was angry about the military and economic price of the war; basic commodity and food prices had soared with devastating results for both the urban poor and landless peasantry. The wartime dislocation of sea and rail communication disrupted the distribution of fuel and food, causing acute hardship when the 1918 monsoon failed in many areas. Though famine was not universal, for tens of thousands of poor people nutrition levels declined from bare subsistence to starvation.[3]

Indian Muslims, especially in Calcutta and the Punjab, were alarmed that the total defeat of Turkey would destroy the temporal influence of Islam. Muslims made alliances with radical Hindus in sensitive provinces such as the Punjab. The Hindus were impatient for more political autonomy for India and agitated against the administration's decision to maintain oppressive war-time legislation, the so-called Rowlatt Acts.[4]

With the notable exception of the Gurkhas, the only troops on whom the Government of India could wholly rely were their British units, who numbered 77,208 all ranks. Not only was this force smaller than the pre-war establishment, it also included 15,186 'D' category troops, classed as non-effective for operational purposes. The majority of British troops were war service volunteers, including territorial and garrison battalions, sent to India as replacements for battalions of regulars who were shipped overseas to aid the wartime offensives.[5]

The authorities acknowledged that about 18,000 of these men had a priority claim for demobilisation but the overwhelming majority of British soldiers stationed in India wanted to be demobilised. Some wished to return to their families, or were disillusioned with army life. Above all, territorials and volunteers who had enlisted to serve on a duration-of-war basis were afraid that delayed demobilisation would jeopardise their chances of resuming or finding work on their return to Britain. They wrote letters home, and it was not long before the men's families, friends and local municipal organisations began to campaign for their return, a refrain echoed in the national press.[6] Politicians were now reminded that at the beginning of the war, when the territorials had volunteered to serve in India, Lord Kitchener had personally guaranteed that: 'The Wessex Division should be brought home before the end of the war, so that the men might resume their employment or get fresh employment before the great rush took place from the colours when the war was over.'[7]

The War Office tried to ease the swelling chorus of discontent by granting pay increases to the armies of occupation and soldiers stationed overseas. However, a pay rise did little to placate the men who remained in India and particularly troops who had survived the gruelling campaign in Mesopotamia.[8] February witnessed a couple of incidents, hinting that the disaffected Mesopotamia veterans were inclined to resort to direct action to remedy grievances.

The first involved Mesopotamian Inland Water Transport (MIWT) personnel, who had originally been part of a multinational force of skilled tradesmen and unskilled labourers based at Basrah. During the war, they had navigated the Tigris and Euphrates, crewing barges and supply vessels that formed part of the lines of communication. Many were granted priority for demobilisation because the Dominions had pressed for the speedy return of their personnel and also because the War Office had ordered the repatriation of all black soldiers from the British West Indies.

A report about British Hondurans of the British West Indies Regiment contained a brief resume about what happened while the MIWT men were in Bombay waiting for their troop ship: 'While there the men seemed to be particularly dissatisfied with having been called on to provide fatigue parties for carrying out work in certain camps which were occupied by European soldiers. During the time we were there… no Europeans came over to our camp to carry out any work in connection with the BWIR. At Deolali certain men were court-martialled for refusing to obey an order which emanated from the dissatisfaction in having to provide fatigues for Europeans stationed in other camps… On arrival at Bombay entraining to Deolali there were a number of Australian troops present. The cars in which the troops were to be conveyed had a very high odour and did not appear to be suited for the purpose. The Australians kicked and refused to go in these cars and the BWI followed. A greater number of cars were put on so that the men agreed to enter them and were conveyed to Deolali.'[9]

The second, more sustained incident involved the thousand war service volunteers of 8 Bn. Welsh Regiment and five hundred garrison troops from India shipped back to Britain on *SS Khiva*. The *Khiva* had been at sea only four days when the fatigue parties went on strike because rations had been cut. When the vessel reached Marseilles, the soldiers overpowered the guard, and went ashore, all efforts by the Quartermaster having failed to control them. They were ordered to vacate that part of the ship reserved for civilian passengers, but they taunted their officers with cries of 'Who's on top now! Tommy. Damn all the Officers and Sergeants. They don't count now.'

Before the *Khiva* left Marseilles, the men had beaten up one of the sergeants, extracted a promise from the Officer Commanding troops on board that rations would improve and forced him to grant shore leave. By the time *Khiva* docked at Gibraltar, the NCOs had also mutinied. Although the Quartermaster of the *Khiva* blamed the insubordination on supine ship's officers and inept embarkation planning at Bombay, it was apparent that the troops were in no mood to put up with military discipline on their journey home.[10]

The Army of India did not attach much importance to these incidents, probably because neither the actions of the MIWT men nor the Khiva incident were particularly uncommon during early 1919. However, in March 1919 the *Bombay Chronicle* published a series of bitterly critical letters from anonymous British territorials awaiting demobilisation in nearby Poona.

One complained: 'The whole scheme as outlined by the Government was one huge bluff from start to finish. If the shortage of transport is the difficulty how is it that papers continue to publish long lists of passengers going home? What prior claim has the civilian over the soldier? None that I can see… For some reason the Government wants to keep us here until October. They say there is some danger to our health in taking us through the tropics in hot weather. Did they say this when they wanted us for gun fodder? No!… I think that if we are not guaranteed to be taken home during say April, May, June, July or August, we express our disappointment in the only way left to us, namely come out on strike on the 11th of May.'[11]

The newspaper's editor, Benjamin Horniman was deported to Britain, and the authorities, worried about unrest by these men, prepared to reduce the garrison of India to 53,000 rather than halt demobilisation altogether.[12] It was a risky decision because the War Office had warned that no drafts of reinforcement were scheduled to reach India until September, and also because of civil unrest.

Anti-Rowlatt Act protests spawned riots in major cities, property was destroyed and some Europeans were murdered. Counter-insurgency forces were over-stretched, and brutal measures were taken against protestors. British control over Northern India was jeopardised after Indian troops commanded by Brigadier General R.B. Dyer massacred hundreds of unarmed civilian demonstrators attending a protest meeting in Amritsar on 13 April.[13] The authorities were cautious about the loyalty of Indian troops in coping with the civil disturbances that followed Dyer's action. The army preferred to employ white troops to suppress unrest but lacked enough reserves. Consequently, demobilisation of British troops was halted, including the disgruntled homeward bound drafts from Mesopotamia who were awaiting transshipment at Indian ports.[14]

On 14 April troops were told: 'The Commander-in-Chief regrets that he is compelled by a serious situation which has arisen in India to ask you to volunteer to remain temporarily in India for a period not exceeding one month, or less if the situation admits of it.'[15]

The following day, C-in-C of the Army in India, Sir Charles Monro informed the War Office that all troops, 'including details from Mesopotamia' at Deolali, had 'volunteered unconditionally.' General Officer Commanding (GOC) Southern Command (Poona), General C.A. Anderson, reported to Army Headquarters, India (AHQI) in Simla that around a third of the 'demobilisers' at Poona 'to prevent trouble with employers ask to be backed by an order,' and added that a few did not volunteer for urgent, but unspecified, personal reasons.[16]

The GOC Karachi reported that all but twenty of the 4,525 men under his command who were awaiting demobilisation had 'volunteered' to stay until the emergency was over. He told Monro that the twenty were refusing 'on compassionate grounds' and recommended that they 'should not be sent to England, as this would have a disastrous effect on the volunteers.' He suggested that they be 'employed elsewhere than Karachi'.[17]

Monro then ordered the Embarkation Officer at Bombay to deploy the transshipment drafts of demobilisees from Mesopotamia at the port to Deolali, Bangalore and Secunderabad.[18] It was intended that these men and those at Karachi would be drafted into composite Special Service infantry battalions. However, the men objected to being classed as volunteers.

From Bombay, and other locations, 'volunteers' protested. At Karachi a communique was issued by a committee of other ranks and forwarded to the British press. The text insisted that the authorities had lied about the availability of homeward bound ships, and insisted that neither they nor the men at Deolali had volunteered to remain in India. The communique added: 'A large number of men here have positions awaiting them in England, and that their families have been since 1914–15 drawing regular allowances from their firms. That these firms now demand their services and have, in many cases, written expressing surprise that they have not been demobilised… We are, and we intend to be still, loyal subjects of His Majesty, but we mistrust the civil and military administration of India, and will not be loyal to such a corrupted system. Moreover we don't respect or esteem the civilian population of India, and considering their pitiful war record we do not see why we should protect them. Mesopotamian Soldiers Committee, Karachi.'[19]

The Special Service battalion at Calcutta was similarly disgruntled, and at Deolali Camp the local Brigade Commander, General Anderson, recommended that Brigadier General Owen Wolley-Dod, a senior staff officer, be authorised to convene courts martial because of 'socialistic ideas and a lack of discipline.' Before matters deteriorated further, a lull in the civil unrest conveniently allowed Monro to announce that demobilisation would resume on 10 May.[20]

However, British troops were warned: 'During the recent disturbances agitators have spread rumours of dissension amongst British Troops with a view to persuade [the] ignorant and excitable Indian population that they may with impunity defy law and order. [The] situation in India though much improved is not yet nearly normal. In order that despatch to the United Kingdom… may proceed steadily without delay, it is essential that no foundation for such rumours be furnished to [the] Indian agitator class, who are very observant and watch closely the attitude of British troops.'[21]

The day after Monro's caution was circulated, Afghan troops crossed the North-West Frontier, declared a *jihad* against the British and called on Indian Muslims to rise in revolt. However, even this incident, which developed into the Third Afghan War, was not sufficient to divert attention from the impression that AHQI had been forced to resume shipping because of collective action by the rank and file. Worse still, men awaiting demobilisation became rightly suspicious that they might be temporarily drafted to fight the Afghans. Matters swiftly came to a head.

In order to obtain enough badly needed lorry drivers, the authorities capitalised on a minor deciphering problem in the text of a telegram which had been sent by the War Office. The telegram initially ordered Simla to retain all demobilisable troops, 'except RASC, invalids, and IWT'. AHQI relayed the order to the troops in India with the addendum, 'other than motor transport'.[22]

When the amended telegram was circulated on 12 May, three-quarters of the 800 Royal Army Service Corps (RASC) troops stationed at Karachi immediately went on strike. Anderson suggested making an example of the strikers by jailing them and deporting them to Britain. The RASC men responded by demanding to know whether the War Office was aware of the predicament in which they were placed by the order. They insisted they had more than done their duty, and were still prepared to carry out fatigue duties at Karachi but flatly refused to entrain for the North-West Frontier.[23]

Army Headquarters' subterfuge was quickly exposed. The General Officer Commanding Karachi reported that the men's retention was dangerous, and that they should immediately be shipped back to Britain. Then the Royal Army Medical Corps soldiers at Poona went on strike, demanding immediate demobilisation. The authorities gave way to the RASC men but stated the War Office had not sanctioned the demobilisation of the RAMC and Ordnance troops.[24]

Again, Simla badgered the War Office to reinforce India with twenty battalions of British infantry and departmental troops. The drafts were urgently needed to relieve the demobilisation crisis, combat the Afghans and meet the threat of civil disorder.[25]

On 5 June the Viceroy forwarded to War Office a statistical summary of the situation. He stated the British forces serving in the Army of India totalled 62,625 all ranks, of whom 14,000 were totally unfit for active service and 2,500 were clerks employed by the Military Accounts Department in Poona. The Viceroy remarked that seven thousand of his force were being retained in India on the same basis as the troubled ex-Mesopotamia veterans – and it was these that AHQI relied on to provide the 1,700 men they needed for reinforcements, reserves and security duties.

The War Office response was blunt and disappointing – no reinforcements could be sent immediately. Yet again, orders were issued to suspend further demobilisation, other than for the repatriation of the RASC men who had refused duties at Karachi.[26]

Further trouble was reported on 6 July when the officer commanding Bombay, Major General Sir Wyndham Knight, warned the Adjutant General, General Sir Havelock Hudson that some more troops would refuse to serve on the North-West frontier. The men concerned were No.6 Special Battalion, ex-Mesopotamia veterans then stationed at Deolali awaiting demobilisation. They were convinced the Army of intended them to be kept in India until April 1920.[27]

The Adjutant General blithely repeated well-worn assurances, and stated that British reinforcements would begin embarking for India at the end of August. It was no good. When No.6 Special Battalion were ordered to entrain, their kit remained unpacked in the barracks and the men refused to budge. They could not be coerced without news being picked up by Indian civilians.

Anderson warned: 'We have to deal with a class of men, which is very discontented and unable to see more than its own point of view; very different from the former class of soldier, and lacking in the old men's sense of discipline.'[28]

Major General Wyndham Knight and Brigadier General Owen Wolley-Dod were despatched to assist Anderson in dealing with the Deolali strike.

Unfortunately no reinforcements were expected to sail until July. Moreover, at Barbhan, further trouble was reported with 240 ex-Mesopotamia veterans, including men from the Queen's Regiment, 'giving trouble collectively, though individually they were quite respectful'. They were persuaded to entrain for Rawalpindi only after officers had given grovelling assurances about their treatment.[29]

At Deolali, the men of No.6 Special Battalion remained obdurate. On 8 July, after having failed yet again to persuade them to entrain for duty on the North-West frontier, Woolley-Dod told Knight: 'They stated that they were not in a mood to listen to the King himself…I paraded the battalion on the morning of the 8th instant and pointed out the serious position in which the men had placed themselves and that they had no grievances which had not been ventilated and replied to.

'Before dismissing the battalion I said that if any men had legitimate grievances which had not been redressed I was prepared to see him in the course of the morning. No men came forward… The mutiny, I believe the men call it passive resistance, has been carefully organised for some time past, and, although warrant and senior NCOs have not openly joined in the movement, and state that they are prepared to go wherever [they are] sent, I feel that some of them must be implicated.'[30]

Instead of parleying with Wolley-Dod, the men sent a written demand, saying they were aggrieved at the army's indifference to their plight. They wanted to go home and would not move other than to be shipped back to Britain.

The predicament in which Anderson, Knight and Wolley-Dod found themselves was analgous with that which had faced the GOC Karachi in April. However, there was one important difference at Deolali – there was no-one with whom the generals could negotiate on a face-to-face basis:

'So far all attempts to discover the instigations [sic] of the trouble have completely failed. The ringleaders keep themselves absolutely in the background and the secret is well kept. Their identity may eventually be disclosed by censorship. With the aid of cadres of the regular units here about 150 strong who are now under orders for embarkation together with about 50 Garrison Artillery cadres totalling 200 it would be possible to disarm the battalion. This number is very small to deal with possible developments and the pitting of Regulars against Territorials and New Army is of very doubtful advisability.'[31]

'Unfortunately on the 12th instant the English mail papers of the 20th June arrived here, giving three instances of collective disobedience amounting to mutiny, at home, by bodies of men ordered to embark for India, in which apparently the men got their own way. This news will have a very bad effect on the 6th Battalion here.'[32]

No sooner had this news reached Monro than intelligence reports suggested that a secret central organisation lay behind the soldiers' action. All senior commanders were ordered to monitor secretly the men's mail to see whether such an organisation could be detected, but no evidence of a conspiracy emerged from their efforts.[33]

On 15 July the Chief of the Indian General Staff, Lieutenant General Sir George Kirkpatrick, transmitted an offer to the Deolali mutineers. They were no longer expected to entrain for the North-West frontier, and from 24 July, ex-Mesopotamia veterans would be shipped out on a man-for-man basis as reinforcements from Britain arrived in India. If their strike persisisted, Kirkpatrick warned, those concerned would be put at the end of the queue for demobilisation.

Privately, Kirkpatrick had his attention drawn by the War Office to the men's terms of enlistment, which would have empowered him to retain them until April 1920. However, as he had already made plain to the Deolali men, he recognised the validity of their grievances and replied to the War Office's advice by drawing attention to the political dangers involved in an open confrontation with the mutineers.

General Anderson personally informed the mutineers of No.6 Special Battalion of Kirkpatrick's offer at a parade on the morning of 16 July. Anderson omitted to include Kirkpatrick's undertaking that No.6 Special Battalion was relieved of further obligation to be sent to the North-West Frontier, because 'its communication might accentuate the idea that men who want to go home have only to mutiny to ensure success'. Nevertheless, the mutineers responded by agreeing to obey orders again.[34]

From Rawalpindi, there then came news of another mutiny by ninety-four soldiers, all Mesopotamia veterans, part of a draft of artillerymen for the North-West Frontier. They were worried because there was no news about the arrival any new artillery drafts in India, and refused to move unless they were accorded the same priority for demobilisation as infantrymen. It was granted but the men's action at the military base depot supporting operations on the North West Frontier meant it would be difficult for the authorities to prevent news of their successful protest being broadcast to other units.[35]

When the authorities' concern was borne out, the ex-Mesopotamia veterans concerned were not disaffected soldiers, but ninety-seven RAMC officers attached to Northern Command. Their contracts having expired, the officers, all of whom were serving on the North-West Frontier, gave notice that they would go on strike on 3 August.

Army Headquarters were told: 'Disciplinary measures are no deterrent and some individuals have announced that in order to gain the publicity they seek they would welcome being cashiered.'

Aside from their rank, the bargaining power of the RAMC officers was impressive. Even had suitably skilled strike-breakers been available, they could have been recruited only from India's British Medical Officers, whose total strength ran to a mere six hundred. The Army capitulated immediately, all were given a pay rise and postings closer to the ports of embarkation were scheduled.[36]

From Baluchistan came news of a short-lived 'failure to parade' by men of No.17 Special Battalion who were worried about demobilisation, but otherwise August witnessed no further trouble.[37]

More generally, tension in India eased, the incidence of civil unrest declined, demobilisation was re-opened and, after protracted negotiations, a peace treaty with Afghanistan was concluded.

Throughout the month, the *Bombay Chronicle* published items that kept British soldiers informed of efforts being made on their behalf by well-wishers in Britain. In a survey of the British press news on 7 August it announced that 'numerous letters are appearing in the press protesting against the detention of territorials in India'. It also reported the heated debate about the soldiers' predicament, which was conducted in the House of Commons on 5 August. *The Bombay Chronicle* also took trouble to print full transcripts of official communiques from Simla regarding details of changes in demobilisation priority.[38]

Almost everything that was published in the *Bombay Chronicle*, except official communiques, was viewed as unwelcome by the authorities. However, one article, reported news of a development that may have had a considerable bearing on what was to develop in September at the British Base at Poona. In a letter from Nariman Lakdawala, readers' attention was drawn to the plight of long-suffering Indian sepoys languishing with various overseas expeditionary forces. Lakdawala unfavourably compared the sepoys 'still sticking on to their posts', to the complaining British Tommies, and pleaded for the return to India of the former.

His final paragraph told those British soldiers who did not already know about the Kantara Mutiny: 'Forty thousand British soldiers appointing their nominees held a conference at Kantara base (in Egypt) in April–May, 1919, where they passed a resolution to the effect that 1914–15 men must be sent back home at the end of May 1919, and that no excuse about the shortage of tonnage available will be accepted. In the meantime they refused to work, though continuing to draw rations, while their officers being without batmen had to do their own washing and prepare their own food.'[39]

Also contributing to a further rash of mutinies by the homesick British Army rank and file was the apparently pedestrian rate at which the resumed demobilisation proceeded. Demobilisation had been re-instituted on 26 July but by the end of August barely 4,600 of the 14,400 Mesopotamia veterans had been shipped out. Worse still, not one of the remaining 38,000 soldiers who were eligible for demobilisation had even been given an embarkation date.[40]

The authorities had planned to ship all the Mesopotamia veterans home by the third week in September. Thereafter, it was intended that demobilisation of the garrison and territorials could commence. However, these plans were restricted by the rate at which British reinforcements arrived in India. To alleviate soldiers' concern about being kept in India until 1920, Sir Charles Monro issued a press communique, assuring those awaiting demobilisation that the process would proceed apace, though on a 'man for man relief' basis. Somewhat ironically, given the Commander-in-Chief's motives, it provoked the most extensive and critical mutiny by the armed forces in India since 1857.[41]

On 16 September, when Monro's communique reached the Military Accounts Depot, Poona, it also listed dates on which various categories of troops eligible for demobilisation would be shipped home. In addition to enunciating the 'man for man relief' principle, it revealed that Mesopotamia veterans, of all departments and lengths of service, would be granted priority over garrison and territorial soldiers.

For the four hundred clerks of the Military Accounts Depot, the scrap of paper proved the ultimate provocation. The clerks had been drafted from various units to serve temporarily at the depot. They were alarmed that their continued absence from their original units might adversely affect their priority for demobilisation. They formed ranks and marched, four abreast, to the Poona Divisional Offices. When a colonel tried to halt their advance, they simply marched past his car, and continued until they finally arrived outside the office of the newly-appointed Divisional Commander, Major-General Nigel Woodyatt.

The following morning Woodyatt was browbeaten by the men's chief spokesman, a powerfully articulate sergeant who rapped the negotiating table with his knuckles and handed over an ultimatum written on a dirty piece of paper. Woodyatt was given eight hours to persuade army headquarters to restore demobilisation priority, otherwise the clerks intended to take further direct action.[42]

Also infuriated by Monro's press communique were the men of Poona's Signal Service Depot. They applied through their Commanding Officer for a meeting between their representatives and the Divisional Commander. The signallers' deputation met Woodyatt on the 19 September and they were, if anything, more angry than the clerks' representatives had been.

The signallers' 'practically mutinous' attitude had been further inflamed by the leisurely response made by Army Headquarters to the clerks' complaints, i.e.: 'The intention is that all shall go home, unless they prefer to remain, and the Military Accountant General would arrive at Poona on 26th September to consult with Generals Woodyatt and Anderson about the situation.'[43]

The signallers' deputation referred to the press communique as a 'challenge to the troops', and prefaced their negotiations by claiming that they were backed by troops at Kirkee. The deputation told Woodyatt they wanted matters settled by 22 September, and demanded: 'That all compassionate cases and all re-enlisted men who are due for furlough, should have sailed by September 30th; 1914 men by October 15th, 1915 men, including men over 37 by October 31st, men of first half of 1916, by 15th November, men of latter half of 1916 by 30 November; duration of war men by 31 December.'[44]

Forwarding the ultimatum to Simla, Anderson commented: 'In my opinion the only thing that will be of any use is [a] definite statement of much accelerated despatch. Recommend also urgent special allotment of compassionate cases up to about 200. In order that Indian Troops should not see mobs of British soldiers marching to insist on interviewing General Officers the only course open had been to receive deputations of representatives.'[45]

Anderson also explained that the signallers believed that men who had enlisted in 1915 were being held back. The ex-Mesopotamia veterans were bitter about having been retained, and retrained as signallers. Anderson explained that the men considered that they were no longer soldiers, and wanted to send a deputation to negotiate with the authorities in Simla.[46]

Hudson responded to Anderson's reports by denying knowledge of any 'broken promises' embodied in the press communique and repeated that the speed of demobilisation depended 'on the rate at which the War Office can despatch reliefs to India'. Priority was to be given to ex-Mesopotamia veterans, followed by compassionate cases and then territorials. The Adjutant General ended by threatening that anyone who caused further trouble would be relegated to the bottom of the demobilisation roster and transferred to units of the post-war army.[47]

Though he admonished the men, it is equally apparent that Hudson was chiding Anderson for his failure to control the troops of Southern Command: 'As regards men who consider themselves civilians these should be advised of the provisions of the Naval Military Service and Air Force Act of 1919 and warned that it is better for them not to compel us, by their unsoldierlike conduct to use the full powers of retention under that Act… Beginnings of indiscipline cannot be countenanced and care must be taken that recent conscripts who are last to go home do not utilise the genuine grievance of older soldiers to become ringleaders in unsubordinate conduct.'[48]

Anderson did not immediately communicate the gist of Hudson's views to the men at Poona. Instead, he persisted in his attempts to persuade Hudson to appreciate the gravity of the crisis in Southern Command.

He wired back: 'Information points to outside influence and funds. I must be in a position to say something before noon 22nd, I can only suggest that I be authorised to inform them that special ships will be taken up forthwith to accelerate the programme. Men's question asking to send deputation to Simla is one on which they lay great stress. Employment of force is most undesirable and other units insufficient even in they could be relied upon to use it.'[49]

Anderson lobbied the Governor of Bombay, Sir George Lloyd. It was a risky ploy for an army officer to try to outflank his superior officer by enlisting the aid of the second most powerful man in the Indian administration. But the Governor was impressed by Anderson's pessimistic estimate of the situation, Lloyd telegraphed the Viceroy, Lord Chelmsford: 'I think it right to inform you of this, for an insurrection or outbreak of mob violence on the part of white troops here would have consequences of the gravest character and we have no troops sufficient for coercive measures. A final and definite reply is demanded by the men by midday tomorrow.'[50]

Hudson made a further effort to encourage Anderson to use force to suppress the Poona protest. The latter refused to countenance such a move but reported that the men's temper had not cooled: 'The attitude of the men in quite respectful but uncompromisingly recalcitrant and in deadly earnest. They again demand to send to Simla a deputation of 15 from all units and state that unless this is sanctioned by Wednesday at 9 a.m. there will be a mass meeting of all troops at Poona and Kirkee… It would be impossible to control such a mass meeting and its probable action could not be gauged.'[51]

Hudson flatly refused to entertain the idea that a deputation of the men could be sent to Army Headquarters, concluding: 'If you think fit you may send an officer who is cognisant with your views.' When he heard that Anderson had enlisted Lloyd's aid, Hudson was furious. However, Lloyd's endorsement finally persuaded Monro to abandon the existing 'man for man' principle and immediately repatriate the men awaiting demobilisation at Bombay.

The Poona mutineers issued a further ultimatum, demanding to send representatives to Simla. Unless the authorities agreed, a mass meeting was scheduled to take place on Simla racecourse, followed by a public protest march. Handicapped by insufficient local military forces to suppress the outbreak, Lloyd identified four options: '(1) That coercion be used to quell the mutiny and troops sent promptly to quell the same, or (2) to take the risk that the men are bluffing and will not in fact act up to their threats, or (3) to meet the men's demands and give [an] early and definite fixed date of sailing, or (4) to allow men's deputation to leave for Simla at once.'

He dismissed (1) as unthinkable ('example to Indians would be serious'); (2) was too risky. He favoured (3), but felt it was impossible to fulfil. After exploring the situation fully with Anderson, Lloyd commended (4) to the Viceroy and the mutineers were subsequently told the Army agreed to negotiate with their representatives at Simla.[52]

When the twenty-five delegates eventually arrived at Simla on 24 October they were chaperoned by four officers from Deolali and Poona. The officers comprised: Lieutenant Donald, MAD; Major Ball, Deolali Camp; Major Sweet, Indian Medical Service; Major Morse, Poona Signal Service Depot. The party was greeted by a small group of British India's most senior military officers. The latter were headed by Monro, Hudson and the Director of Demobilisation, Brigadier General Dennis Deane. Also present were Brigadier General Herbert Browne and Lieutenant Colonel Sir Charles Miles.[53]

Monro formally welcomed the delegates with a brief placatory address and departed. After preliminary verbal sparring with the delegation leader, Sergeant Bowker, Hudson agreed that the men should present their case first.

Hudson had then intended to hand over responsibility for negotiating on behalf of the Army to his subordinate, Brigadier-General Deane. However, the Adjutant General's exit from the proceedings was checked when Bowker unexpectedly took up Hudson's casually expressed offer to remain present. Hudson remained to witness Bowker and Deane quickly agree a seven-point agenda for immediate discussion.[54]

The agenda took the form of a series of questions abstracted from an original list of fourteen grievances made up from demands raised by men of various disaffected units: 'Why did the approximate programme of despatches home, issued as a communique on the 16th September, apparently fall short of the promise of the Secretary of State for War, published in India Army Order No. 68S of 1919?... What is the present programme for the Demobilisation of British troops?... Why cannot exact dates be fixed, by which the last man of each category will have left the country?... Why are civilians going home in airy cabins, while demobilizable soldiers are still detained in India?... Why are Territorials in some cases going home as units and does this hot weather give them an unfair advantage over 1915 men?... Can all 'duration of war' men, or conscript soldiers be sent home by 31st December 1919?... Why are certain individuals, who are apprently doing no useful work in India, retained though they have jobs waiting for them, either at home or in India itself?'

Bowker's opening remarks sketched the origins of the disaffection and reported that the men of Poona and Kirkee would 'keep quiet' pending the outcome of negotiations at Simla. Acknowledging that the delegation was akin to a 'safety valve', Bowker warned: 'While they were reasonable creatures themselves, there were others who were not. Speaking for the Signal Service Depot, one man went down from their Committee because he considered their views were not strong enough. He was for violence out and out, plundering, looting, and burning... Whilst the delegation were at Simla, the men had given their loyal promise that they would keep quiet, but it behoved the Authorities to press forward the matter.'[55]

Though Bowker depicted the delegates as moderate, he ensured that Hudson was left in no doubt about their motives and determination: 'It might be thought strange that men who had conformed to the rules of the military for so long should at last decide to protest. They knew they were pawns in the game, but it must be remembered, as in Chess, pawns were a very powerful combination when working together. They were not, as in Chess mere pawns of wood. They were human, sensitive creatures, and as such they had at least a love of home and kindred, which in the beginning of the war led them to great heights of patriotism, but if this love was going to be prevented from getting back to its object then it was likely to turn into very bitter hatred towards those responsible for their detention. They were men who had volunteered, and the conscription at present was a conscription of the very worst form, for it was keeping men who had volunteered to put themselves into the military hands.'[56]

Bowker considered that distrust of the authorities originated with the scandalous indifference to sick and wounded soldiers in wartime Mesopotamia, and fumed about the sorry litany of official excuses over contemporary demobilisation delays. He warned that if the men's dissatisfaction persisted, unrest would spread, 'and he thought they would agree it would be the death-knell of British prestige in India.' Bowker bluntly reminded the Adjutant General that this failure would attract press criticism, with editors demanding: 'Are we going to lose India through the dilatory methods of the authorities?'[57]

He briefly noted that the ex-Mesopotamia Expeditionary Force details in India had been sent home after their protest. Bowker then explained why the existing protest had been so forceful. If the dates of despatch embodied in the 16 September communique had been allowed to go unchallenged, then those drafts that it was intended should be shipped out in November would be unlikely to reach home before Christmas 1919. Worse still, there was an accompanying impression amongst employers that the men had actually volunteered to remain in India.

'What was India compared with their own country?' he enquired, adding that the men had read in the press about strikes in Britain, and concluded: 'Their place was at home looking after their people. Riots occurred in India. Riots were occurring in England and he considered that at such a time their place was at home.'[58]

Bowker fleshed out his address by presenting a few specific examples of the ways in which individual soldiers had been adversely affected by delayed demobilisation. He concluded that the men he represented wanted justice, and, if the authorities could meet the demands than they would leave India in a less bitter frame of mind.[59]

Bowker's address had been a tour de force, which stressed the responsibility of the army for the situation, but ended far less uncompromisingly than it had begun.

Hudson responded by congratulating Bowker on the 'straightforward and manly manner' in which the sergeant had presented the men's case. The Adjutant General alluded to the difficulties that confronted the Army of India in controlling the country and assured the delegation that they could be certain of a sympathetic response to every detail they wished to raise in the course of their negotiations. After repeatedly insisting that the authorities were doing their utmost to get them demobilised, Hudson departed and left Brigadier General Deane to continue negotiations.[60]

Deane began with a lengthy account of the background to the delays in demobilisation. He stressed army headquarters' genuine committment to accelerating the programme during August 1919, and produced copies of official telegrams to support his argument. The careful, conciliatory tone of the Director of Demobilisation contrasted sharply with Bowker's forceful delivery, but, unlike the latter, Deane was interrupted by his audience. The delegation expressed open disbelief at some of Deane's remarks, and demanded to know whether the officer responsible for publicising the 'volunteering lie' had been removed for his misdemeanour.[61]

The director had little difficulty in coping with such awkward interruptions, mainly because he had already declared that the army agreed to meet the delegation's demand concerning the shipping programme and would accelerate the schedule by a fortnight.[62]

When pressed for further details, Deane replied: 'It was no earthly use giving them the dates of the War Office list because they altered every day. Perhaps the first six or seven ships would be different in names and in dates.'[63]

This technique, of broadly conceding to the men's demands, was similarly employed when Deane came to address the final item on the day's agenda, which concerned the retention in India of men who had jobs waiting for them. Deane simply agreed to their immediate demobilisation, and blamed employers for failing to expedite the associated paperwork. Deane ended his contribution with a caveat. Though men eligible for demobilisation were all to be shipped home immediately, the law still rendered them liable for further retention until 30 April 1920.[64]

The delegates appear to have been pleased with the outcome of their efforts. However, analysis of what had been yielded by the Director of Demobilisation indicates that his apparent concessions amounted far less than outright capitulation to the mutineers' demands. Deane's negotiating strategy was to placate the delegates by focusing their attention on the prospect of being home by Christmas. He accomplished this by his bold initial concession. Thereafter, he avoided any detailed commitments to specific boats and dates by concentrating on the organisational process of demobilisation. The latter was accomplished by Deane's selective presentation of communications to do with shipping and transport to sustain delegates' attention.

Similarly, when agreeing to explore specific cases meriting compassionate consideration, Deane ultimately committed the army to little more than his personal undertaking to 'look into them at once'.

In fact the only material undertaking which appeared to have been made to the men amounted to a fortnight's acceleration in the existing programme for shipping troops back to Britain. More importantly, the delegates' evident satisfaction at hearing the news created an opportunity to counter allegations of widespread discontent in India's garrisons – even though Deane's blanket denial of dissent was supported by scant evidence, namely a solitary letter from the Regimental Sergeant Major, 8 Reserve Battalion, based at the 1/4th Somerset Light Infantry Depot at Bellary.[65]

On 6 October, when negotiations re-opened, in response to an earlier request from Bowker, Deane had drafted a communique for publication in the British press. It was intended to inform British employers of the situation that led to the retention of soldiers in India, and also satisfy the Poona mutineers of the integrity of the Army's intentions. Hudson had ordered Deane to ensure that the text would be worded in a manner that would cover the cases of all soldiers in India, rather than simply the men stationed at the delegates' garrisons.[66] For the Adjutant General, this had the advantage of diluting the significance of the Poona mutiny, and reinforced the impression that accelerated demobilisation had not been due to insubordination.

Bowker wanted the communique amended to include

both men wanting to be demobilised in England and those assured employment in India.[67] However, he was over-ruled by the remainder of the delegation who approved of Deane's draft communique. Classified as a 'Press Communique for Home Papers' and entitled 'Troops in India', it read: 'The Commander-in-Chief in India, Sir Charles Monro regrets that the statement which was made in April last to the effect that large numbers of troops in India eligible for demobilisation had volunteered to remain during the unrest then prevalent for as long as their services were required, has since been ascertained to be incorrect, as the men were anxious to return to their homes and employment.

As considerable apprehension still exists, the Commander-in-Chief would make clear the fact that from 8-5-19, all troops in India were compulsorily retained on instructions from Home Authorities. It is, however, anticipated that all Duration of War troops now in India will be demobilised very shortly, and employers and others are asked to see that the men are not unjustly treated, nor suffer unduly, through the previous unfortunate mistake.'[68]

Deane then turned his attention to answering a succession of questions from individual members of the delegation. The matters on which he was called to respond were numerous but included references to the clerks, Signal Service, and RAMC men stationed at Poona. Even allowing for some advance notice of the issues likely to be raised, Deane displayed his excellent grasp of various issues and was tactful in dealing with his interrogators. He also quite candid in his answers.

For example, he stated the reason why 147 ex-Mesopotamia drivers had been re-trained as signallers and detained since January was because there had been shortage of manpower. However, Deane openly admitted, their continued retention was beyond his comprehension. As for RAMC personnel, they were detained because of the general shortage of trained hospital staff.[69]

These explanations appear to have satisfied the delegation, who then resurrected concern about safeguarding their civilian employment. They wanted the War Office to take up individual cases in which civilian employers had used the delays to renege on pre-war promises that jobs would be held open for volunteers.

Discussion on this issue, about which Bowker seems to have realised Deane could advance no undertakings, was cut short when the former declared that: 'While the Deputation were satisfied that the authorities here were doing their utmost they did think the War Office might be hustled to send the reliefs out quicker.'[70]

Capitalising on this endorsement, Deane concentrated on assuring the delegation that the continued use of shipping for civilians would not impede the accelerated programme of demobilisation for the troops. At this, some of the bitterness felt by the delegation towards British civilians erupted. One anonymous delegate threatened Deane's emollient progress by commenting: 'Unless something was done to stop the civilian traffic there would be trouble. It must be stopped.'[71]

Deane replied by entreating the delegation to trust the authorities' judgement on the question of civilian shipping, when he was cut short by Major Ball, from Deolali Camp. Ball flatly asserted that Deolali could not cope with processing more than twenty to twenty-two thousand soldiers for demobilisation per month. In other words, it was not homeward-bound civilians, but military capacity, that restricted the rate at which men were demobilised.[72] Unlike the vexed issue of the extent to which the army's word was to be trusted, none of the delegates were disposed to challenge Ball's statistics.

The remaining points raised by Bowker and the delegation were speedily disposed of by Deane. The Director of Demobilisation promised them that the army would not hold them responsible for having denuded India of troops. Somewhat superfluously, Deane maintained, that the decision to accelerate the demobilisation programme had been the sole responsibility of the Commander-in-Chief. He added: 'If they were sailing home safely in a month's time and they heard that there was trouble anywhere, the only thing they would then regret would be that they did not set a good example in these last few weeks. Otherwise, they would know that they had played the game not only in 1914 and 1915 when the came forward and saved the British Empire, but also that in 1919 they were asked to 'run another lap' and they had saved the Indian Empire.'[73]

Thereafter the pace of negotiations flagged over the issue of leave for troops awaiting demobilisation. However, Deane swiftly pointed out that even Sir Charles Miles had enjoyed only one weekend off in four years and quashed further discussion.

The procedures entailed in dealing with compassionate cases were also raised but interrupted when Deane was unexpectedly called away to Hudson's office. He returned with a Reuter's telegram:

'Fifty motor lorries today conveyed 2nd Royal Fusiliers and baggage from Aldershot to Tilbury en route to India.'[74]

The news was proof, announced Deane, that the War Office was discharging its duties in spite of strikes in Britain. The positive effect on the delegation of this opportune news became immediately evident. The delegation raised the question of the authority of commanding officers to turn down compassionate cases.

Deane replied: 'Every soldier had the right to appeal to his G.O.C.... He thought the Deputation had shown they understood it by the way they had presented their own case. He was not altogether in favour of increasing the loop-hole for the doubtful compassionate case (hear, hear).'[75]

The Adjutant General returned as Deane ended his contribution to the negotiations with the ringing declaration: "No man would be kept back on the ground that his detention in India was essential.'[76]

It is not possible to estimate the extent to which Deane and his fellow-officers had prepared their negotiating strategy in advance. However, the manner in which Deane used his detailed knowledge of demobilisation to woo the delegation was very apparent. Well before the suspiciously opportune arrival of the Reuter's telegram, Deane, rather than Bowker, held the delegates' interest, and Deane's success in securing vocal endorsement from the delegation testified to his ability as a negotiator. He appeared to be sympathetic, eschewed rhetoric, patiently dealt with every question, and yet made no substantial concessions to the men.

Hudson's re-involvement in the negotiations provided a cue for Bowker to move a formal resolution that had almost certainly been written before the second day's negotiations began.

He thanked Hudson for the unique opportunity to meet with the General Staff and stated: 'This deputation is fully satisfied that everything will be done by the Military Authorities to carry out on general lines the programme demanded by the men. The deputation approve of the general pledge given by the Authorities and expresses its heartiest thanks for the consideration and treatment meted out to its members whilst in Simla, and for the manner in which unrestricted discussion has been allowed.'[77]

Hudson objected to 'demanded', and proposed that it be replaced by 'submitted'. Bowker bridled at the suggestion but was over-ruled by the remainder of the delegation and the Adjutant General's amendment was duly adopted.[78]

It was then Hudson's turn to deliver an extended valedictory address in which he rather ambiguously depicted the Government of India as being 'really in a position of a contractor of labour. He called it labour because it was nothing else. The Govt. of India paid the War Office every year so many million pounds for so many thousands of men.'

On a more personal note, he added 'It was their business to find the men and the Deputation would understand that there were big reasons why they should find the men for they knew the only thing that kept the country were the handful of white men out here.'

Echoing Bowker's opening remarks, Hudson maintained that the officers responsible for the wartime debacle in Mesopotamia had been purged. He blamed the press for depicting the generals as being stupid and insensitive in dealing with the men they commanded, assuring the delegation: 'Army Headquarters and the Government of India although they may have many faults, had not the fault of want of sympathy or want of touch.'.

The Commander-in-Chief joined the gathering to bid farewell: 'We have had our talk and I told you what it would be. It is always the case when Englishmen come together. They talk things over together. You have got commonsense and we have all got sympathy towards one another, and the whole thing arranges itself.'[79]

Bowker conceded that the delegation had all been pleasantly surprised at its reception and almost apologised for the forceful manner in which they had made its case. After an exchange of fulsome farewells the negotiations ended.[80]

Soon after the delegation returned to its depots; the unrest quietened down. Deane's promise was substantially fulfilled on 27 December when the last of the war service volunteers and conscripts from India disembarked at Southampton Docks.[81]

None of the protestors was court martialled, yet their behaviour could hardly have been construed as anything other than mutiny. Their reception, and personal involvement in negotiations by Monro, Hudson and Deane were the tangible fruits of the mutineers' earlier success at Poona and Kirkee.

Whether the outcome of the Simla negotiations may conversely be viewed as a defeat for the authorities is more complex. A week prior to the delegation's arrival in Simla, Lord Chelmsford had expressed superficially modest expectations of the talks: 'I hope that we shall be able to convince the members of the deputation and through them the troops out here that we are doing everything we can to get those due for demobilisation home with the least delay.'[82]

Were this the limit of what was at stake, then the outcome of the negotiations would have been a resounding success, but an affair in which Hudson had to be persuaded to take part. It was, after all, Lloyd's decision to intervene and involve the Viceroy in pressuring possibly Monro and indirectly Hudson to engage in discussions with the Poona mutineers. Lloyd was thus responsible for causing the Adjutant General to withdraw the inflexible policy he had ordered Anderson to adopt towards the Poona mutiny. It was also Lloyd's recommendation to see the men's delegation that was initially taken up by the Viceroy and later endorsed by the Secretary of State for India, Edwin Montagu.

On 7 November, Edwin Montagu informed Chelmsford: 'When men labour under a grievance, as these soldiers obviously did, they may express it in a very regrettable and perhaps in a very dangerous fashion; but what so often turns the scale, especially I should imagine with the British soldier of the New Armies, is the manner in which they find themselves treated. In this case the fact of their being allowed to come into some sort of personal touch with the remote authorities seems to have made all the difference, and Lloyd tells me that the trouble at Poona died down directly the Simla deputation was agreed to.'[83]

The 'remote authorities' to whom Montagu referred were Monro and Hudson. The Simla negotiations were, if not a defeat, at least a sharp reminder by the Viceroy that political priorities took precedence over military matters in British India. In persuading the army hierarchy to engage in face-to-face talks with the Poona mutineers, Anderson, Lloyd and the Viceroy demonstrated their intention to avoid a military crisis leading to civil unrest and possibly a further Amritsar-style massacre.

As for the mutineers, apart from their self-discipline and the consistency with which they pressed their case, it must be admitted that their delegates, particularly Sergeant Bowker, were intelligent and articulate. Their demands were well-drafted and although they lacked the organisational resources and experience of Deane, Bowker and his fellow-delegates acquitted themselves well at Simla. They carefully observed the etiquette of collective bargaining, opting to stress their patriotism, desire to return to their families and demanded consistency in their treatment by the army. They avoided any display of pleasure at staff officers' discomfiture, even though it must have been evident to some delegates that the Army had backed down. As a result they won the prospect of getting back to Britain by Christmas.

Notes

Introduction
1   Dallas & Gill, op. cit., pp. 122-3, 125-30, 164-5; A. Babington, *The Devil to Pay* (Leo Cooper, London, 1991).

Upwey, 1914
1   I.F.W. Beckett & K. Simpson, *A Nation at Arms*, (MUP, 1985), pp. 22–3, 32; Simkins, op. cit..
2   *Weymouth Telegram* 1.1.15.
3   ibid., 4.12.14; Dorchester Mail 4.12.14.
4   *Weymouth Telegram* 15.1.15.

Tidworth, 1915

1 Probably Park House Camp. See N.D.G. James, *Plain Soldiering* (Hobnob Press, Salisbury, 1987), p,59.
2 A.E. Henderson, Ms. memoirs, p. 37. IWM DOCS.
3 ibid., p. 38.
4 ibid.
5. bid.
6 *Gunfire*, 40, pp.49-50.

Blargies North Prison, 1916

1 Institute of Royal Engineers, Chatham, *Work under the Director of Works (France)*, (Mackay & Co., Chatham, 1924), ch. XXV. Captain A. Barker, Deputy Director of Military Prisons in the Field supervised Nos. 1 and 2 prisons, Blargies. His 60-strong staff, controlling circa 600 soldiers undergoing sentence, were the first to wear the distinctive red caps. G.D. Sheffield, op. cit., p.77.
2 ibid; Colonel C.C. Spencer, *Some Recollections of a Base Wallah* (unpub. Ms., 1933), pp. 41, 83, Papers of Major A. Stuart, Liddell Hart Centre (LHC), King's College, London University, Box 7.
3 No.1 diet consisted of, 'Bread and water for three days and compound diet of three days, alternately.' J.W. Graham, op. cit., p. 135. Conscientious objectors separately confirm brutal treatment e.g. Baxter, op. cit., chs. 6–7; *The Tribunal* 4.4.18. Provost staff are more sympathetically appraised in G. Sheffield, op. cit., pp. 80–1.
4 Evidence of Captain A. Barker, GCM of Gunner W.E. Lewis et al, WO 71/510.
5 A/Staff Sergeant S.V. Aves, ibid.
6 ibid.
7 Evidence of Gunner W.E. Lewis, ibid.; N. Boyack, *Behind the Lines* (Allen & Unwin, Wellington, 1989), p. 174.
8 Evidence of Pte. D. McCorkindale and Trooper A.G.Thom, ibid.
9 Lewis, op. cit..
10 Umfreville, op. cit..
11 ibid.
12 C.C. Spencer, op. cit. p.80; Specialist Sanitary Officer, Rouen Base, British Expeditionary Force, Lines of Communication (BEF L of C), *War Diary*, 18.8.16, 29.8.16, WO 95/4044.
13 Evidence of Pte. W. Peden, ibid.
14 (Recalled) evidence of Captain A. Barker. Evidence of A/Sgt. Major G. Gill; Sgt. S.V. Aves; Sgt. P. Currie, ibid.
15 The JAG was Lt. Col. T.G.P. Glynn, OC No.29 Infantry Base Depot (IBD), ibid.
16 The Prisoners' Friend, Capt, J. Lees, OC No. 4 IBD insisted that the disruptive conduct of the Australian prisoners was a major cause of the trouble.
17 *Christchurch Star* (NZ), 31.7.89; C. Pugsley, *On the Fringe of Hell* (Hodder & Stoughton, Auckland, 1991), p. 141. Pugsley, assisted by access to official papers denied Boyack (op. cit.) devotes a chapter to Braithwaite's case.
18 Evidence of Staff Sgt. F.E. Shearing, GCM of Pte. John Braithwaite, Judge Advocate General's Files, Director of Legal Services, HQ NZ Defence Forces (GCM Braithwaite).
19 Evidence of A/Sgt. G. Gill, ibid.
20 Composition of the Court, ibid.
21 Evidence of Pte. J. Braithwaite, ibid.
22 Statement of J. Braithwaite, ibid.
23 Boyack, op. cit., pp. 173, 175; Pugsley op. cit., pp. 144–5; *Wellington Evening Post* (NZ) 7.10.89; *NZ Listener* 14.10.89.
24 Clayton to DJAG, HQ, 16.10.16, 17.10.16., WO 71/510, op. cit..
25 Lewis, a 30 year old Scotsman, had served with 5 Division in France since 1914. For Braithwaite's personal details, see Boyack, op. cit.. pp. 172–3.
26 Courts martial of NZ soldiers increased by 25% in August 1916, Pugsley, op cit. p. 348. Australian soldiers in BEF military prisons proportionally outstripped British and other Imperial troops in September 1919, Military Prisons in the Field,. BEF, France. Showing number of men per thousand in prison. in Statistics, op. cit., India Office Library edition; L/MIL/17/5/2382; Dawnay to Robertson, 15.3.16 and encls., Field Marshal Sir W.Robertson Papers, Robertson 1/32/13/1–3, LHC. P. Charlton, *Pozieres* (Methuen Haynes, North Ryde, 1986), pp. 263–8.
27 BEF L of C, Commander Royal Engineers (CRE), Calais Base, *War Diary*, 20.11.16, 24.11.16, WO 95/4019.

Etaples Base, 1917

1. G. Dallas & D. Gill, *The Unknown Army* (Verso, London, 1985), p.66; J. Putkowski, 'Toplis, Etaples & the Monocled Mutineer', *Stand To!*, 18, Winter 1986, p. 8; M. Healy to Director, IWM, 21.3.85, IWM DOCS.
2 Etaples Base Commandant, *War Diary*, 9.9.17, WO 95/4027.
3 ibid.
4 C. C. Miller, 2 Inniskilling Fusiliers, Ms. memoirs, IWM DOCS.
5 Etaples Base Commandant, *War Diary*, op. cit, 10.9.17.
6 *Manchester Guardian* 18.2.30.
7 ibid.
8 Etaples Base Commandant, *War Diary*, op. cit., 11.9.17.
9 *Manchester Guardian*, 13.2.20.
10 ibid.
11 Etaples Base Commandant, *War Diary*, op. cit., 12.9.17.
12 ibid., 13.9.17.
13 ibid., 13–14.9.17; R.W. Thomas, Ms. diary, 14.9.17, IWM DOCS.
14 ibid., 15.9.17; R.W. Thomas, ibid., 15.9.17.
15 R.N. Gray, , Ms diary, 12.9.17, Gray Family Papers, Alexander Turnbull Library, Wellington, NZ , Ms Papers 4134, Folder 3.
16 Putkowski, *Stand To!* op. cit., pp. 6, 11.
17 M.I. Leared, Ms. memoirs, Sept. 1917, IWM DOCS.
18 W. Allison & J. Fairley, *The Monocled Mutineer* (Quartet Books, London, 1978).
19 Police Superintendent J.L. Cox to Chief Constable, Hants. 17.5.20, Proceedings: Rex vs P. Toplis & H. Fallows, Murder. Department of Public Prosecutions. PRO, DPP 1/62.
20 Collated from WO 213/17. Copy deposited with Musee Quentovic, Etaples-sur-Mer. For personal details about Pte. Short, see Putkowski & Sykes, op.cit., pp. 200-202.
21 Evidence of Capt. E.F. Wilkinson, 2/Lt. C.D. Thompson, 2/Lt. C.D. Critchlow, Sgt. E. Smith, Pte. H. Bilby, FGCM of Cpl. J.R. Short, WO 71/599.
22 Statement, J.R. Short, ibid.
23 Haig Diary, op. cit., 12.9.17, 23.9.17, op. cit.; A.J. Guy et al (eds.), *Military Miscellany 1* (Army Records Society, London, 1977), p. 388.
24 ibid.. Evidence of Capt. E.F. Wilkinson et al, op. cit., WO 71/599.
25 Intelligence Circular No.15, December 1917, pp. 1–5, PRO, AIR 1/720/36/1.
26 G. Pedroncini, *Les Mutineries de 1917* (Presses Universitaires, Paris,1967); L.V. Smith, *Between Mutiny and Obedience* (Princeton University Press, New Jersey, 1994); *Le Monde* 30–31.8.87; J.H. Cockfield, *With Snow on their Boots* (Macmillan, London, 1998).

The Labourers' revolt

1 A.G. 1 to C. in C., British Armies in France, 14.8.16, encl.: Conference to consider proposal that African native labour and Chinese labourers be employed in France, WO 32/11345; Chinese Labour from Wei-hai-wei, WO 107/37.
2 Report on the Work of Labour with the BEF during the War, pt. 2, WO 107/37. Infantrymen from the West Indies Regiment were excluded from combat in Europe and also used as labourers.
3 See memo: Kashi Nath, O.C. 3 Indian Labour Company, July 1917, *War Diary,* Director of Labour (DL), GHQ BEF, WO 95/83.
3 Dallas & Gill, op. cit., p. 85; WO 213/14, op. cit. p. 56; WO 95/83, op. cit., July 1917; Commandant, Dunkirk Base, *War Diary*, 28.5.17.
4 Haig Diary, 11.8.17, WO 256/21.
5 The Cape Coloured Corps, classed as soldiers, were not kept in closed compounds like the South African Native Labour Corps (SANLC). Appendix G, p.3; Appendix F, p.1, WO 107/37, op. cit..
6 With reference to SANLC, see A. Grundlingh, *Fighting their own War* (Ravan Press, Johannesburg, 1987), pp. 101-5; B.P. Willan, 'The South African Native Labour Contingent 1916–1918', *Journal of African History,* XIX, 1 (1978), p.72.
7 WO107/37, op. cit., p 40–1.
8 Historical narrative of the Works Directorate: Hospitals for Coloured Labour, p. 22, WO 161/2.
9 WO 107/73, op. cit, p. 41–3.
10 Commander Royal Engineers (CRE), Dieppe Base, *War Diary*, 21.7.17. Willan , op. cit., p. 79 and Grundlingh, op.cit., p. 113 refer to only one man, 'Charlie'. Director of Labour, GHQ BEF, *War Diary*, July 1917 intimates several men were arrested. Deputy Assistant Director of Medical Services, Dieppe Base, 23.7.17, WO 95/4023. *Haig Dairy*, 26.8.17, WO256/21. WO 213/16, op. cit., p. 151.
11 Deputy Assistant Director of Labour (DADL), Dunkirk Base, 22–3.5.17, 30.5.17, 4.6.17, WO 95/4025.
12 ibid
13 ibid., 16.6.17.
14 Base Commandant, Dunkirk Base, *War Diary*, 2–3.9.17.
15 DADL, Dunkirk Base, op. cit. 22.9.17. For details of CLC contractual issues, see M. Summerskill, *China on the Western Front,* (Summerskill, London, 1982), ch. 10.
16 WO 95/83 op. cit., 5.9.17.
17 ibid.; WO 95/4025, op. cit., 22.9.17.
18 WO 95/83, op. cit., 5.9.17.
19 ibid., September 1917, Annexure : Air Raid on Boulogne on night of 4 and 5 Sept. 1917, War Diary, No.2 Canadian Stationery Hospital, Outreau, 8.9.17, WO 95/4109.
20 A.M. Henniker, *Transportation on the Western Front* (HMSO, London, 1937), p.187.
21 WO 95/83, op. cit., 10.9.17. Commandant, Calais Base, *War Diary*, 10–12.9.17, WO 95/4018.
22 L. Grafftey-Smith, *Bright Levant* (London, J, Murray, 1970), p. 56; B. Carman & J. McPherson, *Bimbashi MacPherson* (BBC Publications, London, 1983), p. 162.
23 Evidence of A/Sergeant-Foreman Selek, FGCM of M.M. Ahmed, WO 71/600.
24 Evidence of Lt. H.V. Diacono, ibid.
25 Evidence of A/Sergeant-Foreman Selek, op. cit..
26 Evidence of A/Corporal-Foreman Richard Obeid, ibid.
27 Evidence of Lt. H.V. Diacono, op. cit..
28 Evidence of A/Corporal-Foreman Mahomed Yosri, ibid..
29 DADL, Marseilles Base, 16.9.17, WO 95/4040; WO 95/83, op. cit., 21.9.17.

30 Statement by Labourer M.M. Ahmed, WO 71/600, op. cit..
31 For 'insubordination' witnessed by Yosri, Ahmed was punished with fifteen lashes on 12.4.17. For 'causing a riot in camp' witnessed by 2/Lt. Turley, Ahmed got ten lashes on 31.5.17, ibid.
32 WO 107/73, op. cit., p. 35.
33 ibid., pp. 36-7.
34 Haig Diary, op. cit. 19.10.17, WO 256/23; WO 95/83, op.cit., 14.10.17, 16.10.17 and Summary, October 1917. R.R. Edgar, 'Lesotho and the First World War: Recruiting Resistance and the South African Native Labour Contingent', *Mohlomi*, iii, 1981, pp.94–108.
35 WO 95/83, op. cit., 18.10.17, 28.10.17, 8.11.17.
36 ibid., 28.10.17, 1.12.17.
37 Summary: October, 1917, op. cit., WO 95/83.
38 Haig Diary, op. cit., 23.12.17, WO 256/25. WO 95/4018, op. cit., 16-17.12.17, 21.12.17, 23.12.17.
39 F. Sayer (ed. W. Turner) *No Tea – No Workee!,* Western Front Association Bulletin, 25, October 1989, p. 15.
40 ibid., p. 17.
41 J.C. Dunn, *The War the Infantry knew* (King, London, 1938), pp. 426.
42 D. Doe, Ms. diary, 25.12.17, IWM DOCS. Commonwealth War Graves Commission Cemetary Register, Westoutre, reveals three labourers were killed in this incident.
43 Fairfax to Gibb, 25.12.17, WO 1971/33.
44 e.g. *Daily News,* 14.9.17; Pekin to FO, 23.2.18, File 191; FO to Pekin, 14.4.18, File 101, Chinese Labour Corps – recruitment and organisation – History of the Corps, WO 106/33.
45 Foreign Office (FO) to J. Jordan, 7.7.17, ibid.. Col. G.D. Gray to FO, 1.1.18, PRO FO371/3178/2699.

India, 1919

1 Telegraph (Tel.) 15248, Chief of the General Staff, Simla (COGS) to General Officer Commanding (GOC), Mesopotamia, 12.11.18. *War Diary,* Army Headquarters (AHQ), India Army Orders, India Office Records and Library (IORL), British Library, L/MIL/17/5/3074.
2 Tel. 102991, CinCI to Director-General, Army Medical Service, London, 7.12.18, L/MIL/17/5/3075; Tel. 97042, WO to Commander-in-Chief, India (CinCI), Delhi, 15.12.18, L/MIL/17/5/3075. Tel. 99302 WO to CinCI, Delhi, 17.1.19, L/MIL/17/5/3076.
3 Statistical Abstract Relating to British India, 1910-11 to 1919-20 (HMSO 1922), pp. 64-5, 67-9, 218-230; H. Tinker, 'India in the First World War and after' *Journal of Contemporary History,* 3, October 1968, pp. 8–107. R.J. Popplewell, *Intelligence and Imperial Defence* (Cass, London, 1995), pp. 297–8.
4 B.R. Nanda, *Gandhi, Pan-Islamism, Imperialism and Nationalism in India* (OUP, 1989) pp. 118, 204–5; A. Rumbold, *Watershed in India* (Athlone Press, London, 1979), pp. 135–8.
5 Tel. 15816 Viceroy, Army Department (VAD) to Secretary of State for India (SOSI), 1.3.19, L/MIL/17/5/3078. Tel. 24636 VAD to SOSI, 7.4.19, L/MIL/17/5/24636.
6 e.g. *Poole, Parkstone & East Dorset Herald,* 9.1.19, 23.1.19; *Daily Express* 21.1.19; *Dartmouth & South Hams Chronicle,* 24.1.19; *Bristol Gazette,* 25.1.19; *Streatham News,* 21.2.19.
7 *Bristol Gazette*, ibid; Tel. 19295, CinCI to WO, 15.3.19, L/MIL/17/5/3078. Tel. 22975, WO to SOSI, 29.3.19, L/MIL/17/5/3079.
8 Tel. 837, SOSI to VAD, Delhi 21.2.17, L/MIL/17/5/3077.
9 Belize: Report of Riot Commission, 1919, p. 294, PRO, CO 123/296/65766.
10 Report of entire lack of discipline on S.S. '*Khiva*', 24.3.19, pp. 1–2. C.T. Price Papers, IWM DOCS.
11 *Bombay Chronicle,* 18.3.19
12 L/MII/17/5/24636, op. cit..
13 M. O'Dwyer, *India as I knew It,* (Constable, London, 1925), ch. 17; R. Furneaux, *Massacre at Amritsar* (Allen & Unwin, London, 1963).
14 Tel. 26289, CinCI to WO, 14.4.19, L/MIL/17/5/3079.
15 Tel. 26239, AHQ, Simla to GOC Brigades, 14.4.19, ibid.
16 Tel. 26944, GOC, Southern Army, Poona (GOC SAP) to War Section, Simla, 16.4.19, ibid..
17 Tel. 27243, GOC, Karachi Bde. to War Section, Simla (WSS), 15.4.19, ibid..
18 Tel. 27814, QMG India, Simla to Embarkation Commandant, Bombay, 17.4.19, ibid..
19 Tel. 30578, GOC, Karachi Bde. and encl. to Adjutant General (AG), AHQ Simla, 23.4.19. Also, Tel. 30086 GOC SAP to AG, AHQ Simla, 25.4.19 and Tel. 29951, GOC SAP to WSS, 28.4.19, ibid..
20 Letter SB-22-14, GOC, Presidency Bde., Calcutta to General Staff, 8 Lucknow Division, 26.4.19; Tel. 30903, C-in-CI, Simla to WO, L/MIL/17/5/3080; Memo. 3107-5-A-1 Major General i.c. Admin, Southern Command to GOCs: 9 Div., Poona Div., Deolali, Bombay Bde., 7.5.19, ibid..
21 Tel. 30903, C-in-CI, Simla to WO, 1.5.19, ibid..
22 Tel. 12484, C-in-CI to WO, 5.5.19, European War, Secret Telegrams, series B, vol. X, WO33/978. Tel. 77807, WO to C-in-CI, Simla, 9.5.19; Tel. 15-9-31 GOC, Karachi,Bde., to WSS, 13.5.19; Tel. 291-3-GS GOC, Karachi Bde, to General Staff Southern Command, Poona, 13.5.19, L/MIL/17/5/3080.
23 Tel. 8159-63-A-1, GOC Southern Command, Poona (GOC SCP) to WSS, 12.5.19; Tel. 291-3-GS, GOC, Karachi Bde to GOC SCP, 13.5.19, L/MIL/17/5/3080.

24 Tel. 291-16-GS-1, GOC, Karachi Bde. to WSS, 17.5.19; Tel. 379-AG-9, WSS to GOC SCP, 17.5.19, ibid..
25 VAD to India Office (IO), 4.6.19, Confidential Telegrams 1919, L/MIL/3/2511.
26 Tel. 48414-AG. Mob-2-B, C-in-CI, Simla to WO, 11.6.19, L/MIL/17/5/3081.
27 Tel. 57729, GOC SCP to AG, Simla, 6.7.19, L/MIL/17/5/3082.
28 Tel. 57730, WS AHQ, Simla to GOC SCP, 6.7.19; Tel. 58799 C-in-CI, Simla to WO, 9.7.19, ibid.
29 Tel. 59749, GOC Northern Command, Muree to WSS, ibid..
30 Memo. 59958, GOC, Deolali to GOC Bde., Bombay, 12.7.19.
31 Tel. 60853, Anderson, Deolali to WS AHQ, Simla, 13.7.19.
32 ibid.
33 Tel. 60823, Chief of the General Staff (COGS), Simla to GOC, Northern & Southern Commands, Secunderabad Div & Bdes., 15.7.19; Tel. 61332, C-in-CI to WO, 16.7.19, ibid..
34 Tel. 60983, COGS, Simla to GOC Southern Command, Deolali, 15.7.19; Tel. D.A-4, Anderson, Deolali to WS, AHQ, Simla, 16.7.19; Tel. 61332, C-in-CI, Simla to WO, 16.7.19, ibid.
35 Tel. 06273-1-A-2, GOC Northern Command, Muree to WS AHQ, Simla, 27.7.19; CGS, Simla to GOC Northern Command, Muree, 28.7.19, ibid..
36 Tel. 68485, GOC, Northern Command, Muree to WSS, 6.8.19; Tel. 68338, C-in-CI to WO, 6.8.19; Tel. 06485, GOC Northern Command, Muree to WSS, 9.8.19; Tel. 3078, SOSI to VAD, 10.8.19; Tel. 10867, Army Dept., Simla to Military Secretary, Viceroy's Camp, 11.8.19; Tel, 70146, War Section, AHQ, Simla to GOC, North-West Frontier Force etc., India, 3.8.19, ibid.; Tel. 12812, CinC1 to WO, 7.8.19, WO 33/978.
37 Tel. 7734-30-27-AG, GOC Baluchistan, Quetta to AG, Simla, 23.8.19, ibid.
38 *Bombay Chronicle*, 2.8.19, 7.8.19, 26.8.19, 28.8.19.
39 ibid., 4.8.19.
40 Tel. 851, VAD, Simla to SOSI, 30.8.19, L/MIL/17/5/3084.
41 Tel. 9950 1.A.I, GOC SCP to AG in India, Simla, 19.9.19, ibid.
42 Tel. 646-X.A-1, GOC Division, Poona to AG in India, Simla, 18.9.19, ibid.; N. Woodyatt, *Under Ten Viceroys,* (London 1922), p. 272.
43 Tel. 028812-9-AG, AG in India, Simla to GOC, Div. Poona, 19.9.19, L/MIL/17/5/3084
44 Tel. 9950 2 AT, GOC SCP to AG in India, Simla, 19.9.19, ibid.
45 ibid.
46 ibid.
47 Tels.: 75235, 75293,75379, AG in India, Simla to GOC SCP, 20-21.9.19. ibid..
48 Tel. 75379, AG in India to GOC SCP, 21.9.19, ibid..
49 Tel. 9950-4-A1, GOC SCP to AG in India, Simla, 21.9.19, ibid.
50 Lloyd to Chelmsford, 21.9.19 in Tel. 494., SOSI to Viceroy, 14.10.19, IORL, Chelmsford Mss. Eur. E. 264/11.
51 Tel. 393, Governor, Bombay to Viceroy, 23.9.19, ibid.
52 ibid
53 Demobilisation (War 1914-1919), L/MIL/17/5/2382. Memo: Simla to I.O. London, 23.10.19, p. 1.
54 ibid., pp. 2-3, 23.
55 ibid., p. 4.
56 Ibid., p. 5.
57 ibid., p. 7.
58 ibid
59 ibid., p. 10.
60 ibid., pp. 10–13.
61 ibid., pp. 13–22.
62 ibid., p. 14.
63 ibid., p. 17.
64 ibid., p. 24.
65 ibid., p. 18.
66 ibid., p. 25.
67 ibid., p. 27.
68 ibid., p. 36.
69 ibid., pp. 29–31.
70 ibid., p. 37.
71 ibid., p. 39.
72 ibid., p. 40.
73 ibid.
74 ibid., p. 42.
75 ibid., p. 43.
76 ibid
77 ibid., p. 44.
78 ibid., p. 47.
79 ibid., p. 46.
80 ibid., p. 47.
81 Tel. 9950, GOC SCP to AG in India, Simla 15.10.19, L/MIL/3/2511, op. cit.; Tel. 13272, C-in-CI to WO, 27.12.19, WO 33/978, op. cit..
82 Chelmsford to Montagu, 25.9.19 Chelmsford Mss. Eur. E. 264, Vol. 5, p. 275.
83 Montagu to Chelmsford, 7.11.19, ibid., p. 141.

The JAG Registers: contents

Guidelines

The data has been tabulated in three ways and divided into sections: The first consists of all men who were charged with mutiny by the British Army, arranged alphabetically by surname. It also records the Public Record Office War Office file number, and the page on which the original entry was written. The second is arranged according to the military units with which the men were recorded as having served. The final section is a chronological arrangement, subdivided into cases tried at Home (i.e. in the United Kingdom) and Abroad. The lists in the last section contain a column of numbers which refer to notes at the end of each list. These notes are intended to assist further research into the mutinies.

The columns are arranged under the following headings, although the order changes in each list.

Reference: This is the reference number of the individual volume and the page on which the information was entered.

Name: This is the name of the man charged with mutiny. Most entries appear to accurately transcribe surnames and initials. In many cases they are more reliable than references that appear in other lists, e.g. WO 93/42 Nominal Roll of Courts Martial Proceedings of the Australian Forces.

Where a man has been awarded a Distinguished Conduct Medal (DCM) or a Military Medal (MM), it has been recorded next to his name.

Rank: This indicates the military rank, or or other title, such as 'Coolie' or 'Native Leader'.

Unit: This refers to the military formation with which the man was serving at the time of his court martial. Battle casualties during the war often led to soldiers being drafted into units, and sometimes corps, which were different to those in which they had originally enlisted. The disruptive effects of demobilising the wartime forces and post-war re-organisation could further complicate an individual soldier's military career. For example, Pte. Joseph Hawes, sentenced to death at Solon, India in June 1920 for his part in the mutiny of 1 Bn. Connaught Rangers, had originally enlisted in the 4 Bn. Royal Munster Fusiliers in January 1916. He served with 6 Bn. Royal Munster Fusiliers in the Middle East during the war and did not begin service with the Connaught Rangers until February 1919.

Date: This is the date when the trial took place. Most mutiny trials were concluded very speedily, especially during the war. For example, the trial of Pte. Jesse Short his role in the Etaples Mutiny could not have taken more than an hour. Sometimes, several dozen men could be tried simultaneously, and their cases disposed of in a single day. Other trials, especially those that took place after the war, might last several days. In the latter cases, the date recorded is the final day of the trial. Other lists, for example WO 93/45 Nominal Roll of Courts Martial of Canadian Forces (all Ranks) 1915-1919, sometimes record different dates. The variations may be explained by the difference between the date of a man's trial and the date on which the sentence was finally confirmed.

The time which elapsed between a mutiny and the courts martial of those respopnsible varied considerably. Some trials took place very quickly. Jesse Short, for example, was arrested at 9.30 p.m. on 10 September 1917, and court martialled the following morning. In other cases men were held in custody for several weeks. For example, a preliminary court of inquiry and a coroner's inquest held up the courts martial of Canadians who mutinied at Kinmel Park Camp in North Wales on 4–5 March 1919 until mid-April.

Offence: This is the charge of mutiny, along with additional charges, such as insubordination or disorderly conduct.

Finding /Punishment: In cases where men were charged with only one offence, the finding and punishment are simple enough to understand. In cases where men faced multiple charges involving mutiny on more than one occasion, or supplementary charges (e.g. disobedience), two sentences may be recorded.

Amendment: This column gives information of any revision to the original sentence.

Location: This gives the location of where the trial took place and may differ from where the offence occurred.

Abbreviations

The registers from which this information has been compiled were written by individuals with differing handwriting styles. Most entries are clearly written, but abbreviations tended to change depending on the writer. I have standardised some of them to make them easier to understand.

1 AM – Airman First Class
2 AM – Airman Second Class
3 AM – Airman Third Class
3 Clerk – Clerk Third Class
A/ – Acting (rank) e.g. A/Sgt. – Acting Sergeant
AASC – Australian Army Service Corps
Ab Regt – Alberta Regiment
Abs – Absent without leave
ABS – Army of the Black Sea
Acquit – Acquitted
AC/RFA – Ammunition Column, Royal Field Artillery
AIF – Australian Imperial Force
AL/Bdr – Acting Lance Bombardier
APM – Assistant Provost Marshal
ASC – Army Service Corps
ASC (SA) – Army Service Corps (South Africa/n)
A & SH – Argyll & Sutherland Highlanders
att – attached
Aus Lt Horse – Australian Light Horse
Aus Mining Coy – Australian Mining Company
Aus Prov Corps – Australian Provost Corps
Aus Sig Troop – Australian Signals Troop
Aust Siege Bty – Australian Siege Battery
Aus Tun Coy – Australian Tunnelling Company
Aust Lt Ry For Coy – Australian Light Railway Company
AWOL – Absent without official leave
Bde – Brigade
BEA – British East Africa
Beds – Bedfordshire Regiment
Bn – Battalion
Border – Border Regiment
Br – Breaking out of barracks or camp
Buffs – East Kent Regiment
BWI – British West Indies Regiment
CAHT – Cape Auxiliary Horse Transport (Corps)
Can – Canadian
Can AMC – Canadian Army Medical Corps
Can Eng - Candian Engineers
Can Engrs – Canadian Engineers
Can For Corps – Canadian Forestry Corps
Can IW Coy – Canadian Inland Waterway Company

Can MG Depot – Canadian Machine Gun (Corps) Depot
Can Mtd Rif – Canadian Mounted Rifles
Can Res Arty – Canadian Reserve Artillery
Can Res Cavy Regt – Canadian Reserve Cavalry Regiment
Can Rail Troops – Canadian Railway Troops
Can Ry Troops – Canadian Railway Troops
Cape Corps – Cape Corps (South African)
Capt – Captain
CARD – Canadian Artillery Remount Depot/Detachment
Causing M – Army Act section 7, para.1 (i.e. causing a mutiny)
Ch – Charge
Ches – Cheshire Regiment
Chinese Lab Corps – Chinese Labour Corps
CM – Army Act section 7, para.1 (i.e. causing a mutiny)
C of Lon Yeo – City of London Yeomanry
Comm – Commuted
Conn Rangers – Connaught Rangers
Coy – Company
Cpl – Corporal
DAC – Divisional Ammunition Column
DCLI – Duke of Cornwall's Light Infantry
Des – Desertion
Detn – Detention
DI – Discharged with ignominy
Disch Igmny – Discharged with ignominy
Dism – (Charge) Dismissed
Disob – Army Act Sec.9 (1) (i.e. showing wilful defiance of authority)
Disob (2) – Army Act Sec. 9 (2) (i.e. disobeying a lawful command)
Div Emp B – Divisional Employment Battalion
Dorsets – Dorsetshire Regiment
DOW – Duke of Wellington's (West Riding) Regiment
Dvr – Driver
dys – Days
(EA)DAC(TF) – East Anglian Divisional Ammunition Column, Territorial Force
E Comm LC – Eastern Command Labour Centre
EEF – Egyptian Expeditionary Force
Egyptian Lab Corps – Egyptian Labour Corps
E Lancs – East Lancashire Regiment
Endeavg M – Army Act section 7, para. 2 (i.e. endeavouring to persuade a person to join a mutiny)
EPM – Army Act section 7, para. 2 (i.e. endeavouring to persuade a person to join a mutiny)
Essex – Essex Regiment
F – Fine
F(arty) – Field Artillery
F of P – Forfeiture of privileges
Field – In the field
FP1 – Field Punishment No.1
FP2 – Field Punishment No.2
Gds – Guards
Glocs – Gloucestershire Regiment
Gloucester – Gloucestershire Regiment
Gn – Garrison
Gnr – Gunner
G of D – Guilty of Desertion
Gordons – Gordon Highlanders
Gordon H'ldrs – Gordon Highlanders
Hants – Hampshire Regiment
HL – Imprisonment with hard labour
HLI – Highland Light Infantry
How – Howitzer
ICC – Imperial Camel Corps
Imp – Imprisonment
Inf – Infantry
Inj pub property – Injuring (damaging) public property
Incit – Inciting
Innis Fus – Royal Inniskilling Fusiliers
Insol – Insolence, Army Act section 8, para.2 (i.e.using insubordinate language)
Insub – Insubordination
Irish Gds – Irish Guards
JM – Army Act section 7, para. 3 (i.e.joining in a mutiny)
Joining M – Army Act section 7, para. 3 (i.e.joining in a mutiny)
KAR – King's African Rifles
K Edw Horse – King Edward's Horse
KO Malta (Militia) – King's Own Malta Militia
KOR Lancs – King's Own Royal Lancaster Regiment
KOSB – King's Own Scottish Borderers
KOYLI – King's Own Yorkshire Light Infantry
KSLI – King's Shropshire Light Infantry
Lab – Labour
Lab Cps – Labour Corps
L/Cpl – Lance Corporal
L/Naik – Lance Naik (Lance Corporal, Indian Army)
Leics – Leicestershire Regiment
Leic – Leicestershire Regiment
Lincs – Lincolnshire Regiment
LN Lancs – Loyal North Lancashire Regiment

43

London – London Regiment
Losing Prop – Army Act section 24 (i.e. Negligently losing property or equipment)
Loss Property – Army Act section 24 (i.e. Negligently losing property or equipment)
L'pool – King's Liverpool Regiment
M – Mutiny
M(2) – Army Act section 7, para. 2 (i.e. persuading a person to join in a mutiny)
M(3a) – Army Act section 7 , 3(a) (i.e. joining in a mutiny)
Malay SG Bty – Malay States Guides (Artillery) Battery
Manch Regt – Manchester Regiment
Maur Lab Bn – Mauritius Labour Battalion
Mddx – Middlesex Regiment (Duke of Cambridge's Own)
MGC – Machine Gun Corps
MGB – Machine Gun Battery
mos – months
Munster Fus – Royal Munster Fusiliers
NC – Not Confirmed
NG – Not Guilty
Norfolk – Norfolk Regiment
North Fus – Northumberland Fusiliers
Not Sup – Army Act section 7, para. 3(b) (i.e. being present, not doing utmost to suppress mutiny)
NSM – Army Act section 7, para. 3(b) (i.e. being present, not doing utmost to suppress mutiny)
NREF – North Russian Expeditionary Force
NZEF – New Zealand Expeditionary Force
NZFA – New Zealand Field Artillery
OBLI – Oxfordshire & Buckinghamshire Light Infantry
Ont Regt – Ontario Regiment
Otago – Otago Rifles
Ox & Bucks LI – Oxfordshire & Buckinghamshire Light Infantry
Penin – Peninsula
Per – Persuading
Pnr – Pioneer/s
POW – Prisoner of war company
P of W Coy – Prisoner of war company
PPCLI – Princess Patricia's Canadian Light Infantry
PS – Penal servitude
Pte – Private
Quebec – Quebec Regiment
Quebec Regt – Quebec Regiment
RAF – Royal Air Force
RAMC – Royal Army Medical Corps
RAOC – Royal Army Ordnance Corps
RASC Royal Army Service Corps
R Berks – Royal Berkshire Regiment
RDC – Royal Defence Corps
R Dub Fus – Royal Dublin Fusiliers
RE – Royal Engineers
Reinf – Reinforcements
Rem – Remitted
Remit – Remitted
Repr – Reprimand
Resist – Resisting arrest

RFA – Royal Field Artillery
R Fus – Royal Fusiliers
RGA – Royal Garrison Artillery
RHGds – Royal Horse Guards
Rif Bde – Rifle Brigade
R Innis Fus – Royal Inniskilling Fusiliers
R Irish – Royal Irish Regiment
Royal Irish – Royal Irish Regiment
R Marines – Royal Marines
R Marine Lab Corps – Royal Marine Labour Corps
Rnks – Reduced to the ranks
R Scots – Royal Scots (Lothian Regiment)
R Sco Fus – Royal Scots Fusiliers
R Sussex TF – Royal Sussex Regiment, Territorial Force
R Wars – Royal Warwickshire Regiment
RWF – Royal Welsh Fusiliers
R W Fus – Royal Welsh Fusiliers
(S) – Service, i.e. war service
S5 – Army Act section 5 (i.e. offences in relation to the enemy not punishable by death)
S7(2) – Army Act section 7, para. 2 (i.e. seducing or persuading others to join in a mutiny)
S7(2b) – Army Act section 7, para.2b (i.e. persuading others to join in a mutiny)
S7(3) – Army Act section 7, para. 3 (i.e. joining in, being present, not doing utmost to suppress mutiny)
S9(1) – Army Act section 9, para.1 (i.e. showing wilful defiance of authority)
S10(3) – Army Act section 10, para.3, (i.e.resisting an escort)
S10(4) – Army Act section 10, para. 4 (i.e.breaking out of barracks, camp or quarters)
S40 – Army Act section 40 (i.e. act conduct, disorder or neglect, to the prejudice of good order)
S12 – Army Act section 12 (i.e. deserting or attempting to desert or persuading others to desert)
S22 – Army Act section 22 (i.e. escaping arrest or confinement)
S40 (2) – Army Act section 40 (2) (i.e. disorderly conduct)
S40 (3) – Army Act section 40 (3) (i.e. disorderly act)
S40 (4) – Army Act section 40 (4) (i.e. negligence to the prejudice of good discipline)
S41 – Army Act section 41 (i.e. serious civil offences, including treason, murder, manslaughter,or rape)
S40(6e) – Army Act section 40, para 6(e) (i.e.improper possession of a comrades' property)
SAASC – South African Army Service Corps
SANLC – South African Native Labour Contingent
SASC – South African Service Corps
Sco Rifs – Scottish Rifles (Cameronians)
Scot Rifles – Scottish Rifles (Cameronians)

Sea Hldrs – Seaforth Highlanders
SEF – Salonika Expeditionary Force
Sher Fstrs – Sherwood Foresters (Nottinghamshire & Derbyshire Regiment)
Slav-Brit Legion – Slavo-British Legion (North Russian Expeditionary Force)
SO – Senior Officer
S/Smith – Shoesmith
Sqdn – Squadron
S Staffs – South Staffordshire Regiment
St – Stoppage of pay
Stoppages – Stoppage of pay or privileges
Striking – Striking or threatening a superior officer
St/V – Striking or using violence to a superior officer
Suffolk – Suffolk Regiment
Susp – Suspended
SWBdrs – South Wales Borderers
Tank – Tank Corps
Thr – Army Act section 8, para. 2 (i.e.using threatening language to a superior officer)
TF – Territorial Force
TMB – Trench Mortar Battery
TR Bn – Training Reserve Battalion
TW – Transport Workers
Viol – Violence, striking or threatening a superior officer
Viol SO – Violence, striking or threatening a superior officer
yr – year
Welsh – Welsh Regiment
W India – West India Regiment
Wellington – Wellington Rifles (New Zealand)
Welsh H – Welsh Horse Yeomanry
West Yorks – West Yorkshire Regiment
Wilts – Wiltshire Regiment
Worc – Worcestershire Regiment
W Riding – Duke of Wellington's (West Riding) Regiment
Yorks – Yorkshire Regiment
York & Lanc – York & Lancaster Regiment
XO – Striking or offering violence to a superior officer
XOS – Striking or offering violence to a superior officer
* – The asterisk denotes a single item in the Finding/Punishment column that has subsequently been amended. See Amendment column.

Alphabetical list of men charged with mutiny

Name	Rank	Unit	Date D/M/Y	Location	Offence	Finding/Punishment	Amendment	PRO Reference File/Piece/Page
1968	Coolie	Chinese Lab Corps	09/05/18	Field	M+Striking	2 yrs HL		WO/213/22/50
25348	Coolie	Chinese Lab Corps	12/05/18	Field	M+Insub+Disob	6 mos HL	Quashed	WO/213/22/111
40749	Coolie	Chinese Lab Corps	09/05/18	Field	M+Striking	1 yr HL		WO/213/22/50
Abdalla Y	Labourer	Egyptian Lab Corps	06/09/17	Boulogne	M+S40	8 mos HL		WO/213/17/41
Aberman P	Pte	39 R Fus	23/08/19	Field EEF	M	5 yrs PS	Comm 1 yr HL	WO/213/31/24
Abrahams R	Gnr	RFA	24/03/19	Field	M	11 yrs PS	Quashed	WO/213/29/91
Acasha A	Labourer	Egyptian Lab Corps	06/09/17	Boulogne	M+S40	8 mos HL		WO/213/17/41
Ackling W	Pte	Can ASC	21/11/17	Bramshott	M+Insub(Lieut)	42 dys Detn	Remit 15 dys	WO/86/79/54
Adams A	Dvr	ASC (SA)	05/08/18	Field	M+S40	18 mos HL		WO/213/24/129
Adams EA	Pte	Quebec Regt	31/07/19	Ripon	M+S7(3b)	1 yr HL+Disch Ignmy		WO/86/88/51
Adendorf M	Dvr	ASC (SA)	05/08/18	Field	M+S40	9 mos HL		WO/213/24/129
Africa Louis	Native Leader	S ASC	31/01/16	Bissil BEA	M	2 yr HL		WO/213/8/132
Aggette F	Spr	RE	09/05/19	Field Italy	M	2 yrs HL	Remit 20 mos/ Quashed	WO/213/29/73
Agnew D	Pte	4 R Scots Greys	09/06/21	Edinburgh	M+V(A/RSM)	18 mos HL		WO/86/91/131
Ahmad [?]	L/Naik	Malay SG Bty	11/03/15	Singapore	M	3 yrs PS	Comm 2 yrs Imp	WO/213/4/17
Ahmad Sultan	Gnr	Malay SG Bty	11/03/15	Singapore	M	3 yrs PS +Disch Ignmy	Comm 18 mos Imp	WO/213/4/17
Ahmed R	Labourer	Egyptian Lab Corps	06/09/17	Boulogne	M+S40	8 mos HL		WO/213/17/41
Ainsworth C	L/Cpl	5 Dragoon Gds	29/09/19	Curragh	M	18 mos H	Comm 9 mos Detn	WO/92/4/83
Alcock MG	Pte	19 AIF	15/02/16	Sinai Penin	M+Disob	18 mos HL		WO/213/8/113
Alexander A	Pte	1 BWI	04/05/19	Field Italy	M	6 mos HL		WO/213/29/37
Alexander F	Dvr	69(EA)DAC(TF)	11/09/16	Killinghall Moor	Joining M	Acquit		WO/92/3/45
Ali A	Labourer	Egyptian Lab Corps	06/09/17	Boulogne	M+S40	8 mos HL		WO/213/17/41
Allam R	L/Bdr	RGA	04/07/19	Aldershot	M	9 mos Detn+Rnks +Disch Ignmy		WO/86/87/188
Allan D	Dvr	372 Coy CAHT	14/05/19	Field	M	5 yrs PS	Comm 1 yr HL	WO/213/30/12
Allcock A	Pte	1 Gn Sher Fstrs	05/06/17	Kantara Egypt	M	2 yrs HL		WO/213/15/176
Allen CH	Pte	5 Dragoon Gds	23/09/19	Curragh	M	84 dys HL	Comm 42 dys Detn	WO/92/4/85
Allen G	Gnr	RFA(att RGA)	13/03/18	Agra	M	1 yr HL	unexpired portion 30/4/18	WO/90/7/190
Allen GH	Gnr	337 Bde RFA	10/01/17	Canterbury	JM	6 mos Detn		WO/92/3/58
Allen J	Pte	2 W India	11/05/19	Field EEF	M	7 yrs PS	Comm 2 yrs HL	WO/213/30/28
Allen JG	Dvr/L/Bdr	RFA	12/05/18	Field	M	1 yr HL	Susp	WO/213/22/153
Allen N	Pte	4 BWI	27/12/18	Field Italy	M+Disob	3 yrs PS	Comm 2 yrs HL	WO/213/27/23
Allen W	Pte	2 W India	11/05/19	Field EEF	M	7 yrs PS	Comm 2 yrs HL	WO/213/30/28
Allmand E	Pte	1 Gn Sher Fstrs	05/06/17	Kantara Egypt	M	2 yrs HL		WO/213/15/176
Alsey A	Pte	3 Essex	09/05/19	Field Italy	M	3 yrs PS	Comm 4 mos HL	WO/213/29/73
Alyward AE	Cpl	1 Inf Bn AIF	15/10/18	Field	M+Des	10 yrs PS+Rnks	Guilty of Des	WO/213/28/180
Ambrose WJ	Pte	K Edw Horse	29/09/19	Curragh	M	1 yr HL+Disch Ignmy	Comm 6 mos	WO/92/4/82
Amey J	Pte	3 Dorsets	29/12/14	Dorchester	Joining M+Viol(Capt)	4 mos HL		WO/92/3/18
Anderson C	Pte	2 MGC	12/06/19	Field	M+Disob(2)+S40	5 yrs PS	Comm 2 yrs HL	WO/213/29/122
Anderson AG	Pte	19 AIF	15/02/16	Sinai Penin	M+Disob	18 mos HL		WO/213/8/113
Anderson EH	Pte	1 Inf Bn AIF	15/10/18	Field	M+Des	3 yrs PS	Guilty of Des	WO/213/28/200
Anderson H	Pte	2 W India	11/05/19	Field EEF	M	5 yrs PS	Comm 1 yr HL	WO/213/30/27
Anderson TG	Pte	25 AIF	24/03/19	Field	M	8 yrs PS		WO/213/29/89
Anderson W	Pte (AL/Cpl)	2/7 R Wars	04/01/19	Field	M	5 yrs PS		WO/213/28/72
Andrews R	Gnr	Can FA[arty]	24/03/19	Field	M	10 yrs PS		WO/213/29/89
Anley H	Pte	Quebec Regt	26/07/19	Ripon	M+S7(3b)+S40	6 mos Detn		WO/86/88/51
Anscombe J	Cpl	3 Dorsets	29/12/14	Dorchester	Joining M+Viol(Capt)	NG		WO/92/3/18
Antoine B	Pte	1 BWI	02/05/19	Field Italy	Mx2+Disob	18 mos HL	Remit 12 mos	WO/213/29/37
April	Pte	SANLC	21/11/17	Field	M+S40	3 yrs PS	Comm 2 yrs HL	WO/213/31/109
Apted A	Pte	2/4 R Sussex TF	23/07/15	Canterbury	JM	84 dys Detn		WO/92/3/20
Arcanthe L	Pte	Labour Bn	16/01/19	Mesopotamia	M	84 dys Detn		WO/90/7/169
Archer E	Pte	6 (S) BWI	24/12/18	Field Italy	M+Disob	3 yrs 6 mos PS		WO/213/27/24
Archibald F	Pte	2/4 R Sussex TF	23/07/15	Canterbury	JM	84 dys Detn		WO/92/3/20
Archie R	Pte	18(R) CEF	22/04/19	Liverpool	M	23 mos HL		WO/92/4/70

45

Name	Rank	Unit	Date D/M/Y	Location	Offence	Finding/Punishment	Amendment	PRO Reference File/Piece/Page
Arlow J	Dvr A/Bdr	234 Bty RFA	15/01/15	Cahir	M+S40+S10(3)	2 yrs HL+Disch Igmny		WO/86/63/137
Armitage E	Pte	9 MGC	09/01/19	Field	M+S40	28 dys x 2	Comm to 2 [dys?]	WO/213/27/200
Arnold G	Pte	71 Lab Coy	04/02/19	Rouen	M	Acquit		WO/90/8/58
Arnold J	Pte	1 Gn Sher Fstrs	05/06/17	Kantara Egypt	M	2 yrs HL		WO/213/15/176
Artemenko G	Pte	1 Slav-Brit Legion	14/07/19	Field NREF	M	NG		WO/213/32/59
Arthur H	Pte	2 R Irish	15/04/18	Field	M	5 yrs PS	Susp	WO/213/21/98
Arthurs E	Pte	5 Dragoon Gds	29/09/19	Curragh	M	1 yr HL+Disch Igmny	Comm 6 mos Detn	WO/92/4/82
Arundale L	Pte	30 MGC	29/07/19	Field	M+Disob	1 yr HL		WO/213/30/119
Arwin A	Pte	7 R Irish	15/04/18	Field	M	5 yrs PS	Susp	WO/213/21/97
Ashenden HE	Tpr(L/Cpl)	5 Aus Lt Horse	28/06/18	Field EEF	M	NG		WO/213/28/138
Aspinall HL	Pte	AASC	22/12/18	Field	M	NG		WO/213/27/184
Atkinson T	Pte	5 Dragoon Gds	29/09/19	Curragh	M	1 yr HL+Disch Igmny	Comm 6 mos Detn	WO/92/4/81
Atoff M	Pte	1 Inf Bn AIF	15/10/18	Field	M+Des	3 yrs PS	Guilty of Des	WO/213/28/199
Auguste A	Pte	Maur Lab Bn	10/05/18	Mespot	M(S7-2B)	3 mos FP1		WO/90/7/151
Austin GW	Pte	7/8 R Innis Fus	15/04/18	Field	M	5 yrs PS	Susp	WO/213/21/96
Austin HC	Pte	1 Inf Bn AIF	15/10/18	Field	M+Des	3 yrs PS	Guilty of Des	WO/213/28/199
Austin J	Pte (L/Cpl)	8 R I Fus	17/06/15	Tipperary	M	84 dys Detn		WO/86/65/77
Aylwin J	Pte	2/4 R Sussex TF	23/07/15	Canterbury	JM	84 dys Detn		WO/92/3/20
Ayres J	Pte	5 Dragoon Gds	29/09/19	Curragh	M	18 mos HL + Disch Igmny	Comm 9 mos Detn	WO/92/4/83
Baayes M	Pte	1 Cape Corps	20/01/19	Mustapha	M+Disob	5 yrs PS	Quashed	WO/213/28/61
Bade B	Pte	10 Hussars	25/01/21	Curragh	Mx2+S9(1)x2	1 yr Detn		WO/92/4/94
Bahit AS	Labourer	Egyptian Lab Corps	06/09/17	Boulogne	M+S40	8 mos HL		WO/213/17/41
Bailey A	Pte	2/4 R Sussex TF	23/07/15	Canterbury	JM	84 dys Detn		WO/92/3/21
Bailey J	Pte	6 KOR Lancs	13/09/15	Gallipoli	M	Death	Comm to 2 yrs HL	WO/213/5/79
Bailey J	Pte	RASC	20/04/20	Field ABS	M+Disob	3 mos FP2		WO/213/31/171
Baines CD	Pte	22 AIF	24/03/19	Field	M	10 yrs PS		WO/213/29/91
Bains VG	L/Bdr	RGA	04/07/19	Aldershot	M	9 mos Detn+Rnks +Disch Igmny		WO/86/87/188
Baker B	Pte	1 Inf Bn AIF	15/10/18	Field	M+Des	3 yrs PS	Guilty of Des	WO/213/28/197
Baker E	Pte	Can ASC	21/11/17	Bramshott	M+Insub(Lieut)	42 dys Detn	Remit 15 dys	WO/86/79/54
Baker HW	Pte	2/6 R Wars	23/01/19	Field	M+Abs+Br	14 dys FP1		WO/213/27/167
Baker NG	Sig	RFA	24/06/19	Field	M+Disob	1 yr HL		WO/213/29/137
Baldwin GE	Pte	17 AIF	24/03/19	Field	M	8 yrs PS		WO/213/29/91
Ball A	Pte	2 KOYLI	14/09/16	Abancourt	M+Insub	3 yrs PS		WO/213/11/31
Ball AT	Pte	2/4 R Sussex TF	23/07/15	Canterbury	JM	84 dys Detn		WO/92/3/20
Ball S	Pte	5 Dragoon Gds	30/09/19	Curragh	M	1 yr HL+Disch Igmny	Comm 6 mos Detn	WO/92/4/87
Balmbro T	Pte	8 KOYLI	10/02/19	Field	M+Disob+S40	10 yrs PS	Quashed	WO/213/28/54
Banbrough W	Pte	65 Coy RDC	21/11/16	Towcester	M	1 yr Detn		WO/92/4/3
Banks JL	Pte	2 Otago NZEF	01/09/17	Field	M	10 yrs PS		WO/213/17/110
Banwell WJ	Cpl	RGA	05/07/19	Aldershot	M	9 mos Detn+Rnks +Disch Igmny		WO/86/87/189
Barber SH	Pte	2 Gn/Beds	04/04/18	Karachi	M+S7(3)	Acquit		WO/90/7/191
Barclay AS	Pte	1 Inf Bn AIF	15/10/18	Field	M+Des	3 yrs PS	Guilty of Des	WO/213/28/197
Bardney R	Pte (L/Cpl)	1 Inf Bn AIF	15/10/18	Field	M+Des	8 yrs PS	Guilty of Des	WO/213/28/199
Barends K	Dvr	ASC (SA)	05/08/18	Field	M+S40	9 mos HL		WO/213/24/129
Barham R	Pte	7/8 R Innis Fus	15/04/18	Field	M	5 yrs PS	Susp	WO/213/21/96
Barker FW	Dvr	RFA	07/03/19	Field	Mx2	1 yr HL	Remit 3 mos	WO/213/29/12
Barker H	Pte	1 Gn Sher Fstrs	05/06/17	Kantara Egypt	M	2 yrs HL		WO/213/15/176
Barker H	Pte	2 MGC	12/06/19	Field	M+Disob(2)+S40	5 yrs PS	Comm 2 yrs HL	WO/213/29/122
Barker JA	Pte	10 Hussars	25/01/21	Curragh	Mx2+S9(1)x2	1 yr Detn	Remit 3 mos	WO/92/4/94
Barkin H	Pte	39 R Fus	23/08/19	Field EEF	M	5 yrs PS	Comm 1 yr HL	WO/213/31/24
Barlow J	Pte	Manch Regt	27/02/19	Field	M+Des	56 dys FP2	Remit 21 dys	WO/213/28/134
Barlow JH	Pte	RASC	20/02/19	Field	Mx2+S40	5 yrs PS		WO/213/28/169
Barnard G	Pte	2/4 R Sussex TF	23/07/15	Canterbury	JM	84 dys Detn		WO/92/3/20
Barnard J	Sgt	2/4 R Sussex TF	23/07/15	Canterbury	NSM	Redu to Cpl		WO/92/3/20
Barnes AG	Pte	26 R Fus	04/02/19	Rouen	M	90 dys Imp		WO/90/8/58
Barnes F	Pte	30 MGC	29/07/19	Field	M+Disob	1 yr HL		WO/213/30/119
Barnes WH	Pte	1 Inf Bn AIF	15/10/18	Field	M+Des	3 yrs PS	Guilty of Des	WO/213/28/196
Barnett A	Pte	1 Inf Bn AIF	15/10/18	Field	M+Des	3 yrs PS	Guilty of Des	WO/213/30/44
Baron A	Spr	101 Field Coy RE	27/03/19	Field Italy	M+Disob	5 yrs PS	Remit 2 yrs	WO/213/28/191
Baron JC	Gnr	RGA	13/03/18	Agra	M	1 yr HL	unexpired portion 30/4/18	WO/90/7/190
Barr R	Pte	2/5 Welsh TF	27/09/16	Cardiff	M	1 yr Detn		WO/86/66/194
Barr WJ	Pte	2 MGC	12/06/19	Field	M+Disob(2)+S40	5 yrs PS		WO/213/29/122
Barrett E	Pte	1/4 KOYLI (att 365 POW Coy)	16/09/19	Field	M+Abs+Disob	3 yrs PS	Comm 1 yr HL	WO/213/31/69
Barrington AV	Dvr	337 Bde RFA	10/01/17	Canterbury	JM	6 mos Detn		WO/92/3/58

Name	Rank	Unit	Date D/M/Y	Location	Offence	Finding/Punishment	Amendment	PRO Reference File/Piece/Page
Bartlett J	Pte	5 Dragoon Gds	29/09/19	Curragh	M	1 yr HL + Disch Igmny	Comm 6 mos Detn	WO/92/4/81
Bass G	Pte	39 R Fus	23/08/19	Field EEF	M	5 yrs PS	Comm 1 yr HL	WO/213/31/24
Batchelor E	Pte	2/4 R Sussex TF	23/07/15	Canterbury	JM	84 dys Detn		WO/92/3/21
Bate R	Pte	21 Manch	08/02/19	Field	M+Abs	6 mos HL		WO/213/28/58
Battersby HM	Pte	2 MGC	12/06/19	Field	M+Disob(2)+S40	5 yrs PS		WO/213/29/122
Baxter J	Pte(L/Cpl)	7/8 R Innis Fus	15/04/18	Field	M	7 yrs PS	Susp	WO/213/21/95
Beal A	Pte	35 MGC	17/01/19	Field	Mx2	2 yrs HL	Remit 6 mos	WO/213/28/121
Beaman T	Pte	58 Coy RDC	21/11/16	Towcester	M	1 yr Detn		WO/92/4/1
Bean HG	Pte	1/1 C of Lon Yeo	17/06/19	Field EEF	M+S40	NG		WO/213/30/104
Beattie RE	Pte	5 Dragoon Gds	23/09/19	Curragh	M	84 dys HL	Comm 42 dys Detn	WO/92/4/85
Beatty L	Pte	Quebec Regt	12/07/19	Ripon	M+S7(3b)	18 mos HL		WO/86/88/29
Beck T	Pte	2 Y[ork] & Lanc	07/11/19	Basrah	M+S40	6 mos HL		WO/90/7/205
Beckford R	Pte	4 BWI	27/12/18	Field Italy	M+Disob	3 yrs PS	Comm 2 yrs HL	WO/213/27/23
Beckman EG	Pte	1 Inf Bn AIF	15/10/18	Field	M+Des	3 yrs PS	Guilty of Des	WO/213/28/200
Bedford W	Pte	West India Regt	29/04/21	Jamaica	M+Abs+Str(Maj)+S9(1)	5 yrs PS+DI	Remit 2 yrs	WO/90/8/87
Beggs R	Pte (L/Cpl)	1 Inf Bn AIF	15/10/18	Field	M+Des	5 yrs PS	Guilty of Des	WO/213/28/199
Beisly HL	Pte (3 AM)	RAF	30/04/18	Swanage	M+Disob	9 mos HL		WO/92/4/41
Bell CG	Pte	30 AIF	24/03/19	Field	M	8 yrs PS		WO/213/29/91
Bell D	Pte	5 Dragoon Gds	29/09/19	Curragh	M	18 mos HL + Disch ignmy	Comm 9 mos Detn	WO/92/4/83
Bell J	Pte	1/4 R Sco Fus	14/01/18	Field	M	10 yrs PS	Comm 2 yrs HL	WO/213/21/34
Bell M	Pte(L/Cpl)	7/8 R Innis Fus	15/04/18	Field	M	7 yrs PS	Susp	WO/213/21/96
Bell WA	Tpr	4 Aust Lt Horse	30/12/15	Malta	M+Not Sup+Disob(APM)	1 yr HL	Remit 1 month	WO/90/6/40
Bell WH	Spr	3 Aus Tun Coy	13/10/18	Field	M+Disob	1 yr HL	NC	WO/213/30/136
Bell WH	Spr	3 Aus Tun Coy	18/10/18	Field	M+Disob	2 yrs HL	Susp	WO/213/26/66
Belmore T	Pte	Quebec Regt	02/08/19	Ripon	M+7(3b)+Abs+S22	1 yr Detn		WO/86/88/53
Bennett C	Pte	1 Inf Bn AIF	15/10/18	Field	M+Des	3 yrs PS	Guilty of Des	WO/213/28/107
Bennett H	Pte	7 Leic	14/10/18	Field	M	Death	Comm 15 yrs PS	WO/213/26/45
Bennett H	Gnr	RGA	08/07/19	Aldershot	M	9 mos Detn + Disch Igmny		WO/86/87/189
Bennett J	Pte	1 Gn Sher Fstrs	05/06/17	Kantara Egypt	M	2 yrs HL		WO/213/15/176
Bentham J	Pte	5 Dragoon Gds	30/09/19	Curragh	M	1 yr HL + Disch Igmny	Comm 6 mos Detn	WO/92/4/87
Bergendorff O	Gnr/L/Bdr	RFA	12/05/18	Field	M	1 yr HL	Susp	WO/213/22/153
Bernard S	Pte	2 W India	11/05/19	Field EEF	M	7 yrs PS	Comm 2 yrs HL	WO/213/30/28
Bernstein AP	Pte	5 Dragoon Gds	22/09/19	Curragh	M	1 yr HL + Disch Igmny	Comm 6 mos Detn	WO/92/4/84
Berry A	Pte	5 Dragoon Gds	26/09/19	Curragh	M	1 yr HL + Disch Igmny	Comm 6 mos Detn	WO/92/4/83
Berry W	Pte (AL/Cpl)	RAMC	10/05/19	Field	M+S40	6 mos HL	Comm 28 dys FP2	WO/213/30/17
Bertucci BG	Pte	1 Can IW Coy	19/05/19	Liverpool	M	Acquit		WO/92/4/68
Besley EA	Pte (L/Cpl)	1 Inf Bn AIF	15/10/18	Field	M+Des	10 yrs PS	Guilty of Des	WO/213/28/200
Best T	Pte	2/4 R Sussex TF	23/07/15	Canterbury	JM	NG		WO/92/3/21
Bestwick C	Pte	17 L'pool	16/05/19	NREF	M	2 yrs HL	Remit 18 mos	WO/213/29/181
Bestwick TC	Pte	1 Gn Sher Fstrs	05/06/17	Kantara Egypt	M	2 yrs HL		WO/213/15/176
Bethuel	Pte	SANLC	21/11/17	Field	M+S40	3 yrs PS	Comm 2 yrs HL	WO/213/31/109
Bexon I	Pte	3 Leics	27/08/14	Portsmouth	M	1 yr HL		WO/213/2/1
Bibb J	Pte	1/4 KOYLI (att 365 POW Coy)	16/09/19	Field	M+Abs+Disob	3 yrs PS	Comm 1 yr HL	WO/213/31/69
Bickerton W	Gnr	RFA	24/04/19	Field	M+Disob	5 mos HL		WO/213/29/160
Biddle C	Pte(A/Cpl)	RAOC	08/10/19	Field	M+S40	NG		WO/213/31/4
Biddle LH	Pte	26 AIF	04/02/19	Rouen	M	56 dys Imp		WO/90/8/59
Biddulph P	Cpl	RGA	04/07/19	Aldershot	M	9 mos Detn+Rnks + Disch Igmny		WO/86/87/188
Biggin A	Pte	58 Coy RDC	21/11/16	Towcester	M	1 yr Detn		WO/92/4/2
Binneker C	Dvr	372 Coy CAHT	14/05/19	Field	M	5 yrs PS		WO/213/30/12
Biram F	Pte	5 Dragoon Gds	22/09/19	Curragh	M	1 yr HL + Disch Igmny	Comm 1 yr Detn	WO/92/4/81
Birkett A	Pte (AL/Cpl)	5(R) L'pool	20/12/18	Pembroke Dock	M+S40	6 mos Detn	2 mos	WO/92/4/59
Bishop C	Gnr	RFA	24/04/19	Field	M+Disob	5 mos HL		WO/213/29/160
Bitel S	Pte	1 Slav-Brit Legion	14/07/19	Field NREF	M	Death		WO/213/32/59
Black T	Bdr	RFA	06/05/19	Leeds	M	1 yr Detn+Rnks		WO/92/4/69
Blackman J	Pte	2/4 R Sussex TF	23/07/15	Canterbury	JM	84 dys Detn		WO/92/3/21
Blackwood PE	Pte	3 AIF	24/03/19	Field	M	11 yrs PS		WO/213/29/91
Blackwood TJ	L/Cpl (T/Cpl)	1 Inf Bn AIF	15/10/18	Field	M+Des	8 yrs PS+Rnks	Guilty of Des	WO/213/28/199
Blair D	Pte	5 Dragoon Gds	25/09/19	Curragh	M	1 yr HL + Disch Igmny	Comm 6 mos Detn	WO/92/4/86
Blair E	Pte	7/8 R Innis Fus	15/04/18	Field	M	5 yrs PS	Susp	WO/213/21/96

Name	Rank	Unit	Date D/M/Y	Location	Offence	Finding/Punishment	Amendment	PRO Reference File/Piece/Page
Blair J	Dvr	RFA	24/04/19	Field	M+Disob	5 mos HL		WO/213/29/160
Blake J	Pte	4 BWI	27/12/18	Field Italy	M+Disob	3 yrs PS	Comm 2 yrs HL	WO/213/27/23
Blumenthal B	Pte	39 R Fus	23/08/19	Field EEF	M	NG		WO/213/31/23
Boland E	Pte	1 Inf Bn AIF	15/10/18	Field	M+Des	3 yrs PS	Guilty of Des	WO/213/28/200
Bolger J	Pte	2 R Irish	15/04/18	Field	M	5 yrs PS	Susp	WO/213/21/98
Bolton JH	Gnr	337 Bde RFA	10/01/17	Canterbury	JM	6 mos Detn		WO/92/3/58
Bonang AW	Pte	43 CEF	23/12/17	Field	M+Disob	2 yrs HL		WO/213/19/116
Boniface A	Pte	2/4 R Sussex TF	23/07/15	Canterbury	JM	84 dys Detn		WO/92/3/24
Bonnana G	Pte	2 KO Malta(Militia)	20/12/15	Malta	M+AWOL +Loss propert	112 dys Detn +Stoppages		WO/86/68/199
Booker A	Pte	2 Ox & Bucks LI	05/05/16	Field	M+Disob	5 yrs PS	Quashed	WO/213/9/46
Boolley WF	Pte	1 Gn Sher Fstrs	05/06/17	Kantara Egypt	M	2 yrs HL		WO/213/15/176
Booth A	Pte(L/Cpl)	1 Manchester	05/09/21	Field (Ireland)	M+Disob(CQMS) +S7(3)	3 yrs PS	2yrs Dtn	WO/213/32/214
Bootle WJ	Pte	1 Inf Bn AIF	15/10/18	Field	M+Des	3 yrs PS	Guilty of Des	WO/213/28/197
Boskett J[V?]	Pte	Can ASC	21/11/17	Bramshott	M+Insub(Lieut)	42 dys Detn	Remit 15 dys	WO/86/79/53
Bostock A	Pte	5 Dragoon Gds	22/09/19	Curragh	M	1 yr HL+Disch Igmny	Comm 6 mos Detn	WO/92/4/83
Boswell W	Tpr(L/Cpl)	NZEF	01/07/18	Field EEF	M	NG		WO/213/28/138
Bothwell W	Pte	7/8 R Innis Fus	15/04/18	Field	M	5 yrs PS	Susp	WO/213/21/94
Boulton GH	Pte	7/8 R Innis Fus	15/04/18	Field	M	5 yrs PS	Susp	WO/213/21/96
Bousset J	Pte	Maur Lab Bn	10/05/18	Mespot	M(S7-2B)	6 mosHL		WO/90/7/151
Bowden WH	Pte	1 Gn Sher Fstrs	05/06/17	Kantara Egypt	M	2 yrs HL		WO/213/15/176
Bowen M	Pte	1/4 KOYLI (att 365 POW Coy)	16/09/19	Field	M+Abs+Disob	5 yrs PS	Comm 2 yrs HL	WO/213/31/68
Bowker J	Pte	5 Dragoon Gds	22/09/19	Curragh	M	1 yr HL+Disch Igmny	Comm 6 mos Detn	WO/92/4/81
Bowley H	Pte(L/Cpl)	2/4 R Sussex TF	23/07/15	Canterbury	NSM	28 dys Detn		WO/92/3/20
Boyce H	Pte	58 Coy RDC	21/11/16	Towcester	M	1 yr Detn		WO/92/4/1
Boyes JF	Pte	58 Coy RDC	21/11/16	Towcester	M	1 yr Detn		WO/92/4/1
Boyle C	Pte	5 Dragoon Gds	30/09/19	Curragh	M	Acquit		WO/92/4/87
Boyle J	Pte	5 Dragoon Gds	29/09/19	Curragh	M	1 yr HL+Disch Igmny	Comm 6 mos Detn	WO/92/4/81
Bozeat WJ	Pte	34 AIF	04/02/19	Rouen	M	90 dys Imp		WO/90/8/59
Brad G	Pte	1 NZ Div Employ Coy	16/10/18	Field	M	6 mos HL	Susp	WO/213/25/165
Bradfield EE	Pte	5 Dragoon Gds	29/09/19	Curragh	M	1 yr HL+Disch Igmny	Comm 6 mos Detn	WO/92/4/82
Bradley FW	Pte	5 Aus Pnrs	04/02/19	Rouen	M	3 yrs 6 mos PS		WO/90/8/59
Bradley S	Pte	West India Regt	29/04/21	Jamaica	M+Abs+S9(1)	6 mos Detn		WO/90/8/87
Bradshaw J	Dvr	RFA	24/03/19	Field	M	15 yrs PS		WO/213/29/89
Bragnell J	Pte	2 R Irish	15/04/18	Field	M	5 yrs PS	Susp	WO/213/21/98
Braithwaite J	Pte	2 Otago NZEF	11/10/16	Rouen	M	Death		WO/90/6/90
Brandall T	Dvr	RFA	27/09/19	Deepcut	M	18 mos HL	Comm to Detn	WO/86/88/138
Brandon CS	Pte	1 Inf Bn AIF	15/10/18	Field	M+Des	3 yrs PS	Guilty of Des	WO/213/28/196
Brandt P	Dvr	372 Coy CAHT	14/05/19	Field	M	5 yrs PS	Remit 2 yrs	WO/213/30/12
Bray E	Spr	Can Engrs	25/01/19	Field	M+Disob	28 dys FP2		WO/213/29/55
Bray J	Pte	3 Leics	27/08/14	Portsmouth	M	1 yr HL		WO/213/2/1
Brealey JW	Pte	7 Dragoon Gds	09/06/21	Edinburgh	M+V(A/RSM)	NG		WO/86/91/131
Brennan JP	Pte	6(R) CEF	19/04/19	Liverpool	M+S40	1 yr HL		WO/92/4/69
Brennan M	Pte	2 MGC	12/06/19	Field	M+Disob(2)+S40	5 yrs PS	Comm 2 yrs HL	WO/213/29/122
Brennan S	Cpl	2/4 R Sussex TF	23/07/15	Canterbury	NSM	Rnks		WO/92/3/20
Brickwood HE	Cpl	8 Lincs	23/12/18	Field	M	4 mos HL+Rnks	Imp	WO/213/28/8
Bridge H	Gnr	RGA	13/03/18	Agra	M	1 yr HL	unexpired portion 30/4/18	WO/90/7/190
Bridge H	Pte	7/8 R Innis Fus	15/04/18	Field	M	5 yrs PS	Susp	WO/213/21/96
Bridle G	Pte	RAMC	10/05/18	Field	M	6 mos HL	Comm 28 dys FP2	WO/213/30/17
Briggs A	Pte	58 Coy RDC	21/11/16	Towcester	M	1 yr Detn		WO/92/4/2
Brighton LC	Pte	34 MGC	17/01/19	Field	Mx2	2 yrs HL	Remit 18 mos	WO/213/28/120
Brissenden CL	Pte	18 AIF	24/03/19	Field	M	10 yrs PS		WO/213/29/90
Brisset J	Cpl	1 Inf Bn AIF	15/10/18	Field	M+Des+Abs	Rnks	G of Abs	WO/213/30/56
Broadhead AS	Pte	50 AIF	24/03/19	Field	M	13 yrs PS		WO0213/29/88
Broadmeadow W	Pte	58 Coy RDC	21/11/16	Towcester	M	1 yr Detn		WO/92/4/2
Brock JJ	Pte	8 AIF	24/03/19	Field	M	12 yrs PS		WO/213/29/90
Brockbank S	Pte	3 Essex	09/05/19	Field Italy	M	3 yrs PS	Comm 4 mos HL	WO/213/29/73
Brodie JN	2/Lt	Welsh H (att 21 Rifle Bde)	06/05/19	Alexandria	M+Drunk	Dism+Repr	NC	WO/90/8/18
Brookes TW	Pte	1 Gn Sher Fstrs	05/06/17	Kantara Egypt	M	2 yrs HL		WO/213/15/176
Brookfield W	Pte	5 Dragoon Gds	23/09/19	Curragh	M	84 dys HL	Comm 42 dys Detn	WO/92/4/85
Brooks RR	Pte	30 MGC	29/07/19	Field	M+Disob	1 yr HL		WO/213/30/119

Name	Rank	Unit	Date D/M/Y	Location	Offence	Finding/Punishment	Amendment	PRO Reference File/Piece/Page
Broom W	Pte(L/Cpl)	7 Suffolk	13/04/17	Arras	M+S40	9 mos HL	Rem 3 mos	WO/213/15/142
Brown A	Pte	5 Berks	13/04/17	Arras	M+S40	3 mos Stop	Rem 2 mos	WO/213/15/142
Brown C	Pte	1 Gn Sher Fstrs	05/06/17	Kantara Egypt	M	2 yrs HL		WO/213/15/176
Broom C	Pte	Quebec Regt	23/07/19	Ripon	M+S7(3b)	22 mos HL +Disch Igmny		WO/86/88/54
Brown E	Pte	6 (S) BWI	24/12/18	Field Italy	M+Disob	3 yrs 6 mos PS		WO/213/27/24
Brown H	Pte	9(S) E Lancs	29/05/18	SEF	M	1 yr HL		WO/213/23/179
Brown HW	Gnr	RGA	13/03/18	Agra	M	1 yr HL	unexpired portion 30/4/18	WO/90/7/190
Brown I	Pte	BWI	04/01/18	Mesopotamia	[M]7(3a)	18 mos HL	Remit 1 yr	WO/90/7/169
Brown J	Pte	9(S) E Lancs	29/05/18	SEF	M	1 yr HL		WO/213/23/179
Brown J	Pte	2 W India	11/05/19	Field EEF	M	7 yrs PS	Comm 2 yrs HL	WO/213/30/28
Brown J	Pte	65 Coy RDC	21/11/16	Towcester	M	1 yr Detn		WO/92/4/3
Brown JE	Pte	58 Coy RDC	21/11/16	Towcester	M	1 yr Detn		WO/92/4/1
Brown JW	Pte	5 Dragoon Gds	24/09/19	Curragh	M	1 yr HL+Disch Igmny	Comm 6 mos Detn	WO/92/4/85
Brown M	Pte	K Edw Horse	22/09/19	Curragh	M	1 yr HL+Disch Igmny	Comm 6 mos Detn	WO/92/3/84
Brown PG	Pte (L/Cpl)	1 Inf Bn AIF	15/10/18	Field	M+Des	NG		WO/213/28/200
Brown R	Pte	17 AIF	24/03/19	Field	M	11 yrs PS		WO/213/29/90
Brown S	Pte	2 W India	11/05/19	Field EEF	M	7 yrs PS	Comm 2 yr HL	WO/213/30/28
Brown W	Pte	2/4 R Sussex TF	23/07/15	Canterbury	J[oin in] M	84 dys Detn		WO/92/3/21
Brown WH	Pte	65 Coy RDC	21/11/16	Towcester	M	1 yr Detn		WO/92/4/2
Browne JE	Pte	2/4 R Sussex TF	23/07/15	Canterbury	J[oin in] M	84 dys Detn		WO/92/3/21
Brownhill FH	Spr	3 Aus Tun Coy	13/10/18	Field	M+Disob	1 yr HL	NC	WO/213/30/136
Brownhill FH	Spr	3 Aus Tun Coy	18/10/18	Field	M+Disob	2 yrs HL	Susp	WO/213/26/66
Browning JB	Pte	54 TR Bn	21/05/17	Kirkcaldy	M+Insub(Cplx2) +Wilful Inj Prop	2 yrs Detn+Stop	Remit 1 yr	WO/86/76/98
Brownsdon S	Pte	5 Dragoon Gds	26/09/19	Curragh	M	1 yr HL+Disch Igmny	Comm 6 mos Detn	WO/92/4/83
Bruce DG	Pte	1 Inf Bn AIF	15/10/18	Field	M+Des	3 yrs PS	Guilty of Des	WO/213/28/197
Bruce JR	Pte	1 Ont Regt	15/07/18	Bramshott	M+S40	18 mos HL+Stoppages		WO/92/4/43
Brunskill A	Pte	5 Dragoon Gds	23/09/19	Curragh	M	1 yr HL+Disch Igmny	Comm 6mos Detn	WO/92/4/85
Bryant CWI	Pte	18 CEF	30/09/18	Seaford	M+S40	6 mos HL		WO/86/84/196
Bryson H	Pte	2 MGC	12/06/19	Field	M+Disob(2)+S40	5 yrs PS	Remit 2 yrs	WO/213/29/122
Buchan GM	Tpr(L/Cpl)	8 Aus Lt Horse	28/06/18	Field EEF	M	NG		WO/213/28/138
Buck O	Spt	3 Aus Tun Coy	13/10/18	Field	M+Disob	1 yr HL	NC	WO/213/30/136
Buck O	Spr	3 Aus Tun Coy	18/10/18	Field	M+Disob	2 yrs HL	Susp	WO/213/26/65
Buckley JJ	Pte	1 Connaught Rangers	04/09/20	Dagshai	M+S7(3b)	Life PS+DI		WO/90/8/188
Buckley M	Pte	13 R Berks	13/04/17	Dunkirk	M	8 mos HL		WO/213/14/138
Budden F	Pte	35 MGC	17/01/19	Field	Mx2	2 yrs HL	Remit 18 mos	WO/213/28/121
Buddle P	Spr	RE	15/05/19	Field	M+Disob	1 yr IHL		WO/213/29/137
Bullen E	Pte	5 Dragoon Gds	26/09/19	Curragh	M	1 yr HL+Disch Igmny	Comm 6 mos Detn	WO/92/4/80
Bullen RG	Pte	R Marine Lab Corps	13/04/17	Dunkirk	M	1 yr HL		WO/213/14/138
Bullock H	Pte	1 Gn Sher Fstrs	05/06/17	Kantara Egypt	M	2 yrs HL		WO/213/15/176
Bundy AE	Pte	35 MGC	17/01/19	Field	Mx2	2 yrs HL	Remit 18 mos	WO/213/28/121
Bundy HG	Pte	Lab Corps (att E Comm LB)	15/06/19	Sutton	M+S7(3b)	Acquit		WO/92/4/74
Bunting C	Pte	23 AIF	24/03/19	Field	M	13 yrs PS +Disch Igmny		WO/213/29/89
Burgess A	Pte	1 Inf Bn AIF	15/10/18	Field	M+Des	3 yrs PS	Guilty of Des	WO/213/28/197
Burland W	Pte	1 Connaught Rangers	04/09/20	Dagshai	M+S7(3b)	5 yrs PS+DI	Remit 2 yrs	WO/90/8/188
Burley H	Pte	2 Dragoon Gds	25/09/19	Curragh	M	1 yr HL+Disch Igmny	Comm 6 mos Detn	WO/92/4/86
Burn AE	Pte	25 AIF	24/03/19	Field	M	12 yrs PS		WO/213/29/89
Burnett A	Gnr	RGA	09/05/21	Field (Ireland)	M+S7(4)	2 yrs HL+DI	Comm to DI Not Conf	WO/213/32/133
Burrows S	S/Smith	337 Bde RFA	10/01/17	Canterbury	JM	6 mos Detn		WO/92/3/58
Burrows G	Pte	1 Gn Sher Fstrs	05/06/17	Kantara Egypt	M	2 yrs HL		WO/213/15/176
Burt A	Pte	2/4 R Sussex TF	23/07/15	Canterbury	J[oin in] M	84 dys Detn		WO/92/3/21
Burton EF	Pte	58 Coy RDC	21/11/16	Towcester	M	1 yr Detn		WO/92/4/1
Burton FA	Pte	1/4 KOYLI (att 365 POW Coy)	16/09/19	Field	M+Abs+Disob	3 yrs PS	Comm 1 yr HL	WO/213/31/69
Burton R	Pte	21 Manch	08/02/19	Field	M+Abs	6 mos HL		WO/213/28/58
Burton W	Pte	11(R) CEF	16/04/19	Liverpool	M+Viol	Acquit		WO/92/4/65
Burton W	L/Bdr	RGA	04/07/19	Aldershot	M	9 mos Detn+Rnks +Disch Igmny		WO/86/87/188
Bushell WJ	Pte	2 Gn/Beds	04/04/18	Karachi	M+S7(3)	1 yr Detn	Comm 6 mos	WO/90/7/191
Butler H	Pte	1 Gn Sher Fstrs	05/06/17	Kantara Egypt	M	2 yrs HL		WO/213/15/176

Name	Rank	Unit	Date D/M/Y	Location	Offence	Finding/punishment	Amendment	PRO Reference File/Piece/Page
Butler PW	Pte	PPCLI	23/01/19	Field	M+Abs	2 yrs HL	Remit/Quashed	WO/213/28/107
Butlin A	Pte	10 Y & Lanc	12/11/17	Field	M+Disob	6 mos HL	Comm 91 dys FP1	WO/213/18/181
Butterick J	L/Cpl	8 KOYLI	10/02/19	Field	M+Disob+S40	Acquit		WO/213/28/54
Butters RE	Pte	23 AIF	04/02/19	Rouen	M	90 dys Imp		WO/90/8/58
Butterworth F	Bdr	RGA	04/07/19	Aldershot	M	9 mos Detn+Rnks +Disch Igmny		WO/86/87/188
Bykoff V	Pte	1 Slav-Brit Legion	17/07/19	Field NREF	M	Death	Comm 10 yrs PS	WO/213/32/59
Byrd J	Pte	1 Gn Sher Fstrs	05/06/17	Kantara Egypt	M	2 yrs HL		WO/213/15/176
Byrne H	Pte	21 Manch	08/02/19	Field	M+Abs	6 mos HL		WO/213/28/58
Byrne J	Pte	7 R Irish	15/04/18	Field	M	NG		WO/213/21/98
Byrne J	Pte	2 R Irish	15/04/18	Field	M	5 yrs PS	Susp	WO/213/21/98
Byrne S	Pte	7 R Irish	15/04/18	Field	M	NG		WO/213/21/97
Cadigan CJ	Pte	33 AIF	24/03/19	Field	M	23 yrs PS		WO/213/29/89
Cain G	Dvr	ASC (SA)	23/07/18	Field	M	2 yrs HL		WO/213/24/168
Cain J	Pte	58 Coy RDC	21/11/16	Towcester	M	1 yr Detn		WO/92/4/1
Cain W	Pte	Can ASC	21/11/17	Bramshott	M+Insub(Lieut)	42 dys Detn	Remit 10 dys	WO/86/79/53
Calden J	Pte	Can ASC	21/11/17	Bramshott	M+Insub(Lieut)	42 dys Detn	Remit 15 dys	WO/86/79/53
Calver LT	Dvr	337 Bde RFA	10/01/17	Canterbury	JM	6 mos Detn		WO/92/3/58
Calvert F	Pte	3 W Yorks	01/08/19	Devizes	M+S40	18 mos HL +Disch Igmny	9 mos	WO/92/4/77
Cambridge JG	Pte	2 AIF	24/03/19	Field	M	10 yrs PS		WO/213/29/91
Cameron A	Tpr(L/Cpl)	1 Aus MG Sqdn	28/06/18	Field EEF	M	NG		WO/213/28/138
Cameron J	Pte	58 Coy RDC	21/11/16	Towcester	M	1 yr Detn		WO/92/4/1
Campbell A	Pte	7 Dragoon Gds	09/06/21	Edinburgh	M+V(A/RSM)	18 mos HL		WO/86/91/131
Campbell M	Pte	2 KOSB	29/10/20	Devonport	M+S40	NG		WO/86/90/187
Campbell S	Pte	6 (S) BWI	24/12/18	Field Italy	M+Disob	3 yrs 6 mos PS		WO/213/27/24
Campbell S	Pte	West India Regt	29/04/21	Jamaica	M+Abs+Disob	112 dys Detn	Remit 56 dys	WO/90/8/87
Campbell W	Pte	65 Coy RDC	21/11/16	Towcester	M	1 yr Detn		WO/92/4/2
Canning J	Pte	Quebec Regt CEF	15/07/18	Bramshott	M+S40	2 yrs HL+Stoppages		WO/92/4/43
Canning W	Pte	58 Coy RDC	21/11/16	Towcester	M	1 yr Detn		WO/92/4/1
Cannon W	Pte	2 R Dublin Fusiliers	05/07/20	Constantinople	M+Disob(Capt)	5 yrs PS	1 yr Detn	WO/90/8/84
Capock H	Pte	Lab Cps	06/01/19	Field	M+S40	NG		WO/213/27/37
Cardonia L	Pte	BWI	27/02/19	Plymouth	M	2 yrs HL+Disch Igmny		WO/86/87/23
Carey G	Pte	2/4 R Sussex TF	23/07/15	Canterbury	J[oin in] M	84 dys Detn		WO/92/3/21
Carey J	Pte	2 R Irish	15/04/18	Field	M	5 yrs PS	Susp	WO/213/21/99
Carey W	Pte	4 BWI	27/12/18	Field Italy	M+Disob	3 yrs PS	Comm 2 yrs HL	WO/213/27/23
Carmichael J	Pte	Bermuda Artillery	31/08/20	Bermuda	M	Acquit		WO/90/8/84
Carmody O	Pte	1 Inf Bn AIF	15/10/18	Field	M+Des	3 yrs PS	Guilty of Des	WO/213/28/197
Carolus F	Pte	1 Cape Corps	18/01/19	Mustapha	M+Disob	28 dys FP1	Quashed	WO/213/28/61
Carpenter A	Cpl	RE	15/05/19	Field	M+Disob	1 yr IHL+Rnks		WO/213/29/137
Carr J	Pte(L/Cpl)	1 Manchester	05/09/21	Field (Ireland)	M+Disob(CQMS) +S7(3)	3 yrs PS	NG	WO/213/32/214
Carr SF	Pte (L/Cpl)	1 Inf Bn AIF	15/10/18	Field	M+Des	5 yrs PS	Guilty of Des	WO/213/28/198
Carroll F	Pte	1 Inf Bn AIF	15/10/18	Field	M+Des	3 yrs PS	Guilty of Des	WO/213/28/198
Carroll W	Pte	5 Dragoon Gds	29/09/19	Curragh	M	1 yr HL+Disch Igmny	Comm 6 mos Detn	WO/92/4/82
Carson R	Pte	21 Manch	08/02/19	Field	M+Abs	6 mos HL		WO/213/28/58
Carson W	Spr	RE	15/05/19	Field	M+Disob	1 yr IHL		WO/213/29/137
Carter A	Pte(L/Cpl)	2/4 R Sussex TF	23/07/15	Canterbury	NSM	28 dys Detn		WO/92/3/20
Carter J	Pte	9(S) E Lancs	29/05/18	SEF	M	1 yr HL		WO/213/23/179
Carter W	Gnr	RGA	13/03/18	Agra	M	1 yr HL	unexpired portion 30/4/18	WO/90/7/190
Carthy J	Gdsn	Irish Gds	04/02/20	Guildhall Wminster	M	5 yrs PS +Disch Igmny		WO/92/4/89
Cartwright A	Dvr	RFA	24/04/19	Field	M+Disob	NG		WO/213/29/160
Case W	Pte	1 Inf Bn AIF	15/10/18	Field	M+Des	3 yrs PS	Guilty of Des	WO/213/28/198
Casey AB	Pte	1 Inf Bn AIF	15/10/18	Field	M+Des	3 yrs PS	Guilty of Des	WO/213/28/199
Casey C	Pte (AL/Cpl)	RAMC	10/05/19	Field	M+S40	6 mos HL	Comm 28 dys FP2	WO/213/30/17
Casey P	Pte	7/8 R Innis Fus	15/04/18	Field	M	5 yrs PS	Susp	WO/213/21/97
Casey W	Pte	26 R Fus	04/02/19	Rouen	M	90 dys Imp		WO/90/8/58
Cash D	Pte	65 Coy RDC	16/11/16	Towcester	CM+JM	1 yr Detn		WO/92/3/55
Cassidy J	Pte	1 Gn Sher Fstrs	05/06/17	Kantara Egypt	M	2 yrs HL		WO/213/15/176
Cassidy T	Pte	58 Coy RDC	21/11/16	Towcester	M	1 yr Detn		WO/92/4/1
Castle J	Pte	3 Leics	27/08/14	Portsmouth	M	1 yr HL		WO/213/2/1
Cattanach M	Pte	35 MGC	17/01/19	Field	Mx2	2 yrs HL	Remit 18 mos	WO/213/28/120
Cattell J	L/Cpl	3 Dorsets	29/12/14	Dorchester	Joining M+Viol(Capt)	4 mos HL		WO/92/3/18
Cattell S	Pte(A/LCpl)	1/7 RW Fus	01/02/19	Field	M+S40	21 dys FP2		WO/213/29/27
Cattenach E	Pte	65 Coy RDC	21/11/16	Towcester	M	1 yr Detn		WO/92/4/3
Cavanagh W	Pte	35 MGC	17/01/19	Field	Mx2	1 yr HL	Remit 6 mos	WO/213/28/121
Cawthan JC	Pte	37 AIF	04/02/19	Rouen	M	90 dys Imp		WO/90/8/59
Chaitman B	Pte	39 R Fus	23/08/19	Field EEF	M	5 yrs PS	Comm 1 yr HL	WO/213/31/24

Name	Rank	Unit	Date D/M/Y	Location	Offence	Finding/punishment	Amendment	PRO Reference File/Piece/Page
Chalmers G	Pte	3 Sea Hldrs	17/06/19	Edinburgh	M+Insub	3 yrs PS+Disch Igmny	NC	WO/92/4/74
Chamberlain F	Pte	8 KOYLI	10/02/19	Field	M+Disob+S40	5 yrs PS	Quashed	WO/213/28/54
Chambers J	Pte	23 (R)CEF	16/05/18	Bramshott	M+Des+Abs +Loss prop+S40	90 dys Detn +Stoppages+G of Abs		WO/86/82/158
Chancellor HKT	Cpl	4 Aus Lt Horse	28/06/18	Field EEF	M	NG		WO/213/28/138
Chapman G	Pte	Lab Corps (att E Comm LB)	15/06/19	Sutton	M+S7(3b)	Acquit		WO/92/4/73
Chapman H	Pte	1 Gn Sher Fstrs	05/06/17	Kantara Egypt	M	2 yrs HL		WO/213/15/176
Chapman HRH	Bdr	RFA	07/03/19	Field	Mx2	1 yr HL+Rnks	Remit 3 mos	WO/213/29/12
Chapman W	Pte	30 MGC	29/07/19	Field	M+Disob	1 yr HL		WO/213/30/119
Chappell J	Pte	RASC	20/04/20	Field ABS	M+Disob	3 mos FP2		WO/213/31/171
Chappell LR	Pte	9 MGC	31/07/19	Field	M+Abs/Br	6 mos HL		WO/213/30/141
Charles J	Dvr	372 Coy CAHT	14/05/19	Field	M	5 yrs PS	Comm 1 yr HL	WO/213/30/12
Charman J	Cpl	RASC	26/07/21	Malta	M+S41+S40	1 yr Detn		WO/90/8/87
Cheeseman CH	Pte	1 Inf Bn AIF	15/10/18	Field	M+Des	3 yrs PS	Guilty of Des	WO/213/28/197
Cherbukin F	Pte	1 Slav-Brit Legion	14/07/19	Field NREF	M	Death		WO/213/32/59
Cherry JE	Pte	58 Coy RDC	21/11/16	Towcester	M	1 yr Detn		WO/92/4/1
Cherry P	Pte	1 Connaught Rangers	04/09/20	Dagshai	M+S7(3b)	15 yrs PS+DI	Remit 2 yrs	WO/90/8/188
Child S	Pte	6 Yorks	16/11/18	Kirkwall	M+Insub(Sgt)	112 dys Detn		WO/86/85/190
Childs FC	AL/Bdr	RGA	08/07/19	Aldershot	M	9 mos Detn+Rnks +Disch Igmny		WO/86/87/189
Chiverrell WH	Pte	28 CEF	04/02/19	Rouen	M	56 dys Imp		WO/90/8/58
Chouinard WA	Pte	Quebec Regt	28/07/19	Ripon	M+S40	NG		WO/86/88/42
Christian C	Dvr	372 Coy CAHT	14/05/19	Field	M	5 yrs PS		WO/213/30/12
Church H	L/Cpl	11 R Fus	23/12/18	Field	M	5 yrs PS		WO/213/28/141
Clarey T	Pte	7 R Irish	15/04/18	Field	M	5 yrs PS	Susp	WO/213/21/98
Clark HL	Pte	28 CEF	24/03/19	Field	M	20 yrs PS		WO/213/29/91
Clark HS	Pte	1 Inf Bn AIF	15/10/18	Field	M+Des	NG		WO/213/28/198
Clarke E	Pte	2 R Irish	15/04/18	Field	M	5 yrs PS	Susp	WO/213/21/98
Clarke F	Pte	5 Dragoon Gds	29/09/19	Curragh	M	1 yr HL+Disch Igmny	Comm 6 mos Detn	WO/92/4/82
Clarke H	Pte	19 AIF	24/03/19	Field	M	11 yrs PS		WO/213/29/89
Clarkson A	Pte	4 HLI(att MGC)	25/04/16	Grantham	NSM	1 dy Detn		WO/92/3/38
Clarkson JR	Pte	4 HLI(att MGC)	25/04/16	Grantham	NSM	1 dy Detn		WO/92/3/38
Clay H	Pte	1 Gn Sher Fstrs	05/06/17	Kantara Egypt	M	2 yrs HL		WO/213/15/176
Claybrook AH	Pte	12 SWBdrs	01/12/16	Field	M+Disob	18 mos HL	Comm 3 mos FP1	WO/213/13/47
Clement F	Pte	20(R) CEF	18/04/19	Liverpool	M	18 mos HL		WO/92/4/69
Clements R	Pte	3 Gn Beds	12/03/18	Meiktila	M+Disob	2 yrs Detn	Comm 1 yr Detn	WO/90/8/199
Clergy C	Pte	43 CEF	11/12/17	Field	M+Disob	18 mos HL		WO/213/19/116
Clift A	Pte	1 Inf Bn AIF	15/10/18	Field	M+Des	3 yrs PS	Guilty of Des	WO/213/28/198
Coats A	Pte	51 Beds	09/10/18	Teverham	M+Theft+S40	28 dys Detn	NC	WO/86/85/9
Cobb A	Pte	Lab Corps (att E Comm LB)	15/06/19	Sutton	M+S7(3b)	Acquit		WO/92/4/73
Codd A	Pte	2 Ches	05/03/20	Field ABS	M+Disob	2 yrs HL	Rem 18 mos	WO/213/31/168
Coffey J	Spr	Aust Mining Coy	19/07/16	[Le] Havre	Per M+Viol SO	5 yrs PS		WO/90/6/66
Coffey W	Cpl	1 MGC	17/07/19	Field	M	5 mos Imp+Rnks		WO/213/30/82
Coffle J	Gnr	2/3 Northern Bde AC/RFA	04/05/16	Bawtry	JM	3 yrs PS + Disch Igmny		WO/92/3/39
Cogger AN	Pte	30 MGC	29/07/19	Field	M+Disob	1 yr HL		WO/213/30/119
Colbert F	Pte	7/8 R Innis Fus	15/04/18	Field	M	5 yrs PS	Susp	WO/213/21/96
Coldwell FH	Gnr	RFA	30/06/19	Field EEF	M	10 yrs PS		WO/213/30/104
Cole FC	Pte	Can ASC	06/09/17	Shorncliffe	M+S40+S7(2)+S41	NG		WO/86/77/169
Cole H	Pte	2 W India	11/05/19	Field EEF	M	7 yrs PS	Comm 2 yrs HL	WO/213/30/27
Cole HA	Pte(L/Cpl)	13 Yorks	16/05/19	NREF	M	2 yrs HL	Remit 18 mos	WO/213/29/181
Cole J	Bdr	RFA	06/05/19	Leeds	M	2 yrs HL	Comm 1 yr Detn	WO/92/4/69
Cole JH	Pnr	RE	23/12/15	Deganwy	Mx2	9 mos Detn	Quashed	WO/86/68/29
Cole RW	Gnr	RFA	24/06/19	Field	M+Abs	NG		WO/213/29/137
Coleman A	L/Bdr	RGA	04/07/19	Aldershot	M	9 mos Detn+Rnks s+Disch Igmny		WO/86/87/188
Coleman J	Pte	Scot Rifles	12/09/18	Field	M(x2)	10 yrs PS	One charge quashed	WO/213/25/177
Coleman P	Cpl	1 Connaught Rangers	23/08/20	Dagshai	M+S7(3)	Acquit		WO/90/8/189
Coley T	Pte	5 Dragoon Gds	22/09/19	Curragh	M	1 yr HL+Disch Igmny	Comm 6 mos Detn	WO/92/4/83
Coley TH	Pte	1/4 KOYLI (att 365 POW Coy)	16/09/19	Field	M+Abs+Disob	3 yrs PS	Comm 1 yr HL	WO/213/31/69
Collier FD	Pte(L/Cpl)	17 L'pool	16/05/19	NREF	M	2 yrs HL	Remit 18 mos	WO/213/29/181
Collings EH	Gnr	RGA	13/03/18	Agra	M	1 yr HL	unexpired portion 30/4/18	WO/90/7/190

51

Name	Rank	Unit	Date D/M/Y	Location	Offence	Finding/Punishment	Amendment	PRO Reference File/Piece/Page
Collins A	Pte	RAMC	25/10/14	Rouen	Incit M+St/V+S40	2 yrs HL	Rem 18 mos	WO/213/2/133
Collins D	Pte	RASC	20/02/19	Field	Mx2+S40	1 yr HL		WO/213/28/169
Collins F	Pte	65 Coy RDC	21/11/16	Towcester	M	1 yr Detn		WO/92/4/2
Collins J	Pte	7 R Irish	15/04/18	Field	M	NG		WO/213/21/98
Collins R	Pte	2 W India	11/05/19	Field EEF	M	5 yrs PS	Comm 1 yr HL	WO/213/30/28
Collins WG	Pte	2 MGC	12/06/19	Field	M+Disob(2)+S40	5 yrs PS	Remit 2 yrs	WO/213/29/122
Colsell H	Pte	41 AIF	22/12/18	Field	M	2 yrs HL		WO/213/27/184
Colwell A	Pte	RASC	20/04/20	Field ABS	M+Disob	3 mos FP2		WO/213/31/171
Coman W	Pte	1 Connaught Rangers	30/08/20	Dagshai	M	15 yrs PS+DI		WO/90/8/188
Commins P	Pte	7 R Irish	15/04/18	Field	M	5 yrs PS	Susp	WO/213/21/97
Comyn A	Pte	58 Coy RDC	16/11/16	Towcester	CM+JM	1 yr Detn		WO/92/3/55
Conley AL	Spr	3(R) Can Eng	27/05/19	Liverpool	M+Res	1 yr HL	Comm Detn	WO/92/4/72
Conlon M	Pte	1 Connaught Rangers	04/09/20	Dagshai	M+S7(3b)	10 yrs PS+DI		WO/90/8/188
Connelly J	Pte	2 R Irish	15/04/18	Field	M	5 yrs PS	Susp	WO/213/21/98
Connor L	Pte	2 R Irish	15/04/18	Field	M	5 yrs PS	Susp	WO/213/21/98
Connor O	Pte	13(R) CEF	28/01/19	Kinmel Pk	M+S7(4)	1 yr Detn		WO/86/86/105
Connors H	Pte	Can ASC	21/11/17	Bramshott	M+Insub(Lieut)	42 dys Detn	Remit 15 dys	WO/86/79/53
Connors J	Pte	7 R Irish	15/04/18	Field	M	5 yrs PS	Susp	WO/213/21/98
Conway D	Gnr	RGA	13/03/18	Agra	M	1 yr HL	unexpired portion 30/4/18	WO/90/7/190
Conway D	Pte	8 R Innis Fus	06/09/15	Eniskillen	M+Inj pub property	1 yr HL		WO/86/66/111
Conway P	Pte	3(R) Munster Fus	19/07/16	[Le] Havre	Persuading M+Insub	Acquit		WO/90/6/67
Cook A	Pte(A/LSgt)	RAOC	08/10/19	Field	M+S40	NG		WO/213/31/4
Cook AJ	Spr	RE	23/12/15	Deganwy	Mx2	15 mos Detn	Remit 3 mos / Quashed	WO/86/68/29
Cook GM	Pte	1 Inf Bn AIF	15/10/18	Field	M+Des	3 yrs PS	Guilty of Des	WO/213/28/200
Cook JR	Pte	18 CEF	30/09/18	Seaford	M+S40	9 mos Imp		WO/86/84/196
Cooke R	Pte	12 SWBdrs	01/12/16	Field	M+Disob	18 mos HL	Comm 3 mos FP1	WO/312/13/46
Cooksey H	Pte	2/6 R Wars	27/05/19	Field	M+S40	2 yrs HL	Remit 1 yr	WO/213/30/64
Cooney R	Cpl	1 Inf Bn AIF	15/10/18	Field	M+Des	8 yrs PS+Rnks	Guilty of Des	WO/213/28/180
Coons L	Pte	21 CEF	05/03/19	Field	M+S40	70 dys FP2	Comm No 2	WO/213/28/202
Cooper AH	Pte	1 Inf Bn AIF	15/10/18	Field	M+Des	3 yrs PS	Guilty of Des	WO/213/28/197
Cooper WJ	Cpl(A/Sgt)	6 R Marines	07/10/19	Field NREF	M(2)+S40	NG		WO/213/30/179
Coote JW	Pte	2/4 R Sussex TF	23/07/15	Canterbury	J[oin in] M	84 dys Detn		WO/92/3/21
Coote WJ	Pte	1 Connaught Rangers	25/08/20	Dagshai	M	1 yr HL+DI		WO/90/8/188
Cope HE	Dvr	RE	04/02/19	Rouen	M	90 dys Imp		WO/90/8/58
Cossey A	Pte	5 Dragoon Gds	29/09/19	Curragh	M	1 yr HL+Disch Igmny	Comm 6 mos Detn	WO/92/4/82
Costello C	Spr	RE	23/12/15	Deganwy	Mx2	2 yrs Detn	Remit 6 mos / Quashed	WO/86/68/29
Coster J	Pte	2 Hants	04/02/19	Rouen	M	90 dys Imp		WO/90/8/58
Costughko V	Pte	12(R) CEF	22/04/19	Liverpool	M	90 dys Detn		WO/92/4/70
Cotter F	Pte	7 R Irish	15/04/18	Field	M	5 yrs PS	Susp	WO/213/21/97
Coughlin HB	Pte	1 Inf Bn AIF	15/10/18	Field	M+Des	3 yrs PS	Guilty of Des	WO/213/28/197
Coulden A	Pte	2 R I Fus	09/06/19	Field EEF	M+XOS+S40	9 mos HL		WO/213/30/126
Couley JJ [MM]	Pte	1 Inf Bn AIF	15/10/18	Field	M+Des	3 yrs PS	Guilty of Des	WO/213/28/196
Covill G	Pte	4 Mddx	12/11/17	Field	M+Disob	6 mos HL	Comm 91 dys FP1	WO/213/18/181
Cowan J	Pte	1 Black Watch	27/09/22	Allahabad	M+Des+Theft+S18(4)	2 yrs HL+DI		WO/90/80/172
Cowley JW	Pte	2/4 R Sussex TF	23/07/15	Canterbury	J[oin in] M	84 dys Detn		WO/92/3/21
Cox P	Pte(L/Cpl)	1 Connaught Rangers	25/08/20	Dagshai	M	Acquit		WO/90/8/188
Cox SG	Bdr	RGA	04/07/19	Aldershot	M	9 mos Detn+Rnks+Disch Igmny		WO/86/87/188
Cox T	L/Bdr	RGA	08/07/19	Aldershot	M	9 mos Detn+Rnks+Disch Igmny		WO/86/87/189
Coxon G	Pte	RAMC	10/05/19	Field	M	6 mos HL	Comm 28 dys FP2	WO/213/30/17
Crabtree EJ	Pte	9(S) E Lancs	29/05/18	SEF	M	1 yr HL		WO/213/23/179
Craig A	Pte	RAOC	29/07/20	Field	M+S7(3b)	4 yrs PS		WO/213/32/22
Craig J	Pte	2 Liverpool	26/04/20	Khartoum	M+S40/S7(3b)	Acquit		WO/90/8/83
Crane J	Pte	Can For Corps	01/05/19	Liverpool	M	6 mos Detn		WO/92/4/69
Cranes CA	Pte	17 AIF	24/03/19	Field	M	11 yrs PS		WO/213/29/90
Cranston HW	Gnr	RGA	13/03/18	Agra	M	1 yr HL	unexpired portion 30/4/18	WO/90/7/190
Crawford A	Dvr	RFA	24/03/19	Field	M	10 yrs PS		WO/213/29/89
Craydon FH	Pte	35 MGC	17/01/19	Field	Mx2	2 yrs HL	Remit 18 mos	WO/213/28/121
Cree T	Pte	65 Coy RDC	21/11/16	Towcester	M	1 yr Detn		WO/92/4/3
Creedy WE	Pte	5 Dragoon Gds	29/09/19	Curragh	M	1 yr HL+Disch Igmny	Comm 6 mos Detn	WO/92/4/81

Name	Rank	Unit	Date D/M/Y	Location	Offence	Finding/Punishment	Amendment	PRO Reference File/Piece/Page
Cregg CD	Pte	10 AIF	24/03/19	Field	M	10 yrs PS		WO213/29/88
Creith BW	Pte	1 Inf Bn AIF	15/10/18	Field	M+Des	3 yrs PS	Guilty of Des	WO/213/28/198
Cresswell E	Cpl	RGA	04/07/19	Aldershot	M	9 mos Detn+Rnks +Disch Igmny		WO/86/87/188
Crisp C	Pte	1 Gn Sher Fstrs	05/06/17	Kantara Egypt	M	2 yrs HL		WO/213/15/176
Crisp W	Pte	45 Royal Fus	21/08/19	NREF	M	Death	2 yrs HL	WO/213/31/27
Crisp WA	Pte	2/6 R Wars	27/05/19	Field	M+S40	2 yrs HL	Remit 1 yr	WO/213/30/64
Crockett AE	Pte	4 Dragoon Gds	09/06/21	Edinburgh	M+V(A/RSM)	2 yrs HL		WO/86/91/131
Crooks R	Pte	2 AIF	24/03/19	Field	M	10 yrs PS		WO/213/29/91
Cross R	Pte	Lab Cps	06/01/19	Field	M+S40	NG		WO/213/27/37
Crouch FE	Pte	2 Buffs	07/10/19	Dover	M	NG		WO/86/88/141
Cruttenden W	Pte	2/4 R Sussex TF	23/07/15	Canterbury	J[oin in] M	84 dys Detn		WO/92/3/21
Cryer W	Dvr	RFA	04/02/19	Rouen	M	56 dys Imp		WO/90/8/58
Cuff SH	Pte	43 CEF	11/12/20	Field	M+Disob	18 mos HL		WO/213/19/116
Cuffy A	Pte	1 BWI	04/05/19	Field Italy	M	6 mos HL		WO/213/29/37
Cummings C	Spr	RE	09/05/19	Field Italy	M	2 yrs HL	Remit 20 mos/ Quashed	WO/213/29/73
Cunningham J	Pte	1/4 R Sco Fus	14/01/18	Field	M	10 yrs PS	Comm 2 yrs HL	WO/213/21/34
Curnew JB	Pte	3 Can MGC	24/03/19	Field	M	Death	Comm PS/Life	WO/213/29/89
Curran RN	Pte	5 Dragoon Gds	26/09/19	Curragh	M	1 yr HL+Disch Igmny	Comm 6 mos Detn	WO/92/4/80
Curtis A	Pte(A/Cpl)	1/4 KOYLI (att RAOC)	08/10/19	Field	M+S40	NG		WO/213/31/4
Curwen T	Pte	5 Dragoon Gds	26/09/19	Curragh	M	1 yr HL+Disch Igmny	Comm 6 mos Detn	WO/92/4/80
Dabell W	Pte	9 MGC	31/07/19	Field	M+Abs/Br	6 mos HL	Quashed	WO/213/30/141
Daley J	Pte	5 Dragoon Gds	24/09/19	Curragh	M	1 yr HL+Disch Igmny	Comm 6 mos Detn	WO/92/4/85
Daly J	Pte	1 Connaught Rangers	04/09/20	Dagshai	M+S7(3b)	3 yrs PS+DI	2 yrs HL	WO/90/8/188
Daly JJ	Pte	1 Connaught Rangers	04/09/20	Dagshai	M+S7(3b)	Death		WO/90/8/188
Daly T	Pte	18 AIF	19/07/16	[Le] Havre	Per M+Viol SO	Acquit		WO/90/6/67
Dancause T	Pte	Quebec Regt	02/08/19	Ripon	M+S40	NG		WO/86/88/42
Dandy W	Pte	2 Liverpool	26/04/20	Khartoum	M+Disob +S40/S7(3b)	6 mos+122 dys Detn + Stop	Remit 122 dys Det+Stop	WO/90/8/83
Daniels C	Pte	2 R Dublin Fusiliers	05/07/20	Constantinople	M+Disob(Capt)	5 yrs PS	2 yrs Detn	WO/90/8/84
Daniels CH	Pte	1 Gn Sher Fstrs	11/06/17	Kantara Egypt	M	2 yrs HL		WO/213/15/175
Danster D	Dvr	ASC (SA)	05/08/18	Field	M+S40	1 yr HL		WO/213/24/129
Davey H	Pte(L/Cpl)	2/4 R Sussex TF	23/07/15	Canterbury	NSM	28 dys Detn		WO/92/3/20
Davi[e?]s JF	Pte	Aus MGC	18/09/17	Etaples	M+Viol+Resist	10 yrs PS		WO/213/17/151
Davids J	Cpl	372 Coy CAHT	14/05/19	Field	M	5 yrs PS		WO/213/30/12
Davidson A	Pte	39 R Fus	23/08/19	Field EEF	M	NG		WO/213/31/25
Davidson L	Pte	R Marine Lab Corps	13/04/17	Dunkirk	M	1 yr HL		WO/213/14/138
Davidson T	Cpl	1/6 HLI	28/12/18	Field	M+Insub+Disob	6 mos HL		WO/213/28/25
Davies B	Pte	5/6 R Welsh Fus	13/01/19	Field EEF	M+S40	90 dys FP2		WO/213/29/42
Davies GH	Gnr	RFA	24/06/19	Field	M+Abs	1 yr HL		WO/213/29/137
Davies HE	Pte	5 Dragoon Gds	29/09/19	Curragh	M	1 yr HL+Disch Igmny	Comm 6 mos Detn	WO/92/4/82
Davies R	Dvr	RASC	18/05/21	Chelsea	M	12 mos HL+DI		WO/92/4/96
Davies W	Pte	26 RW Fus	13/04/19	Field	M+Striking	15 yrs PS	Remit 10 yrs	WO/213/29/177
Davies W	Pte	2/6 R Wars	27/05/19	Field	M+S40	2 yrs HL	Remit 1 yr	WO/213/30/64
Davies WA	Pte	5 Dragoon Gds	22/09/19	Curragh	M	1 yr HL+Disch Igmny	Comm 6 mos Detn	WO/92/4/81
Davis A	Pte	4 BWI	27/12/18	Field Italy	M+Disob	3 yrs PS	Comm 2 yrs HL	WO/213/27/23
Davis C	Pte	3 Leics	27/08/14	Portsmouth	M	1 yr HL		WO/213/2/1
Davis EB	Pte (L/Cpl)	1 Inf Bn AIF	15/10/18	Field	M+Des	3 yrs PS	Guilty of Des	WO/213/28/198
Davis J	Cpl	1 Connaught Rangers	23/08/20	Dagshai	M+S7(3)	2 yrs HL+Rnks+DI		WO/90/8/189
Dawson BE	Pte	3 W Yorks	06/02/18	Wallsend	M+Insub (CSM)	2yrs HL	Comm Detn	WO/86/80/96
Dawson JR	Pte(L/Cpl)	1 Inf Bn AIF	15/10/18	Field	M+Des	5 yrs PS	Guilty of Des	WO/213/28/180
Day G	Pte	9 E Surrey	01/02/19	Field	M+S40	NG		WO/213/28/60
de Vries J	Dvr	372 Coy CAHT	14/05/19	Field	M	5 yrs PS		WO/213/30/12
Deacon PH	Pte	2/4 R Sussex TF	23/07/15	Canterbury	J[oin in] M	84 dys Detn		WO/92/3/21
Dean A	Pte	Lab Cps	06/01/19	Field	M+S40	NG		WO/213/27/37
Dean W	Pte	5 Dragoon Gds	23/09/19	Curragh	M	84 dys HL	Comm 42 dys Detn	WO/92/4/85
Delaney AF	Pte	1 Inf Bn AIF	15/10/18	Field	M+Des	3 yrs PS	Guilty of Des	PRO/213/28/180
Delaney J	Pte	2 A&SH	05/10/16	Rouen	M	Death	Comm 2 yrs PS	WO/90/6/89
Delaney V	Pte	1 Connaught Rangers	30/08/20	Dagshai	M+S7(2)	Death	Life PS	WO/90/8/188
DeLobbe A	Pte	Quebec Regt	23/07/19	Ripon	M+S7(3b)+S40	22mos HL +Disch Igmny		WO/86/88/51
Dennis H	Pte	2/4 R Sussex TF	23/07/15	Canterbury	J[oin in] M	84 dys Detn		WO/92/3/21

53

Name	Rank	Unit	Date D/M/Y	Location	Offence	Finding/Punishment	Amendment	PRO Reference File/Piece/Page
Denton AG	Pte	13 Glouster	16/06/15	Malvern Wells	Incit M+Viol(Sgt)	NG		WO/92/3/18
Derbyshire J	Pte	4(R) LN Lancs	05/02/19	Dublin	M	1 yr Detn		WO/86/86/129
Deriagin I	Pte	1 Slav-Brit Legion	13/07/19	Field	M	Death		WO/213/32/58
Desjardins E	Pte	Quebec Regt	17/07/19	Ripon	M	NG		WO/86/88/12
Desjarlais G	Pte	Can ASC	21/11/17	Bramshott	M+Insub	42 dys Detn	Remit 15 dys	WO/86/79/54
Devenish JE	Pte	20 AIF	24/03/19	Field	M	11 yrs PS		WO/213/29/90
Devers JJ	Pte	1 Connaught Rangers	04/09/20	Dagshai	M+S7(3b)	Life PS+DI	20 yrs PS+DI	WO/90/8/188
Devine J	Pte	6 R Innis Fus	24/03/19	Field	M	11 yrs PS		WO/213/29/89
Devine T	Pte	1 Connaught Rangers	04/09/20	Dagshai	M+S7(3b)	Death	Life PS	WO/90/8/188
Devine TH	Pte	9(S) E Lancs	29/05/18	SEF	M	1 yr HL		WO/213/23/179
Dewhurst G	Pte	9(S) E Lancs	29/05/18	SEF	M	1 yr HL		WO/213/23/179
Diamond F	Pte	Lab Corps (att E Comm LB)	15/06/19	Sutton	M+S7(3b)	Acquit		WO/92/4/73
Dick CE	Pte	1 Inf Bn AIF	15/10/18	Field	M+Des	3 yrs PS	Guilty of Des	WO/213/28/197
Dickenson H	Pte	4 BWI	27/12/18	Field Italy	M+Disob	3 yrs PS	Comm 2 yrs HL	WO/213/27/23
Dickson A	Pte	3(R) CEF	22/04/19	Liverpool	M	23 mos HL		WO/92/4/70
Dickson A	Pte	3(R) CEF	30/05/19	Liverpool	M+S7(3b)	3 yrs HL		WO/92/4/72
Dickson T	Pte	4 R Scots Greys	09/06/21	Edinburgh	M+V(A/RSM)	18 mos HL		WO/86/91/131
Dilworth WF	Pte	5 Dragoon Gds	29/09/19	Curragh	M	1 yr HL+Disch Igmny	Comm 6 mos Detn	WO/92/4/82
Dimelow J	Pte	68 Div Cyclist Coy	17/01/17	Gt Yarmouth	M +Insub(L/Cpl)	NG		WO/86/73/171
Dinneen G	Pte	1 NZ Div Employ Coy	16/10/18	Field	M	6 mos HL	Susp	WO/213/25/165
Dixon SR	Bdr	RGA	04/07/19	Aldershot	M	9 mos Detn+Rnks +Disch Igmny		WO/86/87/188
Dixon T	Pte	2/6 R Wars	27/05/19	Field	M+S40	2 yrs HL	Remit 1 yr	WO/213/30/64
Dixon WT	Pte	58 Coy RDC	21/11/16	Towcester	M	1 yr Detn		WO/92/4/1
Dobbie RR	Pte	1 Inf Bn AIF	15/10/18	Field	M+Des	3 yrs PS	Guilty of Des	WO/213/28/197
Dodds HS	L/Cpl	8 KOYLI	10/02/19	Field	M+Disob+S7(4)	Acquit		WO/213/28/54
Doggrell L	L/Bdr	RGA	04/07/19	Aldershot	M	9 mos Detn+Rnks +Disch Igmny		WO/86/87/188
Donaldson AC	Pte	5 Dragoon Gds	23/09/19	Curragh	M	84 dys HL	Comm 42 dys Detn	WO/92/4/85
Donaldson M	Pte	9 (S) BWI	24/12/18	Field Italy	M+Disob+Esc	5 yrs PS		WO/213/27/25
Donaughey J	Pte	7/8 R Innis Fus	15/04/18	Field	M	5 yrs PS	Susp	WO/213/21/95
Donigan B	Pte	7 R Irish	15/04/18	Field	M	5 yrs PS	Susp	WO/213/21/98
Donkin RB	Pte	21 AIF	04/02/19	Rouen	M	56 dys Imp		WO/90/8/58
Donnell J	Gnr	RGA	13/03/18	Agra	M	1 yr HL	unexpired portion 30/4/18	WO/90/7/190
Donnelly T	Pte	65 Coy RDC	21/11/16	Towcester	M	1 yr Detn		WO/92/4/3
Donohue P	Pte(L/Cpl)	1 Connaught Rangers	23/08/20	Dagshai	M+S7(3)	2 yrs HL+DI		WO/90/8/189
Donovan J	Pte	7 R Irish	15/04/18	Field	M	5 yrs PS	Susp	WO/213/21/97
Dorans H	L/Cpl	5 Dragoon Gds	25/09/19	Curragh	M	Acquit		WO/92/4/86
Doueal A	Cpl	9 Aus Lt Horse	28/06/18	Field EEF	M	NG		WO/213/28/138
Douglas B	Pte	6 (S) BWI	24/12/18	Field Italy	M+Disob	3 yrs 6 mos PS		WO/213/27/24
Douglas G	Pte	65 Coy RDC	16/11/16	Towcester	CM+JM	1 yr Detn		WO/92/3/55
Dowd P	Pte	65 Coy RDC	21/11/16	Towcester	M	1 yr Detn		WO/92/4/3
Downes LA	Pte	58 Coy RDC	21/11/16	Towcester	M	1 yr Detn		WO/92/4/2
Downie A	Pte(L/Cpl)	1 Manchester	05/09/21	Field (Ireland)	M+Disob(CQMS) +S7(3)	3 yrs PS	2yrs Detn	WO/213/32/214
Downton NJ	Pte	1 Inf Bn AIF	15/10/18	Field	M+Des	3 yrs PS	Guilty of Des	WO/213/28/197
Dowse RJ	Pte	5/6 R Welsh Fus	13/01/19	Field EEF	M+S40	90 dys FP2		WO/213/29/42
Dowson W	Cpl	RE	04/02/19	Field	M	10 yrs PS+Rnks	Remit 5 yrs PS	WO/213/28/46
Doxford TR	Pte(L/Cpl)	5 AIF	22/12/18	Field	M	NG		WO/213/27/184
Doyle A	Pte	1 NZ Div Employ Coy	16/10/18	Field	M	6 mos HL	Susp	WO/213/25/165
Doyle D	Pte	14 AIF	24/03/19	Field	M	9 yrs PS		WO/213/29/90
Doyle H	Pte	2 R Dublin Fusiliers	05/07/20	Constantinople	M+Disob(Capt)	5 yrs PS	2 yrs Detn	WO/90/8/84
Doyle NA	Pte	1 Inf Bn AIF	15/10/18	Field	M+Des	3 yrs PS	Guilty of Des	WO/213/29/197
Doyle P	L/Bdr	RGA	05/07/19	Aldershot	M	9 mos Detn+Rnks +Disch Igmny		WO/86/87/189
Drake AJ	Pte	2/4 R Sussex TF	23/07/15	Canterbury	J[oin in] M	84 dys Detn		WO/92/3/21
Draper A	Pte	2 Ches	05/03/20	Field ABS	M+Disob	2 yrs HL	Rem 18 mos	WO/213/31/168
Drew EG	Pte	Lab Corps (att E Comm LB)	15/06/19	Sutton	M+S7(3b)	Acquit		WO/92/4/73
Drury B	Pte	5 Dragoon Gds	26/09/19	Curragh	M	1 yr HL+Disch Igmny	Comm 6 mos Detn	WO/92/4/81
Drury J	Pte	2/4 R Sussex TF	23/07/15	Canterbury	J[oin in] M	84 dys Detn		WO/92/3/21
Du Plessie A	Dvr	ASC (SA)	05/08/18	Field	M+S40	9 mos HL		WO/213/24/129
Duke T	Pte	2 Otago NZEF	01/09/17	Field	M	10 yrs PS		WO/213/17/110

Name	Rank	Unit	Date D/M/Y	Location	Offence	Finding/Punishment	Amendment	PRO Reference File/Piece/Page
Duncan A	Pte	5 Dragoon Gds	22/09/19	Curragh	M	1 yr HL+Disch Igmny	Comm 6 mos Detn	W0/92/3/84
Duncan FT	Pte	65 Coy RDC	21/11/16	Towcester	M	1 yr Detn		W0/92/4/3
Dunlop C	Pte	1/4 R Sco Fus	14/01/18	Field	M	10 yrs PS	Comm 2 yrs HL	W0/213/21/34
Dunn B	Pte(S/Smith)	ASC	30/12/15	Marseilles	Joining M	3 yrs PS	Comm to 2 yrs HL	W0/90/6/44
Dunn ET	A/Cpl	5 Dragoon Gds	03/11/14	At Sea	Endeavg M	56 dys Detn	Comm 14	W0213/1/74
Dunn PS	Pte	Can ASC	21/11/17	Bramshott	M+INsub(Lieut)	42 dys Detn	Remit 10 dys	W0/86/79/54
Dunn R	Pte	30 MGC	29/07/19	Field	M+Disob	1 yr HL		W0/213/30/119
Dunn R	Pte	1 Inf Bn AIF	15/10/18	Field	M+Des	3 yrs PS	Guilty of Des	W0/213/28/199
Dunne AW	Pte(2AM)(A/Cpl)	RAF	30/04/18	Swanage	M+Disob	18 mos HL		W0/92/4/41
Dunse JE		21 Manch	08/02/19	Field	M+Abs	6 mos HL		W0/213/28/58
Durham W	Pte	65 Coy RDC	21/11/16	Towcester	M	1 yr Detn		W0/92/4/3
Dwerryhouse J	Gnr	RFA	24/06/19	Field	M	18 mos HL		W0/213/29/137
Dyer GH	Cpl	1 Connaught Rangers	25/08/20	Dagshai	M	3 yrs PS+Rnks+Dl		W0/90/8/188
Dyer P	Pte	1 Som LI	04/02/19	Rouen	M	90 dys Imp		W0/90/8/58
Dyer S	Pte	7/8 R Innis Fus	15/04/18	Field	M	5 yrs PS	Susp	W0/213/21/95
Eades G	Pte	2/4 R Sussex TF	23/07/15	Canterbury	J[oin in] M	84 dys Detn		W0/92/3/21
Eames J	Pte	1 Inf Bn AIF	15/10/18	Field	Mx2+Des	3 yrs PS	Guilty of Des	W0/213/28/196
Earle J	Pte	2/6 R Wars	27/05/19	Field	M+S40	2 yrs HL	Remit 1 yr	W0/213/30/64
Eden W	Pte	8 (R) CEF	03/09/17	Shorncliffe	Mx2+S40+S41	16 mos HL		W0/86/78/25
Edgar R	Cpl	1 Ox & Bucks LI	04/05/20	Cork	M+V(CSM)	Acquit		W0/92/4/90
Edmeads E	Spr	3 Aus Tun Coy	13/10/18	Field	M+Disob	1 yr HL	NC	W0/213/30/136
Edmonds FW	Spr	3 Aus Tun Coy	18/10/18	Field	M+Disob	2 yrs HL	Susp	W0/213/26/65
Edmonds FW	Pte	Can Res Cav Reg	07/05/19	Liverpool	M	5 yrs PS		W0/92/4/70
Edmondson RH	Spr	RE	15/05/19	Field	M+Disob	1 yr IHL		W0/213/29/137
Edmunds A	Pte	9 (S) BWI	24/12/18	Field Italy	M+Disob+Esc	8 yrs PS		W0/213/27/25
Edwards E	Pte	2/4 R Sussex TF	23/07/15	Canterbury	J[oin in] M	84 dys Detn		W0/92/3/21
Edwards J [aka E]	Pte	8 SWB	02/05/18	Field SEF	M+Disob	10 yrs PS	Comm 2 yrs HL	W0/213/22/30
Edwards T	Pte	RFA	30/05/18	Field Italy	M+Striking	Death	Comm 3 yrs PS	W0/213/22/126
Edwards T	Gnr	1 Connaught Rangers	04/09/20	Dagshai	M+S7(3b)	Death	Life PS	W0/90/8/188
Egan E	Pte	5 Dragoon Gds	26/09/19	Curragh	M	1 yr HL+Disch Igmny	Comm 6 mos Detn	W0/92/4/81
Egglestone JW	Pte	1/13 Lond	04/02/19	Rouen	M	90 dys Imp		W0/90/8/58
Eglinton TR	Pte	39 R Fus	23/08/19	Field EEF	M	NG		W0/213/31/23
Ehrlick L	Pte	39 R Fus	23/08/19	Field EEF	M	5 yrs PS	Comm 1 yr HL	W0/213/31/24
Eisenstat H	Gnr(A/Bdr)	2/3 Northern Bde AC/ RFA	04/05/16	Bawtry	JM	3 yrs PS+Disch Igmny		W0/92/3/39
Eland G	Pte	39 R Fus	23/08/19	Field EEF	M	5 yrs PS	Remit	W0/213/31/25
Elden E	Spr	101 Field Coy RE	27/03/19	Field Italy	M+Disob	5 yrs PS		W0/213/28/191
Elder J	Pte	SANLC	21/11/17	Field	M+S40	3 yrs PS	Comm 2 yrs HL	W0/213/31/109
Elias	Pte	1 Slav-Brit Legion	14/07/19	Field NREF	M	Death		W0/213/32/59
Elisaieff I	Pte	1 Inf Bn AIF	15/10/18	Field	M+Des	3 yrs PS	Guilty of Des	W0/213/28/197
Ellen J	Pte	7/8 R Innis Fus	15/04/18	Field	M	5 yrs PS	Susp	W0/213/21/96
Elliot F	Pte	58 Coy RDC	21/11/16	Towcester	M	1 yr Detn		W0/92/4/1
Elliot J	Cpl	RGA	05/07/19	Aldershot	M	9 mos Detn+Rnks		W0/86/88/1
Elliott F	Pte	5 Dragoon Gds	22/09/19	Curragh	M	1 yr HL+Disch Igmny	Comm 6 mos Detn	W0/92/4/84
Elliott JW	Pte	1 Inf Bn AIF	15/10/18	Field	M+Des	NG		W0/213/28/198
Ellis AJ	Pte	30 MGC	29/07/19	Field	M+Disob	1 yr HL		W0/213/30/119
Ellis EJ	Pte	4/5 Welsh Regt	13/01/19	Field EEF	M+S40	90 dys FP2		W0/213/29/42
Ellis T	Ptr	65 Coy RDC	21/11/16	Towcester	M	1 yr Detn		W0/92/4/2
Ellison E	Pte	2/4 R Sussex TF	23/07/15	Canterbury	J[oin in] M	84 dys Detn		W0/92/3/21
Elphick C	Pte	7 Norfolk	13/04/17	Arras	M+S40	9 mos HL	Rem 3 mos	W0/213/15/142
Elsegood A	Spr	RE	08/08/19	Bordon	M+S40	18 mos Detn	15 mos	W0/92/4/77
Elston A	Spr	Can Ry Troops	22/04/19	Liverpool	M	120 dys Detn		W0/92/4/70
English M	Pte	9(S) E Lancs	29/05/18	SEF	M	1 yr HL		W0/213/23/179
Entwistle E	Pte	45 Royal Fus	21/08/19	NREF	No offence/Mutiny?	Death	2 yrs HL	W0/213/31/27
Enright W	Gnr	Can Res Arty	06/05/19	Liverpool	M	Acquit		W0/92/4/67
Evans E	Pte	1(R) MGC	25/06/18	Grantham	M+S40	1 yr HL		W0/92/4/40
Evans JA	Pte	5 Dragoon Gds	24/09/19	Curragh	M	1 yr HL+Disch Igmny	Comm 6 mos Detn	W0/92/4/85
Evans SW	Pte	4 BWI	27/12/18	Field Italy	M+Disob	3 yrs PS	Comm 2 yrs HL	W0/213/27/23
Evans W	Pte	65 Coy RDC	21/11/16	Towcester	M	1 yr Detn		W0/92/4/2
Evans W	Pte	2/5 Welsh TF	27/09/16	Cardiff	M	1 ytr Detn		W0/86/66/194
Evers (Evens?) T	Pte	65 Coy RDC	21/11/16	Towcester	M	1 yr Detn		W0/92/4/3
Eves R	Pte	1 Slav-Brit Legion	17/07/19	Field NREF	M	Death	Comm 10 yrs PS	W0/213/32/59
Evstraloff P	Pte	5 Dragoon Gds	29/09/19	Curragh	M	1 yr HL+Disch Igmny	Comm 6 mos Detn	W0/92/4/82
Ewington AH	Pte	1/7 Ches	24/03/19	Field	M	18 yrs PS		W0213/29/88
Fagan A	Pte							

Name	Rank	Unit	Date D/M/Y	Location	Offence	Finding/Punishment	Amendment	PRO Reference File/Piece/Page
Failes NC	Pte	2 R Dublin Fusiliers	05/07/20	Constantinople	M+Disob(Capt)	5 yrs PS	2 yrs Detn	WO/90/8/84
Faircrough R	Pte	65 Coy RDC	21/11/16	Towcester	M	1 yr Detn		WO/92/4/2
Faith T	Pte	2/4 R Sussex TF	23/07/15	Canterbury	J[oin in] M	NG		WO/92/3/21
Falkenbury CH	Pte	1 Ont Regt	15/07/18	Bramshott	M+S40	2 yrs HL+Stoppages		WO/92/4/43
Fallon A	Pte	2/4 KOYLI	24/03/19	Field	M	10 yrs PS		WO/213/29/88
Fallon J	Pte(L/Cpl)	1 Connaught Rangers	25/08/20	Dagshai	M	2 yrs HL+DI		WO/90/8/188
Farmer P	Sgt	2/4 R Sussex TF	23/07/15	Canterbury	NSM	Redu to Cpl		WO/92/3/20
Farr WH	Rfn	18 KRRC	22/12/18	Field	M	5 yrs PS		WO/213/27/184
Faulkener H	Pte	2/4 R Sussex TF	23/07/15	Canterbury	J[oin in] M	84 dys Detn		WO/92/3/21
Faulkner JR	Pte	3 W Yorks	01/08/19	Devizes	M+S40	18 mos HL+Disch Igmny	9 mos	WO/92/4/77
Faulkner WH	Pte	1 Inf Bn AIF	15/10/18	Field	M+Des	3 yrs PS	Guilty of Des	WO/213/28/197
Feldman B	Pte	39 R Fus	23/08/19	Field EEF	M	5 yrs PS		WO/213/31/23
Feldman J	Pte	39 R Fus	23/08/19	Field EEF	M	5 yrs PS	Comm 1 yr HL	WO/213/31/25
Fellasters G	Pte	2/7 R Wars	05/01/19	Field	M	NG		WO/213/27/71
Fellows R	Dvr	65 SAASC	04/04/17	Field SEF	M+Insub+S9(1)	10 yrs PS		WO/213/15/5
Fender S	Pte	6 (S) BWI	24/12/18	Field Italy	M+Disob	3 yrs 6 mos PS		WO/213/27/24
Fennell H	Pte	2/4 R Sussex TF	23/07/15	Canterbury	J[oin in] M	84 dys Detn		WO/92/3/22
Fennell S	Pte	2/4 R Sussex TF	23/07/15	Canterbury	J[oin in] M	84 dys Detn		WO/92/3/22
Fennell W	Pte	2/4 R Sussex TF	23/07/15	Canterbury	J[oin in] M	84 dys Detn		WO/92/3/22
Fenwick JL	L/Bdr	RGA	05/07/19	Aldershot	M	9 mos Detn+Rnks		WO/86/88/1
Ferguson WJ	Pte	1 Aus MGB	04/02/19	Rouen	M	90 dys Imp		WO/90/8/59
Ferlander S	Dvr	372 Coy CAHT	14/05/19	Field	M	5 yrs PS	Remit 2 yrs	WO/213/30/12
Ferrington F	Pte	5/6 R Welsh Fus	13/01/19	Field EEF	M+S40	90 dys FP2		WO/213/29/42
Fiander AE	Pte	MGC	05/11/18	Grantham	M+S40	1 yr Detn		WO/86/85/97
Field C	Rfn	3/21 London TF	04/01/16	Winchester	M+Insub(Sgt)	1 yr Detn	Comm 6 mos Detn	WO/86/68/180
Field R	L/Cpl	8 KOYLI	10/02/19	Field	M+Disob+S40	Acquit		WO/213/28/54
Field WH	Pte	65 Coy RDC	21/11/16	Towcester	M	1 yr Detn		WO/92/4/3
Fielder P	Pte	Lab Corps (att E Comm LB)	15/06/19	Sutton	M+S7(3b)	Acquit		WO/92/4/73
Fields W	Pte	12 Lancs Fus	02/05/18	Field SEF	M+Disob	10 yrs PS	Comm 2 yrs HL	WO/213/22/30
Filmar A	Pte	4 Mddx	12/11/17	Field	M+Disob	6 mos HL	Comm 91 dys FP1	WO/213/18/181
Findlay RC	Pte	1 NZ Div Employ Coy	16/10/18	Field	M	6 mos HL	Susp	WO/213/25/165
Finkelstein F	Pte	39 R Fus	23/08/19	Field EEF	M	5 yrs PS	Comm 1 yr HL	WO/213/31/24
Finlan J	Pte	8 R Innis Fus	06/09/15	Eniskillen	M+Inj pub property	1 yr HL		WO/86/66/111
Finlayson R	Pte	1 NZ Div Employ Coy	16/10/18	Field	M	6 mos HL	Susp	WO/213/25/165
Firth J	Pte	10 Y & Lanc	12/11/17	Field	M+Disob	6 mos HL	Comm 91 dys FP1	WO/213/18/181
Fish EW	Pte	1 Inf Bn AIF	15/10/18	Field	M+Des	3 yrs PS	Guilty of Des	WO/213/28/196
Fisher GW	Pte	5 Dragoon Gds	29/09/19	Curragh	M	1 yr HL+Disch Igmny	Comm 6 mos Detn	WO/92/4/82
Fitzgerald M	Pte	1 Connaught Rangers	04/09/20	Dagshai	M+S7(3b)	Death	Life PS	WO/90/8/188
Fitzgerald NJ	Pte	2 AIF	18/06/19	Field	M+Disob	14 mos HL		WO/213/30/131
Fitzgerald P	Pte	2 R I Fus	09/06/19	Field EEF	M+S40	21 dys FP2	Quashed	WO/213/30/126
Fitzpatrick T	Pte	7/8 R Innis Fus	15/04/18	Field	M	5 yrs PS	Susp	WO/213/21/95
Flanagan J	Gdsn	Irish Gds	04/02/20	Guildhall Wminster	M	5 yrs PS+Disch Igmny		WO/92/4/89
Flannery J	Pte	1 Connaught Rangers	30/08/20	Dagshai	M	Death	Life PS	WO/90/8/188
Flannigan J	Pte(L/Cpl)	7/8 R Innis Fus	15/04/18	Field	M	7 yrs PS	Susp	WO/213/21/95
Fletcher C	L/Bdr	RGA	05/07/19	Aldershot	M	9 mos Detn+Rnks		WO/86/88/1
Fletcher WJ	Pte	19 AIF	15/02/16	Sinai Penin	M+Disob	12 mos HL		WO/213/8/113
Flint GH	Tpr	Can Lt Horse	19/09/17	Etaples	M	10 yrs PS	Comm 2 yrs HL	WO/213/17/151
Flores E	Pte	BWI	04/01/18	Mesopotamia	[M]7(2)	3 yrs PS	Comm 1 yr HL	WO/90/7/169
Floyd W	Pte	33 AIF	24/03/19	Field	M	9 yrs PS		WO213/29/88
Flynn G	Pte	R Munster Fus	11/10/14	St Nazaire	M	5 yrs PS	Quashed	WO/213/2/105
Flynn M	Pte	1 Inf Bn AIF	15/10/18	Field	M+Des	3 yrs PS	Guilty of Des	WO/213/28/199
Flynn P	Pte	58 Coy RDC	21/11/16	Towcester	M	1 yr Detn		WO/92/4/1
Forbes J	Pte	RASC	20/04/20	Field ABS	M+Disob	3 mos FP2		WO/213/31/171
Ford B	Pte	Bermuda Artillery	31/08/20	Bermuda	M	Acquit		WO/90/8/84
Ford ES	Cpl	RGA	04/07/19	Aldershot	M	9 mos Detn+Rnks +Disch Igmny		WO/86/87/188
Ford J	Pte	1 Gn Sher Fstrs	05/06/17	Kantara Egypt	M	2 yrs HL		WO/213/15/176
Ford J	Pte	58 AIF	24/03/19	Field	M	10 yrs PS		WO/213/29/90
Ford T	Gnr(AL/Bdr)	RGA	02/03/18	Bettisfield	M[S7(2)]+S40	42 dys Detn		WO/86/80/178
Foreman I	Pte	39 R Fus	23/08/19	Field EEF	M	5 yrs PS		WO/213/31/23
Foreman OG	Pte	West India Regt	29/04/21	Jamaica	M+Abs+S9(1)	5 yrs PS+DI	Remit 2 yrs	WO/90/8/87
Forrest A	Pte	RASC	20/02/19	Field	Mx2+S40	NG		WO/213/28/169

Name	Rank	Unit	Date D/M/Y	Location	Offence	Finding/Punishment	Amendment	PRO Reference File/Piece/Page
Forsyth GH	Pte	18 CEF	30/09/18	Seaford	M+S40	90 dys Detn		WO/86/84/196
Fortin J	Pte	4(R) CEF	02/03/18	Bramshott	M+Abs+S40x2	56 dys Detn	Quashed	WO/86/81/34
Fortis SL	Pte	Lab Corps	24/03/19	Field	M	11 yrs PS		WO/213/29/89
Foster A	Pte	257 P of W Coy	13/05/19	Field	M+S40(2)	6 mos Imp	Comm 90 dys FP2	WO/213/30/31
Foster G	Pte	2/4 R Sussex TF	23/07/15	Canterbury	J[oin in] M	84 dys Detn		WO/92/3/21
Foster JA	Pte	58 Coy RDC	21/11/16	Towcester	M	1 yr Detn		WO/92/4/2
Foster WA	Pte	17 AIF	24/03/19	Field	M	10 yrs PS		WO/213/29/90
Foulkes GJ	Dvr	RFA	27/09/19	Deepcut	M	2 yrs HL	Remit 6 mos +Comm to Detn	WO/86/88/138
Found L	Pte	2/6 R Wars	27/05/19	Field	M+S40	2 yrs HL	Remit 1 yr	WO/213/30/64
Fowler A	Pte	30 MGC	29/07/19	Field	M+Disob	1 yr HL		WO/213/30/119
Fowler F	Gnr	RGA	13/03/18	Agra	M	1 yr HL	unexpired portion 30/4/18	WO/90/7/190
Fox AT	Pte	2/4 R Sussex TF	23/07/15	Canterbury	J[oin in] M	84 dys Detn		WO/92/3/22
Fox H	Cpl	RGA	05/07/19	Aldershot	M	9 mos Detn+Rnks +Disch Igmny		WO/86/87/189
Fox J	Pte	Labour Bn	16/01/19	Mesopotamia	M	84 dys Detn		WO/90/7/169
Fox LF	Pte	9 MGC	31/07/19	Field	M+Abs/Br	6 mos HL		WO/213/30/141
Fradley L	Gnr	337 Bde RFA	10/01/17	Canterbury	JM	6 mos Detn		WO/92/3/58
France W	Pte	11 North Fus	04/02/19	Rouen	M	90 dys Imp		WO/90/8/58
Francis R	Pte	6 (S) BWI	24/12/18	Field Italy	M+Disob	3 yrs 6 mos PS		WO/213/27/24
Frankel A	Pte	39 R Fus	23/08/19	Field EEF	M	5 yrs PS	Comm 1 yr HL	WO/213/31/24
Frans	Pte	SANLC	21/11/17	Field	M+S40	3 yrs PS	Comm 2 yrs HL	WO/213/31/109
Fraser HA	Pte	14 AIF	24/03/19	Field	M	11 yrs PS		WO/213/29/90
Fredericks A	Dvr	372 Coy CAHT	14/05/19	Field	M	5 yrs PS		WO/213/30/12
Free H	Dvr	372 Coy CAHT	14/05/19	Field	M	5 yrs PS	Comm 2 yrs HL	WO/213/30/12
Freeman H	Pte	1 Gn Sher Fstrs	05/06/17	Kantara Egypt	M	2 yrs HL		WO/213/15/176
Freeman W	L/Cpl	35 MGC	17/01/19	Field	M	2 yrs HL	Remit 6 mos	WO/213/28/120
Freestone SG	Dvr	337 Bde RFA	10/01/17	Canterbury	JM	6 mos Detn		WO/92/3/58
French J	Pte	12 SWBdrs	01/12/16	Field	M+Disob	18 mos HL	Comm 3 mos FP1	WO/213/13/46
Frew G	Pte	2 Otago NZEF	01/09/17	Field	M	10 yrs PS		WO/213/17/110
Friar R	Pte(L/Cpl)	2/7 R Wars	04/01/19	Field	M	5 yrs PS		WO/213/28/72
Froom EH	Pte	7/8 R Innis Fus	15/04/18	Field	M	5 yrs PS	Susp	WO/213/21/96
Froude J	Bdr	RGA	05/07/19	Aldershot	M	NG		WO/86/87/189
Fryers W	Pte	21 Manch	08/02/19	Field	M+Abs	6 mos HL		WO/213/28/58
Fulford A	Pte	11 Worc	02/05/18	Field SEF	M+Disob	10 yrs PS	Comm 2 yrs HL	WO/213/22/30
Fullalove JP	Pte	9(S) E Lancs	29/05/18	SEF	M	1 yr HL		WO/213/23/179
Fullerton J	Pte	7/8 R Innis Fus	15/04/18	Field	M	5 yrs PS	Susp	WO/213/21/95
Furlong J	Pte	65 Coy RDC	21/11/16	Towcester	M	1 yr Detn		WO/92/4/3
Gadsby JE	Pte	5 Dragoon Gds	23/09/19	Curragh	M	84 dys HL	Comm 42 dys Detn	WO/92/4/85
Gager SE	Gnr	RGA	13/03/18	Agra	M	1 yr HL	unexpired portion 30/4/18	WO/90/7/190
Gale G	Pte	2 Aus Pnr AIF	24/03/19	Field	M	11 yrs PS		WO/213/29/91
Gale H	Pte	1/1 C of Lon Yeo	17/06/19	Field EEF	M+S40	NG		WO/213/30/104
Gallagher J	Pte(L/Cpl)	1 Connaught Rangers	25/08/20	Dagshai	M	Acquit		WO/90/8/188
Gallagher P	Pte	60 AIF	27/12/16	At Sea	M+Ins+Disob	2 yrs HL+Disch Igmny		WO/213/13/97
Gallagher P	Pte	12 AIF	24/03/19	Field	M	10 yrs PS		WO/213/29/90
Gallimore G	Pte	58 Coy RDC	21/11/16	Towcester	M	1 yr Detn		WO/92/4/1
Galloway JA	Pte	Bermuda Artillery	31/08/20	Bermuda	M	Acquit		WO/90/8/84
Galloway P	Pte	13 Glouster	17/06/15	Malvern Wells	Incit M+Insub(Sgt)+ S40	3 yrs PS		WO/92/3/24
Gamble F	Pte	9 MGC	31/07/19	Field	M+Abs/Br	6 mos HL		WO/213/30/141
Gambrill WJ	Pte	Lab Corps (att E Comm LB)	15/06/19	Sutton	M+S7(3b)	Acquit		WO/92/4/73
Gandy C	Pte	5 Dragoon Gds	29/09/19	Curragh	M	1 yr HL+Disch Igmny	Comm 6 mos Detn	WO/92/4/82
Gandy J	Cpl	11(R) CEF	19/05/19	Liverpool	M+S40	Rnks+1 yr HL		WO/92/4/72
Ganley H	Pte	1 Gn Sher Fstrs	05/06/17	Kantara Egypt	M	2 yrs HL		WO/213/15/176
Gannon C	Gnr	2/3 Northern Bde AC/RFA	04/05/16	Bawtry	JM	3 yrs PS + Disch Igmny		WO/92/3/39
Garadies J	Dvr	372 Coy CAHT	14/05/19	Field	M	5 yrs PS	Comm 2 yrs HL	WO/213/30/12
Garden J	Pte	1 HLI	05/10/16	Rouen	M	Death	Comm 15 yrs PS	WO/90/6/89
Gardener R	Gnr	RFA	24/04/19	Field	M+Disob	5 mos HL		WO/213/29/160
Gardiner GG	Pte	8(R) CEF	05/05/19	Liverpool	M	Acquit		WO/92/4/67
Gardiner J	Pte	Bermuda Artillery	31/08/20	Bermuda	M+Esc+S6(1d)	2 yrs HL+DI		WO/90/8/84
Gardner JT	Pte	3 RWFs	06/06/18	Kinmel Park	M+Disob	6 mos HL		WO/92/4/39
Gareau A	Pte	Quebec Regt	16/07/19	Ripon	M	2o mos+ Disch Igmny		WO/86/88/51
Garner J	Pte	2 York & Lanc	16/07/20	Kasvin	M	1 yr HL		WO/90/7/208

Name	Rank	Unit	Date D/M/Y	Location	Offence	Finding/Punishment	Amendment	PRO Reference File/Piece/Page
Garner VJ	Pte	5 Dragoon Gds	22/09/19	Curragh	M	1 yr HL+Disch Igmny	Comm 6 mos Detn	WO/92/4/84
Garrett JC	Pte	1 Inf Bn AIF	15/10/18	Field	M+Des	3 yrs PS	Guilty of Des	WO/213/28/196
Garton F	Pte	58 Coy RDC	21/11/16	Towcester	M	1 yr Detn		WO/92/4/1
Gates D	Pte	5 Dragoon Gds	22/09/19	Curragh	M	1 yr HL+Disch Igmny	Comm 6 mos Detn	WO/92/4/84
Gatterill D	Pte(L/Cpl)	2/4 R Sussex TF	23/07/15	Canterbury	NSM	28 dys Detn		WO/92/3/20
Gauthier GF	Pte	13(R) CEF	05/05/19	Liverpool	M	Acquit		WO/92/4/67
Gavin AR	Pte (L/Cpl)	1 Inf Bn AIF	15/10/18	Field	M+Des	NG		WO/213/28/200
Gay EH	Pte	27 AIF	24/03/19	Field	M	10 yrs PS		WO213/29/88
Gay G	Pte(S/Smith)	ASC	30/12/15	Marseilles	Joining M	3 yrs PS	Comm to 2 yrs HL	WO/90/6/44
Geary T	Pte/LCpl	2 Royal Irish	05/07/21	Chakrata	M+S7(3b)	3 yrs PS	NC	WO/90/8/170
Gelant F	Dvr	372 Coy CAHT	14/05/19	Field	M	5 yrs PS	Remit 2 yrs	WO/213/30/12
Gibbs JE	Pte	2 W India	11/05/19	Field EEF	M	7 yrs PS	Comm 2 yrs HL	WO/213/30/28
Gilbert J	Pte	5 Dragoon Gds	22/09/19	Curragh	M	1 yr HL+Disch Igmny	Comm 6 mos Detn	WO/92/4/84
Gilkenson J	Pte	1 NZ Div Employ Coy	16/10/18	Field	M	6 mos HL	Susp	WO/213/25/165
Gill J	Pte	5 Dragoon Gds	29/09/19	Curragh	M	1 yr HL+Disch Igmny	Comm 6 mos Detn	WO/92/4/83
Gillespie W	Pte	49 MG Coy	15/04/18	Field	M	NG		WO/213/21/99
Gillett C	Pte	3 W Yorks	01/08/19	Devizes	M+S40	18 mos HL Igmny	9 mos	WO/92/4/77
Gillies R	Pte	R Marine Lab Corps	13/04/17	Dunkirk	M	1 yr HL		WO/213/14/138
Gillingham P	Pte	Lab Cps	06/01/19	Field	M+S40	NG		WO/213/27/37
Gillings WG	Pte	Lab Corps (att E Comm LB)	15/06/19	Sutton	M+S7(3b)	Acquit		WO/92/4/73
Gilmartin J	Spr	RE	04/02/19	Rouen	M	90 dys Imp		WO/90/8/58
Glanister J	L/Bdr	RGA	04/07/19	Aldershot	M	9 mos Detn+Rnks +Disch Igmny		WO/86/87/188
Glass H	L/Bdr	RGA	04/07/19	Aldershot	M	9 mos Detn+Rnks s+Disch Igmny		WO/86/87/188
Gleason JJ	Pte	1 Connaught Rangers	04/09/20	Dagshai	M+S7(3b)	Death	Life PS	WO/90/8/188
Glover JH	Pte	1 Inf Bn AIF	15/10/18	Field	M+Des	3 yrs PS	Guilty of Des	WO/213/28/200
Glover RJ	Dvr	RFA	27/09/19	Deepcut	M	1 yr HL	Comm to Detn	WO/86/88/138
Goden E	Pte(L/Cpl)	7/8 R Innis Fus	15/04/18	Field	M	7 yrs PS	Susp	WO/213/21/96
Gogarty PJ	Pte	1 Connaught Rangers	30/08/20	Dagshai	M	Death	Life PS	WO/90/8/189
Goggins DH	Pte	1 Inf Bn AIF	15/10/18	Field	M+Des	3 yrs PS	Guilty of Des	WO/213/28/199
Golby W	Pte	2/4 R Sussex TF	23/07/15	Canterbury	J[oin in] M	84 dys Detn		WO/92/3/22
Golding D	Pte	6 (S) BWI	24/12/18	Field Italy	M+Disob	3 yrs 6 mos PS		WO/213/27/24
Goldman B	Pte	39 R Fus	23/08/19	Field EEF	M	NG		WO/213/31/23
Goldman M	Pte	39 R Fus	23/08/19	Field EEF	M	5 yrs PS	Comm 1 yr HL	WO/213/31/24
Gonzales BAE	Pte	1 BWI	02/05/19	Field Italy	Mx2+Disob	18 mos HL	Remit 12 mos	WO/213/29/37
Goodman W	Gnr(A/Bdr)	163 (How) Bde RFA	11/12/15	Bulford	M	1 month FP2+Rnks		WO/86/68/23
Goodwin J	Pte	3 RWFs	06/06/18	Kinmel Park	M+Disob	6 mos HL	Comm to Detn Detn	WO/92/4/39
Goodwin J	Pte	5 Dragoon Gds	29/09/19	Curragh	M	1 yr HL+Disch Igmny	Comm 9 mos	WO/92/4/83
Goodwin LR	Pte	19 AIF	24/03/19	Field	M	10 yrs PS		WO/213/29/91
Gordon J	Gnr	RGA	13/03/18	Agra	M	1 yr HL	unexpired portion 30/4/18	WO/90/7/190
Gordon J	Pte	2 W India	11/05/19	Field EEF	M	5 yrs PS	Comm 1 yr HL	WO/213/30/28
Gordon JH	Pte	2 Liverpool	26/04/20	Khartoum	M+S40/S7(3b)	Acquit		WO/90/8/83
Gorman J	Pte	1 Connaught Rangers	04/09/20	Dagshai	M+S7(3b)	7 yrs PS+DI		WO/90/8/188
Gornall R	L/Cpl	5 Dragoon Gds	30/09/19	Curragh	M	18 mos HL +Disch Igmny	Comm 9 mos Dtn	WO/92/4/87
Gough F	Pte	5 Dragoon Gds	29/09/19	Curragh	M	1 yr HL+Disch Igmny	Comm 6 mos Detn	WO/92/4/82
Gough JW	Pte	Lab Corps (att E Comm LB)	15/06/19	Sutton	M+S7(3b)	Acquit		WO/92/4/73
Gould GW	Spr	RE(TF)	24/09/15	Malta	M+S40	NG		WO/90/6/35
Graham JW	Pte	65 Coy RDC	21/11/16	Towcester	M	1 yr Detn		WO/92/4/2
Graham M	Cpl	17 Coy ICC	28/06/18	Field EEF	M	NG		WO/213/28/138
Graham R	Pte	1/4 KOYLI (att 365 POW Coy)	16/09/19	Field	M+Abs+Disob	3 yrs PS	Comm 1 yr HL	WO/213/31/69
Graham WG	Pte	43 CEF	11/12/17	Field	M+Disob	18 mos HL		WO/213/19/116
Grainger L	Pte	11 Sherwood F'sters	30/12/15	Steenbecque	M	28 dys FP1+Rnks		WO/213/7/25
Grant CC	Pte	8 AIF	24/03/19	Field	M	9 yrs PS		WO/213/29/89
Grapes C	Pte	2 MGC	12/06/19	Field	M+Disob(2)+S40	5 yrs PS	Remit 2 yrs	WO/213/29/122
Grasso G	Pte	51 AIF	04/02/19	Rouen	M	Acquit		WO/90/8/59
Gray A	Gnr	RFA	27/09/19	Deepcut	M	NG		WO/86/88/138
Gray FW	S/Smith	1/1 C of Lon Yeo	18/06/19	Field	M+S40	75 dys Stop	Remit 53 dys	WO/213/30/96
Gray G	Gnr	337 Bde RFA	10/01/17	Canterbury	JM	6 mos Detn		WO/92/3/58

Name	Rank	Unit	Date D/M/Y	Location	Offence	Finding/Punishment	Amendment	PRO Reference File/Piece/Page
Greaves H	Pte	9(S) E Lancs	29/05/18	SEF	M	1 yr HL		WO/213/23/179
Green AP	Pte	2 Y[ork] & Lanc	04/11/19	Basrah	M+Disob+Insub Lang	4 yrs PS	Comm 2 yrs HL	WO/90/7/205
Green FC	Pte	2 MGC	12/06/19	Field	M+Disob(2)+S40	5 yrs PS	Remit 2 yrs	WO/213/29/122
Green H	Pte	Labour Bn	16/01/19	Mesopotamia	M	1 yr HL		WO/90/7/169
Green J	Cpl	RGA	04/07/19	Aldershot	M	9 mos Detn+Rnks +Disch Igmny		WO/86/87/188
Green P	Pte	13 E Lancs	04/02/19	Rouen	M	90 dys Imp		WO/90/8/58
Green W	Pte	6 LN Lancs	04/11/17	Mesopotamia	Drunk+Viol+M+S10(3) +Insol	5 yrs PS +DI		WO/90/7/143
Green W	L/Cpl	RE	04/02/19	Field	M+S40	9 mos HL		WO/213/28/46
Greenfield A	Pte	5 Dragoon Gds	26/09/19	Curragh	M	1 yr HL+Disch Igmny	Comm 6 mos Detn	WO/92/4/81
Greenhalgh E	Pte	Quebec Regt	14/07/19	Ripon	M+S7(3b)	18 mos HL		WO/86/88/29
Greenhow WS	Pte	5 Dragoon Gds	29/09/19	Curragh	M	1 yr HL+Disch Igmny	Comm 6 mos Detn	WO/92/4/81
Greenway H	Pte(L/Cpl)	2/7 R Wars	04/01/19	Field	M	5 yrs PS		WO/213/28/72
Gregory W	Pte	2 R Irish	15/04/18	Field	M	5 yrs PS	Susp	WO/213/21/98
Grier A	Spr	RE	15/05/19	Field	M+Disob	1 yr IHL		WO/213/29/137
Griffin AJ	Pte	1/1 C of Lon Yeo	18/06/19	Field	M+S40	NG		WO/213/30/96
Griffin M	Pte	65 Coy RDC	16/11/16	Towcester	CM+JM	1 yr Detn		WO/92/3/55
Griffiths A	Pte	4 BWI	27/12/18	Field Italy	M+Disob	3 yrs PS	Comm 2 yrs HL	WO/213/27/23
Griffiths J	Pte	65 Coy RDC	21/11/16	Towcester	M	1 yr Detn		WO/92/4/2
Griffiths PH	L/Cpl	13 Yorks	17/05/19	Field NREF	M	2 yrs HL		WO/213/29/35
Grimmer FL	Pte	Lab Corps (att E Comm LB)	15/06/19	Sutton	M+S7(3b)	Acquit		WO/92/4/73
Grimshaw H	Pte	21 Manch	08/02/19	Field	M+Abs	6 mos HL		WO/213/28/58
Grimstone H	Dvr	RFA	24/04/19	Field	M+Disob	5 mos HL		WO/213/29/160
Grimwood H	Pte	1 NZ Div Emp B	16/10/18	Field	M	6 mos HL	Susp	WO/213/25/165
Grocott JJ	Dvr	337 Bde RFA	10/01/17	Canterbury	JM	6 mos Detn		WO/92/3/58
Grocutt E	Gnr	RFA	24/06/19	Field	M	NG		WO/213/29/137
Groom W	Pte	1 Border	22/06/16	Louvencourt	M+Insub+Disob	4 yrs PS	Susp	WO/213/10/111
Grove J	Dvr	372 Coy CAHT	14/05/19	Field	M	5 yrs PS		WO/213/30/12
Grubb J	Pte	1 Inf Bn AIF	15/10/18	Field	M+Des	3 yrs PS	Guilty of Des	WO/213/28/199
Guilfoyle H	Pte (L/Cpl)	1 Inf Bn AIF	15/10/18	Field	M+Des	NG		WO/213/28/200
Gummer E	Pte	12 SWBdrs	01/12/16	Field	M+Disob	18 mos HL	Comm 3 mos FP1	WO/213/13/47
Gunchar I	Pte	39 R Fus	23/08/19	Field EEF	M	5 yrs PS	Comm 1yr HL	WO/213/31/24
Gunn F	Pte	4 Mddx	12/11/17	Field	M+Disob	6 mos HL	Comm 91 dys FP1	WO/213/18/181
Gurney P	Gnr	RFA(att RGA)	13/03/18	Agra	M	1 yr HL	unexpired portion 30/4/18	WO/90/7/190
Guthrie A	Bdr	RFA	07/07/19	Field	M+S5+S40(x2)	90 dys FP2		WO/213/30/84
Guthrie M	Pte	8 AIF	04/02/19	Rouen	M	90 dys Imp		WO/90/8/58
Hague A	Dvr	RFA	24/04/19	Field	M+Disob	5 mos HL		WO/213/29/160
Hague T	Pte	68 Div Cyclist Coy	17/01/17	Gt Yarmouth	M + Insub (S/Sgt)	NG		WO/86/73/171
Hague W	Pte	58 Coy RDC	21/11/16	Towcester	M	1 yr Detn		WO/92/4/1
Hale TS	Pte	12 SWBdrs	01/12/16	Field	M+Disob	18 mos HL	Comm 3 mos FP1	WO/213/13/47
Halford T	Pte	1 Leics	28/04/22	Field (Ireland)	M+S40	1 yr HL	Comm 56 dys	WO/213/34/63
Hall A	Spr	RE	09/05/19	Field Italy	M	2 yrs HL	Remit 20 mos/ Quashed	WO/213/29/73
Hall HW	Pte	45 AIF	24/03/19	Field	M	11 yrs PS		WO/213/29/89
Hall J	Pte	21 Manch	08/02/19	Field	M+Abs	6 mos HL		WO/213/28/58
Hall W	L/Cpl	Derby Yeo (att 5 Dragoon Gds)	25/09/19	Curragh	M	1 yr HL + Disch Igmny	6 mos Detn	WO/92/4/86
Hallam G	Pte	1 Gn Sher Fstrs	05/06/17	Kantara Egypt	M	2 yrs HL		WO/213/15/176
Halpin R	Pte	7 Dragoon Gds	09/06/21	Edinburgh	M+V(A/RSM)	2 yrs HL		WO/86/91/131
Halstead EA	Pte	RASC	20/02/19	Field	Mx2+S40	1 yr HL	Remit 6 mos	WO/213/28/169
Ham EH	Pte	1 Inf Bn AIF	15/10/18	Field	M+Des	5 yrs PS	Guilty of Des	WO/213/28/199
Hambrook E	L/Cpl	1/1 C of Lon Yeo	18/06/19	Field EEF	M+S40	NG		WO/213/30/97
Hamelin W	Pte	Can AMC	21/05/19	Liverpool	M+S40	Acquit		WO/92/4/74
Hamilton F	Pte	5 Dragoon Gds	25/09/19	Curragh	M	1 yr HL+Disch Igmny	Comm 6 mos Detn	WO/92/4/87
Hamilton J	Pte	4 BWI	27/12/18	Field Italy	M+Disob	3 yrs PS	Comm 2 yrs HL	WO/213/27/23
Hamilton J	Pte	5 Dragoon Gds	23/09/19	Curragh	M	1 yr HL+Disch Igmny	Comm 6 mos Detn	WO/92/4/84
Hammond H	Pte	1 Gn Sher Fstrs	05/06/17	Kantara Egypt	M	2 yrs HL		WO/213/15/176
Hancock ER	Spr	3 Aus Tun Coy	13/10/18	Field	M+Disob	1 yr HL	NC	WO/213/30/136
Hancock ER	Spr	3 Aus Tun Coy	18/10/18	Field	M+Disob	2 yrs HL	Susp	WO/213/26/66
Hancock GC	Pte	20 AIF	24/03/19	Field	M	11 yrs PS		WO213/29/88
Hancock HT	Pte	1 Inf Bn AIF	15/10/18	Field	M+Des	3 yrs PS	Guilty of Des	WO/213/28/196
Hanrattey B	Pte	7/8 R Innis Fus	15/04/18	Field	M	5 yrs PS	Susp	WO/213/21/95

59

Name	Rank	Unit	Date D/M/Y	Location	Offence	Finding/Punishment	Amendment	PRO Reference File/Piece/Page
Hansen AJ	Pte (L/Cpl)	28 AIF	22/12/18	Field	M	4 yrs PS		WO/213/27/184
Hanson AE	L/Cpl	13 Yorks	17/03/19	Field NREF	M	2 yrs HL		WO/213/29/35
Harber G	Pte	Can R[eserve] C[avy]R[egt]	13/05/19	Liverpool	M+S7(3b)	10 mos HL	NC	WO/92/4/72
Hardcastle W	Pte	3 W Yorks	01/08/19	Devizes	M+S40	18 mos HL + Disch Igmny	9 mos	WO/92/4/76
Harding B	Pte(S/Smith)	ASC	30/12/15	Marseilles	Joining M	3 yrs PS	Comm to 2 yrs HL	WO/90/6/44
Hardwick T	Pte	2/4 R Sussex TF	23/07/15	Canterbury	J[oin in] M	84 dys Detn		WO/92/3/22
Hardy A	Pte	68 Div Cyclist Coy	17/01/17	Gt Yarmouth	M +Insub(L/Cpl)	NG		WO/86/73/171
Hardy D	Bdr	RGA	08/07/19	Aldershot	M	9 mos Detn+Rnks +Disch Igmny		WO/86/87/189
Hardy J	Pte	1 Gn Sher Fstrs	05/06/17	Kantara Egypt	M	2 yrs HL		WO/213/15/176
Hardy PT	Cpl	Ox & Bucks LI	01/02/20	Oxford/Depot	M+Abs+Resisting +S9(1)	2 yrs HL+Rnks+DI	Remit 18 mos	WO/92/4/95
[Harmer?] SW	Pte	2/4 R Sussex TF	23/07/15	Canterbury	J[oin in] M	84 dys Detn		WO/92/3/22
Harragon WL	Pte	1 Inf Bn AIF	15/10/18	Field	M+Des	3 yrs PS	Guilty of Des	WO/213/28/196
Harrigan C	Pte	7/8 R Innis Fus	15/04/18	Field	M	5 yrs PS	Susp	WO/213/21/96
Harrington WR	Pte	Lab Corps (att E Comm LB)	15/06/19	Sutton	M+S7(3b)	Acquit		WO/92/4/73
Harris F	Pte	3 Essex	09/05/19	Field Italy	M	3 yrs PS	Comm 4 mos HL	WO/213/29/73
Harris C	Pte	2/4 R Sussex TF	23/07/15	Canterbury	J[oin in] M	84 dys Detn		WO/92/3/22
Harris C	Pte	Can ASC	21/11/17	Bramshott	M+Insub(Lieut)	42 dys Detn	Remit 15 dys	WO/86/79/54
Harris F	Pte(S/Smith)	ASC	30/12/15	Marseilles	Joining M	3 yrs PS	Comm to 2 yrs HL	WO/90/6/44
Harris F	Pte	Lab Corps	09/06/19	Field	M+S40	1 yr HL		WO/213/30/120
Harris F	Pte	Lab Corps	11/08/19	Field	M+S40	42 dys FP2		WO/213/30/120
Harris L	Tpr	Aus Lt Horse	23/09/15	Malta	M+S40	3 yrs PS+DI		WO/90/6/34
Harris S	Pte	1 W Yorks	24/03/19	Field	M	PS/Life		WO/213/29/90
Harris SJ	Pte	Lab Corps (att E Comm LB)	15/06/19	Sutton	M+S7(3b)	Acquit		WO/92/4/73
Harris T	Dvr	RFA	23/05/21	Hinaidi	M+S9(1)	3 mos FP2		WO/213/33/16
Harrison [?]	A/Bdr	RHA	03/11/14	At Sea	Endeavg M	56 dys Detn	Comm 14	WO213/1/74
Harrison D	Pte	2/7 R Wars	05/01/19	Field	M	3 yrs PS		WO/213/27/122
Harrison GJ	Pte	1 Gn Sher Fstrs	05/06/17	Kantara Egypt	M	2 yrs HL		WO/213/15/176
Harrison J	L/Cpl	8 KOYLI	10/02/19	Field	M+Disob+S7(4)	Acquit		WO/213/28/54
Harrison J	Pte	5 Dragoon Gds	25/09/19	Curragh	M	1 yr HL+Disch Igmny	Comm 6 mos Detn	WO/92/4/86
Harrison JL	Pte	68 Div Cyclist Coy	17/01/17	Gt Yarmouth	M +Insub(L/Cpl)	NG		WO/86/73/171
Harrison JW	Pte	1 Gn Sher Fstrs	05/06/17	Kantara Egypt	M	2 yrs HL		WO/213/15/176
Harrison LR	Pte	7 AIF	24/03/19	Field	M	10 yrs PS		WO/213/29/89
Harrison R	Dvr	RASC	18/05/21	Chelsea	M	9 mos HL+DI		WO/92/4/96
Harrison W	Pte	2 MGC	12/06/19	Field	M+Disob(2)+S40	5 yrs PS	Remit 1 yr	WO/213/29/122
Hart S	Pte	Lab Corps (att E Comm LB)	15/06/19	Sutton	M+S7(3b)	Acquit		WO/92/4/73
Hart T	L/Cpl	35 MGC	17/01/19	Field	M	2 yrs HL	Remit 18 mos	WO/213/28/120
Hartley H	L/Cpl	5 Dragoon Gds	25/09/19	Curragh	M	6 mos HL	Comm 84 dys Detn	WO/92/4/86
Hartley S	Pte	2 Y[ork] & Lanc	06/11/19	Basrah	M+Disob	5 yrs PS	Comm 2 yrs HL	WO/90/7/205
Harvey A	Gnr	RFA	24/04/19	Field	M+Disob	5 mos HL		WO/213/29/160
Harvey AE	Pte	1 Gn Sher Fstrs	05/06/17	Kantara Egypt	M	2 yrs HL		WO/213/15/177
Harvey G	Spr	3 Aus Tun Coy	18/10/18	Field	M+Disob	2 yrs HL	Susp	WO/213/26/66
Harvey L	Pte	6 (S) BWI	24/12/18	Field Italy	M+Disob	3 yrs 6 mos PS		WO/213/27/24
Harvey WA	Pte	46 AIF	24/03/19	Field	M	9 yrs PS		WO/213/29/90
Hasthorpe M	Cpl (L/Sgt)	1 Inf Bn AIF	15/10/18	Field	M+Des	10 yrs PS+Rnks	Guilty of Des	WO/213/28/180
Hastie CE	Cpl	Aus Engrs	29/06/18	Field EEF	M	NG		WO/213/26/112
Haw WE	Pte	2 Yorks att ASC	13/04/17	Dunkirk	M	6 mos HL		WO/213/14/138
Hawes J	Pte	1 Connaught Rangers	30/08/20	Dagshai	M	Death	Life PS	WO/90/8/189
Hawkins A [DCM]	Cpl	RFA	12/05/18	Field	M	1 yr HL	Susp	WO/213/22/153
Hawkins FT	Dvr/L/Bdr	RFA	12/05/18	Field	M	1 yr HL	Susp	WO/213/22/153
Hawkins G	Pte	10 E Yorks	24/03/19	Field	M	18 yrs PS		WO213/29/88
Hawkins WJ	Pte	Lab Corps (att E Comm LB)	15/06/19	Sutton	M+S7(3b)	Acquit		WO/92/4/73
Hawksby T	Pte	5 Dragoon Gds	23/09/19	Curragh	M	6 mos HL +Disch Igmny	Comm 84 dys Dtn	WO/92/4/84
Hayden J	Gnr	RFA	24/04/19	Field	M+Disob	5 mos HL		WO/213/29/160
Hayes A	Pte	1 Connaught Rangers	30/08/20	Dagshai	M	10 yrs PS+DI		WO/90/8/188
Hayes L	Pte	4 AIF	24/03/19	Field	M	10 yrs PS		WO/213/29/89

Name	Rank	Unit	Date D/M/Y	Location	Offence	Finding/Punishment	Amendment	PRO Reference File/Piece/Page
Hayes P	Pte	King Edward Horse (att 5 Dragoon Guards)	25/09/19	Curragh	M	1 yr HL + Disch Igmny	Comm 6 mos Detn	WO/92/4/86
Hayle HV	Pte	35 MGC	17/01/19	Field	Mx2	2 yrs HL	Remit 18 mos	WO/213/28/120
Hayward W	Pte	3 Leics	27/08/14	Portsmouth	M	1 yr HL		WO/213/2/1
Haywood J	Pte	1 Gn Sher Fstrs	05/06/17	Kantara Egypt	M	2 yrs HL		WO/213/15/177
Healy A	Pte	58 Coy RDC	21/11/16	Towcester	M	1 yr Detn		WO/92/4/1
Healy E	Pte	1 Gn Sher Fstrs	05/06/17	Kantara Egypt	M	2 yrs HL		WO/213/15/177
Heath LC	Pte	5 Dragoon Gds	24/09/19	Curragh	M	Acquit		WO/92/4/87
Heffernan PJ	Pte	15 AIF	24/03/19	Field	M	11 yrs PS		WO213/29/88
Heggart TH	Pte	8 AIF	22/12/18	Field	M	5 yrs PS		WO/213/27/184
Heggarty W	Pte	2 R Irish	15/04/18	Field	M	5 yrs PS	Susp	WO/213/21/98
Hellard C	Pte	7 Dragoon Gds	09/06/21	Edinburgh	M+V(A/RSM)	2 yrs HL		WO/86/91/131
Helliker WC	Pte	RASC	20/02/19	Field	Mx2+S40	NG		WO/213/28/169
Hemmings T	Pte	2 W India	11/05/19	Field EEF	M	7 yrs PS	Comm 2 yrs HL	WO/213/30/28
Henderson JJ	Pte	49 AIF	24/03/19	Field	M	11 yrs PS		WO213/29/88
Henderson W	Pte	5 Dragoon Gds	26/09/19	Curragh	M	1 yr HL + Disch Igmny	Comm 6 mos Detn	WO/92/4/81
Hendrick	Pte	SANLC	21/11/17	Field	M+S40	3 yrs PS	Comm 2 yrs HL	WO/213/31/109
Hendricks J	Dvr	372 Coy CAHT	14/05/19	Field	M	5 yrs PS	Comm 2 yrs HL	WO/213/30/12
Hendricks F	Dvr	372 Coy CAHT	14/05/19	Field	M	5 yrs PS	Remit 2 yrs	WO/213/30/12
Henley RE	Pte	20(R) CEF	19/05/19	Liverpool	M+S7(3b)	3 yrs PS		WO/92/4/72
Henry J	Spr	RE	15/05/19	Field	M+Disob	1 yr IHL		WO/213/29/137
Henry R	Pte	9(S) E Lancs	29/05/18	SEF	M	1 yr HL		WO/213/23/179
Henson CE	Pte	Lab Cps	06/01/19	Field	M+S40	NG		WO/213/27/37
Herbert A	Dvr	RFA	24/04/19	Field	M+Disob	NG		WO/213/29/160
Herbert JJ	Gnr	RFA	05/06/19	Field	M+S40	5 yrs HL		WO/213/29/169
Hewett J	Pte	7/8 R Innis Fus	15/04/18	Field	M	5 yrs PS	Susp	WO/213/21/95
Hewson J	Pte	1 Connaught Rangers	04/09/20	Dagshai	M+S7(3b)	7 yrs PS+DI		WO/90/8/188
Heys H	Pte	5 Dragoon Gds	29/09/19	Curragh	M	1 yr HL + Disch Igmny	Comm 6 mos Detn	WO/92/4/83
Hiba J	Spr	Can Rail T[roops]	28/05/19	Liverpool	M+XO(Lt Col)+ XO(Lt)	7 yrs PS		WO/92/4/72
Hidden E	Bdr	RGA	05/07/19	Aldershot	M	9 mos Detn+Rnks +Disch Igmny		WO/86/87/189
Higgins F	Pte	22 AIF	24/03/19	Field	M	No Finding/Sentence		WO/213/29/89
Higgins J	Pte	9(S) E Lancs	29/05/18	SEF	M	1 yr HL		WO/213/23/179
Higgs GH	Pte	5 Dragoon Gds	23/09/19	Curragh	M	1 yr HL + Disch Igmny	Comm 6 mos Detn	WO/92/4/84
Highley D	Pte	5 Dragoon Gds	30/09/19	Curragh	M	1 yr HL + Disch Igmny	Comm 6 mos Detn	WO/92/4/87
Hill E	Pte	10 Hussars	25/01/21	Curragh	Mx2+S9(1)x2	1 yr Detn		WO/92/4/94
Hill N	Cpl	1 MGC	17/07/19	Field	M	5 mos Imp+Rnks		WO/213/30/82
Hill P	Pte	19 AIF	15/02/16	Sinai Penin	M+Disob	18 mos HL		WO/213/8/113
Hilton WG	Pte	RAMC	10/05/19	Field	M	6 mos HL	Comm 28 dys FP2	WO/213/30/17
Hincks W	Pte	1 NZ Div Emp B	16/10/18	Field	M	6 mos HL	Susp	WO/213/25/165
Hinds R	Pte	6 (S) BWI	24/12/18	Field Italy	M+Disob	3 yrs 6 mos PS		WO/213/27/24
Hirst JL	Pte	9(S) E Lancs	29/05/18	SEF	M	1 yr HL		WO/213/23/179
Hiscock C	Pte	1 Inf Bn AIF	15/10/18	Field	M+Des	3 yrs PS	Guilty of Des	WO/213/28/180
Histed T	Pte	2 R Irish	15/04/18	Field	M	5 yrs PS	Susp	WO/213/21/99
Hoaldsworth C	Gnr	155 Bde RFA	13/04/17	Dunkirk	M	8 mos HL		WO/213/14/138
Hobbs C	Dvr	337 Bde RFA	10/01/17	Canterbury	JM	6 mos Detn		WO/92/3/58
Hodge H	Pte	5 Dragoon Gds	22/09/19	Curragh	M	1 yr HL + Disch Igmny	Comm 6 mos Detn	WO/92/4/84
Hodges F	Pte	2/4 R Sussex TF	23/07/15	Canterbury	J[oin in] M	84 dys Detn		WO/92/3/22
Hodges HM	Gnr	4 Aus DAC	24/03/19	Field	M	9 yrs PS		WO/213/29/90
Hodgson JW	Pte	3 W Yorks	01/08/19	Devizes	M+S40	21 mos HL +Disch Igmny	12 mos	WO/92/4/76
Hodgson P	Pte	2 MGC	12/06/19	Field	M+Disob(2)+S40	5 yrs PS	Remit 2 yrs	WO/213/29/122
Hoey G	Pte	5 Dragoon Gds	29/09/19	Curragh	M	18 mos HL +Disch Igmny	Comm 9 mos Detn	WO/92/4/83
Hogg J	Pte	3 Leics	27/08/14	Portsmouth	M	1 yr HL		WO/213/2/1
Hogg E	Pte	5 Dragoon Gds	29/09/19	Curragh	M	1 yr HL + Disch Igmny	Comm 6 mos Detn	WO/92/4/83
Holding A	Pte	5 Dragoon Gds	26/09/19	Curragh	M	1 yr HL + Disch Igmny	Comm 6 mos Detn	WO/92/4/81
Holland JHB	Pte	2 Y[ork] & Lanc	06/11/19	Basrah	M+XSO*	5 yrs PS	Comm 2 yrs+ *Quashed	WO/90/7/205
Holland W	Pte	2/4 R Sussex TF	23/07/15	Canterbury	J[oin in] M	84 dys Detn		WO/92/3/22
Holliday P	Pte	5 Dragoon Gds	23/09/19	Curragh	M	6 mos HL +Disch Igmny	Comm 84 dys Dtn	WO/92/4/84
Hollings F	Pte	4 Mddx	12/11/17	Field	M+Disob	6 mos HL	Comm 91 dys FP1	WO/213/18/181
Holmes S	Pte	1 Gn Sher Fstrs	05/06/17	Kantara Egypt	M	2 yrs HL		WO/213/15/177

Name	Rank	Unit	Date D/M/Y	Location	Offence	Finding/Punishment	Amendment	PRO Reference File/Piece/Page
Holmes WJ	Pte	1 Inf Bn AIF	15/10/18	Field	M+Des	NG		WO/213/28/198
Holt S	A/Bdr	RGA	16/05/19	Field	M	NG		WO/213/29/148
Hooley A	Pte(A/Cpl)	7 S Staffs(att RAOC)	08/10/19	Field	M+S40	NG		WO/213/31/4
Hooper W	L/Bdr	RGA	05/07/19	Aldershot	M	9 mos Detn+ Rnks		WO/86/88/1
Hope AH	Pte	RAMC	10/05/19	Field	M	6 mos HL	Comm 28 dys FP2	WO/213/30/17
Horan T	Dvr	25(R) Bty RFA	25/05/16	Athlone	M+Insub(A/Sgt Maj)	2 yrs HL	Comm 1 yr Detn	WO/86/70/46
Horden TC	Pte	1 Inf Bn AIF	15/10/18	Field	M+Des	3 yrs PS	Guilty of Des	WO/213/28/198
Horowitz J	Pte	39 R Fus	23/08/19	Field EEF	M	5 yrs PS	Comm 1 yr HL	WO/213/31/25
Horton E	Pte	1 Gn Sher Fstrs	05/06/17	Kantara Egypt	M	2 yrs HL		WO/213/15/177
Hosker A	Pte	MG Gds	26/02/18	London	M+Absx2	2 yrs HL		WO/92/4/29
Hotchkiss M	Gnr	RGA	13/03/18	Agra	M	1 yr HL	unexpired portion 30/4/18	WO/90/7/190
Hoult A	Pte	2 York & Lanc	16/07/20	Kasvin	M	1 yr HL		WO/90/7/208
Hounsell EA	Gnr	RGA	13/03/18	Agra	M	1 yr HL	unexpired portion 30/4/18	WO/90/7/190
Houston JP	Pte	Can Res Arty	01/05/19	Liverpool	M	Acquit		WO/92/4/66
Howard C	Pte	7/8 R Innis Fus	15/04/18	Field	M	5 yrs PS	Susp	WO/213/21/96
Howard E	Pte	9 (S) BWI	24/12/18	Field Italy	M+Disob+Esc	5 yrs PS		WO/213/27/25
Howarth R	Pte	5 Dragoon Gds	23/09/19	Curragh	M	84 dys HL	Comm 42 dys Detn	WO/92/4/85
Howe J	Pte	1 Gn Sher Fstrs	05/06/17	Kantara Egypt	M	2 yrs HL		WO/213/15/177
Howe L	Pte	2 MGC	12/06/19	Field	M+Disob(2)+S40	5 yrs PS	Comm 2 yrs HL	WO/213/29/122
Howell E	Pte	7 R Irish	15/04/18	Field	M	5 yrs PS	Susp	WO/213/21/97
Howell TH	Pte	65 Coy RDC	21/11/16	Towcester	M	1 yr Detn		WO/92/4/2
Howells A	Pte	2/6 R Wars	27/05/19	Field	M+S40	2 yrs HL	Remit 1 yr	WO/213/30/64
Howlett H	Spr	RE	09/05/19	Field Italy	M	2 yrs HL	Remit 20 mos/ Quashed	WO/213/29/73
Hudson CE	Pte	3 W Yorks	01/08/19	Devizes	M+S40	18 mos HL +Disch Igmny	9 mos	WO/92/4/76
Hudson E	Pte	2 Y[ork] & Lanc	29/07/19	Clipstone	M+S40	NG		WO/86/88/50
Hudson FWA	Pte	5 Dragoon Gds	25/09/19	Curragh	M	56 dys Detn	NC	WO/92/4/86
Hudson S	Pte	257 P of W Coy	13/05/19	Field	M+S40(2)	92 dys HL		WO/213/30/31
Huggins H	Pte	2 R Irish	15/04/18	Field	M	5 yrs PS	Susp	WO/213/21/99
Hughes D	Pte	11(R) CEF	14/05/19	Liverpool	M+L[eaving] Po[st]	90 dys Detn	NC	WO/92/4/72
Hughes EH	Pte	2/5 RWF(TF)	16/08/15	Bedford	M	Dismissal+Rnks	Remit Dismissal	WO/86/66/80
Hughes J	Pte(L/Cpl)	1 Connaught Rangers	23/08/20	Dagshai	M+S7(3)	1 yr HL+DI		WO/90/8/189
Hughes J	Pte	3 RWFs	06/06/18	Kinmel Park	M+Disob	NG+Acquit		WO/92/4/39
Hughes W	Pte	65 Coy RDC	21/11/16	Towcester	M	1 yr Detn		WO/92/4/3
Humphreys DW	Pte (L/Cpl)	1 Inf Bn AIF	15/10/18	Field	M+Des	5 yrs PS	Guilty of Des	WO/213/28/197
Humpreys B	Pte	30 MGC	29/07/19	Field	M+Disob	1 yr HL		WO/213/30/119
Hunt J	Pte	21 Manch	08/02/19	Field	M+Abs	6 mos HL		WO/213/28/58
Hunt SJ	Pte	1 Inf Bn AIF	15/10/18	Field	M+Des	3 yrs PS	Guilty of Des	WO/213/28/199
Hunter W	Pte	6 Dragoon Gds	23/09/19	Curragh	M	84 dys HL	Comm 42 dys Detn	WO/92/4/85
Hurst F	Pte	5 Dragoon Gds	23/09/19	Curragh	M	84 dys HL	Comm 42 dys Detn	WO/92/4/85
Hurvutz J	Pte	39 R Fus	23/08/19	Field EEF	M	5 yrs PS	Comm 1 yr HL	WO/213/31/25
Hussey A	Pte	7 R Irish	15/04/18	Field	M	5 yrs PS	Susp	WO/213/21/98
Hutchins VG	Spr	Can Engrs	25/01/19	Field	M+Disob	28 dys FP2		WO/213/29/55
Hutchinson G	Pte	22 AIF	04/02/19	Rouen	M	3 yrs 3 mos PS		WO/90/8/59
Hutchinson H	Pte	4 BWI	27/12/18	Field Italy	M+Disob	3 yrs PS	Comm 2 yrs HL	WO/213/27/23
Hutchinson H	Pte	2/4 R Sussex TF	23/07/15	Canterbury	J[oin in] M	84 dys Detn		WO/92/3/22
Hutchinson H	L/Bdr	RGA	05/07/19	Aldershot	M	9 mos Detn+ Rnks		WO/86/88/1
Hutchinson JC	Pte	58 Coy RDC	21/11/16	Towcester	M	1 yr Detn		WO/92/4/1
Hutchinson TJ	Pte	58 AIF	24/03/19	Field	M	15 yrs PS		WO/213/29/89
Hutton A	Pte	20 CEF	11/02/18	Bramshott	M+Abs+Inj property*+S40(2)	112 dys Detn +Quashed*		WO/86/80/139
Huxtable AR	Pte	Lab Corps (att E Comm LB)	15/06/19	Sutton	M+S7(3b)	Acquit		WO/92/4/74
Hyland RG	Pte	2/4 R Sussex TF	23/07/15	Canterbury	J[oin in] M	84 dys Detn		WO/92/3/22
Hyland T	Pte	8 KOYLI	10/02/19	Field	M+Disob+S40	5 yrs PS	Quashed	WO/213/28/54
Hynes P	Pte	1 Connaught Rangers	04/09/20	Dagshai	M+S7(3b)	Death	Life PS	WO/90/8/188
Ibrahim S	Labourer	Egyptian Lab Corps	06/09/17	Boulogne	M+S40	8 mos HL		WO/213/17/41
Illingworth N	Pte	5 Dragoon Gds	29/09/19	Curragh	M	1 yr HL+Disch Igmny	Comm 6 mos Detn	WO/92/4/82
Impey A	Tpr/(L/Cpl)	NZEF	01/07/18	Field EEF	M	NG		WO/213/28/138
Ingalls RA	Pte	12(R) CEF	19/04/19	Liverpool	M	Acquit		WO/92/4/65
Ingram GE	Pte	2/6 R Wars	27/05/19	Field	M+S40	2 yrs HL	Remit 1 yr	WO/213/30/64
Ingram T	Pte	2 Y[ork] & Lanc	05/11/19	Basrah	M+Disob	Acquit		WO/90/7/205

Name	Rank	Unit	Date D/M/Y	Location	Offence	Finding/Punishment	Amendment	PRO Reference File/Piece/Page
Inyani Willie	Native Leader	S ASC	31/01/16	Bissil BEA	M	2 yr HL		WO/213/8/132
Ireland A	Pte(A/Cpl)	16 Rifle Bde	20/11/15	Witley	M+Disob(Capt)	5 yrs PS	Comm 1 yr Det	WO/92/3/29
Ireland GJ	Pte	2/4 R Sussex TF	23/07/15	Canterbury	J[oin in] M	84 dys Detn		WO/92/3/22
Ives GK	Pte	2 Gn/Beds	04/04/18	Karachi	M+S7(3)	3 yrs PS	Comm 2 yrs HL	WO/90/7/191
Jaantyes M	Dvr	ASC (SA)	05/08/18	Field	M+S40	1 yr HL		WO/213/24/129
Jack	Pte	SANLC	21/11/17	Field	M+S40	3 yrs PS	Comm 2 yrs HL	WO/213/31/109
Jack	Pte	SANLC	21/11/17	Field	M+S40	3 yrs PS	Comm 2 yrs HL	WO/213/31/109
Jackman H	Gnr (AL/Bdr)	RFA	24/04/19	Field	M+Disob	5 mos HL		WO/213/29/160
Jackson E	Dvr	337 Bde RFA	10/01/17	Canterbury	JM	6 mos Detn		WO/92/3/58
Jackson F	Gnr	RFA	24/06/19	Field	M+Disob	1 yr HL		WO/213/29/137
Jackson GA	Pte	RAMC	10/05/19	Field	M	6 mos HL	Comm 28 dys FP2	WO/213/30/17
Jackson HB	Pte	5 Dragoon Gds	25/09/19	Curragh	M	Acquit		WO/92/4/86
Jackson J	Pte	2 Ches	05/03/20	Field ABS	M+Disob	2 yrs HL	Rem 18 mos	WO/213/31/168
Jackson T	Dvr	33(R) Bty RFA	13/01/16	Glasgow	M+Viol(Cpl)	NG		WO/86/68/144
Jacob	Pte	SANLC	21/11/17	Field	M+S40	3 yrs PS	Comm 2 yrs HL	WO/213/31/109
Jacob	Pte	SANLC	21/11/17	Field	M+S40	3 yrs PS	Comm 2 yrs HL	WO/213/31/109
Jacob	Pte	SANLC	21/11/17	Field	M+S40	3 yrs PS	Comm 2 yrs HL	WO/213/31/109
Jacobs C	Dvr	372 Coy CAHT	14/05/19	Field	M	5 yrs PS	Remit 2 yrs	WO/213/30/11
Jacobs CP	Dvr	ASC (SA)	23/07/18	Field	M+Ins+Threat	Death	Comm 10 yrs PS	WO/213/24/168
Jacobs J	Dvr	ASC (SA)	05/08/18	Field	M+S40	9 mos HL		WO/213/24/129
Jacobs W	Dvr	372 Coy CAHT	14/05/19	Field	M	5 yrs PS	Remit 2 yrs	WO/213/30/12
James B	Pte	6 (S) BWI	24/12/18	Field Italy	M+Disob	3 yrs 6 mos PS		WO/213/27/24
James D	Dvr	RFA	23/05/21	Hinaidi	M+S9(1)	3 mos FP2		WO/213/33/16
James FA	Pte	5 Dragoon Gds	22/09/19	Curragh	M	1 yr HL + Disch Igmny	Comm 6 mos Detn	WO/92/4/81
James W	Pte	1 Inf Bn AIF	15/10/18	Field	M+Des	3 yrs PS	Guilty of Des	WO/213/28/199
Jansen O	Spr	3 Aust Lt Ry For Coy	24/03/19	Field	M	9 yrs PS		WO213/29/88
January N	Dvr	372 Coy CAHT	14/05/19	Field	M	5 yrs PS	Remit 2 yrs	WO/213/30/12
Jarrod CH	Pte	8 KOYLI	10/02/19	Field	M+Disob+S40	5 yrs PS	Quashed +Rem 2 yrs	WO/213/28/54
Jarvis CA	Pte	8(R) CEF	05/05/19	Liverpool	M	Acquit		WO/92/4/67
Jeffrey EAV	Pte	155 Lab Coy	04/02/19	Rouen	M	90dys Imp		WO/90/8/58
Jeffreys A	Cpl	3 RWFs	06/06/18	Kinmel Park	M+Disob	NG+Acquit		WO/92/4/39
Jeffries F	Pte	RAMC	10/05/19	Field	M	6 mos HL	Comm 28 dys FP2	WO/213/30/17
Jeffries H	Pte	1 Inf Bn AIF	15/10/18	Field	M+Des	3 yrs PS	Guilty of Des	WO/213/28/197
Jelly J	Pnr(A/Lcpl)	RE	27/04/18	Field Italy	M+Disob	Death	Comm 5 yrs PS	WO/213/22/28
Jenkins E	L/Bdr	RGA	05/07/19	Aldershot	M	9 mos Detn + Rnks		WO/86/88/1
Jenkins JH	Gnr	V/38 TMB	10/01/17	Esquelbecq	M+Disob	3 yrs PS		WO/213/13/138
Jenkinson CE	Tpr(L/Cpl)	Aus Prov Corps	29/06/18	Field EEF	M	NG		WO/213/26/112
Jennings A	Pte	1/4 KOYLI (att 265 POW Coy)	16/09/18	Field	M+Abs+Disob	3 yrs PS	Comm 1 yr HL	WO/213/31/69
Jennings A	Pte	3 Leics	27/08/14	Portsmouth	M	1 yr HL		WO/213/2/1
Jepp C	Pte	6 (S) BWI	24/12/18	Field Italy	M+Disob	3 yrs 6 mos PS		WO/213/27/24
Jeremiah W	Dvr	ASC (SA)	23/07/18	Field	M	5 yrs PS		WO/213/24/168
Jim	Pte(L/Cpl)	SANLC	21/11/17	Field	M+S40	3 yrs PS	Comm 2 yrs HL	WO/213/31/109
Jobe C	Pte	11 R Fus	23/12/18	Field	M	5 yrs PS		WO/213/28/141
Johannes	Pte(L/Cpl)	SANLC	21/11/17	Field	M+S40	3 yrs PS	Comm 2 yrs HL	WO/213/31/109
Johnson GL	Pte	7/8 R Innis Fus	15/04/18	Field	M	5 yrs PS	Susp	WO/213/21/95
Johnston J	Pte	11(R) CEF	05/05/19	Liverpool	M	Acquit		WO/92/4/66
Johnston P	Dvr	372 Coy CAHT	14/05/19	Field	M	5 yrs PS	Remit 2 yrs	WO/213/30/12
Johnston R	Pte	5 Dragoon Gds	25/09/19	Curragh	M	56 dys Detn	NC	WO/92/4/86
Johnston T	Cpl	9 MGC	31/07/19	Field	Mx2	12 mos HL+Rnks		WO/213/30/76
Johnstone CJ	Pte	1 Inf Bn AIF	15/10/18	Field	M+Des	3 yrs PS	Guilty of Des	WO/213/28/199
Jones CH	Civilian	att RAOC	29/07/20	Field	M+Disob+S7(3b)	5 yrs PS		WO/213/32/22
Jones E	Dvr	RFA	23/05/21	Hinaidi	M+S9(1)	6 mos Detn		WO/213/33/15
Jones F	Pte	5 Dragoon Gds	24/09/19	Curragh	M	1 yr HL + Disch Igmny	Comm 6 mos Detn	WO/92/4/85
Jones J	Pte	12 Lancs Fus	02/05/18	Field SEF	M+Disob	10 yrs PS	Comm 2 yrs HL	WO/213/22/30
Jones JM	Gnr	V/38 TMB	10/01/17	Esquelbecq	M+Disob	3 yrs PS		WO/213/13/138
Jones JR	Pte	35 MGC	17/01/19	Field	Mx2	2 yrs HL	Remit 18 mos	WO/213/28/120
Jones JW	Pte	2 MGC	12/06/19	Field	M+Disob(2)+S40	5 yrs PS	Comm 2 yrs HL	WO/213/29/122
Jones P	Gnr	V/38 TMB	11/01/17	Esquelbecq	M+S40	56 dys FP1		WO/213/13/138
Jones S	Pte	5 Dragoon Gds	23/09/19	Curragh	M	1 yr HL + Disch Igmny	Comm 6 mos Detn	WO/92/4/84
Jones SH	Pte	2 Gn/Beds	04/04/18	Karachi	M+S7(3)	5 yrs PS	Comm 2 yrs HL	WO/90/7/191
Jones W	Pte	2 Can Mtd Rif	24/03/19	Field	M	7 yrs PS		WO/213/29/91
Jonkers J	Dvr	ASC (SA)	05/08/18	Field	M+S40	1 yr HL		WO/213/24/129
Jowett HW	Pte	5 Dragoon Gds	29/09/19	Curragh	M	1 yr HL + Disch Igmny	Comm 6 mos Detn	WO/92/4/82
Jowett P	Pte	5 Dragoon Gds	22/09/19	Curragh	M	1 yr HL + Disch Igmny	Comm 6 mos Detn	WO/92/4/81

Name	Rank	Unit	Date D/M/Y	Location	Offence	Finding/Punishment	Amendment	PRO Reference File/Piece/Page
Julius A	Dvr	372 Coy CAHT	14/05/19	Field	M	5 yrs PS	Comm 1 yr HL	WO/213/30/12
Junior W	Pte	9 (S) BWI	24/12/18	Field Italy	M+Disob+Esc	5 yrs PS		WO/213/27/25
Justice C	Pte	7 R Irish	15/04/18	Field	M	5 yrs PS	Susp	WO/213/21/97
Kafope A bin	Pte	1/6 KAR	13/08/17	Tabora	Mx2+Striking	15 yrs PS+Disch Igmny		WO/213/23/81
Kalis I	Pte	39 R Fus	23/08/19	Field EEF	M	6 yrs PS	Comm 1 yr HL	WO/213/31/25
Kane T	Pte	7 R Irish	15/04/18	Field	M	5 yrs PS	Susp	WO/213/21/97
Kanieff A	Pte	1 Slav-Brit Legion	13/07/19	Field	M	NG		WO213/32/58
Kanieff P	Cpl	1 Slav-Brit Legion	14/07/19	Field NREF	M	Death		WO/213/32/59
Kay R	Pte	NZEF 3 Reinf	05/04/15	Zeitoun	Incit M+Disob(Lt)	1 yr HL+Disch Igmny		WO/90/6/35
Kay W	Pte	9(S) E Lancs	29/05/18	SEF	M	1 yr HL		WO/213/23/179
Kealley S	Pte	7 R Irish Fus	15/04/18	Field	M	NG		WO/213/21/98
Kearney M	Pte	1 Connaught Rangers	04/09/20	Dagshai	M+S7(3b)	15 yrs PS+DI		WO/90/8/188
Kearns M	Pte	1 Connaught Rangers	04/09/20	Dagshai	M+S7(3b)	3 yrs PS+DI		WO/90/8/188
Keefe A	Pte	334 Coy RDC	17/09/18	Pembroke Dock	M+Disob	84 dys Detn	28 dys	WO/92/4/52
Keenan G	Spr	Can Engrs	25/01/19	Field	M+Disob	NG		WO/213/29/55
Keenan W	Pte	1 Connaught Rangers	30/08/20	Dagshai	M+S7(2)+S7(1)	10 yrs PS+DI		WO/90/8/188
Keighley J	Cpl	2/7 R Wars	04/01/19	Field	M	5 yrs PS		WO/213/28/72
Keith JT	Pte	4(R) CEF	03/09/17	Bramshott	M+Insub(Sgt)+S22	18 mos Detn		WO/86/78/5
Kelleher J	Pte	7 R Irish	15/04/18	Field	M	5 yrs PS	Susp	WO/213/21/97
Kellet A	Spr	RE	15/05/19	Field	M+Disob	1 yr IHL		WO/213/29/137
Kelly A	Pte	5 Dragoon Gds	23/09/19	Curragh	M	6 mos HL	Comm 84 dys Detn	WO/92/4/84
Kelly C	Pte	65 Coy RDC	21/11/16	Towcester	M	1 yr Detn		WO/92/4/3
Kelly D	Pte	2 W India	11/05/19	Field EEF	M	5 yrs PS	Comm 1 yr HL	WO/213/30/28
Kelly DW	Pte	46 AIF	24/03/19	Field	M	11 yrs PS		WO/213/29/90
Kelly E	Dvr	RFA	24/04/19	Field	M+Disob	NG		WO/213/29/160
Kelly J	Pte	1 Connaught Rangers	04/09/20	Dagshai	M+S7(3b)	Death	Life PS	WO/90/8/188
Kelly JJ	Pte	1 NZ Div Emp B	16/10/18	Field	M	6 mos HL	Susp	WO/213/25/165
Kelly P	Pte	1 Connaught Rangers	30/08/20	Dagshai	M+S7(2)+S7(1)	10 yrs PS+DI		WO/90/8/188
Kelly P	Pte	1 Connaught Rangers	04/09/20	Dagshai	M+S7(3b)	10 yrs PS+Rnks+DI	Remit 3 yrs PS	WO/90/8/188
Kelly P	Pte	65 Coy RDC	21/11/16	Towcester	M	1 yr Detn		WO/92/4/3
Kelly SW	Pte	12 SWBdrs	01/12/16	Field	M+Disob	18 mos HL	Comm 3 mos FP1	WO/213/13/47
Kelly T	Pte	Quebec Regt	01/08/19	Ripon	M+7(3b)	2 yr HL+Disch Igmny		WO/86/88/53
Kemble F	Pte(L/Cpl)	7/8 R Innis Fus	15/04/18	Field	M	7 yrs PS	Susp	WO/213/21/96
Kembrey A	Pte	13 AIF	04/02/19	Rouen	M	3 yrs 9 mos PS		WO/90/8/59
Kemp S	Pte	7/8 R Innis Fus	15/04/18	Field	M	5 yrs PS	Susp	WO/213/21/96
Kennedy B	Pte	RAMC	10/05/19	Field	M	6 mos HL	Comm 28 dys FP2	WO/213/30/17
Kennedy J	Pte	5 Dragoon Gds	22/09/19	Curragh	M	1 yr HL+Disch Igmny	Comm 6 mos Detn	WO/92/4/84
Kennedy M	Pte	58 Coy RDC	21/11/16	Towcester	M	1 yr Detn		WO/92/4/1
Kennedy T	Pte	1 Cheshire	23/08/22	Ranikhet	M+Disob(RSM)+S40			WO/90/80/172
Kenny J	Pte	7 R Irish	15/04/18	Field	M	5 yrs PS	Susp	WO/213/21/97
Kent GA	Pte	10 Hussars	25/01/21	Curragh	Mx2+S9(1)x2	1 yr Detn	Remit 3 mos	WO/92/4/94
Kent T	Pte	1/4 KOYLI) (att 365 POW Coy	16/09/19	Field	M+Abs+Disob	3 yrs PS	Comm 1 yr HL	WO/213/31/69
Kenyon TF	Pte	5 Dragoon Gds	30/09/19	Curragh	M	1 yr HL+Disch Igmny	Comm 6 mos Detn	WO/92/4/87
Keogh TE	Cpl(A/Sgt)	Aus Prov Corps	29/06/18	Field EEF	M	NG		WO/213/26/112
Kerr SJ	Cpl	8 Aus Lt Horse	29/06/18	Field EEF	M	NG		WO/213/26/112
Kerrigan C	Pte	1 Connaught Rangers	04/09/20	Dagshai	M+S7(3b)	Death	20 yrs PS	WO/90/8/188
Kershaw J	Pte	2 Dragoon Gds (att RAOC)2	29/07/20	Field	M+S7(3b)	4 yrs PS		WO/213/32/2
Kerwain E	Pte	7/8 R Innis Fus	15/04/18	Field	M	5 yrs PS	Susp	WO/213/21/95
Khan Mozhar	Gnr	Malay SG Bty	11/03/15	Singapore	M	3 yrs PS	Comm 18 mos Imp	WO/213/4/17
Kilpatrick R	Pte	NZEF 3 Reinf	05/04/15	Zeitoun	Incit M+Disob(Lt)	2 yrs HL+Disch Igmny		WO/90/6/35
Kimmit R	Pte	3 HLI(att MGC)	25/04/16	Grantham	M	3 yrs PS		WO/92/3/37
King AE	Pte	45 AIF	24/03/19	Field	M	9 yrs PS		WO/213/29/90
King EJ	Pte	19 AIF	15/02/16	Sinai Penin	M+Disob	18 mos HL		WO/213/8/113
King G	Dvr	372 Coy CAHT	14/05/19	Field	M	5 yrs PS	Remit 2 yrs	WO/213/30/12
King G	Pte	2 Ches	05/03/20	Field ABS	M+Disob	18 mos HL	Rem 1 yr	WO/213/31/168
King J	Pte	7/8 R Innis Fus	15/04/18	Field	M	5 yrs PS	Susp	WO/213/21/96
King J	Pte	5 Dragoon Gds	26/09/19	Curragh	M	1 yr HL+Disch Igmny	Comm 6 mos Detn	WO/92/4/81
Kinney F	Pte	7/8 R Innis Fus	15/04/18	Field	M	5 yrs PS	Susp	WO/213/21/96

Name	Rank	Unit	Date D/M/Y	Location	Offence	Finding/Punishment	Amendment	PRO Reference File/Piece/Page
Kirby G	Pte	MG Gds	2/26/2018 +B321	London	M+Absx2	6 mos Detn		WO/92/4/29
Kirby W	Pte	58 Coy RDC	21/11/16	Towcester	M	1 yr Detn		WO/92/4/1
Kirk D	Pte	2 R I Fus	09/06/19	Field EEF	M+S40	42 dys FP2		WO/213/30/126
Kirkby JK	Pte	8 AIF	24/03/19	Field	M	10 yrs PS		WO/213/29/90
Kirkham D	Pte	65 Coy RDC	21/11/16	Towcester	M	1 yr Detn		WO/92/4/2
Kirkham ST	Pte	35 MGC	17/01/19	Field	Mx2	2 yrs HL	Remit 18 mos	WO/213/28/120
Kirwan N	Pte	8 R Innis Fus	06/09/15	Eniskillen	M+Inj pub property	1 yr HL		WO/86/66/111
Kite FJ	Signlr	RGA	16/05/19	Field	M	6 mos HL	Comm 84 dys FP1 Quashed	WO/213/29/148
Klaas	Pte	SANLC	21/11/17	Field	M+S40	3 yrs PS	Comm 2 yrs HL	WO/213/31/109
Klein M	Pte	39 R Fus	23/08/19	Field EEF	M	5 yrs PS	Comm 1 yr HL	WO/213/31/24
Knapp JJ	Pte	8 KOYLI	10/02/19	Field	M+Disob+S40	5 yrs PS	Quashed +Rem 2 yrs	WO/213/28/54
Knight A	Pte	9 (S) BWI	24/12/18	Field Italy	M+Disob+Esc	5 yrs PS		WO/213/27/25
Knight F	Pte	7 Leic	14/10/18	Field	M	Death	Comm 15 yrs PS	WO/213/26/45
Knight H	Pte	7 Dragoon Gds	09/06/21	Edinburgh	M+V(A/RSM)	NG		WO/86/91/131
Knowles J	Pte	9(S) E Lancs	29/05/18	SEF	M	1 yr HL		WO/213/23/179
Koert J	Dvr	ASC (SA)	23/07/18	Field	M	2 yrs HL		WO/213/24/168
Korr J	Pte	3 HLI(att MGC)	25/04/16	Grantham	M	3 yrs PS		WO/92/3/37
Kosar R	Pte	21(R) CEF	02/05/19	Liverpool	M+S7(3b)	6 mos HL		WO/92/4/71
Kozhin V	Pte	1 Slav-Brit Legion	17/07/19	Field NREF	M	NG		WO/213/32/59
Krantz A	Pte	39 R Fus	23/08/19	Field EEF	M	NG		WO/213/31/24
Lafleur G	Pte	Maur Lab Bn	10/05/18	Mespot	M(S7-2B)	6 mos HL		WO/90/7/151
Laguerre E	Pte	1 BWI	02/05/19	Field Italy	Mx2+Disob	18 mos HL	Remit 12 mos	WO/213/29/37
Lakin W	Pte	1 Gn Sher Fstrs	05/06/17	Kantara Egypt	M	2 yrs HL		WO/213/15/177
Lally S	Pte	1 Connaught Rangers	30/08/20	Dagshai	M	20 yrs PS+DI	Remit 5 yrs	WO/90/8/189
Lamb J	Pte	2 R Dublin Fusiliers	05/07/20	Constantinople	M+Disob(Capt)+S7(3b)	5 yrs PS	1 yr Detn	WO/90/8/84
Lamb W	Pte	1 Gn Sher Fstrs	05/06/17	Kantara Egypt	M	2 yrs HL		WO/213/15/177
Lambert A	Pte	5 Dragoon Gds	26/09/19	Curragh	M	1 yr HL+Disch Igmny	Comm 6 mos Detn	WO/92/4/83
Lamoureux AJ	Pte	20(R) CEF	20/05/19	Liverpool	M+S7(3b)	22 mos HL		WO/92/4/72
Lang PTB	Pte	1 Inf Bn AIF	15/10/18	Field	M+Des	3 yrs PS	Guilty of Des	WO/213/28/196
Langrish JG	Rfn	3 NZ Rifle Bde	17/06/16	Armentieres	M+S40	42 dys FP		WO/213/9/182
Larrad AJ	Dvr	337 Bde RFA	10/01/17	Canterbury	JM	6 mos Detn		WO/92/3/58
Lasheff T	Pte	1 Slav-Brit Legion	13/07/19	Field	M	NG		WO213/32/58
Lashkoff V	Pte	1 Slav-Brit Legion	14/07/19	Field NREF	M	Death		WO/213/32/59
Lasry SH	Pte	39 R Fus	23/08/19	Field EEF	M	5 yrs PS	Comm 1 yr HL	WO/213/31/24
Laughrey GA	Pte	1 Inf Bn AIF	15/10/18	Field	M+Des	3 yrs PS	Guilty of Des	WO/213/28/200
Laurence D	Pte	6 (S) BWI	24/12/18	Field Italy	M+Disob	3 yrs 6 mos PS		WO/213/27/24
Lavendar G	Pte	4 AIF	04/02/19	Rouen	M	90 dys Imp		WO/90/8/58
Lavender TW	Pte (L/Cpl)	1 Inf Bn AIF	15/10/18	Field	M+Des	NG		WO/213/28/200
Laverty J	Pte	1 B Watch	13/04/17	Dunkirk	M	8 mos HL		WO/213/14/138
Lavery F	Pte	7 R Irish	15/04/18	Field	M	5 yrs PS	Susp	WO/213/21/98
Lawler W	Bdr	RGA	05/07/19	Aldershot	M	9 mos Detn+Rnks		WO/86/88/1
Lawrence A	Pte	1 Inf Bn AIF	15/10/18	Field	M+Des	3 yrs PS	Guilty of Des	WO/213/28/196
Lawrence J	Pte	1 Inf Bn AIF	15/10/18	Field	M+Des	3 yrs PS	Guilty of Des	WO/213/28/196
Lawrence JF	Pte	RASC	20/02/19	Field	Mx2+S40	1 yr HL	Remit 3 mos	WO/213/28/169
Lawry W	Pte	2 Aus Pnr	24/03/19	Field	M	12 yrs PS		WO/213/29/91
Lax J	Pte	2 Y[ork] & Lanc	07/11/19	Basrah	M	4 yrs PS	Comm 2 yrs HL	WO/90/7/205
Le Guier B	Pte	14 AIF	11/10/16	Rouen	M	Death	Comm 2 yrs HL	WO/90/6/90
Le Roux G	Dvr	372 Coy CAHT	14/05/19	Field	M	5 yrs PS		WO/213/30/12
Leadbetter R	Pte	2/5 Welsh TF	27/09/16	Cardiff	M	1 yr Detn		WO/86/66/194
Lea E	Pte	68 Div Cyclist Coy	17/07/17	Gt Yarmouth	M	6 mos Detn		WO/86/73/171
Leah J	Pte	2 Dragoon Gds	25/09/19	Curragh	M	1 yr HL+Disch Igmny	Comm 6 mos Detn	WO/92/4/87
Leather AW	Pte	12 SWBdrs	01/12/16	Field	M(2)+Disob	7 yrs PS	Comm 2 yrs HL	WO/213/13/46
Ledicott CF	Sgt	8 Lincs	23/12/18	Field	M+S40	6 mos HL+Rnks	Imp	WO/213/28/8
Lee CEW	L/Cpl	76 Lab Coy	28/10/19	Field	M+Disob+S40	3 yrs PS	Comm 2 yrs HL	WO/213/31/80
Lee CH	Pte	3W Yorks	01/08/19	Devizes	M+S40	18 mos+Disch Igmny	9 mos	WO/92/4/76
Lee HE	Pte	9(S) E Lancs	29/05/18	SEF	M	1 yr HL		WO/213/23/179
Leech E	Pte	46 AIF	04/02/19	Rouen	M	90 dys Imp		WO/90/8/59
Leech H	Spr	RE	15/05/19	Field	M+Disob	1 yr IHL		WO/213/29/137
Leese G	Pte	1 Gn Sher Fstrs	05/06/17	Kantara Egypt	M	2 yrs HL		WO/213/15/177
Leet HJ	Cpl	23(R) CEF	21/02/19	Kinmel Park	M+Str+Drunk	5yrs PS+Rnks+Disch Igmny		WO/92/4/65
Lemon S	Gnr	RGA	05/07/19	Aldershot	M	2 yrs HL+Disch Igmny		WO/86/88/1
Lennox J	Pte	1/4 R Sco Fus	14/01/18	Field	M	10 yrs PS	Comm 2 yrs HL	WO/213/21/34
Lester WH	Pte	2/23 London	19/05/19	Field	M+Insub+S40	6 mos HL		WO/213/30/27

65

Name	Rank	Unit	Date D/M/Y	Location	Offence	Finding/Punishment	Amendment	PRO Reference File/Piece/Page
Lever TG	Pte	2 MGC	12/06/19	Field	M+Disob(2)+S40	5 yrs PS	Comm 2 yrs HL	WO/213/29/122
Levitan B	Pte	39 R Fus	23/08/19	Field EEF	M	5 yrs PS	Comm 1 yr HL	WO/213/31/25
Levitt A	Pte	2 KSLI	04/06/18	Field SEF	M+Disob	10 yrs PS	Comm 2 yrs HL	WO/213/23/40
Lewis AJ	Pte	19 RW Fus	04/02/19	Rouen	M	5 yrs 3 mos PS		WO/90/8/58
Lewis H	Pte	3 Glocs	08/10/15	Gravesend	Mx2+Insub (Sgt)+S10(4)	2 yrs HL + Disch Igmny		WO/86/67/44
Lewis HT	Pte	20 Lancs Fus	13/04/17	Dunkirk	M	6 mos HL		WO/213/14/138
Lewis J	Pte	8 KOYLI	10/02/19	Field	M+Disob+S40	Acquit		WO/213/28/54
Lewis S	Pte	2 W India	11/05/19	Field EEF	M	5 yrs PS	Comm 1 yr HL	WO/213/30/28
Lewis W	Dvr	ASC (SA)	23/07/18	Field	M	5 yrs PS	Comm 2 yrs HL	WO/213/24/168
Lewis WE	Gnr	124 Bde RFA	05/10/16	Rouen	M	Death		WO/90/6/89
Lewis WO	Pte	17 L'pool	16/05/19	NREF	M	2 yrs HL	Remit 18 mos	WO/213/29/181
Leyden JF	Pte	2 Otago NZEF	01/09/17	Field	M	10 yrs PS		WO/213/17/110
Lichenstein I	Pte	39 R Fus	23/08/19	Field EEF	M	5 yrs PS	Comm 1 yr HL	WO/213/31/24
Lievesly H	Pte	8 Lincs	12/11/17	Field	M+Disob	9 mos HL		WO/213/18/180
Lifschitz M	Pte	39 R Fus	23/08/19	Field EEF	M	NG		WO/213/31/24
Lightfoot WJ	Pte	BWI	04/01/18	Mesopotamia	[M]7(3a)x2	5 yrs PS	Comm 2 yrs HL	WO/90/7/169
Limington F	L/Bdr	RGA	05/07/19	Aldershot	M	9 mos Detn+Rnks		WO/86/88/1
Lind CW	Pte	21(R) CEF	05/05/19	Liverpool	M	Acquit		WO/92/4/67
Lindon JS	Spr	RE	15/05/19	Field	M+Disob	1 yr IHL		WO/213/29/137
Lindsay F	Pte	1 Gn Sher Fstrs	05/06/17	Kantara Egypt	M	2 yrs HL		WO/213/15/177
Lindsay GS	Pte	1 Inf Bn AIF	15/10/18	Field	M+Des	3 yrs PS	Guilty of Des	WO/213/28/197
Lingfield G	Gnr	RFA	06/05/19	Leeds	M	Acquit		WO/92/4/69
Lintott JR	Pte	2/4 R Sussex TF	23/07/15	Canterbury	J[oin in] M	84 dys Detn		WO/92/3/22
Little A	Pte	10 AIF	11/10/16	Rouen	M+Striking(Sgt)	Death	Comm 2 yrs HL	WO/90/6/89
Little T	Pte	RASC	20/04/20	Field ABS	M+Disob	3 mos FP2		WO/213/31/171
Little V	Pte (3AM)	RAF	30/04/18	Swanage	M+Disob	9 mos HL		WO/92/4/42
Littlefield GW	Pte	Quebec Regt	25/07/19	Ripon	M+S7(3b)	2 yrs HL+Disch Igmny		WO/86/88/51
Livermore AW	Pte	5 Dragoon Gds	26/09/19	Curragh	M	1 yr HL+Disch Igmny	Comm 6 mos Detn	WO/92/4/81
Livesey HH	AL/Bdr	RGA	16/05/19	Field	M	[No further details recorded]		WO/213/29/148
Livesey J	Pte	9(S) E Lancs	29/05/18	SEF	M	1 yr HL		WO/213/23/179
Livingstone JF	Pte	5 Dragoon Gds	25/09/19	Curragh	M	Acquit		WO/92/4/86
Llewellin L	Pte	4 Mddx	12/11/17	Field	M+Disob	6 mos HL	Comm 91 dys FP1	WO/213/18/181
Lloyd J	Sgt	1 Connaught Rangers	23/08/20	Dagshai	M	Acquit		WO/90/8/189
Lock G	Pte	7/8 R Innis Fus	15/04/18	Field	M	5 yrs PS	Susp	WO/213/21/96
Lodge SJ	Pte (AL/Cpl)	2/7 R Wars	04/01/19	Field	M	5 yrs PS		WO/213/28/72
Loftus JJ	Pte	1 Connaught Rangers	04/09/20	Dagshai	M+S7(3b)	Acquit		WO/90/8/188
Logan T	Pte	3 HLI(att MGC)	25/04/16	Grantham	M	3 yrs PS		WO/92/3/37
Loious T	Pte	6 (S) BWI	24/12/18	Field Italy	M+Disob	3 yrs 6 mos PS		WO/213/27/24
Long D	Pte	58 Coy RDC	21/11/16	Towcester	M	1 yr Detn		WO/92/4/1
Long GH	Pte	7 Can Rail Troops	02/05/19	Liverpool	M+S7(3b)	1 yr HL		WO/92/4/71
Longdon A	Dvr	RFA(att RGA)	13/03/18	Agra	M	1 yr HL	unexpired portion 30/4/18	WO/90/7/190
Lopeman PJ	Pte(L/Cpl)	1 Connaught Rangers	25/08/20	Dagshai	M	2 yrs HL+DI		WO/90/8/188
Lord W	Pte	5 Dragoon Gds	29/09/19	Curragh	M	1 yr HL+Disch Igmny	Comm 6 mos Detn	WO/92/4/83
Lorde G	Pte	9 (S) BWI	24/12/18	Field Italy	M+Disob+Esc	5 yrs PS		WO/213/27/25
Lorenzo FS	Dvr Whlr	ASC (SA)	23/07/18	Field	M	Life PS	Comm 5 yrs	WO/213/24/168
Loud FC	Gnr	V/38 TMB	10/01/17	Esquelbecq	M+Disob	3 yrs PS	Comm 1 yr HL	WO/213/13/138
Louden FH	Pte	4 Tank Bn	17/05/19	Field	M	6 mos HL		WO/213/29/127
Louw J	Dvr	372 Coy CAHT	14/05/19	Field	M	5 yrs PS	Remit 2 yrs	WO/213/30/12
Lovell W	Pte	21 Manch	08/02/19	Field	M+Abs	6 mos HL		WO/213/28/58
Lowe J	Pte	BWI	04/01/18	Mesopotamia	[M]7(3a)x2	10 yrs PS	R[emit?] 7 yrs	WO/90/7/169
Loxley G	Pte	1 Gn Sher Fstrs	05/06/17	Kantara Egypt	M	2 yrs HL		WO/213/15/177
Lucas AF	Pte	9 MGC	31/07/19	Field	M+Abs/Br	6 mos HL		WO/213/30/141
Lucas EC	Dvr	RGA	16/05/19	Field	M	6 mos HL	Comm 84 dys FP1 Quashed	WO/213/29/148
Luckay WW	Pte	Quebec Regt	24/07/19	Ripon	M+S7(3b)	2 yrs HL+Disch Igmny		WO/86/88/51
Lunt S	Ptr	5 Dragoon Gds	23/09/19	Curragh	M	Acquit		WO/92/4/84
Lynch J	Pte	1 Connaught Rangers	30/08/20	Dagshai	M	10 yrs PS+DI	Remit 5 yrs	WO/90/8/189
Lynott J	Pte(L/Cpl)	1 Connaught Rangers	25/08/20	Dagshai	M	2 yrs HL+DI		WO/90/8/188
Lyons P	Pte	18 AIF	04/02/19	Rouen	M	3 yrs 9 mos PS		WO/90/8/59
Lyons SB	Pte	2/6 R Wars	27/05/19	Field	M+S40	2 yrs HL	Remit 1 yr	WO/213/30/64
Lyttle L	Pte	7/8 R Innis Fus	15/04/18	Field	M	5 yrs PS	Susp	WO/213/21/95
Macdonald H	Dvr	RFA	18/08/19	Warlingham	M+S40	1 yr Detn		WO/92/4/78
Macdonald M	Pte(1AM)(A/Cpl)	RAF	30/04/18	Swanage	M+Disob	18 mos HL		WO/92/4/41

Name	Rank	Unit	Date D/M/Y	Location	Offence	Finding/Punishment	Amendment	PRO Reference File/Piece/Page
Macintyre P	Pte	7/8 R Innis Fus	15/04/18	Field	M	5 yrs PS	Susp	WO/213/21/95
Mack	Pte	SANLC	21/11/17	Field	M+S40	3 yrs PS	Comm 2 yrs HL	WO/213/31/109
Mackay W	Pte	7/8 R Innis Fus	15/04/18	Field	M	5 yrs PS	Susp	WO/213/21/94
Mackessy T	Pte	35 MGC	17/01/19	Field	Mx2	2 yrs HL	Remit 6 mos	WO/213/28/120
Mackey M	Pte	B Watch	12/09/18	Field	M(x2)	10 yrs PS	One charge Quashed	WO/213/25/177
Mackey M	Pte	1 Inf Bn AIF	15/10/18	Field	M+Des	3 yrs PS	Guilty of Des	WO/213/28/196
Mackie GE	Pte	5 Dragoon Gds	24/09/19	Curragh	M	84 dys HL	Comm 42 dys Detn	WO/92/4/87
Mademedsha J	Pte	SANLC	17/12/17	Capetown	M	10 yrs PS		WO/213/19/115
Madgwick HJ	Pte	2/4 R Sussex TF	23/07/15	Canterbury	J[oin in] M	84 dys Detn		WO/92/3/22
Madigan D	Pte	1 Connaught Rangers	25/08/20	Dagshai	M	Acquit		WO/90/8/188
Magee M	Pte	7 R Irish	15/04/18	Field	M	5 yrs PS	Susp	WO/213/21/97
Magnusson GD	Gnr	11 Bty NZFA	19/07/16	[Le] Havre	Per M+Viol SO	Acquit		WO/90/6/67
Maher P	Pte	1 Connaught Rangers	30/08/20	Dagshai	M	10 yrs PS+DI	Remit 5 yrs	WO/90/8/189
Makubedi K	Cpl	SANLC	17/12/17	Capetown	M	12 yrs PS+Rnks		WO/213/19/115
Makuku J	Pte	SANLC	17/12/17	Capetown	M	10 yrs PS		WO/213/19/115
Malefa W[illia]m	Native Leader	S ASC	31/01/16	Bissil BEA	M	NG		WO/213/8/132
Malleysi Pohl	Native Leader	S ASC	31/01/16	Bissil BEA	M	NG		WO/213/8/132
Mallon W	Pte	7 R Irish	15/04/18	Field	M	5 yrs PS	Susp	WO/213/21/97
Maloney P	Pte	7 R Irish	15/04/18	Field	M	5 yrs PS	Susp	WO/213/21/98
Maltby GE	Pte	49 AIF	24/03/19	Field	M	11 yrs PS		WO/213/29/91
Malthouse SHJ	Pte	10 AIF Rangers	24/03/19	Field	M	10 yrs PS		WO213/29/88
Mangan PJ	Pte	1 Connaught Rangers	04/09/20	Dagshai	M+S7(3b)	3 yrs PS+DI	2 yrs HL+DI	WO/90/8/188
Maniquois M	Pte	Labour Bn	16/01/19	Mesopotamia	M	84 dys Detn		WO/90/7/169
Manley C	L/Bdr	RGA	04/07/19	Aldershot	M	9 mos Detn+Rnks +Disch Igmny		WO/86/87/188
Mann HG	L/Bdr	RGA	05/07/19	Aldershot	M	9 mos Detn+Rnks		WO/86/88/1
Mannings M	Pte	6 (S) BWI	24/12/18	Field Italy	M+Disob	3 yrs 6 mos PS		WO/213/27/24
Mannion P	Pte(L/Cpl)	1 Connaught Rangers	10/09/20	Dagshai	M+S7(3b)	15 yrs PS+DI		WO/90/8/188
Mannix J	Pte	3 W Yorks	06/02/18	Wallsend	M+Insub (CSM)	1 yr HL		WO/86/80/96
Mansfield E	Pte	1 Suffolk	02/05/18	Field SEF	M+Disob	10 yrs PS	Comm 2 yrs HL	WO/213/22/30
Marchmont J	Dvr	234 Bty RFA	05/01/15	Cahir	M+Viol to Cpl+S40 +S10(3)	2 yrs HL+Disch Igmny		WO/86/63/136
Marlow E	Pte	2 W India	11/05/19	Field EEF	M	7 yrs PS	Comm 2 yrs HL	WO/213/30/28
Marriott A	Pte	7/8 R Innis Fus	15/04/18	Field	M	5 yrs PS	Susp	WO/213/21/94
Marsden E	Pte	12 SWBdrs	01/12/16	Field	M+Disob	18 mos HL	Comm 3 mos FP1	WO/312/13/46
Marsden J	Pte	5 Dragoon Gds	24/09/19	Curragh	M	1 yr HL+Disch Igmny	Comm 6 mos Detn	WO/92/4/86
Marsh B	Pte	30 MGC	29/07/19	Field	M+Disob	1 yr HL		WO/213/30/119
Marsh RE	Dvr	Can Res A[rty]	14/05/19	Liverpool	M+Res+Esc	10 mos HL		WO/92/4/71
Marsh W	Pte	2/4 R Sussex TF	23/07/15	Canterbury	J[oin in] M	84 dys Detn		WO/92/3/22
Marshall A	Pte	9 (S) BWI	24/12/18	Field Italy	M+Disob+Esc	8 yrs PS		WO/213/27/25
Marshall ACO	Pte	1 Inf Bn AIF	15/10/18	Field	M+Des	3 yrs PS	Guilty of Des	WO/213/28/196
Marshall W	Dvr	33(R) Bty RFA	13/01/16	Glasgow	M+Viol(Cpl)	1 yr Detn		WO/86/68/161
Martin F	Pte	2/4 R Sussex TF	23/07/15	Canterbury	J[oin in] M	84 dys Detn		WO/92/3/22
Martin H	Dvr	372 Coy CAHT	14/05/19	Field	M	5 yrs PS		WO/213/30/12
Martin J	Spr	3 Aus Tun Coy	13/10/18	Field	M+Disob	1 yr HL	NC	WO/213/30/136
Martin J	Spr	3 Aus Tun Coy	18/10/18	Field	M+Disob	2 yrs HL	Susp	WO/213/26/66
Martin S	Gnr	RGA	13/03/18	Agra	M	1 yr HL	unexpired portion 30/4/18	WO/90/7/190
Martin S	Pte	6 (S) BWI	24/12/18	Field Italy	M+Disob	3 yrs 6 mos PS		WO/213/27/24
Martin W	Pte	1 Inf Bn AIF	15/10/18	Field	M+Des	3 yrs PS	Guilty of Des	WO/213/28/198
Mason W	Pte	1 Royal Welsh Fus	24/07/20	Ranikhet	M+Insol(L/Cpl)+S40	Death	5 yrs PS	WO/90/8/194
Massey A	Pte	1 Gn Sher Fstrs	05/06/17	Kantara Egypt	M	2 yrs HL		WO/213/15/177
Massey C	Pte	7 Dragoon Gds	09/06/21	Edinburgh	M+V(A/RSM)	NG		WO/86/91/131
Massicote A	Pte	22 Quebec CEF	15/05/19	Liverpool	M	Acquit		WO/92/4/68
Maton J	Dvr	ASC (SA)	05/08/18	Field	M+S40	9 mos HL		WO/213/24/129
Matthews GF	Pte	5 Dragoon Gds	29/09/19	Curragh	M	1 yr HL+Disch Igmny	Comm 6 mos Detn	WO/92/4/82
Matthews J	Pte	RASC	20/04/20	Avonmouth	M	18 mos HL +Disch Igmny	18 mos Detn +Remit Disch	WO/86/90/17
Matume D	Pte	SANLC	17/12/17	Capetown	M	10 yrs PS		WO/213/19/115
Maulson J	Pte	2 Essex (Leics?)	18/07/21	Malta	M+Theft+S18(4b)	1 yr HL+DI		WO/90/8/87
May AE	Spr	RE	09/05/19	Field Italy	M	2 yrs HL	Remit 20 mos/ Quashed	WO/213/29/73
May C	Pte	2 W India	11/05/19	Field EEF	M	5 yrs PS	Comm 1 yr HL	WO/213/30/28

Name	Rank	Unit	Date D/M/Y	Location	Offence	Finding/Punishment	Amendment	PRO Reference File/Piece/Page
May J	Pte	2 Liverpool	26/04/20	Khartoum	M+Disob +S40/S7(3b)	6 mos Dtn + stop 122 dys Dtn + stop	Remit 122 dys Detn+Stop	WO/90/8/83
May M	Dvr	ASC (SA)	23/07/18	Field	M	1 yr HL		WO/213/24/168
May W	Pte	35 MGC	17/01/19	Field	Mx2	2 yrs HL	Remit 18 mos	WO/213/28/121
Mayers C	Pte	9 BWI	28/02/19	Plymouth	M	2 yrs Detn		WO/86/87/17
Mayo J	Dvr	234 Bty RFA	15/01/15	Cahir	M+S40+S10(3)	2 yrs HL+Disch Igmny		WO/86/63/137
McArthur T	Pte	1/4 R Scots	24/03/19	Field	M	12 yrs PS		WO213/29/88
McCabe J	Pte	8 R Innis Fus	06/09/15	Eniskillen	M+Inj pub prop	1 yr HL		WO/86/66/111
McCabe J	Pte	3 W Yorks	01/08/19	Devizes	M+S40	18 mos+HL Igmny	9 mos	WO/92/4/77
McCafferty R	Pte	7 R Irish	15/04/18	Field	M	5 yrs PS	Susp	WO/213/21/97
McCall E	Pte	65 Coy RDC	21/11/16	Towcester	M	1 yr Detn		WO/92/4/3
McCall TM	Pte	30 MGC	29/07/19	Field	M+Disob	1 yr HL		WO/213/30/119
McCallam	Pte	3 HLI att MGC	25/04/16	Grantham	NSM	1 dy Detn		WO/92/3/38
McCallan GH	Pte	9 AIF	24/03/19	Field	M	11 yrs PS		WO/213/29/89
McCallum D	Pte	2(R) MGC	25/06/18	Grantham	M+S40	2yrs HL	Remit 1 yr/ Comm Detn	WO/92/4/41
McCallum S	Pte	6 (S) BWI	24/12/18	Field Italy	M+Disob	3 yrs 6 mos PS		WO/213/27/24
McCann J	Pte	Quebec Regt	21/07/19	Ripon	Mx2+S7[3]b+S40	2 yrs HL+Disch Igmny		WO/86/88/52
McCarthy D	Pte	2 R Mun Fus	24/03/20	Field EEF	M+X0+S2+7(2b)	9 mos HL		WO/213/31/142
McCarthy J	L/Bdr	RGA	05/07/19	Aldershot	M	9 mos Detn+Rnks +Disch Igmny		WO/86/87/189
McCarthy M	Pte	2 R Mun Fus	24/03/20	Field EEF	M+X0+S2+7(2b)	9 mos HL		WO/213/31/142
McCarthy P	Dvr	RFA	07/03/19	Field	M	90 dys FP2		WO/213/29/12
McCauley W	Pte	7 R Irish	15/04/18	Field	M	5 yrs PS	Susp	WO/213/21/98
McClelland A	Pte	5 Dragoon Gds	26/09/19	Curragh	M	1 yr HL+Disch Igmny	Comm 6 mos Detn	WO/92/4/83
McCogg E	Pte	11 BWI	28/02/19	Plymouth	M	2 yrs Detn		WO/86/87/17
McCombie A	Pte	Tank Corps	07/01/21	Ramadi	M	1 yr HL	Comm to Detn	WO/21/33/2
McConaghy D	Pte	R Can	24/03/19	Field	M	10 yrs PS		WO213/29/88
McConnell P	Pte	1 Connaught Rangers	04/09/20	Dagshai	M+S7(3b)	Acquit		WO/90/8/188
McCorkindale D	Pte	11 R Scots	05/10/16	Rouen	M	Death	Comm 15 yrs PS	WO/90/6/89
McCormack C	Pte	KOSB	12/09/18	Field	M(x2)	10 yrs PS	Rem 2 yrs/ one charge NC	WO/213/25/177
McCormack E	Pte	65 Coy RDC	21/11/16	Towcester	M	1 yr Detn		WO/92/4/2
McDonald A	Pte	NZ Pnr	04/02/19	Rouen	M	Acquit		WO/90/8/59
McDonald EC	Pte	25(R) CEF	11/09/17	Bramshott	M+Absx2+S22	2 yrs Detn		WO/86/78/31
McDonald J	Pte	11 R Fus	23/12/18	Field	M	5 yrs PS		WO/213/28/141
McDonald L	Pte	2 R Irish	15/04/18	Field	M	5 yrs PS	Susp	WO/213/21/98
McDonell C	Pte	3 Can MGC	21/01/19	Field	Mx2	5 yrs PS		WO/213/28/189
McDonnell C	Pte	3 Can MGC	24/03/19	Field	M	Death	Comm PS/Life	WO/213/29/90
McDonnell C	Pte	25 AIF	24/03/19	Field	M	11 yrs PS		WO/213/29/91
McDowell S	Pte	5 Dragoon Gds	23/09/19	Curragh	M	6 mos HL	Comm 84 dys Detn	WO/92/4/84
McDowell T	Pte	65 Coy RDC	21/11/16	Towcester	M	1 yr Detn		WO/92/4/3
McElroy J	Pte	2 R I Fus	09/06/19	Field EEF	M+XOS+S40	1 yr HL		WO/213/30/126
McEvoy D	Pte	65 Coy RDC	21/11/16	Towcester	M	1 yr Detn		WO/92/4/3
McFarlane J	Pte	2 R Dublin Fusiliers	05/07/20	Constantinople	M+Disob(Capt) +S7(3b)	5 yrs PS	1 yr Detn	WO/90/8/84
McFarlane R	Pte	18 CEF	30/09/18	Seaford	M+S40	1 yr Imp		WO/86/84/196
McGowan J	Pte	1 Connaught Rangers	30/08/20	Dagshai	M	Life PS+DI		WO/90/8/188
McGrane G	Pte	2 Gor Hdrs	07/01/19	Field	M+S40	1 yr HL		WO/213/27/154
McGrath J	Pte(L/Cpl)	1 Connaught Rangers	25/08/20	Dagshai	M	1 yr HL+DI		WO/90/8/188
McGrath J	Pte	1 Connaught Rangers	04/09/20	Dagshai	M+S7(3b)	5 yrs PS+DI		WO/90/8/188
McGregor A	Pte	46 AIF	24/03/19	Field	M	19 yrs PS		WO213/29/88
McGregor J	Pte	1 NZ Div Emp B	16/10/18	Field	M	6 mos HL	Susp	WO/213/25/165
McGuire EM	Pte	2 Ches	05/03/20	Field ABS	M+Disob	2 yrs HL	Rem 18 mos	WO/213/31/168
McGuire P	Pte	7/8 R Irish Fus	13/04/17	Dunkirk	M	8 mos HL		WO/213/14/138
McIntosh R	Pte	R Sco Fus	18/09/17	Etaples	M	10 yrs PS		WO/213/17/151
McKay RHC	Cpl	1 Inf Bn AIF	15/10/18	Field	M+Des	10 yrs PS+Rnks	Guilty of Des	WO/213/28/199
McKee W	Pte	6 Dragoon Gds (att 5 Dragoon Gds)	30/09/19	Curragh	M	Acquit		WO/92/4/87
McKendry A	Pte	NZEF 3 Reinf	05/04/15	Zeitoun	Incit M+Disob(Lt)	2 yrs HL+Disch Igmny		WO/90/6/35
McKenna JF	Spr	Can Engrs	25/01/19	Field	M+Disob	NG		WO/213/29/55
McKenzie C	Pte	2 W India	11/05/19	Field EEF	M	5 yrs PS	Comm 1 yr HL	WO/213/30/28
McKenzie M	Spr	Can Ry Troops	22/04/19	Liverpool	M	Acquit		WO/92/4/70
McKinley W	Pte	8/10 Gordons (att RE)	28/08/16	Field	M x 2	5 yrs PS	Susp	WO/213/11/9
McLaren R	Pte	24 CEF	08/09/19	Field	M+Des+Esc +S40/S41	2 yrs HL		WO/213/30/141

Name	Rank	Unit	Date D/M/Y	Location	Offence	Finding/Punishment	Amendment	PRO Reference File/Piece/Page
McLaughlin G	Pte	R Marine Lab Corps	13/04/17	Dunkirk	M	1 yr HL		WO/213/14/138
McLaughlin J	Pte	65 Coy RDC	21/11/16	Towcester	M	1 yr Detn		WO/92/4/1
McLean TD	Spr	3 Aus Tun Coy	13/10/18	Field	M+Disob	1 yr HL	NC	WO/213/30/136
McLean TD	Spr	3 Aus Tun Coy	18/10/18	Field	M+Disob	2 yrs HL	Susp	WO/213/26/65
McLeod B	Pte	9 (S) BWI	24/12/18	Field Italy	M+Disob+Esc	5 yrs PS		WO/213/27/25
McLeod GAL	Pte (A/Cpl)	Can Res Arty	22/04/19	Liverpool	M	Acquit		WO/92/4/65
McLeod R	Dvr	10 AIF	18/06/19	Field	M+Disob	19 mos HL		WO/213/30/131
McMeecham M	Pte	1/4 R Sco Fus	14/01/18	Field	M	10 yrs PS	Comm 2 yrs HL	WO/213/21/34
McMillan B	Pte	Quebec Regt	22/07/19	Ripon	M+S7(3b)	20 mos HL +Disch Igmny		WO/86/88/52
McNally J	Pte	14 AIF	04/02/19	Rouen	M	90 dys Imp		WO/90/8/59
McNamee G	Pte	7/8 R Innis Fus	15/04/18	Field	M	5 yrs PS	Susp	WO/213/21/95
McNamee JB	Pte	1 Inf Bn AIF	15/10/18	Field	M+Des	3 yrs PS	Guilty of Des	WO/213/28/199
McNeal P	Pte	A & SH	13/04/17	Dunkirk	M	1 yr HL		WO/213/14/138
McNeill HS	Pte	24 AIF	22/12/18	Field	M	NG		WO/213/27/184
McNicol N	Spr	RE	09/05/19	Field Italy	M	2 yrs HL	Remit 20 mos/ Quashed	WO/213/29/73
McNorvill J	Pte	2/4 R Sussex TF	23/07/15	Canterbury	J[oin in] M	84 dys Detn		WO/92/3/23
McPherson J	Pte	2 R Scots	24/03/19	Field	M	11 yrs PS		WO213/29/88
McQuade F	Pte	1 Gn Sher Fstrs	05/06/17	Kantara Egypt	M	2 yrs HL		WO/213/15/177
McQuillan D	Pte	2 R I Fus	09/06/19	Field EEF	M+S40	NG		WO/213/30/126
McRoberts H	L/Bdr	RGA	05/07/19	Aldershot	M	9 mos Detn+ Rnks		WO/86/88/1
Mead S	Pte	19 AIF	24/03/19	Field	M	11 yrs PS		WO/213/29/90
Meadows J	Dvr	ASC (SA)	05/08/18	Field	M+S40	9 mos HL		WO/213/24/129
Mecklenburgh C	Spr	RE	15/05/19	Field	M+Disob	1 yr IHL		WO/213/29/137
Meek J	Pte	35 MGC	17/01/19	Field	Mx2	2 yrs HL	Remit 18 mos	WO/213/28/120
Mellors H	Pte	1 Gn Sher Fstrs	05/06/17	Kantara Egypt	M	2 yrs HL		WO/213/15/177
Melson J	Pte	2 Y[ork] & Lanc	05/11/19	Basrah	M	4 yrs PS	Comm 2 yrs HL	WO/90/7/205
Mennik N	Dvr	ASC (SA)	23/07/18	Field	M	5 yrs PS	Comm 2 yrs HL	WO/213/24/168
Meres S	Pte	1 Aus MGB	04/02/19	Rouen	M	3 yrs + 3 mos PS		WO/90/8/59
[Merrett?] H	Pte(L/Cpl)	2/4 R Sussex TF	23/07/15	Canterbury	NSM	28 dys Detn		WO/92/3/20
Merritt SG	Pte	Can ASC	21/11/17	Bramshott	M+Insub(Lieut)	42 dys Detn	Remit 15 dys	WO/86/79/54
Merton GA	Rfn	2/5 Sussex	23/06/15	Canterbury	Incit M+Esc Conf +S40	140 dys Detn		WO/92/3/18
Metcalfe JE	Cpl(AL/Sgt)	13 Yorks	16/05/19	NREF	M	2 yrs HL+Rnks		WO/213/29/181
Mettlekamp J	Dvr	ASC (SA)	05/08/18	Field	M+S40	9 mos HL		WO/213/24/129
Miarid G	Pte	1 Slav-Brit Legion	17/07/19	Field NREF	M	Death	Comm 10 yrs PS	WO/213/32/59
Miculka V	Pte	21(R) CEF	19/05/19	Liverpool	M	10 yrs PS		WO/92/4/72
Miles FV	Pte(S/Smith)	ASC	30/12/15	Marseilles	Joining M	3 yrs PS	Comm to 2 yrs HL	WO/90/6/44
Miller AF	Pte	LN Lancs (att RAOC)	08/10/19	Field	M	NG		WO/213/31/6
Miller DM	Pte	1 Inf Bn AIF	15/10/18	Field	M+Des	3 yrs PS	Guilty of Des	WO/213/28/198
Miller G	Pte	2 W India	11/05/19	Field EEF	M	5 yrs PS	Comm 1 yr HL	WO/213/30/28
Miller R	Pte	1/4 KOYLI (att 365 POW Coy)	16/09/19	Field	M+Abs+Disob	3 yrs PS	Comm 1 yr HL	WO/213/31/69
Miller TC	Cpl	43 R Fus	03/02/19	Field	M+S40+S7(2)	5 yrs PS+Rnks		WO/213/28/165
Miller W	Pte	9(S) E Lancs	29/05/18	SEF	M	1 yr HL		WO/213/23/179
Millin GL	Pte	60 AIF	04/02/19	Rouen	M	90 dys Imp		WO/90/8/59
Millings G	Pte	2 W India	11/05/19	Field EEF	M	5 yrs PS	Comm 1 yr HL	WO/213/30/28
Mills A	Spr	RE	15/05/19	Field	M+Disob	1 yr IHL		WO/213/29/137
Mills SC	Dvr	RFA	27/09/19	Deepcut	M	NG		WO/86/88/138
Millward H	Pte	5 Dragoon Gds	29/09/19	Curragh	M	1 yr HL+Disch Igmny	Comm 6 mos Detn	WO/92/4/82
Millward J	Pte	1 Gn Sher Fstrs	05/06/17	Kantara Egypt	M	2 yrs HL		WO/213/15/177
Milne R	Pte	12 SWBdrs	01/12/16	Field	M+Disob	2 yrs HL	Comm 3 mos FP1	WO/213/13/46
Milne RW	Pte	2 MGC	12/06/19	Field	M+Disob(2)+S40	5 yrs PS	Remit 2 yrs	WO/213/29/122
Milner G	Pte	2 Y[ork] & Lanc	07/11/19	Basrah	M+S7(3B)	5 yrs PS	Comm 2 yrs HL	WO/90/7/205
Milson W	Pte	257 P of W Coy	13/05/19	Field	M+S40(2)	112 dys HL	Comm 90 dys FP2	WO/213/30/31
Minto P	Dvr	ASC (SA)	23/07/18	Field	M	5 yrs PS	Comm 2 yrs PS	WO/213/24/168
Mintz N	Pte	39 R Fus	23/08/19	Field EEF	M	NG		WO/213/31/24
Miranda J	Pte	1 Connaught Rangers	25/08/20	Dagshai	M	2 yrs HL+DI		WO/90/8/188
Mitchell BA	Gnr	RHA(att RGA)	13/03/18	Agra	M	1 yr HL	unexpired portion 30/4/18	WO/90/7/190
Mitchell D	Spr	RE	15/05/19	Field	M+Disob	1 yr IHL		WO/213/29/137
Mitchell E	Pte	4 Mddx	12/11/17	Field	M+Disob	6 mos HL	Comm 91 dys FP1	WO/213/18/181
Mitchell FKW	Pte	5 AIF	11/10/16	Rouen	M	Death	Comm 2 yrs HL	WO/90/6/90
Mitchell FW	Pte	2/4 R Sussex TF	23/07/15	Canterbury	J[oin in] M	84 dys Detn		WO/92/3/22
Mitchell G	Pte	2/4 R Sussex TF	23/07/15	Canterbury	J[oin in] M	84 dys Detn		WO/92/3/22

Name	Rank	Unit	Date D/M/Y	Location	Offence	Finding/Punishment	Amendment	PRO Reference File/Piece/Page
Moffatt P	Gdsn	Irish Gds	04/02/20	Guildhall Wminster	M	5 yrs P + Disch Igmny		WO/92/4/89
Mohamed A	Labourer	Egyptian Lab Corps	06/09/17	Boulogne	M+S40	8 mos HL		WO/213/17/41
Moir J	Pte	7/8 R Innis Fus	15/04/18	Field	M	5 yrs PS	Susp	WO/213/21/96
Molloy P	Pte	5 Dragoon Gds	24/09/19	Curragh	M	1 yr HL+Disch Igmny	Comm 6 mos Detn	WO/92/4/87
Monks L	Pte	2 Ches	05/03/20	Field ABS	M+Disob	2 yrs HL	Rem 18 mos	WO/213/31/168
Monteith GJ	Pte(S/Smith)	ASC	30/12/15	Marseilles	Joining M	3 yrs PS	Comm 2yrs HL	WO/90/6/44
Moody WA	Pte	5 Dragoon Gds	22/09/19	Curragh	M	1 yr HL+Disch Igny	Comm 6 mos Detn	WO/92/4/81
Mooney H	Pte	7/8 R Innis Fus	15/04/18	Field	M	5 yrs PS	Susp	WO/213/21/96
Moorcroft AA	Dvr	Aust FA	07/11/18	Field	M+Esc	35 dys FP2		WO/213/26/94
Moore AW	Spr	3 Aus Tun Coy	13/10/18	Field	M+Disob	1 yr HL	NC	WO/213/30/137
Moore AW	Spr	3 Aus Tun Coy	18/10/18	Field	M+Disob	2 yrs HL	Susp	WO/213/26/65
Moore F	Pte	5 Dragoon Gds	25/09/19	Curragh	M	Acquit		WO/92/4/87
Moore GS	Pte	5 Dragoon Gds	29/09/19	Currragh	M	1 yr HL+Disch Igmny	Comm 6 mos Detn	WO/92/4/81
Moore M	Pte	5 Dragoon Gds	24/09/19	Curragh	M	Acquit		WO/92/4/86
Moore R	Pte	RAMC	10/05/19	Field	M	6 mos HL	Comm 28 dys FP2	WO/213/30/17
Moore T	Pte	65 Coy RDC	21/11/16	Towcester	M	1 yr Detn		WO/92/4/3
Moore T	Pte	3 RWFs	08/06/18	Kinmel Park	M+S40	2 yr Imp	Comm Detn	WO/92/4/40
Moore WJ	AL/Bdr	RGA	05/07/19	Aldershot	M	9 mos Detn+Rnks + Disch Igmny		WO/86/87/189
Moorehouse JJ	Pte	1 Connaught Rangers	04/09/20	Dagshai	M+S7(3b)	Life PS+DI	20 yrs PS	WO/90/8/188
Moores TH	Pte	21 Manch	08/02/19	Field	M+Abs	6 mos HL		WO/213/28/58
Moran FJ	Pte(L/Cpl)	1 Connaught Rangers	10/09/20	Dagshai	M+S7(3b)	10 yrs PS+DI		WO/90/8/188
Moran JA	Pte	1 Inf Bn AIF	15/10/18	Field	M+Des	3 yrs PS	Guilty of Des	WO/213/28/198
Moran R	Pte	25 CEF	24/03/19	Field	M	11 yrs PS		WO/213/29/90
Moran T	Pte	1 Connaught Rangers	30/08/20	Dagshai	M	Death	Life PS	WO/90/8/189
Morey J	Pte	1 Black Watch	27/09/22	Allahabad	M+Des+Theft +S18(4)	2 yrs HL+DI		WO/90/80/172
Morgan C	Pte	3 RWFs	06/06/18	Kinmel Park	M+Disob	1 yr HL	Comm to Detn	WO/92/4/39
Morgan J	Pte	21 Manch	08/02/19	Field	M+Abs	6 mos HL		WO/213/28/58
Morgan W	Pte	6 (S) BWI	24/12/18	Field Italy	M+Disob	3 yrs 6 mos PS		WO/213/27/24
Morgan WE	Gnr	V/38 TMB	10/01/17	Esquelbecq	M+Disob	3 yrs PS		WO/213/13/138
Morley J	Pte	65 Coy RDC	21/11/16	Towcester	M	1 yr Detn		WO/92/4/2
Morneau L	Pte	Quebec Regt	22/07/19	Ripon	M	NG		WO/86/88/42
Morphet T	Pte	7/8 R Innis Fus	15/04/18	Field	M	5 yrs PS	Susp	WO/213/21/95
Morris A	Pte	1 Gn Sher Fstrs	05/06/17	Kantara Egypt	M	2 yrs HL		WO/213/15/177
Morris AR	Cpl	1 Aus Lt Horse	29/06/18	Field	M	NG		WO/213/26/112
Morris DJ	Pte	21 RWF	10/01/16	Conway	M+AWOL	1 yr HL+Disch Igmny	Comm/Quashed	WO/86/68/85
Morris H	Pte	5 Dragoon Gds	26/09/19	Curragh	M	1 yr HL+Disch Igmny	Comm 6 mos Detn	WO/92/4/83
Morris HF	Pte	2/5 Welsh TF	27/09/16	Cardiff	M	1 yr Detn		WO/86/66/194
Morris J	Pte	3 Leics	27/08/14	Portsmouth	M	1 yr HL		WO/213/2/1
Morris W	Pte	1 Royal Welsh Fus	24/07/20	Ranikhet	M+Insol(Sgt)+S40	Death	5 yrs PS	WO/90/8/194
Morrison J	Pte	Lab Cps	06/01/19	Field	M+S40	NG		WO/213/27/37
Morrison JB	Pte(A/Cpl)	1(R) CEF	28/04/19	Liverpool	M	5 yrs PS		WO/92/4/70
Moss EJ	Pte	18 AIF	19/07/16	[Le] Havre	Per M+Viol SO	5 yrs PS		WO/90/6/67
Mountford WH	L/Cpl	5 Dragoon Gds	25/09/19	Curragh	M	Acquit		WO/92/4/86
Moxon T	Pte	7/8 R Innis Fus	15/04/18	Field	M	5 yrs PS	Susp	WO/213/21/95
Muir CW	Pte (L/Cpl)	1 Inf Bn AIF	15/10/18	Field	M+Des	5 yrs PS	Guilty of Des	WO/213/28/197
Muir WJC	Spr	Can Engrs	25/01/19	Field	M+Disob	NG		WO/213/29/55
Mullen R	Pte	7/8 R Innis Fus	15/04/18	Field	M	NG		WO/213/21/97
Mullen T	Pte	R Marine Lab Corps	13/04/17	Dunkirk	M	8 mos HL		WO/213/14/138
Mullens C	Dvr	ASC (SA)	05/08/18	Field	M+S40	9 mos HL		WO/213/24/129
Mulligan J	Pte	9(S) E Lancs	29/05/18	SEF	M	1 yr HL		WO/213/23/179
Mullins A	Pte	1 Inf Bn AIF	15/10/18	Field	M+Des	3 yrs PS	Guilty of Des	WO/213/28/195
Mullis WW	Spr	Can Engrs	25/01/19	Field	M+Disob	NG		WO/213/29/55
Mundell J	Pte	3 W Yorks	01/08/19	Devizes	M+S40	18 mos HL Igmny	9 mos	WO/92/4/77
Mundle J	Pte	6 BWI	10/01/19	Field Italy	M	3 yrs PS		WO/213/27/81
Munro DS	Pte	Can O[rdnance] Corps	09/08/19	Witley	M+S40	6 mos Detn		WO/86/88/44
Munroe D	Pnr	RE	07/08/19	Bordon	M+S40	18 mos HL + Disch Igmny	NC	WO/92/4/77
Munroe J	Pte	9 BWI	28/12/18	Field Italy	M+Striking	20 yrs PS	Remit 6 yrs	WO/213/27/25
Murchinson R	Pte	Can ASC	21/11/17	Bramshott	M+Insub(Lieut)	42 dys Detn	Remit 15 dys	WO/86/79/54
Murman I	Pte	39 R Fus	23/08/19	Field EEF	M	NG		WO/213/31/23
Murphy A	Pte	9(S) E Lancs	29/05/18	SEF	M	1 yr HL		WO/213/23/179
Murphy J	Pte	R Marine Lab Corps	13/04/17	Dunkirk	M	1 yr HL		WO/213/14/138

Name	Rank	Unit	Date D/M/Y	Location	Offence	Finding/Punishment	Amendment	PRO Reference File/Piece/Page
Murphy JC	Pte	49 AIF	04/02/19	Rouen	M	90 dys Imp		WO/90/8/59
Murphy JJ	Pte	8 R Innis Fus	06/09/15	Eniskillen	M + Inj pub property	1 yr HL		WO/86/66/111
Murphy M	Pte	7 R Irish	15/04/18	Field	M	NG		WO/213/21/97
Murphy MJ	Pte	6 Conn Rangers	05/10/16	Rouen	M	Death	Comm 10 yrs PS	WO/90/6/89
Murphy R	Pte	18 AIF	19/07/16	[Le] Havre	Per M+Viol SO	5 yrs PS		WO/90/6/67
Murphy T	Pte	1 Inf Bn AIF	15/10/18	Field	M+Des	3 yrs PS	Guilty of Des	WO/213/28/195
Murray T	Gnr	RFA	24/06/19	Field	M+Disob	2 yrs HL		WO/213/29/137
Murray TJ	Cpl	1 Connaught Rangers	25/08/20	Dagshai	M	5 yrs PS+Rnks	Remit 2 yrs	WO/90/8/188
Murray W	Dvr	RFA	24/04/19	Field	M+Disob	5 mos HL		WO/213/29/160
Mutch R	Pte	5 Dragoon Gds	23/09/19	Curragh	M	1 yr HL+Disch Igmny	Comm 6 mos Detn	WO/92/4/84
Mwanyivera A bin	Pte	1/6 KAR	13/08/17	Tabora	Mx2+Striking	15 yrs PS+ Disch Igmny		WO/213/23/81
Myers D	Pte	9 (S) BWI	24/12/18	Field Italy	M+Disob+Esc	10 yrs PS		WO/213/27/25
Napper T	Pte	2/4 R Sussex TF	23/07/15	Canterbury	J[oin in] M	84 dys Detn		WO/92/3/22
Narbey A	Pte	1 NZ Div Emp B	16/10/18	Field	M	6 mos HL	Susp	WO/213/25/165
Nassau H	Pte	15 AIF	04/02/19	Rouen	M	28 dys Imp		WO/90/8/59
Naylor J	Pte	65 Coy RDC	21/11/16	Towcester	M	1 yr Detn		WO/92/4/2
Neale G	Cpl	RGA	05/07/19	Aldershot	M	9 mos Detn+Rnks		WO/86/88/1
Nearin J	Pte	2 CEF	19/07/16	[Le] Havre	Per M+Viol SO	Acquit		WO/90/6/67
Neason WB	Pte	23(R) CEF	28/05/19	Liverpool	M	Acquit		WO/92/4/69
Nelson J	Dvr	RFA	24/04/19	Field	M+Disob	NG		WO/213/29/160
Nelson J	Pte	2 W India	11/05/19	Field EEF	M	5 yrs PS	Comm 1 yr HL	WO/213/30/28
Nelson T	Pte	8/10 Gordons (att RE)	28/08/16	Field	M x 2	5 yrs PS	Susp	WO/213/11/9
Nemcheck M	Pte	39 R Fus	23/08/19	Field EEF	M	5 yrs PS	Comm 1 yr HL	WO/213/31/25
Neve C	Pte	2/4 R Sussex TF	23/07/15	Canterbury	J[oin in] M	84 dys Detn		WO/92/3/23
New B	Pte	4 Mddx	12/11/17	Field	M+Disob	6 mos HL	Comm 91 dys FP1	WO/213/18/181
New[t/l?]on CW	Pte	2 Otago NZEF	01/09/17	Field	M	10 yrs PS		WO/213/17/110
Newbold RF	Dvr	RASC	18/05/21	Chelsea	M	12 mos HL+DI		WO/92/4/96
Newell A	Pte	57 AIF	04/02/19	Rouen	M	90 dys Imp		WO/90/8/59
Newman JJ	Pte	2/4 R Sussex TF	23/07/15	Canterbury	J[oin in] M	NG		WO/92/3/22
Newman L	Gnr	RGA	04/07/19	Aldershot	M	9 mos Detn +Disch Igmny		WO/86/87/189
Newton F	Pte	1 Gn Sher Fstrs	05/06/17	Kantara Egypt	M	2 yrs HL		WO/213/15/177
Nicholas FF	Pte	1/6 L'pool	04/02/19	Rouen	M	56 dys Imp		WO/90/8/58
Nicholls AW	Pte	23 AIF	24/03/19	Field	M	11 yrs PS		WO0213/29/88
Nichols VP	Dvr	69(EA)DAC(TF)	11/09/16	Killinghall Moor	Joining M	Acquit		WO/92/3/45
Nicholson J	Dvr	372 Coy CAHT	14/05/19	Field	M	5 yrs PS	Remit 2 yrs	WO/213/30/12
Nicholson T	Pte	5 Dragoon Gds	24/09/19	Curragh	M	1 yr HL+Disch Igmny	Comm 6 mos Dtn	WO/92/4/86
Nisagie J	Dvr	ASC (SA)	23/07/18	Field	M	2 yrs HL		WO/213/24/168
Niven A	Gnr	RGA	13/03/18	Agra	M	1 yr HL	unexpired portion 30/4/18	WO/90/7/190
Nix A	Pte	3 Leics	27/08/14	Portsmouth	M	1 yr HL		WO/213/2/1
Noakes H	Pte	Lab Corps	24/03/19	Field	M	10 yrs PS		WO/213/29/89
Noble A	Gnr	RGA	13/03/18	Agra	M	1 yr HL	unexpired portion 30/4/18	WO/90/7/190
Noble W	Pte	1 Gn Sher Fstrs	05/06/17	Kantara Egypt	M	2 yrs HL		WO/213/15/177
Nolan J	Bdr	RGA	05/07/19	Aldershot	M	9 mos Detn+Rnks+Disch Igmny		WO/86/87/189
Noon J	Pte	1 Inf Bn AIF	15/10/18	Field	M+Des	3 yrs PS	Guilty of Des	WO/213/28/197
Nordockovitch B	Pte	39 R Fus	23/08/19	Field EEF	M	5 yrs PS	Comm 1 yr HL	WO/213/31/24
Norman AA	Pte	Lab Corps (att E Comm LB)	15/06/19	Sutton	M+S7(3b)	Acquit		WO/92/4/74
Norman J	Pte	West India Regt	29/04/21	Jamaica	M+Abs +S10(3)+S9(1)	5 yrs PS+DI	Remit 2 yrs	WO/90/8/87
Norrish W	Cpl	RGA	04/07/19	Aldershot	M	9 mos Detn+Rnks +Disch Igmny		WO/86/87/188
Norton E	Pte	5 Dragoon Gds	30/09/19	Curragh	M	1 yr HL+Disch Igmny	Comm 6 mos Detn	WO/92/4/87
Noton T	Pte	1 Gn Sher Fstrs	05/06/17	Kantara Egypt	M	2 yrs HL		WO/213/15/177
Nott WH	Pte	5 Dragoon Gds	26/09/19	Curragh	M	1 yr HL+Disch Igmny	Comm 6 mos Detn	WO/92/4/81
Nunan P	Pte	3 Can MGC	27/01/19	Field	M	5 yrs PS		WO/213/28/189
Oakley F	Pte	2 R Mun Fus	24/03/20	Field EEF	M(2)+XO+S2	2 yrs HL		WO/213/31/142
O'Brien T	Pte/LCpl	2 Royal Irish	05/07/21	Chakrata	Mx2+Disob(Lt)+S7(3b)x2	4 yrs PS	Remit 1 yr	WO/90/8/170
O'Brien WO	Pte	Quebec Regt	24/07/19	Ripon	S7(3b)M+S40	6 mos Detn		WO/86/88/51
O'Connell J	Pte	1 Connaught Rangers	30/08/20	Dagshai	M	10 yrs PS+DI		WO/90/8/188

71

Name	Rank	Unit	Date D/M/Y	Location	Offence	Finding/Punishment	Amendment	PRO Reference File/Piece/Page
O'Connell WL	Pte	1 Inf Bn AIF	15/10/18	Field	M+Des	NG		WO/213/28/198
O'Dea B	Pte	7/8 R Innis Fus	15/04/18	Field	M	5 yrs PS	Susp	WO/213/21/95
O'Doherty D	Pte	3 Irish Gds	03/06/16	Brentwood	M	1 yr HL		WO/86/70/108
O'Donnell C	Pte(L/Cpl)	1 Connaught Rangers	23/08/20	Dagshai	M+S7(3)	Acquit		WO/90/8/189
O'Donohue	Cpl	1 Connaught Rangers	23/08/20	Dagshai	M+S7(3)	1 yr HL+Rnks+DI		WO/90/8/189
O'Donoghue D	Pte	7/8 R Innis Fus	15/04/18	Field	M	5 yrs PS	Susp	WO/213/21/95
O'Donohue WM	Pte	46 AIF	24/03/19	Field	M	10 yrs PS		WO/213/29/89
O'Hara T	Pte	65 Coy RDC	21/11/16	Towcester	M	1 yr Detn		WO/92/4/3
O'Keefe D	Pte/LCpl	2 Royal Irish	05/07/21	Chakrata	Mx2+S7(3b)	Acquit		WO/90/8/170
O'Keeffe P	Pte	5 Dragoon Gds	26/09/19	Curragh	M	1 yr HL+Disch Igmny	Comm 6 mos Detn	WO/92/4/83
O'Keefe P	Pte	8 R Innis Fus	06/09/15	Eniskillen	M+ Inj pub property	1 yr HL		WO/86/66/111
Oliver AE	Spr (L/Cpl)	101 Field Coy RE	27/03/19	Field Italy	M+Disob	5 yrs PS		WO/213/28/191
Oliver J	Pte	1 Connaught Rangers	04/09/20	Dagshai	M+S7(3b)	Death	Life PS	WO/90/8/188
O'Malley M	Pte	7 R Irish	15/04/18	Field	M	5 yrs PS	Susp	WO/213/21/97
O'Neall W	Pte	7/8 R Innis Fus	15/04/18	Field	M	5 yrs PS	Susp	WO/213/21/96
O'Neil W	Pte	54 TR Bn	31/05/17	Kirkcaldy	M+Insub(Cplx2)	2 yrs Detn	Remit 1 yr	WO/86/76/98
O'Neill J	Pte	ASC	13/04/17	Dunkirk	M	1 yr HL		WO/213/14/138
O'Neill M	Pte	R Munster Fus	11/10/14	St Nazaire	M	3 yrs PS	Quashed	WO/213/2/105
O'Neill P	Pte	18 AIF	24/03/19	Field	M	9 yrs PS		WO/213/29/91
O'Neill T	Pte	NZEF 3 Reinf	05/04/15	Zeitoun	Incit M+Disob(Lt)	1 yr HL+Disch Igmny		WO/90/6/35
Onslow R	Pte(L/Cpl)	1 Manchester	05/09/21	Field (Ireland)	M+Disob(CQMS)+S7(3)	3 yrs PS	2yrs Detn	WO/213/32/214
O'Riley J	Spr	Can Engrs	25/01/19	Field	M+Disob	NG		WO/213/29/55
O'Rourke C	Bdr	RGA	05/07/19	Aldershot	M	NG		WO/86/88/1
O'Rourke J	Pte	5 Dragoon Gds	26/09/19	Curragh	M	1 yr HL+Disch Igmny	Comm 6 mos Detn	WO/92/4/83
Orr A	Spr	Can Engrs	25/01/19	Field	M+Disob	NG		WO/213/29/55
Orr D	Pte	65 Coy RDC	21/11/16	Towcester	M	1 yr Detn		WO/92/4/2
Orr E	Pte	1 Inf Bn AIF	15/10/18	Field	M+Des	3 yrs PS	Guilty of Des	WO/213/28/200
Orr R	Pte	1/10 Manch	01/01/19	Field	M+Abs+S40(2)	5 yrs PS	Comm 3 yrs HL	WO/213/28/106
Osborne H	Pte	21 CEF	12/05/19	Witley	M+S40	NG		WO/86/87/124
O'Shea J	Bdr	RGA	04/07/19	Aldershot	M	9 mos Detn+Rnks +Disch Igmny		WO/86/87/188
Osmond OG	Bdr	RGA	08/07/19	Aldershot	M	9 mos Detn+Rnks +Disch Igmny		WO/86/87/189
O'Sullivan C	Pte	2 AIF	04/02/19	Rouen	M	3 yrs 6 mos PS		WO/90/8/59
O'Sullivan J	Pte	8/10 Gordons (att RE)	28/08/16	Field	M x 2	Death	Comm 5 yrs PS	WO/213/11/9
Owen EL	Pte (A/Cpl)	1 MGC	17/07/19	Field	M	5 mos Imp		WO/213/30/82
Owens JW	Pte	5 Dragoon Gds	24/09/19	Curragh	M	1 yr HL+Disch Igmny	Comm 6mos Detn	WO/92/4/86
Oxley W	Pte	9 (S) BWI	24/12/18	Field Italy	M+Disob+Esc	5 yrs PS		WO/213/27/25
Oxley W	Pte(L/Cpl)	2 Worc	01/07/18	Perham Down	M+S40	Acquit		WO/92/4/41
Page A	Pte	2/4 R Sussex TF	23/07/15	Canterbury	J[oin in] M	84 dys Detn		WO/92/3/23
Page AE	Pte	Lab Corps	15/06/19	Sutton	M+S7(3b)	Acquit		WO/92/4/73
Page AJ	Pte	2/4 R Sussex TF (att E Comm LB)	23/07/15	Canterbury	J[oin in] M	84 dys Detn		WO/92/3/23
Page EE	Pte	30 MGC	29/07/19	Field	M+Disob	1 yr HL		WO/213/30/119
Page FT	AL/Bdr	RGA	16/05/19	Field	M	9 mos HL	Remit 3 mos	WO/213/29/148
Page G	Pte	1 Inf Bn AIF	15/10/18	Field	M+Des	3 yrs PS	Guilty of Des	WO/213/28/198
Pain J	Pte	2/4 R Sussex TF	23/07/15	Canterbury	J[oin in] M	84 dys Detn		WO/92/3/23
Palfrey WR	Pte	1 Gn Sher Fstrs	05/06/17	Kantara Egypt	M	2 yrs HL		WO/213/15/177
Pallister JF	Pte	5 Dragoon Gds	26/09/19	Curragh	M	1 yr HL+Disch Igmny	Comm 6 mos Detn	WO/92/4/81
Palmer AE	Gnr	RGA	13/03/18	Agra	M	1 yr HL	unexpired portion 30/4/18	WO/90/7/190
Palmer C	Pte	6 (S) BWI	24/12/18	Field Italy	M+Disob	3 yrs 6 mos PS		WO/213/27/24
Palmer TG	Pte	1 Inf Bn AIF	15/10/18	Field	M+Des	3 yrs PS	Guilty of Des	WO/213/28/199
Palmer TH	Pte	Lab Corps (att E Comm LB)	15/06/19	Sutton	M+S7(3b)	Acquit		WO/92/4/73
Palmer W	Dvr	RFA	23/05/21	Hinaidi	M+S9(1)	3 mos FP2		WO/213/33/15
Pannell A	Pte	5 Dragoon Gds	23/09/19	Curragh	M	84 dys HL	Comm 42 dys Detn	WO/92/4/85
Parish EC	Pte	1 Inf Bn AIF	15/10/18	Field	M+Des	3 yrs PS	Guilty of Des	WO/213/28/198
Park JR	Pte	21 Manch	08/02/19	Field	M+Abs	6 mos HL		WO/213/28/58
Parker G	Pte	1 Gn Sher Fstrs	05/06/17	Kantara Egypt	M	2 yrs HL		WO/213/15/177
Parker JL	Pte	Can Reserve Cavy Regt	11/09/17	Shorncliffe	M+S40+S22+S41	[No entry - 1 yr Detn?]		WO/86/78/19
Parks JJ	Pte	Can ASC	21/11/17	Bramshott	M+Insub	42 dys Detn	Remit 15 dys	WO/86/79/53
Parris HN	Cpl	1 BWI	10/05/19	Field	M+S40	90 dys FP2+Rnks	Remit 62 dys	WO/213/29/49

Name	Rank	Unit	Date D/M/Y	Location	Offence	Finding/Punishment	Amendment	PRO Reference File/Piece/Page
Parrish D	Pte	3 Gn Beds	12/03/18	Meiktila	M+Disob	2 yrs Detn	Comm 1 yr Detn	WO/90/8/199
Parsons A	Pte	3 Dorsets	29/12/14	Dorchester	Joining M+Viol(Capt)	4 mos HL		WO/92/3/18
Parsons J	Pte	2/4 R Sussex TF	23/07/15	Canterbury	J[oin in] M	84 dys Detn		WO/92/3/23
Partington A	Pte	5 Dragoon Gds	22/09/19	Curragh	M	1 yr HL+Disch Igmny	Comm 6 mos Detn	WO/92/4/84
Partington WE	Pte	2 Dragoon Gds	30/09/19	Curragh	M	84 dys HL	Comm 42 dys Detn	WO/92/4/87
Pascoe EJ	Pte	4 AIF	24/03/19	Field	M	9 yrs PS		WO/213/29/91
Patching CW	Pte	2/4 R Sussex TF	23/07/15	Canterbury	J[oin in] M	84 dys Detn		WO/92/3/23
Paterson P	Fitter	AFA	11/09/18	Fovant	M+Absx2	1 yr Detn	NC	WO/86/85/9
Paton PP	Pte	1 Inf Bn AIF	15/10/18	Field	M+Des	NG		WO/213/28/198
Patten JC	Pte	1 Inf Bn AIF	15/10/18	Field	M+Des	3 yrs PS	Guilty of Des	WO/213/28/196
Patton GL	Pte(2AM)	RAF	30/04/18	Swanage	M+Disob	1 yr HL		WO/92/4/41
Paul HJ	Pte	RAMC	10/05/19	Field	M	6 mos HL	Comm 28 dys FP2	WO/213/30/17
Payne GW	Pte	2/4 R Sussex TF	23/07/15	Canterbury	J[oin in] M	84 dys Detn		WO/92/3/23
Payne JA	Pte(A/Cpl)	8(R) CEF	02/05/19	Liverpool	M+S7(3b)	1 yr HL		WO/92/4/71
Payne WE	Pte	3 W Yorks	01/08/19	Devizes	M+S40	18 mos HL+Disch Igmny	9 mos	WO/92/4/76
Peacock A	Pte	Can ASC	21/11/17	Bramshott	M+Insub(Lieut)	42 dys Detn	Remit 15 dys	WO/86/79/53
Peacock A	Bdr	RGA	04/07/19	Aldershot	M	9 mos Detn+Rnks+Disch Igmny		WO/86/87/188
Peacock H	Pte	35 MGC	17/01/19	Field	Mx2	2 yrs HL	Remit 18 mos	WO/213/28/120
Peacock W	Pte	Lab Corps (att E Comm LB)	15/06/19	Sutton	M+S7(3b)	Acquit		WO/92/4/74
Pearl E	Pte	Lab Corps (att E Comm LB)	15/06/19	Sutton	M+S7(3b)	Acquit		WO/92/4/74
Pearman A	Pte	2/6 R Wars	27/05/19	Field	M+S40	2 yrs HL	Remit 1 yr	WO/213/30/64
Pearson H	Pte	2 Ches	05/03/20	Field ABS	M+Disob	2 yrs HL	Rem 18 mos	WO/213/31/168
Pearson JH	Pte	20 CEF	11/02/18	Bramshott	M+Inj property*+S40(2)	112 dys Detn + Quashed*		WO/86/80/139
Peden W	Dvr	ASC	05/10/16	Rouen	M	Death	Comm 2 yrs HL	WO/90/6/89
Peden W	Dvr	ASC	10/12/17	Field	M	5 yrs PS		WO/213/19/52
Pedley J	Pte	21 Manch	08/02/19	Field	M+Abs	6 mos HL		WO/213/28/58
Peers F	Pte	6 (S) BWI	24/12/18	Field Italy	M+Disob	3 yrs 6 mos PS		WO/213/27/24
Penman WTC	Cpl	1/6 HLI	28/12/18	Field	M+Disob	6 mos HL		WO/213/28/25
Penneall AA	Pte	Quebec Regt	11/07/19	Ripon	M+S7(3b)+S40	1 yr HL		WO/86/88/54
Peregrine JB	Pte	1/4 KOYLI (att 365 POW Coy)	16/09/19	Field	M+Abs+Disob	3 yrs PS	Comm 1 yr HL	WO/213/31/69
Perring G	Pte	2 Gn/Beds	04/04/18	Karachi	M+S7(3)	5 yrs PS	Comm 1yr	WO/90/7/191
Pesochnikoff J	Sgt	1 Slav-Brit Legion	13/07/19	Field NREF	M	Death		WO/213/32/59
Peterkin J	Pte	3/6 Gordon H'ldrs (TF)	13/01/16	Hawick	M+Viol(Sgt)+S40	6 mos Detn+Rnks		WO/86/68/95
Peters H	Gnr/L/Bdr	RFA	12/05/18	Field	M	1yr HL	Susp	WO/213/22/153
Petersen J	Dvr	372 Coy CAHT	14/05/19	Field	M	5 yrs PS	Remit 2 yrs	WO/213/30/12
Peterson A	Dvr	ASC (SA)	23/07/18	Field	M	6 mos HL		WO/213/24/168
Peterson J	Dvr	ASC (SA)	05/08/18	Field	M+S40	9 mos HL		WO/213/24/129
Petonhoff M	Pte	1 Slav-Brit Legion	14/07/19	Field NREF	M	Death	Comm 10 yrs PS	WO/213/32/59
Petrofsky P	Pte	39 R Fus	23/08/19	Field EEF	M	NG		WO/213/31/25
Petter W	Pte	2/4 R Sussex TF	23/07/15	Canterbury	J[oin in] M	84 dys Detn		WO/92/3/23
Pettit LW	Pte (L/Cpl)	1 Inf Bn AIF	15/10/18	Field	M+Des	5 yrs PS	Guilty of Des	WO/213/28/199
Phillimore H	Pte	2/4 R Sussex TF	23/07/15	Canterbury	J[oin in] M	84 dys Detn		WO/92/3/23
Phillips F	Pte	13 Glouster	16/06/15	Malvern Wells	Incit M+Insub(Maj)+Resist+Esc	3 yrs PS		WO/92/3/24
Phillips F	Pte	5 Dragoon Gds	23/09/19	Curragh	M	84 dys HL	Comm 42 dys Detn	WO/92/4/85
Phillips H	Pte	1 Inf Bn AIF	15/10/18	Field	M+Des	3 yrs PS	Guilty of Des	WO/213/28/198
Phillips JE	Pte	Can Reserve Cavy	30/08/17	Shorncliffe	Mx2+S40(4)+S41	2 yrs HL		WO/86/78/8
Phillips K	Dvr L/Cpl	ASC (SA)	23/07/18	Field	M	6 mos HL		WO/213/24/168
Phillips R	Pte	58 Coy RDC	21/11/16	Towcester	M	1 yr Detn		WO/92/4/2
Phillips R	Gnr	RGA	05/07/19	Aldershot	M	NG		WO/86/88/1
Phillis W	Pte	3 W Yorks	01/08/19	Devizes	M+S40	18 mos HL+Disch Igmny	9 mos	WO/92/4/76
Piasosky A	Pte	1 Slav-Brit Legion	17/07/19	Field NREF	M	NG		WO/213/32/59
Pickles JR	Pte	1 Gn Sher Fstrs	05/06/17	Kantara Egypt	M	2 yrs HL		WO/213/15/177
Pickstone G	Bdr	RFA	12/05/18	Field	M	1 yr HL	Susp	WO/213/22/153
Pierce HE	Pte	4 AIF	24/03/19	Field	M	12 yrs PS		WO/213/29/89
Pitt FL	Pte	4 CEF	08/01/18	Bramshott	M+Desx2+Abs+Loss Pub Prop+S22	2 yrs Detn	Remit 1 yr Dtn/ Quashed	WO/86/79/171
Pittock WH	Cpl	1 Inf Bn AIF	15/10/18	Field	M+Des	8 yrs PS+Rnks	Guilty of Des	WO/213/28/197
Plant F	Gnr	RGA	13/03/18	Agra	M	1 yr HL	unexpired portion 30/4/18	WO/90/7/190

Name	Rank	Unit	Date D/M/Y	Location	Offence	Finding/Punishment	Amendment	PRO Reference File/Piece/Page
Plumbley AM	Pte	2/6 R Wars	27/05/19	Field	M+S40	2 yrs HL	Remit 1 yr	WO/213/30/64
Plumtree W	Pte	Lab Corps (att E Comm LB)	15/06/19	Sutton	M+S7(3b)	Acquit		WO/92/4/74
Plunkett J	Pte	2 Otago NZEF	01/09/17	Field	M	1 yr HL		WO/213/17/110
Pocock E	Pte	35 MGC	17/01/19	Field	Mx2	2 yrs HL	Remit 18 mos	WO/213/28/121
Podger HC	Pte	1 DCLI	01/09/20	Belfast	M	1 yr Detn		WO/86/90/140
Pole J	Pte	3 HLI(att MGC)	25/04/16	Grantham	NSM	1 dy Detn		WO/92/3/38
Pollentine G	L/Bdr	RGA	05/07/19	Aldershot	M	9 mos Detn+Rnks		WO/86/87/189
Pontefract JV	Pte	58 Coy RDC	21/11/16	Towcester	M	1 yr Detn		WO/92/4/1
Poole FC	Pte	9 Middx	15/03/16	Guildhall West	E P(ersuade) M +Disob	1 yr HL		WO/92/3/34
Poole WD	Pte	RE	04/02/19	Field	M+S40	9 mos HL+Rnks		WO/213/28/46
Popham HH	Pte	5 Dragoon Gds	24/09/19	Curragh	M	1 yr HL+Disch Igmny	Comm 6 mos Detn	WO/92/4/86
Popple JE	Pte(S/Smith)	ASC	30/12/15	Marseilles	Joining M	Acquit		WO/90/6/44
Porter EM	Pte (L/Cpl)	1 Inf Bn AIF	15/10/18	Field	M+Des	3 yrs PS	Guilty of Des	WO/213/28/199
Porter GE	Pte	35 MGC	17/01/19	Field	M	NG		WO/213/28/121
Porter T	Pte	A&S Hdrs	12/09/18	Field	M(x2)	10 yrs PS	One charge quashed	WO/213/25/177
Portman HE	Pte	2 Y[ork] & Lanc	07/11/19	Basrah	M+S9(1)	4 yrs PS	Comm 2 yrs HL	WO/90/7/205
Posdjeef N	Pte	1 Slav-Brit Legion	14/07/19	Field NREF	M	Death		WO/213/32/59
Potter EC	Pte	Lab Corps (att E Comm LB)	15/06/19	Sutton	M+S7(3b)	Acquit		WO/92/4/73
Potter T	Pte	5 Dragoon Gds	22/09/19	Curragh	M	1 yr HL+Disch Igmny	Comm 6 mos Detn	WO/92/4/81
Potts C	Pte	RAMC	10/05/19	Field	M	6 mos HL	Comm 28 dys FP2	WO/213/30/17
Powardy HR	Pte	50 AIF	24/03/19	Field	M	12 yrs PS		WO/213/29/89
Powell CT	Pte	7/8 R Innis Fus	15/04/18	Field	M	NG		WO/213/21/97
Powell L	Pte	6 (S) BWI	24/12/18	Field Italy	M+Disob	3 yrs 6 mos PS		WO/213/27/24
Powell R	L/Bdr	RGA	05/07/19	Aldershot	M	9 mos Detn+Rnks +Disch Igmny		WO/86/87/189
Pownall WD	Pte	5 Dragoon Gds	29/09/19	Curragh	M	1 yr HL+Disch Igmny	Comm 6 mos Detn	WO/92/4/82
Prangley W	Pte	9(S) E Lancs	29/05/18	SEF	M	1 yr HL		WO/213/23/179
Pratt O	Pte	7/8 R Innis Fus	15/04/18	Field	M	5 yrs PS	Susp	WO/213/21/96
Precious F	Pte	58 Coy RDC	21/11/16	Towcester	M	1 yr Detn		WO/92/4/2
Preece W	Gnr	RGA	13/03/18	Agra	M	Acquit		WO/90/7/190
Prendergast F	Pte	1 Connaught Rangers	04/09/20	Dagshai	M+S7(3b)	3 yrs PS+DI		WO/90/8/188
Prentice W	Pte	7/8 R Innis Fus	15/04/18	Field	M	5 yrs PS	Susp	WO/213/21/96
Prescott B	Pte	10 BWI	28/02/19	Plymouth	M	2 yrs Detn		WO/86/87/17
Preston EC	Pte (L/Cpl)	1 Inf Bn AIF	15/10/18	Field	M+Des	5 yrs PS	Guilty of Des	WO/213/28/196
Preston S	Pte	50 AIF	24/03/19	Field	M	10 yrs PS		WO213/29/88
Price CR	Pte(L/Cpl)	12 SWBdrs	01/12/16	Field	M+Disob	NG		WO/213/13/46
Price E	Gnr	RGA	13/03/18	Agra	M	1 yr HL	unexpired portion 30/4/18	WO/90/7/190
Price J	Pte	7/8 R Innis Fus	15/04/18	Field	M	5 yrs PS	Susp	WO/213/21/96
Priest FC	Pte	7/8 R Innis Fus	15/04/18	Field	M	5 yrs PS	Susp	WO/213/21/97
Primett H	Pte	43 CEF	11/12/17	Field	M+Disob	18 mos HL		WO/213/19/116
Primm J	Rfn	3 Rif Bde	24/03/19	Field	M	11 yrs PS		WO213/29/88
Prince J	Pte	5 Dragoon Gds	24/09/19	Curragh	M	Acquit		WO/92/4/87
Prince N	Pte	39 R Fus	23/08/19	Field EEF	M	NG		WO/213/31/24
Prior G	Pte	3 W Yorks	01/08/19	Devizes	M+S40	1 yr HL+Disch Igmny	3 mos	WO/92/4/77
Pritchard SP	Pte	6 KSLI	24/03/19	Field	M	Death	Comm PS/Life	WO/213/29/90
Proctor E	Gnr	RGA	13/03/18	Agra	M	1 yr HL	unexpired portion 30/4/18	WO/90/7/190
Puckeridge J	Pte	55 AIF	04/02/19	Rouen	M	90 dys Imp		WO/90/8/58
Purcell J	Pte	2 R Irish	15/04/18	Field	M	5 yrs PS	Susp	WO/213/21/98
Purcell W	Gnr	Aust Siege Bty	19/07/16	[Le] Havre	Per M+Viol SO	5 yrs PS		WO/90/6/67
Purchase W	Pte	11 Worc	02/05/18	Field SEF	M+Disob	10 yrs PS	Comm 2 yrs HL	WO/213/22/30
Quarton H	Pte	10 Hussars	04/02/19	Rouen	M	3 yrs PS		WO/90/8/58
Quenelle W	Pte	Alb Regt CEF	15/07/18	Bramshott	M+S40	2 yrs HL+Stoppages		WO/92/4/43
Quinn D	Pte	1 KOSB	30/12/15	Malta	M+Not Sup +Disob(APM)	1 yr HL	Remit 1 month	WO/90/6/40
Radcliffe G	Pte	9 MGC	31/07/19	Field	M+Abs/Br	6 mos HL		WO/213/30/141
Raddock NG	Pte	7/8 R Innis Fus	15/04/18	Field	M	5 yrs PS	Susp	WO/213/21/95
Rahman Abdul	Gnr	Malay SG Bty	11/03/15	Singapore	M	3 yrs PS	Comm 18 mos Imp	WO/213/4/17
Raines J	Spr	RE	08/08/19	Bordon	M+S40	2 yrs HL+Disch Igmny	15 mos	WO/92/4/77
Ramsey JGS	Pte	5 Dragoon Gds	26/09/19	Curragh	M	1 yr HL+Disch Igmny	Comm 6 mos Detn	WO/92/4/83
Randall H	Pte	2 MGC	12/06/19	Field	M+Disob(2)+S40	5 yrs PS		WO/213/29/122

Name	Rank	Unit	Date D/M/Y	Location	Offence	Finding/Punishment	Amendment	PRO Reference File/Piece/Page
Randell G	L/Bdr	RGA	04/07/19	Aldershot	M	9 mos Detn+Rnks +Disch Igmny		WO/86/87/188
Rapatele A	L/Cpl	SANLC	17/12/17	Capetown	M	10 yrs PS		WO/213/19/115
Ratcliffe H	Pte	1 Gn Sher Fstrs	05/06/17	Kantara Egypt	M	2 yrs HL		WO/213/15/177
Rathbone H	Pte	1 Gn Sher Fstrs	05/06/17	Kantara Egypt	M	2 yrs HL		WO/213/15/177
Rattigan F	Pte	10 Bn AIF	24/09/15	Malta	M+S40	NG		WO/90/6/35
Rawlinson E	Spr	RE	15/05/19	Field	M+Disob	1 yr IHL		WO/213/29/137
Rawlinson F	Pte	21 Manch	08/02/19	Field	M+Abs	6 mos HL		WO/213/28/58
Read H	Spr	101 Field Coy RE	27/03/19	Field Italy	M+Disob	5 yrs PS		WO/213/28/191
Reddin H	Cpl	1/6 HLI	28/12/18	Field	M+Insub+Disob	6 mos HL		WO/213/28/62
Redding G	Bdr	RGA	05/07/19	Aldershot	M	9 mos Detn+Rnks		WO/86/88/1
Redgrave J	Pte	51 Rif Bde (att 2 MGC)	12/06/19	Field	M+Disob(2)+S40	5 yrs PS	Comm 2 yrs HL	WO/213/29/122
Reed E	Pte	2 R Irish	15/04/18	Field	M	5 yrs PS	Susp	WO/213/21/99
Reed T	Pte	Lab Corps (att E Comm LB)	15/06/19	Sutton	M+S7(3b)	Acquit		WO/92/4/74
Rees TR	Spr	RE	07/08/19	Bordon	M+S40	1 yr Detn	9 mos	WO/92/4/77
Reeve C	Pte	69(EA)DAC(TF)	11/09/16	Killinghall Moor	Joining M	Acquit		WO/92/3/45
Regan D	Pte	1 Connaught Rangers	25/08/20	Dagshai	M	5 yrs PS+DI		WO/90/8/188
Reid C	Pte	2 W India	11/05/19	Field EEF	M	7 yrs PS	Comm 2 yrs HL	WO/213/30/28
Reid H	Pte	Can Reserve Cavy	06/09/17	Shorncliffe	Mx2+S40+S41	16 mos HL		WO/86/78/8
Reid J	Pte	65 Coy RDC	21/11/16	Towcester	M	1 yr Detn		WO/92/4/2
Reid S	Pte	2 Otago NZEF	01/09/17	Field	M	10 yrs PS		WO/213/17/110
Reid WHV	Pte	32 AIF	24/03/19	Field	M	11 yrs PS		WO213/29/88
Remfrey S	Pte	1 DCLI	01/09/20	Belfast	M	2 yrs Detn		WO/86/90/140
Renelle E	Pte	Labour Bn	16/01/19	Mesopotamia	M	84 dys Detn		WO/90/7/169
Renelle J	Pte	Labour Bn	16/01/19	Mesopotamia	M	84 dys Detn		WO/90/7/169
Resnik S	Pte	39 R Fus	23/08/19	Field EEF	M	5 yrs PS	Comm 1 yr HL	WO/213/31/25
Reynolds JH	Pte	2/6 R Wars	27/05/19	Field	M+S40	2 yrs HL	Remit 1 yr	WO/213/30/64
Reynolds P	Pte	7/8 R Innis Fus	15/04/18	Field	M	5 yrs PS	Susp	WO/213/21/97
Reynolds W	Pte	21 Manch	08/02/19	Field	M+Abs	NG		WO/213/28/58
Richards AA	Pte	5 AIF	18/06/19	Field	M+Disob	5 mos HL		WO/213/30/131
Richards JH	Pte	2 Y[ork] & Lanc	05/11/19	Basrah	M+Disob	5 yrs PS	Comm 2 yrs HL	WO/90/7/205
Ricketts R	Pte	2 W India	11/05/19	Field EEF	M	5 yrs PS	Comm 1 yr HL	WO/213/30/27
Riddell TJ	Pte	5 Dragoon Gds	23/09/19	Curragh	M	1 yr HL+Disch Igmny	Comm 6 mos Detn	WO/92/4/84
Riley B	Pte	Quebec Regt	30/07/19	Ripon	M+S7(3b)	6 mos Detn		WO/86/88/51
Riley JJ	Pte	68 Div Cyclist Coy	17/01/17	Gt Yarmouth	M +Insub(L/Cpl)	NG		WO/86/73/171
Riley W	Pte	1 Gn Sher Fstrs	05/06/17	Kantara Egypt	M	2 yrs HL		WO/213/15/177
Rimmer F	Pte	5 Dragoon Gds	30/09/19	Curragh	M	1 yr HL+Disch Igmny	Comm 6 mos Detn	WO/92/4/87
Ringrose R	Pte	35 MGC	17/01/19	Field	Mx2	2 yrs HL	Remit 18 mos	WO/213/28/120
Rispel A	Dvr	372 Coy CAHT	14/05/19	Field	M	5 yrs PS	Remit 2 yrs	WO/213/30/11
Roast J	Cpl	RGA	05/07/19	Aldershot	M	9 mos Detn+Rnks		WO/86/88/1
Roberts A	Pte	2 Ches	05/03/20	Field ABS	M+Disob	18 mos HL	Rem 1 yr	WO/213/31/168
Roberts C	Pte	21 Manch	08/02/19	Field	M+Abs	6 mos HL		WO/213/28/58
Roberts F	Pte	21 Manch	08/02/19	Field	M+Abs	6 mos HL		WO/213/28/58
Roberts G	Pte	2 W India	11/05/19	Field EEF	M	7 yrs PS	Comm 2 yrs HL	WO/213/30/28
Roberts J	Bdr	RGA	04/07/19	Aldershot	M	9 mos Detn+Rnks +Disch Igmny		WO/86/87/188
Roberts PC	Pte	Lab Corps (att E Comm LB)	15/06/19	Sutton	M+S7(3b)	Acquit		WO/92/4/73
Roberts W	Pte	3 Can MGC	23/01/19	Field	M+Abs+S40	2 yrs HL		WO/213/28/108
Roberts WH	Pte	Lab Corps (att E Comm LB)	15/06/19	Sutton	M+S7(3b)	Acquit		WO/92/4/73
Roberts WR	Pte	1 Inf Bn AIF	15/10/18	Field	M+Des	3 yrs PS	Guilty of Des	WO/213/28/198
Robertshaw G	Spr	RE	15/05/19	Field	M+Disob	1 yr IHL		WO/213/29/137
Robertson H	Pte	5 Dragoon Gds	22/09/19	Curragh	M	1 yr HL+Disch Igmny	Comm 6 mos Detn	WO/92/4/84
Robinson AW	Pte	1 Inf Bn AIF	15/10/18	Field	M+Des	3 yrs PS	Guilty of Des	WO/213/28/199
Robinson B	Pte	3 Leics	27/08/14	Portsmouth	M	1 yr HL		WO/213/2/2
Robinson E	Pte	2 W India	11/05/19	Field EEF	M	5 yrs PS	Comm 1 yr HL	WO/213/30/28
Robinson E	Pte	2 York & Lanc	16/07/20	Kasvin	M	1 yr HL		WO/90/7/208
Robinson E	Pte	3 W Yorks	01/08/19	Devizes	M+S40	18 mos HL +Disch Igmny	9 mos	WO/92/4/76
Robinson F	Pte	4(R) CEF	14/09/17	Bramshott	M+Abs+S22+S40	1 yr Detn		WO/86/78/17
Robinson G	Pte	58 Coy RDC	21/11/16	Towcester	M	1 yr Detn		WO/92/4/2
Robinson H	Pte	5 Dragoon Gds	29/09/19	Curragh	M	1 yr HL+Disch Igmny	Comm 6 mos Detn	WO/92/4/82
Robinson J	Pte(AL/Cpl)	2/7 R Wars	04/01/19	Field	M	5 yrs PS		WO/213/28/72
Robinson J	AL/Bdr	RGA	16/05/19	Field	M	NG		WO/213/29/148
Robinson JEG	Pte	1 Gn Sher Fstrs	05/06/17	Kantara Egypt	M	2 yrs HL		WO/213/15/177

Name	Rank	Unit	Date D/M/Y	Location	Offence	Finding/Punishment	Amendment	PRO Reference File/Piece/Page
Robinson MH	Pte	1 R Berks	04/02/19	Rouen	M	Acquit		WO/90/8/58
Robinson W	Pte	1/4 KOYLI (att 365 POW Coy)	16/09/19	Field	M+Abs+Disob	3 yrs PS	Comm 1 yr HL	WO/213/31/69
Robson H	Pte	21 Manch	08/02/19	Field	M+Abs	6 mos HL		WO/213/28/58
Robson PL	Pte	8 SA Infantry	23/12/16	Potchefstroom	M+S40	20 dys Detn+Rnks+Stop		WO/213/11/179
Robson WJ	Pte	1 Inf Bn AIF	15/10/18	Field	M+Des	3 yrs PS	Guilty of Des	WO/213/28/196
Roche GR	Pte	45 AIF	24/03/19	Field	M	11 yrs PS		WO/213/29/90
Rodbourne A	Gnr	234 Bty	15/01/15	Cahir	M+Insub(Cpl)+S40(2)	2 yrs HL+Disch Igmny		WO/86/63/137
Roddy S	Pte	1 KOYLI	02/05/18	Field SEF	M+Disob	10 yrs PS	Comm 2 yrs HL	WO/213/22/30
Roden GW	Pte	5 Dragoon Gds	26/09/19	Curragh	M	1 yr HL+Disch Igmny	Comm 6 mos Detn	WO/92/4/83
Rodgers P	Pte	21 Manch	08/02/19	Field	M+Abs	9 mos HL		WO/213/28/58
Roe F	Pte	3 W Yorks	01/08/19	Devizes	M	Acquit		WO/92/4/75
Roffey R	Bdr	RFA	12/05/18	Field	M	1 yr HL	Susp	WO/213/22/153
Rogers E	Pte	18 AIF	24/03/19	Field	M	11 yrs PS		WO/213/29/89
Rogers R	Pte	65 Coy RDC	21/11/16	Towcester	M	1 yr Detn		WO/92/4/2
Rogers RS	Pte	1 Inf Bn AIF	15/10/18	Field	M+Des	3 yrs PS	Guilty of Des	WO/213/28/199
Rollason HH	Pte	15 AIF	24/03/19	Field	M	9 yrs PS		WO/213/29/91
Ronson C	Pte	1 Inf Bn AIF	15/10/18	Field	M+Des	3 yrs PS	Guilty of Des	WO/213/28/196
Rook AJ	Pte	1 Inf Bn AIF	15/10/18	Field	M+Des	3 yrs PS	Guilty of Des	WO/213/28/198
Rooke GB	Pte(S/Smith)	ASC	30/12/15	Marseilles	Joining M	3 yrs PS	Comm to 2 yrs HL	WO/90/6/44
Roond I	Pte	1 Slav-Brit Legion	17/07/19	Field NREF	M	NG		WO/213/31/59
Roper C	Pte	11 Worc	02/05/18	Field SEF	M+Disob	10 yrs PS	Comm 2 yrs HL	WO/213/22/30
Rosen J	Pte(L/Cpl)	2/4 R Sussex TF	23/07/15	Canterbury	NSM	28 dys Detn		WO/92/3/20
Rosenwig M	Pte	53 Welsh	25/01/19	Shoreham	M+S40	112 dys Detn		WO/86/86/103
Roser WG	Pte	2/4 R Sussex TF	23/07/15	Canterbury	J[oin in] M	84 dys Detn		WO/92/3/23
Ross A	Pte	King Edw Horse (att 5 Dragoon Gds)	24/09/19	Curragh	M	56 dys Detn	Remit 21dys	WO/92/4/86
Ross AS	Pte	1 Inf Bn AIF	15/10/18	Field	M+Des	NG		WO/213/28/198
Ross F	Pte	2/4 R Sussex TF	23/07/15	Canterbury	NSM	Redu to Cpl		WO/92/3/20
Ross G	Pte	2 MGC	12/06/19	Field	M+Disob(2)+S40	5 yrs PS	Remit 2 yrs	WO/213/29/122
Rowan T	Pte	7/8 R Innis Fus	15/04/18	Field	M	5 yrs PS	Susp	WO/213/21/97
Rowe FB	Cpl	Aus ASC	01/07/18	Field EEF	M	NG		WO/213/28/138
Rowe T	Pte	58 Coy RDC	21/11/16	Towcester	M	1 yr Detn		WO/92/4/1
Rowlands TJ	Pte	19 AIF	15/02/16	Sinai Penin	M+Disob	12 mos HL		WO/213/8/113
Rowling K	Cpl	Aus ASC	01/07/18	Field EEF	M	NG		WO/213/28/138
Rozell H	Spr	Can Engrs	25/01/19	Field	M+Disob	NG		WO/213/29/55
Rueben [?]	Pte	SANLC	17/12/20	Capetown	M	10 yrs PS		WO/213/19/115
Rump S	Pte	Lab Corps (att E Comm LB)	15/06/19	Sutton	M+S7(3b)	Acquit		WO/92/4/74
Rush EW	Pte	7/8 R Innis Fus	15/04/18	Field	M	5 yrs PS	Susp	WO/213/21/96
Rush JA	Pte	21 Manch	08/02/19	Field	M+Abs	6 mos HL		WO/213/28/58
Rush P	Pte	7/8 R Innis Fus	15/04/18	Field	M	5 yrs PS	Susp	WO/213/21/96
Russell J	Pte(L/Cpl)	1/6 HLI	28/12/18	Field	M+Disob	6 mos HL		WO/213/28/25
Russell J	Pte	2/5 Welsh TF	27/09/16	Cardiff	M	2 yrs HL+Disch Igmny		WO/86/66/194
Rustage VA	Pte	12 SWBdrs	01/12/16	Field	M+Disob	18 mos HL	Comm 3 mos FP1	WO/213/13/47
Rutter S	Pte	5 Dragoon Gds	23/09/19	Curragh	M	1 yr HL+Disch Igmny	Comm 6 mos Detn	WO/92/4/84
Ryan JH	Pte	59 AIF	24/03/19	Field	M	9 yrs PS		WO/213/29/88
Ryan S	Pte	65 Coy RDC	21/11/16	Towcester	M	1 yr Detn		WO/92/4/3
Sababies J	Dvr	372 Coy CAHT	14/05/19	Field	M	5 yrs PS		WO/213/30/11
Sadler LC	Cpl	11 KRRC	09/12/18	Field	M+S40	6 mos HL+Rnks	Comm 90dys FP2	WO/213/27/42
Sager WG	Pte	5 CEF	19/07/16	[Le] Havre	Per M + Insub	Acquit		WO/90/6/67
Sakharoff F	Pte	1 Slav-Brit Legion	13/07/19	Field	M	Death		WO0213/32/58
Sallam C	Labourer	Egyptian Lab Corps	06/09/17	Boulogne	M+S40	8 mos HL		WO/213/17/41
Salmon W	Pte	2 W India	11/05/19	Field EEF	M	7 yrs PS	Comm 2 yrs HL	WO/213/30/28
Sam	Pte	SANLC	21/11/17	Field	M+S40	3 yrs PS	Comm 2 yrs HL	WO/213/31/109
Samarzich L	Spr	Can Engrs	01/02/19	Field	M+Disob	28 dys FP2		WO/213/28/71
Samanne R	Pte	Maur Lab Bn	10/05/18	Mespot	M(S7-2B)	18 mos HL		WO/90/7/151
Sampson F	Gnr	RGA	13/03/18	Agra	M	1 yr HL	unexpired portion 30/4/18	WO/90/7/190
Sampson WR	Pte	Can Res A[rty]	12/05/19	Liverpool	M+Res+Esc	30 dys Detn		WO/92/4/71
Samuel J	Pte	10 B Watch	02/05/18	Field SEF	M+Disob	10 yrs PS	Comm 2 yrs HL	WO/213/22/30
Samuel V	Pte	12 SWBdrs	01/12/16	Field	M+Disob	18 mos HL	Comm 3 mos FP1	WO/213/13/4
Sanches A	Pte	9 BWI	27/12/18	Field Italy	M	Death	Comm 20 yrs PS	WO/213/27/81

Name	Rank	Unit	Date D/M/Y	Location	Offence	Finding/Punishment	Amendment	PRO Reference File/Piece/Page
Sandercott W	Spr	3 Aus Tun Coy	18/10/18	Field	M+Disob	2 yrs HL	Susp	WO/213/26/66
Sandercourt W	Spr	3 Aus Tun Coy	13/10/18	Field	M+Disob	1 yr HL	NC	WO/213/30/136
Sanders EW	Gnr	RGA	13/03/18	Agra	M	1 yr HL	unexpired portion 30/4/18	WO/90/7/190
Sandieson J	Pte	65 Coy RDC	21/11/16	Towcester	M	1 yr Detn		WO/92/4/3
Sands WH	Pte	5 Dragoon Gds	30/09/19	Curragh	M	1 yr HL+Disch Igmny	Comm 6 mos Detn	WO/92/4/87
Sankey J	L/Cpl	35 MGC	17/01/19	Field	M	2 yrs HL	Remit 18 mos	WO/213/28/120
Sargeant A	Pte	7/8 R Innis Fus	15/04/18	Field	M	5 yrs PS	Susp	WO/213/21/95
Sarhan M	Labourer	Egyptian Lab Corps	06/09/17	Boulogne	M+S40	8 mos HL		WO/213/17/41
Sauber A	Pte	39 R Fus	23/08/19	Field EEF	M	NG		WO/213/31/24
Saunders HP	Pte	2 MGC	12/06/19	Field	M+Disob(2)+S40	5 yrs PS	Comm 2 yrs HL	WO/213/29/122
Savchok A	Spr	Can Engrs	25/01/19	Field	M+Disob	NG		WO/213/29/55
Sayers C	Cpl(L/Sgt)	2/4 R Sussex TF	23/07/15	Canterbury	NSM	Rnks		WO/92/3/20
Scally P	Pte	1 Connaught Rangers	04/09/20	Dagshai	M+S7(3b)	10 yrs PS+DI	Remit 3 yrs	WO/90/8/188
Scanlon J	Pte	1 Connaught Rangers	30/08/20	Dagshai	M	20 yrs PS+DI	Remit 5 yrs	WO/90/8/189
Scannell G	Pte	R Munster Fus	11/10/14	St Nazaire	M+Forcing Guard	4 yrs PS	Rem 1 yr/ Quashed	WO/213/2/105
Scarborough J	Dvr	RFA	07/03/19	Field	M	90 dys FP2		WO/213/29/12
Schmidt J	Dvr	372 Coy CAHT	14/05/19	Field	M	5 yrs PS	Remit 2 yrs	WO/213/30/11
Schmidt J	Pte	Can MG Depot	02/06/19	Liverpool	M+XO(Lt)+S7(3b)	22 mos Detn		WO/92/4/72
Schofield S	Pte	3 W Yorks	01/08/19	Devizes	M+S40	18 mos HL +Disch Igmny	9 mos	WO/92/4/77
Scholtz J	Dvr L/Cpl	ASC (SA)	23/07/18	Field	M	2 yrs HL		WO/213/24/168
Schorr H	Pte	39 R Fus	23/08/19	Field EEF	M	NG		WO/213/31/24
Schrader PF	Pte	1 NZ Div Employ Coy	16/10/18	Field	M	6 mos HL	Susp	WO/213/25/165
Scoffham W	Pte	1 Gn Sher Fstrs	05/06/17	Kantara Egypt	M	2 yrs HL		WO/213/15/178
Scott J	Pte	Can F[orestry] C[orps]	26/05/19	Liverpool	M+S7(3b)	22 mos HL		WO/92/4/71
Seaborn N	Pte	Lab Corps (att E Comm LB)	15/06/19	Sutton	M+S7(3b)	Acquit		WO/92/4/74
Sealey C	Pte	1 BWI	04/05/19	Field Italy	M	6 mos HL		WO/213/29/37
Searson S	Pte	7/8 R Innis Fus	15/04/18	Field	M	5 yrs PS	Susp	WO/213/21/95
Seddon TG	Pte	5 Dragoon Gds	23/09/19	Curragh	M	1 yr HL+Disch Igmny	Comm 6 mos Detn	WO/92/4/85
Sekgoba C	Pte	SANLC	17/12/17	Capetown	M	10 yrs PS		WO/213/19/115
Self TE	Pnr	RE	08/08/19	Bordon	M+Disob (CSM) +Res+Esc+S40	2 yrs HL + Disch Igmny	15 mos	WO/92/4/77
Selmes LJ	Pte	1 Inf Bn AIF	15/10/18	Field	M+Des	3 yrs PS	Guilty of Des	WO/213/28/196
Settle J	Pte	1 Inf Bn AIF	15/10/18	Field	M+Des	3 yrs PS	Guilty of Des	WO/213/28/198
Seymour J	Pte	58 Coy RDC	21/11/16	Towcester	M	1 yr Detn		WO/92/4/1
Shallow W	Pte	1 Connaught Rangers	04/09/20	Dagshai	M+S7(3b)	10 yrs PS+DI	Remit 3 yrs	WO/90/8/188
Shanks AG	Pte	Quebec Regt	15/07/19	Ripon	M	NG		WO/86/88/41
Sharoff V	Pte	1 Slav-Brit Legion	17/07/19	Field NREF	M	Death	Comm 10 yrs PS	WO/213/32/59
Sharp J	Pte	58 Coy RDC	21/11/16	Towcester	M	1 yr Detn		WO/92/4/1
Shaw A	Pte	2 W India	11/05/19	Field EEF	M	7 yrs PS	Comm 2 yrs HL	WO/213/30/27
Shaw C	Pte	9 (S) BWI	24/12/18	Field Italy	M+Disob+Esc	5 yrs PS		WO/213/27/25
Sheffield S	Pte	4 AIF	11/10/16	Rouen	M	Death	Comm 2 yrs HL	WO/90/6/90
Sheffield W	Gnr	RGA	09/05/21	Field (Ireland)	M+S7(4)	2 yrs HL+DI	Comm to DI Not Conf	WO/213/32/133
Shelly F	Pte	2 Ches	05/03/20	Field ABS	M+7(2b)	2 yrs HL		WO/213/31/168
Shepherd AE	Pte	9 MGC	31/07/19	Field	M+Abs/Br	6 mos HL	Quashed	WO/213/30/141
Sheppard H	Pte	23 AIF	04/02/19	Rouen	M	90 dys Imp		WO/90/8/58
Sherenitz D	Pte	39 R Fus	23/08/19	Field EEF	M	5 yrs PS	Comm 1 yr HL	WO/213/31/24
Sherring J	Pte	2 MGC	12/06/19	Field	M+Disob(2)+S40	5 yrs PS	Comm 2 yrs HL	WO/213/29/122
Sherstotoff F	Pte	Can For[estry] Corps	18/04/19	Liverpool	M+Striking	2 yrs HL		WO/92/4/69
Shields T	Pte	65 Coy RDC	21/11/16	Towcester	M	1 yr Detn		WO/92/4/2
Shields W	Pte	65 Coy RDC	21/11/16	Towcester	M	1 yr Detn		WO/92/4/3
Shilton T	Dvr	337 Bde RFA	10/01/17	Canterbury	JM	6 mos Detn		WO/92/3/58
Shirvington C	Pte	1 Inf Bn AIF	15/10/18	Field	M+Des	3 yrs PS	Guilty of Des	WO/213/28/197
Short JR	Cpl	24 North Fus	12/09/17	Etaples	M	Death		WO/213/17/119
Shoubridge T	Pte	2/4 R Sussex TF	23/07/15	Canterbury	J[oin in] M	84 dys Detn		WO/92/3/23
Shouliatieff T	Pte	1 Slav-Brit Legion	13/07/19	Field	M	Death	Comm 10 yrs PS	WO213/32/58
Shrivell C	Pte(L/Cpl)	2/4 R Sussex TF	23/07/15	Canterbury	NSM	28 dys Detn		WO/92/3/20
Shuttleworth G	L/Cpl	RE	04/02/19	Field	M	10 yrs PS+Rnks	Remit 5 yrs PS	WO/213/28/46
Sibbald JS	Pte	5 Dragoon Gds	29/09/19	Curragh	M	1 yr HL+Disch Igmny	Comm 6 mos Detn	WO/92/4/82

Name	Rank	Unit	Date D/M/Y	Location	Offence	Finding/Punishment	Amendment	PRO Reference File/Piece/Page
Sickles W	Pte	Quebec Regt	18/07/19	Ripon	S7(3b)[M]	6 mos Detn		WO/86/88/51
Sidebotham WE	Pte	1 Inf Bn AIF	15/10/18	Field	M+Des	NG		WO/213/28/198
Sidwell W	Pte	2/6 R Wars	27/05/19	Field	M+S40	2 yrs HL	Remit 1 yr	WO/213/30/64
Silva P	Pte	3 NZ Rifles	30/12/15	Malta	M+Not Sup+Disob (APM)	1 yr HL	Remit 1 month	WO/90/6/40
Simeon	Pte	SANLC	21/11/17	Field	M+S40	3 yrs PS	Comm 2 yrs HL	WO/213/31/109
Simm J	Pte	7/8 R Innis Fus	15/04/18	Field	M	5 yrs PS	Susp	WO/213/21/94
Simmonds JF	Pte	5 Dragoon Gds	25/09/19	Curragh	M	56 dys Detn	NC	WO/92/4/86
Simon R	Pte	Can For Corps	28/04/19	Liverpool	M	5 yrs PS		WO/92/4/70
Simpson A	Pte(3 Clerk)	RAF	02/05/18	Swanage	M	Acquit		WO/92/4/37
Simpson J	Pte	5 Dragoon Gds	29/09/19	Curragh	M	1 yr HL+Disch Igmny	Comm 6 mos Detn	WO/92/4/82
Sims W	Pte(S/Smith)	ASC	30/12/15	Marseilles	Joining M	3 yrs PS	Comm to 2 yrs HL	WO/90/6/44
Sinclair C	Pte	1 NZ Div Emp B	16/10/18	Field	M	6 mos HL	Susp	WO/213/25/165
Singer A	Pte	39 R Fus	23/08/19	Field EEF	M	5 ys PS	Comm 1 yr HL	WO/213/31/24
Skeels A	Pte	Lab Corps (att E Comm LB)	15/06/19	Sutton	M+S7(3b)	Acquit		WO/92/4/73
Skene H	Gnr	RFA(att RGA)	13/03/18	Agra	M	1 yr HL	unexpired portion 30/4/18	WO/90/7/190
Skipp WH	Pte	5 Dragoon Gds	26/09/19	Curragh	M	1 yr HL+Disch Igmny	Comm 6 mos Detn	WO/92/4/83
Slater H	L/Cpl (T/Cpl)	1 Inf Bn AIF	15/10/18	Field	M+Des	7 yrs PS+Rnks	Guilty of Des	WO/213/28/198
Slater H	Gnr	RFA	03/02/19	Field	M+Insub+S7(2)	90 dys FP1		WO/213/28/165
Slater JE	Pte	1 Gn Sher Fstrs	05/06/17	Kantara Egypt	M	2 yrs HL		WO/213/15/178
Slater W	Pte	5 Dragoon Gds	26/09/19	Curragh	M	1 yr HL+Disch Igmny	Comm 6 mos Detn	WO/92/4/81
Slattery M	Pte	7 R Irish	15/04/18	Field	M	5 yrs PS	Susp	WO/213/21/97
Slinger J	Dvr	372 Coy CAHT	14/05/19	Field	M	5 yrs PS	Remit 2 yrs	WO/213/30/11
Slowgrove AR	Pte	Lab Corps (att E Comm LB)	15/06/19	Sutton	M+S7(3b)	Acquit		WO/92/4/74
Smallbone GW	Pte	1/1 C of Lon Yeo	18/06/19	Field	M+S40	NG		WO/213/30/96
Smalley J	Pte	2 Manch	04/02/19	Rouen	M	3 yrs + 9 mos PS		WO/90/8/58
Smart WH	Pte	2/4 R Sussex TF	23/07/15	Canterbury	J[oin in] M	84 dys Detn		WO/92/3/23
Smith AE	Pte	Alb Regt CEF	15/07/18	Bramshott	M+S40	Acquit		WO/92/4/43
Smith B	Dvr	337 Bde RFA	10/01/17	Canterbury	JM	6 mos Detn		WO/92/3/58
Smith C	Spr	Can Engrs	01/02/19	Field	M+Disob	28 dys FP2		WO/213/28/71
Smith D	Pte	6 (S) BWI	24/12/18	Field Italy	M+Disob	3 yrs 6 mos PS		WO/213/27/24
Smith D	Pte	2 Ches	05/03/20	Field ABS	M+Disob	2 yrs HL	Rem 18 mos	WO/213/31/168
Smith E	Pte	3 Essex	09/05/19	Field Italy	M	3 yrs PS	Comm 4 mos HL	WO/213/29/72
Smith E	Pte	RGA	24/04/18		Mx2	10 yrs PS	2 yrs HL	WO/213/22/30
Smith EH	Pte	5 Dragoon Gds	23/09/19	Curragh	M	84 dys HL	Comm 42 dys Detn	WO/92/4/85
Smith EN	Pte	20(R) CEF	15/06/19	Liverpool	M+S40	Acquit		WO/92/4/74
Smith FR	Cpl	1 Inf Bn AIF	15/10/18	Field	M+Des	8 yrs PS+Rnks	Guilty of Des	WO/213/28/199
Smith GWP	Spr	RE	15/05/19	Field	M+Disob	1 yr IHL		WO/213/29/137
Smith HG	Pte	Lab Corps (att E Comm LB)	15/06/19	Sutton	M+S7(3b)	Acquit		WO/92/4/73
Smith HJ	Pte	5 Dragoon Gds	23/09/19	Curragh	M	6 mos HL	Comm 84 dys Detn	WO/92/4/85
Smith JI	Pte	1 HLI	09/02/16	Field (Mespot)	[M]S7(2b)	18 mos HL		WO/90/7/70
Smith J	Pte	1 Gn Sher Fstrs	05/06/17	Kantara Egypt	M	2 yrs HL		WO/213/15/178
Smith J	Gnr	RGA	13/03/18	Agra	M	1 yr HL	unexpired portion 30/4/18	WO/90/7/190
Smith J	Pte	21 Manch	08/02/19	Field	M+Abs	6 mos HL		WO/213/28/58
Smith J	Pte	234 Bde RFA	15/01/15	Cahir	M+Viol to Cpl +S40+S10(3)	2 yr HL+Disch ignmy		WO/86/63/136
Smith L	Gnr	RGA	13/03/18	Agra	M	1 yr HL	unexpired portion 30/4/18	WO/90/7/190
Smith LE	AL/Bdr	RGA	16/05/19	Field	M	9 mos HL	Remit 3 mos/ Quashed	WO/213/29/148
Smith N	Pte	39 R Fus	23/08/19	Field EEF	M	NG		WO/213/31/24
Smith R	Pte	35 MGC	17/01/19	Field	Mx2	2 yrs HL	Remit 18 mos	WO/213/28/121
Smith RA	Pte	5 Dragoon Gds	24/09/19	Curragh	M	1 yr HL+Ignmy	Comm 6 mos Detn	WO/92/4/86
Smith RH	Boy	King Edward Horse	24/09/19	Curragh	M	6 mos HL	Comm 84 dys Detn	WO/92/4/87
Smith RW	Dvr	ASC (SA)	23/07/18	Field	M	Life PS	Comm 5 yrs	WO/213/24/168
Smith S	Pte	334 Coy RDC	17/09/18	Pembroke Dock	M + Disob	112 dys Detn	28 dys	WO/92/4/52
Smith TR	Pte	1 Inf Bn AIF	15/10/18	Field	M+Des	3 yrs PS	Guilty of Des	WO/213/28/196
Smith W	Pte	5 Dragoon Gds	24/09/19	Curragh	M	1 yr HL+Disch Ignmy	Comm 6 mos Detn	WO/92/4/87

Name	Rank	Unit	Date D/M/Y	Location	Offence	Finding/Punishment	Amendment	PRO Reference File/Piece/Page
Smith W	Pte	5 Dragoon Gds	30/09/19	Curragh	M	1 yr HL+Disch Igmny	Comm 6 mos Detn	WO/92/4/87
Smyth GH	Pte	Can ASC	27/02/19	Witley	M+S40(2)	2 yrs Detn		WO/86/87/14
Snell A	Dvr	RFA	24/04/19	Field	M+Disob	5 mos HL		WO/213/29/160
Snell FJ	Pte (A/Cpl)	1 MGC	17/07/19	Field	M	5 mos Imp		WO/213/30/82
Snelling A	Pte	2/4 R Sussex TF	23/07/15	Canterbury	J[oin in] M	84 dys Detn		WO/92/3/23
Snow W	Pte	35 MGC	17/01/19	Field	Mx2	2 yrs HL	Remit 18 mos	WO/213/28/121
Snowden J	Pte	Lab Corps (att E Comm LB)	15/06/19	Sutton	M+S7(3b)	Acquit		WO/92/4/73
Soames W	Pte	Lab Corps (att E Comm LB)	15/06/19	Sutton	M+S7(3b)	Acquit		WO/92/4/74
Solari L	L/Bdr	RGA	05/07/19	Aldershot	M	9 mos Detn+Rnks +Disch Igmny		WO/86/87/189
Somerville A	Pte	2/4 R Sussex TF	23/07/15	Canterbury	J[oin in] M	84 dys Detn		WO/92/3/23
Sophie E	Pte(A/Cpl)	Labour Bn	16/01/19	Mesopotamia	M	2 yrs HL		WO/90/7/169
Souliere V	Pte	21 CEF	11/05/19	Witley	M+S40(2)	2 yrs HL+Disch Igmny		WO/86/87/169
Southwick S	Gnr	RFA	24/04/19	Field	M+Disob	NG		WO/213/29/160
Sova S	Pte	17 Worc	23/07/19	Field	M+S40	1 yr HL		WO/213/30/135
Spence A	Pte	4 BWI	27/12/18	Field Italy	M+Disob	3 yrs PS	Comm 2 yrs HL	WO/213/27/23
Spence HA	Pte	Can ASC	21/11/17	Bramshott	M+Insub(Lieut)	42 dys Detn	Remit 15 dys	WO/86/79/53
Spence JD	Pte	5 Dragoon Gds	23/09/19	Curragh	M	84 dys HL	Comm 42 dys Detn	WO/92/4/85
Spencer H	Pte	4 BWI	28/02/19	Plymouth	M	2 yrs Detn		WO/86/87/17
Spriggs A	Pte	1/4 KOYLI (att 365 POW Coy)	16/09/19	Field	M+Abs+Disob	3 yrs PS	Comm 1 yr HL	WO/213/31/69
Springer J	Cpl	NZEF 3 Reinf	05/04/15	Zeitoun	Incit M+Disob(Lt)	3 yrs PS+DI		WO/90/6/35
Stacey EW	Pte	2 Y[ork] & Lanc	06/11/19	Basrah	M	4 yrs PS	Comm 2 yrs HL	WO/90/7/205
Stafford J	Pte	RAMC	10/05/19	Field	M	6 mos HL	Comm 28 dys FP2	WO/213/30/17
Stafford R	Pte	1 Inf Bn AIF	15/10/18	Field	M+Des	3 yrs PS	Guilty of Des	WO/213/28/198
Stanworth H	Pte	5 Dragoon Gds	23/09/19	Curragh	M	1 yr HL+Disch Igmny	Comm 6 mos Detn	WO/92/4/85
Staples G	Pte	7/8 R Innis Fus	15/04/18	Field	M	5 yrs PS	Susp	WO/213/21/94
Stapley LJ	Pte	Lab Corps (att E Comm LB)	15/06/19	Sutton	M+S7(3b)	Acquit		WO/92/4/74
Statton T	Pte	Can ASC	21/11/17	Bramshott	M+Insub(Lieut)	42 dys Detn	Remit 15 dys	WO/86/79/53
Steele DN	Pte (L/Cpl)	1 Inf Bn AIF	15/10/18	Field	M+Des	5 yrs PS	Guilty of Des	WO/213/28/196
Steele FJ	Pte	5 Dragoon Gds	24/09/19	Curragh	M	1 yr HL+Disch Igmny	Comm 6 mos Detn	WO/92/4/86
Stenning H	Pte	2/4 R Sussex TF	23/07/15	Canterbury	J[oin in] M	84 dys Detn		WO/92/3/23
Stephens E	Pte	2 MGC	12/06/19	Field	M+Disob(2)+S40	5 yrs PS	Comm 2 yrs HL	WO/213/29/122
Stephenson L	Pte	1 Gn Sher Fstrs	05/06/17	Kantara Egypt	M	2 yrs HL		WO/213/15/178
Stephenson WA	Pte	13 AIF	24/03/19	Field	M	11 yrs PS		WO/213/29/89
Sterrett W	Pte	9(S) E Lancs	29/05/18	SEF	M	1 yr HL		WO/213/23/179
Stevens DM	Pte	5 Dragoon Gds	26/09/19	Curragh	M	1 yr HL+Disch Igmny	Comm 6 mos Detn	WO/92/4/83
Stevens SH	Gnr	RGA	13/03/18	Agra	M	1 yr HL	unexpired portion 30/4/18	WO/90/7/190
Stevens WA	Pte	Can ASC	21/11/17	Bramshott	M+Insub(Lieut)	42 dys Detn	Remit 15 dys	WO/86/79/53
Stevenson J	Pte	3 Leics	27/08/14	Portsmouth	M	1 yr HL		WO/213/2/1
Stevenson J	Pte	7/8 R Innis Fus	15/04/18	Field	M	5 yrs PS	Susp	WO/213/21/95
Stevenson W	Pte	30 MGC	29/07/19	Field	M+Disob	1 yr HL		WO/213/30/119
Stirling H	Pte	9 AIF	24/03/19	Field	M	10 yrs PS		WO/213/29/90
Stocks WA	Rfn	51 Rif Bde (att 2 MGC)	12/06/19	Field	M+Disob(2)+S40	5 yrs PS	Comm 2 yrs HL	WO/213/29/122
Stokes EF	Pte	1 Inf Bn AIF	15/10/18	Field	M+Des	3 yrs PS	Guilty of Des	WO/213/28/198
Stone F	Pte	Lab Corps (att E CommLB)	15/06/19	Sutton	M+S7(3b)	Acquit		WO/92/4/73
Stone HF	Pte	5 Dragoon Gds	25/09/19	Curragh	M	1 yr HL+Disch Igmny	Comm 6 mos Detn	WO/92/4/86
Stones D	Pte	5 Dragoon Gds	29/09/19	Curragh	M	1 yr HL+Disch Igmny	Comm 6 mos Detn	WO/92/4/82
Stothard GW	Pte	5 Dragoon Gds	24/09/19	Curragh	M	1 yr HL+Disch Igmny	Comm 6 mos Detn	WO/92/4/86
Strasburg J	Pte	39 R Fus	29/03/19	Field EEF	M+Insub	1 yr HL	Remit 6 mos	WO/213/29/86
Strauss H	Pte	39 R Fus	23/08/19	Field EEF	M	NG		WO/213/31/24
Street GS	Pte	1 Gn Sher Fstrs	05/06/17	Kantara Egypt	M	2 yrs HL		WO/213/15/178
Street V	L/Bdr	RGA	04/07/19	Aldershot	M	9 mos Detn+Rnks +Disch Igmny		WO/86/87/188
Stringer S	Pte	5 Dragoon Gds	23/09/19	Curragh	M	1 yr HL+Disch Igmny	Comm 6 mos Detn	WO/92/4/85
Stringer T	Dvr	RFA	08/10/18	Field	M+Disob	5 yrs PS	Susp	WO/213/25/158
Stringer T	Dvr	523 Bty RFA	25/09/16	Ewshott Camp	M	2 yrs Detn	Remit 18 mos	WO/86/70/219
Stubbs W	Pte	21 Manch	08/02/19	Field	M+Abs	6 mos HL		WO/213/28/58

Name	Rank	Unit	Date D/M/Y	Location	Offence	Finding/Punishment	Amendment	PRO Reference File/Piece/Page
Suleiman M	Labourer	Egyptian Lab Corps	06/09/17	Boulogne	M+S40	8 mos HL		WO/213/17/41
Sullivan FG	Pte	10 Hussars	25/01/21	Curragh	Mx2+S9(1)x2	1 yr Detn	Remit 3 mos	WO/92/4/94
Sullivan RP	Pte	10 Ruyal Fus	31/01/17	Field	M+Sleeping	Death	NC	WO/213/13/172
Summers J	Pte	65 Coy RDC	21/11/16	Towcester	M	1 yr Detn		WO/92/4/3
Summersby W	Spr	RE	15/05/19	Field	M+Disob	1 yr IHL		WO/213/29/137
Supple DR	Pte	Can Ry Troops	05/05/19	Liverpool	M	Acquit		WO/92/4/67
Susans W	Dvr	337 Bde RFA	10/01/17	Canterbury	JM	6 mos Detn		WO/92/3/58
Sutherland AG	Spr	RE	09/05/19	Field Italy	M	2 yrs HL	Remit 20 mos/ Quashed	WO/213/29/73
Sutton W	Pte	12 SWBdrs	01/12/16	Field	M+Disob	18 mos HL	Comm 3 mos FP1	WO/213/13/47
Sutton WW	Pte	5 Dragoon Gds	30/09/19	Curragh	M	1 yr HL+Disch Igmny	Comm 6 mos Detn	WO/92/4/87
Swallow L	Pte	5 Dragoon Gds	24/09/19	Curragh	M	1 yr HL+Disch Igmny	Comm 6 mos Detn	WO/92/4/87
Swatridge G	Cpl	RGA	04/07/19	Aldershot	M	9 mos Detn+Rnks +Disch Igmny		WO/86/87/188
Sweeney E	Spr	Can Engrs	01/02/19	Field	M+Disob	28 dys FP2		WO/213/28/71
Sweeney P	Pte	1 Connaught Rangers	30/08/20	Dagshai	M	Life PS+DI	20 yrs PS	WO/90/8/189
Sweeney T	Pte	7 R Irish	15/04/18	Field	M	5 yrs PS	Susp	WO/213/21/97
Sykes H	Pte	9 Northumberland Fus	05/07/19	Field	M+S40	3 yrs PS	Comm 1 yr HL	WO/213/30/109
Sykes J	Pte	5 Dragoon Gds	23/09/19	Curragh	M	1 yr HL+Disch Igmny	Comm 6 mos Detn	WO/92/4/85
Synnott P	Bdr	RGA	04/07/19	Aldershot	M	9 mos Detn+Rnks +Disch Igmny		WO/86/87/188
Syring A	Spr	101 Field Coy RE	27/03/19	Field Italy	M+Disob	5 yrs PS	Remit 2 yrs	WO/213/28/191
Taffe J	L/Bdr	RGA	04/07/19	Aldershot	M	9 mos Detn+Rnks +Disch Igmny		WO/86/87/188
Tailby J	Bdr	RGA	08/07/19	Aldershot	M	9 mos Detn+Rnks +Disch Igmny		WO/86/87/189
Tandet J	Pte	39 R Fus	23/08/19	Field EEF	M	6 yrs PS	Comm 1 yr HL	WO/213/31/24
Taplin RC	Cpl	1 Inf Bn AIF	15/10/18	Field	M+Des	10 yrs PS+Rnks	Guilty of Des	WO/213/28/199
Taratin P	Pte	1 Slav-Brit Legion	14/07/19	Field NREF	M	Death		WO/213/32/59
Tarren F	L/Cpl	2 Y[ork] & Lanc	04/11/19	Basrah	M+Drunk	60 dys FP2		WO/90/7/205
Taylor A	Pte	1 Gn Sher Fstrs	05/06/17	Kantara Egypt	M	2 yrs HL		WO/213/15/178
Taylor A	Dvr	Can Res A[rty]	13/05/19	Liverpool	M	120 dys Detn	NC	WO/92/4/71
Taylor B	Pte	21 Manch	08/02/19	Field	M+Abs	6 mos HL		WO/213/28/58
Taylor CM	L/Cpl	Can Engrs	21/01/19	Field	M+S7(3b)	2 yrs HL+Rnks		WO/213/28/108
Taylor E	Pte	2 W India	11/05/19	Field EEF	M	5 yrs PS	Comm 1 yr HL	WO/213/30/28
Taylor ES	Pte	5 Dragoon Gds	26/09/19	Curragh	M	1 yr HL+Disch Igmny	Comm 6 mos Detn	WO/92/4/83
Taylor FH	Gnr	RGA	13/03/18	Agra	M	1 yr HL	unexpired portion 30/4/18	WO/90/7/190
Taylor FJ	Pte	65 Coy RDC	21/11/16	Towcester	M	1 yr Detn		WO/92/4/3
Taylor H	Pte	344 Coy RDC	17/09/18	Pembroke Dock	M+Insub	112 dys Detn	28 dys	WO/92/4/52
Taylor H	Pte	5 Dragoon Gds	30/09/19	Curragh	M	1 yr HL+Disch Igmny	Comm 6 mos Detn	WO/92/4/87
Taylor J	Pte(L/Cpl)	1/6 HLI	28/12/18	Field	M+Disob	42 dys FP1		WO/213/28/25
Taylor JA	Pte	Lab Corps	24/03/19	Field	M	10 yrs PS		WO213/29/88
Taylor JN	Pte	8 (R)CEF	30/07/19	Witley	M	Not Guilty		WO/86/88/30
Taylor N	Pte	2 W India	11/05/19	Field EEF	M	7 yrs PS	Comm 2 yrs HL	WO/213/30/28
Taylor R	Pte	3 HLI(att MGC)	25/04/16	Grantham	M	2 yrs Detn		WO/92/3/37
Taylor S	Pte	1 Gn Sher Fstrs	05/06/17	Kantara Egypt	M	2 yrs HL		WO/213/15/178
Taylor W	Pte	Lab Corps (att E Comm LB)	15/06/19	Sutton	M+S7(3b)	Acquit		WO/92/4/74
Tenentieff H	Pte	1 Slav-Brit Legion	13/07/19	Field	M	NG		WO213/32/58
Tepoorten JE	Pte	Can ASC	19/07/16	[Le] Havre	M+Insub	5 yrs PS		WO/90/6/67
Terrell SJ	Spr	3 Aus Tun Coy	13/10/18	Field	M+Disob	1 yr HL	NC	WO/213/30/136
Terrell SJ	Spr	3 Aus Tun Coy	18/10/18	Field	M+Disob	2 yrs HL	Susp	WO/213/26/66
Tetley JW	Pte	3W Yorks	01/08/19	Devizes	M+S40	18 mos HL +Disch Igmny	9 mos	WO/92/4/77
Thacker GH	Gnr	RGA	13/03/18	Agra	M	1 yr HL	unexpired portion 30/4/18	WO/90/7/190
Theirens RH	Pte	5 Dragoon Gds	26/09/19	Curragh	M	5 yrs PS+Disch Igmny	Comm 2 yrs Detn	WO/92/4/83
Thom AG	Tpr	6 Dragoon (att RHGds)	05/10/16	Rouen	M	5 yrs PS	Comm 2 yrs HL	WO/90/6/89
Thomas D	Gnr	V/38 TMB	10/01/17	Esquelbecq	M+Disob	3 yrs PS		WO/213/13/138
Thomas EL	Pte	1/7 RW Fus	05/12/18	Field	M+S40(6e)	NG		WO/213/27/171
Thomas R	Spr	RE	09/05/19	Field Italy	M	2 yrs HL	Remit 20 mos/ Quashed	WO/213/29/73

Name	Rank	Unit	Date D/M/Y	Location	Offence	Finding/Punishment	Amendment	PRO Reference File/Piece/Page
Thomas RG [DCM]	Spr	3 Aus Tun Coy	13/10/18	Field	M+Disob	1 yr HL	NC	WO/213/30/136
Thomas RG [DCM]	Spr	3 Aus Tun Coy	18/10/18	Field	M+Disob	2 yrs HL	Susp	WO/213/26/66
Thomas T	Pte	12 SWBdrs	01/12/16	Field	M+Disob	18 mos HL	Comm 3 mos FP1	WO/213/13/47
Thomas W	Dvr	ASC (SA)	05/08/18	Field	M+S40	18 mos HL		WO/213/24/129
Thomas W	Dvr	337 Bde RFA	10/01/17	Canterbury	JM	6 mos Detn		WO/92/3/58
Thomas W	Pte	334 Coy RDC	17/09/18	Pembroke Dock	M+Disob	90 dys Detn	28 dys	WO/92/4/52
Thomasson WP	Pte	RASC	20/02/19	Field	Mx2+S40	3 yrs PS		WO/213/28/169
Thompson AS	Pte	21 Manch	08/02/19	Field	M+Abs	6 mos HL		WO/213/28/58
Thompson AW	Pte	Quebec Regt	18/07/19	Ripon	M+S7(3b)	18 mos HL		WO/86/88/29
Thompson H	Pte	11 R Fus	02/08/19	Field	M+Viol+Thr+Insol	10 yrs PS		WO/213/30/160
Thompson J	Pte	2/4 R Sussex TF	23/07/15	Canterbury	J[oin in] M	84 dys Detn		WO/92/3/23
Thompson J	Cpl	RGA	05/07/19	Aldershot	M	9 mos Detn+Rnks+Disch Igmny		WO/86/87/189
Thompson R	Pte	7/8 R Innis Fus	15/04/18	Field	M	5 yrs PS	Susp	WO/213/21/95
Thompson T	Pte	2 East Yorks	05/07/20	Constantinople	M	5 yrs PS	Comm 1 yr Detn	WO/90/8/84
Thomson C	Cpl	3 Aus Sig Troop	01/07/18	Field EEF	M	NG		WO/213/28/138
Thomson F	Pte	7 Dragoon Gds	09/06/21	Edinburgh	M+V(A/RSM)	2 yrs HL		WO/86/91/131
Thomson J	Pte	257 P of W Coy	13/05/19	Field	M+S40(2)	6 mos HL	56 dys FP1	WO/213/30/31
Thomson W	Pte	58 Coy RDC	21/11/16	Towcester	M	1 yr Detn		WO/92/4/1
Thorton W	Pte	1/4 KOYLI (att 365 POW Coy)	16/09/19	Field	M+Abs+Disob	3 yrs PS	Comm 1 yr HL	WO/213/31/69
Threlfell E	Pte	2 MGC	12/06/19	Field	M+Disob(2)+S40	5 yrs PS		WO/213/29/122
Tickner HH	Pte	1 Inf Bn AIF	15/10/18	Field	M+Des	3 yrs PS	Guilty of Des	WO/213/28/195
Timmon F	Pte	15(TW) Worc	12/04/17	Swindon	M+S40	9 mos Detn		WO/86/75/125
Timms W	Pte	5 Dragoon Gds	24/09/19	Curragh	M	1 yr HL+Disch Igmny	Comm 6 mos Detn	WO/92/4/87
Tobin D	Pte	39 R Fus	23/08/19	Field EEF	M	6 yrs PS	Rem 3 yrs/Comm 1 yr HL	WO/213/31/24
Tobin JE	Pte	25 CEF	11/02/18	Bramshott	M+Inj property*+S40(2)	112 dys Detn Quashed*		WO/86/80/139
Tonk DE	Pte	56 AIF	22/12/18	Field	M	4 yrs PS		WO/213/27/184
Tonkikh V	Pte	1 Slav-Brit Legion	17/07/19	Field NREF	M	Death	Comm 10 yrs PS	WO/213/32/59
Topley TC	Pte	2 Gn/Beds	04/04/18	Karachi	M+S7(3)	3 yrs PS	Comm 2 yrs HL	WO/90/7/191
Tough TF	Pte	12 SWBdrs	01/12/16	Field	M+Disob	18 mos HL	Comm 3 mos FP1	WO/213/13/47
Towlson H	Dvr	337 Bde RFA	10/01/17	Canterbury	JM	6 mos Detn		WO/92/3/58
Town GT	Pte(S/Smith)	ASC	30/12/15	Marseilles	Joining M	3 yrs PS	Comm to 2 yrs HL	WO/90/6/44
Townend R	Pte	9(S) E Lancs	29/05/18	SEF	M	1 yr HL		WO/213/23/179
Townsend J	Pte(L/Cpl)	2/4 R Sussex TF	23/07/15	Canterbury	NSM	28 dys Detn		WO/92/3/20
Travers WF	Pte	1 Inf Bn AIF	15/10/18	Field	M+Des	3 yrs PS	Guilty of Des	WO/213/28/196
Travis R	Pte	2 AIF	18/06/19	Field	M+Disob	2 yrs HL		WO/213/30/131
Treadwell HW	Dvr	RGA	16/05/19	Field	M	6 mos HL	Comm 84 dys FP1/Quashed	WO/213/29/148
Treisler GW	Pte	2/4 R Sussex TF	23/07/15	Canterbury	J[oin in] M	84 dys Detn		WO/92/3/23
Trenholm AE	Pte	3 RWFs	06/06/18	Kinmel Park	M+Disob	NG+Acquit		WO/92/4/39
Troy J	Pte	2 Liverpool	26/04/20	Khartoum	M+Resist+Esc+S40+S7(3b)	14 dys Detn	Remit Sentence	WO/90/8/83
Truby JT	Pte	35 MGC	17/01/19	Field	Mx2	1 yr HL	Remit 6 mos	WO/213/28/120
Tucker W	Dvr	337 Bde RFA	10/01/17	Canterbury	JM	6 mos Detn		WO/92/3/58
Tuckman B	Pte	Can Fores(try) Corps	02/05/19	Liverpool	M+S7(3b)	6 mos HL		WO/92/4/71
Tudor F	Pte	7 R Irish	15/04/18	Field	M	5 yrs PS	Susp	WO/213/21/97
Tugby P	Pte	2 R Irish	15/04/18	Field	M	5 yrs PS	Susp	WO/213/21/98
[Tuislick?] TN	Pte	2/4 R Sussex TF	23/07/15	Canterbury	J[oin in] M	84 dys Detn		WO/92/3/23
Tulley M	Pte	7 R Irish	15/04/18	Field	M	5 yrs PS	Susp	WO/213/21/97
Turks AJ	Pte	5 Dragoon Gds	26/09/19	Curragh	M	2 yrs HL+Disch Igmny	Comm 1 yr Detn	WO/92/4/81
Turner A	Pte	7/8 R Innis Fus	15/04/18	Field	M	NG		WO/213/21/95
Turner AE	Pte	Lab Corps (att E Comm LB)	15/06/19	Sutton	M+S7(3b)	Acquit		WO/92/4/74
Turner E	Pte	12 SWBdrs	01/12/16	Field	M+Disob	18 mos HL	Comm 3 mos FP1	WO/312/13/46
Turner G	Pte	1/4 KOYLI (att 365 POW Coy)	16/09/19	Field	M+Abs+Disob	3 yrs PS	Comm 1 yr HL	WO/213/31/69
Turner J	Pte	8/10 Gordons (att RE)	28/08/16	Field	M x 2	2 yrs HL	Susp	WO/213/11/9
Turner J	Pte	29 MGC	01/02/19	Field	M+S40	1 yr HL	Remit 6 mo	WO/213/28/73
Turner JW	Dvr	RFA	07/03/19	Field	M+Des+Drunk+Losing property	2 yrs HL		WO/213/29/169

Name	Rank	Unit	Date D/M/Y	Location	Offence	Finding/Punishment	Amendment	PRO Reference File/Piece/Page
Turton H	Pte	68 Div Cyclist Coy	17/01/17	Gt Yarmouth	M	NG		WO/96/73/171
Twaits R	Pte	50 AIF	24/03/19	Field	M	11 yrs PS		WO/213/29/90
Twist M	Pte	65 Coy RDC	21/11/16	Towcester	M	1 yr Detn		WO/92/4/3
Tyrrell A	Pte	6 (S) BWI	24/12/18	Field Italy	M+Disob	3 yrs 6 mos PS		WO/213/27/24
Ulph RW	Spr	3 Aus Tun Coy	13/10/18	Field	M+Disob	1 yr HL	NC	WO/213/30/136
Ulph RW	Spr	3 Aus Tun Coy	18/10/18	Field	M+Disob	2 yrs HL	Susp	WO/213/26/65
Underwood CA	Pte(S/Smith)	ASC	30/12/15	Marseilles	Joining M	3 yrs PS	Comm to 2 yrs HL	WO/90/6/44
Urquhart S	Pte	Gordon Hdrs	12/09/18	Field	M(x2)	10 yrs PS	One charge quashed	WO/213/25/177
Uys E	Dvr	ASC (SA)	05/08/18	Field	M+S40	1 yr HL		WO/213/24/129
Van Diemen F	Dvr	372 Coy CAHT	14/05/19	Field	M	5 yrs PS	Comm 2 yrs HL	WO/213/30/11
Vance H	Pte	5 Dragoon Gds	22/09/19	Curragh	M	Acquit		WO/92/4/84
Varieur EL	Pte	Quebec Regt	26/07/19	Ripon	M	2 yrs HL+Disch Igmny		WO/86/88/51
Vaught R	Pte	1 Inf Bn AIF	15/10/18	Field	M+Des	3 yrs PS	Guilty of Des	WO/213/28/200
Veale W	Pte	7/8 R Irish Fus	13/04/17	Dunkirk	M	8 mos HL		WO/213/14/138
Vidler W	Cpl	2/4 R Sussex TF	23/07/15	Canterbury	NSM	Rnks		WO/92/3/20
Vidler WT	Pte	1 Inf Bn AIF	15/10/18	Field	M+Des	3 yrs PS	Guilty of Des	WO/213/28/196
Villalard C	Pte	6 York & Lanc	24/03/19	Field	M	10 yrs PS		WO/213/29/89
Vieillese W	Pte	Maur Lab Bn	10/05/18	Mespot	M(S7-2B)	2 yrs HL		WO/90/7/151
Vincent W	Pte	47 R Fus (att 29 L'pool)	14/04/20	Field	M+S40	6 mos HL		WO/213/142
Vine JW	Pte	2/4 R Sussex TF	23/07/15	Canterbury	J[oin in] M	84 dys Detn		WO/92/3/23
Vizard J	Pte(S/Smith)	ASC	30/12/15	Marseilles	Joining M	3 yrs PS	Comm to 2 yrs HL	WO/90/6/44
Vizer HC	Pte	47 R Fus (att 29 L'pool)	14/04/20	Field	M+S40	6 mos HL		WO/213/142
Volkoff P	Pte	1 Slav-Brit Legion	14/07/19	Field NREF	M	Death		WO/213/32/59
Voysey E	Pte	1 Inf Bn AIF	15/10/18	Field	M+Des	3 yrs PS	Guilty of Des	WO/213/28/199
Wadman W	Pte	2 Gn/Beds	04/04/18	Karachi	M+S7(3)	5 yrs PS	Comm 2 yrs HL	WO/90/7/191
Wain J	Pte	7/8 R Innis Fus	15/04/18	Field	M	5 yrs PS	Susp	WO/213/21/94
Wake N	Pte	2 Y[ork] & Lanc	05/11/19	Basrah	M+S9(1)	4 yrs PS	Comm 2 yrs HL	WO/90/7/205
Wakefield W	Pte	35 MGC	17/01/19	Field	Mx2	2 yrs HL	Remit 6 mos	WO/213/28/121
Waldron M	Pte	Lab Corps	15/06/19	Sutton	M+S7(3b)	Acquit		WO/92/4/74
Walker E	Pte (L/Cpl)	1 Inf Bn AIF	15/10/18	Field	M+Des	5 yrs PS	Guilty of Des	WO/213/28/199
Walker H	Pte	334 Coy RDC	17/09/18	Pembroke Dock	M+Disob	112 dys Detn	28 dys	WO/92/4/52
Walker JA	Cpl	19 AIF	15/02/16	Sinai Penin	M+Disob	3 yrs HL		WO/213/8/113
Walker T	Pte	9 Middx	15/03/16	Guildhall West	P(ersuade) M+Disob	1 yr HL		WO/92/3/34
Wallace E	Pte	5 Dragoon Gds	29/09/19	Curragh	M	1 yr HL+Disch Igmny	Comm 6 mos Detn	WO/92/4/82
Wallace J	Pte	14 AIF	24/03/19	Field	M	11 yrs PS		WO/213/29/90
Wallace J	Pte	Can For Corps	22/04/19	Liverpool	M	90 dys Detn		WO/92/4/70
Wallcutt H	Pte	2 W India	11/05/19	Field EEF	M	5 yrs PS	Comm 1 yr HL	WO/213/30/27
Waller GH	Pte(L/Cpl))	7/8 R Innis Fus	15/04/18	Field	M	7 yrs PS	Susp	WO/213/21/95
Wallis P	Pte	10 AIF	24/03/19	Field	M	11 yrs PS		WO/213/29/91
Walmsley J	Pte	9(S) E Lancs	29/05/18	SEF	M	1 yr HL		WO/213/23/179
Walsh J	Pte	1 Connaught Rangers	25/08/20	Dagshai	M	5 yrs PS+DI		WO/90/8/188
Walsh MJ	Pte	Lab Corps (att E Comm LB)	15/06/19	Sutton	M+S7(3b)	Acquit		WO/92/4/73
Walsh T	Pte	47 R Fus (att 29 L'pool)	14/04/20	Field	M+S40	6 mos HL		WO/213/142
Walsh WP	Spr	Can Eng	02/06/19	Liverpool	M	Acquit		WO/92/4/69
Walters W	Sgt	18 Bn Scot Rifs	03/02/19	Field	M+Insub+S7(2)	12 mos HL+Rnks		WO/213/28/165
Walton R	Pte	12 SWBdrs	01/12/16	Field	M+Disob	18 mos HL	Comm 3 mos FP1	WO/312/13/46
Warbrick J	Pte	RASC	20/04/20	Field ABS	M+Disob	3 mos FP2		WO/213/31/171
Ward HC	Dvr	RGA	09/05/21	Field (Ireland)	M+S7(2b)	2 yrs HL+DI	Comm to DI Not Conf	WO/213/32/133
Ward J	Pte	2 R I Fus	09/06/19	Field EEF	M+XOS+S40	6 mos HL		WO/213/30/126
Ward JWH	Dvr	175 Bde RFA	16/07/16	Field	M+Disob	28 dys FP1		WO/213/11/24
Ward W	Pte	1 Gn Sher Fstrs	05/06/17	Kantara Egypt	M	2 yrs HL		WO/213/15/178
Warn A	L/Bdr	RGA	04/07/19	Aldershot	M	9 mos Detn+Rnks+Disch Igmny		WO/86/87/18
Warner C	Pte	3 Leics	27/08/14	Portsmouth	M	1 yr HL		WO/213/2/2
Warnes EE	Pte	3 W Yorks	01/08/19	Devizes	M+S40	18 mos HL+Disch Igmny	9 mos	WO/92/4/76
Warr B	Pte	5 Worc	11/08/19	Dublin	M+S40	Acquit		WO/92/4/76

Name	Rank	Unit	Date D/M/Y	Location	Offence	Finding/Punishment	Amendment	PRO Reference File/Piece/Page
Warren WC	Bdr(A/LCpl)	RGA	08/07/19	Aldershot	M	9 mos Detn+Rnks +Disch Igmny		WO/86/87/189
Warrener EG	Gnr	RGA	13/03/18	Agra	M	1 yr HL	unexpired portion 30/4/18	WO/90/7/191
Warsdale H	Pte	RASC	20/04/20	Field ABS	M+Disob	3 mos FP2		WO/213/31/171
Waterman H	Pte	2/4 R Sussex TF	23/07/15	Canterbury	J[oin in] M	84 dys Detn		WO/92/3/24
Waters F	Sgt	R Berks (att 1/0BLI)	26/07/19	Field NREF	M+S40	6 mos HL+Rnks	Comm 91 dys Imp	WO/213/30/106
Watkins F	Pte	12 SWBdrs	01/12/16	Field	M+Disob	18 mos HL	Comm 3 mos FP1	WO/312/13/46
Watkins JB	Pte	23 AIF	24/03/19	Field	M	11 yrs PS		WO/213/29/90
Watkinson W	Pte	5 Dragoon Gds	29/09/19	Curragh	M	1 yr HL+Disch Igmny	Comm 6 mos Detn	WO/92/4/82
Watley J	Pte	6 (S) BWI	24/12/18	Field Italy	M+Disob	3 yrs 6 mos PS		WO/213/27/24
Watson H	Cpl	2/7 R Wars	04/01/19	Field	M	5 yrs PS		WO/213/28/72
Watson J	Pte	2 W India	11/05/19	Field EEF	M	7 yrs PS	Comm 2 yrs HL	WO/213/30/28
Watts A	Pte	344 Coy RDC	17/09/18	Pembroke Dock	M+Disob	90 dys Detn	28 dys	WO/92/4/52
Watts SC	Pte	47 R Fus (att 29 L'pool)	14/04/20	Field	M+S40	6 mos HL		WO/213/142
Way R	Spr	Can Engrs	25/01/19	Field	M+Disob	28 dys FP2		WO/213/29/55
Weallens JH	Pte	1(R) Gn HLI	04/10/18	Glasgow	M+Theft	6 mos Detn	NC	WO/86/85/9
Weatherley J	Pte	4 Mddx	12/11/17	Field	M+Disob	6 mos HL	Comm 91 dys FP1	WO/213/18/181
Webb WH	Dvr	Aus[t] FA[rty]	24/03/19	Field	M	10 yrs PS		WO213/29/88
Webber S	Pte(3AM)	RAF	02/05/18	Swanage	M	Acquit		WO/92/4/37
Webster A	Pte	257 P of W Coy	12/05/19	Field	M+S40(2)	6 mos Imp	Comm 90 dys FP2	WO/213/30/31
Webster T	Pte(A/Cpl)	RAOC	08/10/19	Field	M+S40	NG		WO/213/31/4
Weikel F	Pte	21(R) CEF	22/05/19	Liverpool	M+S7(3b)	22 mos HL		WO/92/4/71
Wein H	Pte	39 R Fus	23/08/19	Field EEF	M	5 yrs PS	Comm 1 yr HL	WO/213/31/24
Weinberg S	Pte	2 MGC	12/06/19	Field	M+Disob(2)+S40	5 yrs PS	Remit 2 yrs	WO/213/29/122
Weir W	Pte	2/4 R Sussex TF	23/07/15	Canterbury	J[oin in] M	84 dys Detn		WO/92/3/24
Weldon E	Gnr	RGA	08/07/19	Aldershot	M	9 mos Detn		WO/86/87/189
Weller P	Pte	Can ASC	21/11/17	Bramshott	M+Insub(Lieut)	42 dys Detn	Remit 15 dys	WO/86/79/53
Wellington FA	Spr	RE	15/05/19	Field	M+Disob	1 yr IHL		WO/213/29/137
Wells J	Pte	2 R Irish	15/04/18	Field	M	5 yrs PS	Susp	WO/213/21/98
Welsh T	Pte	2 R Irish	15/04/18	Field	M	5 yrs PS	Susp	WO/213/21/98
Wesman W	Pte	1 Gn Sher Fstrs	05/06/17	Kantara Egypt	M	2 yrs HL		WO/213/15/178
West NF	Spr	Aus[t] Engrs	24/03/19	Field	M	12 yrs PS		WO213/29/88
Westmoreland G	Pte	8 Lincs	12/11/17	Field	M+Disob	6 mos HL	Comm 91 dys FP1	WO/213/18/180
Wethered GF	Cpl	1 Inf Bn AIF	15/10/18	Field	M+Des	8 yrs PS+Rnks	Guilty of Des	WO/213/28/195
Whalley H	Pte	7 Wilts	02/05/18	Field SEF	M+Disob	10 yrs PS	Comm 2 yrs HL	WO/213/22/30
Whatmore T	Pte	1 Inf Bn AIF	15/10/18	Field	M+Des	3 yrs PS	Guilty of Des	WO/213/28/197
Wheeler W	Pte	2/4 R Sussex TF	23/07/15	Canterbury	J[oin in] M	84 dys Detn		WO/92/3/24
Whelan D	Pte	9(S) E Lancs	29/05/18	SEF	M	1 yr HL		WO/213/23/179
Whincop AG	Dvr	337 Bde RFA	10/01/17	Canterbury	JM	6 mos Detn		WO/92/3/58
White A	Bdr	RGA	05/07/19	Aldershot	M	9 mos Detn+Rnks +Disch Igmny		WO/86/87/189
White A	Pte	5 Dragoon Gds	22/09/19	Curragh	M	1 yr HL+Disch Igmny	Comm 6 mos Detn	WO/92/4/81
White GE	Pte	1 Inf Bn AIF	15/10/18	Field	M+Des	3 yrs PS	Guilty of Des	WO/213/28/197
White HT	Pte	20 AIF	08/07/16	Field	M+Drunk	18 mos HL		WO/213/10/145
White J	Pte	2 W India	11/05/19	Field EEF	M	7 yrs PS	Comm 2 yrs HL	WO/213/30/28
White JE	Spr	Can Engrs	25/01/19	Field	M+Disob	NG		WO/213/29/55
White JH	L/Cpl	5 Dragoon Gds	29/09/19	Curragh	M	1 yr HL+Disch Igmny	Comm 6 mos Detn	WO/92/4/81
White JJ	Pte	RAOC	29/07/20	Field	M+S7(3b)	4 yrs PS		WO/213/32/22
White JK	Pte	5 Dragoon Gds	29/09/19	Curragh	M	1 yr HL+Disch Igmny	Comm 6 mos Detn	WO/92/4/82
White R	Pte	CARD	15/07/19	Witley	M+S40	2 mos Imp	Comm Detn	WO/86/88/19
White JW	Pte	1 R Dub Fus	24/03/19	Field	M	10 yrs PS		WO213/29/88
White W	Pte	4 Mddx	04/02/19	Rouen	M	Acquit		WO/90/8/58
Whitehall J	L/Bdr	RGA	04/07/19	Aldershot	M	9 mos Detn+Rnks +Disch Igmny		WO/86/87/188
Whitehead J	Pte	5 Dragoon Gds	22/09/19	Curragh	M	1 yr HL+Disch Igmny	Comm 6 mos Detn	WO/92/4/84
Whitehead W	Pte	5 Dragoon Gds	24/09/19	Curragh	M	1 yr HL+Disch Igmny	Comm 6 mos Detn	WO/92/4/86
Whitehouse AJ	Pte	30 MGC	29/07/19	Field	M+Disob	1 yr HL		WO/213/30/119
Whitelam G	Pte	Lab Corps (att E Comm LB)	15/06/19	Sutton	M+S7(3b)	Acquit		WO/92/4/73
Whiteman A	Pte	9 MGC	31/07/19	Field	M+Abs/Br	6 mos HL	Quashed	WO/213/30/141

Name	Rank	Unit	Date D/M/Y	Location	Offence	Finding/Punishment	Amendment	PRO Reference File/Piece/Page
Whitewood HF	Pte(2AM)	RAF	30/04/18	Swanage	M+Disob	9 mos HL		WO/92/4/42
Whittaker J	Pte	5 Dragoon Gds	22/09/19	Curragh	M	1 yr HL+Disch Igmny	Comm 6 mos Detn	WO/92/4/84
Whittaker T	Pte	5 Dragoon Gds	23/09/19	Curragh	M	1 yr HL+Disch Igmny	Comm 6 mos Detn	WO/92/4/85
Whittle J	Pte	21 Manch	08/02/19	Field	M+Abs	6 mos HL		WO/213/28/59
Whitton R	Pte	8 KOYLI	10/02/19	Field	M+Disob+S40	6 mos Imp	Quashed	WO/213/28/54
Wickham J	Pte	7 R Irish	15/04/18	Field	M	5 yrs PS	Susp	WO/213/21/98
Wild P	Pte	10 Hussars	25/01/21	Curragh	Mx2+S9(1)	1 yr Detn	Remit 3 mos	WO/92/4/94
Wiles C	Pte	2 W India	11/05/19	Field EEF	M	7 yrs PS	Comm 2 yrs HL	WO/213/30/27
Wilkinson A	Pte(2AM)	RAF	02/05/18	Swanage	M	Acquit		WO/92/4/37
Wilkinson J	Pte	1 Gn Sher Fstrs	05/06/17	Kantara Egypt	M	2 yrs HL		WO/213/15/178
Williams A	Pte	2 Gn/Beds	04/04/18	Karachi	M+S7(3)	2 yrs PS	Comm 12 mos Detn	WO/90/7/191
Williams A	Pte	4 BWI	27/12/18	Field Italy	M+Disob	3 yrs PS	Comm 2 yrs HL	WO/213/27/23
Williams B	Pte	5 Dragoon Gds	26/09/19	Curragh	M	1 yr HL+Disch Igmny	Comm 6 mos Detn	WO/92/4/83
Williams D	Dvr	RFA	23/05/21	Hinaidi	M+S9(1)	3 mos FP2		WO/213/33/16
Williams EJ	Pte	1 NZ Div Emp B	16/10/18	Field	M	NG		WO/213/25/165
Williams F	Pte	65 Coy RDC	21/11/16	Towcester	M	1 yr Detn		WO/92/4/3
Williams H	Dvr	ASC (SA)	23/07/18	Field	M	Life PS	Comm 5 yrs PS	WO/213/24/168
Williams J	Pte	1 Cape Corps	18/01/19	Mustapha	M+Disob	10 yrs PS	Comm 3 mos FP1	WO/213/28/61
Williams JA	Pte	RAMC	10/05/19	Field	M	6 mos HL	Comm 28 dys FP2	WO/213/30/17
Williams PH	Pte	5 Dragoon Gds	23/09/19	Curragh	M	84 dys HL	Comm 42 dys Detn	WO/92/4/85
Williams SG	Pte	1 Wellington NZEF	19/07/16	[Le] Havre	Per M+Viol SO	Acquit		WO/90/6/67
Williams T	Pte	47 R Fus (att 29 L'pool)	14/04/20	Field	M+S40	6 mos HL		WO/213/142
Williams TR	Pte	RGA	23/09/15	RGA	M+S40	1 yr HL		WO/90/6/35
Williams W	Pte(S/Smith)	ASC	30/12/15	Marseilles	Joining M	3 yrs PS	Comm to 2 yrs HL	WO/90/6/44
Williamson H	Gnr	RFA(att RGA)	13/03/18	Agra	M	1 yr HL	unexpired portion 30/4/18	WO/90/7/191
Williamson T	Pte	21 Manch	08/02/19	Field	M+Abs	NG		WO/213/28/59
Williamson T	Pte	8 KOYLI	10/02/19	Field	M+Disob+S40	5 yrs PS	Quashed	WO/213/28/54
Willis F	Pte	7 R Irish	15/04/18	Field	M	5 yrs PS	Susp	WO/213/21/97
Willis P	Pte(L/Cpl)	1 Connaught Rangers	25/08/20	Dagshai	M	3 yrs PS+DI		WO/90/8/188
Willis T	Dvr	2/3 Northern Bde AC/RFA	04/05/16	Bawtry	JM	3 yrs PS +Disch Igmny		WO/92/3/39
Willmott F	Pte	2/4 R Sussex TF	23/07/15	Canterbury	J[oin in] M	84 dys Detn		WO/92/3/24
Wilmot E	Pte	21 Manch	08/02/19	Field	M+Abs	6 mos HL		WO/213/28/58
Wilmot E	Dvr	372 Coy CAHT	14/05/19	Field	M	5 yrs PS	Remit 2 yrs	WO/213/30/11
Wilson A	L/Cpl	RE	04/02/19	Field	M+S40	15 mos HL		WO/213/28/46
Wilson A	Cpl	3 Dorsets	29/12/14	Dorchester	Joining M+Viol(Capt)	6 mos HL		WO/92/3/18
Wilson A	Pte	8 R Innis Fus	06/09/15	Eniskillen	M+Inj pub property	1 yr HL		WO/86/66/111
Wilson C	Pte	2/4 R Sussex TF	23/07/15	Canterbury	J[oin in] M	84 dys Detn		WO/92/3/24
Wilson D	Spr	RE	09/05/19	Field Italy	M	2 yrs HL	Remit 20 mos/ Quashed	WO/213/29/73
Wilson D	Pte	5 Dragoon Gds	22/09/19	Curragh	M	1 yr HL+Disch Igmny	Comm 6 mos Detn	WO/92/4/84
Wilson F	Pte	Can ASC	28/02/19	Bramshott	M	6 mos Detn	Comm 28 dys Detn	WO/86/87/17
Wilson G	Pte	2 W India	11/05/19	Field EEF	M	7 yrs PS	Comm 1 yr HL	WO/213/30/28
Wilson JHC	Pte	4 AIF	24/03/19	Field	M	11 yrs PS		WO/213/29/90
Wilson RH	Spr	Can Engrs	25/01/19	Field	M+Disob	NG		WO/213/29/55I
Wilson W	Cpl	7/8 R Innis Fus	15/04/18	Field	M	10 yrs PS	Susp	WO/213/21/95
Wilson W	Pte	7 R Irish	15/04/18	Field	M	5 yrs PS	Susp	WO/213/21/98
Winchester R	Pte	1 Inf Bn AIF	15/10/18	Field	M+Des	3 yrs PS	Guilty of Des	WO/213/28/197
Winder T	Pte	2/4 R Sussex TF	23/07/15	Canterbury	J[oin in] M	84 dys Detn		WO/92/3/24
Winter C	Gnr	RGA	13/03/18	Agra	M	1 yr HL	unexpired portion 30/4/18	WO/90/7/191
Wirth J	Spr	Can Eng	05/05/19	Liverpool	M	Acquit		WO/92/4/67
Woiters FC	Pte	2 R Sussex Regt	28/02/19	Field	M+Esc	1 yr HL		WO/213/28/157
Wolfe WG	Pte	30 MGC	29/07/19	Field	M+Disob	1 yr HL		WO/213/30/11
Wood R	Bdr	RGA	05/07/19	Aldershot	M	NG		WO/86/88/1
Wood A	Gnr	RGA	13/03/18	Agra	M	1 yr HL	unexpired portion 30/4/18	WO/90/7/190
Wood GW	Pte	2/6 R Wars	27/05/19	Field	M+S40	2 yrs HL	Remit 1 yr	WO/213/30/64
Wood H	Pte	5 Dragoon Gds	29/09/19	Curragh	M	1 yr HL+Disch Igmny	Comm 6 mos Detn	WO/92/4/82

Name	Rank	Unit	Date D/M/Y	Location	Offence	Finding/Punishment	Amendment	PRO Reference File/Piece/Page
Wood LS	Gnr	RGA	13/03/18	Agra	M	1 yr HL	unexpired portion 30/4/18	WO/90/7/190
Wood W	Pte	12 SWBdrs	05/12/16	Field	M+Disob	NG		WO/312/13/30
Woodbury PA	Pte	1 Aus Pnr Bn	24/03/19	Field	M	9 yrs PS		WO/213/29/89
Woodford A	Pte	1 Inf Bn AIF	15/10/18	Field	M+Des	3 yrs PS	Guilty of Des	WO/213/28/196
Woodgate F	Pte	2/4 R Sussex TF	23/07/15	Canterbury	J[oin in] M	84 dys Detn		WO/92/3/24
Woodhead E	Cpl	257 P of W Coy	13/05/19	Field	M+S40(2)	9 mos HL+Rnks		WO/213/30/31
Woodietts H	Pte	2/4 R Sussex TF	23/07/15	Canterbury	J[oin in] M	84 dys Detn		WO/92/3/24
Woodman C	L/Bdr	RGA	04/07/19	Aldershot	M	9 mos Detn+Rnks +Disch Igmny		WO/86/87/189
Woods G	Pte	65 Coy RDC	21/11/16	Towcester	M	1 yr Detn		WO/92/4/2
Woods H	L/Bdr	RGA	05/07/19	Aldershot	M	9 mos Detn+Rnks +Disch Igmny		WO/86/87/189
Woods J	Pte(L/Cpl)	7/8 R Innis Fus	15/04/18	Field	M	7 yrs PS	Susp	WO/213/21/95
Woods J	Sgt	1 Connaught Rangers	25/08/20	Dagshai	M	10 yrs PS+Rnks +DI+Forfeit MM	Remit 2 yrs	WO/90/8/188
Woodworth GW	Gnr	RGA	13/03/18	Agra	M	Acquit		WO/90/7/191
Wormald S	Pte	2 MGC	12/06/19	Field	M+Disob(2)+S40	5 yrs PS	Remit 2 yrs	WO/213/29/122
Wragg GW	Pte	5 Dragoon Gds	24/09/19	Curragh	M	1 yr HL+Disch Igmny	Comm 6 mos Detn	WO/92/4/87
Wraith E	Pte	2 York & Lanc	16/07/20	Kasvin	M	1 yr HL		WO/90/7/208
Wright A	Dvr	RFA	23/05/21	Hinaidi	M+S9(1)	3 mos FP2		WO/213/33/15
Wright F	Pte	3 Essex	09/05/19	Field Italy	M	3 yrs PS	Comm 4 mos HL	WO/213/29/73
Wright GCM	Bdr (A/Cpl)	RFA	14/07/19	Field	M+7(2)	6 mos HL+Rnks		WO/213/30/81
Wright H	Pte	Can ASC	28/02/19	Bramshott	M	NG		WO/86/87/17
Wright J	Gnr/L/Bdr	RFA	12/05/18	Field	M	1 yr HL	Susp	WO/213/22/153
Wright M	Pte	3 Leics	27/08/14	Portsmouth	M	1 yr HL		WO/213/2/2
Wright W	Pnr	RE	09/05/19	Field Italy	M	2 yrs HL	Remit 20 mos/ Quashed	WO/213/29/73
Wright WS	Pte	5 Dragoon Gds	23/09/19	Curragh	M	84 dys HL	Comm 42 dys Detn	WO/92/4/85
Wrigley L	Rfn	12(S) Rifle Bde	19/11/18	Field	M+Abs+S40	28 dys FP1		WO/213/26/49
Wtsoane G	Pte	SANLC	17/12/17	Capetown	M	10 yrs PS		WO/213/19/115
Yard B	Pte	9 (S) BWI	24/12/18	Field Italy	M+Disob+Esc	5 yrs PS		WO/213/27/25
Yard F	Pte	7/8 R Innis Fus	15/04/18	Field	M	5 yrs PS	Susp	WO/213/21/94
Yates F	Pte	Lab Corps	24/03/19	Field	M	10 yrs PS		WO/213/29/91
Yates J	Pte	1 Gn Sher Fstrs	05/06/17	Kantara Egypt	M	2 yrs HL		WO/213/15/178
Yates J	Pte	2/4 R Sussex TF	23/07/15	Canterbury	J[oin in] M	84 dys Detn		WO/92/3/24
Yeadon C[A/R?]	Pte	19 AIF	15/02/16	Sinai Penin	M+Disob	18 mos HL		WO/213/8/113
Young A	Pte	5 Dragoon Gds	24/09/19	Curragh	M	1 yr HL+Disch Igmny	Comm 6 mos Detn	WO/92/4/86
Young B	Pte	Can ASC	21/11/17	Bramshott	M+Insub(Lieut)	42 dys Detn	Remit 15 dys	WO/86/79/53
Young C	L/Bdr	RGA	05/07/19	Aldershot	M	9 mos Detn+Rnks +Disch Igmny		WO/86/87/189
Young CF	Pte	5 Dragoon Gds	29/09/19	Curragh	M	1 yr HL+Disch Igmny	Comm 6 mos Detn	WO/92/4/82
Young FG	Pte	7/8 R Innis Fus	15/04/18	Field	M	NG		WO/213/21/96
Young LS	Pte	1 Inf Bn AIF	15/10/18	Field	M+Des	3 yrs PS	Guilty of Des	WO/213/28/195
Yoxall T	Pte	7/8 R Innis Fus	15/04/18	Field	M	5 yrs PS	Susp	WO/213/21/94
Zamasthansky N	Pte	39 R Fus	23/08/19	Field EEF	M	5 yrs PS		WO/213/31/23
Zorowski N	Pte	39 R Fus	23/08/19	Field EEF	M	5 yrs PS		WO/213/31/23
Zotzman A	Pte	8(R) CEF	11/09/17	Shorncliffe	M+S40(3)	9 mos Detn	Quashed	WO/86/78/26
Zouev AM	2 Lt	1 Slav-Brit Legion	15/07/19	Field	M	Acquit	No evidence	WO/90/8/85

List by unit of men charged with mutiny

Unit	Rank	Name	Location	Date D/M/Y	Offence	Finding/Punishment	Amendment	PRO Reference File/Piece/Page
Australian								
1 Inf Bn AIF	Cpl	Alyward AE	Field	15/10/18	M+Des	10 yrs PS+Rnks	Guilty of Des	WO/213/28/180
1 Inf Bn AIF	Pte	Anderson EH	Field	15/10/18	M+Des	3 yrs PS	Guilty of Des	WO/213/28/200
1 Inf Bn AIF	Pte	Atoff M	Field	15/10/18	M+Des	3 yrs PS	Guilty of Des	WO/213/28/199
1 Inf Bn AIF	Pte	Austin HC	Field	15/10/18	M+Des	3 yrs PS	Guilty of Des	WO/213/28/199
1 Inf Bn AIF	Pte	Baker B	Field	15/10/18	M+Des	3 yrs PS	Guilty of Des	WO/213/28/197
1 Inf Bn AIF	Pte	Barclay AS	Field	15/10/18	M+Des	3 yrs PS	Guilty of Des	WO/213/28/197
1 Inf Bn AIF	Pte (L/Cpl)	Bardney R	Field	15/10/18	M+Des	8 yrs PS	Guilty of Des	WO/213/28/199
1 Inf Bn AIF	Pte	Barnes WH	Field	15/10/18	M+Des	3 yrs PS	Guilty of Des	WO/213/28/196
1 Inf Bn AIF	Pte	Barnett A	Field	15/10/18	M+Des	3 yrs PS	Guilty of Des	WO/213/30/44
1 Inf Bn AIF	Pte	Beckman EG	Field	15/10/18	M+Des	3 yrs PS	Guilty of Des	WO/213/28/200
1 Inf Bn AIF	Pte (L/Cpl)	Beggs R	Field	15/10/18	M+Des	5 yrs PS	Guilty of Des	WO/213/28/199
1 Inf Bn AIF	Pte	Bennett C	Field	15/10/18	M+Des	3 yrs PS	Guilty of Des	WO/213/28/107
1 Inf Bn AIF	Pte (L/Cpl)	Besley EA	Field	15/10/18	M+Des	10 yrs PS	Guilty of Des	WO/213/28/200
1 Inf Bn AIF	L/Cpl (T/Cpl)	Blackwood TJ	Field	15/10/18	M+Des	8 yrs PS+Rnks	Guilty of Des	WO/213/28/199
1 Inf Bn AIF	Pte	Boland E	Field	15/10/18	M+Des	3 yrs PS	Guilty of Des	WO/213/28/200
1 Inf Bn AIF	Pte	Bootle WJ	Field	15/10/18	M+Des	3 yrs PS	Guilty of Des	WO/213/28/197
1 Inf Bn AIF	Cpl	Brisset J	Field	15/10/18	M+Des+Abs	Rnks	G of Abs	WO/213/30/56
1 Inf Bn AIF	Pte	Brandon CS	Field	15/10/18	M+Des	3 yrs PS	Guilty of Des	WO/213/28/196
1 Inf Bn AIF	Pte (L/Cpl)	Brown PG	Field	15/10/18	M+Des	NG		WO/213/28/200
1 Inf Bn AIF	Pte	Bruce DG	Field	15/10/18	M+Des	3 yrs PS	Guilty of Des	WO/213/28/197
1 Inf Bn AIF	Pte	Burgess A	Field	15/10/18	M+Des	3 yrs PS	Guilty of Des	WO/213/28/197
1 Inf Bn AIF	Pte	Carmody O	Field	15/10/18	M+Des	3 yrs PS	Guilty of Des	WO/213/28/197
1 Inf Bn AIF	Pte (L/Cpl)	Carr SF	Field	15/10/18	M+Des	5 yrs PS	Guilty of Des	WO/213/28/198
1 Inf Bn AIF	Pte	Carroll F	Field	15/10/18	M+Des	3 yrs PS	Guilty of Des	WO/213/28/198
1 Inf Bn AIF	Pte	Case W	Field	15/10/18	M+Des	3 yrs PS	Guilty of Des	WO/213/28/198
1 Inf Bn AIF	Pte	Casey AB	Field	15/10/18	M+Des	3 yrs PS	Guilty of Des	WO/213/28/199
1 Inf Bn AIF	Pte	Cheeseman CH	Field	15/10/18	M+Des	3 yrs PS	Guilty of Des	WO/213/28/197
1 Inf Bn AIF	Pte	Clark HS	Field	15/10/18	M+Des	NG		WO/213/28/198
1 Inf Bn AIF	Pte	Clift A	Field	15/10/18	M+Des	3 yrs PS	Guilty of Des	WO/213/28/198
1 Inf Bn AIF	Pte	Cook GM	Field	15/10/18	M+Des	3 yrs PS	Guilty of Des	WO/213/28/198
1 Inf Bn AIF	Cpl	Cooney R	Field	15/10/18	M+Des	8 yrs PS+Rnks	Guilty of Des	WO/213/28/200
1 Inf Bn AIF	Pte	Cooper AH	Field	15/10/18	M+Des	3 yrs PS	Guilty of Des	WO/213/28/180
1 Inf Bn AIF	Pte	Coughlin HB	Field	15/10/18	M+Des	3 yrs PS	Guilty of Des	WO/213/28/197
1 Inf Bn AIF	Pte	Couley JJ [MM]	Field	15/10/18	M+Des	3 yrs PS	Guilty of Des	WO/213/28/197
1 Inf Bn AIF	Pte	Creith BW	Field	15/10/18	M+Des	3 yrs PS	Guilty of Des	WO/213/28/196
1 Inf Bn AIF	Pte (L/Cpl)	Davis EB	Field	15/10/18	M+Des	3 yrs PS	Guilty of Des	WO/213/28/198
1 Inf Bn AIF	Pte(L/Cpl)	Dawson JR	Field	15/10/18	M+Des	5 yrs PS	Guilty of Des	WO/213/28/180
1 Inf Bn AIF	Pte	Delaney AF	Field	15/10/18	M+Des	3 yrs PS	Guilty of Des	WO/213/28/180
1 Inf Bn AIF	Pte	Dick CE	Field	15/10/18	M+Des	3 yrs PS	Guilty of Des	WO/213/28/197
1 Inf Bn AIF	Pte	Dobbie RR	Field	15/10/18	M+Des	3 yrs PS	Guilty of Des	WO/213/28/197
1 Inf Bn AIF	Pte	Downton NJ	Field	15/10/18	M+Des	3 yrs PS	Guilty of Des	WO/213/28/197
1 Inf Bn AIF	Pte	Doyle NA	Field	15/10/18	M+Des	3 yrs PS	Guilty of Des	WO/213/28/197
1 Inf Bn AIF	Pte	Dunne AW	Field	15/10/18	M+Des	3 yrs PS	Guilty of Des	WO/213/28/199
1 Inf Bn AIF	Pte	Earle J	Field	15/10/18	Mx2+Des	3 yrs PS	Guilty of Des	WO/213/28/196
1 Inf Bn AIF	Pte	Ellen J	Field	15/10/18	M+Des	3 yrs PS	Guilty of Des	WO/213/28/197
1 Inf Bn AIF	Pte	Ellis AJ	Field	15/10/18	M+Des	NG		WO/213/28/198
1 Inf Bn AIF	Pte	Faulkner WH	Field	15/10/18	M+Des	3 yrs PS	Guilty of Des	WO/213/28/197
1 Inf Bn AIF	Pte	Fish EW	Field	15/10/18	M+Des	3 yrs PS	Guilty of Des	WO/213/28/196
1 Inf Bn AIF	Pte	Flynn M	Field	15/10/18	M+Des	3 yrs PS	Guilty of Des	WO/213/28/199
1 Inf Bn AIF	Pte	Garrett JC	Field	15/10/18	M+Des	3 yrs PS	Guilty of Des	WO/213/28/196
1 Inf Bn AIF	Pte (L/Cpl)	Gavin AR	Field	15/10/18	M+Des	NG		WO/213/28/200
1 Inf Bn AIF	Pte	Glover JH	Field	15/10/18	M+Des	3 yrs PS	Guilty of Des	WO/213/28/200
1 Inf Bn AIF	Pte	Goggins DH	Field	15/10/18	M+Des	3 yrs PS	Guilty of Des	WO/213/28/199
1 Inf Bn AIF	Pte	Grubb J	Field	15/10/18	M+Des	3 yrs PS	Guilty of Des	WO/213/28/199
1 Inf Bn AIF	Pte (L/Cpl)	Guilfoyle H	Field	15/10/18	M+Des	NG		WO/213/28/200
1 Inf Bn AIF	Pte	Ham EH	Field	15/10/18	M+Des	5 yrs PS	Guilty of Des	WO/213/28/196
1 Inf Bn AIF	Pte	Hancock HT	Field	15/10/18	M+Des	3 yrs PS	Guilty of Des	WO/213/28/196
1 Inf Bn AIF	Pte	Harragon WL	Field	15/10/18	M+Des	3 yrs PS	Guilty of Des	WO/213/28/196
1 Inf Bn AIF	Cpl (L/Sgt)	Hasthorpe M	Field	15/10/18	M+Des	10 yrs PS+Rnks	Guilty of Des	WO/213/28/180
1 Inf Bn AIF	Pte	Hiscock C	Field	15/10/18	M+Des	3 yrs PS	Guilty of Des	WO/213/28/180

Unit	Rank	Name	Location	Date D/M/Y	Offence	Finding/Punishment	Amendment	PRO Reference File/Piece/Page
1 Inf Bn AIF	Pte	Holmes WJ	Field	15/10/18	M+Des	NG		WO/213/28/198
1 Inf Bn AIF	Pte	Horden TC	Field	15/10/18	M+Des	3 yrs PS	Guilty of Des	WO/213/28/198
1 Inf Bn AIF	Pte (L/Cpl)	Humphreys DW	Field	15/10/18	M+Des	5 yrs PS	Guilty of Des	WO/213/28/197
1 Inf Bn AIF	Pte	Hunt SJ	Field	15/10/18	M+Des	3 yrs PS	Guilty of Des	WO/213/28/199
1 Inf Bn AIF	Pte	James W	Field	15/10/18	M+Des	3 yrs PS	Guilty of Des	WO/213/28/199
1 Inf Bn AIF	Pte	Jeffries H	Field	15/10/18	M+Des	3 yrs PS	Guilty of Des	WO/213/28/197
1 Inf Bn AIF	Pte	Johnstone CJ	Field	15/10/18	M+Des	3 yrs PS	Guilty of Des	WO/213/28/199
1 Inf Bn AIF	Pte	Lang PTB	Field	15/10/18	M+Des	3 yrs PS	Guilty of Des	WO/213/28/196
1 Inf Bn AIF	Pte	Laughrey GA	Field	15/10/18	M+Des	3 yrs PS	Guilty of Des	WO/213/28/200
1 Inf Bn AIF	Pte (L/Cpl)	Lavendar G	Field	15/10/18	M+Des	NG		WO/213/28/200
1 Inf Bn AIF	Pte	Lawrence A	Field	15/10/18	M+Des	3 yrs PS	Guilty of Des	WO/213/28/196
1 Inf Bn AIF	Pte	Lawrence J	Field	15/10/18	M+Des	3 yrs PS	Guilty of Des	WO/213/28/196
1 Inf Bn AIF	Pte	Lindsay GS	Field	15/10/18	M+Des	3 yrs PS	Guilty of Des	WO/213/28/197
1 Inf Bn AIF	Pte	Mackey M	Field	15/10/18	M+Des	3 yrs PS	Guilty of Des	WO/213/28/196
1 Inf Bn AIF	Pte	Marshall ACO	Field	15/10/18	M+Des	3 yrs PS	Guilty of Des	WO/213/28/196
1 Inf Bn AIF	Pte	Martin W	Field	15/10/18	M+Des	3 yrs PS	Guilty of Des	WO/213/28/198
1 Inf Bn AIF	Cpl	McKay RHC	Field	15/10/18	M+Des	10 yrs PS+Rnks	Guilty of Des	WO/213/28/199
1 Inf Bn AIF	Pte	McNamee JB	Field	15/10/18	M+Des	3 yrs PS	Guilty of Des	WO/213/28/199
1 Inf Bn AIF	Pte	Miller DM	Field	15/10/18	M+Des	3 yrs PS	Guilty of Des	WO/213/28/198
1 Inf Bn AIF	Pte	Moran JA	Field	15/10/18	M+Des	3 yrs PS	Guilty of Des	WO/213/28/198
1 Inf Bn AIF	Pte (L/Cpl)	Muir CW	Field	15/10/18	M+Des	5 yrs PS	Guilty of Des	WO/213/28/197
1 Inf Bn AIF	Pte	Mullins A	Field	15/10/18	M+Des	3 yrs PS	Guilty of Des	WO/213/28/195
1 Inf Bn AIF	Pte	Murphy T	Field	15/10/18	M+Des	3 yrs PS	Guilty of Des	WO/213/28/195
1 Inf Bn AIF	Pte	Noon J	Field	15/10/18	M+Des	3 yrs PS	Guilty of Des	WO/213/28/197
1 Inf Bn AIF	Pte	O'Connell WL	Field	15/10/18	M+Des	NG		WO/213/28/198
1 Inf Bn AIF	Pte	Orr E	Field	15/10/18	M+Des	3 yrs PS	Guilty of Des	WO/213/28/200
1 Inf Bn AIF	Pte	Page G	Field	15/10/18	M+Des	3 yrs PS	Guilty of Des	WO/213/28/198
1 Inf Bn AIF	Pte	Palmer TG	Field	15/10/18	M+Des	3 yrs PS	Guilty of Des	WO/213/28/199
1 Inf Bn AIF	Pte	Parish EC	Field	15/10/18	M+Des	3 yrs PS	Guilty of Des	WO/213/28/198
1 Inf Bn AIF	Pte	Paton PP	Field	15/10/18	M+Des	NG		WO/213/28/198
1 Inf Bn AIF	Pte	Patten JC	Field	15/10/18	M+Des	3 yrs PS	Guilty of Des	WO/213/28/196
1 Inf Bn AIF	Pte (L/Cpl)	Pettit LW	Field	15/10/18	M+Des	5 yrs PS	Guilty of Des	WO/213/28/198
1 Inf Bn AIF	Pte	Phillips H	Field	15/10/18	M+Des	3 yrs PS	Guilty of Des	WO/213/28/198
1 Inf Bn AIF	Cpl	Pittock WH	Field	15/10/18	M+Des	8 yrs PS+Rnks	Guilty of Des	WO/213/28/197
1 Inf Bn AIF	Pte (L/Cpl)	Porter EM	Field	15/10/18	M+Des	3 yrs PS	Guilty of Des	WO/213/28/199
1 Inf Bn AIF	Pte (L/Cpl)	Preston EC	Field	15/10/18	M+Des	5 yrs PS	Guilty of Des	WO/213/28/196
1 Inf Bn AIF	Pte	Roberts WR	Field	15/10/18	M+Des	3 yrs PS	Guilty of Des	WO/213/28/198
1 Inf Bn AIF	Pte	Robinson AW	Field	15/10/18	M+Des	3 yrs PS	Guilty of Des	WO/213/28/199
1 Inf Bn AIF	Pte	Robson WJ	Field	15/10/18	M+Des	3 yrs PS	Guilty of Des	WO/213/28/196
1 Inf Bn AIF	Pte	Rogers RS	Field	15/10/18	M+Des	3 yrs PS	Guilty of Des	WO/213/28/199
1 Inf Bn AIF	Pte	Ronson C	Field	15/10/18	M+Des	3 yrs PS	Guilty of Des	WO/213/28/196
1 Inf Bn AIF	Pte	Rook AJ	Field	15/10/18	M+Des	3 yrs PS	Guilty of Des	WO/213/28/198
1 Inf Bn AIF	Pte	Ross AS	Field	15/10/18	M+Des	NG		WO/213/28/198
1 Inf Bn AIF	Pte	Selmes LJ	Field	15/10/18	M+Des	3 yrs PS	Guilty of Des	WO/213/28/196
1 Inf Bn AIF	Pte	Settle J	Field	15/10/18	M+Des	3 yrs PS	Guilty of Des	WO/213/28/198
1 Inf Bn AIF	Pte	Shirvington C	Field	15/10/18	M+Des	3 yrs PS	Guilty of Des	WO/213/28/197
1 Inf Bn AIF	Pte	Sidebotham WE	Field	15/10/18	M+Des	NG		WO/213/28/198
1 Inf Bn AIF	L/Cpl (T/Cpl)	Slater H	Field	15/10/18	M+Des	7 yrs PS+Rnks	Guilty of Des	WO/213/28/198
1 Inf Bn AIF	Cpl	Smith FR	Field	15/10/18	M+Des	8 yrs PS+Rnks	Guilty of Des	WO/213/28/199
1 Inf Bn AIF	Pte	Smith TR	Field	15/10/18	M+Des	3 yrs PS	Guilty of Des	WO/213/28/196
1 Inf Bn AIF	Pte	Stafford R	Field	15/10/18	M+Des	3 yrs PS	Guilty of Des	WO/213/28/198
1 Inf Bn AIF	Pte (L/Cpl)	Steele DN	Field	15/10/18	M+Des	5 yrs PS	Guilty of Des	WO/213/28/196
1 Inf Bn AIF	Pte	Stokes EF	Field	15/10/18	M+Des	3 yrs PS	Guilty of Des	WO/213/28/198
1 Inf Bn AIF	Cpl	Taplin RC	Field	15/10/18	M+Des	10 yrs PS+Rnks	Guilty of Des	WO/213/28/199
1 Inf Bn AIF	Pte	Tickner HH	Field	15/10/18	M+Des	3 yrs PS	Guilty of Des	WO/213/28/195
1 Inf Bn AIF	Pte	Travers WF	Field	15/10/18	M+Des	3 yrs PS	Guilty of Des	WO/213/28/196
1 Inf Bn AIF	Pte	Vaught R	Field	15/10/18	M+Des	3 yrs PS	Guilty of Des	WO/213/28/200
1 Inf Bn AIF	Pte	Vidler WT	Field	15/10/18	M+Des	3 yrs PS	Guilty of Des	WO/213/28/196
1 Inf Bn AIF	Pte	Voysey E	Field	15/10/18	M+Des	3 yrs PS	Guilty of Des	WO/213/28/199
1 Inf Bn AIF	Pte (L/Cpl)	Walker E	Field	15/10/18	M+Des	5 yrs PS	Guilty of Des	WO/213/28/199
1 Inf Bn AIF	Cpl	Wethered GF	Field	15/10/18	M+Des	8 yrs PS+Rnks	Guilty of Des	WO/213/28/195
1 Inf Bn AIF	Pte	Whatmore T	Field	15/10/18	M+Des	3 yrs PS	Guilty of Des	WO/213/28/197
1 Inf Bn AIF	Pte	White GE	Field	15/10/18	M+Des	3 yrs PS	Guilty of Des	WO/213/28/197
1 Inf Bn AIF	Pte	Winchester R	Field	15/10/18	M+Des	3 yrs PS	Guilty of Des	WO/213/28/197
1 Inf Bn AIF	Pte	Woodford A	Field	15/10/18	M+Des	3 yrs PS	Guilty of Des	WO/213/28/196
1 Inf Bn AIF	Pte	Young LS	Field	15/10/18	M+Des	3 yrs PS	Guilty of Des	WO/213/28/195
2 AIF	Pte	Cambridge JG	Rouen	24/03/19	M	10 yrs PS		WO/90/8/59
2 AIF	Pte	Crooks R	Field	24/03/19	M	10 yrs PS		WO/213/29/91
2 AIF	Pte	Fitzgerald NJ	Field	18/06/19	M+Disob	14 mos HL		WO/213/29/91
2 AIF	Pte	O'Sullivan C	Field	04/02/19	M	3 yrs 6 mos PS		WO/213/30/131
2 AIF	Pte	Travis R	Field	18/06/19	M+Disob	2 yrs HL		WO/213/30/131
3 AIF	Pte	Blackwood PE	Field	24/03/19	M	11 yrs PS		WO/213/29/91
4 AIF	Pte	Hayes L	Field	24/03/19	M	10 yrs PS		WO/213/29/89
4 AIF	Pte	Lavender G	Rouen	04/02/19	M	90 dys Imp		WO/90/8/58

Unit	Rank	Name	Location	Date D/M/Y	Offence	Finding/Punishment	Amendment	PRO Reference File/Piece/Page
4 AIF	Pte	Pascoe EJ	Field	24/03/19	M	9 yrs PS		WO/213/29/91
4 AIF	Pte	Pierce HE	Field	24/03/19	M	12 yrs PS		WO/213/29/89
4 AIF	Pte	Sheffield S	Rouen	11/10/16	M	Death	Comm 2 yrs HL	WO/90/6/90
4 AIF	Pte	Wilson JHC	Field	24/03/19	M	11 yrs PS		WO/213/29/90
5 AIF	Pte(L/Cpl)	Doxford TR	Field	22/12/18	M	NG		WO/213/27/184
5 AIF	Pte	Mitchell FKW	Rouen	11/10/16	M	Death	Comm 2 yrs HL	WO/90/6/90
5 AIF	Pte	Richards AA	Field	18/06/19	M+Disob	5 mos HL		WO/213/30/131
7 AIF	Pte	Harrison LR	Field	24/03/19	M	10 yrs PS		WO/213/29/89
8 AIF	Pte	Heggart TH	Field	22/12/18	M	5 yrs PS		WO/213/29/90
8 AIF	Pte	Guthrie M	Field	04/02/19	M	90 dys Imp		WO/213/27/184
8 AIF	Pte	Kirkby JK	Rouen	24/03/19	M	10 yrs PS		WO/90/8/58
8 AIF	Pte	Brock JJ	Field	24/03/19	M	12 yrs PS		WO/213/29/90
8 AIF	Pte	Grant CC	Field	24/03/19	M	9 yrs PS		WO/213/29/89
9 AIF	Pte	McCallan GH	Field	24/03/19	M	11 yrs PS		WO/213/29/89
9 AIF	Pte	Stirling H	Field	24/03/19	M	10 yrs PS		WO/213/29/90
10 AIF	Pte	Rattigan F	Malta	24/09/15	M+S40	NG		WO/90/6/35
10 AIF	Pte	Cregg CD	Field	24/03/19	M	10 yrs PS		WO213/29/88
10 AIF	Pte	Little A	Rouen	11/10/16	M+Striking(Sgt)	Death	Comm 2 yrs HL	WO/90/6/89
10 AIF	Pte	Malthouse SHJ	Field	24/03/19	M	10 yrs PS		WO213/29/88
10 AIF	Dvr	McLeod R	Field	18/06/19	M+Disob	19 mos HL		WO/213/30/131
10 AIF	Pte	Wallis P	Field	24/03/19	M	11 yrs PS		WO/213/29/91
12 AIF	Pte	Gallagher P	Field	24/03/19	M	10 yrs PS		WO/213/29/90
13 AIF	Pte	Kembrey A	Rouen	04/02/19	M	3 yrs 9 mos PS		WO/90/8/59
13 AIF	Pte	Stephenson WA	Field	24/03/19	M	11 yrs PS		WO/213/29/89
14 AIF	Pte	Doyle D	Field	24/03/19	M	9 yrs PS		WO/213/29/90
14 AIF	Pte	Fraser HA	Field	24/03/19	M	11 yrs PS		WO/213/29/90
14 AIF	Pte	Le Guier B	Rouen	11/10/16	M	Death	Comm 2 yrs HL	WO/90/6/90
14 AIF	Pte	McNally J	Rouen	04/02/19	M	90 dys Imp		WO/90/8/59
14 AIF	Pte	Wallace J	Field	24/03/19	M	11 yrs PS		WO/213/29/90
15 AIF	Pte	Heffernan PJ	Field	24/03/19	M	11 yrs PS		WO213/29/88
15 AIF	Pte	Nassau H	Rouen	04/02/19	M	28 dys Imp		WO/90/8/59
15 AIF	Pte	Rollason HH	Field	24/03/19	M	9 yrs PS		WO/213/29/91
17 AIF	Pte	Baldwin GE	Field	24/03/19	M	8 yrs PS		WO/213/29/91
17 AIF	Pte	Brown R	Field	24/03/19	M	11 yrs PS		WO/213/29/90
17 AIF	Pte	Cranes CA	Field	24/03/19	M	11 yrs PS		WO/213/29/90
17 AIF	Pte	Foster WA	Field	24/03/19	M	10 yrs PS		WO/213/29/90
18 AIF	Pte	Daly T	[Le] Havre	19/07/16	Per M+Viol SO	Acquit		WO/90/6/67
18 AIF	Pte	Moss EJ	[Le] Havre	19/07/16	Per M+Viol SO	5 yrs PS		WO/90/6/67
18 AIF	Pte	Murphy R	[Le] Havre	19/07/16	Per M+Viol SO	5 yrs PS		WO/90/6/67
18 AIF	Pte	Lyons P	Rouen	04/02/19	M	3 yrs 9 mos PS		WO/90/8/59
18 AIF	Pte	Brissenden CL	Field	24/03/19	M	10 yrs PS		WO/213/29/90
18 AIF	Pte	O'Neill P	Field	24/03/19	M	9 yrs PS		WO/213/29/91
18 AIF	Pte	Rogers E	Field	24/03/19	M	11 yrs PS		WO/213/29/89
19 AIF	Pte	Alcock MG	Sinai Penin	15/02/16	M+Disob	18 mos HL		WO/213/8/113
19 AIF	Pte	Anderson AG	Sinai Penin	15/02/16	M+Disob	18 mos HL		WO/213/8/113
19 AIF	Pte	Clarke H	Sinai Penin	24/03/19	M	11 yrs PS		WO/213/8/113
19 AIF	Pte	Fletcher WJ	Sinai Penin	15/02/16	M+Disob	12 mos HL		WO/213/8/113
19 AIF	Pte	Goodwin LR	Sinai Penin	24/03/19	M	10 yrs PS		WO/213/8/113
19 AIF	Pte	Hill P	Sinai Penin	15/02/16	M+Disob	18 mos HL		WO/213/8/113
19 AIF	Pte	King EJ	Sinai Penin	15/02/16	M+Disob	18 mos HL		WO/213/8/113
19 AIF	Pte	Mead S	Sinai Penin	24/03/19	M	11 yrs PS		WO/213/8/113
19 AIF	Pte	Rowlands TJ	Field	15/02/16	M+Disob	12 mos HL		WO/213/29/89
19 AIF	Cpl	Walker JA	Field	15/02/16	M+Disob	3 yrs HL		WO/213/29/91
19 AIF	Pte	Yeadon C[A/R?]	Field	15/02/16	M+Disob	18 mos HL		WO/213/29/90
20 AIF	Pte	Devenish JE	Field	24/03/19	M	11 yrs PS		WO/213/29/90
20 AIF	Pte	Hancock GC	Field	24/03/19	M	11 yrs PS		WO213/29/88
20 AIF	Pte	White HT	Field	08/07/16	M+Drunk	18 mos HL		WO/213/10/145
21 AIF	Pte	Donkin RB	Rouen	04/02/19	M	56 dys Imp		WO/90/8/58
22 AIF	Pte	Baines CD	Field	24/03/19	M	10 yrs PS		WO/213/29/91
22 AIF	Pte	Hutchinson G	Rouen	04/02/19	M	3 yrs 3 mos PS		WO/90/8/59
22 AIF	Pte	Higgins F	Field	24/03/19	M	No Finding/Sentence		WO/213/29/89
23 AIF	Pte	Bunting C	Rouen	24/03/19	M	13 yrs PS		WO/90/8/58
23 AIF	Pte	Butters RE	Rouen	04/02/19	M	90 dys Imp		WO/90/8/58
23 AIF	Pte	Nicholls AW	Field	24/03/19	M	11 yrs PS		WO/213/29/89
23 AIF	Pte	Sheppard H	Field	04/02/19	M	90 dys Imp		WO213/28/88
23 AIF	Pte	Watkins JB	Field	24/03/19	M	11 yrs PS		WO/213/29/90
24 AIF	Pte	McNeill HS	Field	22/12/18	M	NG		WO/213/27/184
25 AIF	Pte	Anderson TG	Field	24/03/19	M	8 yrs PS		WO/213/29/89
25 AIF	Pte	Burn AE	Field	24/03/19	M	12 yrs PS		WO/213/29/89
25 AIF	Pte	McDonnell C	Field	24/03/19	M	11 yrs PS		WO/213/29/91
26 AIF	Pte	Biddle LH	Rouen	04/02/19	M	56 dys Imp		WO/90/8/59
27 AIF	Pte	Gay EH	Field	24/03/19	M	10 yrs PS		WO213/29/88
28 AIF	Pte (L/Cpl)	Hansen AJ	Field	22/12/18	M	4 yrs PS		WO/213/27/184
30 AIF	Pte	Bell CG	Field	24/03/19	M	8 yrs PS		WO/213/29/91

Unit	Rank	Name	Location	Date D/M/Y	Offence	Finding/Punishment	Amendment	PRO Reference File/Piece/Page
32 AIF	Pte	Reid WHV	Field	24/03/19	M	11 yrs PS		WO/213/29/88
33 AIF	Pte	Cadigan CJ	Field	24/03/19	M	23 yrs PS		WO/213/29/89
33 AIF	Pte	Floyd W	Field	24/03/19	M	9 yrs PS		WO/213/29/88
34 AIF	Pte	Bozeat WJ	Rouen	04/02/19	M	90 dys Imp		WO/90/8/59
37 AIF	Pte	Cawthan JC	Rouen	04/02/19	M	90 dys Imp		WO/90/8/59
41 AIF	Pte	Colsell H	Field	22/12/18	M	2 yrs HL		WO/213/27/184
45 AIF	Pte	Hall HW	Field	24/03/19	M	11 yrs PS		WO/213/29/90
45 AIF	Pte	King AE	Field	24/03/19	M	9 yrs PS		WO/213/29/90
45 AIF	Pte	Roche GR	Rouen	24/03/19	M	11 yrs PS		WO/90/8/59
46 AIF	Pte	Harvey WA	Field	24/03/19	M	9 yrs PS		WO/213/29/90
46 AIF	Pte	Kelly DW	Field	24/03/19	M	11 yrs PS		WO/213/29/90
46 AIF	Pte	Leech E	Field	04/02/19	M	90 dys Imp		WO/213/29/89
46 AIF	Pte	McGregor A	Field	24/03/19	M	19 yrs PS		WO/213/29/88
46 AIF	Pte	O'Donohue WM	Field	24/03/19	M	10 yrs PS		WO/213/29/89
49 AIF	Pte	Henderson JJ	Field	24/03/19	M	11 yrs PS		WO/213/29/88
49 AIF	Pte	Maltby GE	Field	24/03/19	M	11 yrs PS		WO/213/29/91
49 AIF	Pte	Murphy JC	Rouen	04/02/19	M	90 dys Imp		WO/90/8/59
50 AIF	Pte	Broadhead AS	Field	24/03/19	M	13 yrs PS		WO/213/29/88
50 AIF	Pte	Powardy HR	Field	24/03/19	M	12 yrs PS		WO/213/29/89
50 AIF	Pte	Preston S	Field	24/03/19	M	10 yrs PS		WO/213/29/88
50 AIF	Pte	Twaits R	Field	24/03/19	M	11 yrs PS		WO/213/29/90
51 AIF	Pte	Grasso G	Rouen	04/02/19	M	Acquit		WO/90/8/59
55 AIF	Pte	Puckeridge J	Rouen	04/02/19	M	90 dys Imp		WO/90/8/58
56 AIF	Pte	Tonk DE	Field	22/12/18	M	4 yrs PS		WO/213/27/184
57 AIF	Pte	Newell A	Rouen	04/02/19	M	90 dys Imp		WO/90/8/59
58 AIF	Pte	Ford J	Field	24/03/19	M	10 yrs PS		WO/213/29/90
58 AIF	Pte	Hutchinson TJ	Field	24/03/19	M	15 yrs PS		WO/213/29/89
59 AIF	Pte	Ryan JH	Field	24/03/19	M	9 yrs PS		WO/213/29/88
60 AIF	Pte	Gallagher P	At Sea	27/12/16	M+Ins+Disob	2 yrs HL+Disch Igmny		WO/213/13/97
60 AIF	Pte	Millin GL	Rouen	04/02/19	M	90 dys Imp		WO/90/8/59
AASC	Pte	Aspinall HL	Field	22/12/18	M	NG		WO/213/27/184
Aus ASC	Cpl	Rowe FB	Field EEF	01/07/18	M	NG		WO/213/28/138
Aus ASC	Cpl	Rowling K	Field EEF	01/07/18	M	NG		WO/213/28/138
4 Aus DAC	Gnr	Hodges HM	Field	24/03/19	M	9 yrs PS		WO/213/29/90
Aus Engrs	Cpl	Hastie CE	Field EEF	29/06/18	M	NG		WO/213/26/112
Aus[t] Engrs	Spr	West NF	Field	24/03/19	M	12 yrs PS		WO/213/29/88
Aus[t] FA[rty]	Dvr	Webb WH	Field	24/03/19	M	10 yrs PS		WO/213/29/88
Aust FA	Dvr	Moorcroft AA	Field	07/11/18	M+Esc	35 dys FP2		WO/213/26/94
Aus Lt Horse	Tpr	Harris L	Malta	23/09/15	M+S40	3 yrs PS+DI		WO/90/6/34
1 Aus Lt Horse	Cpl	Morris AR	Field	29/06/18	M	NG		WO/213/26/112
4 Aus Lt Horse	Cpl	Chancellor HKT	Field EEF	28/06/18	M	NG		WO/213/28/138
4 Aust Lt Horse	Tpr	Bell WA	Malta	30/12/15	M+Not Sup+Disob(APM)	1 yr HL	Remit 1 month	WO/90/6/40
5 Aus Lt Horse	Tpr(L/Cpl)	Ashenden HE	Field EEF	28/06/18	M	NG		WO/213/28/138
8 Aus Lt Horse	Tpr(L/Cpl)	Buchan GM	Field EEF	28/06/18	M	NG		WO/213/28/138
8 Aus Lt Horse	Cpl	Kerr SJ	Field EEF	29/06/18	M	NG		WO/213/26/112
9 Aus Lt Horse	Cpl	Doueal A	Field EEF	28/06/18	M	NG		WO/213/28/138
3 Aust Lt Ry For Coy	Spr	Jansen O	Field	24/03/19	M	9 yrs PS		WO/213/29/88
1 Aus MGB	Pte	Ferguson WJ	Rouen	04/02/19	M	90 dys Imp		WO/90/8/59
1 Aus MGB	Pte	Meres S	Rouen	04/02/19	M	3 yrs + 3 mos PS		WO/90/8/59
Aus MGC	Pte	Davi[e?]s JF	Etaples	18/09/17	M+Viol+Resist	10 yrs PS		WO/213/17/151
1 Aus MG Sqdn	Tpr(L/Cpl)	Cameron A	Field EEF	28/06/18	M	NG		WO/213/28/138
Aust Mining Coy	Spr	Coffey J	[Le] Havre	19/07/16	Per M+Viol SO	5 yrs PS		WO/90/6/66
1 Aus Pnr Bn	Pte	Woodbury PA	Field	24/03/19	M	9 yrs PS		WO/213/29/89
2 Aus Pnr AIF	Pte	Gale G	Field	24/03/19	M	11 yrs PS		WO/213/29/91
2 Aus Pnr	Pte	Lawry W	Field	24/03/19	M	12 yrs PS		WO/213/29/91
5 Aus Pnrs	Pte	Bradley FW	Rouen	04/02/19	M	3 yrs 6 mos PS		WO/90/8/59
Aus Prov Corps	Tpr(L/Cpl)	Jenkinson CE	Field EEF	29/06/18	M	NG		WO/213/26/112
Aus Prov Corps	Cpl(A/Sgt)	Keogh TE	Field EEF	29/06/18	M	NG		WO/213/26/112
Aust Siege Bty	Gnr	Purcell W	[Le] Havre	19/07/16	Per M+Viol SO	5 yrs PS		WO/90/6/67
3 Aus Sig Troop	Cpl	Thomson C	Field EEF	01/07/18	M	NG		WO/213/28/138
3 Aus Tun Coy	Spr	Bell WH	Field	13/10/18	M+Disob	1 yr HL	NC	WO/213/30/136
3 Aus Tun Coy	Spr	Bell WH	Field	18/10/18	M+Disob	2 yrs HL	Susp	WO/213/26/66
3 Aus Tun Coy	Spr	Brownhill FH	Field	13/10/18	M+Disob	1 yr HL	NC	WO/213/30/136
3 Aus Tun Coy	Spr	Brownhill FH	Field	18/10/18	M+Disob	2 yrs HL	Susp	WO/213/26/66
3 Aus Tun Coy	Spt	Buck O	Field	13/10/18	M+Disob	1 yr HL	NC	WO/213/30/136
3 Aus Tun Coy	Spr	Buck O	Field	18/10/18	M+Disob	2 yrs HL	Susp	WO/213/26/65
3 Aus Tun Coy	Spr	Edmonds FW	Field	13/10/18	M+Disob	1 yr HL	NC	WO/213/30/136
3 Aus Tun Coy	Spr	Edmonds FW	Field	18/10/18	M+Disob	2 yrs HL	Susp	WO/213/26/65
3 Aus Tun Coy	Spr	Hancock ER	Field	13/10/18	M+Disob	1 yr HL	NC	WO/213/30/136
3 Aus Tun Coy	Spr	Hancock ER	Field	18/10/18	M+Disob	2 yrs HL	Susp	WO/213/26/66
3 Aus Tun Coy	Spr	Harvey G	Field	18/10/18	M+Disob	2 yrs HL	Susp	WO/213/26/66
AFA	Pte	Paterson P	Fovant	11/09/18	M+Absx2	1 yr Detn	NC	WO/86/85/9

Unit	Rank	Name	Location	Date D/M/Y	Offence	Finding/Punishment	Amendment	PRO Reference File/Piece/Page
3 Aus Tun Coy	Spr	Martin J	Field	13/10/18	M+Disob	1 yr HL	NC	WO/213/30/136
3 Aus Tun Coy	Spr	Martin J	Field	18/10/18	M+Disob	2 yrs HL	Susp	WO/213/26/66
3 Aus Tun Coy	Spr	McLean TD	Field	13/10/18	M+Disob	1 yr HL	NC	WO/213/30/136
3 Aus Tun Coy	Spr	McLean TD	Field	18/10/18	M+Disob	2 yrs HL	Susp	WO/213/26/65
3 Aus Tun Coy	Spr	Moore AW	Field	13/10/18	M+Disob	1 yr HL	NC	WO/213/30/137
3 Aus Tun Coy	Spr	Moore AW	Field	18/10/18	M+Disob	2 yrs HL	Susp	WO/213/26/65
3 Aus Tun Coy	Spr	Sandercott W	Field	18/10/18	M+Disob	2 yrs HL	Susp	WO/213/26/66
3 Aus Tun Coy	Spr	Sandercourt W	Field	13/10/18	M+Disob	1 yr HL	NC	WO/213/30/136
3 Aus Tun Coy	Spr	Terrell SJ	Field	13/10/18	M+Disob	1 yr HL	NC	WO/213/30/136
3 Aus Tun Coy	Spr	Terrell SJ	Field	18/10/18	M+Disob	2 yrs HL	Susp	WO/213/26/66
3 Aus Tun Coy	Spr	Thomas RG [DCM]	Field	13/10/18	M+Disob	1 yr HL	NC	WO/213/30/136
3 Aus Tun Coy	Spr	Thomas RG [DCM]	Field	18/10/18	M+Disob	2 yrs HL	Susp	WO/213/26/66
3 Aus Tun Coy	Spr	Ulph RW	Field	13/10/18	M+Disob	1 yr HL	NC	WO/213/30/136
3 Aus Tun Coy	Spr	Ulph RW	Field	18/10/18	M+Disob	2 yrs HL	Susp	WO/213/26/65
17 Coy ICC	Cpl	Graham M	Field EEF	28/06/18	M	NG		WO/213/28/138

Canadian

Unit	Rank	Name	Location	Date D/M/Y	Offence	Finding/Punishment	Amendment	PRO Reference File/Piece/Page
Alb Regt CEF	Pte	Quenelle W	Bramshott	15/07/18	M+S40	2 yrs HL+Stoppages		WO/92/4/43
Alb Regt CEF	Pte	Smith AE	Bramshott	15/07/18	M+S40	Acquit		WO/92/4/43
Quebec Regt	Pte	Adams EA	Ripon	31/07/19	M+S7(3b)	1 yr HL+Disch Igmny		WO/86/88/51
Quebec Regt	Pte	Anley H	Ripon	26/07/19	M+S7(3b)+S40	6 mos Detn		WO/86/88/43
Quebec Regt	Pte	Beatty L	Ripon	12/07/19	M+S7(3b)	1 yr HL		WO/86/88/54
Quebec Regt	Pte	Belmore T	Ripon	02/08/19	M+7(3b)+Abs+S22	1 yr Detn		WO/86/88/53
Quebec Regt	Pte	Broom C	Ripon	23/07/19	M+S7(3b)	22 mos HL+Disch Igmny		WO/86/88/29
Quebec Regt	Cpl	Bureau H	Ripon	05/08/19	M+7(3b)	2 yr HL+Rnks+Disch Igmny		WO/86/88/53
Quebec Regt CEF	Pte	Canning J	Bramshott	15/07/18	M+S40	2 yrs HL+Stoppages		WO/86/88/29
Quebec Regt	Pte	Chouinard WA	Ripon	28/07/19	M+S40	NG		WO/86/88/41
Quebec Regt	Pte	Dancause T	Ripon	02/08/19	M+S40	NG		WO/86/88/42
Quebec Regt	Pte	DeLobbe A	Ripon	23/07/19	M+S7(3b)+S40	22mos HL+Disch Igmny		WO/86/88/12
Quebec Regt	Pte	Desjardins E	Ripon	17/07/19	M	NG		WO/86/88/12
Quebec Regt	Pte	Gareau A	Ripon	16/07/19	M	20 mos+Disch Igmny		WO/86/88/51
Quebec Regt	Pte	Greenhalgh E	Ripon	14/07/19	M+S7(3b)	18 mos HL		WO/86/88/29
Quebec Regt	Pte	Kelly T	Ripon	01/08/19	M+7(3b)	2 yr HL+Disch Igmny		WO/86/88/53
Quebec Regt	Pte	Littlefield GW	Ripon	25/07/19	M+S7(3b)	2 yrs HL+Disch Igmny		WO/86/88/51
Quebec Regt	Pte	Luckay WW	Ripon	24/07/19	M+S7(3b)	2 yrs HL+Disch Igmny		WO/86/88/51
Quebec Regt	Pte	McCann J	Ripon	21/07/19	Mx2+S7[3]b+S40	2 yrs HL+Disch Igmny		WO/86/88/52
Quebec Regt	Pte	McMillan B	Ripon	22/07/19	M+S7(3b)	20 mos HL+Disch Igmny		WO/86/88/52
Quebec Regt	Pte	Morneau L	Ripon	22/07/19	M	NG		WO/86/88/51
Quebec Regt	Pte	O'Brien WO	Ripon	24/07/19	S7(3b)M+S40	6 mos Detn		WO/86/88/51
Quebec Regt	Pte	Penneall AA	Ripon	11/07/19	M+S7(3b)+S40	1 yr HL		WO/86/88/51
Quebec Regt	Pte	Shanks AG	Ripon	15/07/19	M	NG		WO/86/88/51
Quebec Regt	Pte	Sickles W	Ripon	18/07/19	S7(3b)[M]	6 mos Detn		WO/86/88/51
Quebec Regt	Pte	Thompson AW	Ripon	18/07/19	M+S7(3b)	18 mos HL		WO/86/88/51
Quebec Regt	Pte	Varieur EL	Ripon	26/07/19	M	2 yrs HL+Disch Igmny		WO/86/88/42
Quebec Regt	Pte	Riley B	Ripon	30/07/19	M+S7(3b)	6 mos Detn		WO/86/88/51
1 Ont Regt	Pte	Bruce JR	Bramshott	15/07/18	M+S40	18 mos HL+Stoppages		WO/92/4/43
1 Ont Regt	Pte	Falkenbury CH	Bramshott	15/07/18	M+S40	2 yrs HL+Stoppages		WO/92/4/43
1(R) CEF	Pte(A/Cpl)	Morrison JB	Liverpool	28/04/19	M	5 yrs PS		WO/92/4/70
2 CEF	Pte	Nearin J	[Le] Havre	19/07/16	Per M+Viol SO	Acquit		WO/90/6/67
3(R) CEF	Pte	Dickson A	Liverpool	22/04/19	M	23 mos HL		WO/92/4/70
3(R) CEF	Pte	Dickson A	Liverpool	30/05/19	M+S7(3b)	3 yrs HL		WO/92/4/72
4 CEF	Pte	Pitt FL	Bramshott	08/01/18	M+Desx2+Abs+loss pub prop+S2	2 yrs Detn	Remit 1 yr Detn Quashed	WO/86/79/171
4(R) CEF	Pte	Fortin J	Bramshott	02/03/18	M+Abs+S40x2	56 dys Detn	Quashed	WO/86/81/34
4(R) CEF	Pte	Keith JT	Bramshott	03/09/17	M+Insub(Sgt)+S22	18 mos Detn		WO/86/78/5
4(R) CEF	Pte	Robinson F	Bramshott	14/09/17	M+Abs+S22+S40	1 yr Detn		WO/86/78/1
5 CEF	Pte	Sager WG	[Le] Havre	19/07/16	Per M+Insub	Acquit		WO/90/6/67
6(R) CEF	Pte	Brennan JP	Liverpool	19/04/19	M+S40	1 yr HL		WO/92/4/69
8(R) CEF	Pte	Edgar R	Shorncliffe	03/09/17	Mx2+S40+S41	16 mos HL		WO/86/78/25
8(R) CEF	Pte	Gardiner GG	Liverpool	05/05/19	M	Acquit		WO/92/4/67
8(R) CEF	Pte	Jarvis CA	Liverpool	05/05/19	M	Acquit		WO/92/4/67
8(R) CEF	Pte(A/Cpl)	Payne JA	Liverpool	02/05/19	M+S7(3b)	1 yr HL		WO/92/4/71
8(R) CEF	Pte	Taylor JN	Witley	30/07/19	M	Not Guilty		WO/86/88/30
8(R) CEF	Pte	Zotzman A	Shorncliffe	11/09/17	M+S40(3)	9 mos Detn	Quashed	WO/86/78/26
11(R) CEF	Pte	Burton W	Liverpool	16/04/19	M+Viol	Acquit		WO/92/4/65
11(R) CEF	Cpl	Gandy J	Liverpool	19/05/19	M+S40	Rnks+1 yr HL		WO/92/4/72
11(R) CEF	Pte	Hughes D	Liverpool	14/05/19	M+L[eaving] Po[st]	90 dys Detn	NC	WO/92/4/72
11(R) CEF	Pte	Johnston J	Liverpool	05/05/19	M	Acquit		WO/92/4/66
12(R) CEF	Pte	Costughko V	Liverpool	22/04/19	M	90 dys Detn		WO/92/4/70
12(R) CEF	Pte	Ingalls RA	Liverpool	19/04/19	M	Acquit		WO/92/4/65

Unit	Rank	Name	Location	Date D/M/Y	Offence	Finding/Punishment	Amendment	PRO Reference File/Piece/Page
13(R) CEF	Pte	Connor O	Kinmel Pk	28/01/19	M+S7(4)	1 yr Detn		WO/86/86/105
13(R) CEF	Pte	Gauthier GF	Liverpool	05/05/19	M	Acquit		WO/92/4/67
18(R) CEF	Pte	Archie R	Liverpool	22/04/19	M	23 mos HL		WO/92/4/70
18 CEF	Pte	Bryant CWI	Seaford	30/09/18	M+S40	6 mos HL		WO/86/84/196
18 CEF	Pte	Cook JR	Seaford	30/09/18	M+S40	9 mos HL		WO/86/84/196
18 CEF	Pte	Forsyth GH	Seaford	30/09/18	M+S40	90 dys Detn		WO/86/84/196
18 CEF	Pte	McFarlane R	Seaford	30/09/18	M+S40	1 yr HL		WO/86/84/196
20(R) CEF	Pte	Clement F	Liverpool	18/04/19	M	18 mos HL		WO/92/4/69
20(R) CEF	Pte	Henley RE	Liverpool	19/05/19	M+S7(3b)	3 yrs PS		WO/92/4/72
20(R) CEF	Pte	Lamoureux AJ	Liverpool	20/05/19	M+S7(3b)	22 mos HL		WO/92/4/72
21 CEF	Pte	Coons L	Field	05/03/19	M+S40	70 dys FP2	Comm No 2	WO/213/28/202
21(R) CEF	Pte	Kosar R	Liverpool	02/05/19	M+S7(3b)	6 mos HL		WO/92/4/71
21(R) CEF	Pte	Lind CW	Liverpool	05/05/19	M	Acquit		WO/92/4/67
21(R) CEF	Pte	Miculka V	Liverpool	19/05/19	M	10 yrs PS		WO/92/4/72
21 CEF	Pte	Osborne H	Witley	12/05/19	M+S40	NG		WO/86/87/124
21 CEF	Pte	Souliere V	Witley	11/05/19	M+S40(2)	2 yrs HL+Disch Igmny		WO/86/87/169
21(R) CEF	Pte	Weikel F	Liverpool	22/05/19	M+S7(3b)	22 mos HL		WO/92/4/71
22 Quebec CEF	Pte	Massicote A	Liverpool	15/05/19	M	Acquit		WO/92/4/68
23(R)CEF	Pte	Chambers J	Bramshott	16/05/18	M+Des+Abs+Loss prop+S40	90 dys Detn Stoppages+G of Abs		WO/86/82/158
23(R) CEF	Cpl	Leet HJ	Kinmel Park	21/02/19	M+Str+Drunk	5yrs PS+RnkS +Disch Igmny		WO/92/4/65
23(R) CEF	Pte	Neason WB	Liverpool	28/05/19	M	Acquit		WO/92/4/69
24 CEF	Pte	McLaren R	Field	08/09/19	M+Des+Esc +S40/S41	2 yrs HL		WO/213/30/141
25 CEF	Pte	Hutton A	Bramshott	11/02/18	M+Abs+Inj property* +S40(2)	112 dys Detn +Quashed*		WO/86/80/139
25 CEF	Pte	Pearson JH	Bramshott	11/02/18	M+Inj property* +S40(2)	112 dys Detn +Quashed*		WO/86/80/139
25 CEF	Pte	Tobin JE	Bramshott	11/02/18	M+Inj property* +S40(2)	112 dys Detn Quashed*		WO/86/80/139
25 CEF	Pte	Moran R	Field	24/03/19	M	11 yrs PS		WO/213/29/90
25(R) CEF	Pte	McDonald EC	Bramshott	11/09/17	M+Absx2+S22	2 yrs Detn		WO/86/78/31
28 CEF	Pte	Chiverrell WH	Rouen	04/02/19	M	56 dys Imp		WO/90/8/58
28 CEF	Pte	Clark HL	Field	24/03/19	M	20 yrs PS		WO/213/29/91
43 CEF	Pte	Clergy C	Field	11/12/17	M+Disob	18 mos HL		WO/213/19/116
43 CEF	Pte	Cuff SH	Field	11/12/17	M+Disob	18 mos HL		WO/213/19/116
43 CEF	Pte	Graham WG	Field	11/12/17	M+Disob	18 mos HL		WO/213/19/116
43 CEF	Pte	Primett H	Field	11/12/17	M+Disob	18 mos HL		WO/213/19/116
43 CEF	Pte	Bonang AW	Field	23/12/17	M+Disob	2 yrs HL		WO/213/19/116
PPCLI	Pte	Butler PW	Field	23/01/19	M+Abs	2 yrs HL	Remit/Quashed	WO/213/28/107
R Can	Pte	McConaghy D	Field	24/03/19	M	10 yrs PS		WO213/29/88
Can AMC	Pte	Hamelin W	Liverpool	21/05/19	M+S40	Acquit		WO/92/4/74
Can ASC	Pte	Ackling W	Bramshott	21/11/17	M+Insub(Lieut)	42 dys Detn	Remit 15 dys	WO/86/79/54
Can ASC	Pte	Baker E	Bramshott	21/11/17	M+Insub(Lieut)	42 dys Detn	Remit 15 dys	WO/86/79/54
Can ASC	Pte	Boskett J[V?]	Bramshott	21/11/17	M+Insub(Lieut)	42 dys Detn	Remit 15 dys	WO/86/79/53
Can ASC	Pte	Cain W	Bramshott	21/11/17	M+Insub(Lieut)	42 dys Detn	Remit 10 dys	WO/86/79/53
Can ASC	Pte	Calden J	Bramshott	21/11/17	M+Insub(Lieut)	42 dys Detn	Remit 15 dys	WO/86/79/53
Can ASC	Pte	Cole FC	Shorncliffe	06/09/17	M+S40+S7(2)+S41	NG		WO/86/77/169
Can ASC	Pte	Connors H	Bramshott	21/11/17	M+Insub(Lieut)	42 dys Detn	Remit 15 dys	WO/86/79/53
Can ASC	Pte	Desjarlais G	Bramshott	21/11/17	M+Insub	42 dys Detn	Remit 15 dys	WO/86/79/54
Can ASC	Pte	Dunn PS	Bramshott	21/11/17	M+INsub(Lieut)	42 dys Detn	Remit 10 dys	WO/86/79/54
Can ASC	Pte	Harris C	Bramshott	21/11/17	M+Insub(Lieut)	42 dys Detn	Remit 15 dys	WO/86/79/54
Can ASC	Pte	Merritt SG	Bramshott	21/11/17	M+Insub(Lieut)	42 dys Detn	Remit 15 dys	WO/86/79/54
Can ASC	Pte	Murchinson R	Bramshott	21/11/17	M+Insub(Lieut)	42 dys Detn	Remit 15 dys	WO/86/79/54
Can ASC	Pte	Parks JJ	Bramshott	21/11/17	M+Insub	42 dys Detn	Remit 15 dys	WO/86/79/53
Can ASC	Pte	Peacock A	Bramshott	21/11/17	M+Insub(Lieut)	42 dys Detn	Remit 15 dys	WO/86/79/53
Can ASC	Pte	Smyth GH	Witley	27/02/19	M+S40(2)	2 yrs Detn		WO/86/87/14
Can ASC	Pte	Spence HA	Bramshott	21/11/17	M+Insub(Lieut)	42 dys Detn	Remit 15 dys	WO/86/79/53
Can ASC	Pte	Statton T	Bramshott	21/11/17	M+Insub(Lieut)	42 dys Detn	Remit 15 dys	WO/86/79/53
Can ASC	Pte	Stevens WA	Bramshott	21/11/17	M+Insub(Lieut)	42 dys Detn	Remit 15 dys	WO/86/79/53
Can ASC	Pte	Tepoorten JE	[Le] Havre	19/07/16	M+Insub	5 yrs PS		WO/90/6/67
Can ASC	Pte	Weller E	Bramshott	21/11/17	M+Insub(Lieut)	42 dys Detn	Remit 15 dys	WO/86/79/53
Can ASC	Pte	Wilson F	Bramshott	28/02/19	M	6 mos Detn	Comm to 28 dys Detn	WO/86/87/17
Can ASC	Pte	Wright H	Bramshott	28/02/19	M	NG		WO/86/87/17
Can ASC	Pte	Young B	Bramshott	21/11/17	M+Insub(Lieut)	42 dys Detn	Remit 15 dys	WO/86/79/53
Can Engrs	L/Cpl	Taylor CM	Field	21/01/19	M+S7(3b)	2 yrs HL+Rnks		WO/213/28/108
Can Engrs	Spr	Bray E	Field	25/01/19	M+Disob	28 dys FP2		WO/213/29/55
Can Engrs	Spr	Hutchins VG	Field	25/01/19	M+Disob	28 dys FP2		WO/213/29/55
Can Engrs	Spr	Keenan G	Field	25/01/19	M+Disob	NG		WO/213/29/55
Can Engrs	Spr	McKenna JF	Field	25/01/19	M+Disob	NG		WO/213/29/55
Can Engrs	Spr	Muir WJC	Field	25/01/19	M+Disob	NG		WO/213/29/55
Can Engrs	Spr	Mullis WW	Field	25/01/19	M+Disob	NG		WO/213/29/55

Unit	Rank	Name	Location	Date D/M/Y	Offence	Finding/Punishment	Amendment	PRO Reference File/Piece/Page
Can Engrs	Spr	O'Riley J	Field	25/01/19	M+Disob	NG		WO/213/29/55
Can Engrs	Spr	Orr A	Field	25/01/19	M+Disob	NG		WO/213/29/55
Can Engrs	Spr	Rozell H	Field	25/01/19	M+Disob	NG		WO/213/29/55
Can Engrs	Spr	Savchok A	Field	25/01/19	M+Disob	NG		WO/213/29/55
Can Engrs	Spr	Way R	Field	25/01/19	M+Disob	28 dys FP2		WO/213/29/55
Can Eng	Spr	Walsh WP	Liverpool	02/06/19	M	Acquit		WO/92/4/69
Can Engrs	Spr	White JE	Field	25/01/19	M+Disob	NG		WO/213/29/55
Can Engrs	Spr	Wilson RH	Field	25/01/19	M+Disob	NG		WO/213/29/55
Can Engrs	Spr	Samarzich L	Field	01/02/19	M+Disob	28 dys FP2		WO/213/28/71
Can Engrs	Spr	Smith C	Field	01/02/19	M+Disob	28 dys FP2		WO/213/28/71
Can Engrs	Spr	Sweeney E	Field	01/02/19	M+Disob	28 dys FP2		WO/213/28/71
Can Engrs	Pte	Taylor CM	Field	24/03/19	M	PS/Life		WO213/28/88
Can Eng	Spr	Wirth J	Liverpool	05/05/19	M	Acquit		WO/92/4/67
3(R) Can Eng	Spr	Conley AL	Liverpool	27/05/19	M+Res	1 yr HL	Comm Detn	WO/92/4/72
Can FA[arty]	Gnr	Andrews R	Field	24/03/19	M	10 yrs PS		WO/213/29/89
Can For Corps	Pte	Crane J	Liverpool	01/05/19	M	6 mos Detn		WO/92/4/69
CARD	Pte	White R	Witley	15/07/19	M + S40	2 mos Imp	Comm Detn	WO/86/88/19
Can Rail T[roops]	Spr	Hiba J	Liverpool	28/05/19	M+XO(Lt Col)+ XO(Lt)	7 yrs PS		WO/92/4/72
Can F[orestry] C[orps]	Pte	Scott J	Liverpool	26/05/19	M+S7(3b)	22 mos HL		WO/92/4/71
Can s For[estry] Corp	Pte	Sherstotoff F	Liverpool	18/04/19	M+Striking	2 yrs HL		WO/92/4/69
Can For Corps	Pte	Simon R	Liverpool	28/04/19	M	5 yrs PS		WO/92/4/70
Can Fores[try] Corps	Pte	Tuckman B	Liverpool	02/05/19	M+S7(3b)	6 mos HL		WO/92/4/71
Can For Corps	Pte	Wallace J	Liverpool	22/04/19	M	90 dys Detn		WO/92/4/70
1 Can IW Coy	Pte	Bertucci BG	Liverpool	19/05/19	M	Acquit		WO/92/4/68
Can Lt Horse	Tpr	Flint GH	Etaples	19/09/17	M	10 yrs PS	Comm 2 yrs HL	WO/213/17/151
2 Can Mtd Rif	Pte	Jones W	Field	24/03/19	M	7 yrs PS		WO/213/29/91
Can O[rdnance] Corps	Pte	Munro DS	Witley	09/08/19	M+S40	6 mos Detn		WO/86/88/44
Can Ry Troops	Spr	English M	Liverpool	22/04/19	M	120 dys Detn		WO/92/4/70
Can Ry Troops	Spr	Mckenzie M	Liverpool	22/04/19	M	Acquit		WO/92/4/70
7 Can Rail Troops	Pte	Long GH	Liverpool	02/05/19	M+S7(3b)	1 yr HL		WO/92/4/71
Can Ry Troops	Pte	Supple DR	Liverpool	05/05/19	M	Acquit		WO/92/4/67
Can Res Arty	Gnr	Evans E	Liverpool	06/05/19	M	Acquit		WO/92/4/67
Can Res Arty	Pte	Houston JP	Liverpool	01/05/19	M	Acquit		WO/92/4/66
Can Res A[rty]	Dvr	Marsh RE	Liverpool	14/05/19	M+Res+Esc	10 mos HL		WO/92/4/71
Can Res Arty	Pte	McLeod GAL	Liverpool	22/04/19	M	Acquit		WO/92/4/65
Can Res A[rty]	Pte	Sampson WR	Liverpool	12/05/19	M+Res+Esc	30 dys Detn		WO/92/4/71
Can Res A[rty]	Dvr	Taylor A	Liverpool	13/05/19	M	120 dys Detn	NC	WO/92/4/71
Can Res Cav Reg	Pte	Edmondson RH	Liverpool	07/05/19	M	5 yrs PS		WO/92/4/70
Can R[eserve]C[avy]R[egt]	Pte	Harber G	Liverpool	13/05/19	M+S7(3b)	10 mos HL	NC	WO/92/4/72
Can Reserve Cavy Regt	Pte	Parker JL	Shorncliffe	11/09/17	M+S40+S22+S41	[No entry - 1 yr Detn?]		WO/86/78/19
Can Reserve Cavy	Pte	Phillips JE	Shorncliffe	30/08/17	Mx2+S40(4)+S41	2 yrs HL		WO/86/78/8
Can Reserve Cavy	Pte	Reid H	Shorncliffe	06/09/17	Mx2+S40+S41	16 mos HL		WO/86/78/8
Can MG Depot	Pte	Schmidt J	Liverpool	02/06/19	M+XO(Lt)+S7(3b)	22 mos Detn		WO/92/4/72
3 Can MGC	Pte	Curnew JB	Field	24/03/19	M	Death	Comm PS/Life	WO/213/29/89
3 Can MGC	Pte	McDonell C	Field	21/01/19	Mx2	5 yrs PS		WO/213/28/189
3 Can MGC	Pte	McDonnell C	Field	24/03/19	M	Death	Comm PS/Life	WO/213/29/90
3 Can MGC	Pte	Nunan P	Field	27/01/19	M	5 yrs PS		WO/213/28/189
3 Can MGC	Pte	Roberts W	Field	23/01/19	M+Abs+S40	2 yrs HL		WO/213/28/108
Caribbean								
[?] BWI	Pte	Cardonia L	Plymouth	27/02/19	M	2 yrs HL+Disch Igmny		WO/86/87/23
BWI	Pte	Brown I	Mesopot	04/01/18	[M]7(3a)	18 mos HL	Remit 1 yr	WO/90/7/169
BWI	Pte	Flores E	Mesopot	04/01/18	[M]7(2)	3 yrs PS	Comm 1 yr HL	WO/90/7/169
BWI	Pte	Lightfoot WJ	Mesopot	04/01/18	[M]7(3a)x2	5 yrs PS	Comm 2 yrs HL	WO/90/7/169
BWI	Pte	Lowe J	Mesopot	04/01/18	[M]7(3a)x2	10 yrs PS	R[emit?] 7 yrs	WO/90/7/169
1 BWI	Pte	Alexander A	Field Italy	04/05/19	M	6 mos HL		WO/213/29/37
1 BWI	Pte	Antoine B	Field Italy	02/05/19	Mx2+Disob	18 mos HL	Remit 12 mos	WO/213/29/37
1 BWI	Pte	Cuffy A	Field Italy	04/05/19	M	6 mos HL		WO/213/29/37
1 BWI	Pte	Gonzales BAE	Field Italy	02/05/19	Mx2+Disob	18 mos HL	Remit 12 mos	WO/213/29/37
1 BWI	Pte	Laguerre E	Field Italy	02/05/19	Mx2+Disob	18 mos HL	Remit 12 mos	WO/213/29/37
1 BWI	Cpl	Parris HN	Field	10/05/19	M+S40	90 dys FP2+Rnks	Remit 62 dys	WO/213/29/49
1 BWI	Pte	Sealey C	Field Italy	04/05/19	M	6 mos HL		WO/213/29/37
4 BWI	Pte	Allen N	Field Italy	27/12/18	M+Disob	3 yrs PS	Comm 2 yrs HL	WO/213/27/23
4 BWI	Pte	Beckford R	Field Italy	27/12/18	M+Disob	3 yrs PS	Comm 2 yrs HL	WO/213/27/23

Unit	Rank	Name	Location	Date D/M/Y	Offence	Finding/Punishment	Amendment	PRO Reference File/Piece/Page
4 BWI	Pte	Blake J	Field Italy	27/12/18	M+Disob	3 yrs PS	Comm 2 yrs HL	WO/213/27/23
4 BWI	Pte	Carey W	Field Italy	27/12/18	M+Disob	3 yrs PS	Comm 2 yrs HL	WO/213/27/23
4 BWI	Pte	Davis A	Field Italy	27/12/18	M+Disob	3 yrs PS	Comm 2 yrs HL	WO/213/27/23
4 BWI	Pte	Dickenson H	Field Italy	27/12/18	M+Disob	3 yrs PS	Comm 2 yrs HL	WO/213/27/23
4 BWI	Pte	Evans W	Field Italy	27/12/18	M+Disob	3 yrs PS	Comm 2 yrs HL	WO/213/27/23
4 BWI	Pte	Griffiths A	Field Italy	27/12/18	M+Disob	3 yrs PS	Comm 2 yrs HL	WO/213/27/23
4 BWI	Pte	Hamilton J	Field Italy	27/12/18	M+Disob	3 yrs PS	Comm 2 yrs HL	WO/213/27/23
4 BWI	Pte	Hutchinson H	Field Italy	27/12/18	M+Disob	3 yrs PS	Comm 2 yrs HL	WO/213/27/23
4 BWI	Pte	Spence A	Field Italy	27/12/18	M+Disob	3 yrs PS	Comm 2 yrs HL	WO/213/27/23
4 BWI	Pte	Spencer H	Plymouth	28/02/19	M	2 yrs Detn		WO/86/87/17
4 BWI	Pte	Williams A	Field Italy	27/12/18	M+Disob	3 yrs PS	Comm 2 yrs HL	WO/213/27/23
6 (S) BWI	Pte	Archer E	Field Italy	24/12/18	M+Disob	3 yrs 6 mos PS		WO/213/27/24
6 (S) BWI	Pte	Brown E	Field Italy	24/12/18	M+Disob	3 yrs 6 mos PS		WO/213/27/24
6 (S) BWI	Pte	Campbell S	Field Italy	24/12/18	M+Disob	3 yrs 6 mos PS		WO/213/27/24
6 (S) BWI	Pte	Douglas B	Field Italy	24/12/18	M+Disob	3 yrs 6 mos PS		WO/213/27/24
6 (S) BWI	Pte	Fender S	Field Italy	24/12/18	M+Disob	3 yrs 6 mos PS		WO/213/27/24
6 (S) BWI	Pte	Francis R	Field Italy	24/12/18	M+Disob	3 yrs 6 mos PS		WO/213/27/24
6 (S) BWI	Pte	Golding D	Field Italy	24/12/18	M+Disob	3 yrs 6 mos PS		WO/213/27/24
6 (S) BWI	Pte	Harvey L	Field Italy	24/12/18	M+Disob	3 yrs 6 mos PS		WO/213/27/24
6 (S) BWI	Pte	Hinds R	Field Italy	24/12/18	M+Disob	3 yrs 6 mos PS		WO/213/27/24
6 (S) BWI	Pte	James B	Field Italy	24/12/18	M+Disob	3 yrs 6 mos PS		WO/213/27/24
6 (S) BWI	Pte	Jepp C	Field Italy	24/12/18	M+Disob	3 yrs 6 mos PS		WO/213/27/24
6 (S) BWI	Pte	Laurence D	Field Italy	24/12/18	M+Disob	3 yrs 6 mos PS		WO/213/27/24
6 (S) BWI	Pte	Loious T	Field Italy	24/12/18	M+Disob	3 yrs 6 mos PS		WO/213/27/24
6 (S) BWI	Pte	Mannings M	Field Italy	24/12/18	M+Disob	3 yrs 6 mos PS		WO/213/27/24
6 (S) BWI	Pte	Martin S	Field Italy	24/12/18	M+Disob	3 yrs 6 mos PS		WO/213/27/24
6 (S) BWI	Pte	McCallum S	Field Italy	24/12/18	M+Disob	3 yrs 6 mos PS		WO/213/27/24
6 (S) BWI	Pte	Morgan W	Field Italy	24/12/18	M+Disob	3 yrs 6 mos PS		WO/213/27/24
6 (S) BWI	Pte	Palmer C	Field Italy	24/12/18	M+Disob	3 yrs 6 mos PS		WO/213/27/24
6 (S) BWI	Pte	Peers F	Field Italy	24/12/18	M+Disob	3 yrs 6 mos PS		WO/213/27/24
6 (S) BWI	Pte	Powell L	Field Italy	24/12/18	M+Disob	3 yrs 6 mos PS		WO/213/27/24
6 (S) BWI	Pte	Smith D	Field Italy	24/12/18	M+Disob	3 yrs 6 mos PS		WO/213/27/24
6 (S) BWI	Pte	Tyrrell A	Field Italy	24/12/18	M+Disob	3 yrs 6 mos PS		WO/213/27/24
6 (S) BWI	Pte	Watley J	Field Italy	24/12/18	M+Disob	3 yrs 6 mos PS		WO/213/27/24
6 BWI	Pte	Mundle J	Field Italy	10/01/19	M	3 yrs PS		WO/213/27/81
9 (S) BWI	Pte	Donaldson M	Field Italy	24/12/18	M+Disob+Esc	5 yrs PS		WO/213/27/25
9 (S) BWI	Pte	Edwards E	Field Italy	24/12/18	M+Disob+Esc	8 yrs PS		WO/213/27/25
9 (S) BWI	Pte	Howard E	Field Italy	24/12/18	M+Disob+Esc	5 yrs PS		WO/213/27/25
9 (S) BWI	Pte	Junior W	Field Italy	24/12/18	M+Disob+Esc	5 yrs PS		WO/213/27/25
9 (S) BWI	Pte	Knight A	Field Italy	24/12/18	M+Disob+Esc	5 yrs PS		WO/213/27/25
9 (S) BWI	Pte	Lorde G	Field Italy	24/12/18	M+Disob+Esc	5 yrs PS		WO/213/27/25
9 (S) BWI	Pte	Marshall A	Field Italy	24/12/18	M+Disob+Esc	8 yrs PS		WO/213/27/25
9 (S) BWI	Pte	McLeod B	Field Italy	24/12/18	M+Disob+Esc	5 yrs PS		WO/213/27/25
9 BWI	Pte	Mayers C	Plymouth	28/02/19	M	2 yrs Detn		WO/86/87/17
9 BWI	Pte	Munroe J	Field Italy	28/12/18	M+Striking	20 yrs PS	Remit 6 yrs	WO/213/27/25
9 (S) BWI	Pte	Myers D	Field Italy	24/12/18	M+Disob+Esc	10 yrs PS		WO/213/27/25
9 (S) BWI	Pte	Oxley W	Field Italy	24/12/18	M+Disob+Esc	5 yrs PS		WO/213/27/25
9 BWI	Pte	Sanches A	Field Italy	27/12/18	M	Death	Comm 20 yrs PS	WO/213/27/81
9 (S) BWI	Pte	Shaw C	Field Italy	24/12/18	M+Disob+Esc	5 yrs PS		WO/213/27/25
9 (S) BWI	Pte	Yard B	Field Italy	24/12/18	M+Disob+Esc	5 yrs PS		WO/213/27/25
10 BWI	Pte	Prescott B	Plymouth	28/02/19	M	2 yrs Detn		WO/86/87/17
11 BWI	Pte	McCogg E	Plymouth	28/02/19	M	2 yrs Detn		WO/86/87/17
West India Regt	Pte	Bedford W	Jamaica	29/04/21	M+Abs+Striking(Maj)+S9(1)	5 yrs PS+DI	Remit 2 yrs	WO/90/8/87
West India Regt	Pte	Bradley S	Jamaica	29/04/21	M+Abs+S9(1)	6 mos Detn		WO/90/8/87
West India Regt	Pte	Campbell S	Jamaica	29/04/21	M+Abs+Disob	112 dys Detn	Remit 56 dys	WO/90/8/87
West India Regt	Pte	Foreman OG	Jamaica	29/04/21	M+Abs+S9(1)	5 yrs PS+DI	Remit 2 yrs	WO/90/8/87
West India Regt	Pte	Norman J	Jamaica	29/04/21	M+Abs+S10(3)+S9(1)	5 yrs PS+DI	Remit 2 yrs	WO/90/8/87
2 W India	Pte	Allen J	Field EEF	11/05/19	M	7 yrs PS	Comm 2 yrs HL	WO/213/30/28
2 W India	Pte	Allen W	Field EEF	11/05/19	M	7 yrs PS	Comm 2 yrs HL	WO/213/30/28
2 W India	Pte	Bernard S	Field EEF	11/05/19	M	7 yrs PS	Comm 2 yrs HL	WO/213/30/28
2 W India	Pte	Brown J	Field EEF	11/05/19	M	7 yrs PS	Comm 2 yrs HL	WO/213/30/28
2 W India	Pte	Brown S	Field EEF	11/05/19	M	7 yrs PS	Comm 2 yr HL	WO/213/30/28
2 W India	Pte	Cole H	Field EEF	11/05/19	M	7 yrs PS	Comm 2 yrs HL	WO/213/30/27
2 W India	Pte	Collins R	Field EEF	11/05/19	M	5 yrs PS	Comm 1 yr HL	WO/213/30/28
2 W India	Pte	Gibbs JE	Field EEF	11/05/19	M	7 yrs PS	Comm 2 yrs HL	WO/213/30/28
2 W India	Pte	Gordon J	Field EEF	11/05/19	M	5 yrs PS	Comm 1 yr HL	WO/213/30/28
2 W India	Pte	Hemmings T	Field EEF	11/05/19	M	7 yrs PS	Comm 2 yrs HL	WO/213/30/28
2 W India	Pte	Kelly D	Field EEF	11/05/19	M	5 yrs PS	Comm 1 yr HL	WO/213/30/28
2 W India	Pte	Lewis S	Field EEF	11/05/19	M	5 yrs PS	Comm 1 yr HL	WO/213/30/28
2 W India	Pte	Marlow E	Field EEF	11/05/19	M	7 yrs PS	Comm 2 yrs HL	WO/213/30/28
2 W India	Pte	May C	Field EEF	11/05/19	M	5 yrs PS	Comm 1 yr HL	WO/213/30/28

Unit	Rank	Name	Location	Date D/M/Y	Offence	Finding/Punishment	Amendment	PRO Reference File/Piece/Page
2 W India	Pte	McKenzie C	Field EEF	11/05/19	M	5 yrs PS	Comm 1 yr HL	WO/213/30/28
2 W India	Pte	Miller G	Field EEF	11/05/19	M	5 yrs PS	Comm 1 yr HL	WO/213/30/28
2 W India	Pte	Millings G	Field EEF	11/05/19	M	5 yrs PS	Comm 1 yr HL	WO/213/30/28
2 W India	Pte	Nelson J	Field EEF	11/05/19	M	5 yrs PS	Comm 1 yr HL	WO/213/30/28
2 W India	Pte	Reid C	Field EEF	11/05/19	M	7 yrs PS	Comm 2 yrs HL	WO/213/30/28
2 W India	Pte	Ricketts R	Field EEF	11/05/19	M	5 yrs PS	Comm 1 yr HL	WO/213/30/27
2 W India	Pte	Roberts G	Field EEF	11/05/19	M	7 yrs PS	Comm 2 yrs HL	WO/213/30/28
2 W India	Pte	Robinson E	Field EEF	11/05/19	M	5 yrs PS	Comm 1 yr HL	WO/213/30/28
2 W India	Pte	Salmon W	Field EEF	11/05/19	M	7 yrs PS	Comm 2 yrs HL	WO/213/30/28
2 W India	Pte	Shaw A	Field EEF	11/05/19	M	7 yrs PS	Comm 2 yrs HL	WO/213/30/27
2 W India	Pte	Taylor E	Field EEF	11/05/19	M	5 yrs PS	Comm 1 yr HL	WO/213/30/28
2 W India	Pte	Taylor N	Field EEF	11/05/19	M	7 yrs PS	Comm 2 yrs HL	WO/213/30/28
2 W India	Pte	Wallcutt H	Field EEF	11/05/19	M	5 yrs PS	Comm 1 yr HL	WO/213/30/27
2 W India	Pte	Watson J	Field EEF	11/05/19	M	7 yrs PS	Comm 2 yrs HL	WO/213/30/28
2 W India	Pte	White J	Field EEF	11/05/19	M	7 yrs PS	Comm 2 yrs HL	WO/213/30/28
2 W India	Pte	Wiles C	Field EEF	11/05/19	M	7 yrs PS	Comm 2 yrs HL	WO/213/30/27
2 W India	Pte	Wilson G	Field EEF	11/05/19	M	7 yrs PS	Comm 1 yr HL	WO/213/30/28
2 W India	Pte	Anderson H	Field EEF	11/05/19	M	5 yrs PS	Comm 1 yr HL	WO/213/30/27
Bermuda Royal Artillery	Gnr	Carmichael J	Bermuda	31/08/20	M	Acquit		WO/90/8/84
Bermuda Royal Artillery	Gnr	Ford B	Bermuda	31/08/20	M	Acquit		WO/90/8/84
Bermuda Royal Artillery	Gnr	Galloway JA	Bermuda	31/08/20	M	Acquit		WO/90/8/84
Bermuda Royal Artillery	Gnr	Gardiner J	Bermuda	01/09/20	M+Esc+S6(1d)	2 yrs HL+DI		WO/90/8/84

Chinese

Unit	Rank	Name	Location	Date	Offence	Finding/Punishment	Amendment	PRO Reference
Chinese Lab Corps	Coolie	1968	Field	09/05/18	M+Striking	2 yrs HL		WO/213/22/50
Chinese Lab Corps	Coolie	40749	Field	09/05/18	M+Striking	1 yr HL		WO/213/22/50
Chinese Lab Corps	Coolie	25348	Field	12/05/18	M+Insub+Disob	6 mos HL	Quashed	WO/213/22/111

Egyptian

Unit	Rank	Name	Location	Date	Offence	Finding/Punishment	Amendment	PRO Reference
Egyptian Lab Corps	Labourer	Abdalla Y	Boulogne	06/09/17	M+S40	8 mos HL		WO/213/17/41
Egyptian Lab Corps	Labourer	Acasha A	Boulogne	06/09/17	M+S40	8 mos HL		WO/213/17/41
Egyptian Lab Corps	Labourer	Ahmed R	Boulogne	06/09/17	M+S40	8 mos HL		WO/213/17/41
Egyptian Lab Corps	Labourer	Ali A	Boulogne	06/09/17	M+S40	8 mos HL		WO/213/17/41
Egyptian s Lab Corp	Labourer	Bahit AS	Boulogne	06/09/17	M+S40	8 mos HL		WO/213/17/41
Egyptian Lab Corps	Labourer	Ibrahim S	Boulogne	06/09/17	M+S40	8 mos HL		WO/213/17/41
Egyptian Lab Corps	Labourer	Mohamed A	Boulogne	06/09/17	M+S40	8 mos HL		WO/213/17/41
Egyptian Lab Corps	Labourer	Sallam O	Boulogne	06/09/17	M+S40	8 mos HL		WO/213/17/41
Egyptian Lab Corps	Labourer	Sarhan M	Boulogne	06/09/17	M+S40	8 mos HL		WO/213/17/41
Egyptian Lab Corps	Labourer	Suleiman M	Boulogne	06/09/17	M+S40	8 mos HL		WO/213/17/41

English and British Corps and Royal Air Force

Unit	Rank	Name	Location	Date	Offence	Finding/Punishment	Amendment	PRO Reference
2 Gn/Beds	Pte	Barber SH	Karachi	04/04/18	M+S7(3)	Acquit		WO/90/7/191
2 Gn/Beds	Pte	Bushell WJ	Karachi	04/04/18	M+S7(3)	1 yr Detn	Comm 6 mos	WO/90/7/191
2 Gn/Beds	Pte	Ives GK	Karachi	04/04/18	M+S7(3)	3 yrs PS	Comm 2 yrs HL	WO/90/7/191
2 Gn/Beds	Pte	Jones SH	Karachi	04/04/18	M+S7(3)	5 yrs PS	Comm 2 yrs HL	WO/90/7/191
2 Gn/Beds	Pte	Perring G	Karachi	04/04/18	M+S7(3)	5 yrs PS	Comm 1yr	WO/90/7/191
2 Gn/Beds	Pte	Topley TC	Karachi	04/04/18	M+S7(3)	3 yrs PS	Comm 2 yrs HL	WO/90/7/191
2 Gn/Beds	Pte	Wadman W	Karachi	04/04/18	M+S7(3)	5 yrs PS	Comm 2 yrs HL	WO/90/7/191
2 Gn/Beds	Pte	Williams A	Karachi	04/04/18	M+S7(3)	2 yrs PS	Comm 12 mos Detn	WO/90/7/191
3 Gn Beds	Pte	Clements R	Meiktila	12/03/18	M+Disob	2 yrs Detn	Comm 1 yr Detn	WO/90/8/199
3 Gn Beds	Pte	Parrish D	Meiktila	12/03/18	M+Disob	2 yrs Detn	Comm 1 yr Detn	WO/90/8/199
51 Beds	Pte	Coats A	Teverham	09/10/18	M+Theft+S40	28 dys Detn	NC	WO/86/85/9
R Berks (att 1/OBLI)	Sgt	Waters F	Field NREF	26/07/19	M+S40	6 mos HL+Rnks	Comm 91 dys Imp	WO/213/30/106
1 R Berks	Pte	Robinson MH	Rouen	04/02/19	M	Acquit		WO/90/8/58
5 Berks	Pte	Brown A	Arras	13/04/17	M+S40	3 mos Stop	Rem 2 mos	WO/213/15/142
13 R Berks	Pte	Buckley M	Dunkirk	13/04/17	M	8 mos HL		WO/213/14/138

Unit	Rank	Name	Location	Date D/M/Y	Offence	Finding/Punishment	Amendment	PRO Reference File/Piece/Page
1 Border	Pte	Groom W	Louvencourt	22/06/16	M+Insub+Disob	4 yrs PS	Susp	WO/213/10/111
2 Buffs	Pte	Crouch FE	Dover	07/10/19	M	NG		WO/86/88/141
1 Cheshire	Pte	Kennedy T	Ranikhet	23/08/22	M+Disob(Sgt Maj)+S40	1 yr Detn		WO/90/8/172
1/7 Ches	Pte	Fagan A	Field	24/03/19	M	18 yrs PS		WO213/29/88
2 Ches	Pte	Codd A	Field ABS	05/03/20	M+Disob	2 yrs HL	Rem 18 mos	WO/213/31/168
2 Ches	Pte	Draper A	Field ABS	05/03/20	M+Disob	2 yrs HL	Rem 18 mos	WO/213/31/168
2 Ches	Pte	Jackson J	Field ABS	05/03/20	M+Disob	2 yrs HL	Rem 18 mos	WO/213/31/168
2 Ches	Pte	King G	Field ABS	05/03/20	M+Disob	9 mos HL	Rem 3 mos	WO/213/31/168
2 Ches	Pte	McGuire EM	Field ABS	05/03/20	M+Disob	2 yrs HL	Rem 18 mos	WO/213/31/168
2 Ches	Pte	Monks L	Field ABS	05/03/20	M+Disob	2 yrs HL	Rem 18 mos	WO/213/31/168
2 Ches	Pte	Pearson H	Field ABS	05/03/20	M+Disob	2 yrs HL	Rem 18 mos	WO/213/31/168
2 Ches	Pte	Roberts A	Field ABS	05/03/20	M+Disob	18 mos HL	Rem 1 yr	WO/213/31/168
2 Ches	Pte	Shelly F	Field ABS	05/03/20	M+7(2b)	2 yrs HL		WO/213/31/168
2 Ches	Pte	Smith D	Field ABS	05/03/20	M+Disob	2 yrs HL	Rem 18 mos	WO/213/31/168
1/1 C of Lon Yeo	Pte	Bean HG	Field EEF	17/06/19	M+S40	NG		WO/213/30/104
1/1 C of Lon Yeo	Pte	Gale H	Field EEF	17/06/19	M+S40	NG		WO/213/30/104
1/1 C of Lon Yeo	S/Smith	Gray FW	Field	18/06/19	M+S40	75 dys Stop	Remit 53 dys	WO/213/30/96
1/1 C of Lon Yeo	Pte	Griffin AJ	Field	18/06/19	M+S40	NG		WO/213/30/96
1/1 C of Lon Yeo	L/Cpl	Hambrook E	Field EEF	18/06/19	M+S40	NG		WO/213/30/97
1/1 C of Lon Yeo	Pte	Smallbone GW	Field	18/06/19	M+S40	NG		WO/213/30/96
68 Div Cyclist Co	Pte	Lea E	Gt Yarmouth	17/07/17	M	6 mos Detn		WO/86/73/171
68 Div Cyclist Co	Pte	Hague T	Gt Yarmouth	17/07/17	M+Insub(S/Sgt)	NG		WO/86/73/171
68 Div Cyclist Co	Pte	Turton H	Gt Yarmouth	17/07/17	M	NG		WO/86/73/171
68 Div Cyclist Co	Pte	Dimelow	Gt Yarmouth	17/07/17	M+Insub(L/Cpl)	NG		WO/86/73/171
68 Div Cyclist Co	Pte	Hardy A	Gt Yarmouth	17/07/17	M+Insub(L/Cpl)	NG		WO/86/73/171
68 Div Cyclist Co	Pte	Harrison JL	Gt Yarmouth	17/07/17	M+Insub(L/Cpl)	NG		WO/86/73/171
68 Div Cyclist Co	Pte	Riley JJ	Gt Yarmouth	17/07/17	M+Insub(L/Cpl)	NG		WO/86/73/171
Derby Yeo (att 5 Dragoon Gds)	L/Cpl	Hall W	Curragh	25/09/19	M	1 yr HL+Disch Igmny	6 mos Detn	WO/92/4/86
3 Dorsets	Pte	Amey J	Dorchester	29/12/14	Joining M+Viol(Capt)	4 mos HL		WO/92/3/18
3 Dorsets	Cpl	Anscombe J	Dorchester	29/12/14	Joining M+Viol(Capt)	NG		WO/92/3/18
3 Dorsets	L/Cpl	Cattell J	Dorchester	29/12/14	Joining M+Viol(Capt)	4 mos HL		WO/92/3/18
3 Dorsets	Pte	Parsons A	Dorchester	29/12/14	Joining M+Viol(Capt)	4 mos HL		WO/92/3/18
3 Dorsets	Cpl	Wilson A	Dorchester	29/12/14	Joining M+Viol(Capt)	6 mos HL		WO/92/3/18
4 Dragoon Gds	Pte	Crockett AE	Edinburgh	09/06/21	M+V(A/RSM)	2 yrs HL		WO/86/91/131
5 Dragoon Gds	L/Cpl	Ainsworth C	Curragh	29/09/19	M	18 mos HL+Disch Igmny	Comm 9 mos Dtn	WO/92/4/83
5 Dragoon Gds	Pte	Allen CH	Curragh	23/09/19	M	84 dys HL	Comm 42 dys Detn	WO/92/4/85
5 Dragoon Gds	Pte	Arthurs E	Curragh	29/09/19	M	1 yr HL+Disch Igmny	Comm 6 mos Detn	WO/92/4/82
5 Dragoon Gds	Pte	Atkinson T	Curragh	29/09/19	M	1 yr HL+Disch Igmny	Comm 6 mos Detn	WO/92/4/81
5 Dragoon Gds	Pte	Ayres J	Curragh	29/09/19	M	18 mos HL+Disch Igmny	Comm 9 mos Dtn	WO/92/4/83
5 Dragoon Gds	Pte	Ball S	Curragh	30/09/19	M	1 yr HL+Disch Igmny	Comm 6 mos Detn	WO/92/4/87
5 Dragoon Gds	Pte	Bartlett J	Curragh	29/09/19	M	1 yr HL+Disch Igmny	Comm 6 mos Detn	WO/92/4/81
5 Dragoon Gds	Pte	Beattie RE	Curragh	23/09/19	M	84 dys HL	Comm 42 dys Detn	WO/92/4/85
5 Dragoon Gds	Pte	Bell D	Curragh	29/09/19	M	18 mos HL+Disch Igmny	Comm 9 mos Dtn	WO/92/4/83
5 Dragoon Gds	Pte	Bentham	Currasgh		M	1yr HL+Disch Igmny	Comm 6 mos Dtn	WO/92/4/87
5 Dragoon Gds	Pte	Bernstein AP	Curragh	22/09/19	M	1 yr HL+Disch Igmny	Comm 6 mos Detn	WO/92/4/84
5 Dragoon Gds	Pte	Berry A	Curragh	26/09/19	M	1 yr HL+Disch Igmny	Comm 6 mos Detn	WO/92/4/83
5 Dragoon Gds	Pte	Biram F	Curragh	22/09/19	M	1 yr HL+Disch Igmny	Comm 1 yr Detn	WO/92/4/81
5 Dragoon Gds	Pte	Blair D	Curragh	25/09/19	M	1 yr HL+Disch Igmny	Comm 6 mos Detn	WO/92/4/86
5 Dragoon Gds	Pte	Bostock A	Curragh	22/09/19	M	1 yr HL+Disch Igmny	Comm 6 mos Detn	WO/92/4/83
5 Dragoon Gds	Pte	Bowker J	Curragh	22/09/19	M	1 yr HL+Disch Igmny	Comm 6 mos Detn	WO/92/4/81
5 Dragoon Gds	Pte	Boyle C	Curragh	30/09/19	M	Acquit		WO/92/4/87
5 Dragoon Gds	Pte	Boyle J	Curragh	29/09/19	M	1 yr HL+Disch Igmny	Comm 6 mos Detn	WO/92/4/81
5 Dragoon Gds	Pte	Bradfield EE	Curragh	29/09/19	M	1 yr HL+Disch Igmny	Comm 6 mos Detn	WO/92/4/82

Unit	Rank	Name	Location	Date D/M/Y	Offence	Finding/Punishment	Amendment	PRO Reference File/Piece/Page
5 Dragoon Gds	Pte	Brookfield W	Curragh	23/09/19	M	84 dys HL	Comm 42 dys Detn	WO/92/4/85
5 Dragoon Gds	Pte	Brown JW	Curragh	24/09/19	M	1 yr HL+Disch Igmny	Comm 6 mos Detn	WO/92/4/85
5 Dragoon Gds	Pte	Brownsdon S	Curragh	26/09/19	M	1 yr HL+Disch Igmny	Comm 6 mos Detn	WO/92/4/83
5 Dragoon Gds	Pte	Brunskill A	Curragh	23/09/19	M	1 yr HL+Disch Igmny	Comm 6mos Detn	WO/92/4/85
5 Dragoon Gds	Pte	Bullen E	Curragh	26/09/19	M	1 yr HL+Disch Igmny	Comm 6 mos Detn	WO/92/4/80
2 Dragoon Gds	Pte	Burley H	Curragh	25/09/19	M	1 yr HL+Disch Igmny	Comm 6 mos Detn	WO/92/4/86
5 Dragoon Gds	Pte	Carroll W	Curragh	29/09/19	M	1 yr HL+Disch Igmny	Comm 6 mos Detn	WO/92/4/82
5 Dragoon Gds	Pte	Clarke F	Curragh	29/09/19	M	1 yr HL+Disch Igmny	Comm 6 mos Detn	WO/92/4/82
5 Dragoon Gds	Pte	Coley T	Curragh	22/09/19	M	1 yr HL+Disch Igmny	Comm 6 mos Detn	WO/92/4/83
5 Dragoon Gds	Pte	Cossey A	Curragh	29/09/19	M	1 yr HL+Disch Igmny	Comm 6 mos Detn	WO/92/4/82
5 Dragoon Gds	Pte	Creedy WE	Curragh	29/09/19	M	1 yr HL+Disch Igmny	Comm 6 mos Detn	WO/92/4/81
5 Dragoon Gds	Pte	Curran RN	Curragh	26/09/19	M	1 yr HL+Disch Igmny	Comm 6 mos Detn	WO/92/4/80
5 Dragoon Gds	Pte	Curwen T	Curragh	26/09/19	M	1 yr HL+Disch Igmny	Comm 6 mos Detn	WO/92/4/80
5 Dragoon Gds	Pte	Daley J	Curragh	24/09/19	M	1 yr HL+Disch Igmny	Comm 6 mos Detn	WO/92/4/85
5 Dragoon Gds	Pte	Davies HE	Curragh	29/09/19	M	1 yr HL+Disch Igmny	Comm 6 mos Detn	WO/92/4/82
5 Dragoon Gds	Pte	Davies WA	Curragh	22/09/19	M	1 yr HL+Disch Igmny	Comm 6 mos Detn	WO/92/4/81
5 Dragoon Gds	Pte	Dean W	Curragh	23/09/19	M	84 dys HL	Comm 42 dys Detn	WO/92/4/85
5 Dragoon Gds	Pte	Dilworth WF	Curragh	29/09/19	M	1 yr HL+Disch Igmny	Comm 6 mos Detn	WO/92/4/82
5 Dragoon Gds	Pte	Donaldson AC	Curragh	23/09/19	M	84 dys HL	Comm 42 dys Detn	WO/92/4/85
5 Dragoon Gds	L/Cpl	Dorans H	Curragh	25/09/19	M	Acquit		WO/92/4/86
5 Dragoon Gds	Pte	Drury B	Curragh	26/09/19	M	1 yr HL+Disch Igmny	Comm 6 mos Detn	WO/92/4/81
5 Dragoon Gds	Pte	Duncan A	Curragh	22/09/19	M	1 yr HL+Disch Igmny	Comm 6 mos Detn	WO/92/3/84
5 Dragoon Gds	Pte	Egglestone JW	Curragh	26/09/19	M	1 yr HL+Disch Igmny	Comm 6 mos Detn	WO/92/4/81
5 Dragoon Gds	Pte	Elliott JW	Curragh	22/09/19	M	1 yr HL+Disch Igmny	Comm 6 mos Detn	WO/92/4/84
5 Dragoon Gds	Pte	Evans SW	Curragh	24/09/19	M	1 yr HL+Disch Igmny	Comm 6 mos Detn	WO/92/4/85
5 Dragoon Gds	Pte	Ewington AH	Curragh	29/09/19	M	1 yr HL+Disch Igmny	Comm 6 mos Detn	WO/92/4/82
5 Dragoon Gds	Pte	Fisher GW	Curragh	29/09/19	M	1 yr HL+Disch Igmny	Comm 6 mos Detn	WO/92/4/82
5 Dragoon Gds	Pte	Gadsby JE	Curragh	23/09/19	M	84 dys HL	Comm 42 dys Detn	WO/92/4/85
5 Dragoon Gds	Pte	Gandy C	Curragh	29/09/19	M	1 yr HL+Disch Igmny	Comm 6 mos Detn	WO/92/4/82
5 Dragoon Gds	Pte	Garner VJ	Curragh	22/09/19	M	1 yr HL+Disch Igmny	Comm 6 mos Detn	WO/92/4/84
5 Dragoon Gds	Pte	Gates D	Curragh	22/09/19	M	1 yr HL+Disch Igmny	Comm 6 mos Detn	WO/92/4/84
5 Dragoon Gds	Pte	Gilbert J	Curragh	22/09/19	M	1 yr HL+Disch Igmny	Comm 6 mos Detn	WO/92/4/84
5 Dragoon Gds	Pte	Gill J	Curragh	29/09/19	M	1 yr HL+Disch Igmny	Comm 6 mos Detn	WO/92/4/83
5 Dragoon Gds	Pte	Goodwin J	Curragh	29/09/19	M	1 yr HL+Disch Igmny	Comm 9 mos Detn	WO/92/4/83
5 Dragoon Gds	L/Cpl	Gornall R	Curragh	30/09/19	M	18 mos HL +Disch Igmny	Comm 9 mos Dtn	WO/92/4/87
5 Dragoon Gds	Pte	Gough F	Curragh	29/09/19	M	1 yr HL+Disch Igmny	Comm 6 mos Detn	WO/92/4/82
5 Dragoon Gds	Pte	Greenfield A	Curragh	26/09/19	M	1 yr HL+Disch Igmny	Comm 6 mos Detn	WO/92/4/81

Unit	Rank	Name	Location	Date D/M/Y	Offence	Finding/Punishment	Amendment	PRO Reference File/Piece/Page
5 Dragoon Gds	Pte	Greenhow WS	Curragh	29/09/19	M	1 yr HL+Disch Igmny	Comm 6 mos Detn	WO/92/4/81
5 Dragoon Gds	Pte	Hamilton F	Curragh	25/09/19	M	1 yr HL+Disch Igmny	Comm 6 mos Detn	WO/92/4/87
5 Dragoon Gds	Pte	Hamilton J	Curragh	23/09/19	M	1 yr HL+Disch Igmny	Comm 6 mos Detn	WO/92/4/84
5 Dragoon Gds	Pte	Harrison J	Curragh	25/09/19	M	1 yr HL+Disch Igmny	Comm 6 mos Detn	WO/92/4/86
5 Dragoon Gds	L/Cpl	Hartley H	Curragh	25/09/19	M	6 mos HL	Comm 84 dys Detn	WO/92/4/86
5 Dragoon Gds	Pte	Hawksby T	Curragh	23/09/19	M	6 mos HL +Disch Igmny	Comm 84 dys Dtn	WO/92/4/84
5 Dragoon Gds	Pte	Heath LC	Curragh	24/09/19	M	Acquit		WO/92/4/87
5 Dragoon Gds	Pte	Henderson W	Curragh	26/09/19	M	1 yr HL+Disch Igmny	Comm 6 mos Detn	WO/92/4/81
5 Dragoon Gds	Pte	Heys H	Curragh	29/09/19	M	1 yr HL+Disch Igmny	Comm 6 mos Detn	WO/92/4/83
5 Dragoon Gds	Pte	Higgs GH	Curragh	23/09/19	M	1 yr HL+Disch Igmny	Comm 6 mos Detn	WO/92/4/84
5 Dragoon Gds	Pte	Highley D	Curragh	30/09/19	M	1 yr HL+Disch Igmny	Comm 6 mos Detn	WO/92/4/87
5 Dragoon Gds	Pte	Hodge H	Curragh	22/09/19	M	1 yr HL+Disch Igmny	Comm 6 mos Detn	WO/92/4/84
5 Dragoon Gds	Pte	Hoey G	Curragh	29/09/19	M	18 mos HL +Disch Igmny	Comm 9 mos Dtn	WO/92/4/83
5 Dragoon Gds	Pte	Hogg E	Curragh	29/09/19	M	1 yr HL+Disch Igmny	Comm 6 mos Detn	WO/92/4/83
5 Dragoon Gds	Pte	Holding A	Curragh	26/09/19	M	1 yr HL+Disch Igmny	Comm 6 mos Detn	WO/92/4/81
5 Dragoon Gds	Pte	Holliday P	Curragh	23/09/19	M	6 mos HL +Disch Igmny	Comm 84 dys Dtn	WO/92/4/84
5 Dragoon Gds	Pte	Howarth R	Curragh	23/09/19	M	84 dys HL	Comm 42 dys Detn	WO/92/4/85
5 Dragoon Gds	Pte	Hudson FWA	Curragh	25/09/19	M	56 dys Detn	NC	WO/92/4/86
6 Dragoon Gds	Pte	Hunter W	Curragh	23/09/19	M	84 dys HL	Comm 42 dys Detn	WO/92/4/85
5 Dragoon Gds	Pte	Hurst F	Curragh	23/09/19	M	84 dys HL	Comm 42 dys Detn	WO/92/4/85
5 Dragoon Gds	Pte	Illingworth N	Curragh	29/09/19	M	1 yr HL+Disch Igmny	Comm 6 mos Detn	WO/92/4/82
5 Dragoon Gds	Pte	Jackson HB	Curragh	25/09/19	M	Acquit		WO/92/4/86
5 Dragoon Gds	Pte	James FA	Curragh	22/09/19	M	1 yr HL+Disch Igmny	Comm 6 mos Detn	WO/92/4/81
5 Dragoon Gds	Pte	Johnston R	Curragh	25/09/19	M	56 dys Detn	NC	WO/92/4/86
5 Dragoon Gds	Pte	Jones F	Curragh	24/09/19	M	1 yr HL +Disch Igmny	Comm 6 mos Detn	WO/92/4/85
5 Dragoon Gds	Pte	Jones S	Curragh	23/09/19	M	1 yr HL+Disch Igmny	Comm 6 mos Detn	WO/92/4/84
5 Dragoon Gds	Pte	Jowett HW	Curragh	29/09/19	M	1 yr HL+Disch Igmny	Comm 6 mos Detn	WO/92/4/82
5 Dragoon Gds	Pte	Jowett P	Curragh	22/09/19	M	1 yr HL+Disch Igmny	Comm 6 mos Detn	WO/92/4/81
5 Dragoon Gds	Pte	Kelly A	Curragh	23/09/19	M	6 mos HL	Comm 84 dys Detn	WO/92/4/84
5 Dragoon Gds	Pte	Kennedy J	Curragh	22/09/19	M	1 yr HL+Disch Igmny	Comm 6 mos Detn	WO/92/4/84
5 Dragoon Gds	Pte	Kenyon TF	Curragh	30/09/19	M	1 yr HL+Disch Igmny	Comm 6 mos Detn	W 0/92/4/87
5 Dragoon Gds	Pte	King J	Curragh	26/09/19	M	1 yr HL+Disch Igmny	Comm 6 mos Detn	WO/92/4/81
5 Dragoon Gds	Pte	Lambert A	Curragh	26/09/19	M	1 yr HL+Disch Igmny	Comm 6 mos Detn	WO/92/4/83
2 Dragoon Gds	Pte	Leah J	Curragh	25/09/19	M	1 yr HL+Disch Igmny	Comm 6 mos Detn	WO/92/4/87
5 Dragoon Gds	Pte	Livermore AW	Curragh	26/09/19	M	1 yr HL+Disch Igmny	Comm 6 mos Detn	WO/92/4/81
5 Dragoon Gds	Pte	Livingstone JF	Curragh	25/09/19	M	Acquit		WO/92/4/86
5 Dragoon Gds	Pte	Lord W	Curragh	29/09/19	M	1 yr HL+Disch Igmny	Comm 6 mos Detn	WO/92/4/83
5 Dragoon Gds	Ptr	Lunt S	Curragh	23/09/19	M	Acquit		WO/92/4/84
5 Dragoon Gds	Pte	Mackie GE	Curragh	24/09/19	M	84 dys HL	Comm 42 dys Detn	WO/92/4/87
5 Dragoon Gds	Pte	Marsden J	Curragh	24/09/19	M	1 yr HL+Disch Igmny	Comm 6 mos Detn	WO/92/4/86

Unit	Rank	Name	Location	Date D/M/Y	Offence	Finding/Punishment	Amendment	PRO Reference File/Piece/Page
5 Dragoon Gds	Pte	Matthews GF	Curragh	29/09/19	M	1 yr HL + Disch Igmny	Comm 6 mos Detn	WO/92/4/82
5 Dragoon Gds	Pte	McClelland A	Curragh	26/09/19	M	1 yr HL + Disch Igmny	Comm 6 mos Detn	WO/92/4/83
5 Dragoon Gds	Pte	McDowell S	Curragh	23/09/19	M	6 mos HL	Comm 84 dys Detn	WO/92/4/84
5 Dragoon Gds	Pte	Millward H	Curragh	29/09/19	M	1 yr HL + Disch Igmny	Comm 6 mos Detn	WO/92/4/82
5 Dragoon Gds	Pte	Molloy P	Curragh	24/09/19	M	1 yr HL + Disch Igmny	Comm 6 mos Detn	WO/92/4/87
5 Dragoon Gds	Pte	Moody WA	Curragh	22/09/19	M	1 yr HL + Disch Igny	Comm 6 mos Detn	WO/92/4/81
5 Dragoon Gds	Pte	Moore F	Curragh	25/09/19	M	Acquit		WO/92/4/87
5 Dragoon Gds	Pte	Moore GS	Currragh	29/09/19	M	1 yr HL + Disch Igmny	Comm 6 mos Detn	WO/92/4/81
5 Dragoon Gds	Pte	Moore M	Curragh	24/09/19	M	Acquit		WO/92/4/86
5 Dragoon Gds	Pte	Morris H	Curragh	26/09/19	M	1 yr HL + Disch Igmny	Comm 6 mos Detn	WO/92/4/83
5 Dragoon Gds	L/Cpl	Mountford WH	Curragh	25/09/19	M	Acquit		WO/92/4/86
5 Dragoon Gds	Pte	Mutch R	Curragh	23/09/19	M	1 yr HL + Disch Igmny	Comm 6 mos Detn	WO/92/4/84
5 Dragoon Gds	Pte	Nicholson T	Curragh	24/09/19	M	1 yr HL + Disch Igmny	Comm 6 mos Detn	WO/92/4/86
5 Dragoon Gds	Pte	Norton E	Curragh	30/09/19	M	1 yr HL + Disch Igmny	Comm 6 mos Detn	WO/92/4/87
5 Dragoon Gds	Pte	Nott WH	Curragh	26/09/19	M	1 yr HL + Disch Igmny	Comm 6 mos Detn	WO/92/4/81
5 Dragoon Gds	Pte	O'Keeffe P	Curragh	26/09/19	M	1 yr HL + Disch Igmny	Comm 6 mos Detn	WO/92/4/83
5 Dragoon Gds	Pte	O'Rourke J	Curragh	26/09/19	M	1 yr HL + Disch Igmny	Comm 6 mos Detn	WO/92/4/83
5 Dragoon Gds	Pte	Owens JW	Curragh	24/09/19	M	1 yr HL + Disch Igmny	Comm 6mos Detn	WO/92/4/86
5 Dragoon Gds	Pte	Pallister JF	Curragh	26/09/19	M	1 yr HL + Disch Igmny	Comm 6 mos Detn	WO/92/4/81
5 Dragoon Gds	Pte	Pannell A	Curragh	23/09/19	M	84 dys HL	Comm 42 dys Detn	WO/92/4/85
5 Dragoon Gds	Pte	Partington A	Curragh	22/09/19	M	1 yr HL + Disch Igmny	Comm 6 mos Detn	WO/92/4/84
2 Dragoon Gds	Pte	Partington WE	Curragh	30/09/19	M	84 dys HL	Comm 42 dys Detn	WO/92/4/87
5 Dragoon Gds	Pte	Phillips F	Curragh	23/09/19	M	84 dys HL	Comm 42 dys Detn	WO/92/4/85
5 Dragoon Gds	Pte	Popham HH	Curragh	24/09/19	M	1 yr HL + Disch Igmny	Comm 6 mos Detn	WO/92/4/86
5 Dragoon Gds	Pte	Potter T	Curragh	22/09/19	M	1 yr HL + Disch Igmny	Comm 6 mos Detn	WO/92/4/81
5 Dragoon Gds	Pte	Pownall WD	Curragh	29/09/19	M	1 yr HL + Disch Igmny	Comm 6 mos Detn	WO/92/4/82
5 Dragoon Gds	Pte	Prince J	Curragh	24/09/19	M	Acquit		WO/92/4/87
5 Dragoon Gds	Pte	Ramsey JGS	Curragh	26/09/19	M	1 yr HL + Disch Igmny	Comm 6 mos Detn	WO/92/4/83
5 Dragoon Gds	Pte	Riddell TJ	Curragh	23/09/19	M	1 yr HL + Disch Igmny	Comm 6 mos Detn	WO/92/4/84
5 Dragoon Gds	Pte	Rimmer F	Curragh	30/09/19	M	1 yr HL + Disch Igmny	Comm 6 mos Detn	WO/92/4/87
5 Dragoon Gds	Pte	Robertson H	Curragh	22/09/19	M	1 yr HL + Disch Igmny	Comm 6 mos Detn	WO/92/4/84
5 Dragoon Gds	Pte	Robinson H	Curragh	29/09/19	M	1 yr HL + Disch Igmny	Comm 6 mos Detn	WO/92/4/82
5 Dragoon Gds	Pte	Roden GW	Curragh	26/09/19	M	1 yr HL + Disch Igmny	Comm 6 mos Detn	WO/92/4/83
5 Dragoon Gds	Pte	Rutter S	Curragh	23/09/19	M	1 yr HL + Disch Igmny	Comm 6 mos Detn	WO/92/4/84
5 Dragoon Gds	Pte	Sands WH	Curragh	30/09/19	M	1 yr HL + Disch Igmny	Comm 6 mos Detn	WO/92/4/87
5 Dragoon Gds	Pte	Seddon TG	Curragh	23/09/19	M	1 yr HL + Disch Igmny	Comm 6 mos Detn	WO/92/4/85
5 Dragoon Gds	Pte	Sibbald JS	Curragh	29/09/19	M	1 yr HL + Disch Igmny	Comm 6 mos Detn	WO/92/4/82
5 Dragoon Gds	Pte	Simmonds JF	Curragh	25/09/19	M	56 dys Detn	NC	WO/92/4/86
5 Dragoon Gds	Pte	Simpson J	Curragh	29/09/19	M	1 yr HL + Disch Igmny	Comm 6 mos Detn	WO/92/4/82

Unit	Rank	Name	Location	Date D/M/Y	Offence	Finding/Punishment	Amendment	PRO Reference File/Piece/Page
5 Dragoon Gds	Pte	Skipp WH	Curragh	26/09/19	M	1 yr HL+Disch Igmny	Comm 6 mos Detn	WO/92/4/83
5 Dragoon Gds	Pte	Slater W	Curragh	26/09/19	M	1 yr HL+Disch Igny	Comm 6 mos Detn	WO/92/4/81
5 Dragoon Gds	Pte	Smith EH	Curragh	23/09/19	M	84 dys HL	Comm 42 dys Detn	WO/92/4/85
5 Dragoon Gds	Pte	Smith HJ	Curragh	23/09/19	M	6 mos HL	Comm 84 dys Detn	WO/92/4/85
5 Dragoon Gds	Pte	Smith RA	Curragh	24/09/19	M	1 yr HL+Igmny	Comm 6 mos Detn	WO/92/4/86
5 Dragoon Gds	Pte	Smith W	Curragh	24/09/19	M	1 yr HL+Disch Igmny	Comm 6 mos Detn	WO/92/4/87
5 Dragoon Gds	Pte	Smith W	Curragh	30/09/19	M	1 yr HL+Disch Igmny	Comm 6 mos Detn	WO/92/4/87
5 Dragoon Gds	Pte	Spence JD	Curragh	23/09/19	M	84 dys HL	Comm 42 dys Detn	WO/92/4/85
5 Dragoon Gds	Pte	Stanworth H	Curragh	23/09/19	M	1 yr HL+Disch Igmny	Comm 6 mos Detn	WO/92/4/85
5 Dragoon Gds	Pte	Steele FJ	Curragh	24/09/19	M	1 yr HL+Disch Igmny	Comm 6 mos Detn	WO/92/4/86
5 Dragoon Gds	Pte	Stevens DM	Curragh	26/09/19	M	1 yr HL+Disch Igmny	Comm 6 mos Detn	WO/92/4/83
5 Dragoon Gds	Pte	Stone HF	Curragh	25/09/19	M	1 yr HL+Disch Igmny	Comm 6 mos Detn	WO/92/4/86
5 Dragoon Gds	Pte	Stones D	Curragh	29/09/19	M	1 yr HL+Disch Igmny	Comm 6 mos Detn	WO/92/4/82
5 Dragoon Gds	Pte	Stothard GW	Curragh	24/09/19	M	1 yr HL+Disch Igmny	Comm 6 mos Detn	WO/92/4/86
5 Dragoon Gds	Pte	Stringer S	Curragh	23/09/19	M	1 yr HL+Disch Igmny	Comm 6 mos Detn	WO/92/4/85
5 Dragoon Gds	Pte	Sutton WW	Curragh	30/09/19	M	1 yr HL+Disch Igmny	Comm 6 mos Detn	WO/92/4/87
5 Dragoon Gds	Pte	Swallow L	Curragh	24/09/19	M	1 yr HL+Disch Igmny	Comm 6 mos Detn	WO/92/4/87
5 Dragoon Gds	Pte	Sykes J	Curragh	23/09/19	M	1 yr HL+Disch Igmny	Comm 6 mos Detn	WO/92/4/85
5 Dragoon Gds	Pte	Taylor ES	Curragh	26/09/19	M	1 yr HL+Disch Igmny	Comm 6 mos Detn	WO/92/4/83
5 Dragoon Gds	Pte	Taylor H	Curragh	30/09/19	M	1 yr HL+Disch Igmny	Comm 6 mos Detn	WO/92/4/87
5 Dragoon Gds	Pte	Theirens RH	Curragh	26/09/19	M	5 yrs PS+Disch Igmny	Comm 2 yrs Detn	WO/92/4/83
5 Dragoon Gds	Pte	Timms W	Curragh	24/09/19	M	1 yr HL+Disch Igmny	Comm 6 mos Detn	WO/92/4/87
5 Dragoon Gds	Pte	Turks AJ	Curragh	26/09/19	M	2 yrs HL+Disch Igny	Comm 1 yr Detn	WO/92/4/81
5 Dragoon Gds	Pte	Vance H	Curragh	22/09/19	M	Acquit		WO/92/4/84
5 Dragoon Gds	Pte	Wallace E	Curragh	29/09/19	M	1 yr HL+Disch Igmny	Comm 6 mos Detn	WO/92/4/82
5 Dragoon Gds	Pte	Watkinson W	Curragh	29/09/19	M	1 yr HL+Disch Igmny	Comm 6 mos Detn	WO/92/4/82
5 Dragoon Gds	Pte	White A	Curragh	22/09/19	M	1 yr HL+Disch Igmny	Comm 6 mos Detn	WO/92/4/81
5 Dragoon Gds	L/Cpl	White JH	Curragh	29/09/19	M	1 yr HL+Disch Igmny	Comm 6 mos Detn	WO/92/4/81
5 Dragoon Gds	Pte	White JK	Curragh	29/09/19	M	1 yr HL+Disch Igmny	Comm 6 mos Detn	WO/92/4/82
5 Dragoon Gds	Pte	Whitehead J	Curragh	22/09/19	M	1 yr HL+Disch Igmny	Comm 6 mos Detn	WO/92/4/84
5 Dragoon Gds	Pte	Whitehead W	Curragh	24/09/19	M	1 yr HL+Disch Igmny	Comm 6 mos Detn	WO/92/4/86
5 Dragoon Gds	Pte	Whittaker J	Curragh	22/09/19	M	1 yr HL+Disch Igmny	Comm 6 mos Detn	WO/92/4/84
5 Dragoon Gds	Pte	Whittaker T	Curragh	23/09/19	M	1 yr HL+Disch Igmny	Comm 6 mos Detn	WO/92/4/85
5 Dragoon Gds	Pte	Williams B	Curragh	26/09/19	M	1 yr HL+Disch Igmny	Comm 6 mos Detn	WO/92/4/83
5 Dragoon Gds	Pte	Williams PH	Curragh	23/09/19	M	84 dys HL	Comm 42 dys Detn	WO/92/4/85
5 Dragoon Gds	Pte	Wilson D	Curragh	22/09/19	M	1 yr HL+Disch Igmny	Comm 6 mos Detn	WO/92/4/84
5 Dragoon Gds	Pte	Wood H	Curragh	29/09/19	M	1 yr HL+Disch Igmny	Comm 6 mos Detn	WO/92/4/82

Unit	Rank	Name	Location	Date D/M/Y	Offence	Finding/Punishment	Amendment	PRO Reference File/Piece/Page
5 Dragoon Gds	Pte	Wragg GW	Curragh	24/09/19	M	1 yr HL+Disch Igmny	Comm 6 mos Detn	WO/92/4/87
5 Dragoon Gds	Pte	Wright WS	Curragh	23/09/19	M	84 dys HL	Comm 42 dys	WO/92/4/85
5 Dragoon Gds	Pte	Young A	Curragh	24/09/19	M	1 yr HL+Disch Igmny	Comm 6 mos Detn	WO/92/4/86
5 Dragoon Gds	Pte	Young CF	Curragh	29/09/19	M	1 yr HL+Disch Igmny	Comm 6 mos Detn	WO/92/4/82
6 Dragoon Gds (att 5 Dragoon Gds)	Pte	McKee W	Curragh	30/09/19	M	Acquit		WO/92/4/87
7 Dragoon Gds	Pte	Brealey JW	Edinburgh	09/06/21	M+V(A/RSM)	NG		WO/86/91/131
7 Dragoon Gds	Pte	Campbell A	Edinburgh	09/06/21	M+V(A/RSM)	18 mos HL		WO/86/91/131
7 Dragoon Gds	Pte	Halpin R	Edinburgh	09/06/21	M+V(A/RSM)	2 yrs HL		WO/86/91/131
7 Dragoon Gds	Pte	Hellard C	Edinburgh	09/06/21	M+V(A/RSM)	2 yrs HL		WO/86/91/131
7 Dragoon Gds	Pte	Knight H	Edinburgh	09/06/21	M+V(A/RSM)	NG		WO/86/91/131
7 Dragoon Gds	Pte	Massey C	Edinburgh	09/06/21	M+V(A/RSM)	NG		WO/86/91/131
7 Dragoon Gds	Pte	Thomson F	Edinburgh	09/06/21	M+V(A/RSM)	2 yrs HL		WO/86/91/131
1 DCLI	Pte	Podger HC	Belfast	01/09/20	M	1 yr Detn		WO/86/90/140
1 DCLI	Pte	Remfrey S	Belfast	01/09/20	M	2 yrs Detn		WO/86/90/140
9(S) E Lancs	Pte	Brown H	SEF	29/05/18	M	1 yr HL		WO/213/23/179
9(S) E Lancs	Pte	Brown J	SEF	29/05/18	M	1 yr HL		WO/213/23/179
9(S) E Lancs	Pte	Carter J	SEF	29/05/18	M	1 yr HL		WO/213/23/179
9(S) E Lancs	Pte	Crabtree EJ	SEF	29/05/18	M	1 yr HL		WO/213/23/179
9(S) E Lancs	Pte	Devine TH	SEF	29/05/18	M	1 yr HL		WO/213/23/179
9(S) E Lancs	Pte	Dewhurst G	SEF	29/05/18	M	1 yr HL		WO/213/23/179
9(S) E Lancs	Pte	Entwistle E	SEF	29/05/18	M	1 yr HL		WO/213/23/179
9(S) E Lancs	Pte	Fullalove JP	SEF	29/05/18	M	1 yr HL		WO/213/23/179
9(S) E Lancs	Pte	Greaves H	SEF	29/05/18	M	1 yr HL		WO/213/23/179
9(S) E Lancs	Pte	Henry R	SEF	29/05/18	M	1 yr HL		WO/213/23/179
9(S) E Lancs	Pte	Higgins J	SEF	29/05/18	M	1 yr HL		WO/213/23/179
9(S) E Lancs	Pte	Hirst JL	SEF	29/05/18	M	1 yr HL		WO/213/23/179
9(S) E Lancs	Pte	Kay W	SEF	29/05/18	M	1 yr HL		WO/213/23/179
9(S) E Lancs	Pte	Knowles J	SEF	29/05/18	M	1 yr HL		WO/213/23/179
9(S) E Lancs	Pte	Lee HE	SEF	29/05/18	M	1 yr HL		WO/213/23/179
9(S) E Lancs	Pte	Livesey J	SEF	29/05/18	M	1 yr HL		WO/213/23/179
9(S) E Lancs	Pte	Miller W	SEF	29/05/18	M	1 yr HL		WO/213/23/179
9(S) E Lancs	Pte	Mulligan J	SEF	29/05/18	M	1 yr HL		WO/213/23/179
9(S) E Lancs	Pte	Murphy A	SEF	29/05/18	M	1 yr HL		WO/213/23/179
9(S) E Lancs	Pte	Prangley W	SEF	29/05/18	M	1 yr HL		WO/213/23/179
9(S) E Lancs	Pte	Sterrett W	SEF	29/05/18	M	1 yr HL		WO/213/23/179
9(S) E Lancs	Pte	Townend R	SEF	29/05/18	M	1 yr HL		WO/213/23/179
9(S) E Lancs	Pte	Walmsley J	SEF	29/05/18	M	1 yr HL		WO/213/23/179
9(S) E Lancs	Pte	Whelan D	SEF	29/05/18	M	1 yr HL		WO/213/23/179
13 E Lancs	Pte	Green P	Rouen	04/02/19	M	90 dys Imp		WO/90/8/58
9 E Surrey	Pte	Day G	Field	01/02/19	M+S40	NG		WO/213/28/60
2 East Yorks	Pte	Thompson T	Constantinople	05/07/20	M+Disob(Capt)	5 yrs PS	Comm 1 yr Detn	WO/90/8/84
10 E Yorks	Pte	Hawkins G	Field	24/03/19	M	18 yrs PS		WO213/29/88
2 Essex	Pte	Maulson J	Malta	18/07/21	M+Theft+S18(4b)	1 yr HL+DI		WO/90/8/87
3 Essex	Pte	Alsey A	Field Italy	09/05/19	3 yrs PS	Comm 4 mos HL		WO/213/29/73
3 Essex	Pte	Brockbank S	Field Italy	09/05/19	3 yrs PS	Comm 4 mos HL		WO/213/29/73
3 Essex	Pte	Harris F	Field Italy	09/05/19	M	3 yrs PS	Comm 4 mos HL	WO/213/29/72
3 Essex	Pte	Smith E	Field Italy	09/05/19	3 yrs PS	Comm 4 mos HL		WO/213/29/73
3 Essex	Pte	Wright F	Field Italy	09/05/19	3 yrs PS	Comm 4 mos HL		WO/213/29/73
3 Glocs	Pte	Lewis H	Gravesend	08/10/15	Mx2+Insub (Sgt)+S10(4)	2 yrs HL + Disch Igmny		WO/86/67/44
13 Glouster	Pte	Phillips F	Malvern Wells	16/06/15	Incit M+Insub(Maj)+Resist+Esc	3 yrs PS		WO/92/3/24
13 Glouster	Pte	Denton AG	Malvern Wells	16/06/15	Incit M+Viol(Sgt)	NG		WO/92/3/18
13 Glouster	Pte	Galloway P	Malvern Wells	17/06/15	Incit M+Insub(Sgt)+S40	3 yrs PS		WO/92/3/24
2 Hants	Pte	Coster J	Rouen	04/02/19	M	90 dys Imp		WO/90/8/58
10 Hussars	Pte	Bade B	Curragh	25/01/21	Mx2+S9(1)x2	1 yr Detn		WO/92/4/94
10 Hussars	Pte	Barker JA	Curragh	25/01/21	Mx2+S9(1)x2	1 yr Detn	Remit 3 mos	WO/92/4/94
10 Hussars	Pte	Hill E	Curragh	25/01/21	Mx2+S9(1)x2	1 yr Detn		WO/92/4/94
10 Hussars	Pte	Kent GA	Curragh	25/01/21	Mx2+S9(1)x2	1 yr Detn	Remit 3 mos	WO/92/4/94
10 Hussars	Pte	Quarton H	Rouen	04/02/19	M	3 yrs PS		WO/90/8/58
10 Hussars	Pte	Sullivan FG	Curragh	25/01/21	Mx2+S9(1)x2	1 yr Detn	Remit 3 mos	F/O/92/4/94
10 Hussars	Pte	Wild P	Curragh	25/01/21	Mx2+S9(1)	1 yr Detn	Remit 3 mos	WO/92/4/94
K Edw Horse	Pte	Ambrose WJ	Curragh	29/09/19	M	1 yr HL+Disch Igmny	Comm 6 mos Detn	WO/92/4/82
K Edw Horse	Pte	Brown M	Curragh	22/09/19	M	1 yr HL+Disch Igmny	Comm 6 mos Detn	WO/92/3/84

Unit	Rank	Name	Location	Date D/M/Y	Offence	Finding/Punishment	Amendment	PRO Reference File/Piece/Page
King Edward Horse (att 5 Dragoon Gds)	Pte	Hayes P	Curragh	25/09/19	M	1 yr HL	WO/92/4/86 +Disch Igmny	
King Edw Horse)Pte (att 5 Dragoon Gds		Ross A	Curragh	24/09/19	M	56 dys Detn	Remit 21dys Dtn	WO/92/4/86
King Edw Horse	Boy	Smith RH	Curragh	24/09/19	M	6 mos HL	Comm 84 dys	WO/92/4/87
6 KOR Lancs	Pte	Bailey J	Gallipoli	13/09/15	M	Death	Comm 2 yrs HL	WO/213/5/79
1 KOYLI	Pte	Roddy S	Field SEF	02/05/18	M+Disob	10 yrs PS	Comm 2 yrs HL	WO/213/22/30
1/4 KOYLI (att 265 POW Coy)	Pte	Jennings A	Field	16/09/19	M+Abs+Disob	3 yrs PS	Comm 1 yr HL	WO/213/31/69
1/4 KOYLI (att 365 POW Coy)	Pte	Barrett E	Field	16/09/19	M+Abs+Disob	3 yrs PS	Comm 1 yr HL	WO/213/31/69
1/4 KOYLI (att 365 POW Coy)	Pte	Bibb J	Field	16/09/19	M+Abs+Disob	3 yrs PS	Comm 1 yr HL	WO/213/31/69
1/4 KOYLI (att 365 POW Coy)	Pte	Bowen M	Field	16/09/19	M+Abs+Disob	5 yrs PS	Comm 2 yrs HL	WO/213/31/68
1/4 KOYLI (att 365 POW Coy)	Pte	Burton FA	Field	16/09/19	M+Abs+Disob	3 yrs PS	Comm 1 yr HL	WO/213/31/69
1/4 KOYLI (att 365 POW Coy)	Pte	Coley TH	Field	16/09/19	M+Abs+Disob	3 yrs PS	Comm 1 yr HL	WO/213/31/69
1/4 KOYLI (att 365 POW Coy)	Pte	Graham R	Field	16/09/19	M+Abs+Disob	3 yrs PS	Comm 1 yr HL	WO/213/31/69
1/4 KOYLI (att 365 POW Coy)	Pte	Kent T	Field	16/09/19	M+Abs+Disob	3 yrs PS	Comm 1 yr HL	WO/213/31/69
1/4 KOYLI (att 365 POW Coy)	Pte	Miller R	Field	16/09/19	M+Abs+Disob	3 yrs PS	Comm 1 yr HL	WO/213/31/69
1/4 KOYLI (att 365 POW Coy)	Pte	Peregrine JB	Field	16/09/19	M+Abs+Disob	3 yrs PS	Comm 1 yr HL	WO/213/31/69
1/4 KOYLI (att 365 POW Coy)	Pte	Robinson W	Field	16/09/19	M+Abs+Disob	3 yrs PS	Comm 1 yr HL	WO/213/31/69
1/4 KOYLI (att 365 POW Coy)	Pte	Spriggs A	Field	16/09/19	M+Abs+Disob	3 yrs PS	Comm 1 yr HL	WO/213/31/69
1/4 KOYLI (att 365 POW Coy)	Pte	Thorton W	Field	16/09/19	M+Abs+Disob	3 yrs PS	Comm 1 yr HL	WO/213/31/69
1/4 KOYLI (att 365 POW Coy)9	Pte	Turner G	Field	16/09/19	M+Abs+Disob	3 yrs PS	Comm 1 yr HL	WO/213/31/6
1/4 KOYLI (att RAOC)	Pte(A/Cpl)	Curtis A	Field	08/10/19	M+S40	NG		WO/213/31/4
2 KOYLI	Pte	Ball A	Abancourt	14/09/16	M+Insub	3 yrs PS		WO/213/11/31
2/4 KOYLI	Pte	Fallon A	Field	24/03/19	M	10 yrs PS		WO213/29/88
8 KOYLI	Pte	Balmbro T	Field	10/02/19	M+Disob+S40	10 yrs PS	Quashed	WO/213/28/54
8 KOYLI	L/Cpl	Butterick J	Field	10/02/19	M+Disob+S40	Acquit		WO/213/28/54
8 KOYLI	Pte	Chamberlain F	Field	10/02/19	M+Disob+S40	5 yrs PS	Quashed	WO/213/28/54
8 KOYLI	L/Cpl	Dodds HS	Field	10/02/19	M+Disob+S7(4)	Acquit		WO/213/28/54
8 KOYLI	L/Cpl	Field R	Field	10/02/19	M+Disob+S40	Acquit		WO/213/28/54
8 KOYLI	L/Cpl	Harrison J	Field	10/02/19	M+Disob+S7(4)	Acquit		WO/213/28/54
8 KOYLI	Pte	Hyland T	Field	10/02/19	M+Disob+S40	5 yrs PS	Quashed	WO/213/28/54
8 KOYLI	Pte	Jarrod CH	Field	10/02/19	M+Disob+S40	5 yrs PS	Quashed +Rem 2 yrs	WO/213/28/54
8 KOYLI	Pte	Knapp JJ	Field	10/02/19	M+Disob+S40	5 yrs PS	Quashed +Rem 2 yrs	WO/213/28/54
8 KOYLI	Pte	Lewis J	Field	10/02/19	M+Disob+S40	Acquit		WO/213/28/54
8 KOYLI	Pte	Whitton R	Field	10/02/19	M+Disob+S40	6 mos Imp	Quashed	WO/213/28/54
8 KOYLI	Pte	Williamson T	Field	10/02/19	M+Disob+S40	5 yrs PS	Quashed	WO/213/28/54
11 KRRC	Cpl	Sadler LC	Field	09/12/18	M+S40	6 mos HL+Rnks	Comm 90dys FP2	WO/213/27/42
18 KRRC	Rfn	Farr WH	Field	22/12/18	M	5 yrs PS		WO/213/27/184
2 KSLI	Pte	Levitt A	Field SEF	04/06/18	M+Disob	10 yrs PS	Comm 2 yrs HL	WO/213/23/40
6 KSLI	Pte	Pritchard SP	Field	24/03/19	M	Death	Comm PS/Life	WO/213/29/90
12 Lancs Fus	Pte	Fields W	Field SEF	02/05/18	M+Disob	10 yrs PS	Comm 2 yrs HL	WO/213/22/30
12 Lancs Fus	Pte	Jones J	Field SEF	02/05/18	M+Disob	10 yrs PS	Comm 2 yrs HL	WO/213/22/30
20 Lancs Fus	Pte	Lewis HT	Dunkirk	13/04/17	M	6 mos HL		WO/213/14/138
1 Leics	Pte	Halford T	Field (Ireland)	28/04/22	M+S40	1 yr HL	Comm 56 dys	WO/213/34/63
3 Leics	Pte	Bexon I	Portsmouth	27/08/14	M	1 yr HL		WO/213/2/2
3 Leics	Pte	Bray J	Portsmouth	27/08/14	M	1 yr HL		WO/213/2/2
3 Leics	Pte	Castle J	Portsmouth	27/08/14	M	1 yr HL		WO/213/2/2
3 Leics	Pte	Davis C	Portsmouth	27/08/14	M	1 yr HL		WO/213/2/2
3 Leics	Pte	Hayward W	Portsmouth	27/08/14	M	1 yr HL		WO/213/2/2
3 Leics	Pte	Hogg J	Portsmouth	27/08/14	M	1 yr HL		WO/213/2/2
3 Leics	Pte	Jennings A	Portsmouth	27/08/14	M	1 yr HL		WO/213/2/2
3 Leics	Pte	Morris J	Portsmouth	27/08/14	M	1 yr HL		WO/213/2/2
3 Leics	Pte	Nix A	Portsmouth	27/08/14	M	1 yr HL		WO/213/2/2
3 Leics	Pte	Robinson B	Portsmouth	27/08/14	M	1 yr HL		WO/213/2/2
3 Leics	Pte	Stevenson J	Portsmouth	27/08/14	M	1 yr HL		WO/213/2/2

Unit	Rank	Name	Location	Date D/M/Y	Offence	Finding/Punishment	Amendment	PRO Reference File/Piece/Page
3 Leics	Pte	Warner C	Portsmouth	27/08/14	M	1 yr HL		WO/213/2/2
3 Leics	Pte	Wright M	Portsmouth	27/08/14	M	1 yr HL		WO/213/2/2
7 Leic	Pte	Bennett H	Field	14/10/18	M	Death	Comm 15 yrs PS	WO/213/26/45
7 Leic	Pte	Knight F	Field	14/10/18	M	Death	Comm 15 yrs PS	WO/213/26/45
8 Lincs	Cpl	Brickwood HE	Field	23/12/18	M	4 mos HL+Rnks	Imp	WO/213/28/8
8 Lincs	Sgt	Ledicott CF	Field	23/12/18	M+S40	6 mos HL+Rnks	Imp	WO/213/28/8
8 Lincs	Pte	Lievesley H	Field	12/11/17	M+Disob	9 mos HL		WO/213/18/180
8 Lincs	Pte	Westmoreland G	Field	12/11/17	M+Disob	6 mos HL	Comm 91 dys FP1	WO/213/18/180
1/6 L'pool	Pte	Nicholas FF	Rouen	04/02/19	M	56 dys Imp		WO/90/8/58
2 Liverpool	Pte	Craig J	Khartoum	26/04/20	M+S40/S7(3b)	Acquit		WO/90/8/83
2 Liverpool	Pte	Dandy W	Khartoum	26/04/20	M+Disob+S40/S7(3b)	6 mos Detn+Stop;122 dys Detn+Stop	Remit 122 dys Detn + Stop	WO/90/8/83
2 Liverpool	Pte	Gordon JH	Khartoum	26/04/20	M+S40/S7(3b)	Acquit		WO/90/8/83
2 Liverpool	Pte	May J	Khartoum	26/04/20	M+Disob+S40/S7(3b)	6 mos Detn+Stop;122 dys Detn+Stop	Remit 122 dys Detn + Stop	WO/90/8/83
2 Liverpool	Pte	Troy J	Khartoum	26/04/20	M+Resist+Esc+S40+S7(3B)	14 dys Detn	Remit Sentence	WO/90/8/83
5(R) L'pool	Pte (AL/Cpl)	Birkett A	Pembroke Dock	20/12/18	M+S40	6 mos Detn	2 mos	WO/92/4/5
17 L'pool	Pte	Bestwick C	NREF	16/05/19	M	2 yrs HL	Remit 18 mos	WO/213/29/181
17 L'pool	Pte(L/Cpl)	Collier FD	NREF	16/05/19	M	2 yrs HL	Remit 18 mos	WO/213/29/181
17 L'pool	Pte	Lewis WO	NREF	16/05/19	M	2 yrs HL	Remit 18 mos	WO/213/29/181
1/13 Lond	Pte	Eglinton TR	Rouen	04/02/19	M	90 dys Imp		WO/90/8/58
2/23 London	Pte	Lester WH	Field	19/05/19	M+Insub+S40	6 mos HL		WO/213/30/27
3/21 London TF	Rfn	Field C	Winchester	04/01/16	M+Insub(Sgt)	1 yr Detn	Comm 6 mos Detn	WO/86/68/180
LN Lancs (att RAOC)	Pte	Miller AF	Field	08/10/19	M	NG		WO/213/31/6
4(R) LN Lancs	Pte	Derbyshire J	Dublin	05/02/19	M	1 yr Detn		WO/86/86/129
6 LN Lancs	Pte	Green W	Mesopotamia	04/11/17	Drunk+Viol+M+S10(3)+Insol	5 yrs PS+DI		WO/90/7/143
Manch Regt	Pte	Barlow J	Field	27/02/19	M+Des	56 dys FP2	Remit 21 dys	WO/213/28/134
1 Manchester	Pte(L/Cpl)	Booth A	Field (Ireland)	05/09/21	M+Disob(CQMS)+S7(3)4	3 yrs PS	2yrs Dtn	WO/213/32/21
1 Manchester	Pte(L/Cpl)	Carr J	Field (Ireland)	05/09/21	M+Disob(CQMS)+S7(3)4	3 yrs PS	NG	WO/213/32/21
1 Manchester	Pte(L/Cpl)	Downie A	Field (Ireland)	05/09/21	M+Disob(CQMS)+S7(3)	3 yrs PS	2yrs Detn	WO/213/32/214
1 Manchester	Pte(L/Cpl)	Onslow R	Field (Ireland)	05/09/21	M+Disob(CQMS)+S7(3)	3 yrs PS	2yrs Detn	WO/213/32/214
1/10 Manch	Pte	Orr R	Field	01/01/19	M+Abs+S40(2)	5 yrs PS	Comm 3 yrs HL	WO/213/28/106
2 Manch	Pte	Smalley J	Rouen	04/02/19	M	3 yrs + 9 mos PS		WO/90/8/58
21 Manch	Pte	Bate R	Field	08/02/19	M+Abs	6 mos HL		WO/213/28/58
21 Manch	Pte	Burton R	Field	08/02/19	M+Abs	6 mos HL		WO/213/28/58
21 Manch	Pte	Byrne H	Field	08/02/19	M+Abs	6 mos HL		WO/213/28/58
21 Manch	Pte	Carson R	Field	08/02/19	M+Abs	6 mos HL		WO/213/28/58
21 Manch	Pte	Durham W	Field	08/02/19	M+Abs	6 mos HL		WO/213/28/58
21 Manch	Pte	Fryers W	Field	08/02/19	M+Abs	6 mos HL		WO/213/28/58
21 Manch	Pte	Grimshaw H	Field	08/02/19	M+Abs	6 mos HL		WO/213/28/58
21 Manch	Pte	Hall J	Field	08/02/19	M+Abs	6 mos HL		WO/213/28/58
21 Manch	Pte	Hunt J	Field	08/02/19	M+Abs	6 mos HL		WO/213/28/58
21 Manch	Pte	Lovell W	Field	08/02/19	M+Abs	6 mos HL		WO/213/28/58
21 Manch	Pte	Moores TH	Field	08/02/19	M+Abs	6 mos HL		WO/213/28/58
21 Manch	Pte	Morgan J	Field	08/02/19	M+Abs	6 mos HL		WO/213/28/58
21 Manch	Pte	Park JR	Field	08/02/19	M+Abs	6 mos HL		WO/213/28/58
21 Manch	Pte	Pedley J	Field	08/02/19	M+Abs	6 mos HL		WO/213/28/58
21 Manch	Pte	Rawlinson F	Field	08/02/19	M+Abs	6 mos HL		WO/213/28/58
21 Manch	Pte	Reynolds W	Field	08/02/19	M+Abs	NG		WO/213/28/58
21 Manch	Pte	Roberts C	Field	08/02/19	M+Abs	6 mos HL		WO/213/28/58
21 Manch	Pte	Roberts F	Field	08/02/19	M+Abs	6 mos HL		WO/213/28/58
21 Manch	Pte	Robson H	Field	08/02/19	M+Abs	6 mos HL		WO/213/28/58
21 Manch	Pte	Rodgers P	Field	08/02/19	M+Abs	9 mos HL		WO/213/28/58
21 Manch	Pte	Rush JA	Field	08/02/19	M+Abs	6 mos HL		WO/213/28/58
21 Manch	Pte	Smith J	Field	08/02/19	M+Abs	6 mos HL		WO/213/28/58
21 Manch	Pte	Stubbs W	Field	08/02/19	M+Abs	6 mos HL		WO/213/28/58
21 Manch	Pte	Taylor B	Field	08/02/19	M+Abs	6 mos HL		WO/213/28/58
21 Manch	Pte	Thompson AS	Field	08/02/19	M+Abs	6 mos HL		WO/213/28/58
21 Manch	Pte	Whittle J	Field	08/02/19	M+Abs	6 mos HL		WO/213/28/50
21 Manch	Pte	Williamson T	Field	08/02/19	M+Abs	NG		WO/213/28/59
21 Manch	Pte	Wilmot E	Field	08/02/19	M+Abs	6 mos HL		WO/213/28/58

Unit	Rank	Name	Location	Date D/M/Y	Offence	Finding/Punishment	Amendment	PRO Reference File/Piece/Page
4 Mddx	Pte	Covill G	Field	12/11/17	M+Disob	6 mos HL	Comm 91 dys Imp	WO/213/18/181
4 Mddx	Pte	Filmar A	Field	12/11/17	M+Disob	6 mos HL	Comm 91 dys FP1	WO/213/18/181
4 Mddx	Pte	Gunn F	Field	12/11/17	M+Disob	6 mos HL	Comm 91 dys FP1	WO/213/18/181
4 Mddx	Pte	Hollings F	Field	12/11/17	M+Disob	6 mos HL	Comm 91 dys FP1	WO/213/18/181
4 Mddx	Pte	Llewellin L	Field	12/11/17	M+Disob	6 mos HL	Comm 91 dys FP1	WO/213/18/181
4 Mddx	Pte	Mitchell E	Field	12/11/17	M+Disob	6 mos HL	Comm 91 dys FP1	WO/213/18/181
4 Mddx	Pte	New B	Field	12/11/17	M+Disob	6 mos HL	Comm 91 dys FP1	WO/213/18/181
4 Mddx	Pte	Weatherley J	Field	12/11/17	M+Disob	6 mos HL	Comm 91 dys FP1	WO/213/18/181
4 Mddx	Pte	White W	Rouen	04/02/19	M	Acquit		WO/90/8/58
9 Middx	Pte	Poole FC	Guildhall West	15/03/16	E P(ersuade) M+Disob	1 yr HL		WO/92/3/34
9 Middx	Pte	Walker T	Guildhall West	15/03/16	E P(ersuade) M+Disob	1 yr HL		WO/92/3/34
7 Norfolk	Pte	Elsegood A	Arras	13/04/17	M+S40	9 mos HL	Rem 3 mos	WO/213/15/142
9 Northumberland Fus	Pte	Sykes H	Field	05/07/19	M+S40	3 yrs PS	Comm 1 yr HL	WO/213/30/109
11 North Fus	Pte	France W	Rouen	04/02/19	M	90 dys Imp		WO/90/8/58
24 North Fus	Cpl	Short JR	Etaples	12/09/17	M	Death		WO/213/17/119
Ox & Bucks LI	Cpl	Hardy PT	Oxford	01/02/20	M+Abs+Resisting+S9(1)	2 yrs HL+Rnks+Dl	Remit 18 mos	WO/92/4/95
1 Ox & Bucks LI	Cpl	Edmeads E	Cork	04/05/20	M+V(CSM)	Acquit		WO/92/4/90
2 Ox & Bucks LI	Pte	Booker A	Field	05/05/16	M+Disob	5 yrs PS	Quashed	WO/213/9/46
3 Rif Bde	Rfn	Primm J	Field	24/03/19	M	11 yrs PS		WO213/29/88
12(S) Rifle Bde	Rfn	Wrigley L	Field	19/11/18	M+Abs+S40	28 dys FP1		WO/213/26/49
16 Rifle Bde	Pte(A/Cpl)	Ireland A	Witley	20/11/15	M+Disob(Capt)	5 yrs PS	Comm 1 yr Detn	WO/92/3/29
51 Rif Bde (att 2 MGC)	Pte	Redgrave J	Field	12/06/19	M+Disob(2)+S40	4 yrs PS	Comm 2 yrs HL	WO/213/29/122
51 Rif Bde (att 2 MGC)	Rfn	Stocks WA	Field	12/06/19	M+Disob(2)+S40	4 yrs PS	Comm 2 yrs HL	WO/213/29/122
10 Royal Fus	Pte	Sullivan RP	Fiield	31/01/17	M+Sleeping	Death	NC	WO/213/13/172
11 R Fus	L/Cpl	Church H	Field	23/12/18	M	5 yrs PS		WO/213/28/141
11 R Fus	Pte	Jobe C	Field	23/12/18	M	5 yrs PS		WO/213/28/141
11 R Fus	Pte	McDonald J	Field	23/12/18	M	5 yrs PS		WO/213/28/141
11 R Fus	Pte	Thompson H	Field	02/08/19	M+Viol+Thr+Insol	10 yrs PS		WO/213/30/160
26 R Fus	Pte	Barnes AG	Rouen	04/02/19	M	90 dys Imp		WO/90/8/58
26 R Fus	Pte	Casey W	Rouen	04/02/19	M	90 dys Imp		WO/90/8/58
39 R Fus	Pte	Strasburg J	Field EEF	29/03/19	M+Insub	1 yr HL	Remit 6 mos	WO/213/29/86
39 R Fus	Pte	Aberman P	Field EEF	23/08/19	M	5 yrs PS	Comm 1 yr HL	WO/213/31/24
39 R Fus	Pte	Barkin H	Field EEF	23/08/19	M	5 yrs PS	Comm 1 yr HL	WO/213/31/24
39 R Fus	Pte	Bass G	Field EEF	23/08/19	M	5 yrs PS	Comm 1 yr HL	WO/213/31/24
39 R Fus	Pte	Blumenthal B	Field EEF	23/08/19	M	NG		WO/213/31/23
39 R Fus	Pte	Chaitman B	Field EEF	23/08/19	M	5 yrs PS	Comm 1 yr HL	WO/213/31/24
39 R Fus	Pte	Davidson A	Field EEF	23/08/19	M	NG		WO/213/31/25
39 R Fus	Pte	Ehrlick L	Field EEF	23/08/19	M	NG		WO/213/31/23
39 R Fus	Pte	Eisenstat H	Field EEF	23/08/19	M	5 yrs PS	Comm 1 yr HL	WO/213/31/24
39 R Fus	Pte	Elden E	Field EEF	23/08/19	M	5 yrs PS	Remit	WO/213/31/25
39 R Fus	Pte	Feldman B	Field EEF	23/08/19	M	5 yrs PS		WO/213/31/23
39 R Fus	Pte	Feldman J	Field EEF	23/08/19	M	5 yrs PS	Comm 1 yr HL	WO/213/31/25
39 R Fus	Pte	Finkelstein F	Field EEF	23/08/19	M	5 yrs PS	Comm 1 yr HL	WO/213/31/24
39 R Fus	Pte	Foreman I	Field EEF	23/08/19	M	5 yrs PS		WO/213/31/23
39 R Fus	Pte	Frankel A	Field EEF	23/08/19	M	5 yrs PS	Comm 1 yr HL	WO/213/31/24
39 R Fus	Pte	Goldman B	Field EEF	23/08/19	M	NG		WO/213/31/23
39 R Fus	Pte	Goldman M	Field EEF	23/08/19	M	5 yrs PS	Comm 1 yr HL	WO/213/31/24
39 R Fus	Pte	Gunchar I	Field EEF	23/08/19	M	5 yrs PS	Comm 1 yr HL	WO/213/31/24
39 R Fus	Pte	Horowitz J	Field EEF	23/08/19	M	5 yrs PS	Comm 1 yr HL	WO/213/31/25
39 R Fus	Pte	Hurvutz J	Field EEF	23/08/19	M	5 yrs PS	Comm 1 yr HL	WO/213/31/25
39 R Fus	Pte	Kalis I	Field EEF	23/08/19	M	6 yrs PS	Comm 1 yr HL	WO/213/31/25
39 R Fus	Pte	Klein M	Field EEF	23/08/19	M	5 yrs PS	Comm 1 yr HL	PO/213/31/24
39 R Fus	Pte	Krantz A	Field EEF	23/08/19	M	NG		W/0/213/31/24
39 R Fus	Pte	Lasry SH	Field EEF	23/08/19	M	5 yrs PS	Comm 1 yr HL	WO/213/31/24
39 R Fus	Pte	Levitan B	Field EEF	23/08/19	M	5 yrs PS	Comm 1 yr HL	WO/213/31/25
39 R Fus	Pte	Lichenstein I	Field EEF	23/08/19	M	5 yrs PS	Comm 1 yr HL	WO/213/31/24
39 R Fus	Pte	Lifschitz M	Field EEF	23/08/19	M	NG		WO/213/31/24
39 R Fus	Pte	Mintz N	Field EEF	23/08/19	M	NG		WO/213/31/24

Unit	Rank	Name	Location	Date D/M/Y	Offence	Finding/Punishment	Amendment	PRO Reference File/Piece/Page
39 R Fus	Pte	Murman I	Field EEF	23/08/19	M	NG		WO/213/31/23
39 R Fus	Pte	Nemcheck M	Field EEF	23/08/19	M	5 yrs PS	Comm 1 yr HL	WO/213/31/25
39 R Fus	Pte	Nordockovitch B	Field EEF	23/08/19	M	5 yrs PS	Comm 1 yr HL	WO/213/31/24
39 R Fus	Pte	Petrofsky P	Field EEF	23/08/19	M	NG		WO/213/31/25
39 R Fus	Pte	Prince N	Field EEF	23/08/19	M	NG		WO/213/31/24
39 R Fus	Pte	Resnik S	Field EEF	23/08/19	M	5 yrs PS	Comm 1 yr HL	WO/213/31/25
39 R Fus	Pte	Sauber A	Field EEF	23/08/19	M	NG		WO/213/31/24
39 R Fus	Pte	Schorr H	Field EEF	23/08/19	M	NG		WO/213/31/24
39 R Fus	Pte	Sherenitz D	Field EEF	23/08/19	M	5 yrs PS	Comm 1 yr HL	WO/213/31/24
39 R Fus	Pte	Singer A	Field EEF	23/08/19	M	5 ys PS	Comm 1 yr HL	WO/213/31/24
39 R Fus	Pte	Smith N	Field EEF	23/08/19	M	NG		WO/213/31/24
39 R Fus	Pte	Strauss H	Field EEF	23/08/19	M	NG		WO/213/31/24
39 R Fus	Pte	Tandet J	Field EEF	23/08/19	M	6 yrs PS	Comm 1 yr HL	WO/213/31/24
39 R Fus	Pte	Tobin D	Field EEF	23/08/19	M	6 yrs PS	Rem 3 yrs/ Comm 1 yr HL	WO/213/31/24
39 R Fus	Pte	Wein H	Field EEF	23/08/19	M	5 yrs PS	Comm 1 yr HL	WO/213/31/24
39 R Fus	Pte	Zamasthansky N	Field EEF	23/08/19	M	5 yrs PS		WO/213/31/23
39 R Fus	Pte	Zorowski N	Field EEF	23/08/19	M	5 yrs PS		WO/213/31/23
43 R Fus	Cpl	Miller TC	Field	03/02/19	M+S40+S7(2)	5 yrs PS+Rnks		WO/213/28/165
45 Royal Fus	Pte	Crisp W	NREF	21/08/19	No offence/Mutiny?	Death	2 yrs HL	WO/213/31/27
45 Royal Fus	Pte	Enright W	NREF	21/08/19	No offence/Mutiny?	Death	2 yrs HL	WO/213/31/27
47 R Fus (att 29 Liverpool)	Pte	Vincent W	Field	14/04/20	M+S40	6 mos HL		WO/213/31/142
47 R Fus (att 29 Liverpool)	Pte	Vizer HC	Field	14/04/20	M+S40	6 mos HL		WO/213/31/142
47 R Fus (att 29 Liverpool)	Pte	Walsh T	Field	14/04/20	M+S40	6 mos HL		WO/213/31/142
47 R Fus (att 29 Liverpool)2	Pte	Watts SC	Field	14/04/20	M+S40	6 mos HL		WO/213/31/142
47 R Fus) (att 29 Liverpool	Pte	Williams T	Field	14/04/20	M+S40	6 mos HL		WO/213/31/142
1 Gn Sher Fstrs	Pte	Allcock A	Kantara Egypt	05/06/17	M	2 yrs HL		WO/213/15/176
1 Gn Sher Fstrs	Pte	Allmand E	Kantara Egypt	05/06/17	M	2 yrs HL		WO/213/15/176
1 Gn Sher Fstrs	Pte	Arnold J	Kantara Egypt	05/06/17	M	2 yrs HL		WO/213/15/176
1 Gn Sher Fstrs	Pte	Barker H	Kantara Egypt	05/06/17	M	2 yrs HL		WO/213/15/176
1 Gn Sher Fstrs	Pte	Bennett J	Kantara Egypt	05/06/17	M	2 yrs HL		WO/213/15/176
1 Gn Sher Fstrs	Pte	Bestwick TC	Kantara Egypt	05/06/17	M	2 yrs HL		WO/213/15/176
1 Gn Sher Fstrs	Pte	Boolley WF	Kantara Egypt	05/06/17	M	2 yrs HL		WO/213/15/176
1 Gn Sher Fstrs	Pte	Bowden WH	Kantara Egypt	05/06/17	M	2 yrs HL		WO/213/15/176
1 Gn Sher Fstrs	Pte	Brookes TW	Kantara Egypt	05/06/17	M	2 yrs HL		WO/213/15/176
1 Gn Sher Fstrs	Pte	Brown C	Kantara Egypt	05/06/17	M	2 yrs HL		WO/213/15/176
1 Gn Sher Fstrs	Pte	Bullock H	Kantara Egypt	05/06/17	M	2 yrs HL		WO/213/15/176
1 Gn Sher Fstrs	Pte	Burrows G	Kantara Egypt	05/06/17	M	2 yrs HL		WO/213/15/176
1 Gn Sher Fstrs	Pte	Butler H	Kantara Egypt	05/06/17	M	2 yrs HL		WO/213/15/176
1 Gn Sher Fstrs	Pte	Byrd J	Kantara Egypt	05/06/17	M	2 yrs HL		WO/213/15/176
1 Gn Sher Fstrs	Pte	Cassidy J	Kantara Egypt	05/06/17	M	2 yrs HL		WO/213/15/176
1 Gn Sher Fstrs	Pte	Chapman H	Kantarat Egypt	05/06/17	M	2 yrs HL		WO/213/15/176
1 Gn Sher Fstrs	Pte	Clay H	Kantara Egypt	05/06/17	M	2 yrs HL		WO/213/15/176
1 Gn Sher Fstrs	Pte	Crisp C	Kantara Egypt	05/06/17	M	2 yrs HL		WO/213/15/176
1 Gn Sher Fstrs	Pte	Daniels CH	Kantara Egypt	11/06/17	M	2 yrs HL		WO/213/15/175
1 Gn Sher Fstrs	Pte	Ford J	Kantara Egypt	05/06/17	M	2 yrs HL		WO/213/15/176

Unit	Rank	Name	Location	Date D/M/Y	Offence	Finding/Punishment	Amendment	PRO Reference File/Piece/Page
1 Gn Sher Fstrs	Pte	Freeman H	Kantara Egypt6	05/06/17	M	2 yrs HL		WO/213/15/17
1 Gn Sher Fstrs	Pte	Ganley H	Kantara Egypt	05/06/17	M	2 yrs HL		WO/213/15/176
1 Gn Sher Fstrs	Pte	Hallam G	Kantara Egypt	05/06/17	M	2 yrs HL		WO/213/15/176
1 Gn Sher Fstrs	Pte	Hammond H	Kantara Egypt	05/06/17	M	2 yrs HL		WO/213/15/176
1 Gn Sher Fstrs	Pte	Hardy J	Kantara Egypt	05/06/17	M	2 yrs HL		WO/213/15/176
1 Gn Sher Fstrs	Pte	Harrison GJ	Kantara Egypt	05/06/17	M	2 yrs HL		WO/213/15/176
1 Gn Sher Fstrs	Pte	Harrison JW	Kantara Egypt	05/06/17	M	2 yrs HL		WO/213/15/176
1 Gn Sher Fstrs	Pte	Harvey AE	Kantara Egypt	05/06/17	M	2 yrs HL		WO/213/15/177
1 Gn Sher Fstrs	Pte	Haywood J	Kantara Egypt	05/06/17	M	2 yrs HL		WO/213/15/177
1 Gn Sher Fstrs	Pte	Healy E	Kantara Egypt	05/06/17	M	2 yrs HL		WO/213/15/177
1 Gn Sher Fstrs	Pte	Holmes S	Kantara Egypt	05/06/17	M	2 yrs HL		WO/213/15/177
1 Gn Sher Fstrs	Pte	Horton E	Kantara Egypt	05/06/17	M	2 yrs HL		WO/213/15/177
1 Gn Sher Fstrs	Pte	Howe J	Kantara Egypt	05/06/17	M	2 yrs HL		WO/213/15/177
1 Gn Sher Fstrs	Pte	Lakin W	Kantara Egypt	05/06/17	M	2 yrs HL		WO/213/15/177
1 Gn Sher Fstrs	Pte	Lamb W	Kantara Egypt	05/06/17	M	2 yrs HL		WO/213/15/177
1 Gn Sher Fstrs	Pte	Leese G	Kantara Egypt	05/06/17	M	2 yrs HL		WO/213/15/177
1 Gn Sher Fstrs	Pte	Lindsay F	Kantara Egypt	05/06/17	M	2 yrs HL		WO/213/15/177
1 Gn Sher Fstrs	Pte	Loxley G	Kantara Egypt	05/06/17	M	2 yrs HL		WO/213/15/177
1 Gn Sher Fstrs	Pte	Massey A	Kantara Egypt	05/06/17	M	2 yrs HL		WO/213/15/177
1 Gn Sher Fstrs	Pte	McQuade F	Kantara Egypt	05/06/17	M	2 yrs HL		WO/213/15/177
1 Gn Sher Fstrs	Pte	Mellors H	Kantara Egypt	05/06/17	M	2 yrs HL		WO/213/15/177
1 Gn Sher Fstrs	Pte	Millward J	Kantara Egypt	05/06/17	M	2 yrs HL		WO/213/15/177
1 Gn Sher Fstrs	Pte	Morris A	Kantara Egypt	05/06/17	M	2 yrs HL		WO/213/15/177
1 Gn Sher Fstrs	Pte	Newton F	Kantara Egypt	05/06/17	M	2 yrs HL		WO/213/15/177
1 Gn Sher Fstrs	Pte	Noble W	Kantara Egypt	05/06/17	M	2 yrs HL		WO/213/15/177
1 Gn Sher Fstrs	Pte	Noton T	Kantara Egypt	05/06/17	M	2 yrs HL		WO/213/15/177
1 Gn Sher Fstrs	Pte	Palfrey WR	Kantara Egypt	05/06/17	M	2 yrs HL		WO/213/15/177
1 Gn Sher Fstrs	Pte	Parker G	Kantara Egypt	05/06/17	M	2 yrs HL		WO/213/15/177
1 Gn Sher Fstrs	Pte	Pickles JR	Kantara Egypt	05/06/17	M	2 yrs HL		WO/213/15/177
1 Gn Sher Fstrs	Pte	Ratcliffe H	Kantara Egypt	05/06/17	M	2 yrs HL		WO/213/15/177
1 Gn Sher Fstrs	Pte	Rathbone H	Kantara Egypt	05/06/17	M	2 yrs HL		WO/213/15/177
1 Gn Sher Fstrs	Pte	Riley W	Kantara Egypt	05/06/17	M	2 yrs HL		WO/213/15/177
1 Gn Sher Fstrs	Pte	Robinson JEG	Kantara Egypt	05/06/17	M	2 yrs HL		WO/213/15/177
1 Gn Sher Fstrs	Pte	Scoffham W	Kantara Egypt	05/06/17	M	2 yrs HL		WO/213/15/178
1 Gn Sher Fstrs	Pte	Slater JE	Kantara Egypt	05/06/17	M	2 yrs HL		WO/213/15/178
1 Gn Sher Fstrs	Pte	Smith J	Kantara Egypt	05/06/17	M	2 yrs HL		WO/213/15/178
1 Gn Sher Fstrs	Pte	Stephenson L	Kantara Egypt	05/06/17	M	2 yrs HL		WO/213/15/178

Unit	Rank	Name	Location	Date D/M/Y	Offence	Finding/Punishment	Amendment	PRO Reference File/Piece/Page
1 Gn Sher Fstrs	Pte	Street GS	Kantara Egypt	05/06/17	M	2 yrs HL		WO/213/15/178
1 Gn Sher Fstrs	Pte	Taylor A	Kantara Egypt	05/06/17	M	2 yrs HL		WO/213/15/178
1 Gn Sher Fstrs	Pte	Taylor S	Kantara Egypt	05/06/17	M	2 yrs HL		WO/213/15/178
1 Gn Sher Fstrs	Pte	Ward W	Kantara Egypt	05/06/17	M	2 yrs HL		WO/213/15/178
1 Gn Sher Fstrs	Pte	Wesman W	Kantara Egypt	05/06/17	M	2 yrs HL		WO/213/15/178
1 Gn Sher Fstrs	Pte	Wilkinson J	Kantara Egypt	05/06/17	M	2 yrs HL		WO/213/15/178
1 Gn Sher Fstrs	Pte	Yates J	Kantara Egypt	05/06/17	M	2 yrs HL		WO/213/15/178
11 Sherwood Fstrs	Pte	Grainger L	Steenbecque	30/12/15	M	28 dys FP1+Rnks		WO/213/7/25
1 Som LI	Pte	Dyer S	Rouen	04/02/19	M	90 dys Imp		WO/90/8/58
2 S Lancs	Rfn	Merton GA	Canterbury	23/06/14	Incit M+Esc Conf+S40	140 dys Detn		WO/92/3/18
7 S Staffs (att RAOC)	Pte(A/Cpl)	Hooley A	Field	08/10/19	M+S40	NG		WO/213/31/4
7 Suffolk	Pte(L/Cpl)	Broom W	Arras	13/04/17	M+S40	9 mos HL	Rem 3 mos	WO/213/15/142
12 SWBdrs	Pte	Claybrook AH	Field	01/12/16	M+Disob	18 mos HL	Comm 3 mos FP1	WO/213/13/47
12 SWBdrs	Pte	Cooke R	Field	01/12/16	M+Disob	18 mos HL	Comm 3 mos FP1	WO/312/13/46
12 SWBdrs	Pte	French J	Field	01/12/16	M+Disob	18 mos HL	Comm 3 mos FP1	WO/213/13/46
12 SWBdrs	Pte	Gummer E	Field	01/12/16	M+Disob	18 mos HL	Comm 3 mos FP1	WO/213/13/47
12 SWBdrs	Pte	Hale TS	Field	01/12/16	M+Disob	18 mos HL	Comm 3 mos FP1	WO/213/13/47
12 SWBdrs	Pte	Kelly SW	Field	01/12/16	M+Disob	18 mos HL	Comm 3 mos FP1	WO/213/13/47
12 SWBdrs	Pte	Leather AW	Field	01/12/16	M(2)+Disob	7 yrs PS	Comm 2 yrs HL	WO/213/13/46
12 SWBdrs	Pte	Marsden E	Field	01/12/16	M+Disob	18 mos HL	Comm 3 mos FP1	WO/312/13/46
12 SWBdrs	Pte	Milne R	Field	01/12/16	M+Disob	2 yrs HL	Comm 3 mos FP1	WO/213/13/46
12 SWBdrs	Pte(L/Cpl)	Price CR	Field	01/12/16	M+Disob	NG		WO/213/13/46
12 SWBdrs	Pte	Rustage VA	Field	01/12/16	M+Disob	18 mos HL	Comm 3 mos FP1	WO/213/13/47
12 SWBdrs	Pte	Samuel V	Field	01/12/16	M+Disob	18 mos HL	Comm 3 mos FP1	WO/213/13/47
12 SWBdrs	Pte	Sutton W	Field	01/12/16	M+Disob	18 mos HL	Comm 3 mos FP1	WO/213/13/47
12 SWBdrs	Pte	Thomas T	Field	01/12/16	M+Disob	18 mos HL	Comm 3 mos FP1	WO/213/13/47
12 SWBdrs	Pte	Tough TF	Field	01/12/16	M+Disob	18 mos HL	Comm 3 mos FP1	WO/213/13/47
12 SWBdrs	Pte	Turner E	Field	01/12/16	M+Disob	18 mos HL	Comm 3 mos FP1	WO/312/13/46
12 SWBdrs	Pte	Walton R	Field	01/12/16	M+Disob	18 mos HL	Comm 3 mos FP1	WO/312/13/46
12 SWBdrs	Pte	Watkins F	Field	01/12/16	M+Disob	18 mos HL	Comm 3 mos FP1	WO/312/13/46
12 SWBdrs	Pte	Wood W	Field	05/12/16	M+Disob	NG		WO/312/13/30
6 R Marines	Cpl(A/Sgt)	Cooper WJ	Field NREF	07/10/19	M(2)+S40	NG		WO/213/30/179
1 Suffolk	Pte	Mansfield E	Field SEF	02/05/18	M+Disob	10 yrs PS	Comm 2 yrs HL	WO/213/22/30
2/5 Sussex	Rfn	Merton	Canterbury	23/06/15	Incit M+Esc Conf+S40	140 dys Detn		WO/92/3/18
2 R Sussex Regt	Pte	Woiters FC	Field	28/02/19	M+Esc	1 yr HL		WO/213/28/157
2/4 R Sussex TF	Pte	Apted A	Canterbury	23/07/15	JM	84 dys Detn		WO/92/3/20
2/4 R Sussex TF	Pte	Archibald F	Canterbury	23/07/15	JM	84 dys Detn		WO/92/3/20
2/4 R Sussex TF	Pte	Aylwin J	Canterbury	23/07/15	JM	84 dys Detn		WO/92/3/20
2/4 R Sussex TF	Pte	Bailey A	Canterbury	23/07/15	JM	84 dys Detn		WO/92/3/21
2/4 R Sussex TF	Pte	Ball AT	Canterbury	23/07/15	JM	84 dys Detn		WO/92/3/20
2/4 R Sussex TF	Pte	Barnard G	Canterbury	23/07/15	JM	84 dys Detn		WO/92/3/20
2/4 R Sussex TF	Sgt	Barnard J	Canterbury	23/07/15	NSM	Redu to Cpl		WO/92/3/20
2/4 R Sussex TF	Pte	Batchelor E	Canterbury	23/07/15	JM	84 dys Detn		PRO/92/3/21
2/4 R Sussex TF	Pte	Best T	Canterbury	23/07/15	JM	NG		WO/92/3/21
2/4 R Sussex TF	Pte	Blackman J	Canterbury	23/07/15	JM	84 dys Detn		WO/92/3/21
2/4 R Sussex TF	Pte	Boniface A	Canterbury	23/07/15	JM	84 dys Detn		WO/92/3/24
2/4 R Sussex TF	Pte(L/Cpl)	Bowley H	Canterbury	23/07/15	NSM	28 dys Detn		WO/92/3/20
2/4 R Sussex TF	Cpl	Brennan S	Canterbury	23/07/15	NSM	Rnks		WO/92/3/20
2/4 R Sussex TF	Pte	Brown W	Canterbury	23/07/15	J[oin in] M	84 dys Detn		WO/92/3/21

Unit	Rank	Name	Location	Date D/M/Y	Offence	Finding/Punishment	Amendment	PRO Reference File/Piece/Page
2/4 R Sussex TF	Pte	Browne JE	Canterbury	23/07/15	J[oin in] M	84 dys Detn		WO/92/3/21
2/4 R Sussex TF	Pte	Burt A	Canterbury	23/07/15	J[oin in] M	84 dys Detn		WO/92/3/21
2/4 R Sussex TF	Pte	Carey G	Canterbury	23/07/15	J[oin in] M	84 dys Detn		WO/92/3/21
2/4 R Sussex TF	Pte(L/Cpl)	Carter A	Canterbury	23/07/15	NSM	28 dys Detn		WO/92/3/20
2/4 R Sussex TF	Pte	Coote JW	Canterbury	23/07/15	J[oin in] M	84 dys Detn		WO/92/3/21
2/4 R Sussex TF	Pte	Cowley JW	Canterbury	23/07/15	J[oin in] M	84 dys Detn		WO/92/3/21
2/4 R Sussex TF	Pte	Cruttenden W	Canterbury	23/07/15	J[oin in] M	84 dys Detn		WO/92/3/21
2/4 R Sussex TF	Pte(L/Cpl)	Davey H	Canterbury	23/07/15	NSM	28 dys Detn		WO/92/3/20
2/4 R Sussex TF	Pte	Deacon PH	Canterbury	23/07/15	J[oin in] M	84 dys Detn		WO/92/3/21
2/4 R Sussex TF	Pte	Dennis H	Canterbury	23/07/15	J[oin in] M	84 dys Detn		WO/92/3/21
2/4 R Sussex TF	Pte	Drake AJ	Canterbury	23/07/15	J[oin in] M	84 dys Detn		WO/92/3/21
2/4 R Sussex TF	Pte	Drury J	Canterbury	23/07/15	J[oin in] M	84 dys Detn		WO/92/3/21
2/4 R Sussex TF	Pte	Eames J	Canterbury	23/07/15	J[oin in] M	84 dys Detn		WO/92/3/21
2/4 R Sussex TF	Pte	Edwards J [aka E]	Canterbury	23/07/15	J[oin in] M	84 dys Detn		WO/92/3/21
2/4 R Sussex TF	Pte	Elphick C	Canterbury	23/07/15	J[oin in] M	84 dys Detn		WO/92/3/21
2/4 R Sussex TF	Pte	Faith T	Canterbury	23/07/15	J[oin in] M	NG		WO/92/3/21
2/4 R Sussex TF	Sgt	Farmer P	Canterbury	23/07/15	NSM	Redu to Cpl		WO/92/3/20
2/4 R Sussex TF	Pte	Faulkener H	Canterbury	23/07/15	J[oin in] M	84 dys Detn		WO/92/3/21
2/4 R Sussex TF	Pte	Fennell H	Canterbury	23/07/15	J[oin in] M	84 dys Detn		WO/92/3/22
2/4 R Sussex TF	Pte	Fennell S	Canterbury	23/07/15	J[oin in] M	84 dys Detn		WO/92/3/22
2/4 R Sussex TF	Pte	Fennell W	Canterbury	23/07/15	J[oin in] M	84 dys Detn		WO/92/3/22
2/4 R Sussex TF	Pte	Foster G	Canterbury	23/07/15	J[oin in] M	84 dys Detn		WO/92/3/21
2/4 R Sussex TF	Pte	Fox AT	Canterbury	23/07/15	J[oin in] M	84 dys Detn		WO/92/3/22
2/4 R Sussex TF	Pte(L/Cpl)	Gatterill D	Canterbury	23/07/15	NSM	28 dys Detn		WO/92/3/20
2/4 R Sussex TF	Pte	Golby W	Canterbury	23/07/15	J[oin in] M	84 dys Detn		WO/92/3/22
2/4 R Sussex TF	Pte	Hardwick T	Canterbury	23/07/15	J[oin in] M	84 dys Detn		WO/92/3/22
2/4 R Sussex TF	Pte	[Harmer?] SW	Canterbury	23/07/15	J[oin in] M	84 dys Detn		WO/92/3/22
2/4 R Sussex TF	Pte	Harris C	Canterbury	23/07/15	J[oin in] M	84 dys Detn		WO/92/3/22
2/4 R Sussex TF	Pte	Hodges F	Canterbury	23/07/15	J[oin in] M	84 dys Detn		WO/92/3/22
2/4 R Sussex TF	Pte	Holland W	Canterbury	23/07/15	J[oin in] M	84 dys Detn		WO/92/3/22
2/4 R Sussex TF	Pte	Hutchinson H	Canterbury	23/07/15	J[oin in] M	84 dys Detn		WO/92/3/22
2/4 R Sussex TF	Pte	Hyland RG	Canterbury	23/07/15	J[oin in] M	84 dys Detn		WO/92/3/22
2/4 R Sussex TF	Pte	Ireland GJ	Canterbury	23/07/15	J[oin in] M	84 dys Detn		WO/92/3/22
2/4 R Sussex TF	Pte	Lintott JR	Canterbury	23/07/15	J[oin in] M	84 dys Detn		WO/92/3/22
2/4 R Sussex TF	Pte	Madgwick HJ	Canterbury	23/07/15	J[oin in] M	84 dys Detn		WO/92/3/22
2/4 R Sussex TF	Pte	Marsh W	Canterbury	23/07/15	J[oin in] M	84 dys Detn		WO/92/3/22
2/4 R Sussex TF	Pte	Martin F	Canterbury	23/07/15	J[oin in] M	84 dys Detn		WO/92/3/22
2/4 R Sussex TF	Pte	McNorvill J	Canterbury	23/07/15	J[oin in] M	84 dys Detn		WO/92/3/23
2/4 R Sussex TF	Pte(L/Cpl)	[Merrett?] H	Canterbury	23/07/15	NSM	28 dys Detn		WO/92/3/20
2/4 R Sussex TF	Pte	Mitchell FW	Canterbury	23/07/15	J[oin in] M	84 dys Detn		WO/92/3/22
2/4 R Sussex TF	Pte	Mitchell G	Canterbury	23/07/15	J[oin in] M	84 dys Detn		WO/92/3/22
2/4 R Sussex TF	Pte	Napper T	Canterbury	23/07/15	J[oin in] M	84 dys Detn		WO/92/3/22
2/4 R Sussex TF	Pte	Neve C	Canterbury	23/07/15	J[oin in] M	84 dys Detn		File/92/3/23
2/4 R Sussex TF	Pte	Newman JJ	Canterbury	23/07/15	J[oin in] M	NG		WO/92/3/22
2/4 R Sussex TF	Pte	Page A	Canterbury	23/07/15	J[oin in] M	84 dys Detn		WO/92/3/23
2/4 R Sussex TF	Pte	Page AJ	Canterbury	23/07/15	J[oin in] M	84 dys Detn		WO/92/3/23
2/4 R Sussex TF	Pte	Pain J	Canterbury	23/07/15	J[oin in] M	84 dys Detn		WO/92/3/23
2/4 R Sussex TF	Pte	Parsons J	Canterbury	23/07/15	J[oin in] M	84 dys Detn		WO/92/3/23
2/4 R Sussex TF	Pte	Patching CW	Canterbury	23/07/15	J[oin in] M	84 dys Detn		WO/92/3/23
2/4 R Sussex TF	Pte	Payne GW	Canterbury	23/07/15	J[oin in] M	84 dys Detn		WO/92/3/23
2/4 R Sussex TF	Pte	Petter W	Canterbury	23/07/15	J[oin in] M	84 dys Detn		WO/92/3/23
2/4 R Sussex TF	Pte	Phillimore H	Canterbury	23/07/15	J[oin in] M	84 dys Detn		WO/92/3/23
2/4 R Sussex TF	Pte(L/Cpl)	Rosen J	Canterbury	23/07/15	NSM	28 dys Detn		WO/92/3/20
2/4 R Sussex TF	Pte	Roser WG	Canterbury	23/07/15	J[oin in] M	84 dys Detn		WO/92/3/23
2/4 R Sussex TF	Pte	Ross F	Canterbury	23/07/15	NSM	Redu to Cpl		WO/92/3/20
2/4 R Sussex TF	Cpl(L/Sgt)	Sayers C	Canterbury	23/07/15	NSM	Rnks		WO/92/3/20
2/4 R Sussex TF	Pte	Shoubridge T	Canterbury	23/07/15	J[oin in] M	84 dys Detn		WO/92/3/23
2/4 R Sussex TF	Pte(L/Cpl)	Shrivell C	Canterbury	23/07/15	NSM	28 dys Detn		WO/92/3/20
2/4 R Sussex TF	Pte	Smart WH	Canterbury	23/07/15	J[oin in] M	84 dys Detn		WO/92/3/23
2/4 R Sussex TF	Pte	Snelling A	Canterbury	23/07/15	J[oin in] M	84 dys Detn		WO/92/3/23
2/4 R Sussex TF	Pte	Somerville A	Canterbury	23/07/15	J[oin in] M	84 dys Detn		WO/92/3/23
2/4 R Sussex TF	Pte	Stenning H	Canterbury	23/07/15	J[oin in] M	84 dys Detn		WO/92/3/23
2/4 R Sussex TF	Pte	Thompson J	Canterbury	23/07/15	J[oin in] M	84 dys Detn		WO/92/3/23
2/4 R Sussex TF	Pte(L/Cpl)	Townsend J	Canterbury	23/07/15	NSM	28 dys Detn		WO/92/3/20
2/4 R Sussex TF	Pte	Treisler GW	Canterbury	23/07/15	J[oin in] M	84 dys Detn		WO/92/3/23
2/4 R Sussex TF	Pte	[Tuislick?] TN	Canterbury	23/07/15	J[oin in] M	84 dys Detn		WO/92/3/23
2/4 R Sussex TF	Cpl	Vidler W	Canterbury	23/07/15	NSM	Rnks		WO/92/3/20
2/4 R Sussex TF	Pte	Vine JW	Canterbury	23/07/15	J[oin in] M	84 dys Detn		WO/92/3/23
2/4 R Sussex TF	Pte	Waterman H	Canterbury	23/07/15	J[oin in] M	84 dys Detn		WO/92/3/24
2/4 R Sussex TF	Pte	Weir W	Canterbury	23/07/15	J[oin in] M	84 dys Detn		WO/92/3/24
2/4 R Sussex TF	Pte	Wheeler W	Canterbury	23/07/15	J[oin in] M	84 dys Detn		WO/92/3/24
2/4 R Sussex TF	Pte	Willmott F	Canterbury	23/07/15	J[oin in] M	84 dys Detn		WO/92/3/24
2/4 R Sussex TF	Pte	Wilson C	Canterbury	23/07/15	J[oin in] M	84 dys Detn		WO/92/3/24
2/4 R Sussex TF	Pte	Winder T	Canterbury	23/07/15	J[oin in] M	84 dys Detn		WO/92/3/24

Unit	Rank	Name	Location	Date D/M/Y	Offence	Finding/Punishment	Amendment	PRO Reference File/Piece/Page
2/4 R Sussex TF	Pte	Woodgate F	Canterbury	23/07/15	J[oin in] M	84 dys Detn		WO/92/3/24
2/4 R Sussex TF	Pte	Woodietts H	Canterbury	23/07/15	J[oin in] M	84 dys Detn		WO/92/3/24
2/4 R Sussex TF	Pte	Yates J	Canterbury	23/07/15	J[oin in] M	84 dys Detn		WO/92/3/24
54 TR Bn	Pte	Browning JB	Kirkcaldy	21/05/17	M+Insub(Cplx2) +Wilful Inj Prop	2 yrs Detn+Stop	Remit 1 yr	WO/86/76/98
54 TR Bn	Pte	O'Neil W	Kirkcaldy	31/05/17	M+Insub(Cplx2)	2 yrs Detn	Remit 1 yr	WO/86/76/98
2/6 R Wars	Pte	Baker HW	Field	23/01/19	M+Abs+Br	14 dys FP1		WO/213/27/167
2/6 R Wars	Pte	Cooksey H	Field	27/05/19	M+S40	2 yrs HL	Remit 1 yr	WO/213/30/64
2/6 R Wars	Pte	Crisp WA	Field	27/05/19	M+S40	2 yrs HL	Remit 1 yr	WO/213/30/64
2/6 R Wars	Pte	Davies W	Field	27/05/19	M+S40	2 yrs HL	Remit 1 yr	WO/213/30/64
2/6 R Wars	Pte	Dixon T	Field	27/05/19	M+S40	2 yrs HL	Remit 1 yr	WO/213/30/64
2/6 R Wars	Pte	Eden W	Field	27/05/19	M+S40	2 yrs HL	Remit 1 yr	WO/213/30/64
2/6 R Wars	Pte	Found L	Field	27/05/19	M+S40	2 yrs HL	Remit 1 yr	WO/213/30/64
2/6 R Wars	Pte	Howells A	Field	27/05/19	M+S40	2 yrs HL	Remit 1 yr	WO/213/30/64
2/6 R Wars	Pte	Ingram GE	Field	27/05/19	M+S40	2 yrs HL	Remit 1 yr	WO/213/30/64
2/6 R Wars	Pte	Lyons SB	Field	27/05/19	M+S40	2 yrs HL	Remit 1 yr	WO/213/30/64
2/6 R Wars	Pte	Pearman A	Field	27/05/19	M+S40	2 yrs HL	Remit 1 yr	WO/213/30/64
2/6 R Wars	Pte	Plumbley AM	Field	27/05/19	M+S40	2 yrs HL	Remit 1 yr	WO/213/30/64
2/6 R Wars	Pte	Reynolds JH	Field	27/05/19	M+S40	2 yrs HL	Remit 1 yr	WO/213/30/64
2/6 R Wars	Pte	Sidwell W	Field	27/05/19	M+S40	2 yrs HL	Remit 1 yr	WO/213/30/64
2/6 R Wars	Pte	Wood GW	Field	27/05/19	M+S40	2 yrs HL	Remit 1 yr	WO/213/30/64
2/7 R Wars	Pte (AL/Cpl)	Anderson W	Field	04/01/19	M	5 yrs PS		WO/213/28/72
2/7 R Wars	Pte(L/Cpl)	Friar R	Field	04/01/19	M	5 yrs PS		WO/213/28/72
2/7 R Wars	Pte(L/Cpl)	Greenway H	Field	04/01/19	M	5 yrs PS		WO/213/28/72
2/7 R Wars	Cpl	Keighley J	Field	04/01/19	M	5 yrs PS		WO/213/28/72
2/7 R Wars	Pte (AL/Cpl)	Lodge SJ	Field	04/01/19	M	5 yrs PS		WO/213/28/72
2/7 R Wars	Pte(AL/Cpl)	Robinson J	Field	04/01/19	M	5 yrs PS		WO/213/28/72
2/7 R Wars	Cpl	Watson H	Field	04/01/19	M	5 yrs PS		WO/213/28/72
2/7 R Wars	Pte	Fellasters G	Field	05/01/19	M	NG		WO/213/27/71
2/7 R Wars	Pte	Harrison D	Field	05/01/19	M	3 yrs PS		WO/213/27/122
1 W Yorks	Pte	Harris S	Field	24/03/19	M	PS/Life		WO/213/29/90
3 W Yorks	Pte	Calvert F	Devizes	01/08/19	M+S40	18 mos HL +Disch Igmny	9 mos	WO/92/4/77
3 W Yorks	Pte	Dawson BE	Wallsend	06/02/18	M+Insub(CSM)	2 yrs HL	Comm Detn	WO/86/88/96
3 W Yorks	Pte	Faulkner JR	Devizes	01/08/19	M+S40	18 mos HL +Disch Igmny	9 mos	WO/92/4/77
3 W Yorks	Pte	Gillett C	Devizes	01/08/19	M+S40	18 mos HL Igmny	9 mos	WO/92/4/77
3 W Yorks	Pte	Hardcastle W	Devizes	01/08/19	M+S40	18 mos HL +Disch Igmny	9 mos	WO/92/4/76
3 W Yorks	Pte	Hodgson JW	Devizes	01/08/19	M+S40	21 mos HL +Disch Igmny	12 mos	WO/92/4/76
3 W Yorks	Pte	Hudson CE	Devizes	01/08/19	M+S40	18 mos HL +Disch Igmny	9 mos	WO/92/4/76
3 W Yorks	Pte	Lee CH	Devizes	01/08/19	M+S40	18 mos+Disch Igmny	9 mos	WO/92/4/76
3 W Yorks	Pte	Mannix J	Wallsend	06/02/18	M+Insub(CSM)	1 yr HL		WO/86/80/96
3 W Yorks	Pte	McCabe J	Devizes	01/08/19	M+S40	18 mos+HL Igmny	9 mos	WO/92/4/77
3 W Yorks	Pte	Mundell J	Devizes	01/08/19	M+S40	18 mos HL Igmny	9 mos	WO/92/4/77
3 W Yorks	Pte	Payne WE	Devizes	01/08/19	M+S40	18 mos HL +Disch Igmny	9 mos	WO/92/4/76
3 W Yorks	Pte	Phillis W	Devizes	01/08/19	M+S40	18 mos HL +Disch Igmny	9 mos	WO/92/4/76
3 W Yorks	Pte	Prior G	Devizes	01/08/19	M+S40	1 yr HL+Disch Igmny	3 mos	WO/92/4/77
3 W Yorks	Pte	Robinson E	Devizes	01/08/19	M+S40	18 mos HL +Disch Igmny	9 mos	WO/92/4/76
3 W Yorks	Pte	Roe F	Devizes	01/08/19	M	Acquit		WO/92/4/75
3 W Yorks	Pte	Schofield S	Devizes	01/08/19	M+S40	18 mos HL +Disch Igmny	9 mos	WO/92/4/77
3 W Yorks	Pte	Tetley JW	Devizes	01/08/19	M+S40	18 mos HL +Disch Igmny	9 mos	WO/92/4/77
3 W Yorks	Pte	Warnes EE	Devizes	01/08/19	M+S40	18 mos HL +Disch Igmny	9 mos	WO/92/4/76
7 Wilts	Pte	Whalley H	Field SEF	02/05/18	M+Disob	10 yrs PS	Comm 2 yrs HL	WO/213/22/30
2 Worc	Pte(L/Cpl)	Oxley W	Perham Down	01/07/18	M+S40	Acquit		WO/92/4/41
5 Worc	Pte	Warr B	Dublin	11/08/19	M+S40	Acquit		WO/92/4/76
11 Worc	Pte	Fulford A	Field SEF	02/05/18	M+Disob	10 yrs PS	Comm 2 yrs HL	WO/213/22/30
11 Worc	Pte	Purchase W	Field SEF	02/05/18	M+Disob	10 yrs PS	Comm 2 yrs HL	WO/213/22/30
11 Worc	Pte	Roper C	Field SEF	02/05/18	M+Disob	10 yrs PS	Comm 2 yrs HL	WO/213/22/30
17 Worc	Pte	Sova S	Field	23/07/19	M+S40	1 yr HL		WO/213/30/135
15(TW) Worc	Pte	Timmon F	Swindon	12/04/17	M+S40	9 mos Detn		WO/86/75/125
2 Yorks att ASC	Pte	Haw WE	Dunkirk	13/04/17	M	6 mos HL		WO/213/14/138
6 Yorks	Pte	Child S	Kirkwall	16/11/18	M+Insub(Sgt)	112 dys Detn		WO/86/85/190
13 Yorks	Pte(L/Cpl)	Cole HA	NREF	16/05/19	M	2 yrs HL	Remit 18 mos	WO/213/29/181
13 Yorks	Cpl(AL/Sgt)	Metcalfe JE	NREF	16/05/19	M	2 yrs HL+Rnks		WO/213/29/181

Unit	Rank	Name	Location	Date D/M/Y	Offence	Finding/Punishment	Amendment	PRO Reference File/Piece/Page
2 Y[ork] & Lanc	Pte	Beck T	Basrah	07/11/19	M+S40	6 mos HL		WO/90/7/205
2 Y[ork] & Lanc	Pte	Green AP	Basrah	04/11/19	M+Disob+Insub Lang	4 yrs PS	Comm 2 yrs HL	WO/90/7/205
2 Y[ork] & Lanc	Pte	Hartley S	Basrah	06/11/19	M+Disob	5 yrs PS	Comm 2 yrs HL	WO/90/7/205
2 Y[ork] & Lanc	Pte	Holland JHB	Basrah	06/11/19	M+XSO*	5 yrs PS	Comm 2 yrs +*Quashed	WO/90/7/205
2 Y[ork] & Lanc	Pte	Hudson E	Clipstone	29/07/19	M+S40	NG		WO/86/88/50
2 Y[ork] & Lanc	Pte	Ingram T	Basrah	05/11/19	M+Disob	Acquit		WO/90/7/205
2 Y[ork] & Lanc	Pte	Lax J	Basrah	07/11/19	M	4 yrs PS	Comm 2 yrs HL	WO/90/7/205
2 Y[ork] & Lanc	Pte	Melson J	Basrah	05/11/19	M	4 yrs PS	Comm 2 yrs HL	WO/90/7/205
2 Y[ork] & Lanc	Pte	Milner G	Basrah	07/11/19	M+S7(3B)	5 yrs PS	Comm 2 yrs HL	WO/90/7/205
2 Y[ork] & Lanc	Pte	Portman HE	Basrah	07/11/19	M+S9(1)	4 yrs PS	Comm 2 yrs HL	WO/90/7/205
2 Y[ork] & Lanc	Pte	Richards JH	Basrah	05/11/19	M+Disob	5 yrs PS	Comm 2 yrs HL	WO/90/7/205
2 Y[ork] & Lanc	Pte	Stacey EW	Basrah	06/11/19	M	4 yrs PS	Comm 2 yrs HL	WO/90/7/205
2 Y[ork] & Lanc	L/Cpl	Tarren F	Basrah	04/11/19	M+Drunk	60 dys FP2		WO/90/7/20
2 Y[ork] & Lanc	Pte	Wake N	Basrah	05/11/19	M+S9(1)	4 yrs PS	Comm 2 yrs HL	WO/90/7/205
2 York & Lanc	Pte	Garner J	Kasvin	16/07/20	M	1 yr HL		WO/90/7/208
2 York & Lanc	Pte	Hoult A	Kasvin	16/07/20	M	1 yr HL		WO/90/7/208
2 York & Lanc	Pte	Robinson E	Kasvin	16/07/20	M	1 yr HL		WO/90/7/208
2 York & Lanc	Pte	Wraith E	Kasvin	16/07/20	M	1 yr HL		WO/90/7/208
6 York & Lanc	Pte	Villalard C	Field	24/03/19	M	10 yrs PS		WO/213/29/89
10 Y & Lanc	Pte	Butlin A	Field	12/11/17	M+Disob	6 mos HL	Comm 91 dy FP1	WO/213/18/181
10 Y & Lanc	Pte	Firth J	Field	12/11/17	M+Disob	6 mos HL	Comm 91 dys FP1	WO/213/18/181
ASC	Pte(S/Smith)	Dunn B	Marseilles	30/12/15	Joining M	3 yrs PS	Comm 2 yrs HL	WO/90/6/44
ASC	Pte(S/Smith)	Gay G	Marseilles	30/12/15	Joining M	3 yrs PS	Comm 2 yrs HL	WO/90/6/
ASC	Pte(S/Smith)	Harding B	Marseilles	30/12/15	Joining M	3 yrs PS	Comm 2 yrs HL	WO/90/6/44
ASC	Pte(S/Smith)	Harris F	Marseilles	30/12/15	Joininh M	3 yrs PS	Comm 2 yrsHL	WO/90/6/44
ASC	Pte(S/Smith)	Miles FV	Marseilles	30/12/15	Joining M	3 yrs PS	Comm 2 yrs HL	WO/90/6/44
ASC	Pte(S/Smith)	Monteith GJ	Marseilles	30/12/15	Joining M	3 yrs PS	Comm 2 yrs PS	WO/90/6/44
ASC	Pte	O'Neill J	Dunkirk	13/04/17	M	1 yr HL		WO/213/14/138
ASC	Dvr	Peden W	Rouen	05/10/16	M	Death	Comm 2 yrs HL	WO/90/6/89
ASC	Dvr	Peden W	Field	10/12/17	M	5 yrs PS		WO/213/19/52
ASC	Pte(S/Smith)	Popple JE	Marseilles	30/12/15	Joining M	Acquit		WO/90/6/44
ASC	Pte(S/Smith)	Rooke GB	Marseilles	30/12/15	Joining M	3 yrs PS	Comm 2 yrs HL	WO/90/6/44
ASC	Pte(S/Smith)	Sims W	Marseilles	30/12/15	Joining M	3 yrs PS	Comm 2 yrs HL	WO/90/6/44
ASC	Pte(S/Smith)	Town GT	Marseilles	30/12/15	Joining M	3 yrs PS	Comm 2 yrs HL	WO/90/6/44
ASC	Pte(S/Smith)	Underwood CA	Marseilles	30/12/15	Joining M	3 yrs PS	Comm 2 yrs HL	WO/90/6/44
ASC	Pte(S/Smith)	Vizard J	Marseilles	30/12/15	Joining M	3 yrs PS	Comm 2 yrs HL	WO/90/6/44
ASC	Pte(S/Smith)	Williams W	Marseilles	30/12/15	Joining M	3 yrs PS	Comm 2 yrs HL	WO/90/6/44
65 Coy RDC	Pte	Cash D	Towcester	16/11/16	CM+JM	1 yr Detn		WO/92/3/55
58 Coy RDC	Pte	Comyn A	Towcester	16/11/16	CM+JM	1 yr Detn		WO/92/3/55
65 Coy RDC	Pte	Douglas G	Towcester	16/11/16	CM+JM	1 yr Detn		WO/92/3/55
65 Coy RDC	Pte	Griffin M	Towcester	16/11/16	CM+JM	1 yr Detn		WO/92/3/55
65 Coy RDC	Pte	Banbrough W	Towcester	21/11/16	M	1 yr Detn		WO/92/4/3
58 Coy RDC	Pte	Beaman T	Towcester	21/11/16	M	1 yr Detn		WO/92/4/1
58 Coy RDC	Pte	Biggin A	Towcester	21/11/16	M	1 yr Detn		WO/92/4/2
58 Coy RDC	Pte	Boyce H	Towcester	21/11/16	M	1 yr Detn		WO/92/4/1
58 Coy RDC	Pte	Boyes JF	Towcester	21/11/16	M	1 yr Detn		WO/92/4/1
58 Coy RDC	Pte	Briggs A	Towcester	21/11/16	M	1 yr Detn		WO/92/4/2
58 Coy RDC	Pte	Broadmeadow W	Towcester	21/11/16	M	1 yr Detn		WO/92/4/2
65 Coy RDC	Pte	Brown J	Towcester	21/11/16	M	1 yr Detn		WO/92/4/3
58 Coy RDC	Pte	Brown JE	Towcester	21/11/16	M	1 yr Detn		WO/92/4/1
65 Coy RDC	Pte	Brown WH	Towcester	21/11/16	M	1 yr Detn		WO/92/4/2
58 Coy RDC	Pte	Burton EF	Towcester	21/11/16	M	1 yr Detn		WO/92/4/1
58 Coy RDC	Pte	Cain J	Towcester	21/11/16	M	1 yr Detn		WO/92/4/1
58 Coy RDC	Pte	Cameron J	Towcester	21/11/16	M	1 yr Detn		WO/92/4/1
65 Coy RDC	Pte	Campbell W	Towcester	21/11/16	M	1 yr Detn		WO/92/4/2
58 Coy RDC	Pte	Canning W	Towcester	21/11/16	M	1 yr Detn		WO/92/4/1
58 Coy RDC	Pte	Cassidy T	Towcester	21/11/16	M	1 yr Detn		WO/92/4/1
65 Coy RDC	Pte	Cattenach E	Towcester	21/11/16	M	1 yr Detn		WO/92/4/3

Unit	Rank	Name	Location	Date D/M/Y	Offence	Finding/Punishment	Amendment	PRO Reference File/Piece/Page
58 Coy RDC	Pte	Cherry JE	Towcester	21/11/16	M	1 yr Detn		WO/92/4/1
65 Coy RDC	Pte	Collins F	Towcester	21/11/16	M	1 yr Detn		WO/92/4/2
65 Coy RDC	Pte	Cree T	Towcester	21/11/16	M	1 yr Detn		WO/92/4/3
58 Coy RDC	Pte	Dixon WT	Towcester	21/11/16	M	1 yr Detn		WO/92/4/1
65 Coy RDC	Pte	Donnelly T	Towcester	21/11/16	M	1 yr Detn		WO/92/4/3
65 Coy RDC	Pte	Dowd P	Towcester	21/11/16	M	1 yr Detn		WO/92/4/3
58 Coy RDC	Pte	Downes LA	Towcester	21/11/16	M	1 yr Detn		WO/92/4/2
65 Coy RDC	Pte	Duncan FT	Towcester	21/11/16	M	1 yr Detn		WO/92/4/3
65 Coy RDC	Pte	Dwerryhouse J	Towcester	21/11/16	M	1 yr Detn		WO/92/4/3
58 Coy RDC	Pte	Elliot J	Towcester	21/11/16	M	1 yr Detn		WO/92/4/1
65 Coy RDC	Ptr	Ellison E	Towcester	21/11/16	M	1 yr Detn		WO/92/4/2
65 Coy RDC	Pte	Evans W	Towcester	21/11/16	M	1 yr Detn		WO/92/4/2
65 Coy RDC	Pte	Eves R	Towcester	21/11/16	M	1 yr Detn		WO/92/4/3
65 Coy RDC	Pte	Faircrough R	Towcester	21/11/16	M	1 yr Detn		WO/92/4/2
65 Coy RDC	Pte	Field WH	Towcester	21/11/16	M	1 yr Detn		WO/92/4/3
58 Coy RDC	Pte	Flynn P	Towcester	21/11/16	M	1 yr Detn		WO/92/4/1
58 Coy RDC	Pte	Foster JA	Towcester	21/11/16	M	1 yr Detn		WO/92/4/1
65 Coy RDC	Pte	Furlong J	Towcester	21/11/16	M	1 yr Detn		WO/92/4/3
58 Coy RDC	Pte	Gallimore G	Towcester	21/11/16	M	1 yr Detn		WO/92/4/1
58 Coy RDC	Pte	Garton F	Towcester	21/11/16	M	1 yr Detn		WO/92/4/1
65 Coy RDC	Pte	Graham JW	Towcester	21/11/16	M	1 yr Detn		WO/92/4/2
65 Coy RDC	Pte	Griffiths J	Towcester	21/11/16	M	1 yr Detn		WO/92/4/2
58 Coy RDC	Pte	Hague W	Towcester	21/11/16	M	1 yr Detn		WO/92/4/1
58 Coy RDC	Pte	Healy A	Towcester	21/11/16	M	1 yr Detn		WO/92/4/1
65 Coy RDC	Pte	Howell TH	Towcester	21/11/16	M	1 yr Detn		WO/92/4/2
65 Coy RDC	Pte	Hughes W	Towcester	21/11/16	M	1 yr Detn		WO/92/4/3
58 Coy RDC	Pte	Hutchinson JC	Towcester	21/11/16	M	1 yr Detn		WO/92/4/1
65 Coy RDC	Pte	Kelly C	Towcester	21/11/16	M	1 yr Detn		WO/92/4/3
65 Coy RDC	Pte	Kelly P	Towcester	21/11/16	M	1 yr Detn		WO/92/4/3
58 Coy RDC	Pte	Kennedy M	Towcester	21/11/16	M	1 yr Detn		WO/92/4/1
58 Coy RDC	Pte	Kirby W	Towcester	21/11/16	M	1 yr Detn		WO/92/4/1
65 Coy RDC	Pte	Kirkham D	Towcester	21/11/16	M	1 yr Detn		WO/92/4/2
58 Coy RDC	Pte	Long D	Towcester	21/11/16	M	1 yr Detn		WO/92/4/1
65 Coy RDC	Pte	McCall E	Towcester	21/11/16	M	1 yr Detn		WO/92/4/3
65 Coy RDC	Pte	McCormack E	Towcester	21/11/16	M	1 yr Detn		WO/92/4/2
65 Coy RDC	Pte	McDowell T	Towcester	21/11/16	M	1 yr Detn		WO/92/4/3
65 Coy RDC	Pte	McEvoy D	Towcester	21/11/16	M	1 yr Detn		WO/92/4/3
65 Coy RDC	Pte	Mclaughlin J	Towcester	21/11/16	M	1 yr Detn		WO/92/4/4
65 Coy RDC	Pte	Moore T	Towcester	21/11/16	M	1 yr Detn		WO/92/4/3
65 Coy RDC	Pte	Morley J	Towcester	21/11/16	M	1 yr Detn		WO/92/4/2
65 Coy RDC	Pte	Naylor J	Towcester	21/11/16	M	1 yr Detn		WO/92/4/2
65 Coy RDC	Pte	O'Hara T	Towcester	21/11/16	M	1 yr Detn		WO/92/4/3
65 Coy RDC	Pte	Orr D	Towcester	21/11/16	M	1 yr Detn		WO/92/4/3
58 Coy RDC	Pte	Phillips R	Towcester	21/11/16	M	1 yr Detn		WO/92/4/2
58 Coy RDC	Pte	Pontefract JV	Towcester	21/11/16	M	1 yr Detn		WO/92/4/1
58 Coy RDC	Pte	Precious F	Towcester	21/11/16	M	1 yr Detn		WO/92/4/2
65 Coy RDC	Pte	Reid J	Towcester	21/11/16	M	1 yr Detn		WO/92/4/2
58 Coy RDC	Pte	Robinson G	Towcester	21/11/16	M	1 yr Detn		WO/92/4/2
65 Coy RDC	Pte	Rogers R	Towcester	21/11/16	M	1 yr Detn		WO/92/4/2
58 Coy RDC	Pte	Rowe T	Towcester	21/11/16	M	1 yr Detn		WO/92/4/1
65 Coy RDC	Pte	Ryan S	Towcester	21/11/16	M	1 yr Detn		WO/92/4/3
65 Coy RDC	Pte	Sandieson J	Towcester	21/11/16	M	1 yr Detn		WO/92/4/3
58 Coy RDC	Pte	Seymour J	Towcester	21/11/16	M	1 yr Detn		WO/92/4/1
58 Coy RDC	Pte	Sharp J	Towcester	21/11/16	M	1 yr Detn		WO/92/4/1
65 Coy RDC	Pte	Shields T	Towcester	21/11/16	M	1 yr Detn		WO/92/4/2
65 Coy RDC	Pte	Shields W	Towcester	21/11/16	M	1 yr Detn		WO/92/4/3
65 Coy RDC	Pte	Summers J	Towcester	21/11/16	M	1 yr Detn		WO/92/4/3
65 Coy RDC	Pte	Taylor FJ	Towcester	21/11/16	M	1 yr Detn		WO/92/4/3
58 Coy RDC	Pte	Thomson W	Towcester	21/11/16	M	1 yr Detn		WO/92/4/1
65 Coy RDC	Pte	Twist M	Towcester	21/11/16	M	1 yr Detn		WO/92/4/3
65 Coy RDC	Pte	Williams F	Towcester	21/11/16	M	1 yr Detn		WO/92/4/3
65 Coy RDC	Pte	Woods G	Towcester	21/11/16	M	1 yr Detn		WO/92/4/2
334 Coy RDC	Pte	Keefe A	Pembroke Dock	17/09/18	M+Disob	84 dys Detn	28 dys	WO/92/4/52
334 Coy RDC	Pte	Smith S	Pembroke Dock	17/09/18	M+Disob	112 dys Detn	28 dys	WO/92/4/52
344 Coy RDC	Pte	Taylor H	Pembroke Dock	17/09/18	M+Insub	112 dys Detn	28 dys	WO/92/4/52
334 Coy RDC	Pte	Thomas W	Pembroke Dock	17/09/18	M+Disob	90 dys Detn	28dys	WO/92/4/52
334 Coy RDC	Pte	Walker H	Pembroke Dock	17/09/18	M+Disob	112 dys Detn	28 dys	WO/92/4/52
344 Coy RDC	Pte	Watts A	Pembroke Dock	17/09/18	M+Disob	90 dys Detn	28 dys	WO/92/4/52

Unit	Rank	Name	Location	Date D/M/Y	Offence	Finding/Punishment	Amendment	PRO Reference File/Piece/Page
2 Dragoon Gds (att RAOC)	Pte	Kershaw J	Field	29/07/20	M+S7(3b)	4 yrs PS		WO/213/32/22
5 Dragoon Gds	A/Cpl	Dunn ET	At Sea	03/11/14	Endeavg M	56 dys Detn	Comm 14	WO213/1/74
6 Dragoon RHGds)	Tpr	Thom AG	Rouen	05/10/16	M	5 yrs PS	Comm 2 yrs HL	WO/90/6/89((att
71 Lab Coy	Pte	Arnold G	Rouen	04/02/19	M	Acquit		WO/90/8/58
76 Lab Coy	L/Cpl	Lee CEW	Field	28/10/19	M+Disob+S40	3 yrs PS	Comm 2 yrs HL	WO/213/31/80
Lab Corps (att E Comm LB)	Pte	Bundy HG	Sutton	15/06/19	M+S7(3b)	Acquit		WO/92/4/74
Lab Cps	Pte	Capock H	Field	06/01/19	M+S40	NG		WO/213/29/89
Lab Corps (att E Comm LB)	Pte	Chapman G	Sutton	15/06/19	M+S7(3b)	Acquit		WO/92/4/73
Lab Corps (att E Comm LB)	Pte	Cobb A	Sutton	15/06/19	M+S7(3b)	Acquit		WO/92/4/73
Lab Cps	Pte	Cross R	Field	06/01/19	M+S40	NG		WO/213/29/89
Lab Cps	Pte	Dean A	Field	06/01/19	M+S40	NG		WO213/28/88
Lab Corps (att E Comm LB)	Pte	Diamond F	Sutton	15/06/19	M+S7(3b)	Acquit		WO/92/4/73
Lab Corps (att E Comm LB)	Pte	Drew EG	Sutton	15/06/19	M+S7(3b)	Acquit		WO/92/4/73
Lab Corps (att E Comm LB)	Pte	Fielder P	Sutton	15/06/19	M+S7(3b)	Acquit		WO/92/4/73
Lab Corps	Pte	Fortis SL	Field	24/03/19	M	11 yrs PS		WO/213/29/91
Lab Corps (att E Comm LB)	Pte	Gambrill WJ	Sutton	15/06/19	M+S7(3b)	Acquit		WO/92/4/73
Lab Cps	Pte	Gillingham P	Field	06/01/19	M+S40	NG		WO/213/30/120
Lab Corps (att E Comm LB)	Pte	Gillings WG	Sutton	15/06/19	M+S7(3b)	Acquit		WO/92/4/73
Lab Corps (att E Comm LB)	Pte	Gough JW	Sutton	15/06/19	M+S7(3b)	Acquit		WO/92/4/73
Lab Corps (att E Comm LB)	Pte	Grimmer FL	Sutton	15/06/19	M+S7(3b)	Acquit		WO/92/4/73
Lab Corps (att E Comm LB)	Pte	Harrington WR	Sutton	15/06/19	M+S7(3b)	Acquit		WO/92/4/73
Lab Corps	Pte	Harris F	Field	09/06/19	M+S40	1 yr HL		WO/213/27/37
Lab Corps	Pte	Harris	Field	11/08/19	M+S40	42 dys FP2		WO/213/30/120
Lab Corps (att E Comm LB)	Pte	Harris SJ	Sutton	15/06/19	M+S7(3b)	Acquit		WO/92/4/73
Lab Corps (att E Comm LB)	Pte	Hart S	Sutton	15/06/19	M+S7(3b)	Acquit		WO/92/4/73
Lab Corps (att E Comm LB)	Pte	Hawkins WJ	Sutton	15/06/19	M+S7(3b)	Acquit		WO/92/4/73
Lab Cps	Pte	Henson CE	Field	06/01/19	M+S40	NG		WO/213/27/37
Lab Corps (att E Comm LB)	Pte	Huxtable AR	Sutton	15/06/19	M+S7(3b)	Acquit		WO/92/4/74
Lab Cps	Pte	Morrison J	Field	06/01/19	M+S40	NG		WO/213/27/37
Lab Corps	Pte	Noakes H	Field	24/03/19	M	10 yrs PS		WO/213/27/37
Lab Corps (att E Comm LB)	Pte	Norman AA	Sutton	15/06/19	M+S7(3b)	Acquit		WO/92/4/74
Lab Corps (att E Comm LB)	Pte	Page AE	Sutton	15/06/19	M+S7(3b)	Acquit		WO/92/4/73
Lab Corps (att E Comm LB)	Pte	Palmer TH	Sutton	15/06/19	M+S7(3b)	Acquit		WO/92/4/73
Lab Corps (att E Comm LB)	Pte	Peacock W	Sutton	15/06/19	M+S7(3b)	Acquit		WO/92/4/74
Lab Corps (att E Comm LB)	Pte	Pearl E	Sutton	15/06/19	M+S7(3b)	Acquit		WO/92/4/74
Lab Corps (att E Comm LB)	Pte	Plumtree W	Sutton	15/06/19	M+S7(3b)	Acquit		WO/92/4/74
Lab Corps (att E Comm LB)	Pte	Potter EC	Sutton	15/06/19	M+S7(3b)	Acquit		WO/92/4/73
Lab Corps (att E Comm LB)	Pte	Reed T	Sutton	15/06/19	M+S7(3b)	Acquit		WO/92/4/74
Lab Corps (att E Comm LB)	Pte	Roberts PC	Sutton	15/06/19	M+S7(3b)	Acquit		WO/92/4/73
Lab Corps (att E Comm LB)	Pte	Roberts WH	Sutton	15/06/19	M+S7(3b)	Acquit		WO/92/4/73
Lab Corps (att E Comm LB)	Pte	Rump S	Sutton	15/06/19	M+S7(3b)	Acquit		WO/92/4/74
Lab Corps (att E Comm LB)	Pte	Seaborn N	Sutton	15/06/19	M+S7(3b)	Acquit		WO/92/4/74
Lab Corps (att E Comm LB)	Pte	Skeels A	Sutton	15/06/19	M+S7(3b)	Acquit		WO/92/4/73

Unit	Rank	Name	Location	Date D/M/Y	Offence	Finding/Punishment	Amendment	PRO Reference File/Piece/Page
Lab Corps (att E Comm LB)	Pte	Slowgrove AR	Sutton	15/06/19	M+S7(3b)	Acquit		WO/92/4/74
20(R) CEF	Pte	Smith EN	Liverpool	15/06/19	M+S40	Acquit		WO/92/4/74
Lab Corps (att E Comm LB)	Pte	Smith HG	Sutton	15/06/19	M+S7(3b)	Acquit		WO/92/4/73
Lab Corps (att E Comm LB)	Pte	Snowden J	Sutton	15/06/19	M+S7(3b)	Acquit		WO/92/4/73
Lab Corps (att E Comm LB)	Pte	Soames W	Sutton	15/06/19	M+S7(3b)	Acquit		WO/92/4/74
Lab Corps (att E Comm LB)	Pte	Stapley LJ	Sutton	15/06/19	M+S7(3b)	Acquit		WO/92/4/74
Lab Corps (att E Comm LB)	Pte	Stone F	Sutton	15/06/19	M+S7(3b)	Acquit		WO/92/4/73
Lab Corps	Pte	Taylor JA	Field	24/03/19	M	10 yrs PS		WO/213/29/88
Lab Corps (att E Comm LB)	Pte	Taylor W	Sutton	15/06/19	M+S7(3b)	Acquit		WO/92/4/74
Lab Corps (att E Comm LB)	Pte	Turner AE	Sutton	15/06/19	M+S7(3b)	Acquit		WO/92/4/74
Lab Corps (att E Comm LB)	Pte	Waldron M	Sutton	15/06/19	M+S7(3b)	Acquit		WO/92/4/74
Lab Corps (att E Comm LB)	Pte	Walsh MJ	Sutton	15/06/19	M+S7(3b)	Acquit		WO/92/4/73
Lab Corps) (att E Comm LB	Pte	Whitelam G	Sutton	15/06/19	M+S7(3b)	Acquit		WO/92/4/73
Lab Corps	Pte	Yates F	Field	24/03/19	M	10 yrs PS		WO/213/27/37
257 P of W Coy	Pte	Foster A	Field	13/05/19	M+S40(2)	6 mos Imp	Comm 90 dys FP2	WO/213/30/31
257 P of W Coy	Pte	Hudson S	Field	13/05/19	M+S40(2)	92 dys HL		WO/213/30/3i
257 P of W Coy	Pte	Milson W	Field	13/05/19	M+S40(2)	112 dys HL	Comm 90 dys FP2	WO/213/30/31
257 P of W Coy	Pte	Thomson J	Field	13/05/19	M+S40(2)	6 mos HL	56 dys FP1	WO/213/30/31
257 P of W Coy	Pte	Webster A	Field	13/05/19	M+S40(2)	6 mos Imp	Comm 90 dys FP2	WO/213/30/31
257 P of W Coy	Cpl	Woodhead E	Field	13/05/19	M+S40(2)	9 mos HL+Rnks		WO/213/30/31
MGC	Pte	Fiander AE	Grantham	05/11/18	M+S40	1 yr Detn		WO/86/85/97
MG Gds	Pte	Hosker A	London	26/02/18	M+Absx2	2 yrs HL		WO/92/4/29
MG Gds	Pte	Kirby G	London	26/02/18	M+Absx2	6 mos Detn		WO/92/4/29
1 MGC	Cpl	Coffey W	Field	17/07/19	M	5 mos Imp+Rnks		WO/213/30/82
1 MGC	Cpl	Hill N	Field	17/07/19	M	5 mos Imp+Rnks		WO/213/30/82
1 MGC	Pte (A/Cpl)	Owen EL	Field	17/07/19	M	5 mos Imp		WO/213/30/82
1 MGC	Pte (A/Cpl)	Snell FJ	Field	17/07/19	M	5 mos Imp		WO/213/30/82
1(R) MGC	Pte	Evans JA	Grantham	25/06/18	M+S40	1 yr HL		WO/92/4/40
2 MGC	Pte	Anderson C	Field	12/06/19	M+Disob(2)+S40	5 yrs PS	Comm 2 yrs HL	WO/213/29/122
2 MGC	Pte	Barker H	Field	12/06/19	M+Disob(2)+S40	5 yrs PS	Comm 2 yrs HL	WO/213/29/122
2 MGC	Pte	Barr WJ	Field	12/06/19	M+Disob(2)+S40	5 yrs PS		WO/213/29/122
2 MGC	Pte	Battersby HM	Field	12/06/19	M+Disob(2)+S40	5 yrs PS		WO/213/29/122
2 MGC	Pte	Brennan M	Field	12/06/19	M+Disob(2)+S40	5 yrs PS	Comm 2 yrs HL	WO/213/29/122
2 MGC	Pte	Bryson H	Field	12/06/19	M+Disob(2)+S40	5 yrs PS	Remit 2 yrs	WO/213/29/122
2 MGC	Pte	Collins WG	Field	12/06/19	M+Disob(2)+S40	5 yrs PS	Remit 2 yrs	WO/213/29/122
2 MGC	Pte	Grapes C	Field	12/06/19	M+Disob(2)+S40	5 yrs PS	Remit 2 yrs	WO/213/29/122
2 MGC	Pte	Green FC	Field	12/06/19	M+Disob(2)+S40	5 yrs PS	Remit 2 yrs	WO/213/29/122
2 MGC	Pte	Harrison W	Field	12/06/19	M+Disob(2)+S40	5 yrs PS	Remit 1 yr	WO/213/29/122
2 MGC	Pte	Hodgson P	Field	12/06/19	M+Disob(2)+S40	5 yrs PS	Remit 2 yrs	WO/213/29/122
2 MGC	Pte	Howe L	Field	12/06/19	M+Disob(2)+S40	5 yrs PS	Comm 2 yrs HL	WO/213/29/122
2 MGC	Pte	Jones JW	Field	12/06/19	M+Disob(2)+S40	5 yrs PS	Comm 2 yrs HL	WO/213/29/122
2 MGC	Pte	Lever TG	Field	12/06/19	M+Disob(2)+S40	5 yrs PS	Comm 2 yrs HL	WO/213/29/122
2 MGC	Pte	Milne RW	Field	12/06/19	M+Disob(2)+S40	5 yrs PS	Remit 2 yrs	WO/213/29/122
2 MGC	Pte	Randall H	Field	12/06/19	M+Disob(2)+S40	5 yrs PS		WO/213/29/122
2 MGC	Pte	Ross G	Field	12/06/19	M+Disob(2)+S40	5 yrs PS	Remit 2 yrs	WO/213/29/122
2 MGC	Pte	Saunders HP	Field	12/06/19	M+Disob(2)+S40	5 yrs PS	Comm 2 yrs HL	WO/213/29/122
2 MGC	Pte	Sherring J	Field	12/06/19	M+Disob(2)+S40	5 yrs PS	Comm 2 yrs HL	WO/213/29/122
2 MGC	Pte	Stephens E	Field	12/06/19	M+Disob(2)+S40	5 yrs PS	Comm 2 yrs HL	WO/213/29/122
2 MGC	Pte	Threlfell E	Field	12/06/19	M+Disob(2)+S40	5 yrs PS		WO/213/29/122
2 MGC	Pte	Weinberg S	Field	12/06/19	M+Disob(2)+S40	5 yrs PS	Remit 2 yrs	WO/213/29/122
2 MGC	Pte	Wormald S	Field	12/06/19	M+Disob(2)+S40	5 yrs PS	Remit 2 yrs	WO/213/29/122
2(R) MGC	Pte	McCallum D	Grantham	25/06/18	M+S40	2yrs HL	Remit 1 yr/ Comm Detn	WO/92/4/41
9 MGC	Pte	Armitage E	Field	09/01/19	M+S40	28 dys x 2	Comm to 2 [dys?]	WO/213/27/200
9 MGC	Pte	Chappell LR	Field	31/07/19	M+Abs/Br	6 mos HL		WO/213/30/141
9 MGC	Pte	Dabell W	Field	31/07/19	M+Abs/Br	6 mos HL	Quashed	WO/213/30/141
9 MGC	Pte	Fox LF	Field	31/07/19	M+Abs/Br	6 mos HL		WO/213/30/141
9 MGC	Pte	Gamble F	Field	31/07/19	M+Abs/Br	6 mos HL		WO/213/30/141
9 MGC	Cpl	Johnston T	Field	31/07/19	Mx2	12 mos HL+Rnks		WO/213/30/76

Unit	Rank	Name	Location	Date D/M/Y	Offence	Finding/Punishment	Amendment	PRO Reference File/Piece/Page
9 MGC	Pte	Lucas AF	Field	31/07/19	M+Abs/Br	6 mos HL		WO/213/30/141
9 MGC	Pte	Radcliffe G	Field	31/07/19	M+Abs/Br	6 mos HL		WO/213/30/141
9 MGC	Pte	Shepherd AE	Field	31/07/19	M+Abs/Br	6 mos HL	Quashed	WO/213/30/141
9 MGC	Pte	Whiteman A	Field	31/07/19	M+Abs/Br	6 mos HL	Quashed	WO/213/30/141
29 MGC	Pte	Turner J	Field	01/02/19	M+S40	1 yr HL	Remit 6 mos	WO/213/28/73
30 MGC	Pte	Arundale L	Field	29/07/19	M+Disob	1 yr HL		WO/213/30/119
30 MGC	Pte	Barnes F	Field	29/07/19	M+Disob	1 yr HL		WO/213/30/119
30 MGC	Pte	Brooks RR	Field	29/07/19	M+Disob	1 yr HL		WO/213/30/119
30 MGC	Pte	Chapman W	Field	29/07/19	M+Disob	1 yr HL		WO/213/30/119
30 MGC	Pte	Cogger AN	Field	29/07/19	M+Disob	1 yr HL		WO/213/30/119
30 MGC	Pte	Dunn R	Field	29/07/19	M+Disob	1 yr HL		WO/213/30/119
30 MGC	Pte	Ellis EJ	Field	29/07/19	M+Disob	1 yr HL		WO/213/30/119
30 MGC	Pte	Fowler A	Field	29/07/19	M+Disob	1 yr HL		WO/213/30/119
30 MGC	Pte	Humpreys B	Field	29/07/19	M+Disob	1 yr HL		WO/213/30/119
30 MGC	Pte	Marsh B	Field	29/07/19	M+Disob	1 yr HL		WO/213/30/119
30 MGC	Pte	McCall TM	Field	29/07/19	M+Disob	1 yr HL		WO/213/30/119
30 MGC	Pte	Page EE	Field	29/07/19	M+Disob	1 yr HL		WO/213/30/119
30 MGC	Pte	Stevenson W	Field	29/07/19	M+Disob	1 yr HL		WO/213/30/119
30 MGC	Pte	Whitehouse AJ	Field	29/07/19	M+Disob	1 yr HL		WO/213/30/119
30 MGC	Pte	Wolfe WG	Field	29/07/19	M+Disob	1 yr HL		WO/213/30/119
34 MGC	Pte	Brighton LC	Field	17/01/19	Mx2	2 yrs HL	Remit 18 mos	WO/213/28/120
35 MGC	Pte	Beal A	Field	17/01/19	Mx2	2 yrs HL	Remit 6 mos	WO/213/28/121
35 MGC	Pte	Budden F	Field	17/01/19	Mx2	2 yrs HL	Remit 18 mos	WO/213/28/121
35 MGC	Pte	Bundy AE	Field	17/01/19	Mx2	2 yrs HL	Remit 18 mos	WO/213/28/121
35 MGC	Pte	Cattanach M	Field	17/01/19	Mx2	2 yrs HL	Remit 6 mos	WO/213/28/120
35 MGC	Pte	Cavanagh W	Field	17/01/19	Mx2	1 yr HL	Remit 6 mos	WO/213/28/121
35 MGC	Pte	Craydon FH	Field	17/01/19	Mx2	2 yrs HL	Remit 18 mos	WO/213/28/120
35 MGC	L/Cpl	Freeman W	Field	17/01/19	M	2 yrs HL	Remit 6 mos	WO/213/28/120
35 MGC	L/Cpl	Hart T	Field	17/01/19	M	2 yrs HL	Remit 18 mos	WO/213/28/120
35 MGC	Pte	Hayle HV	Field	17/01/19	Mx2	2 yrs HL	Remit 18 mos	WO/213/28/120
35 MGC	Pte	Jones JR	Field	17/01/19	Mx2	2 yrs HL	Remit 18 mos	WO/213/28/120
35 MGC	Pte	Kirkham ST	Field	17/01/19	Mx2	2 yrs HL	Remit 18 mos	WO/213/28/120
35 MGC	Pte	Mackessy T	Field	17/01/19	Mx2	2 yrs HL	Remit 6 mos	WO/213/28/120
35 MGC	Pte	May W	Field	17/01/19	Mx2	2 yrs HL	Remit 18 mos	WO/213/28/121
35 MGC	Pte	Meek J	Field	17/01/19	Mx2	2 yrs HL	Remit 18 mos	WO/213/28/120
35 MGC	Pte	Peacock H	Field	17/01/19	Mx2	2 yrs HL	Remit 18 mos	WO/213/28/120
35 MGC	Pte	Pocock E	Field	17/01/19	Mx2	2 yrs HL	Remit 18 mos	WO/213/28/121
35 MGC	Pte	Porter GE	Field	17/01/19	M	NG		WO/213/28/121
35 MGC	Pte	Ringrose R	Field	17/01/19	Mx2	2 yrs HL	Remit 18 mos	WO/213/28/120
35 MGC	L/Cpl	Sankey J	Field	17/01/19	M	2 yrs HL	Remit 18 mos	WO/213/28/120
35 MGC	Pte	Smith R	Field	17/01/19	Mx2	2 yrs HL	Remit 18 mos	WO/213/28/121
35 MGC	Pte	Snow W	Field	17/01/19	Mx2	2 yrs HL	Remit 18 mos	WO/213/28/121
35 MGC	Pte	Truby JT	Field	17/01/19	Mx2	1 yr HL	Remit 6 mos	WO/213/28/120
35 MGC	Pte	Wakefield W	Field	17/01/19	Mx2	2 yrs HL	Remit 6 mos	WO/213/28/121
49 MG Coy	Pte	Gillespie W	Field	15/04/18	M	NG		WO/213/21/99
RAMC	Pte (AL/Cpl)	Berry W	Field	10/05/19	M+S40	6 mos HL	Comm 28 dys FP2	WO/213/30/17
RAMC	Pte	Bridle G	Field	10/05/19	M	6 mos HL	Comm 28 dys FP2	WO/213/30/17
RAMC	Pte (AL/Cpl)	Casey C	Field	10/05/19	M+S40	6 mos HL	Comm 28 dys FP2	WO/213/30/17
RAMC	Pte	Collins A	Rouen	25/10/14	Incit M+St/V+S40	2 yrs HL	Rem 18 mos	WO/213/2/133
RAMC	Pte	Coxon G	Field	10/05/19	M	6 mos HL	Comm 28 dys FP2	WO/213/30/17
RAMC	Pte	Hilton WG	Field	10/05/19	M	6 mos HL	Comm 28 dys FP2	WO/213/30/17
RAMC	Pte	Hope AH	Field	10/05/19	M	6 mos HL	Comm 28 dys FP2	WO/213/30/17
RAMC	Pte	Jackson GA	Field	10/05/19	M	6 mos HL	Comm 28 dys FP2	WO/213/30/17
RAMC	Pte	Jeffries F	Field	10/05/19	M	6 mos HL	Comm 28 dys FP2	WO/213/30/17
RAMC	Pte	Kennedy B	Field	10/05/19	M	6 mos HL	Comm 28 dys FP2	WO/213/30/17
RAMC	Pte	Moore R	Field	10/05/19	M	6 mos HL	Comm 28 dys FP2	WO/213/30/17
RAMC	Pte	Paul HJ	Field	10/05/19	M	6 mos HL	Comm 28 dys FP2	WO/213/30/17
RAMC	Pte	Potts C	Field	10/05/19	M	6 mos HL	Comm 28 dys FP2	WO/213/30/17
RAMC	Pte	Stafford J	Field	10/05/19	M	6 mos HL	Comm 28 dys FP2	WO/213/30/17
RAMC	Pte	Williams JA	Field	10/05/19	M	6 mos HL	Comm 28 dys FP2	WO/213/30/17

Unit	Rank	Name	Location	Date D/M/Y	Offence	Finding/Punishment	Amendment	PRO Reference File/Piece/Page
RAOC	Pte(A/Cpl)	Biddle C	Field	08/10/19	M+S40	NG		WO/213/31/4
RAOC	Pte(A/LSgt)	Cook A	Field	08/10/19	M+S40	NG		WO/213/31/4
RAOC	Pte	Craig A	Field	29/07/20	M+S7(3b)	4 yrs PS		WO/213/31/4
RAOC	Pte(A/Cpl)	Webster T	Field	08/10/19	M+S40	NG		WO/213/32/22
RAOC	Pte	White JJ	Field	29/07/20	M+S7(3b)	4 yrs PS		WO/213/32/22
att RAOC	Civilian	Jones CH	Field	29/07/20	M+Disob+S7(3b)	5 yrs PS		WO/213/32/22
RASC	Pte	Bailey J	Field ABS	20/04/20	M+Disob	3 mos FP2		WO/213/31/171
RASC	Pte	Barlow JH	Field	20/02/19	Mx2+S40	5 yrs PS		WO/213/28/169
RASC	Pte	Chappell J	Field ABS	20/04/20	M+Disob	3 mos FP2		WO/213/31/171
RASC	Cpl	Charman J	Malta	26/07/21	M+S41+S40	1 yr HL+Rnks+DI		WO/90/8/87
RASC	Pte	Collins D	Field	20/02/19	Mx2+S40	1 yr HL		WO/213/28/169
RASC	Pte	Colwell A	Field ABS	20/04/20	M+Disob	3 mos FP2		WO/213/31/171
RASC	Dvr	Davies R	Chelsea	18/05/21	M	12 mos HL+DI		WO/92/4/96
RASC	Pte	Forbes J	Field ABS	20/04/20	M+Disob	3 mos FP2		WO/213/31/171
RASC	Pte	Forrest A	Field	20/02/19	Mx2+S40	NG		WO/213/28/169
RASC	Pte	Halstead EA	Field	20/02/19	Mx2+S40	1 yr HL	Remit 6 mos	WO/213/28/169
RASC	Dvr	Harrison R	Chelsea	18/05/21	M	9 mos HL+DI		WO/92/4/96
RASC	Pte	Helliker WC	Field	20/02/19	Mx2+S40	NG		WO/213/28/169
RASC	Pte	Lawrence JF	Field	20/02/19	Mx2+S40	1 yr HL	Remit 3 mos	WO/213/28/169
RASC	Pte	Little T	Field ABS	20/04/20	M+Disob	3 mos FP2		WO/213/31/171
RASC	Pte	Matthews J	Avonmouth	20/04/20	M	18 mos HL * Disch Igmny	18 mos Detn +Remit Disch	WO/86/90/17
RASC	Dvr	Newbold RF	Chelsea	18/05/21	M	12 mos HL+DI		WO/92/4/96
RASC	Pte	Thomasson WP	Field	20/02/19	Mx2+S40	3 yrs PS		WO/213/28/169
RASC	Pte	Warbrick J	Field ABS	20/04/20	M+Disob	3 mos FP2		WO/213/31/171
RASC	Pte	Warsdale H	Field ABS	20/04/20	M+Disob	3 mos FP2		WO/213/31/171
RE	Spr	Aggette F	Field Italy	09/05/19	M	2 yrs HL	Remit 20 mos/ Quashed	WO/213/29/73
RE	Spr	Buddle P	Field	15/05/19	M+Disob	1 yr IHL		WO/213/29/137
RE	Cpl	Carpenter A	Field	15/05/19	M+Disob	1 yr IHL+Rnks		WO/213/29/137
RE	Spr	Carson W	Field	15/05/19	M+Disob	1 yr IHL		WO/213/29/137
RE	Pnr	Cole JH	Deganwy	23/12/15	Mx2	9 mos Detn	Quashed	WO/86/68/29
RE	Spr	Cook AJ	Deganwy	23/12/15	Mx2	15 mos Detn	Remit 3 mos/ Quashed	WO/86/68/29
RE	Dvr	Cope HE	Rouen	04/02/19	M	90 dys Imp		WO/90/8/58
RE	Spr	Costello C	Deganwy	23/12/15	Mx2	2 yrs Detn	Remit 6 mos/ Quashed	WO/86/68/29
RE	Spr	Cummings C	Field Italy	09/05/19	M	2 yrs HL	Remit 20 mos/ Quashed	WO/213/29/73
RE	Cpl	Dowson W	Field	04/02/19	M	10 yrs PS+Rnks	Remit 5 yrs PS	WO/213/28/46
RE	Spr	Edmunds A	Field	15/05/19	M+Disob	1 yr IHL		WO/213/29/137
RE	Spr	Elston A	Bordon	08/08/19	M+S40	18 mos Detn	15 mos	WO/92/4/77
RE	Spr	Gilmartin J	Rouen	04/02/19	M	90 dys Imp		WO/90/8/58
RE(TF)	Spr	Gould GW	Malta	24/09/15	M+S40	NG		WO/90/6/35
RE	L/Cpl	Green W	Field	04/02/19	M+S40	9 mos HL		WO/213/28/46
RE	Spr	Grier A	Field	15/05/19	M+Disob	1 yr IHL		WO/213/29/137
RE	Spr	Hall A	Field Italy	09/05/19	M	2 yrs HL		WO/213/29/73
RE	Spr	Henry J	Field	15/05/19	M+Disob	1 yr IHL		WO/213/29/137
RE	Spr	Howlett H	Field Italy	09/05/19	M	2 yrs HL	Remit 20 mos/ Quashed	WO/213/29/73
RE	Pnr(A/LCpl)	Jelly J	Field Italy	27/04/18	M+Disob	Death	Comm 5 yrs PS	WO/213/22/28
RE	Spr	Kellet A	Field	15/05/19	M+Disob	1 yr IHL		WO/213/29/137
RE	Spr	Leech H	Field	15/05/19	M+Disob	1 yr IHL		WO/213/29/137
RE	Spr	Lindon JS	Field	15/05/19	M+Disob	1 yr IHL		WO/213/29/137
RE	Spr	May AE	Field Italy	09/05/19	M	2 yrs HL	Remit 20 mos/ Quashed	WO/213/29/73
RE	Spr	McNicol N	Field Italy	09/05/19	M	2 yrs HL	Remit 20 mos/ Quashed	WO/213/29/73
RE	Spr	Mecklenburgh C	Field	15/05/19	M+Disob	1 yr IHL		WO/213/29/137
RE	Spr	Mills A	Field	15/05/19	M+Disob	1 yr IHL		WO/213/29/137
RE	Spr	Mitchell D	Field	15/05/19	M+Disob	1 yr IHL		WO/213/29/137
RE	Pnr	Munroe D	Bordon	07/08/19	M+S40	18 mos HL +Disch Igmny	NC	WO/92/4/77
RE	Pte	Poole WD	Field	04/02/19	M+S40	9 mos HL+Rnks		WO/213/28/46
RE	Spr	Raines J	Bordon	08/08/19	M+S40	2 yrs HL+Disch Igmny	15 mos	WO/92/4/77
RE	Spr	Rawlinson E	Field	15/05/19	M+Disob	1 yr IHL		WO/213/29/137
RE	Spr	Rees TR	Bordon	07/08/19	M+S40	1 yr Detn	9 mos	WO/92/4/77
RE	Spr	Robertshaw G	Field	15/05/19	M+Disob	1 yr IHL		WO/213/29/137
RE	Pnr	Self TE	Bordon	08/08/19	M+Disob(CSM)+Res +Esc+S40	2 yrs HL +Disch Igmny	15 mos	WO/92/4/77
RE	L/Cpl	Shuttleworth G	Field	04/02/19	M	10 yrs PS+Rnks	Remit 5 yrs PS	WO/213/28/46
RE	Spr	Smith GWP	Field	15/05/19	M+Disob	1 yr IHL		WO/213/29/137
RE	Spr	Summersby W	Field	15/05/19	M+Disob	1 yr IHL		WO/213/29/137

Unit	Rank	Name	Location	Date D/M/Y	Offence	Finding/Punishment	Amendment	PRO Reference File/Piece/Page
RE	Spr	Sutherland AG	Field Italy	09/05/19	M	2 yrs HL	Remit 20 mos/ Quashed	WO/213/29/73
RE	Spr	Thomas R	Field Italy	09/05/19	M	2 yrs HL	Remit 20 mos/ Quashed	WO/213/29/73
RE	Spr	Wellington FA	Field	15/05/19	M+Disob	1 yr IHL		WO/213/29/137
RE	L/Cpl	Wilson A	Field	04/02/19	M+S40	15 mos HL		WO/213/28/46
RE	Spr	Wilson D	Field Italy	09/05/19	M	2 yrs HL	Remit 20 mos/ Quashed	WO/213/29/73
RE	Pnr	Wright W	Field Italy	09/05/19	M	2 yrs HL	Remit 20 mos/ Quashed	WO/213/29/73
101 Field Coy RE	Spr	Baron A	Field Italy	27/03/19	M+Disob	5 yrs PS	Remit 2 yrs	WO/213/28/191
101 Field Coy RE	Spr	Elder J	Field Italy	27/03/19	M+Disob	5 yrs PS		WO/213/28/191
101 Field Coy RE	Spr (L/Cpl)	Oliver AE	Field Italy	27/03/19	M+Disob	5 yrs PS		WO/213/28/191
101 Field Coy RE	Spr	Read H	Field Italy	27/03/19	M+Disob	5 yrs PS		WO/213/28/191
101 Field Coy RE1	Spr	Syring A	Field Italy	27/03/19	M+Disob	5 yrs PS	Remit 2 yrs	WO/213/28/19
155 Lab Coy	Pte	Jeffrey EAV	Rouen	04/02/19	M	90dys Imp		WO/90/8/58
69(EA)DAC(TF)	Dvr	Alexander F	Killinghall Moor	11/09/16	Joining M	Acquit		WO/92/3/45
69(EA)DAC(TF)	Dvr	Nichols VP	Killinghall Moor	11/09/16	Joining M	Acquit		WO/92/3/45
69(EA)DAC(TF)	Pte	Reeve C	Killinghall Moor	11/09/16	Joining M	Acquit		WO/92/3/45
RFA	Gnr	Abrahams R	Field	24/03/19	M	11 yrs PS	Quashed	WO/213/29/91
RFA	Dvr/L/Bdr	Allen JG	Field	12/05/18	M	1 yr HL	Susp	WO/213/22/153
RFA	Sig	Baker NG	Field	24/06/19	M+Disob	1 yr HL		WO/213/29/137
RFA	Dvr	Barker FW	Field	07/03/19	Mx2	1 yr HL	Remit 3 mos	WO/213/29/12
RFA	Gnr/L/Bdr	Bergendorff O	Field	12/05/18	M	1 yr HL	Susp	WO/213/22/153
RFA	Gnr	Bickerton W	Field	24/04/19	M+Disob	5 mos HL		WO/213/29/160
RFA	Gnr	Bishop C	Field	24/04/19	M+Disob	5 mos HL		WO/213/29/160
RFA	Bdr	Black T	Leeds	06/05/19	M	1 yr Detn+Rnks		WO/92/4/69
RFA	Dvr	Blair J	Field	24/04/19	M+Disob	5 mos HL		WO/213/29/160
RFA	Dvr	Bradshaw J	Field	24/03/19	M	15 yrs PS		WO/213/29/89
RFA	Dvr	Brandall T	Deepcut	27/09/19	M	18 mos HL	Comm to Detn	WO/86/88/138
RFA	Dvr	Cartwright A	Field	24/04/19	M+Disob	NG		WO/213/29/160
RFA	Bdr	Chapman HRH	Field	07/03/19	Mx2	1 yr HL+Rnks	Remit 3 mos	WO/213/29/12
RFA	Gnr	Coldwell FH	Field EEF	30/06/19	M	10 yrs PS		WO/213/30/104
RFA	Bdr	Cole J	Leeds	06/05/19	M	2 yrs HL	Comm 1 yr Detn	WO/92/4/69
RFA	Gnr	Cole RW	Field	24/06/19	M+Abs	NG		WO/213/29/137
RFA	Dvr	Crawford A	Field	24/03/19	M	10 yrs PS		WO/213/29/89
RFA	Dvr	Cryer W	Rouen	04/02/19	M	56 dys Imp		WO/90/8/58
RFA	Gnr	Davies GH	Field	24/06/19	M+Abs	1 yr HL		WO/213/29/137
RFA	Gnr	Dyer GH	Field	24/06/19	M	18 mos HL		WO/213/29/137
RFA	Gnr	Edwards T	Field Italy	30/05/18	M+Striking	Death	Comm 3 yrs PS	WO/213/22/126
RFA	Dvr	Foulkes GJ	Deepcut	27/09/19	M	2 yrs HL	Remit 6 mos +Comm to Detn	WO/86/88/138
RFA	Gnr	Gardener R	Field	24/04/19	M+Disob	5 mos HL		WO/213/29/160
RFA	Dvr	Glover RJ	Deepcut	27/09/19	M	1 yr HL	Comm to Detn	WO/86/88/138
RFA	Gnr	Gray A	Deepcut	27/09/19	M	NG		WO/86/88/138
RFA	Dvr	Grimstone H	Field	24/04/19	M+Disob	5 mos HL		WO/213/29/160
RFA	Gnr	Grocutt E	Field	24/06/19	M	NG		WO/213/29/137
RFA	Bdr	Guthrie A	Field	07/07/19	M+S5+S40(x2)	90 dys FP2		WO/213/30/84
RFA	Dvr	Hague A	Field	24/04/19	M+Disob	5 mos HL		WO/213/29/160
RFA	Dvr	Harris T	Hinaidi	23/05/21	M+S9(1)	3 mos FP2		WO/213/33/16
RFA	Gnr	Harvey A	Field	24/04/19	M+Disob	5 mos HL		WO/213/29/160
RFA	Cpl	Hawkins A [DCM]	Field	12/05/18	M	1 yr HL	Susp	WO/213/22/153
RFA	Dvr/L/Bdr	Hawkins FT	Field	12/05/18	M	1 yr HL	Susp	WO/213/22/153
RFA	Gnr	Hayden J	Field	24/04/19	M+Disob	5 mos HL		WO/213/29/160
RFA	Dvr	Herbert A	Field	24/04/19	M+Disob	NG		WO/213/29/160
RFA	Gnr	Herbert JJ	Field	05/06/19	M+S40	5 yrs HL		WO/213/29/169
RFA	Gnr (AL/Bdr)	Jackman H	Field	24/04/19	M+Disob	5 mos HL		WO/213/29/160
RFA	Gnr	Jackson F	Field	24/06/19	M+Disob	1 yr HL		WO/213/29/137
RFA	Dvr	James D	Hinaidi	23/05/21	M+S9(1)	3 mos FP2		WO/213/33/16
RFA	Dvr	Jones E	Hinaidi	23/05/21	M+S9(1)	6 mos Detn		WO/213/33/15
RFA	Dvr	Kelly E	Field	24/04/19	M+Disob	NG		WO/213/29/160
RFA	Gnr	Lingfield G	Leeds	06/05/19	M	Acquit		WO/92/4/69
RFA	Dvr	McCarthy P	Field	07/03/19	M	90 dys FP2		WO/213/29/12
RFA	Dvr	Macdonald H	Warlingham	18/08/19	M+S40	1 yr Detn		WO/92/4/78
RFA	Dvr	Mills SC	Deepcut	27/09/19	M	NG		WO/86/88/138
RFA	Gnr	Murray T	Field	24/06/19	M+Disob	2 yrs HL		WO/213/29/137

Unit	Rank	Name	Location	Date D/M/Y	Offence	Finding/Punishment	Amendment	PRO Reference File/Piece/Page
RFA	Dvr	Murray W	Field	24/04/19	M+Disob	5 mos HL		WO/213/29/160
RFA	Dvr	Nelson J	Field	24/04/19	M+Disob	NG		WO/213/29/160
RFA	Dvr	Palmer W	Hinaidi	23/05/21	M+S9(1)	3 mos FP2		WO/213/33/15
RFA	Gnr/L/Bdr	Peters H	Field	12/05/18	M	1yr HL	Susp	WO/213/22/153
RFA	Bdr	Pickstone G	Field	12/05/18	M	1 yr HL	Susp	WO/213/22/153
RFA	Bdr	Roffey R	Field	12/05/18	M	1 yr HL	Susp	WO/213/22/153
RFA	Dvr	Scarborough J	Field	07/03/19	M	90 dys FP2		WO/213/29/12
RFA	Gnr	Slater H	Field	03/02/19	M+Insub+S7(2)	90 dys FP1		WO/213/28/165
RFA	Dvr	Snell A	Field	24/04/19	M+Disob	5 mos HL		WO/213/29/160
RFA	Gnr	Southwick S	Field	24/04/19	M+Disob	NG		WO/213/29/160
RFA	Dvr	Stringer T	Field	08/10/18	M+Disob	5 yrs PS	Susp	WO/213/25/158
RFA	Dvr	Turner JW	Field	07/03/19	M+Des+Drunk +Losing Prop	2 yrs HL		WO/213/29/169
RFA	Dvr	Williams D	Hinaidi	23/05/21	M+S9(1)	3 mos FP2		WO/213/33/16
RFA	Dvr	Wright A	Hinaidi	23/05/21	M+S9(1)	3 mos FP2		WO/213/33/15
RFA	Bdr (A/Cpl)	Wright GCM	Field	14/07/19	M+7(2)	6 mos HL + Rnks		WO/213/30/81
RFA	Gnr/L/Bdr	Wright J	Field	12/05/18	M	1 yr HL	Susp	WO/213/22/153
2/3 Northern Bde AC/RFA	Gnr	Gannon C	Bawtry	04/05/16	JM	3 yrs PS Disch Igmny		WO/92/3/39
2/3 Northern Bde AC/RFA	Gnr	Coffle J	Bawtry	04/05/16	JM	3 yrs PS +Disch Igmny		WO/92/3/39
2/3 Northern e Bde AC/RFA	Gnr(A/Bdr)	Eland G	Bawtry	04/05/16	JM	3 yrs PS +Disch Igmny		WO/92/3/39
2/3 Northern Bde Bd AC/RFA	Dvr	Willis T	Bawtry	04/05/16	JM	+Disch Igmny	3 yrs PS	WO/92/3/39
124 Bde RFA	Gnr	Lewis WE	Rouen	05/10/16	M	Death		WO/90/6/89
155 Bde RFA	Gnr	Hoaldsworth C	Dunkirk	13/04/17	M	8 mos HL		WO/213/14/138
163 (How) Bde RFA	Gnr(A/Bdr)	Goodman W	Bulford	11/12/15	M	1 month FP2+Rnks		WO/86/68/23
175 Bde RFA	Dvr	Ward JWH	Field	16/07/16	M+Disob	28 dys FP1		WO/213/11/9
337 Bde RFA	Gnr	Allen GH	Canterbury	10/01/17	JM	6 mos Detn		WO/92/3/58
337 Bde RFA	Dvr	Barrington AV	Canterbury	10/01/17	JM	6 mos Detn		WO/92/3/58
337 Bde RFA	Gnr	Bolton JH	Canterbury	10/01/17	JM	6 mos Detn		WO/92/3/58
337 Bde RFA	S/Smith	Burrows S	Canterbury	10/01/17	JM	6 mos Detn		WO/92/3/58
337 Bde RFA	Dvr	Calver LT	Canterbury	10/01/17	JM	6 mos Detn		WO/92/3/58
337 Bde RFA	Gnr	Fradley L	Canterbury	10/01/17	JM	6 mos Detn		WO/92/3/58
337 Bde RFA	Dvr	Freestone SG	Canterbury	10/01/17	JM	6 mos Detn		WO/92/3/58
337 Bde RFA	Gnr	Gray G	Canterbury	10/01/17	JM	6 mos Detn		WO/92/3/58
337 Bde RFA	Dvr	Grocott JJ	Canterbury	10/01/17	JM	6 mos Detn		WO/92/3/58
337 Bde RFA	Dvr	Hobbs C	Canterbury	10/01/17	JM	6 mos Detn		WO/92/3/58
337 Bde RFA	Dvr	Jackson E	Canterbury	10/01/17	JM	6 mos Detn		WO/92/3/58
337 Bde RFA	Dvr	Larrad AJ	Canterbury	10/01/17	JM	6 mos Detn		WO/92/3/58
337 Bde RFA	Dvr	Shilton T	Canterbury	10/01/17	JM	6 mos Detn		WO/92/3/58
337 Bde RFA	Dvr	Smith B	Canterbury	10/01/17	JM	6 mos Detn		WO/92/3/58
337 Bde RFA	Dvr	Susans W	Canterbury	10/01/17	JM	6 mos Detn		WO/92/3/58
337 Bde RFA	Dvr	Thomas W	Canterbury	10/01/17	JM	6 mos Detn		WO/92/3/58
337 Bde RFA	Dvr	Towlson H	Canterbury	10/01/17	JM	6 mos Detn		WO/92/3/58
337 Bde RFA	Dvr	Tucker W	Canterbury	10/01/17	JM	6 mos Detn		WO/92/3/58
337 Bde RFA	Dvr	Whincop AG	Canterbury	10/01/17	JM	6 mos Detn		WO/92/3/58
25(R) Bty RFA	Dvr	Horan T	Athlone	25/05/16	M+Insub(A/Sgt Maj)	2 yrs HL	Comm 1 yr Detn	WO/86/70/46
33(R) Bty RFA	Dvr	Jackson T	Glasgow	13/01/16	M+Viol(Cpl)	NG		WO/86/68/144
33(R) Bty RFA	Dvr	Marshall W	Glasgow	13/01/16	M+Viol(Cpl)	1 yr Detn		WO/86/68/161
234 Bty RFA	Dvr	Marchmont J	Cahir	05/01/15	M+Viol to Cpl+S40 +S10(3)	2 yrs HL +Disch Igmny		WO/86/63/136
234 Bty RFA	Gnr	Rodbourne A	Cahir	15/01/15	M+Insub(Cpl)+S40(2)	2 yrs HL+Disch Igmny		WO/86/63/137
234 Bty RFA	Dvr A/Bdr	Arlow J	Cahir	15/01/15	M+S40+S10(3)	2 yrs HL+Disch Igmny		WO/86/63/137
234 Bty RFA	Dvr	Mayo J	Cahir	15/01/15	M+S40+S10(3)	2 yrs HL+Disch Igmny		WO/86/63/137
4 W Riding/234 Bty RFA	Pte	Smith J	Cahir	15/01/15	M+Viol to Cpl+S40 +S10(3)	2 yrs HL+Disch Igmny		WO/86/63/136
523 Bty RFA	Dvr	Stringer T	Ewshott Camp	25/09/16	M	2 yrs Detn	Remit 18 mos	WO/86/70/219
RFA(att RGA)	Gnr	Allen G	Agra	13/03/18	M	1 yr HL	unexpired portion 30/4/18	WO/90/7/190
RFA(att RGA)	Gnr	Gurney P	Agra	13/03/18	M	1 yr HL	unexpired portion 30/4/18	WO/90/7/190
RFA(att RGA)	Dvr	Longdon A	Agra	13/03/18	M	1 yr HL	unexpired portion 30/4/18	WO/90/7/190
RFA(att RGA)	Gnr	Skene H	Agra	13/03/18	M	1 yr HL	unexpired portion 30/4/18	WO/90/7/190
RFA(att RGA)	Gnr	Williamson H	Agra	13/03/18	M	1 yr HL	unexpired portion 30/4/18	WO/90/7/191
RGA	L/Bdr	Allam R	Aldershot	04/07/19	M	9 mos Detn+Rnks +Disch Igmny		WO/86/87/188

Unit	Rank	Name	Location	Date D/M/Y	Offence	Finding/Punishment	Amendment	PRO Reference File/Piece/Page
RGA	L/Bdr	Bains VG	Aldershot	04/07/19	M	9 mos Detn+Rnks +Disch Igmny		WO/86/87/188
RGA	Cpl	Banwell WJ	Aldershot	05/07/19	M	9 mos Detn+Rnks +Disch Igmny		WO/86/87/189
RGA	Gnr	Baron JC	Agra	13/03/18	M	1 yr HL	unexpired portion 30/4/18	WO/90/7/190
RGA	Gnr	Bennett H	Aldershot	08/07/19	M	9 mos Detn +Disch Igmny		WO/86/87/189
RGA	Cpl	Biddulph P	Aldershot	04/07/19	M	9 mos Detn+Rnks +Disch Igmny		WO/86/87/188
RGA	Gnr	Bridge H	Agra	13/03/18	M	1 yr HL	unexpired portion 30/4/18	WO/90/7/190
RGA	Gnr	Brown HW	Agra	13/03/18	M	1 yr HL	unexpired portion 30/4/18	WO/90/7/190
RGA	Gnr	Burnett A	Field (Ireland)	09/05/21	M+S7(4)	2 yrs HL+DI	Comm to DI Not Conf	WO/213/32/133
RGA	L/Bdr	Burton W	Aldershot	04/07/19	M	9 mos Detn+Rnks +Disch Igmny		WO/86/87/188
RGA	Bdr	Butterworth F	Aldershot	04/07/19	M	9 mos Detn+Rnks +Disch Igmny		WO/86/87/188
RGA	Gnr	Carter W	Agra	13/03/18	M	1 yr HL	unexpired portion 30/4/18	WO/90/7/190
RGA	AL/Bdr	Childs FC	Aldershot	08/07/19	M	9 mos Detn+Rnks +Disch Igmny		WO/86/87/189
RGA	L/Bdr	Coleman A	Aldershot	04/07/19	M	9 mos Detn+Rnks +Disch Igmny		WO/86/87/188
RGA	Gnr	Collings EH	Agra	13/03/18	M	1 yr HL	unexpired portion 30/4/18	WO/90/7/190
RGA	Gnr	Conway D	Agra	13/03/18	M	1 yr HL	unexpired portion 30/4/18	WO/90/7/190
RGA	Bdr	Cox SG	Aldershot	04/07/19	M	9 mos Detn+Rnks +Disch Igmny		WO/86/87/188
RGA	L/Bdr	Cox T	Aldershot	08/07/19	M	9 mos Detn+Rnks +Disch Igmny		WO/86/87/189
RGA	Gnr	Cranston HW	Agra	13/03/18	M	1 yr HL	unexpired portion 30/4/18	WO/90/7/190
RGA	Cpl	Cresswell E	Aldershot	04/07/19	M	9 mos Detn+Rnks +Disch Igmny		WO/86/87/188
RGA	Bdr	Dixon SR	Aldershot	04/07/19	M	9 mos Detn+Rnks +Disch Igmny		WO/86/87/188
RGA	L/Bdr	Doggrell L	Aldershot	04/07/19	M	9 mos Detn+Rnks +Disch Igmny		WO/86/87/188
RGA	Gnr	Donnell J	Agra	13/03/18	M	1 yr HL	unexpired portion 30/4/18	WO/90/7/190
RGA	L/Bdr	Doyle P	Aldershot	05/07/19	M	9 mos Detn+Rnks +Disch Igmny		WO/86/87/189
RGA	Cpl	Elliott F	Aldershot	05/07/19	M	9 mos Detn+Rnks		WO/86/88/1
RGA	L/Bdr	Fenwick JL	Aldershot	05/07/19	M	9 mos Detn+ Rnks		WO/86/88/1
RGA	L/Bdr	Fletcher C	Aldershot	05/07/19	M	9 mos Detn+Rnks		WO/86/88/1
RGA	Cpl	Ford ES	Aldershot	04/07/19	M	9 mos Detn+Rnks +Disch Igmny		WO/86/87/188
RGA	Gnr(AL/Bdr)	Ford T	Bettisfield	02/03/18	M[S7(2)]+S40	42 dys Detn		WO/86/80/178
RGA	Gnr	Fowler F	Agra	13/03/18	M	1 yr HL	unexpired portion 30/4/18	WO/90/7/190
RGA	Cpl	Fox H	Aldershot	05/07/19	M	9 mos Detn+Rnks +Disch Igmny		WO/86/87/189
RGA	Bdr	Froude J	Aldershot	05/07/19	M	NG		WO/86/87/189
RGA	Gnr	Gager SE	Agra	13/03/18	M	1 yr HL	unexpired portion 30/4/18	WO/90/7/190
RGA	L/Bdr	Glanister J	Aldershot	04/07/19	M	9 mos Detn+Rnks +Disch Igmny		WO/86/87/188
RGA	L/Bdr	Glass H	Aldershot	04/07/19	M	9 mos Detn+Rnks+Disch Igmny		WO/86/87/188
RGA	Gnr	Gordon J	Agra	13/03/18	M	1 yr HL	unexpired portion 30/4/18	WO/90/7/190
RGA	Cpl	Green J	Aldershot	04/07/19	M	9 mos Detn+Rnks +Disch Igmny		WO/86/87/188
RGA	Bdr	Hardy D	Aldershot	08/07/19	M	9 mos Detn+Rnks +Disch Igmny		WO/86/87/189
RGA	Bdr	Hidden E	Aldershot	05/07/19	M	9 mos Detn+Rnks +Disch Igmny		WO/86/87/189
RGA	A/Bdr	Holt S	Field	16/05/19	M	NG		WO/213/29/148
RGA	L/Bdr	Hooper W	Aldershot	05/07/19	M	9 mos Detn+Rnks		WO/86/88/1

Unit	Rank	Name	Location	Date D/M/Y	Offence	Finding/Punishment	Amendment	PRO Reference File/Piece/Page
RGA	Gnr	Hotchkiss M	Agra	13/03/18	M	1 yr HL	unexpired portion 30/4/18	WO/90/7/190
RGA	Gnr	Hounsell EA	Agra	13/03/18	M	1 yr HL	unexpired portion 30/4/18	WO/90/7/190
RGA	L/Bdr	Hutchinson H	Aldershot	05/07/19	M	9 mos Detn+Rnks		WO/86/88/1
RGA	L/Bdr	Jenkins E	Aldershot	05/07/19	M	9 mos Detn+Rnks		WO/86/88/1
RGA	Signlr	Kite FJ	Field	16/05/19	M	6 mos HL	Comm 84 dys FP1 Quashed	WO/213/29/148
RGA	Bdr	Lawler W	Aldershot	05/07/19	M	9 mos Detn+Rnks		WO/86/88/1
RGA	Gnr	Lemon S	Aldershot	05/07/19	M	2 yrs HL+Disch Igmny		WO/86/88/1
RGA	L/Bdr	Limington F	Aldershot	05/07/19	M	9 mos Detn+Rnks		WO/86/88/1
RGA	AL/Bdr	Livesey HH	Field	16/05/19	M	[No further details recorded]		WO/213/29/148
RGA	Dvr	Lucas EC	Field	16/05/19	M	6 mos HL	Comm 84 dys FP1/Quashed	WO/213/29/148
RGA	L/Bdr	Manley C	Aldershot	04/07/19	M	9 mos Detn+Rnks +Disch Igmny		WO/86/87/188
RGA	L/Bdr	Mann HG	Aldershot	05/07/19	M	9 mos Detn+Rnks		WO/86/88/1
RGA	Gnr	Martin S	Agra	13/03/18	M	1 yr HL	unexpired portion 30/4/18	WO/90/7/190
RGA	L/Bdr	McCarthy J	Aldershot	05/07/19	M	9 mos Detn+Rnks +Disch Igmny		WO/86/87/189
RGA	L/Bdr	McRoberts H	Aldershot	05/07/19	M	9 mos Detn+Rnks		WO/86/88/1
RGA	AL/Bdr	Moore WJ	Aldershot	05/07/19	M	9 mos Detn+Rnks +Disch Igmny		WO/86/87/189
RGA	Cpl	Neale G	Aldershot	05/07/19	M	9 mos Detn+Rnks		WO/86/88/1
RGA	Gnr	Newman L	Aldershot	04/07/19	M	9 mos Detn +Disch Igmny		WO/86/87/189
RGA	Gnr	Niven A	Agra	13/03/18	M	1 yr HL	unexpired portion 30/4/18	WO/90/7/190
RGA	Gnr	Noble A	Agra	13/03/18	M	1 yr HL	unexpired portion 30/4/18	WO/90/7/190
RGA	Bdr	Nolan J	Aldershot	05/07/19	M	9 mos Detn+Rnks +Disch Igmny		WO/86/87/189
RGA	Cpl	Norrish W	Aldershot	04/07/19	M	9 mos Detn+Rnks +Disch Igmny		WO/86/87/188
RGA	Bdr	O'Rourke C	Aldershot	05/07/19	M	NG		WO/86/88/1
RGA	Bdr	O'Shea J	Aldershot	04/07/19	M	9 mos Detn+Rnks +Disch Igmny		WO/86/87/188
RGA	Bdr	Osmond OG	Aldershot	08/07/19	M	9 mos Detn+Rnks +Disch Igmny		WO/86/87/189
RGA	AL/Bdr	Page FT	Field	16/05/19	M	9 mos HL	Remit 3 mos	WO/213/29/148
RGA	Gnr	Palmer AE	Agra	13/03/18	M	1 yr HL	unexpired portion 30/4/18	WO/90/7/190
RGA	Bdr	Peacock A	Aldershot	04/07/19	M	9 mos Detn+Rnks +Disch Igmny		WO/86/87/188
RGA	Gnr	Phillips R	Aldershot	05/07/19	M	NG		WO/86/88/1
RGA	Gnr	Plant F	Agra	13/03/18	M	1 yr HL	unexpired portion 30/4/18	WO/90/7/190
RGA	L/Bdr	Pollentine G	Aldershot	05/07/19	M	9 mos Detn+Rnks		WO/86/87/189
RGA	L/Bdr	Powell R	Aldershot	05/07/19	M	9 mos Detn+Rnks +Disch Igmny		WO/86/87/189
RGA	Gnr	Preece W	Agra	13/03/18	M	Acquit		WO/90/7/190
RGA	Gnr	Price E	Agra	13/03/18	M	1 yr HL	unexpired portion 30/4/18	WO/90/7/190
RGA	Gnr	Proctor E	Agra	13/03/18	M	1 yr HL	unexpired portion 30/4/18	WO/90/7/190
RGA	L/Bdr	Randell G	Aldershot	04/07/19	M	9 mos Detn+Rnks +Disch Igmny		WO/86/87/188
RGA	Bdr	Redding G	Aldershot	05/07/19	M	9 mos Detn+Rnks		WO/86/88/1
RGA	Cpl	Roast J	Aldershot	05/07/19	M	9 mos Detn+Rnks		WO/86/88/1
RGA	Bdr	Roberts J	Aldershot	04/07/19	M	9 mos Detn+Rnks +Disch Igmny		WO/86/87/188
RGA	AL/Bdr	Robinson J	Field	16/05/19	M	NG		WO/213/29/148
RGA	Gnr	Sampson F	Agra	13/03/18	M	1 yr HL	unexpired portion 30/4/18	WO/90/7/190
RGA	Gnr	Sanders EW	Agra	13/03/18	M	1 yr HL	unexpired portion 30/4/18	WO/90/7/190
RGA	Gnr	Sheffield W	Field (Ireland)	09/05/21	M+S7(4)	2 yrs HL+DI	Comm to DI Not Conf	WO/213/32/133
RGA	Gnr	Smith J	Agra	13/03/18	M	1 yr HL	unexpired portion 30/4/18	WO/90/7/190
RGA	Gnr	Smith L	Agra	13/03/18	M	1 yr HL	unexpired portion 30/4/18	WO/90/7/190

Unit	Rank	Name	Location	Date D/M/Y	Offence	Finding/Punishment	Amendment	PRO Reference File/Piece/Page
RGA	Pte	Smith E	Field Italy	24/04/18	Mx2	10 yrs PS	2 yrsHL	WO/213/22/30
RGA	AL/Bdr	Smith LE	Field	16/05/19	M	9 mos HL	Remit 3 mos/ Quashed	WO/213/29/148
RGA	L/Bdr	Solari L	Aldershot	05/07/19	M	9 mos Detn+Rnks +Disch Igmny		WO/86/87/189
RGA	Gnr	Stevens SH	Agra	13/03/18	M	1 yr HL	unexpired portion 30/4/18	WO/90/7/190
RGA	L/Bdr	Street V	Aldershot	04/07/19	M	9 mos Detn+Rnks +Disch Igmny		WO/86/87/188
RGA	Cpl	Swatridge G	Aldershot	04/07/19	M	9 mos Detn+Rnks +Disch Igmny		WO/86/87/188
RGA	Bdr	Synnott P	Aldershot	04/07/19	M	9 mos Detn+Rnks +Disch Igmny		WO/86/87/188
RGA	L/Bdr	Taffe J	Aldershot	04/07/19	M	9 mos Detn+Rnks +Disch Igmny		WO/86/87/188
RGA	Bdr	Tailby J	Aldershot	08/07/19	M	9 mos Detn+Rnks +Disch Igmny		WO/86/87/189
RGA	Gnr	Taylor FH	Agra	13/03/18	M	1 yr HL	unexpired portion 30/4/18	WO/90/7/190
RGA	Gnr	Thacker GH	Agra	13/03/18	M	1 yr HL	unexpired portion 30/4/18	WO/90/7/190
RGA	Cpl	Thompson J	Aldershot	05/07/19	M	9 mos Detn+Rnks +Disch Igmny		WO/86/87/189
RGA	Dvr	Treadwell HW	Field	16/05/19	M	6 mos HL	Comm 84 dys FP1 Quashed	WO/213/29/148
RGA	Dvr	Ward HC	Field (Ireland)	09/05/21	M+S7(2b)	2 yrs HL+DI	Comm to DI Not Conf	WO/213/32/133
RGA	L/Bdr	Warn A	Aldershot	04/07/19	M	9 mos Detn+Rnks +Disch Igmny		WO/86/87/188
RGA	Bdr(A/LCpl)	Warren WC	Aldershot	08/07/19	M	9 mos Detn+Rnks +Disch Igmny		WO/86/87/189
RGA	Gnr	Warrener EG	Agra	13/03/18	M	1 yr HL	unexpired portion 30/4/18	WO/90/7/191
RGA	Gnr	Weldon E	Aldershot	08/07/19	M	9 mos Detn		WO/86/87/189
RGA	Bdr	White A	Aldershot	05/07/19	M	9 mos Detn+Rnks +Disch Igmny		WO/86/87/189
RGA	L/Bdr	Whitehall J	Aldershot	04/07/19	M	9 mos Detn+Rnks +Disch Igmny		WO/86/87/188
RGA	Pte	Williams TR	Malta	23/09/15	M+S40	1 yr HL		WO/90/6/35
RGA	Gnr	Winter C	Agra	13/03/18	M	1 yr HL	unexpired portion 30/4/18	WO/90/7/191
RGA	Bdr	Wood R	Aldershot	05/07/19	M	NG		WO/86/88/1
RGA	Gnr	Wood A	Agra	13/03/18	M	1 yr HL	unexpired portion 30/4/18	WO/90/7/190
RGA	Gnr	Wood LS	Agra	13/03/18	M	1 yr HL	unexpired portion 30/4/18	WO/90/7/190
RGA	L/Bdr	Woodman C	Aldershot	04/07/19	M	9 mos Detn+Rnks +Disch Igmny		WO/86/87/189
RGA	L/Bdr	Woods H	Aldershot	05/07/19	M	9 mos Detn+Rnks +Disch Igmny		WO/86/87/189
RGA	Gnr	Woodworth GW	Agra	13/03/18	M	Acquit		WO/90/7/191
RGA	L/Bdr	Young C	Aldershot	05/07/19	M	9 mos Detn+Rnks +Disch Igmny		WO/86/87/189
RHA	A/Bdr	Harrison [?]	At Sea	03/11/14	Endeavg M	56 dys Detn	Comm 14	WO213/1/74
RHA(att RGA)	Gnr	Mitchell BA	Agra	13/03/18	M	1 yr HL	unexpired portion 30/4/18	WO/90/7/190
R Marine Lab Corps	Pte	Bullen RG	Dunkirk	13/04/17	M	1 yr HL		WO/213/14/138
R Marine Lab Corps	Pte	Davidson L	Dunkirk	13/04/17	M	1 yr HL		WO/213/14/138
R Marine Lab Corps	Pte	Gillies R	Dunkirk	13/04/17	M	1 yr HL		WO/213/14/138
R Marine Lab Corps8	Pte	McLaughlin G	Dunkirk	13/04/17	M	1 yr HL		WO/213/14/13
R Marine Lab Corps	Pte	Mullen T	Dunkirk	13/04/17	M	8 mos HL		WO/213/14/138
R Marine Lab Corps	Pte	Murphy J	Dunkirk	13/04/17	M	1 yr HL		WO/213/14/138
4 Tank Bn	Pte	Louden FH	Field	17/05/19	M	6 mos HL		WO/213/29/127
Tank Corps	Pte	McCombie A	Ramadi	07/01/21	M	1 yr HL	Comm to Detn	WO/213/33/2
RAF	Pte (3 AM)	Beisly HL	Swanage	30/04/18	M+Disob	9 mos HL		WO/92/4/41
RAF	Pte(2AM)(A/Cpl)	Dunse JE	Swanage	30/04/18	M+Disob	18 mos HL		WO/92/4/41
RAF	Pte (3AM)	Little V	Swanage	30/04/18	M+Disob	9 mos HL		WO/92/4/42

Unit	Rank	Name	Location	Date D/M/Y	Offence	Finding/Punishment	Amendment	PRO Reference File/Piece/Page
RAF	Pte(1AM)(A/Cpl)	Macdonald M	Swanage	30/04/18	M+Disob	18 mos HL		WO/92/4/41
RAF	Pte(2AM)	Patton GL	Swanage	30/04/18	M+Disob	1 yr HL		WO/92/4/41
RAF	Pte(2AM)	Whitewood HF	Swanage	30/04/18	M+Disob	9 mos HL		WO/92/4/42
RAF	Pte(3 Clerk)	Simpson A	Swanage	02/05/18	M	Acquit		WO/92/4/37
RAF	Pte(3AM)	Webber S	Swanage	02/05/18	M	Acquit		WO/92/4/37
RAF	Pte(2AM)	Wilkinson A	Swanage	02/05/18	M	Acquit		WO/92/4/37
Indian								
Malay SG Bty	L/Naik	Ahmad [?]	Singapore	11/03/15	M	3 yrs PS	Comm 2 yrs Imp	WO/213/4/17
Malay SG Bty	Gnr	Ahmad Sultan	Singapore	11/03/15	M	3 yrs PS	Comm 18 mos Imp	WO/213/4/17
Malay SG Bty	Gnr	Khan Mozhar	Singapore	11/03/15	M	3 yrs PS	Comm 18 mos Imp	WO/213/4/17
Malay SG Bty	Gnr	Rahman Abdul	Singapore	11/03/15	M	3 yrs PS	Comm 18 mos Imp	WO/213/4/17
Irish								
1 Connaught Rangers	Pte	Buckley JJ	Dagshai	04/09/20	M+S7(3b)	Life PS+DI		WO/90/8/187
1 Connaught Rangers	Pte	Burland W	Dagshai	04/09/20	M+S7(3b)	5 yrs PS+DI	Remit 2 yrs	WO/90/8/187
1 Connaught Rangers	Pte	Cherry P	Dagshai	04/09/20	M+S7(3b)	15 yrs PS+DI	Remit 2 yrs	WO/90/8/187
1 Connaught Rangers	Cpl	Coleman P	Dagshai	23/08/20	M+S7(3)	Acquit		WO/90/8/189
1 Connaught Rangers	Pte	Coman W	Dagshai	30/08/20	M	15 yrs PS+DI		WO/90/8/188
1 Connaught Rangers	Boy	Conlon M	Dagshai	04/09/20	M+S7(3b)	10 yrs PS+DI		WO/90/8/188
1 Connaught Rangers	Pte	Coote WJ	Dagshai	25/08/20	M	1 yr HL+DI		WO/90/8/188
1 Connaught Rangers	Pte(L/Cpl)	Cox P	Dagshai	25/08/20	M	Acquit		WO/90/8/188
1 Connaught Rangers	Pte	Daly J	Dagshai	04/09/20	M+S7(3b)	3 yrs PS+DI	2 yrs HL	WO/90/8/187
1 Connaught Rangers	Pte	Daly JJ	Dagshai	04/09/20	M+S7(3b)	Death		WO/90/8/187
1 Connaught Rangers	Cpl	Davis J	Dagshai	23/08/20	M+S7(3)	2 yrs HL+Ranks+DI		WO/90/8/189
1 Connaught Rangers	Pte	Delaney V	Dagshai	30/08/20	M+S7(2)	Death	Life PS	WO/90/8/188
1 Connaught Rangers	Pte	Devers JJ	Dagshai	04/09/20	M+S7(3b)	Life PS+DI	20 yrs PS+DI	WO/90/8/187
1 Connaught Rangers	Pte	Devine T	Dagshai	04/09/20	M+S7(3b)	Death	Life PS	WO/90/8/187
1 Connaught Rangers	Pte(L/Cpl)	Donohue P	Dagshai	23/08/20	M+S7(3)	2 yrs HL+DI		WO/90/8/189
1 Connaught Rangers	Cpl	Dyer P	Dagshai	25/08/20	M	3 yrs PS+Rnks+DI		WO/90/8/188
1 Connaught Rangers	Pte	Egan E	Dagshai	04/09/20	M+S7(3b)	Death	Life PS	WO/90/8/187
1 Connaught Rangers	Pte(L/Cpl)	Fallon J	Dagshai	25/08/20	M	2 yrs HL+DI		WO/90/8/188
1 Connaught Rangers	Pte	Fitzgerald M	Dagshai	04/09/20	M+S7(3b)	Death	Life PS	WO/90/8/187
1 Connaught Rangers	L/Cpl	Flannery J	Dagshai	30/08/20	M	Death	Life PS	WO/90/8/188
1 Connaught Rangers	Pte(L/Cpl)	Gallagher J	Dagshai	25/08/20	M	Acquit		WO/90/8/188
1 Connaught Rangers	Pte	Gleeson JJ	Dagshai	04/09/20	M+S7(3b)	Death	Life PS	WO/90/8/187
1 Connaught Rangers	Pte	Gogarty PJ	Dagshai	30/08/20	M	Death	Life PS	WO/90/8/189
1 Connaught Rangers	Pte	Gorman J	Dagshai	04/09/20	M+S7(3b)	7 yrs PS+DI		WO/90/8/187
1 Connaught Rangers	Pte	Hawes J	Dagshai	30/08/20	M	Death	Life PS	WO/90/8/189
1 Connaught Rangers	Pte	Hayes A	Dagshai	30/08/20	M	10 yrs PS+DI		WO/90/8/188
1 Connaught Rangers	L/Cpl	Hewson J	Dagshai	04/09/20	M+S7(3b)	7 yrs PS+DI		WO/90/8/187
1 Connaught Rangers	Pte(L/Cpl)	Hughes J	Dagshai	23/08/20	M+S7(3)	1 yr HL+DI		WO/90/8/189
1 Connaught Rangers	Pte	Hynes P	Dagshai	04/09/20	M+S7(3b)	Death	Life PS	WO/90/8/187

Unit	Rank	Name	Location	Date D/M/Y	Offence	Finding/Punishment	Amendment	PRO Reference File/Piece/Page
1 Connaught Rangers	Pte	Kearney M	Dagshai	04/09/20	M+S7(3b)	15 yrs PS+DI		WO/90/8/187
1 Connaught Rangers	Pte	Kearns M	Dagshai	04/09/20	M+S7(3b)	3 yrs PS+DI		WO/90/8/187
1 Connaught Rangers	Pte	Keenan W	Dagshai	30/08/20	M+S7(2)+S7(1)	10 yrs PS+DI		WO/90/8/188
1 Connaught Rangers	Pte	Kelly J	Dagshai	04/09/20	M+S7(3b)	Death	Life PS	WO/90/8/187
1 Connaught Rangers	Pte	Kelly P	Dagshai	30/08/20	M+S7(2)+S7(1)	10 yrs PS+DI		WO/90/8/188
1 Connaught Rangers	Cpl	Kelly P	Dagshai	04/09/20	M+S7(3b)	10 yrs PS+Rnks+DI	Remit 3 yrs PS	WO/90/8/187
1 Connaught Rangers	Pte	Kerrigan C	Dagshai	04/09/20	M+S7(3b)	Death	20 yrs PS	WO/90/8/188
1 Connaught Rangers	Pte	Lally S	Dagshai	30/08/20	M	20 yrs PS+DI	Remit 5 yrs	WO/90/8/189
1 Connaught Rangers	Sgt	Lloyd J	Dagshai	23/08/20	M	Acquit		WO/90/8/189
1 Connaught Rangers	Pte	Loftus JJ	Dagshai	04/09/20	M+S7(3b)	Acquit		WO/90/8/187
1 Connaught Rangers	Pte(L/Cpl)	Lopeman PJ	Dagshai	25/08/20	M	2 yrs HL+DI		WO/90/8/188
1 Connaught Rangers	Pte	Lynch J	Dagshai	30/08/20	M	10 yrs PS+DI	Remit 5 yrs	WO/90/8/189
1 Connaught Rangers	Pte(L/Cpl)	Lynott J	Dagshai	25/08/20	M	2 yrs HL+DI		WO/90/8/188
1 Connaught Rangers	Pte	Madigan D	Dagshai	25/08/20	M	Acquit		WO/90/8/188
1 Connaught Rangers	Pte	Maher P	Dagshai	30/08/20	M	10 yrs PS+DI	Remit 5 yrs	WO/90/8/189
1 Connaught Rangers	Pte	Mangan PJ	Dagshai	04/09/20	M+S7(3b)	3 yrs PS+DI	2 yrs HL+DI	WO/90/8/187
1 Connaught Rangers	Pte(L/Cpl)	Mannion P	Dagshai	10/09/20	M+S7(3b)	15 yrs PS+DI		WO/90/8/189
1 Connaught Rangers	Pte	McConnell P	Dagshai	04/09/20	M+S7(3b)	Acquit		WO/90/8/187
1 Connaught Rangers	Pte	McGowan J	Dagshai	30/08/20	M	Life PS+DI		WO/90/8/188
1 Connaught Rangers	Pte(L/Cpl)	McGrath J	Dagshai	25/08/20	M	1 yr HL+DI		WO/90/8/188
1 Connaught Rangers	Pte	McGrath J	Dagshai	04/09/20	M+S7(3b)	5 yrs PS+DI		WO/90/8/187
1 Connaught Rangers	Pte	Miranda J	Dagshai	25/08/20	M	2 yrs HL+DI		WO/90/8/188
1 Connaught Rangers	Pte	Moorehouse JJ	Dagshai	04/09/20	M+S7(3b)	Life PS+DI	20 yrs PS	WO/90/8/187
1 Connaught Rangers	Pte(L/Cpl)	Moran FJ	Dagshai	10/09/20	M+S7(3b)	10 yrs PS+DI		WO/90/8/189
1 Connaught Rangers	Pte	Moran T	Dagshai	30/08/20	M	Death	Life PS	WO/90/8/189
1 Connaught Rangers	Cpl	Murray TJ	Dagshai	25/08/20	M	5 yrs PS+Rnks+	Remit 2 yrs	WO/90/8/188
1 Connaught Rangers	Pte	O'Connell J	Dagshai	30/08/20	M	10 yrs PS+DI		WO/90/8/188
1 Connaught Rangers	Pte(L/Cpl)	O'Donnell C	Dagshai	23/08/20	M+S7(3)	Acquit		WO/90/8/189
1 Connaught Rangers	Cpl	O'Donohue	Dagshai	23/08/20	M+S7(3)	1 yr HL+Ranks+DI		WO/90/8/189
1 Connaught Rangers	Pte	Oliver J	Dagshai	04/09/20	M+S7(3b)	Death	Life PS	WO/90/8/187
1 Connaught Rangers	Pte	Prendergast F	Dagshai	04/09/20	M+S7(3b)	3 yrs PS+DI		WO/90/8/187
1 Connaught Rangers	Pte	Regan D	Dagshai	25/08/20	M	5 yrs PS+DI	Remit 1 yr	WO/90/8/188
1 Connaught Rangers	Pte	Scally P	Dagshai	04/09/20	M+S7(3b)	10 yrs PS+DI	Remit 3 yrs	WO/90/8/187
1 Connaught Rangers	Pte	Scanlon J	Dagshai	30/08/20	M	20 yrs PS+DI	Remit 5 yrs	WO/90/8/189
1 Connaught Rangers	Pte	Shallow W	Dagshai	04/09/20	M+S7(3b)	10 yrs PS+DI	Remit 3 yrs	WO/90/8/187
1 Connaught Rangers	Pte	Sweeney P	Dagshai	30/08/20	M	Life PS+DI	20 yrs PS	WO/90/8/189
1 Connaught Rangers	Pte	Walsh J	Dagshai	25/08/20	M	5 yrs PS+DI		WO/90/8/188

Unit	Rank	Name	Location	Date D/M/Y	Offence	Finding/Punishment	Amendment	PRO Reference File/Piece/Page
1 Connaught Rangers	Pte(L/Cpl)	Willis P	Dagshai	25/08/20	M	3 yrs PS+DI		WO/90/8/188
1 Connaught Rangers	Sgt	Woods J	Dagshai	25/08/20	M	10 yrs PS+Rnks+DI +Forfeits MM	Remit 2 yrs	WO/90/8/188
6 Conn Rangers	Pte	Murphy MJ	Rouen	05/10/16	M	Death	Comm 10 yrs PS	WO/90/6/89
1 R Dub Fus	Pte	White JW	Field	24/03/19	M	10 yrs PS		WO213/29/88
2 R Dublin Fusiliers	Pte	Cannon W	Constantinople	05/07/20	M+Disob(Capt)	5 yrs PS	1 yr Detn	WO/90/8/84
2 R Dublin Fusiliers	Pte	Daniels C	Constantinople	05/07/20	M+Disob(Capt)	12 yrs PS	2 yrs Detn	WO/90/8/84
2 R Dublin Fusiliers	Pte	Doyle H	Constantinople	05/07/20	M+Disob(Capt)	12 yrs PS	2 yrs Detn	WO/90/8/84
2 R Dublin Fusiliers	Pte	Failes NC	Constantinople	05/07/20	M+Disob(Capt)	12 yrs PS	2 yrs Detn	WO/90/8/84
2 R Dublin Fusiliers	Gnr	Lamb J	Constantinople	05/07/20	M+Disob(Capt) +S7(3b)	5 yrs PS	1 yr Detn	WO/90/8/84
2 R Dublin Fusiliers	Pte	McFarlane J	Constantinople	05/07/20	M+Disob(Capt) +S7(3b)	5 yrs PS	1 yr Detn	WO/90/8/84
Irish Gds	Gdsn	Carthy J	Guildhall Westnnster	04/02/20	M	5 yrs PS+Disch Igmny		WO/92/4/89
Irish Gds	Gdsn	Flanagan J	Guildhall Westminster	04/02/20	M	5 yrs PS+Disch Igmny		WO/92/4/89
Irish Gds	Gdsn	Moffatt P	Guildhall Wminster	04/02/20	M	5 yrs PS+Disch Igmny		WO/92/4/89
6 R Innis Fus	Pte	Devine J	Field	24/03/19	M	11 yrs PS		WO/213/29/89
7/8 R Innis Fus	Pte	Austin GW	Field	15/04/18	M	5 yrs PS	Susp	WO/213/21/96
7/8 R Innis Fus	Pte	Barham R	Field	15/04/18	M	5 yrs PS	Susp	WO/213/21/96
7/8 R Innis Fus	Pte(L/Cpl)	Baxter J	Field	15/04/18	M	7 yrs PS	Susp	WO/213/21/95
7/8 R Innis Fus	Pte(L/Cpl)	Bell M	Field	15/04/18	M	7 yrs PS	Susp	WO/213/21/96
7/8 R Innis Fus	Pte	Blair E	Field	15/04/18	M	5 yrs PS	Susp	WO/213/21/96
7/8 R Innis Fus	Pte	Bothwell W	Field	15/04/18	M	5 yrs PS	Susp	WO/213/21/94
7/8 R Innis Fus	Pte	Boulton GH	Field	15/04/18	M	5 yrs PS	Susp	WO/213/21/96
7/8 R Innis Fus	Pte	Bridge H	Field	15/04/18	M	5 yrs PS	Susp	WO/213/21/96
7/8 R Innis Fus	Pte	Casey P	Field	15/04/18	M	5 yrs PS	Susp	WO/213/21/97
7/8 R Innis Fus	Pte	Colbert F	Field	15/04/18	M	5 yrs PS	Susp	WO/213/21/96
7/8 R Innis Fus	Pte	Donaughey J	Field	15/04/18	M	5 yrs PS	Susp	WO/213/21/95
7/8 R Innis Fus	Pte	Eades G	Field	15/04/18	M	5 yrs PS	Susp	WO/213/21/95
7/8 R Innis Fus	Pte	Elliot F	Field	15/04/18	M	5 yrs PS	Susp	WO/213/21/96
7/8 R Innis Fus	Pte	Fitzpatrick T	Field	15/04/18	M	5 yrs PS	Susp	WO/213/21/95
7/8 R Innis Fus	Pte(L/Cpl)	Flannigan J	Field	15/04/18	M	7 yrs PS	Susp	WO/213/21/95
7/8 R Innis Fus	Pte	Froom EH	Field	15/04/18	M	5 yrs PS	Susp	WO/213/21/96
7/8 R Innis Fus	Pte	Fullerton J	Field	15/04/18	M	5 yrs PS	Susp	WO/213/21/95
7/8 R Innis Fus	Pte(L/Cpl)	Goden E	Field	15/04/18	M	7 yrs PS	Susp	WO/213/21/96
7/8 R Innis Fus	Pte	Hanrattey B	Field	15/04/18	M	5 yrs PS	Susp	WO/213/21/95
7/8 R Innis Fus	Pte	Harrigan C	Field	15/04/18	M	5 yrs PS	Susp	WO/213/21/96
7/8 R Innis Fus	Pte	Hewett J	Field	15/04/18	M	5 yrs PS	Susp	WO/213/21/95
7/8 R Innis Fus	Pte	Howard C	Field	15/04/18	M	5 yrs PS	Susp	WO/213/21/96
7/8 R Innis Fus	Pte	Johnson GL	Field	15/04/18	M	5 yrs PS	Susp	WO/213/21/95
7/8 R Innis Fus	Pte(L/Cpl)	Kemble F	Field	15/04/18	M	7 yrs PS	Susp	WO/213/21/96
7/8 R Innis Fus	Pte	Kemp S	Field	15/04/18	M	5 yrs PS	Susp	WO/213/21/96
7/8 R Innis Fus	Pte	Kerwain E	Field	15/04/18	M	5 yrs PS	Susp	WO/213/21/95
7/8 R Innis Fus	Pte	King J	Field	15/04/18	M	5 yrs PS	Susp	WO/213/21/96
7/8 R Innis Fus	Pte	Kinney F	Field	15/04/18	M	5 yrs PS	Susp	WO/213/21/96
7/8 R Innis Fus	Pte	Lock G	Field	15/04/18	M	5 yrs PS	Susp	WO/213/21/96
7/8 R Innis Fus	Pte	Lyttle L	Field	15/04/18	M	5 yrs PS	Susp	WO/213/21/95
7/8 R Innis Fus	Pte	Macintyre P	Field	15/04/18	M	5 yrs PS	Susp	WO/213/21/95
7/8 R Innis Fus	Pte	Mackay W	Field	15/04/18	M	5 yrs PS	Susp	WO/213/21/94
7/8 R Innis Fus	Pte	Marriott A	Field	15/04/18	M	5 yrs PS	Susp	WO/213/21/94
7/8 R Innis Fus	Pte	McNamee G	Field	15/04/18	M	5 yrs PS	Susp	WO/213/21/95
7/8 R Innis Fus	Pte	Moir J	Field	15/04/18	M	5 yrs PS	Susp	WO/213/21/96
7/8 R Innis Fus	Pte	Mooney H	Field	15/04/18	M	5 yrs PS	Susp	WO/213/21/96
7/8 R Innis Fus	Pte	Morphet T	Field	15/04/18	M	5 yrs PS	Susp	WO/213/21/95
7/8 R Innis Fus	Pte	Moxon T	Field	15/04/18	M	5 yrs PS	Susp	WO/213/21/95
7/8 R Innis Fus	Pte	Mullen R	Field	15/04/18	M	NG		WO/213/21/97
7/8 R Innis Fus	Pte	O'Dea B	Field	15/04/18	M	5 yrs PS	Susp	WO/213/21/95
7/8 R Innis Fus	Pte	O'Donoghue D	Field	15/04/18	M	5 yrs PS	Susp	WO/213/21/95
7/8 R Innis Fus	Pte	O'Neall W	Field	15/04/18	M	5 yrs PS	Susp	WO/213/21/96
7/8 R Innis Fus	Pte	Powell CT	Field	15/04/18	M	NG		WO/213/21/97
7/8 R Innis Fus	Pte	Pratt O	Field	15/04/18	M	5 yrs PS	Susp	WO/213/21/96
7/8 R Innis Fus	Pte	Prentice W	Field	15/04/18	M	5 yrs PS	Susp	WO/213/21/96
7/8 R Innis Fus	Pte	Price J	Field	15/04/18	M	5 yrs PS	Susp	WO/213/21/96
7/8 R Innis Fus	Pte	Priest FC	Field	15/04/18	M	5 yrs PS	Susp	WO/213/21/97
7/8 R Innis Fus	Pte	Raddock NG	Field	15/04/18	M	5 yrs PS	Susp	WO/213/21/95

Unit	Rank	Name	Location	Date D/M/Y	Offence	Finding/Punishment	Amendment	PRO Reference File/Piece/Page
7/8 R Innis Fus	Pte	Reynolds P	Field	15/04/18	M	5 yrs PS	Susp	WO/213/21/97
7/8 R Innis Fus	Pte	Rowan T	Field	15/04/18	M	5 yrs PS	Susp	WO/213/21/97
7/8 R Innis Fus	Pte	Rush EW	Field	15/04/18	M	5 yrs PS	Susp	WO/213/21/96
7/8 R Innis Fus	Pte	Rush P	Field	15/04/18	M	5 yrs PS	Susp	WO/213/21/96
7/8 R Innis Fus	Pte	Sargeant A	Field	15/04/18	M	5 yrs PS	Susp	WO/213/21/95
7/8 R Innis Fus	Pte	Searson S	Field	15/04/18	M	5 yrs PS	Susp	WO/213/21/95
7/8 R Innis Fus	Pte	Simm J	Field	15/04/18	M	5 yrs PS	Susp	WO/213/21/94
7/8 R Innis Fus	Pte	Staples G	Field	15/04/18	M	5 yrs PS	Susp	WO/213/21/94
7/8 R Innis Fus	Pte	Stevenson J	Field	15/04/18	M	5 yrs PS	Susp	WO/213/21/95
7/8 R Innis Fus	Pte	Thompson R	Field	15/04/18	M	5 yrs PS	Susp	WO/213/21/95
7/8 R Innis Fus	Pte	Turner A	Field	15/04/18	M	NG		WO/213/21/95
7/8 R Innis Fus	Pte	Wain J	Field	15/04/18	M	5 yrs PS	Susp	WO/213/21/94
7/8 R Innis Fus	Pte(L/Cpl))	Waller GH	Field	15/04/18	M	7 yrs PS	Susp	WO/213/21/95
7/8 R Innis Fus	Cpl	Wilson W	Field	15/04/18	M	10 yrs PS	Susp	WO/213/21/95
7/8 R Innis Fus	Pte(L/Cpl)	Woods J	Field	15/04/18	M	7 yrs PS	Susp	WO/213/21/95
7/8 R Innis Fus	Pte	Yard F	Field	15/04/18	M	5 yrs PS	Susp	WO/213/21/94
7/8 R Innis Fus	Pte	Young FG	Field	15/04/18	M	NG		WO/213/21/96
7/8 R Innis Fus	Pte	Yoxall T	Field	15/04/18	M	5 yrs PS	Susp	WO/213/21/94
8 R Innis Fus	Pte	Conway D	Eniskillen	06/09/15	M+Inj pub property	1 yr HL		WO/86/66/111
8 R Innis Fus	Pte	Finlan J	Eniskillen	06/09/15	M+Inj pub property	1 yr HL		WO/86/66/111
8 R Innis Fus	Pte	Kirwan N	Eniskillen	06/09/15	M+Inj pub property	1 yr HL		WO/86/66/111
8 R Innis Fus	Pte	McCabe J	Eniskillen	06/09/15	M+Inj Pub Property	1 yr HL		WO/86/66/111
8 R Innis Fus	Pte	Murphy JJ	Eniskillen	06/09/15	M+Inj pub property	1 yr HL		WO/86/66/111
8 R Innis Fus	Pte	OíKeefe P	Eniskillen	06/09/15	M+Inj pub property	1 yr HL		WO/86/66/111
8 R Innis Fus	Pte	Wilson A	Eniskillen	06/09/15	M+Inj pub property	1 yr HL		WO/86/66/111
7/8 R Irish Fus	Pte	McGuire P	Dunkirk	13/04/17	M	8 mos HL		WO/213/14/138
7/8 R Irish Fus	Pte	Veale W	Dunkirk	13/04/17	M	8 mos HL		WO/213/14/138
2 R I Fus	Pte	Coulden A	Field EEF	09/06/19	M+XOS+S40	9 mos HL		WO/213/30/126
2 R I Fus	Pte	Fitzgerald P	Field EEF	09/06/19	M+S40	21 dys FP2	Quashed	WO/213/30/126
2 R I Fus	Pte	Kirk D	Field EEF	09/06/19	M+S40	42 dys FP2		WO/213/30/126
2 R I Fus	Pte	McElroy J	Field EEF	09/06/19	M+XOS+S40	1 yr HL		WO/213/30/126
2 R I Fus	Pte	McQuillan D	Field EEF	09/06/19	M+S40	NG		WO/213/30/126
2 R I Fus	Pte	Ward J	Field EEF	09/06/19	M+XOS+S40	6 mos HL		WO/213/30/126
8 R I Fus	Pte (L/Cpl)	Austin J	Tipperary	17/06/15	M	84 dys Detn		WO/86/65/77
3 Irish Gds	Pte	O'Doherty D	Brentwood	03/06/16	M	1 yr HL		WO/86/70/108
2 R Irish	Pte	Arthur H	Field	15/04/18	M	5 yrs PS	Susp	WO/213/21/98
2 R Irish	Pte	Bolger J	Field	15/04/18	M	5 yrs PS	Susp	WO/213/21/98
2 R Irish	Pte	Bragnell J	Field	15/04/18	M	5 yrs PS	Susp	WO/213/21/98
2 R Irish	Pte	Byrne J	Field	15/04/18	M	5 yrs PS	Susp	WO/213/21/98
2 R Irish	Pte	Carey J	Field	15/04/18	M	5 yrs PS	Susp	WO/213/21/99
2 R Irish	Pte	Clarke E	Field	15/04/18	M	5 yrs PS	Susp	WO/213/21/98
2 R Irish	Pte	Connelly J	Field	15/04/18	M	5 yrs PS	Susp	WO/213/21/98
2 R Irish	Pte	Connor L	Field	15/04/18	M	5 yrs PS	Susp	WO/213/21/98
2 Royal Irish	Pte/LCpl	Geary T	Chakrata	05/07/21	M+S7(3b)	3 yrs PS	NC	WO/90/8/170
2 R Irish	Pte	Gregory W	Field	15/04/18	M	5 yrs PS	Susp	WO/213/21/98
2 R Irish	Pte	Heggarty W	Field	15/04/18	M	5 yrs PS	Susp	WO/213/21/98
2 R Irish	Pte	Histed T	Field	15/04/18	M	5 yrs PS	Susp	WO/213/21/99
2 R Irish	Pte	Huggins H	Field	15/04/18	M	5 yrs PS	Susp	WO/213/21/99
2 R Irish	Pte	McDonald L	Field	15/04/18	M	5 yrs PS	Susp	WO/213/21/98
2 Royal Irish	Pte/LCpl	O'Brien T	Chakrata	05/07/21	Mx2+Disob(Lt)+S7(3b)x2	4 yrs PS	Remit 1 yr	WO/90/8/170
2 Royal Irish	Pte/LCpl	O'Keefe D	Chakrata	05/07/21	Mx2+S7(3b)	Acquit		WO/90/8/170
2 R Irish	Pte	Purcell J	Field	15/04/18	M	5 yrs PS	Susp	WO/213/21/98
2 R Irish	Pte	Reed E	Field	15/04/18	M	5 yrs PS	Susp	WO/213/21/99
2 R Irish	Pte	Tugby P	Field	15/04/18	M	5 yrs PS	Susp	WO/213/21/98
2 R Irish	Pte	Wells J	Field	15/04/18	M	5 yrs PS	Susp	WO/213/21/98
2 R Irish	Pte	Welsh T	Field	15/04/18	M	5 yrs PS	Susp	WO/213/21/98
7 R Irish	Pte	Arwin A	Field	15/04/18	M	5 yrs PS	Susp	WO/213/21/97
7 R Irish	Pte	Byrne J	Field	15/04/18	M	NG		WO/213/21/97
7 R Irish	Pte	Byrne S	Field	15/04/18	M	NG		WO/213/21/97
7 R Irish	Pte	Clarey T	Field	15/04/18	M	5 yrs PS	Susp	WO/213/21/98
7 R Irish	Pte	Collins J	Field	15/04/18	M	NG		WO/213/21/98
7 R Irish	Pte	Commins P	Field	15/04/18	M	5 yrs PS	Susp	WO/213/21/97
7 R Irish	Pte	Connors J	Field	15/04/18	M	5 yrs PS	Susp	WO/213/21/98
7 R Irish	Pte	Cotter F	Field	15/04/18	M	5 yrs PS	Susp	WO/213/21/97
7 R Irish	Pte	Donigan B	Field	15/04/18	M	5 yrs PS	Susp	WO/213/21/98
7 R Irish	Pte	Donovan J	Field	15/04/18	M	5 yrs PS	Susp	WO/213/21/97
7 R Irish	Pte	Howell E	Field	15/04/18	M	5 yrs PS	Susp	WO/213/21/97
7 R Irish	Pte	Hussey A	Field	15/04/18	M	5 yrs PS	Susp	WO/213/21/98
7 R Irish	Pte	Justice C	Field	15/04/18	M	5 yrs PS	Susp	WO/213/21/97
7 R Irish	Pte	Kane T	Field	15/04/18	M	5 yrs PS	Susp	WO/213/21/97
7 R Irish	Pte	Kelleher J	Field	15/04/18	M	5 yrs PS	Susp	WO/213/21/97
7 R Irish	Pte	Kenny J	Field	15/04/18	M	5 yrs PS	Susp	WO/213/21/97
7 R Irish	Pte	Lavery F	Field	15/04/18	M	5 yrs PS	Susp	WO/213/21/98

Unit	Rank	Name	Location	Date D/M/Y	Offence	Finding/Punishment	Amendment	PRO Reference File/Piece/Page
7 R Irish	Pte	Magee M	Field	15/04/18	M	5 yrs PS	Susp	WO/213/21/97
7 R Irish	Pte	Mallon W	Field	15/04/18	M	5 yrs PS	Susp	WO/213/21/97
7 R Irish	Pte	Maloney P	Field	15/04/18	M	5 yrs PS	Susp	WO/213/21/98
7 R Irish	Pte	McCafferty R	Field	15/04/18	M	5 yrs PS	Susp	WO/213/21/97
7 R Irish	Pte	McCauley W	Field	15/04/18	M	5 yrs PS	Susp	WO/213/21/98
7 R Irish	Pte	Murphy M	Field	15/04/18	M	NG		WO/213/21/97
7 R Irish	Pte	O'Malley M	Field	15/04/18	M	5 yrs PS	Susp	WO/213/21/97
7 R Irish	Pte	Slattery M	Field	15/04/18	M	5 yrs PS	Susp	WO/213/21/97
7 R Irish	Pte	Sweeney T	Field	15/04/18	M	5 yrs PS	Susp	WO/213/21/97
7 R Irish	Pte	Tudor F	Field	15/04/18	M	5 yrs PS	Susp	WO/213/21/97
7 R Irish	Pte	Tulley M	Field	15/04/18	M	5 yrs PS	Susp	WO/213/21/97
7 R Irish	Pte	Wickham J	Field	15/04/18	M	5 yrs PS	Susp	WO/213/21/98
7 R Irish	Pte	Willis F	Field	15/04/18	M	5 yrs PS	Susp	WO/213/21/97
7 R Irish	Pte	Wilson W	Field	15/04/18	M	5 yrs PS	Susp	WO/213/21/98
7 R Irish Fus	Pte	Kealley S	Field	15/04/18	M	NG		WO/213/21/98
R Munster Fus	Pte	Flynn G	St Nazaire	11/10/14	M	5 yrs PS	Quashed	WO/213/2/105
R Munster Fus	Pte	O'Neill M	St Nazaire	11/10/14	M	3 yrs PS	Quashed	WO/213/2/105
R Munster Fus	Pte	Scannell G	St Nazaire	11/10/14	M+Forcing Guard	4 yrs PS	Rem 1 yr/ Quashed	WO/213/2/105
2 R Mun Fus	Pte	McCarthy D	Field EEF	24/03/20	M+XO+S2+7(2b)	9 mos HL		WO/213/31/142
2 R Mun Fus	Pte	McCarthy M	Field EEF	24/03/20	M+XO+S2+7(2b)	9 mos HL		WO/213/31/142
2 R Mun Fus	Pte	Oakley F	Field EEF	24/03/20	M(2)+XO+S2	2 yrs HL		WO/213/31/142
3(R) Munster Fus	Pte	Conway P	[Le] Havre	19/07/16	Persuading M+Insub	Acquit		WO/90/6/67
Kenyan								
1/6 KAR	Pte	Kafope A bin	Tabora	13/08/17	Mx2+Striking	15 yrs PS+Disch IgmnyDI		WO/213/23/81
1/6 KAR	Pte	Mwanyivera A bin	Tabora	13/08/17	Mx2+Striking	15 yrs PS+Disch IgmnyDI		WO/213/23/81
Maltese								
2 KO Malta Militia	Pte	Bonnana G	Malta	20/12/15	M+AWOL+Loss prop	112 dys Detn +Stoppages		WO/86/68/199
Mauritian								
Labour Bn	Pte	Arcanthe L	Mesopotamia	16/01/19	M	84 dys Detn		WO/90/7/169
Maur Lab Bn	Pte	Auguste A	Mespot	10/05/18	M(S7-2B)	3 mos FP1		WO/90/7/151
Maur Lab Bn	Pte	Bousset J	Mespot	10/05/18	M(S7-2B)	6 mos HL		WO/90/7/151
Labour Bn	Pte	Fox J	Mesopotamia	16/01/19	M	84 dys Detn		WO/90/7/169
Labour Bn	Pte	Green H	Mesopotamia	16/01/19	M	1 yr HL		WO/90/7/169
Maur Lab Bn	Pte	Lafleur G	Mespot	10/05/18	M	6 mos HL		WO/90/7/151t
Labour Bn	Pte	Maniquois M	Mesopotamia	16/01/19	M	84 dys Detn		WO/90/7/169
Labour Bn	Pte	Renelle E	Mesopotamia	16/01/19	M	84 dys Detn		WO/90/7/169
Labour Bn	Pte	Renelle J	Mesopotamia	16/01/19	M	84 dys Detn		WO/90/7/169
Maur Lab Bn	Pte	Samanne R	Mespot	10/05/18	M	18 mos HL		WO/90/7/151
Labour Bn	Pte(A/Cpl)	Sophie E	Mesopotamia	16/01/19	M	2 yrs HL		WO/90/7/169
Maur Lab Bn	Pte	Vieillese W	Mespot	10/05/18	M(S7-2B)	2 yrs HL		WO/90/7/151
New Zealand								
NZEF	Tpr(L/Cpl)	Boswell W	Field EEF	01/07/18	M	NG		WO/213/28/138
NZEF	Tpr/(L/Cpl)	Impey A	Field EEF	01/07/18	M	NG		WO/213/28/138
NZEF 3 Reinf	Pte	Kay R	Zeitoun	05/04/15	Incit M+Disob(Lt)	1 yr HL+DI		WO/90/6/35
NZEF 3 Reinf	Pte	Kilpatrick R	Zeitoun	05/04/15	Incit M+Disob(Lt)	2 yrs HL+DI		WO/90/6/35
NZEF 3 Reinf	Pte	McKendry A	Zeitoun	05/04/15	Incit M+Disob(Lt)	2 yrs HL+DI		WO/90/6/35
NZEF 3 Reinf	Pte	O'Neill T	Zeitoun	05/04/15	Incit M+Disob(Lt)	1 yr HL+DI		WO/90/6/35
NZEF 3 Reinf	Cpl	Springer J	Zeitoun	05/04/15	Incit M+Disob(Lt)	3 yrs PS+DI		WO/90/6/35
3 NZ Rifles	Pte	Silva P	Malta	30/12/15	M+Not Sup+Disob(APM)	1 yr HL	Remit 1 month	WO/90/6/40
3 NZ Rifle Bde	Rfn	Langrish JG	Armenieres	17/06/16	M+S40	42 dys FP		WO/213/9/182
2 Otago NZEF	Pte	Banks JL	Rouen	01/09/17	M	10 yrs PS		WO/90/6/90
2 Otago NZEF	Pte	Braithwaite J	Field	11/10/16	M	Death		WO/213/17/110
2 Otago NZEF	Pte	Duke T	Field	01/09/17	M	10 yrs PS		WO/213/17/110
2 Otago NZEF	Pte	Frew G	Field	01/09/17	M	10 yrs PS		WO/213/17/110
2 Otago NZEF	Pte	Leyden JF	Field	01/09/17	M	10 yrs PS		WO/213/17/110
2 Otago NZEF	Pte	New[t/l?]on CW	Field	01/09/17	M	10 yrs PS		WO/213/17/110
2 Otago NZEF	Pte	Plunkett J	Field	01/09/17	M	10 yrs HL		WO/213/17/110
2 Otago NZEF	Pte	Reid S	Field	01/09/17	M	10 yrs PS		WO/213/17/110

Unit	Rank	Name	Location	Date D/M/Y	Offence	Finding/Punishment	Amendment	PRO Reference File/Piece/Page
1 Wellington NZEF	Pte	Williams SG	[Le] Havre	19/07/16	Per M+Viol SO	Acquit		WO/90/6/67
1 NZ Div B Employ Coy	Pte	Brad G	Field	16/10/18	M	6 mos HL	Susp	WO/213/25/165
1 NZ Div Employ Coy	Pte	Dinneen G	Field	16/10/18	M	6 mos HL	Susp	WO/213/25/165
1 NZ Div Employ Coy	Pte	Doyle A	Field	16/10/18	M	6 mos HL	Susp	WO/213/25/165
1 NZ Div Employ Coy	Pte	Findlay RC	Field	16/10/18	M	6 mos HL	Susp	WO/213/25/165
1 NZ Div Employ Coy	Pte	Finlayson R	Field	16/10/18	M	6 mos HL	Susp	WO/213/25/165
1 NZ Div Employ Coy	Pte	Gilkenson J	Field	16/10/18	M	6 mos HL	Susp	WO/213/25/165
1 NZ Div Emp B	Pte	Grimwood H	Field	16/10/18	M	6 mos HL	Susp	WO/213/25/165
1 NZ Div Emp B	Pte	Hincks W	Field	16/10/18	M	6 mos HL	Susp	WO/213/25/165
1 NZ Div Emp B	Pte	Kelly JJ	Field	16/10/18	M	6 mos HL	Susp	WO/213/25/165
1 NZ Div Emp B	Pte	McGregor J	Field	16/10/18	M	6 mos HL	Susp	WO/213/25/165
1 NZ Div Emp B	Pte	Narbey A	Field	16/10/18	M	6 mos HL	Susp	WO/213/25/165
1 NZ Div Empl B	Pte	Schrader PF	Field	16/10/18	M	6 mos HL	Susp	WO/213/25/165
1 NZ Div Emp B	Pte	Sinclair C	Field	16/10/18	M	6 mos HL	Susp	WO/213/25/165
1 NZ Div Emp B	Pte	Williams EJ	Field	16/10/18	M	NG		WO/213/25/165
11 Bty NZFA	Gnr	Magnusson GD	[Le] Havre	19/07/16	Per M+Viol SO	Acquit		WO/90/6/67
NZ Pnr	Pte	McDonald A	Rouen	04/02/19	M	Acquit		WO/90/8/59

Russian

Unit	Rank	Name	Location	Date	Offence	Finding/Punishment	Amendment	PRO Reference
1 Slav-Brit	Pte	Artemenko G	Field NREF	14/07/19	M	NG		WO/213/32/59
1 Slav-Brit	Pte	Bitel S	Field NREF	14/07/19	M	Death		WO/213/32/59
1 Slav-Brit	Pte	Bykoff V	Field NREF	17/07/19	M	Death	Comm 10 yrs PS	WO/213/32/59
1 Slav-Brit	Pte	Cherbukin F	Field NREF	14/07/19	M	Death		WO/213/32/59
1 Slav-Brit Legion	Pte	Deriagin I	Field	13/07/19	M	Death		WO213/32/58
1 Slav-Brit	Pte	Elisaieff I	Field NREF	14/07/19	M	Death		WO/213/32/59
1 Slav-Brit Legion	Pte	Evstraloff P	Field NREF	17/07/19	M	Death	Comm 10 yrs PS	WO/213/32/59
1 Slav-Brit Legion	Pte	Kanieff A	Field	13/07/19	M	NG		WO213/32/58
1 Slav-Brit Legion	Cpl	Kanieff P	Field NREF	14/07/19	M	Death		WO/213/32/59
1 Slav-Brit Legion	Pte	Kozhin V	Field NREF	17/07/19	M	NG		WO/213/32/59
1 Slav-Brit Legion	Pte	Lasheff T	Field	13/07/19	M	NG		WO213/32/58
1 Slav-Brit Legion	Pte	Lashkoff V	Field NREF	14/07/19	M	Death		WO/213/32/59
1 Slav-Brit Legion	Pte	Miarid G	Field NREF	17/07/19	M	Death	Comm 10 yrs PS	WO/213/32/59
1 Slav-Brit Legion	Sgt	Pesochnikoff J	Field NREF	13/07/19	M	Death		WO/213/32/59
1 Slav-Brit Legion	Pte	Petonhoff M	Field NREF	14/07/19	M	Death	Comm 10 yrs PS	WO/213/32/5 9
1 Slav-Brit Legion	Pte	Piasosky A	Field NREF	17/07/19	M	NG		WO/213/32/59
1 Slav-Brit Legion	Pte	Posdjeef N	Field NREF	14/07/19	M	Death		WO/213/32/59
1 Slav-Brit Legion	Pte	Roond I	Field NREF	17/07/19	M	NG		WO/213/31/59
1 Slav-Brit Legion	Pte	Sakharoff F	Field	13/07/19	M	Death		WO213/32/58
1 Slav-Brit Legion	Pte	Sharoff V	Field NREF	17/07/19	M	Death	Comm 10 yrs PS	WO/213/32/59
1 Slav-Brit Legion	Pte	Shouliatieff T	Field	13/07/19	M	Death	Comm 10 yrs PS	WO213/32/58
1 Slav-Brit Legion	Pte	Taratin P	Field NREF	14/07/19	M	Death		WO/213/32/59
1 Slav-Brit Legion	Pte	Tenentieff H	Field	13/07/19	M	NG		WO213/32/58
1 Slav-Brit Legion	Pte	Tonkikh V	Field NREF	17/07/19	M	Death	Comm 10 yrs P	WO/213/32/ 59
1 Slav-Brit Legion	Pte	Volkoff P	Field NREF	14/07/19	M	Death		WO/213/32/59
1 Slav-Brit Legion	2 Lt	Zouev AM	Field	15/07/19	M	Acquit	No evidence	WO/90/8/85

Date D/M/Y	Name	Rank	Unit	Offence		Finding/Punishment	Amendment	Location	PRO Reference File/Piece/Page	Note:
Scottish										
A & SH	Pte	McNeal P	Dunkirk	13/04/17	M	1 yr HL			WO/213/14/138	
A&S Hdrs	Pte	Porter T	Field	12/09/18	M(x2)	10 yrs PS	One charge quashed		WO/213/25/177	
2 A&SH	Pte	Delaney J	Rouen	05/10/16	M	Death	Comm 2 yrs PS		WO/90/6/89	
B Watch	Pte	Mackey M	Field	12/09/18	M(x2)	10 yrs PS	One charge quashed		WO/213/25/177	
1 Black Watch	Pte	Cowan J	Allahabad	27/09/22	M+Des+Theft+S18(4)	2 yrs HL+DI			WO/90/8/172	
1 B Watch	Pte	Laverty J	Dunkirk	13/04/17	M	8 mos HL			WO/213/14/138	
1 Black Watch	Pte	Morey J	Allahabad	27/09/22	M+Des+Theft+S18(4)	2 yrs HL+DI			WO/90/8/172	
10 B Watch	Pte	Samuel J	Field SEF	02/05/18	M+Disob	10 yrs PS	Comm 2 yrs HL		WO/213/22/30	
Gordon Hdrs	Pte	Urquhart S	Field	12/09/18	M(x2)	10 yrs PS	One charge quashed		WO/213/25/177	
2 Gor Hdrs	Pte	McGrane G	Field	07/01/19	M+S40	1 yr HL			WO/213/27/154	
3/6 Gordon H'ldrs(YTF)	Pte	Peterkin J	Hawick	13/01/16	M+Viol(Sgt)+S40	6 mos Detn+Rnks			WO/86/68/95	
8/10 Gordons (att RE)	Pte	McKinley W	Field	28/08/16	M x 2	5 yrs PS	Susp		WO/213/11/9	
8/10 Gordons (att RE)	Pte	Nelson T	Field	28/08/16	M x 2	5 yrs PS	Susp		WO/213/11/9	
8/10 Gordons (att RE)	Pte	O'Sullivan J	Field	28/08/16	M x 2	Death	Comm 5 yrs PS		WO/213/11/9	
8/10 Gordons (att RE)	Pte	Turner J	Field	28/08/16	M x 2	2 yrs HL	Susp		WO/213/11/9	
1 HLI	Pte	Garden J	Rouen	05/10/16	M	Death	Comm 15 yrs PS		WO/90/6/89	
1 HLI	Pte	Smith JI	Field (Mespot)	09/02/16	[M]S7(2b)	18 mos HL			WO/90/7/70	
1(R) Gn HLI	Pte	Weallens JH	Glasgow	04/10/18	M+Theft	6 mos Detn	NC		WO/86/85/9	
1/6 HLI	Cpl	Davidson T	Field	28/12/18	M+Insub+Disob	6 mos HL			WO/213/28/25	
1/6 HLI	Cpl	Penman WTC	Field	28/12/18	M+Disob	6 mos HL			WO/213/28/25	
1/6 HLI	Cpl	Reddin H	Field	28/12/18	M+Insub+Disob	6 mos HL			WO/213/28/62	
1/6 HLI	Pte(L/Cpl)	Russell J	Field	28/12/18	M+Disob	6 mos HL			WO/213/28/25	
1/6 HLI	Pte(L/Cpl)	Taylor J	Field	28/12/18	M+Disob	42 dys FP1			WO/213/28/25	
3 HLI(att MGC)	Pte	Kimmit R	Grantham	25/04/16	M	3 yrs PS			WO/92/3/37	
3 HLI(att MGC)	Pte	Korr J	Grantham	25/04/16	M	3 yrs PS			WO/92/3/37	
3 HLI(att MGC)	Pte	Logan T	Grantham	25/04/16	M	3 yrs PS			WO/92/3/37	
3 HLI(att MGC)	Pte	McCallam	Grantham	25/04/16	NSM	1 dy Detn			WO/92/3/38	
3 HLI(att MGC)	Pte	Pole J	Grantham	25/04/16	NSM	1 dy Detn			WO/92/3/38	
3 HLI(att MGC)	Pte	Taylor R	Grantham	25/04/16	M	2 yrs Detn			WO/92/3/37	
4 HLI(att MGC)	Pte	Clarkson A	Grantham	25/04/16	NSM	1 dy Detn			WO/92/3/38	
4 HLI(att MGC)	Pte	Clarkson JR	Grantham	25/04/16	NSM	1 dy Detn			WO/92/3/38	
KOSB	Pte	McCormack C	Field	12/09/18	M(x2)	10 yrs PS	Rem 2 yrs/ one charge NC		WO/213/25/177	
1 KOSB	Pte	Quinn D	Malta	30/12/15	M+Not Sup +Disob(APM)	1 yr HL	Remit 1 month		WO/90/6/40	
1/4 R Scots	Pte	McArthur T	Field	24/03/19	M	12 yrs PS			WO213/29/88	
2 KOSB	Pte	Campbell M	Devonport	29/10/20	M+S40	NG			WO/86/90/187	
2 R Scots	Pte	McPherson J	Field	24/03/19	M	11 yrs PS			WO213/29/88	
11 R Scots	Pte	McCorkindale D	Rouen	05/10/16	M	Death	Comm 15 yrs PS		WO/90/6/89	
R Sco Fus	Pte	McIntosh R	Etaples	18/09/17	M	10 yrs PS			WO/213/17/151	
1/4 R Sco Fus	Pte	Bell J	Field	14/01/18	M	10 yrs PS	Comm 2 yrs HL		WO/213/21/34	
1/4 R Sco Fus	Pte	Cunningham J	Field	14/01/18	M	10 yrs PS	Comm 2 yrs HL		WO/213/21/34	
1/4 R Sco Fus	Pte	Dunlop C	Field	14/01/18	M	10 yrs PS	Comm 2 yrs HL		WO/213/21/34	
1/4 R Sco Fus	Pte	Lennox J	Field	14/01/18	M	10 yrs PS	Comm 2 yrs HL		WO/213/21/34	
1/4 R Sco Fus	Pte	McMeecham M	Field	14/01/18	M	10 yrs PS	Comm 2 yrs HL		WO/213/21/34	
4 R Scots Greys	Pte	Agnew D	Edinburgh	09/06/21	M+V(A/RSM)	18 mos HL			WO/86/91/131	
4 R Scots Greys	Pte	Dickson T	Edinburgh	09/06/21	M+V(A/RSM)	18 mos HL			WO/86/91/131	
Scot Rifles	Pte	Coleman J	Field	12/09/18	M(x2)	10 yrs PS	One charge quashed		WO/213/25/177	
18 Bn Scot Rifs	Sgt	Walters W	Field	03/02/19	M+Insub+S7(2)	12 mos HL+Rnks			WO/213/28/165	
3 Sea Hldrs	Pte	Chalmers G	Edinburgh	17/06/19	M+Insub	3 yrs PS+Dis Igmny	NC		WO/92/4/74	
South African										
8 SA Infantry	Pte	Robson PL	Potchefstroom	23/12/15	M+S40	20 dys Detn +Rnks +Stop			WO/213/11/179	
372 Coy CAHT	Dvr	Allan D	Field	14/05/19	M	5 yrs PS	Comm 1 yr HL		WO/213/30/12	
372 Coy CAHT	Dvr	Binneker C	Field	14/05/19	M	5 yrs PS			WO/213/30/12	
372 Coy CAHT	Dvr	Brandt P	Field	14/05/19	M	5 yrs PS	Remit 2 yrs		WO/213/30/12	
372 Coy CAHT	Dvr	Charles J	Field	14/05/19	M	5 yrs PS	Comm 1 yr HL		WO/213/30/12	
372 Coy CAHT	Dvr	Christian C	Field	14/05/19	M	5 yrs PS			WO/213/30/12	
372 Coy CAHT	Cpl	Davids J	Field	14/05/19	M	5 yrs PS			WO/213/30/12	
372 Coy CAHT	Dvr	de Vries J	Field	14/05/19	M	5 yrs PS			WO/213/30/12	
372 Coy CAHT	Dvr	Ferlander S	Field	14/05/19	M	5 yrs PS	Remit 2 yrs		WO/213/30/12	

Date D/M/Y	Name	Rank	Unit	Offence		Finding/Punishment	Amendment	Location	PRO Reference File/Piece/Page
372 Coy CAHT	Dvr	Fredericks A	Field	14/05/19	M	5 yrs PS			WO/213/30/12
372 Coy CAHT	Dvr	Free H	Field	14/05/19	M	5 yrs PS	Comm 2 yrs HL		WO/213/30/12
372 Coy CAHT	Dvr	Garadies J	Field	14/05/19	M	5 yrs PS	Comm 2 yrs HL		WO/213/30/12
372 Coy CAHT	Dvr	Gelant F	Field	14/05/19	M	5 yrs PS	Remit 2 yrs		WO/213/30/12
372 Coy CAHT	Dvr	Grove J	Field	14/05/19	M	5 yrs PS			WO/213/30/12
372 Coy CAHT	Dvr	Hendricks J	Field	14/05/19	M	5 yrs PS	Comm 2 yrs HL		WO/213/30/12
372 Coy CAHT	Dvr	Hendricks T	Field	14/05/19	M	5 yrs PS	Remit 2 yrs		WO/213/30/12
372 Coy CAHT	Dvr	Jacobs C	Field	14/05/19	M	5 yrs PS	Remit 2 yrs		WO/213/30/11
372 Coy CAHT	Dvr	Jacobs W	Field	14/05/19	M	5 yrs PS	Remit 2 yrs		WO/213/30/12
372 Coy CAHT	Dvr	January N	Field	14/05/19	M	5 yrs PS	Remit 2 yrs		WO/213/30/12
372 Coy CAHT	Dvr	Johnson P	Field	14/05/19	M	5 yrs PS	Remit 2 yrs		WO/213/30/12
372 Coy CAHT	Dvr	Julius A	Field	14/05/19	M	5 yrs PS	Comm 1 yr HL		WO/213/30/12
372 Coy CAHT	Dvr	King G	Field	14/05/19	M	5 yrs PS	Remit 2 yrs		WO/213/30/12
372 Coy CAHT	Dvr	Le Roux G	Field	14/05/19	M	5 yrs PS			WO/213/30/12
372 Coy CAHT	Dvr	Louw J	Field	14/05/19	M	5 yrs PS	Remit 2 yrs		WO/213/30/12
372 Coy CAHT	Dvr	Martin H	Field	14/05/19	M	5 yrs PS			WO/213/30/12
372 Coy CAHT	Dvr	Nicholson J	Field	14/05/19	M	5 yrs PS	Remit 2 yrs		WO/213/30/12
372 Coy CAHT	Dvr	Petersen J	Field	14/05/19	M	5 yrs PS	Remit 2 yrs		WO/213/30/12
372 Coy CAHT	Dvr	Rispel A	Field	14/05/19	M	5 yrs PS	Remit 2 yrs		WO/213/30/11
372 Coy CAHT	Dvr	Sababies J	Field	14/05/19	M	5 yrs PS			WO/213/30/11
372 Coy CAHT	Dvr	Schmidt J	Field	14/05/19	M	5 yrs PS	Remit 2 yrs		WO/213/30/11
372 Coy CAHT	Dvr	Slinger J	Field	14/05/19	M	5 yrs PS	Remit 2 yrs		WO/213/30/11
372 Coy CAHT	Dvr	Van Diemen F	Field	14/05/19	M	5 yrs PS	Comm 2 yrs HL		WO/213/30/11
372 Coy CAHT	Dvr	Wilmot E	Field	14/05/19	M	5 yrs PS	Remit 2 yrs		WO/213/30/11
ASC (SA)	Dvr	Adams A	Field	05/08/18	M+S40	18 mos HL			WO/213/24/129
ASC (SA)	Dvr	Adendorf M	Field	05/08/18	M+S40	9 mos HL			WO/213/24/129
S ASC	Native Leader	Africa Louis	Bissil BEA	31/01/16	M	2 yr HL			WO/213/8/132
ASC (SA)	Dvr	Barends K	Field	05/08/18	M+S40	9 mos HL			WO/213/24/129
ASC (SA)	Dvr	Cain G	Field	23/07/18	M	2 yrs HL			WO/213/24/168
ASC (SA)	Dvr	Danster D	Field	05/08/18	M+S40	1 yr HL			WO/213/24/129
ASC (SA)	Dvr	Du Plessie A	Field	05/08/18	M+S40	9 mos HL			WO/213/24/129
65 SAASC	Dvr	Fellows R	Field SEF	04/04/17	M+Insub+S9(1)	10 yrs PS			WO/213/15/5
S ASC	Native Leader	Inyani Willie	Bissil BEA	31/01/16	M	2 yr HL			WO/213/8/132
ASC (SA)	Dvr	Jaantyes M	Field	05/08/18	M+S40	1 yr HL			WO/213/24/129
ASC (SA)	Dvr	Jacobs CP	Field	23/07/18	M+Ins+Threat	Death	Comm 10 yrs PS		WO/213/24/168
ASC (SA)	Dvr	Jacobs J	Field	05/08/18	M+S40	9 mos HL			WO/213/24/129
ASC (SA)	Dvr	Jeremiah W	Field	23/07/18	M	5 yrs PS			WO/213/24/168
ASC (SA)	Dvr	Jonkers J	Field	05/08/18	M+S40	1 yr HL			WO/213/24/129
ASC (SA)	Dvr	Koert J	Field	23/07/18	M	2 yrs HL			WO/213/24/168
ASC (SA)	Dvr	Lewis W	Field	23/07/18	M	5 yrs PS	Comm 2 yrs HL		WO/213/24/168
ASC (SA)	Dvr Whlr	Lorenzo FS	Field	23/07/18	M	Life PS	Comm 5 yrs		WO/213/24/168
S ASC	Native Leader	Malefa W[illia]m	Bissil BEA	31/01/16	M	NG			WO/213/8/132
S ASC	Native Leader	Malleysi Pohl	Bissil BEA	31/01/16	M	NG			WO/213/8/132
ASC (SA)	Dvr	Maton J	Field	05/08/18	M+S40	9 mos HL			WO/213/24/129
ASC (SA)	Dvr	May M	Field	23/07/18	M	1 yr HL			WO/213/24/168
ASC (SA)	Dvr	Meadows J	Field	05/08/18	M+S40	9 mos HL			WO/213/24/129
ASC (SA)	Dvr	Mennik N	Field	23/07/18	M	5 yrs PS	Comm 2 yrs HL		WO/213/24/168
ASC (SA)	Dvr	Mettlekamp J	Field	05/08/18	M+S40	9 mos HL			WO/213/24/129
ASC (SA)	Dvr	Minto P	Field	23/07/18	M	5 yrs PS	Comm 2 yrs PS		WO/213/24/168
ASC (SA)	Dvr	Mullens C	Field	05/08/18	M+S40	9 mos HL			WO/213/24/129
ASC (SA)	Dvr	Nisagie J	Field	23/07/18	M	2 yrs HL			WO/213/24/168
ASC (SA)	Dvr	Peterson A	Field	23/07/18	M	6 mos HL			WO/213/24/168
ASC (SA)	Dvr	Peterson J	Field	05/08/18	M+S40	9 mos HL			WO/213/24/129
ASC (SA)	Dvr L/Cpl	Phillips K	Field	23/07/18	M	6 mos HL			WO/213/24/168
ASC (SA)	Dvr L/Cpl	Scholtz J	Field	23/07/18	M	2 yrs HL			WO/213/24/168
ASC (SA)	Dvr	Smith RW	Field	23/07/18	M	Life PS	Comm 5 yrs		WO/213/24/168
ASC (SA)	Dvr	Thomas W	Field	05/08/18	M+S40	18 mos HL			WO/213/24/129
ASC (SA)	Dvr	Uys E	Field	05/08/18	M+S40	1 yr HL			WO/213/24/129
ASC (SA)	Dvr	Williams H	Field	23/07/18	M	Life PS	Comm 5 yrs PS		WO/213/24/168
1 Cape Corps	Pte	Baatjes M	Mustapha	20/01/19	M+Disob	5 yrs PS	Quashed		WO/213/28/61
1 Cape Corps	Pte	Carolus F	Mustapha	18/01/19	M+Disob	28 dys FP1	Quashed		WO/213/28/61
1 Cape Corps	Pte	Williams J	Mustapha	18/01/19	M+Disob	10 yrs PS	Comm 3 mos FP1/Quashed		WO/213/28/61
SANLC	Pte	April	Field	21/11/17	M+S40	3 yrs PS	Comm 2 yrs HL		WO/213/31/109
SANLC	Pte	Bethuel	Field	21/11/17	M+S40	3 yrs PS	Comm 2 yrs HL		WO/213/31/109
SANLC	Pte	Elias	Field	21/11/17	M+S40	3 yrs PS	Comm 2 yrs HL		WO/213/31/109
SANLC	Pte	Frans	Field	21/11/17	M+S40	3 yrs PS	Comm 2 yrs HL		WO/213/31/109
SANLC	Pte	Hendrick	Field	21/11/17	M+S40	3 yrs PS	Comm 2 yrs HL		WO/213/31/109
SANLC	Pte	Jack	Field	21/11/17	M+S40	3 yrs PS	Comm 2 yrs HL		WO/213/31/109
SANLC	Pte	Jack	Field	21/11/17	M+S40	3 yrs PS	Comm 2 yrs HL		WO/213/31/109
SANLC	Pte	Jacob	Field	21/11/17	M+S40	3 yrs PS	Comm 2 yrs HL		WO/213/31/109
SANLC	Pte	Jacob	Field	21/11/17	M+S40	3 yrs PS	Comm 2 yrs HL		WO/213/31/109
SANLC	Pte	Jacob	Field	21/11/17	M+S40	3 yrs PS	Comm 2 yrs HL		WO/213/31/109

Date D/M/Y	Name	Rank	Unit	Offence		Finding/punishment	Amendment	Location	PRO Reference File/Piece/Page	Note
SANLC	Pte(L/Cpl)	Jim	Field	21/11/17	M+S40	3 yrs PS	Comm 2 yrs HL	WO/213/31/109		
SANLC	Pte(L/Cpl)	Johannes	Field	21/11/17	M+S40	3 yrs PS	Comm 2 yrs HL	WO/213/31/109		
SANLC	Pte	Klaas	Field	21/11/17	M+S40	3 yrs PS	Comm 2 yrs HL	WO/213/31/109		
SANLC	Pte	Mack	Field	21/11/17	M+S40	3 yrs PS	Comm 2 yrs HL	WO/213/31/109		
SANLC	Pte	Sam	Field	21/11/17	M+S40	3 yrs PS	Comm 2 yrs HL	WO/213/31/109		
SANLC	Pte	Simeon	Field	21/11/17	M+S40	3 yrs PS	Comm 2 yrs HL	WO/213/31/109		
SANLC	Pte	Mademedsha J	Capetown	17/12/17	M	10 yrs PS		WO/213/19/115		
SANLC	Cpl	Makubedi K	Capetown	17/12/17	M	12 yrs PS+Rnks		WO/213/19/115		
SANLC	Pte	Makuku J	Capetown	17/12/17	M	10 yrs PS		WO/213/19/115		
SANLC	Pte	Matume D	Capetown	17/12/17	M	10 yrs PS		WO/213/19/115		
SANLC	L/Cpl	Rapatele A	Capetown	17/12/17	M	10 yrs PS		WO/213/19/115		
SANLC	Pte	Rueben [?]	Capetown	17/12/17	M	10 yrs PS		WO/213/19/115		
SANLC	Pte	Sekgoba C	Capetown	17/12/17	M	10 yrs PS		WO/213/19/115		
SANLC	Pte	Wtsoane G	Capetown	17/12/17	M	10 yrs PS		WO/213/19/115		

Welsh

Date	Name	Rank	Unit	Offence		Finding/punishment	Amendment	Location	PRO Reference	
1 Royal Welsh Fus	Pte	Mason W	Ranikhet	24/07/20	M+Insol(L/Cpl)+S40	Death	5yrs PS	WO/90/8/194		
1 Royal Welsh Fus	Pte	Morris W	Ranikhet	26/07/20	M+Insol(Sgt)+S40	Death	5yrs PS	WO/90/8/194		
1/7 RW Fus	Pte(A/LCpl)	Cattell S	Field	01/02/19	M+S40	21 dys FP2		WO/213/29/27		
1/7 RW Fus	Pte	Thomas EL	Field	05/12/18	M+S40(6e)	NG		WO/213/27/171		
2/5 RWF(TF)	Pte	Hughes EH	16/08/15	Bedford	M	Dismissal+Rnks	Remit Dismissal	WO/86/66/80		
3 RWFs	Pte	Gardner JT	Kinmel Park	06/06/18	M+Disob	6 mos HL		WO/92/4/39		
3 RWFs	Pte	Goodwin J	Kinmel Park	06/06/18	M+Disob	6 mos HL	Comm to Detn	WO/92/4/39		
3 RWFs	Pte	Hughes J	Kinmel Park	06/06/18	M+Disob	NG+Acquit		WO/92/4/39		
3 RWFs	Cpl	Jeffreys A	Kinmel Park	06/06/18	M+Disob	NG+Acquit		WO/92/4/39		
3 RWFs	Pte	Morgan C	Kinmel Park	06/06/18	M+Disob	1 yr HL	Comm to Detn	WO/92/4/39		
3 RWFs	Pte	Trenholm AE	Kinmel Park	06/06/18	M+Disob	NG+Acquit		WO/92/4/39		
3 RWFs	Pte	Moore T	Kinmel Park	08/06/18	M+S40	2 yr Imp	Comm Detn	WO/92/4/40		
5/6 R Welsh Fus	Pte	Davies B	Field EEF	13/01/19	M+S40	90 dys FP2		WO/213/29/42		
5/6 R Welsh Fus	Pte	Dowse RJ	Field EEF	13/01/19	M+S40	90 dys FP2		WO/213/29/42		
5/6 R Welsh Fus	Pte	Ferrington F	Field EEF	13/01/19	M+S40	90 dys FP2		WO/213/29/42		
19 RW Fus	Pte	Lewis AJ	Rouen	04/02/19	M	5 yrs + 3mos PS		WO/90/8/58		
21 RWF	Pte	Morris DJ	Conway	10/01/16	M+AWOL	1 yr HL+Disch Igmny	Comm/Quashed	WO/86/68/85		
26 RW Fus	Pte	Davies W	Field	13/04/19	M+Striking	15 yrs PS	Remit 10 yrs	WO/213/29/177		
8 SWB	Pte	Edwards T	Field SEF	02/05/18	M+Disob	10 yrs PS	Comm 2 yrs HL	WO/213/22/30		
2/5 Welsh TF	Pte	Barr R	Cardiff	27/09/16	M	1 yr Detn		WO/86/66/194		
2/5 Welsh TF	Pte	Evers (Evens?) T	Cardiff	27/09/16	M	1 ytr Detn		WO/86/66/194		
2/5 Welsh TF	Pte	Leadbetter R	Cardiff	27/09/16	M	1 yr Detn		WO/86/66/194		
2/5 Welsh TF	Pte	Morris HF	Cardiff	27/09/16	M	1 yr Detn		WO/86/66/194		
2/5 Welsh TF	Pte	Russell J	Cardiff	27/09/16	M	2 yrs HL +Disch Igmny		WO/86/66/194		
4/5 Welsh Regt	Pte	Ellis T	Field EEF	13/01/19	M+S40	90 dys FP2		WO/213/29/42		
53 Welsh	Pte	Rosenwig M	Shoreham	25/01/19	M+S40	112 dys Detn		WO/86/86/103		
Welsh H (att 21 Rifle Bde)	2/Lt	Brodie JN	Alexandria	06/05/18	M+Drunk	Dism+Repr	NC	WO/90/8/18		
V/38 TMB	Gnr	Jenkins JH	Esquelbecq	10/01/17	M+Disob	3 yrs PS		WO/213/13/138		
V/38 TMB	Gnr	Jones JM	Esquelbecq	10/01/17	M+Disob	3 yrs PS		WO/213/13/138		
V/38 TMB	Gnr	Loud FC	Esquelbecq	10/01/17	M+Disob	3 yrs PS	Comm 1 yr HL	WO/213/13/138		
V/38 TMB	Gnr	Morgan WE	Esquelbecq	10/01/17	M+Disob	3 yrs PS		WO/213/13/138		
V/38 TMB	Gnr	Thomas D	Esquelbecq	10/01/17	M+Disob	3 yrs PS		WO/213/13/138		
V/38 TMB	Gnr	Jones P	Esquelbecq	11/01/17	M+S40	56 dys FP1		WO/213/13/138		

Chronological list of men charged with mutiny – Home

Date D/M/Y	Name	Rank	Unit	Offence	Finding/Punishment	Amendment	Location	PRO Reference File/Piece/Page	Note:
27/08/14	Bexon I	Pte	3 Leics	M	1 yr HL		Portsmouth	WO/213/2/1	1
27/08/14	Bray J	Pte	3 Leics	M	1 yr HL		Portsmouth	WO/213/2/1	
27/08/14	Castle J	Pte	3 Leics	M	1 yr HL		Portsmouth	WO/213/2/1	
27/08/14	Davis C	Pte	3 Leics	M	1 yr HL		Portsmouth	WO/213/2/1	
27/08/14	Hayward W	Pte	3 Leics	M	1 yr HL		Portsmouth	WO/213/2/1	
27/08/14	Hogg J	Pte	3 Leics	M	1 yr HL		Portsmouth	WO/213/2/1	
27/08/14	Jennings A	Pte	3 Leics	M	1 yr HL		Portsmouth	WO/213/2/1	
27/08/14	Morris J	Pte	3 Leics	M	1 yr HL		Portsmouth	WO/213/2/1	
27/08/14	Nix A	Pte	3 Leics	M	1 yr HL		Portsmouth	WO/213/2/1	
27/08/14	Robinson B	Pte	3 Leics	M	1 yr HL		Portsmouth	WO/213/2/2	
27/08/14	Stevenson J	Pte	3 Leics	M	1 yr HL		Portsmouth	WO/213/2/1	
27/08/14	Warner C	Pte	3 Leics	M	1 yr HL		Portsmouth	WO/213/2/2	
27/08/14	Wright M	Pte	3 Leics	M	1 yr HL		Portsmouth	WO/213/2/2	
29/12/14	Amey J	Pte	3 Dorsets	Joining M+Viol(Capt)	4 mos HL		Dorchester	WO/92/3/18	2
29/12/14	Anscombe J	Cpl	3 Dorsets	Joining M+Viol(Capt)	NG		Dorchester	WO/92/3/18	
29/12/14	Cattell J	L/Cpl	3 Dorsets	Joining M+Viol(Capt)	4 mos HL		Dorchester	WO/92/3/18	
29/12/14	Parsons A	Pte	3 Dorsets	Joining M+Viol(Capt)	4 mos HL		Dorchester	WO/92/3/18	
29/12/14	Wilson A	Cpl	3 Dorsets	Joining M+Viol(Capt)	6 mos HL		Dorchester	WO/92/3/18	
05/01/15	Marchmont J	Dvr	234 Bty RFA	M+Viol to Cpl+S40 +S10(3)	2 yrs HL + Disch Igmny		Cahir	WO/86/63/136	3
15/01/15	Rodbourne A	Gnr	234 Bty RFA	M+Insub(Cpl)+S40(2)	2 yrs HL+Disch Igmny		Cahir	WO/86/63/137	
15/01/15	Arlow J	Dvr A/Bdr	234 Bty RFA	M+S40+S10(3)	2 yrs HL+Disch Igmny		Cahir	WO/86/63/137	
15/01/15	Mayo J	Dvr	234 Bty RFA	M+S40+S10(3)	2 yrs HL+Disch Igmny		Cahir	WO/86/63/137	
15/01/15	Smith J	Pte	234 Bty RFA	M+Viol to Cpl+S40 +S10(3)	2 yr HL + Disch Igmny		Cahir	WO/86/63/136	
16/06/15	Phillips F	Pte	13 Glouster	Incit M+Insub(Maj) +Resist+Esc	3 yrs PS		Malvern Wells	WO/92/3/24	4
16/06/15	Denton AG	Pte	13 Glouster	Incit M+Viol(Sgt)	NG		Malvern Wells	WO/92/3/18	
17/06/15	Galloway P	Pte	13 Glouster	Incit M+Insub(Sgt)+ S40	3 yrs PS		Malvern Wells	WO/92/3/24	
17/06/15	Austin J	Pte (L/Cpl)	8 R I Fus	M	84 dys Detn		Tipperary	WO/86/65/77	5
23/06/15	Merton GA	Rfn	2/5 Sussex	Incit M+Esc Conf+S40	140 dys Detn		Canterbury	WO/92/3/18	6
23/07/15	Apted A	Pte	2/4 R Sussex TF JM		84 dys Detn		Canterbury	WO/92/3/20	
23/07/15	Archibald F	Pte	2/4 R Sussex TF JM		84 dys Detn		Canterbury	WO/92/3/20	
23/07/15	Aylwin J	Pte	2/4 R Sussex TF JM		84 dys Detn		Canterbury	WO/92/3/20	
23/07/15	Bailey A	Pte	2/4 R Sussex TF JM		84 dys Detn		Canterbury	WO/92/3/21	
23/07/15	Ball AT	Pte	2/4 R Sussex TF JM		84 dys Detn		Canterbury	WO/92/3/20	
23/07/15	Barnard G	Pte	2/4 R Sussex TF JM		84 dys Detn		Canterbury	WO/92/3/20	
23/07/15	Barnard J	Sgt	2/4 R Sussex TF NSM		Redu to Cpl		Canterbury	WO/92/3/21	
23/07/15	Batchelor E	Pte	2/4 R Sussex TF JM		84 dys Detn		Canterbury	WO/92/3/21	
23/07/15	Best T	Pte	2/4 R Sussex TF JM		NG		Canterbury	WO/92/3/21	
23/07/15	Blackman J	Pte	2/4 R Sussex TF JM		84 dys Detn		Canterbury	WO/92/3/21	
23/07/15	Boniface A	Pte	2/4 R Sussex TF JM		84 dys Detn		Canterbury	WO/92/3/24	
23/07/15	Bowley H	Pte(L/Cpl)	2/4 R Sussex TF NSM		28 dys Detn		Canterbury	WO/92/3/20	
23/07/15	Brennan S	Cpl	2/4 R Sussex TF NSM		Rnks		Canterbury	WO/92/3/20	
23/07/15	Brown W	Pte	2/4 R Sussex TF J[oin in] M		84 dys Detn		Canterbury	WO/92/3/21	
23/07/15	Browne JE	Pte	2/4 R Sussex TF J[oin in] M		84 dys Detn		Canterbury	WO/92/3/21	
23/07/15	Burt A	Pte	2/4 R Sussex TF J[oin in] M		84 dys Detn		Canterbury	WO/92/3/21	
23/07/15	Carey G	Pte	2/4 R Sussex TF J[oin in] M		84 dys Detn		Canterbury	WO/92/3/21	
23/07/15	Carter A	Pte(L/Cpl)	2/4 R Sussex TF NSM		28 dys Detn		Canterbury	WO/92/3/20	
23/07/15	Coote JW	Pte	2/4 R Sussex TF J[oin in] M		84 dys Detn		Canterbury	WO/92/3/21	
23/07/15	Cowley JW	Pte	2/4 R Sussex TF J[oin in] M		84 dys Detn		Canterbury	WO/92/3/21	
23/07/15	Cruttenden W	Pte	2/4 R Sussex TF J[oin in] M		84 dys Detn		Canterbury	WO/92/3/21	
23/07/15	Davey H	Pte(L/Cpl)	2/4 R Sussex TF NSM		28 dys Detn		Canterbury	WO/92/3/20	
23/07/15	Deacon PH	Pte	2/4 R Sussex TF J[oin in] M		84 dys Detn		Canterbury	WO/92/3/21	
23/07/15	Dennis H	Pte	2/4 R Sussex TF J[oin in] M		84 dys Detn		Canterbury	WO/92/3/21	

Date D/M/Y	Name	Rank	Unit	Offence	Finding/Punishment	Amendment	Location	PRO Reference File/Piece/Page	Note:
23/07/15	Drake AJ	Pte	2/4 R Sussex TF	J[oin in] M	84 dys Detn		Canterbury	WO/92/3/21	
23/07/15	Drury J	Pte	2/4 R Sussex TF	J[oin in] M	84 dys Detn		Canterbury	WO/92/3/21	
23/07/15	Eames J	Pte	2/4 R Sussex TF	J[oin in] M	84 dys Detn		Canterbury	WO/92/3/21	
23/07/15	Edwards J [aka E]	Pte	2/4 R Sussex TF	J[oin in] M	84 dys Detn		Canterbury	WO/92/3/21	
23/07/15	Elphick C	Pte	2/4 R Sussex TF	J[oin in] M	84 dys Detn		Canterbury	WO/92/3/21	
23/07/15	Faith T	Pte	2/4 R Sussex TF	J[oin in] M	NG		Canterbury	WO/92/3/21	
23/07/15	Farmer P	Sgt	2/4 R Sussex TF	NSM	Redu to Cpl		Canterbury	WO/92/3/20	
23/07/15	Faulkener H	Pte	2/4 R Sussex TF	J[oin in] M	84 dys Detn		Canterbury	WO/92/3/21	
23/07/15	Fennell H	Pte	2/4 R Sussex TF	J[oin in] M	84 dys Detn		Canterbury	WO/92/3/22	
23/07/15	Fennell S	Pte	2/4 R Sussex TF	J[oin in] M	84 dys Detn		Canterbury	WO/92/3/22	
23/07/15	Fennell W	Pte	2/4 R Sussex TF	J[oin in] M	84 dys Detn		Canterbury	WO/92/3/22	
23/07/15	Foster G	Pte	2/4 R Sussex TF	J[oin in] M	84 dys Detn		Canterbury	WO/92/3/21	
23/07/15	Fox AT	Pte	2/4 R Sussex TF	J[oin in] M	84 dys Detn		Canterbury	WO/92/3/22	
23/07/15	Gatterill D	Pte(L/Cpl)	2/4 R Sussex TF	NSM	28 dys Detn		Canterbury	WO/92/3/20	
23/07/15	Golby W	Pte	2/4 R Sussex TF	J[oin in] M	84 dys Detn		Canterbury	WO/92/3/22	
23/07/15	Hardwick T	Pte	2/4 R Sussex TF	J[oin in] M	84 dys Detn		Canterbury	WO/92/3/22	
23/07/15	[Harmer?] SW	Pte	2/4 R Sussex TF	J[oin in] M	84 dys Detn		Canterbury	WO/92/3/22	
23/07/15	Harris C	Pte	2/4 R Sussex TF	J[oin in] M	84 dys Detn		Canterbury	WO/92/3/22	
23/07/15	Hodges F	Pte	2/4 R Sussex TF	J[oin in] M	84 dys Detn		Canterbury	WO/92/3/22	
23/07/15	Holland W	Pte	2/4 R Sussex TF	J[oin in] M	84 dys Detn		Canterbury	WO/92/3/22	
23/07/15	Hutchinson H	Pte	2/4 R Sussex TF	J[oin in] M	84 dys Detn		Canterbury	WO/92/3/22	
23/07/15	Hyland RG	Pte	2/4 R Sussex TF	J[oin in] M	84 dys Detn		Canterbury	WO/92/3/22	
23/07/15	Ireland GJ	Pte	2/4 R Sussex TF	J[oin in] M	84 dys Detn		Canterbury	WO/92/3/22	
23/07/15	Lintott JR	Pte	2/4 R Sussex TF	J[oin in] M	84 dys Detn		Canterbury	WO/92/3/22	
23/07/15	Madgwick HJ	Pte	2/4 R Sussex TF	J[oin in] M	84 dys Detn		Canterbury	WO/92/3/22	
23/07/15	Marsh W	Pte	2/4 R Sussex TF	J[oin in] M	84 dys Detn		Canterbury	WO/92/3/22	
23/07/15	Martin F	Pte	2/4 R Sussex TF	J[oin in] M	84 dys Detn		Canterbury	WO/92/3/22	
23/07/15	McNorvill J	Pte	2/4 R Sussex TF	J[oin in] M	84 dys Detn		Canterbury	WO/92/3/23	
23/07/15	[Merrett?] H	Pte(L/Cpl)	2/4 R Sussex TF	NSM	28 dys Detn		Canterbury	WO/92/3/20	
23/07/15	Mitchell FW	Pte	2/4 R Sussex TF	J[oin in] M	84 dys Detn		Canterbury	WO/92/3/22	
23/07/15	Mitchell G	Pte	2/4 R Sussex TF	J[oin in] M	84 dys Detn		Canterbury	WO/92/3/22	
23/07/15	Napper T	Pte	2/4 R Sussex TF	J[oin in] M	84 dys Detn		Canterbury	WO/92/3/22	
23/07/15	Neve C	Pte	2/4 R Sussex TF	J[oin in] M	84 dys Detn		Canterbury	WO/92/3/23	
23/07/15	Newman JJ	Pte	2/4 R Sussex TF	J[oin in] M	NG		Canterbury	WO/92/3/22	
23/07/15	Page A	Pte	2/4 R Sussex TF	J[oin in] M	84 dys Detn		Canterbury	WO/92/3/23	
23/07/15	Page AJ	Pte	2/4 R Sussex TF	J[oin in] M	84 dys Detn		Canterbury	WO/92/3/23	
23/07/15	Pain J	Pte	2/4 R Sussex TF	J[oin in] M	84 dys Detn		Canterbury	WO/92/3/23	
23/07/15	Parsons J	Pte	2/4 R Sussex TF	J[oin in] M	84 dys Detn		Canterbury	WO/92/3/23	
23/07/15	Patching CW	Pte	2/4 R Sussex TF	J[oin in] M	84 dys Detn		Canterbury	WO/92/3/23	
23/07/15	Payne GW	Pte	2/4 R Sussex TF	J[oin in] M	84 dys Detn		Canterbury	WO/92/3/23	
23/07/15	Petter W	Pte	2/4 R Sussex TF	J[oin in] M	84 dys Detn		Canterbury	WO/92/3/23	
23/07/15	Phillimore H	Pte	2/4 R Sussex TF	J[oin in] M	84 dys Detn		Canterbury	WO/92/3/23	
23/07/15	Rosen J	Pte(L/Cpl)	2/4 R Sussex TF	NSM	28 dys Detn		Canterbury	WO/92/3/20	
23/07/15	Roser WG	Pte	2/4 R Sussex TF	J[oin in] M	84 dys Detn		Canterbury	WO/92/3/20	
23/07/15	Ross F	Pte	2/4 R Sussex TF	NSM	Redu to Cpl		Canterbury	WO/92/3/20	
23/07/15	Sayers C	Cpl(L/Sgt)	2/4 R Sussex TF	NSM	Rnks		Canterbury	WO/92/3/20	
23/07/15	Shoubridge T	Pte	2/4 R Sussex TF	J[oin in] M	84 dys Detn		Canterbury	WO/92/3/23	
23/07/15	Shrivell C	Pte(L/Cpl)	2/4 R Sussex TF	NSM	28 dys Detn		Canterbury	WO/92/3/20	
23/07/15	Smart WH	Pte	2/4 R Sussex TF	J[oin in] M	84 dys Detn		Canterbury	WO/92/3/23	
23/07/15	Snelling A	Pte	2/4 R Sussex TF	J[oin in] M	84 dys Detn		Canterbury	WO/92/3/23	
23/07/15	Somerville A	Pte	2/4 R Sussex TF	J[oin in] M	84 dys Detn		Canterbury	WO/92/3/23	
23/07/15	Stenning H	Pte	2/4 R Sussex TF	J[oin in] M	84 dys Detn		Canterbury	WO/92/3/23	
23/07/15	Thompson J	Pte	2/4 R Sussex TF	J[oin in] M	84 dys Detn		Canterbury	WO/92/3/23	
23/07/15	Townsend J	Pte(L/Cpl)	2/4 R Sussex TF	NSM	28 dys Detn		Canterbury	WO/92/3/20	
23/07/15	Treisler GW	Pte	2/4 R Sussex TF	J[oin in] M	84 dys Detn		Canterbury	WO/92/3/23	
23/07/15	[Tuislick?] TN	Pte	2/4 R Sussex TF	J[oin in] M	84 dys Detn		Canterbury	WO/92/3/23	
23/07/15	Vidler W	Cpl	2/4 R Sussex TF	NSM	Rnks		Canterbury	WO/92/3/20	
23/07/15	Vine JW	Pte	2/4 R Sussex TF	J[oin in] M	84 dys Detn		Canterbury	WO/92/3/23	
23/07/15	Waterman H	Pte	2/4 R Sussex TF	J[oin in] M	84 dys Detn		Canterbury	WO/92/3/24	
23/07/15	Weir W	Pte	2/4 R Sussex TF	J[oin in] M	84 dys Detn		Canterbury	WO/92/3/24	
23/07/15	Wheeler W	Pte	2/4 R Sussex TF	J[oin in] M	84 dys Detn		Canterbury	WO/92/3/24	
23/07/15	Willmott F	Pte	2/4 R Sussex TF	J[oin in] M	84 dys Detn		Canterbury	WO/92/3/24	
23/07/15	Wilson C	Pte	2/4 R Sussex TF	J[oin in] M	84 dys Detn		Canterbury	WO/92/3/24	
23/07/15	Winder T	Pte	2/4 R Sussex TF	J[oin in] M	84 dys Detn		Canterbury	WO/92/3/24	
23/07/15	Woodgate F	Pte	2/4 R Sussex TF	J[oin in] M	84 dys Detn		Canterbury	WO/92/3/24	
23/07/15	Woodietts H	Pte	2/4 R Sussex TF	J[oin in] M	84 dys Detn		Canterbury	WO/92/3/24	
23/07/15	Yates J	Pte	2/4 R Sussex TF	J[oin in] M	84 dys Detn		Canterbury	WO/92/3/24	
16/08/15	Hughes EH	Pte	2/5 RWF(TF)	M	Dismissal+Rnks	Remit Dismissal	Bedford	WO/86/66/80	7
06/09/15	Conway D	Pte	8 R Innis Fus	M+Inj pub property	1 yr HL		Eniskillen	WO/86/66/111	8
06/09/15	Finlan J	Pte	8 R Innis Fus	M+Inj pub property	1 yr HL		Eniskillen	WO/86/66/111	
06/09/15	Kirwan N	Pte	8 R Innis Fus	M+Inj pub property	1 yr HL		Eniskillen	WO/86/66/111	

Date D/M/Y	Name	Rank	Unit	Offence	Finding/Punishment	Amendment	Location	PRO Reference File/Piece/Page	Note:
06/09/15	McCabe J	Pte	8 R Innis Fus	M+Inj pub property	1 yr HL		Eniskillen	WO/86/66/111	
06/09/15	Murphy JJ	Pte	8 R Innis Fus	M+Inj pub property	1 yr HL		Eniskillen	WO/86/66/111	
06/09/15	O'Keefe P	Pte	8 R Innis Fus	M+Inj pub property	1 yr HL		Eniskillen	WO/86/66/111	
06/09/15	Wilson A	Pte	8 R Innis Fus	M+Inj pub property	1 yr HL		Eniskillen	WO/86/66/111	
08/10/15	Lewis H	Pte	3 Glocs	Mx2+Insub (Sgt)+S10(4)	2 yrs HL+Disch Igmny		Gravesend	WO/86/67/44	9
20/11/15	Ireland A	Pte(A/Cpl)	16 Rifle Bde	M+Disob(Capt)	5 yrs PS	Comm 1 yr Detn	Witley	WO/92/3/29	10
11/12/15	Goodman W	Gnr(A/Bdr)	163 (How) Bde RFA	M	1 month FP2+Rnks		Bulford	WO/86/68/23	11
23/12/15	Cole JH	Pnr	RE	Mx2	9 mos Detn	Quashed	Deganwy	WO/86/68/29	
23/12/15	Cook AJ	Spr	RE	Mx2	15 mos Detn	Remit 3 mos / Quashed	Deganwy	WO/86/68/29	
23/12/15	Costello C	Spr	RE	Mx2	2 yrs Detn	Remit 6 mos / Quashed	Deganwy	WO/86/68/29	
04/01/16	Field C	Rfn	3/21 London TF	M+Insub(Sgt)	1 yr Detn	Comm 6 mos Detn	Winchester	WO/86/68/180	12
10/01/16	Morris DJ	Pte	21 RWF	M+AWOL	1 yr HL+Disch Igmny	Comm/Quashed	Conway	WO/86/68/85	13
13/01/16	Peterkin J	Pte	3/6 Gordon H'ldrs (TF)	M+Viol(Sgt)+S40	6 mos Detn+Rnks		Hawick	WO/86/68/95	14
13/01/16	Jackson T	Dvr	33(R) Bty RFA	M+Viol(Cpl)	NG		Glasgow	WO/86/68/144	15
13/01/16	Marshall W	Dvr	33(R) Bty RFA	M+Viol(Cpl)	1 yr Detn		Glasgow	WO/86/68/161	
15/03/16	Poole FC	Pte	9 Middx	E P(ersuade) M+Disob	1 yr HL		Guildhall West	WO/92/3/34	16
15/03/16	Walker T	Pte	9 Middx	E P(ersuade) M+Disob	1 yr HL		Guildhall West	WO/92/3/34	
25/04/16	Clarkson A	Pte	4 HLI(att MGC)	NSM	1 dy Detn		Grantham	WO/92/3/38	17
25/04/16	Clarkson JR	Pte	4 HLI(att MGC)	NSM	1 dy Detn		Grantham	WO/92/3/38	
25/04/16	Kimmit R	Pte	3 HLI(att MGC)	M	3 yrs PS		Grantham	WO/92/3/37	
25/04/16	Korr J	Pte	3 HLI(att MGC)	M	3 yrs PS		Grantham	WO/92/3/37	
25/04/16	Logan T	Pte	3 HLI(att MGC)	M	3 yrs PS		Grantham	WO/92/3/37	
25/04/16	McCallam	Pte	3 HLI att MGC	NSM	1 dy Detn		Grantham	WO/92/3/38	
25/04/16	Pole J	Pte	3 HLI(att MGC)	NSM	1 dy Detn		Grantham	WO/92/3/38	
25/04/16	Taylor R	Pte	3 HLI(att MGC)	M	2 yrs Detn		Grantham	WO/92/3/37	
04/05/16	Coffie J	Gnr	2/3 Northern Bde		3 yrs PS+Disch Igmny		Bawtry	WO//92/3/39	18
04/05/16	Eland G	Gnr(A/Bdr)	2/3 Northern Bde AC/ RFA	JM	3 yrs PS+Disch Igmny		Bawtry	WO/92/3/39	
4/05/16	Gannon C	Gnr	2/3 Northern Bde AC/RFA	JM	3 yrs PS+Disch Igmny		Bawtry	WO/92/3/39	
04/05/16	Willis T	Dvr	2/3 Northern Bde AC/RFA	JM	3 yrs PS+Disch Igmny		Bawtry	WO/92/3/39	
25/05/16	Horan T	Dvr	25(R) Bty RFA	M+Insub(A/Sgt Maj)	2 yrs HL	Comm 1 yr Detn	Athlone	WO/86/70/46	19
03/06/16	O'Doherty D	Pte	3 Irish Gds	M	1 yr HL		Brentwood	WO/86/70/108	20
11/09/16	Alexander F	Dvr	69(EA)DAC(TF)	Joining M	Acquit		Killinghall Moor	WO/92/3/45	21
11/09/16	Nichols VP	Dvr	69(EA)DAC(TF)	Joining M	Acquit		Killinghall Moor	WO/92/3/45	
11/09/16	Reeve C	Pte	69(EA)DAC(TF)	Joining M	Acquit		Killinghall Moor	WO//92/3/45	
25/09/16	Stringer T	Dvr	523 Bty RFA	M	2 yrs Detn	Remit 18 mos	Ewshott Camp	WO/86/70/219	
27/09/16	Barr R	Pte	2/5 Welsh TF	M	1 yr Detn		Cardiff	WO/86/66/194	22
27/09/16	Evers (Evens?) T	Pte	2/5 Welsh TF	M	1 ytr Detn		Cardiff	WO/86/66/194	
27/09/16	Leadbetter R	Pte	2/5 Welsh TF	M	1 yr Detn		Cardiff	WO/86/66/194	
27/09/16	Morris HF	Pte	2/5 Welsh TF	M	1 yr Detn		Cardiff	WO/86/66/194	
27/09/16	Russell J	Pte	2/5 Welsh TF	M	2 yrs HL +Disch Igmny		Cardiff	WO/86/66/194	
16/11/16	Cash D	Pte	65 Coy RDC	CM+JM	1 yr Detn		Towcester	WO/92/3/55	23
16/11/16	Comyn A	Pte	58 Coy RDC	CM+JM	1 yr Detn		Towcester	WO/92/3/55	
16/11/16	Douglas G	Pte	65 Coy RDC	CM+JM	1 yr Detn		Towcester	WO/92/3/55	
16/11/16	Griffin M	Pte	65 Coy RDC	CM+JM	1 yr Detn		Towcester	WO/92/3/55	
21/11/16	Banbrough W	Pte	65 Coy RDC	M	1 yr Detn		Towcester	WO/92/4/3	
21/11/16	Beaman T	Pte	58 Coy RDC	M	1 yr Detn		Towcester	WO/92/4/1	
21/11/16	Biggin A	Pte	58 Coy RDC	M	1 yr Detn		Towcester	WO/92/4/2	

Date D/M/Y	Name	Rank	Unit	Offence	Finding/Punishment	Amendment	Location	PRO Reference File/Piece/Page
21/11/16	Boyce H	Pte	58 Coy RDC	M	1 yr Detn		Towcester	WO/92/4/1
21/11/16	Boyes JF	Pte	58 Coy RDC	M	1 yr Detn		Towcester	WO/92/4/1
21/11/16	Briggs A	Pte	58 Coy RDC	M	1 yr Detn		Towcester	WO/92/4/2
21/11/16	Broadmeadow W	Pte	58 Coy RDC	M	1 yr Detn		Towcester	WO/92/4/2
21/11/16	Brown J	Pte	65 Coy RDC	M	1 yr Detn		Towcester	WO/92/4/3
21/11/16	Brown JE	Pte	58 Coy RDC	M	1 yr Detn		Towcester	WO/92/4/1
21/11/16	Brown WH	Pte	65 Coy RDC	M	1 yr Detn		Towcester	WO/92/4/2
21/11/16	Burton EF	Pte	58 Coy RDC	M	1 yr Detn		Towcester	WO/92/4/1
21/11/16	Cain J	Pte	58 Coy RDC	M	1 yr Detn		Towcester	WO/92/4/1
21/11/16	Cameron J	Pte	58 Coy RDC	M	1 yr Detn		Towcester	WO/92/4/1
21/11/16	Campbell W	Pte	65 Coy RDC	M	1 yr Detn		Towcester	WO/92/4/2
21/11/16	Canning W	Pte	58 Coy RDC	M	1 yr Detn		Towcester	WO/92/4/1
21/11/16	Cassidy T	Pte	58 Coy RDC	M	1 yr Detn		Towcester	WO/92/4/1
21/11/16	Cattenach E	Pte	65 Coy RDC	M	1 yr Detn		Towcester	WO/92/4/3
21/11/16	Cherry JE	Pte	58 Coy RDC	M	1 yr Detn		Towcester	WO/92/4/1
21/11/16	Collins F	Pte	65 Coy RDC	M	1 yr Detn		Towcester	WO/92/4/2
21/11/16	Cree T	Pte	65 Coy RDC	M	1 yr Detn		Towcester	WO/92/4/3
21/11/16	Dixon WT	Pte	58 Coy RDC	M	1 yr Detn		Towcester	WO/92/4/1
21/11/16	Donnelly T	Pte	65 Coy RDC	M	1 yr Detn		Towcester	WO/92/4/3
21/11/16	Dowd P	Pte	65 Coy RDC	M	1 yr Detn		Towcester	WO/92/4/3
21/11/16	Downes LA	Pte	58 Coy RDC	M	1 yr Detn		Towcester	WO/92/4/2
21/11/16	Duncan FT	Pte	65 Coy RDC	M	1 yr Detn		Towcester	WO/92/4/3
21/11/16	Dwerryhouse J	Pte	65 Coy RDC	M	1 yr Detn		Towcester	WO/92/4/3
21/11/16	Elliot J	Pte	58 Coy RDC	M	1 yr Detn		Towcester	WO/92/4/1
21/11/16	Ellison E	Ptr	65 Coy RDC	M	1 yr Detn		Towcester	WO/92/4/2
21/11/16	Evans W	Pte	65 Coy RDC	M	1 yr Detn		Towcester	WO/92/4/2
21/11/16	Eves R	Pte	65 Coy RDC	M	1 yr Detn		Towcester	WO/92/4/3
21/11/16	Faircrough R	Pte	65 Coy RDC	M	1 yr Detn		Towcester	WO/92/4/2
21/11/16	Field WH	Pte	65 Coy RDC	M	1 yr Detn		Towcester	WO/92/4/3
21/11/16	Flynn P	Pte	58 Coy RDC	M	1 yr Detn		Towcester	WO/92/4/1
21/11/16	Foster JA	Pte	58 Coy RDC	M	1 yr Detn		Towcester	WO/92/4/2
21/11/16	Furlong J	Pte	65 Coy RDC	M	1 yr Detn		Towcester	WO/92/4/3
21/11/16	Gallimore G	Pte	58 Coy RDC	M	1 yr Detn		Towcester	WO/92/4/1
21/11/16	Garton F	Pte	58 Coy RDC	M	1 yr Detn		Towcester	WO/92/4/1
21/11/16	Graham JW	Pte	65 Coy RDC	M	1 yr Detn		Towcester	WO/92/4/2
21/11/16	Griffiths J	Pte	65 Coy RDC	M	1 yr Detn		Towcester	WO/92/4/2
21/11/16	Hague W	Pte	58 Coy RDC	M	1 yr Detn		Towcester	WO/92/4/1
21/11/16	Healy A	Pte	58 Coy RDC	M	1 yr Detn		Towcester	WO/92/4/1
21/11/16	Howell TH	Pte	65 Coy RDC	M	1 yr Detn		Towcester	WO/92/4/2
21/11/16	Hughes W	Pte	65 Coy RDC	M	1 yr Detn		Towcester	WO/92/4/3
21/11/16	Hutchinson JC	Pte	58 Coy RDC	M	1 yr Detn		Towcester	WO/92/4/1
21/11/16	Kelly C	Pte	65 Coy RDC	M	1 yr Detn		Towcester	File/92/4/3
21/11/16	Kelly P	Pte	65 Coy RDC	M	1 yr Detn		Towcester	WO/92/4/3
21/11/16	Kennedy M	Pte	58 Coy RDC	M	1 yr Detn		Towcester	WO/92/4/1
21/11/16	Kirby W	Pte	58 Coy RDC	M	1 yr Detn		Towcester	WO/92/4/1
21/11/16	Kirkham D	Pte	65 Coy RDC	M	1 yr Detn		Towcester	WO/92/4/2
21/11/16	Long D	Pte	58 Coy RDC	M	1 yr Detn		Towcester	WO/92/4/1
21/11/16	McCall E	Pte	65 Coy RDC	M	1 yr Detn		Towcester	WO/92/4/3
21/11/16	McCormack E	Pte	65 Coy RDC	M	1 yr Detn		Towcester	WO/92/4/2
21/11/16	McDowell T	Pte	65 Coy RDC	M	1 yr Detn		Towcester	WO/92/4/3
21/11/16	McEvoy D	Pte	65 Coy RDC	M	1 yr Detn		Towcester	WO/92/4/3
21/11/16	Mclaughlin J	Pte	65 Coy RDC	M	1 yr Detn		Towcester	WO/92/4/4
21/11/16	Moore T	Pte	65 Coy RDC	M	1 yr Detn		Towcester	WO/92/4/3
21/11/16	Morley J	Pte	65 Coy RDC	M	1 yr Detn		Towcester	WO/92/4/2
21/11/16	Naylor J	Pte	65 Coy RDC	M	1 yr Detn		Towcester	WO/92/4/2
21/11/16	O'Hara T	Pte	65 Coy RDC	M	1 yr Detn		Towcester	WO/92/4/3
21/11/16	Orr D	Pte	65 Coy RDC	M	1 yr Detn		Towcester	WO/92/4/2
21/11/16	Phillips R	Pte	58 Coy RDC	M	1 yr Detn		Towcester	WO/92/4/2
21/11/16	Pontefract JV	Pte	58 Coy RDC	M	1 yr Detn		Towcester	WO/92/4/1
21/11/16	Precious F	Pte	58 Coy RDC	M	1 yr Detn		Towcester	WO/92/4/2
21/11/16	Reid J	Pte	65 Coy RDC	M	1 yr Detn		Towcester	WO/92/4/2
21/11/16	Robinson G	Pte	58 Coy RDC	M	1 yr Detn		Towcester	WO/92/4/2
21/11/16	Rogers R	Pte	65 Coy RDC	M	1 yr Detn		Towcester	WO/92/4/2
21/11/16	Rowe T	Pte	58 Coy RDC	M	1 yr Detn		Towcester	WO/92/4/1
21/11/16	Ryan S	Pte	65 Coy RDC	M	1 yr Detn		Towcester	WO/92/4/3
21/11/16	Sandieson J	Pte	65 Coy RDC	M	1 yr Detn		Towcester	WO/92/4/3
21/11/16	Seymour J	Pte	58 Coy RDC	M	1 yr Detn		Towcester	WO/92/4/1
21/11/16	Sharp J	Pte	58 Coy RDC	M	1 yr Detn		Towcester	WO/92/4/1
21/11/16	Shields T	Pte	65 Coy RDC	M	1 yr Detn		Towcester	WO/92/4/2
21/11/16	Shields W	Pte	65 Coy RDC	M	1 yr Detn		Towcester	WO/92/4/3
21/11/16	Summers J	Pte	65 Coy RDC	M	1 yr Detn		Towcester	WO/92/4/3
21/11/16	Taylor FJ	Pte	65 Coy RDC	M	1 yr Detn		Towcester	WO/92/4/3
21/11/16	Thomson W	Pte	58 Coy RDC	M	1 yr Detn		Towcester	WO/92/4/1

Date D/M/Y	Name	Rank	Unit	Offence	Finding/Punishment	Amendment	Location	PRO Reference File/Piece/Page	Note:
21/11/16	Twist M	Pte	65 Coy RDC	M	1 yr Detn		Towcester	WO/92/4/3	
21/11/16	Williams F	Pte	65 Coy RDC	M	1 yr Detn		Towcester	WO/92/4/3	
21/11/16	Woods G	Pte	65 Coy RDC	M	1 yr Detn		Towcester	WO/92/4/2	
10/01/17	Allen GH	Gnr	337 Bde RFA	JM	6 mos Detn		Canterbury	WO/92/3/58	24
10/01/17	Barrington AV	Dvr	337 Bde RFA	JM	6 mos Detn		Canterbury	WO/92/3/58	
10/01/17	Bolton JH	Gnr	337 Bde RFA	JM	6 mos Detn		Canterbury	WO/92/3/58	
10/01/17	Burrows S	Gnr	337 Bde RFA	JM	6 mos Detn		Canterbury	WO/92/3/58	
10/01/17	Calver LT	Dvr	337 Bde RFA	JM	6 mos Detn		Canterbury	WO/92/3/58	
10/01/17	Fradley L	Gnr	337 Bde RFA	JM	6 mos Detn		Canterbury	WO/92/3/58	
10/01/17	Freestone SG	Dvr	337 Bde RFA	JM	6 mos Detn		Canterbury	WO/92/3/58	
10/01/17	Gray G	Gnr	337 Bde RFA	JM	6 mos Detn		Canterbury	WO/92/3/58	
10/01/17	Grocott JJ	Dvr	337 Bde RFA	JM	6 mos Detn		Canterbury	WO/92/3/58	
10/01/17	Hobbs C	Dvr	337 Bde RFA	JM	6 mos Detn		Canterbury	WO/92/3/58	
10/01/17	Jackson E	Dvr	337 Bde RFA	JM	6 mos Detn		Canterbury	WO/92/3/58	
10/01/17	Larrad AJ	Dvr	337 Bde RFA	JM	6 mos Detn		Canterbury	WO/92/3/58	
10/01/17	Shilton T	Dvr	337 Bde RFA	JM	6 mos Detn		Canterbury	WO/92/3/58	
10/01/17	Smith B	Dvr	337 Bde RFA	JM	6 mos Detn		Canterbury	WO/92/3/58	
10/01/17	Susans W	Dvr	337 Bde RFA	JM	6 mos Detn		Canterbury	WO/92/3/58	
10/01/17	Thomas W	Dvr	337 Bde RFA	JM	6 mos Detn		Canterbury	WO/92/3/58	
10/01/17	Towlson H	Dvr	337 Bde RFA	JM	6 mos Detn		Canterbury	WO/92/3/58	
10/01/17	Tucker W	Dvr	337 Bde RFA	JM	6 mos Detn		Canterbury	WO/92/3/58	
10/01/17	Whincop AG	Dvr	337 Bde RFA	JM	6 mos Detn		Canterbury	WO/92/3/58	
17/07/17	Lea E	Pte	68 Div Cyclist Co	M	6 mos Detn		Gt Yarmouth	WO/86/73/171	25
17/07/17	Hague T	Pte	68 Div Cyclist Co	M + Insub (S/Sgt)	NG		Gt Yarmouth	WO/86/73/171	
17/07/17	Turton H	Pte	68 Div Cyclist Co	M	NG		Gt Yarmouth	WO/86/73/171	
17/07/17	Dimelow J	Pte	68 Div Cyclist Co	M + Insub (L/Cpl)	NG		Gt Yarmouth	WO/86/73/171	
17/07/17	Hardy A	Pte	68 Div Cyclist Co	M + Insub (L/Cpl)	NG		Gt Yarmouth	WO/86/73/171	
17/07/17	Harrison JL	Pte	68 Div Cyclist Co	M + Insub (L/Cpl)	NG		Gt Yarmouth	WO/86/73/171	
17/07/17	Riley JJ	Pte	68 Div Cyclist Co	M + Insub (L/Cpl)	NG		Gt Yarmouth	WO/86/73/171	
12/04/17	Timmon F	Pte	15(TW) Worc	M+S40	9 mos Detn		Swindon	WO/86/75/125	26
21/05/17	Browning JB	Pte	54 TR Bn	M+Insub(Cplx2) +Wilful Inj Prop	2 yrs Detn+Stop	Remit 1 yr	Kirkcaldy	WO/86/76/98	27
31/05/17	O'Neil W	Pte	54 TR Bn	M+Insub(Cplx2)	2 yrs Detn	Remit 1 yr	Kirkcaldy	WO/86/76/98	
30/08/17	Phillips JE	Pte	Can Reserve Cavy	Mx2+S40(4)+S41	2 yrs HL		Shorncliffe	WO/86/78/8	28
03/09/17	Keith JT	Pte	4(R) CEF	M+Insub(Sgt)+S22	18 mos Detn		Bramshott	WO/86/78/5	
03/09/17	Edgar R	Pte	8 (R) CEF	Mx2+S40+S41	16 mos HL		Shorncliffe	WO/86/78/25	29
06/09/17	Cole FC	Pte	Can ASC	M+S40+S7(2)+S41	NG		Shorncliffe	WO/86/77/169	
06/09/17	Reid H	Pte	Can Reserve Cavy	Mx2+S40+S41	16 mos HL		Shorncliffe	WO/86/78/8	
11/09/17	Parker JL	Pte	Can Res Cavy	M+S40+S22+S41	[No entry - 1 yr Detn?]		Shorncliffe	WO/86/78/19	
11/09/17	Zotzman A	Pte	8(R) CEF	M+S40(3)	9 mos Detn	Quashed	Shorncliffe	WO/86/78/26	
11/09/17	McDonald EC	Pte	25(R) CEF	M+Absx2+S22	2 yrs Detn		Bramshott	WO/86/78/31	
14/09/17	Robinson F	Pte	4(R) CEF	M+Abs+S22+S40	1 yr Detn		Bramshott	WO/86/78/17	
21/11/17	Ackling W	Pte	Can ASC	M+Insub(Lieut)	42 dys Detn	Remit 15 dys	Bramshott	WO/86/79/54	30
21/11/17	Baker E	Pte	Can ASC	M+Insub(Lieut)	42 dys Detn	Remit 15 dys	Bramshott	WO/86/79/54	
21/11/17	Boskett J[V?]	Pte	Can ASC	M+Insub(Lieut)	42 dys Detn	Remit 10 dys	Bramshott	WO/86/79/53	
21/11/17	Cain W	Pte	Can ASC	M+Insub(Lieut)	42 dys Detn	Remit 15 dys	Bramshott	WO/86/79/53	
21/11/17	Calden J	Pte	Can ASC	M+Insub(Lieut)	42 dys Detn	Remit 15 dys	Bramshott	WO/86/79/53	
21/11/17	Connors H	Pte	Can ASC	M+Insub(Lieut)	42 dys Detn	Remit 15 dys	Bramshott	WO/86/79/53	
21/11/17	Desjarlais G	Pte	Can ASC	M+Insub	42 dys Detn	Remit 15 dys	Bramshott	WO/86/79/54	
21/11/17	Dunn PS	Pte	Can ASC	M+INsub(Lieut)	42 dys Detn	Remit 10 dys	Bramshott	WO/86/79/54	
21/11/17	Harris C	Pte	Can ASC	M+Insub(Lieut)	42 dys Detn	Remit 15 dys	Bramshott	WO/86/79/54	
21/11/17	Merritt SG	Pte	Can ASC	M+Insub(Lieut)	42 dys Detn	Remit 15 dys	Bramshott	WO/86/79/54	
21/11/17	Murchinson R	Pte	Can ASC	M+Insub(Lieut)	42 dys Detn	Remit 15 dys	Bramshott	WO/86/79/54	
21/11/17	Parks JJ	Pte	Can ASC	M+Insub	42 dys Detn	Remit 15 dys	Bramshott	WO/86/79/53	
21/11/17	Peacock A	Pte	Can ASC	M+Insub(Lieut)	42 dys Detn	Remit 15 dys	Bramshott	PRO/86/79/53	
21/11/17	Spence HA	Pte	Can ASC	M+Insub(Lieut)	42 dys Detn	Remit 15 dys	Bramshott	WO/86/79/53	
21/11/17	Statton T	Pte	Can ASC	M+Insub(Lieut)	42 dys Detn	Remit 15 dys	Bramshott	WO/86/79/53	
21/11/17	Stevens WA	Pte	Can ASC	M+Insub(Lieut)	42 dys Detn	Remit 15 dys	Bramshott	WO/86/79/53	
21/11/17	Weller E	Pte	Can ASC	M+Insub(Lieut)	42 dys Detn	Remit 15 dys	Bramshott	WO/86/79/53	
21/11/17	Young B	Pte	Can ASC	M+Insub(Lieut)	42 dys Detn	Remit 15 dys	Bramshott	WO/86/79/53	

Date D/M/Y	Name	Rank	Unit	Offence	Finding/Punishment	Amendment	Location	PRO Reference File/Piece/Page	Note:
08/01/18	Pitt FL	Pte	4 CEF	M+Desx2+Abs +Loss Pub Prop+S22	2 yrs Detn	Remit 1 yr Detn/ Quashed	Bramshott	WO/86/79/171	31
06/02/18	Dawson BE	Pte	3 W Yorks	M+Insub (CSM)	2yrs HL	Comm Detn	Wallsend	WO/86/80/96	32
06/02/18	Mannix J	Pte	3 W Yorks	M+Insub (CSM)	1 yr		Wallsend	WO/86/80/96	
11/02/18	Hutton A	Pte	25 CEF	M+Abs+Inj property* +S40(2)	112 dys Detn +Quashed*		Bramshott	WO/86/80/139	33
11/02/18	Pearson JH	Pte	25 CEF	M+Inj property*+S40(2)	112 dys Detn + Quashed*		Bramshott	WO/86/80/139	
11/02/18	Tobin JE	Pte	25 CEF	M+Inj property*+S40(2)	112 dys Detn +Quashed*		Bramshott	WO/86/80/139	
26/02/18	Hosker A	Pte	MG Gds	M+Absx2	2 yrs HL		London	WO/92/4/29	34
26/02/18	Kirby G	Pte	MG Gds	M+Absx2	6 mos Detn		London	WO/92/4/29	
02/03/18	Fortin J	Pte	4(R) CEF	M+Abs+S40x2	56 dys Detn	Quashed	Bramshott	WO/86/81/34	35
02/03/18	Ford T	Gnr (AL/Bdr)	RGA	M[S7(2)]+S40	42 dys Detn		Bettisfield	WO/86/80/178	
30/04/18	Beisly HL	Pte (3 AM)	RAF	M+Disob	9 mos HL		Swanage	WO/92/4/41	36
30/04/18	Dunse JE	Pte(2AM) (A/Cpl)	RAF	M+Disob	18 mos HL		Swanage	WO/92/4/41	
30/04/18	Little V	Pte (3AM)	RAF	M+Disob	9 mos HL		Swanage	WO/92/4/42	
30/04/18	Macdonald M	Pte(1AM) (A/Cpl)	RAF	M+Disob	18 mos HL		Swanage	WO/92/4/41	
30/04/18	Patton GL	Pte(2AM)	RAF	M+Disob	1 yr HL		Swanage	WO/92/4/41	
30/04/18	Whitewood HF	Pte(2AM)	RAF	M+Disob	9 mos HL		Swanage	WO/92/4/42	
02/05/18	Simpson A	Pte (3 Clerk)	RAF	M	Acquit		Swanage	WO/92/4/37	
02/05/18	Webber S	Pte(3AM)	RAF	M	Acquit		Swanage	WO/92/4/37	
02/05/18	Wilkinson A	Pte(2AM)	RAF	M	Acquit		Swanage	WO/92/4/37	
16/05/18	Chambers J	Pte	23 (R) CEF	M+Des+Abs +Loss of Prop +S40	90 dys Detn + Stoppages+G of Abs		Bramshott	WO/86/82/158	37
06/06/18	Gardner JT	Pte	3 RWFs	M+Disob	6 mos HL		Kinmel Park	WO/92/4/39	38
06/06/18	Goodwin J	Pte	3 RWFs	M+Disob	6 mos HL	Comm to Detn	Kinmel Park	WO/92/4/39	
06/06/18	Hughes J	Pte	3 RWFs	M+Disob	NG+Acquit		Kinmel Park	WO/92/4/39	
06/06/18	Jeffreys A	Cpl	3 RWFs	M+Disob	NG+Acquit		Kinmel Park	WO/92/4/39	
06/06/18	Morgan C	Pte	3 RWFs	M+Disob	1 yr HL	Comm to Detn	Kinmel Park	WO/92/4/39	
06/06/18	Trenholm AE	Pte	3 RWFs	M+Disob	NG+Acquit		Kinmel Park	WO/92/4/39	
08/06/18	Moore T	Pte	3 RWFs	M+S40	2 yr Imp	Comm Detn	Kinmel Park	WO/92/4/40	
25/06/18	Evans JA	Pte	1(R) MGC	M+S40	1 yr HL	Comm Detn	Grantham	WO/92/4/40	
25/06/18	McCallum D	Pte	2(R) MGC	M+S40	2yrs HL	Remit 1 yr/ Comm Detn	Grantham	WO/92/4/41	
01/07/18	Oxley W	Pte(L/Cpl)	2 Worc	M+S40	Acquit		Perham Down	WO/92/4/41	39
15/07/18	Bruce JR	Pte	1 Ont Regt	M+S40	18 mos HL+Stoppages		Bramshott	WO/92/4/43	40
15/07/18	Canning J	Pte	Quebec Regt CEF	M+S40	2 yrs HL +Stoppages		Bramshott	WO/92/4/43	
15/07/18	Falkenbury CH	Pte	1 Ont Regt	M+S40	2 yrs HL+Stoppages		Bramshott	WO/92/4/43	
15/07/18	Quenelle W	Pte	Alb Regt CEF	M+S40	2 yrs HL+Stoppages		Bramshott	WO/92/4/43	
15/07/18	Smith AE	Pte	Alb Regt CEF	M+S40	Acquit		Bramshott	WO/92/4/43	
11/09/18	Paterson P	Fitter	AFA	M+Absx2	1 yr Detn	NC	Fovant	WO/86/85/9	
17/09/18	Keefe A	Pte	334 Coy RDC	M+Disob	84 dys Detn	28 dys	Pembroke Dock	WO/92/4/52	
17/09/18	Smith S	Pte	334 Coy RDC	M+Disob	112 dys Detn	28 dys	Pembroke Dock	WO/92/4/52	
17/09/18	Taylor H	Pte	344 Coy RDC	M+Insub	112 dys Detn	28 dys	Pembroke Dock	WO/92/4/52	
17/09/18	Thomas W	Pte	334 Coy RDC	M+Disob	90 dys Detn	28 dys	Pembroke Dock	WO/92/4/52	
17/09/18	Walker H	Pte	334 Coy RDC	M+Disob	112 dys Detn	28 dys	Pembroke Dock	WO/92/4/52	
17/09/18	Watts A	Pte	344 Coy RDC	M+Disob	90 dys Detn	28 dys	Pembroke Dock	WO/92/4/52	
30/09/18	Bryant CWI	Pte	18 CEF	M+S40	6 mos HL		Seaford	WO/86/84/196	41
30/09/18	Cook JR	Pte	18 CEF	M+S40	9 mos HL		Seaford	WO/86/84/196	
30/09/18	Forsyth GH	Pte	18 CEF	M+S40	90 dys Detn		Seaford	WO/86/84/196	
30/09/18	McFarlane R	Pte	18 CEF	M+S40	1 yr HL		Seaford	WO/86/84/196	
04/10/18	Weallens JH	Pte	1(R) Gn HLI	M+Theft	6 mos Detn	NC	Glasgow	WO/86/85/9	42

Date D/M/Y	Name	Rank	Unit	Offence	Finding/Punishment	Amendment	Location	PRO Reference File/Piece/Page	Note:
09/10/18	Coats A	Pte	51 Beds	M+Theft+S40	28 dys Detn	NC	Teverham	WO/86/85/9	43
05/11/18	Fiander AE	Pte	MGC	M+S40	1 yr Detn		Grantham	WO/86/85/97	
16/11/18	Child S	Pte	6 Yorks	M+Insub(Sgt)	112 dys Detn		Kirkwall	WO/86/85/190	44
20/12/18	Birkett A	Pte (AL/Cpl)	5(R) L'pool	M+S40	6 mos Detn	Remit 2 mos	Pembroke Dock	WO/92/4/59	45
25/01/19	Rosenwig M	Pte	53 Welsh	M+S40	112 dys Detn		Shoreham	WO/86/86/103	46
28/01/19	Connor O	Pte	13(R) CEF	M+S7(4)	1 yr Detn		Kinmel Pk	WO/86/86/105	47
05/02/19	Derbyshire J	Pte	4(R) LN Lancs	M	1 yr Detn		Dublin	WO/86/86/129	48
21/02/19	Leet HJ	Cpl	23(R) CEF	M+Str+Drunk	5yrs PS+Rnks +Disch Igmny		Kinmel Park	WO/92/4/65	49
27/02/19	Smyth GH	Pte	Can ASC	M+S40(2)	2 yrs Detn		Witley	WO/86/87/14	50
27/02/19	Cardonia L	Pte	BWI	M	2 yrs HL+Disch Igmny		Plymouth	WO/86/87/23	51
28/02/19	Mayers C	Pte	9 BWI	M	2 yrs Detn		Plymouth	WO/86/87/17	
28/02/19	McCogg E	Pte	11 BWI	M	2 yrs Detn		Plymouth	WO/86/87/17	
28/02/19	Prescott B	Pte	10 BWI	M	2 yrs Detn		Plymouth	WO/86/87/17	
28/02/19	Spencer H	Pte	4 BWI	M	2 yrs Detn		Plymouth	WO/86/87/17	
28/02/19	Wilson F	Pte	Can ASC	M	6 mos Detn	Comm to 28 dys Detn	Bramshott	WO/86/87/17	52
28/02/19	Wright H	Pte	Can ASC	M	NG		Bramshott	WO/86/87/17	
16/04/19	Burton W	Pte	11(R) CEF	M+Viol	Acquit		Liverpool	WO/92/4/65	53
18/04/19	Clement F	Pte	20(R) CEF	M	18 mos HL		Liverpool	WO/92/4/69	
18/04/19	Sherstotoff F	Pte	Can For[estry] Corps	M+Striking	2 yrs HL		Liverpool	WO/92/4/69	
19/04/19	Brennan JP	Pte	6(R) CEF	M+S40	1 yr HL		Liverpool	WO/92/4/69	
19/04/19	Ingalls RA	Pte	12(R) CEF	M	Acquit		Liverpool	WO/92/4/65	
22/04/19	McLeod GAL	Pte(A/Cpl)	Can Res Arty	M	Acquit		Liverpool	WO/92/4/65	
22/04/19	Archie R	Pte	18(R) CEF	M	23 mos HL		Liverpool	WO/92/4/70	
22/04/19	Costughko V	Pte	12(R) CEF	M	90 dys Detn		Liverpool	WO/92/4/70	
22/04/19	Dickson A	Pte	3(R) CEF	M	23 mos HL		Liverpool	WO/92/4/70	
22/04/19	English M	Spr	Can Ry Troops	M	120 dys Detn		Liverpool	WO/92/4/70	
22/04/19	Mckenzie M	Spr	Can Ry Troops	M	Acquit		Liverpool	WO/92/4/70	
22/04/19	Wallace J	Pte	Can For Corps	M	90 dys Detn		Liverpool	WO/92/4/70	
28/04/19	Morrison JB	Pte(A/Cpl)	1(R) CEF	M	5 yrs PS		Liverpool	WO/92/4/70	
28/04/19	Simon R	Pte	Can For Corps	M	5 yrs PS		Liverpool	WO/92/4/70	
01/05/19	Crane J	Pte	Can For Corps	M	6 mos Detn		Liverpool	WO/92/4/69	
01/05/19	Houston JP	Pte	Can Res Arty	M	Acquit		Liverpool	WO/92/4/66	
02/05/19	Kosar R	Pte	21(R) CEF	M+S7(3b)	6 mos HL		Liverpool	WO/92/4/71	
02/05/19	Long GH	Pte	7 Can Rail Troops	M+S7(3b)	1 yr HL		Liverpool	WO/92/4/71	
02/05/19	Payne JA	Pte(A/Cpl)	8(R) CEF	M+S7(3b)	1 yr HL		Liverpool	WO/92/4/71	
02/05/19	Tuckman B	Pte	Can Fores(try) Corps	M+S7(3b)	6 mos HL		Liverpool	WO/92/4/71	
05/05/19	Gardiner GG	Pte	8(R) CEF	M	Acquit		Liverpool	WO/92/4/67	
05/05/19	Gauthier GF	Pte	13(R) CEF	M	Acquit		Liverpool	WO/92/4/67	
05/05/19	Jarvis CA	Pte	8(R) CEF	M	Acquit		Liverpool	WO/92/4/67	
05/05/19	Johnston J	Pte	11(R) CEF	M	Acquit		Liverpool	WO/92/4/66	
05/05/19	Lind CW	Pte	21(R) CEF	M	Acquit		Liverpool	WO/92/4/67	
05/05/19	Supple DR	Pte	Can Ry Troops	M	Acquit		Liverpool	WO/92/4/67	
05/05/19	Wirth J	Spr	Can Eng	M	Acquit		Liverpool	WO/92/4/67	
06/05/19	Evans E	Gnr	Can Res Arty	M	Acquit		Liverpool	WO/92/4/67	
06/05/19	Black T	Bdr	RFA	M	1 yr Detn+Rnks		Leeds	WO/92/4/69	54
06/05/19	Cole J	Bdr	RFA	M	2 yrs HL	Comm 1 yr Detn	Leeds	WO/92/4/69	
06/05/19	Lingfield G	Gnr	RFA	M	Acquit		Leeds	WO/92/4/69	
07/05/19	Edmondson RH	Pte	Can Res Cav Reg	M	5 yrs PS		Liverpool	WO/92/4/70	55
11/05/19	Souliere V	Pte	21 CEF	M+S40(2)	2 yrs HL+Disch Igmny		Witley	WO/86/87/169	56
12/05/19	Osborne H	Pte	21 CEF	M+S40	NG		Witley	WO/86/87/124	

135

Date D/M/Y	Name	Rank	Unit	Offence	Finding/Punishment	Amendment	Location	PRO Reference File/Piece/Page	Note:
12/05/19	Sampson WR	Pte	Can Res A[rty]	M+Res+Esc	30 dys Detn		Liverpool	WO/92/4/71	57
13/05/19	Harber G	Pte	Can R[eserve] C[avy]R[egt]	M+S7(3b)	10 mos HL	NC	Liverpool	WO/92/4/72	
13/05/19	Taylor A	Dvr	Can Res A[rty]	M	120 dys Detn	NC	Liverpool	WO/92/4/71	
14/05/19	Hughes D	Pte	11(R) CEF	M+L[eaving] Po[st]	90 dys Detn	NC	Liverpool	WO/92/4/72	
14/05/19	Marsh RE	Dvr	Can Res A[rty]	M+Res+Esc	10 mos HL		Liverpool	WO/92/4/71	
15/05/19	Massicote A	Pte	22 Quebec CEF	M	Acquit		Liverpool	WO/92/4/68	
19/05/19	Bertucci BG	Pte	1 Can IW Coy	M	Acquit		Liverpool	WO/92/4/68	
19/05/19	Gandy J	Cpl	11(R) CEF	M+S40	Rnks+1 yr HL		Liverpool	WO/92/4/72	
19/05/19	Henley RE	Pte	20(R) CEF	M+S7(3b)	3 yrs PS		Liverpool	WO/92/4/72	
19/05/19	Miculka V	Pte	21(R) CEF	M	10 yrs PS		Liverpool	WO/92/4/72	
20/05/19	Lamoureux AJ	Pte	20(R) CEF	M+S7(3b)	22 mos HL		Liverpool	WO/92/4/72	
21/05/19	Hamelin W	Pte	Can AMC	M+S40	Acquit		Liverpool	WO/92/4/74	
22/05/19	Weikel F	Pte	21(R) CEF	M+S7(3b)	22 mos HL		Liverpool	WO/92/4/71	
26/05/19	Scott J	Pte	Can F[orestry] C[orps]	M+S7(3b)	22 mos HL		Liverpool	WO/92/4/71	
27/05/19	Conley AL	Spr	3(R) Can Eng	M+Res	1 yr HL	Comm Detn	Liverpool	WO/92/4/72	
28/05/19	Hiba J	Spr	Can Rail T[roops]	M+XO(Lt Col)+XO(Lt)	7 yrs PS		Liverpool	WO/92/4/72	
28/05/19	Neason WB	Pte	23(R) CEF	M	Acquit		Liverpool	WO/92/4/69	
30/05/19	Dickson A	Pte	3(R) CEF	M+S7(3b)	3 yrs HL		Liverpool	WO/92/4/72	
02/06/19	Schmidt J	Pte	Can MG Depot	M+XO(Lt)+S7(3b)	22 mos Detn		Liverpool	WO/92/4/72	
02/06/19	Walsh WP	Spr	Can Eng	M	Acquit		Liverpool	WO/92/4/69	
15/06/19	Bundy HG	Pte	Lab Corps (att E Comm LB)	M+S7(3b)	Acquit		Sutton	WO/92/4/74	58
15/06/19	Chapman G	Pte	Lab Corps (att E Comm LB)	M+S7(3b)	Acquit		Sutton	WO/92/4/73	
15/06/19	Cobb A	Pte	Lab Corps (att E Comm LB)	M+S7(3b)	Acquit		Sutton	WO/92/4/73	
15/06/19	Diamond F	Pte	Lab Corps (att E Comm LB)	M+S7(3b)	Acquit		Sutton	WO/92/4/73	
15/06/19	Drew EG	Pte	Lab Corps (att E Comm LB)	M+S7(3b)	Acquit		Sutton	WO/92/4/73	
15/06/19	Fielder P	Pte	Lab Corps (att E Comm LB)	M+S7(3b)	Acquit		Sutton	WO/92/4/73	
15/06/19	Gambrill WJ	Pte	Lab Corps (att E Comm LB)	M+S7(3b)	Acquit		Sutton	WO/92/4/73	
15/06/19	Gillings WG	Pte	Lab Corps (att E Comm LB)	M+S7(3b)	Acquit		Sutton	WO/92/4/73	
15/06/19	Gough JW	Pte	Lab Corps (att E Comm LB)	M+S7(3b)	Acquit		Sutton	WO/92/4/73	
15/06/19	Grimmer FL	Pte	Lab Corps (att E Comm LB)	M+S7(3b)	Acquit		Sutton	WO/92/4/73	
15/06/19	Harrington WR	Pte	Lab Corps (att E Comm LB)	M+S7(3b)	Acquit		Sutton	WO/92/4/73	
15/06/19	Harris SJ	Pte	Lab Corps (att E Comm LB)	M+S7(3b)	Acquit		Sutton	WO/92/4/73	
15/06/19	Hart S	Pte	Lab Corps (att E Comm LB)	M+S7(3b)	Acquit		Sutton	WO/92/4/73	
15/06/19	Hawkins WJ	Pte	Lab Corps (att E Comm LB)	M+S7(3b)	Acquit		Sutton	WO/92/4/73	
15/06/19	Huxtable AR	Pte	Lab Corps (att E Comm LB)	M+S7(3b)	Acquit		Sutton	WO/92/4/74	
15/06/19	Norman AA	Pte	Lab Corps (att E Comm LB)	M+S7(3b)	Acquit		Sutton	WO/92/4/74	
15/06/19	Page AE	Pte	Lab Corps (att E Comm LB)	M+S7(3b)	Acquit		Sutton	WO/92/4/73	
15/06/19	Palmer TH	Pte	Lab Corps (att E Comm LB)	M+S7(3b)	Acquit		Sutton	WO/92/4/73	
15/06/19	Peacock W	Pte	Lab Corps (att E Comm LB)	M+S7(3b)	Acquit		Sutton	WO/92/4/74	
15/06/19	Pearl E	Pte	Lab Corps (att E Comm LB)	M+S7(3b)	Acquit		Sutton	WO/92/4/74	
15/06/19	Plumtree W	Pte	Lab Corps (att E Comm LB)	M+S7(3b)	Acquit		Sutton	WO/92/4/74	
15/06/19	Potter EC	Pte	Lab Corps (att E Comm LB)	M+S7(3b)	Acquit		Sutton	WO/92/4/73	
15/06/19	Reed T	Pte	Lab Corps (att E Comm LB)	M+S7(3b)	Acquit		Sutton	WO/92/4/74	
15/06/19	Roberts PC	Pte	Lab Corps (att E Comm LB)	M+S7(3b)	Acquit		Sutton	WO/92/4/73	
15/06/19	Roberts WH	Pte	Lab Corps (att E Comm LB)	M+S7(3b)	Acquit		Sutton	WO/92/4/73	

Date D/M/Y	Name	Rank	Unit	Offence	Finding/Punishment	Amendment	Location	PRO Reference File/Piece/Page	Note:
15/06/19	Rump S	Pte	Lab Corps (att E Comm LB)	M+S7(3b)	Acquit		Sutton	WO/92/4/74	
15/06/19	Seaborn N	Pte	Lab Corps (att E Comm LB)	M+S7(3b)	Acquit		Sutton	WO/92/4/74	
15/06/19	Skeels A	Pte	Lab Corps (att E Comm LB)	M+S7(3b)	Acquit		Sutton	WO/92/4/73	
15/06/19	Slowgrove AR	Pte	Lab Corps (att E Comm LB)	M+S7(3b)	Acquit		Sutton	WO/92/4/74	
15/06/19	Smith EN	Pte	20(R) CEF	M+S40	Acquit		Liverpool	WO/92/4/74	
15/06/19	Smith HG	Pte	Lab Corps (att E Comm LB)	M+S7(3b)	Acquit		Sutton	WO/92/4/73	
15/06/19	Snowden J	Pte	Lab Corps (att E Comm LB)	M+S7(3b)	Acquit		Sutton	WO/92/4/73	
15/06/19	Soames W	Pte	Lab Corps (att E Comm LB)	M+S7(3b)	Acquit		Sutton	WO/92/4/74	
15/06/19	Stapley LJ	Pte	Lab Corps (att E Comm LB)	M+S7(3b)	Acquit		Sutton	WO/92/4/74	
15/06/19	Stone F	Pte	Lab Corps (att E Comm LB)	M+S7(3b)	Acquit		Sutton	WO/92/4/73	
15/06/19	Taylor W	Pte	Lab Corps (att E Comm LB)	M+S7(3b)	Acquit		Sutton	WO/92/4/74	
15/06/19	Turner AE	Pte	Lab Corps (att E Comm LB)	M+S7(3b)	Acquit		Sutton	WO/92/4/74	
15/06/19	Waldron M	Pte	Lab Corps (att E Comm LB)	M+S7(3b)	Acquit		Sutton	WO/92/4/74	
15/06/19	Walsh MJ	Pte	Lab Corps (att E Comm LB)	M+S7(3b)	Acquit		Sutton	WO/92/4/73	
15/06/19	Whitelam G	Pte	Lab Corps (att E Comm LB)	M+S7(3b)	Acquit		Sutton	WO/92/4/73	
17/06/19	Chalmers G	Pte	3 Sea Hldrs	M+Insub	3 yrs PS+Dis Igmny	NC	Edinburgh	WO/92/4/74	59
04/07/19	Allam R	L/Bdr	RGA	M	9 mos Detn+Rnks +Disch Igmny		Aldershot	WO/86/87/188	60
04/07/19	Bains VG	L/Bdr	RGA	M	9 mos Detn+Rnks +Disch Igmny		Aldershot	WO/86/87/188	
04/07/19	Biddulph P	Cpl	RGA	M	9 mos Detn+Rnks +Disch Igmny		Aldershot	WO/86/87/188	
04/07/19	Burton W	L/Bdr	RGA	M	9 mos Detn+Rnks +Disch Igmny		Aldershot	WO/86/87/188	
04/07/19	Butterworth F	Bdr	RGA	M	9 mos Detn+Rnks +Disch Igmny		Aldershot	WO/86/87/188	
04/07/19	Coleman A	L/Bdr	RGA	M	9 mos Detn+Rnks +Disch Igmny		Aldershot	WO/86/87/188	
04/07/19	Cox SG	Bdr	RGA	M	9 mos Detn+Rnks +Disch Igmny		Aldershot	WO/86/87/188	
04/07/19	Cresswell E	Cpl	RGA	M	9 mos Detn+Rnks +Disch Igmny		Aldershot	WO/86/87/188	
04/07/19	Dixon SR	Bdr	RGA	M	9 mos Detn+Rnks +Disch Igmny		Aldershot	WO/86/87/188	
04/07/19	Doggrell L	L/Bdr	RGA	M	9 mos Detn+Rnks +Disch Igmny		Aldershot	WO/86/87/188	
04/07/19	Ford ES	Cpl	RGA	M	9 mos Detn+Rnks +Disch Igmny		Aldershot	WO/86/87/188	
04/07/19	Glanister J	L/Bdr	RGA	M	9 mos Detn+Rnks +Disch Igmny		Aldershot	WO/86/87/188	
04/07/19	Glass H	L/Bdr	RGA	M	9 mos Detn+Rnks +Disch Igmny		Aldershot	WO/86/87/188	
04/07/19	Green J	Cpl	RGA	M	9 mos Detn+Rnks +Disch Igmny		Aldershot	WO/86/87/188	
04/07/19	Manley C	L/Bdr	RGA	M	9 mos Detn+Rnks +Disch Igmny		Aldershot	WO/86/87/188	
04/07/19	Newman L	Gnr	RGA	M	9 mos Detn +Disch Igmny		Aldershot	WO/86/87/189	
04/07/19	Norrish W	Cpl	RGA	M	9 mos Detn+Rnks +Disch Igmny		Aldershot	WO/86/87/188	
04/07/19	O'Shea J	Bdr	RGA	M	9 mos Detn+Rnks +Disch Igmny		Aldershot	WO/86/87/188	
04/07/19	Peacock A	Bdr	RGA	M	9 mos Detn+Rnks +Disch Igmny		Aldershot	WO/86/87/188	
04/07/19	Randell G	L/Bdr	RGA	M	9 mos Detn+Rnks +Disch Igmny		Aldershot	WO/86/87/188	

Date D/M/Y	Name	Rank	Unit	Offence	Finding/Punishment	Amendment	Location	PRO Reference File/Piece/Page	Note:
04/07/19	Roberts J	Bdr	RGA	M	9 mos Detn+Rnks +Disch Igmny		Aldershot	WO/86/87/188	
04/07/19	Street V	L/Bdr	RGA	M	9 mos Detn+Rnks +Disch Igmny		Aldershot	WO/86/87/188	
04/07/19	Swatridge G	Cpl	RGA	M	9 mos Detn+Rnks +Disch Igmny		Aldershot	WO/86/87/188	
04/07/19	Synnott P	Bdr	RGA	M	9 mos Detn+Rnks +Disch Igmny		Aldershot	WO/86/87/188	
04/07/19	Taffe J	L/Bdr	RGA	M	9 mos Detn+Rnks +Disch Igmny		Aldershot	WO/86/87/188	
04/07/19	Warn A	L/Bdr	RGA	M	9 mos Detn+Rnks +Disch Igmny		Aldershot	WO/86/87/188	
04/07/19	Whitehall J	L/Bdr	RGA	M	9 mos Detn+Rnks +Disch Igmny		Aldershot	WO/86/87/188	
04/07/19	Woodman C	L/Bdr	RGA	M	9 mos Detn+Rnks +Disch Igmny		Aldershot	WO/86/87/189	
05/07/19	Banwell WJ	Cpl	RGA	M	9 mos Detn+Rnks +Disch Igmny		Aldershot	WO/86/87/189	
05/07/19	Doyle P	L/Bdr	RGA	M	9 mos Detn+Rnks +Disch Igmny		Aldershot	WO/86/87/189	
05/07/19	Elliott F	Cpl	RGA	M	9 mos Detn+Rnks		Aldershot	WO/86/88/1	
05/07/19	Fenwick JL	L/Bdr	RGA	M	9 mos Detn+ Rnks		Aldershot	WO/86/88/1	
05/07/19	Fletcher C	L/Bdr	RGA	M	9 mos Detn+Rnks		Aldershot	WO/86/88/1	
05/07/19	Fox H	Cpl	RGA	M	9 mos Detn+Rnks +Disch Igmny		Aldershot	WO/86/87/189	
05/07/19	Froude J	Bdr	RGA	M	NG		Aldershot	WO/86/87/189	
05/07/19	Hidden E	Bdr	RGA	M	9 mos Detn+Rnks +Disch Igmny		Aldershot	WO/86/87/189	
05/07/19	Hooper W	L/Bdr	RGA	M	9 mos Detn+ Rnks		Aldershot	WO/86/88/1	
05/07/19	Hutchinson H	L/Bdr	RGA	M	9 mos Detn+ Rnks		Aldershot	WO/86/88/1	
05/07/19	Jenkins E	L/Bdr	RGA	M	9 mos Detn+ Rnks		Aldershot	WO/86/88/1	
05/07/19	Lawler W	Bdr	RGA	M	9 mos Detn+Rnks		Aldershot	WO/86/88/1	
05/07/19	Lemon S	Gnr	RGA	M	2 yrs HL+Disch Igmny		Aldershot	WO/86/88/1	
05/07/19	Limington F	L/Bdr	RGA	M	9 mos Detn+Rnks		Aldershot	WO/86/88/1	
05/07/19	Mann HG	L/Bdr	RGA	M	9 mos Detn+Rnks		Aldershot	WO/86/88/1	
05/07/19	McCarthy J	L/Bdr	RGA	M	9 mos Detn+Rnks +Disch Igmny		Aldershot	WO/86/87/189	
05/07/19	McRoberts H	L/Bdr	RGA	M	9 mos Detn+ Rnks		Aldershot	WO/86/88/1	
05/07/19	Moore WJ	AL/Bdr	RGA	M	9 mos Detn+Rnks +Disch Igmny		Aldershot	WO/86/87/189	
05/07/19	Neale G	Cpl	RGA	M	9 mos Detn+Rnks		Aldershot	WO/86/88/1	
05/07/19	Nolan J	Bdr	RGA	M	9 mos Detn+Rnks +Disch Igmny		Aldershot	WO/86/87/189	
05/07/19	O'Rourke C	Bdr	RGA	M	NG		Aldershot	WO/86/88/1	
05/07/19	Phillips R	Gnr	RGA	M	NG		Aldershot	WO/86/88/1	
05/07/19	Pollentine G	L/Bdr	RGA	M	9 mos Detn+Rnks		Aldershot	WO/86/87/189	
05/07/19	Powell R	L/Bdr	RGA	M	9 mos Detn+Rnks +Disch Igmny		Aldershot	WO/86/87/189	
05/07/19	Redding G	Bdr	RGA	M	9 mos Detn+Rnks		Aldershot	WO/86/88/1	
05/07/19	Roast J	Cpl	RGA	M	9 mos Detn+Rnks		Aldershot	WO/86/88/1	
05/07/19	Solari L	L/Bdr	RGA	M	9 mos Detn+Rnks +Disch Igmny		Aldershot	WO/86/87/189	
05/07/19	Thompson J	Cpl	RGA	M	9 mos Detn+Rnks +Disch Igmny		Aldershot	WO/86/87/189	
05/07/19	White A	Bdr	RGA	M	9 mos Detn+Rnks +Disch Igmny		Aldershot	WO/86/87/189	
05/07/19	Wood R	Bdr	RGA	M	NG		Aldershot	WO/86/88/1	
05/07/19	Woods H	L/Bdr	RGA	M	9 mos Detn+Rnks +Disch Igmny		Aldershot	WO/86/87/189	
05/07/19	Young C	L/Bdr	RGA	M	9 mos Detn+Rnks +Disch Igmny		Aldershot	WO/86/87/189	
08/07/19	Bennett H	Gnr	RGA	M	9 mos Detn +Disch Igmny		Aldershot	WO/86/87/189	
08/07/19	Childs FC	AL/Bdr	RGA	M	9 mos Detn+Rnks +Disch Igmny		Aldershot	WO/86/87/189	
08/07/19	Cox T	L/Bdr	RGA	M	9 mos Detn+Rnks +Disch Igmny		Aldershot	WO/86/87/189	
08/07/19	Hardy D	Bdr	RGA	M	9 mos Detn+Rnks +Disch Igmny		Aldershot	WO/86/87/189	
08/07/19	Osmond OG	Bdr	RGA	M	9 mos Detn+Rnks +Disch Igmny		Aldershot	WO/86/87/189	
08/07/19	Tailby J	Bdr	RGA	M	9 mos Detn+Rnks +Disch Igmny		Aldershot	WO/86/87/189	

Date D/M/Y	Name	Rank	Unit	Offence	Finding/Punishment	Amendment	Location	PRO Reference File/Piece/Page	Note:
08/07/19	Warren WC	Bdr (A/LCpl)	RGA	M	9 mos Detn + Rnks + Disch Igmny		Aldershot	WO/86/87/189	
08/07/19	Weldon E	Gnr	RGA	M	9 mos Detn		Aldershot	WO/86/87/189	
11/07/19	Penneall AA	Pte	Quebec Regt	M+S7(3b)+S40	1 yr HL		Ripon	WO/86/88/54	61
12/07/19	Beatty L	Pte	Quebec Regt	M+S7(3b)	18 mos HL		Ripon	WO/86/88/29	
14/07/19	Greenhalgh E	Pte	Quebec Regt	M+S7(3b)	18 mos HL		Ripon	WO/86/88/29	
15/07/19	White R	Pte	CARD	M+S40	20 mos Imp	Comm to Detn	Witley	WO/86/88/19	
15/07/19	Shanks AG	Pte	Quebec Regt	M	NG		Ripon	WO/86/88/41	
16/07/19	Gareau A	Pte	Quebec Regt	M	20 mos + Disch Igmny		Ripon	WO/86/88/51	
17/07/19	Desjardins E	Pte	Quebec Regt	M	NG		Ripon	WO/86/88/12	
18/07/19	Sickles W	Pte	Quebec Regt	S7(3b)[M]	6 mos Detn		Ripon	WO/86/88/51	
18/07/19	Thompson AW	Pte	Quebec Regt	M+S7(3b)	18 mos HL		Ripon	WO/86/88/29	
21/07/19	McCann J	Pte	Quebec Regt	Mx2+S7[3]b+S40	2 yrs HL+Disch Igmny		Ripon	WO/86/88/52	
22/07/19	McMillan B	Pte	Quebec Regt	M+S7(3b)	20 mos HL + Disch Igmny		Ripon	WO/86/88/52	
22/07/19	Morneau L	Pte	Quebec Regt	M	NG		Ripon	WO/86/88/42	
23/07/19	Broom C	Pte	Quebec Regt	M+S7(3b)	22 mos HL + Disch Igmny		Ripon	WO/86/88/54	
23/07/19	DeLobbe A	Pte	Quebec Regt	M+S7(3b)+S40	22 mos HL + Disch Igmny		Ripon	WO/86/88/51	
24/07/19	Luckay WW	Pte	Quebec Regt	M+S7(3b)	2 yrs HL+Disch Igmny		Ripon	WO/86/88/51	
24/07/19	O'Brien WO	Pte	Quebec Regt	M+S7(3b)M+S40	6 mos Detn		Ripon	WO/86/88/51	
25/07/19	Littlefield GW	Pte	Quebec Regt	M+S7(3b)	2 yrs HL+Disch Igmny		Ripon	WO/86/88/51	
26/07/19	Anley H	Pte	Quebec Regt	M+S7(3b)+S40	6 mos Detn		Ripon	WO/86/88/51	
26/07/19	Varieur EL	Pte	Quebec Regt	M	2 yrs HL+Disch Igmny		Ripon	WO/86/88/51	
28/07/19	Chouinard WA	Pte	Quebec Regt	M+S40	NG		Ripon	WO/86/88/42	
29/07/19	Hudson E	Pte	2 Y[orks] & Lancs	M+S40	NG		Clipstone	WO/86/88/50	
30/07/19	Riley B	Pte	Quebec Regt	M+S7(3b)	6 mos Detn		Ripon	WO/86/88/51	62
30/07/19	Taylor JN	Pte	8(R) CEF	M	Not Guilty		Witley	W)/86/88/30	
31/07/19	Adams EA	Pte	Quebec Regt	M+S7(3b)	1 yr HL+Disch Igmny		Ripon	WO/86/88/51	
01/08/19	Calvert F	Pte	3 W Yorks	M+S40	18 mos HL + Disch Igmny	9 mos	Devizes	WO/92/4/77	63
01/08/19	Faulkner JR	Pte	3 W Yorks	M+S40	18 mos HL + Disch Igmny	9 mos	Devizes	WO/92/4/77	
01/08/19	Gillett C	Pte	3 W Yorks	M+S40	18 mos HL Igmny	9 mos	Devizes	WO/92/4/77	
01/08/19	Hardcastle W	Pte	3 W Yorks	M+S40	18 mos HL + Disch Igmny	9 mos	Devizes	WO/92/4/76	
01/08/19	Hodgson JW	Pte	3 W Yorks	M+S40	21 mos HL + Disch Igmny	12 mos	Devizes	WO/92/4/76	
01/08/19	Hudson CE	Pte	3 W Yorks	M+S40	18 mos HL + Disch Igmny	9 mos	Devizes	WO/92/4/76	
01/08/19	Lee CH	Pte	3 W Yorks	M+S40	18 mos + Disch Igmny	9 mos	Devizes	WO/92/4/76	
01/08/19	McCabe J	Pte	3 W Yorks	M+S40	18 mos+HL Igmny	9 mos	Devizes	WO/92/4/77	
01/08/19	Mundell J	Pte	3 W Yorks	M+S40	18 mos HL Igmny	9 mos	Devizes	WO/92/4/77	
01/08/19	Payne WE	Pte	3 W Yorks	M+S40	18 mos HL + Disch Igmny	9 mos	Devizes	WO/92/4/76	
01/08/19	Phillis W	Pte	3 W Yorks	M+S40	18 mos HL + Disch Igmny	9 mos	Devizes	WO/92/4/76	
01/08/19	Prior G	Pte	3 W Yorks	M+S40	1 yr HL+Disch Igmny	3 mos	Devizes	WO/92/4/77	
01/08/19	Robinson E	Pte	3 W Yorks	M+S40[M]	18 mos HL + Disch Igmny	9 mos	Devizes	WO/92/4/76	
01/08/19	Roe F	Pte	3 W Yorks	M	Acquit		Devizes	WO/92/4/75	
01/08/19	Schofield S	Pte	3 W Yorks	M+S40	18 mos HL + Disch Igmny	9 mos	Devizes	WO/92/4/77	
01/08/19	Tetley JW	Pte	3 W Yorks	M+S40	18 mos HL + Disch Igmny	9 mos	Devizes	WO/92/4/77	
01/08/19	Warnes EE	Pte	3 W Yorks	M+S40	18 mos HL + Disch Igmny	9 mos	Devizes	WO/92/4/76	
01/08/19	Kelly T	Pte	Quebec Regt	M+7(3b)	2 yr HL+Disch Igmny		Ripon	WO/86/88/53	64
02/08/19	Belmore T	Pte	Quebec Regt	M+7(3b)+Abs+S22	1 yr Detn		Ripon	WO/86/88/53	
02/08/19	Dancause T	Pte	Quebec Regt	M+S40	NG		Ripon	WO/86/88/42	
05/08/19	Bureau H	Cpl	Quebec Regt	M+7(3b)	2 yr HL+Rnks + Disch Igmny		Ripon	WO/86/88/53	
07/08/19	Munroe D	Pnr	RE	M+S40	18 mos HL + Disch Igmny	NC	Bordon	WO/92/4/77	
07/08/19	Rees TR	Spr	RE	M+S40	1 yr Detn	9 mos	Bordon	WO/92/4/77	
08/08/19	Elston A	Spr	RE	M+S40	18 mos Detn	15 mos	Bordon	WO/92/4/77	

Date D/M/Y	Name	Rank	Unit	Offence	Finding/Punishment	Amendment	Location	PRO Reference File/Piece/Page	Note:
08/08/19	Raines J	Spr	RE	M+S40	2 yrs HL+Disch Igmny	15 mos	Bordon	WO/92/4/77	
08/08/19	Self TE	Pnr	RE	M+Disob (CSM)+Res+Esc+S40)	2 yrs HL +Disch Igmny	15 mos	Bordon	WO/92/4/77	
09/08/19	Munro DS	Pte	Can O[rdnance] Corps	M+S40	6 mos Detn		Witley	WO/86/88/44	
11/08/19	Warr B	Pte	5 Worc	M+S40	Acquit		Dublin	WO/92/4/76	65
18/08/19	Macdonald H	Dvr	RFA	M+S40	1 yr Detn		Warlingham	WO/92/4/78	
22/09/19	Bernstein AP	Pte	5 Dragoon Gds	M	1 yr HL+Disch Igmny	Comm 6 mos Detn Curragh		WO/92/4/84	66
22/09/19	Biram F	Pte	5 Dragoon Gds	M	1 yr HL+Disch Igmny	Comm 1 yr Detn Curragh		WO/92/4/81	
22/09/19	Bostock A	Pte	5 Dragoon Gds	M	1 yr HL+Disch gmny	Comm 6 mos Detn Curragh		WO/92/4/83	
22/09/19	Bowker J	Pte	5 Dragoon Gds	M	1 yr HL+Disch Igmny	Comm 6 mos Detn Curragh		WO/92/4/81	
22/09/19	Brown M	Pte	K Edw Horse	M	1 yr HL+Disch Igmny	Comm 6 mos Detn Curragh		WO/92/3/84	
22/09/19	Coley T	Pte	5 Dragoon Gds	M	1 yr HL+Disch Igmny	Comm 6 mos Detn Curragh		WO/92/4/83	
22/09/19	Davies WA	Pte	5 Dragoon Gds	M	1 yr HL+Disch Igmny	Comm 6 mos Detn Curragh		WO/92/4/81	
22/09/19	Duncan A	Pte	5 Dragoon Gds	M	1 yr HL+Disch Igmny	Comm 6 mos Detn Curragh		WO/92/3/84	
22/09/19	Elliott JW	Pte	5 Dragoon Gds	M	1 yr HL+Disch Igmny	Comm 6 mos Detn Curragh		WO/92/4/84	
22/09/19	Garner VJ	Pte	5 Dragoon Gds	M	1 yr HL+Disch Igmny	Comm 6 mos Detn Curragh		WO/92/4/84	
22/09/19	Gates D	Pte	5 Dragoon Gds	M	1 yr HL+Disch Igmny	Comm 6 mos Detn Curragh		WO/92/4/84	
22/09/19	Gilbert J	Pte	5 Dragoon Gds	M	1 yr HL+Disch Igmny	Comm 6 mos Detn Curragh		WO/92/4/84	
22/09/19	Hodge H	Pte	5 Dragoon Gds	M	1 yr HL+Disch Igmny	Comm 6 mos Detn Curragh		WO/92/4/84	
22/09/19	James FA	Pte	5 Dragoon Gds	M	1 yr HL+Disch Igmny	Comm 6 mos Detn Curragh		WO/92/4/81	
22/09/19	Jowett P	Pte	5 Dragoon Gds	M	1 yr HL+Disch Igmny	Comm 6 mos Detn Curragh		WO/92/4/81	
22/09/19	Kennedy J	Pte	5 Dragoon Gds	M	1 yr HL+Disch Igmny	Comm 6 mos Detn Curragh		WO/92/4/84	
22/09/19	Moody WA	Pte	5 Dragoon Gds	M	1 yr HL+Disch Igmny	Comm 6 mos Detn Curragh		WO/92/4/81	
22/09/19	Partington A	Pte	5 Dragoon Gds	M	1 yr HL+Disch Igmny	Comm 6 mos Detn Curragh		WO/92/4/84	
22/09/19	Potter T	Pte	5 Dragoon Gds	M	1 yr HL+Disch Igmny	Comm 6 mos Detn Curragh		WO/92/4/81	
22/09/19	Robertson H	Pte	5 Dragoon Gds	M	1 yr HL+Disch Igmny	Comm 6 mos Detn Curragh		WO/92/4/84	
22/09/19	Vance H	Pte	5 Dragoon Gds	M	Acquit		Curragh	WO/92/4/84	
22/09/19	White A	Pte	5 Dragoon Gds	M	1 yr HL+Disch Igmny	Comm 6 mos Detn Curragh		WO/92/4/81	
22/09/19	Whitehead J	Pte	5 Dragoon Gds	M	1 yr HL+Disch Igmny	Comm 6 mos Detn Curragh		WO/92/4/84	
22/09/19	Whittaker J	Pte	5 Dragoon Gds	M	1 yr HL+Disch Igmny	Comm 6 mos Detn Curragh		WO/92/4/84	
22/09/19	Wilson D	Pte	5 Dragoon Gds	M	1 yr HL+Disch Igmny	Comm 6 mos Detn Curragh		WO/92/4/84	
23/09/19	Allen CH	Pte	5 Dragoon Gds	M	84 dys HL	Comm 42 dys DetnCurragh		WO/92/4/85	
23/09/19	Beattie RE	Pte	5 Dragoon Gds	M	84 dys HL	Comm 42 dys DetnCurragh		WO/92/4/85	
23/09/19	Brookfield W	Pte	5 Dragoon Gds	M	84 dys HL	Comm 42 dys DetnCurragh		WO/92/4/85	
23/09/19	Brunskill A	Pte	5 Dragoon Gds	M	1 yr HL+Disch Igmny	Comm 6mos Detn Curragh		WO/92/4/85	
23/09/19	Dean W	Pte	5 Dragoon Gds	M	84 dys HL	Comm 42 dys DetnCurragh		WO/92/4/85	
23/09/19	Donaldson AC	Pte	5 Dragoon Gds	M	84 dys HL	Comm 42 dys DetnCurragh		WO/92/4/85	
23/09/19	Gadsby JE	Pte	5 Dragoon Gds	M	84 dys HL	Comm 42 dys DetnCurragh		WO/92/4/85	
23/09/19	Hamilton J	Pte	5 Dragoon Gds	M	1 yr HL+Disch Igmny	Comm 6 mos Detn Curragh		WO/92/4/84	
23/09/19	Hawksby T	Pte	5 Dragoon Gds	M	6 mos HL +Disch Igmny	Comm 84 dys DetnCurragh		WO/92/4/84	
23/09/19	Higgs GH	Pte	5 Dragoon Gds	M	1 yr HL+Disch Igmny	Comm 6 mos Detn Curragh		WO/92/4/84	
23/09/19	Holliday P	Pte	5 Dragodn Gds	M	6 mos HL +Disch Igmny	Comm 84 dys DetnCurragh		WO/92/4/84	
23/09/19	Howarth R	Pte	5 Dragoon Gds	M	84 dys HL	Comm 42 dys DetnCurragh		WO/92/4/85	
23/09/19	Hunter W	Pte	6 Dragoon Gds	M	84 dys HL	Comm 42 dys DetnCurragh		WO/92/4/85	
23/09/19	Hurst F	Pte	5 Dragoon Gds	M	84 dys HL	Comm 42 dys DetnCurragh		WO/92/4/85	
23/09/19	Jones S	Pte	5 Dragoon Gds	M	1 yr HL+Disch Igmny	Comm 6 mos Detn Curragh		WO/92/4/84	
23/09/19	Kelly A	Pte	5 Dragoon Gds	M	6 mos HL	Comm 84 dys DetnCurragh		WO/92/4/84	
23/09/19	Lunt S	Pte	5 Dragoon Gds	M	Acquit		Curragh	WO/92/4/84	
23/09/19	McDowell S	Pte	5 Dragoon Gds	M	6 mos HL	Comm 84 dys DetnCurragh		WO/92/4/84	
23/09/19	Mutch R	Pte	5 Dragoon Gds	M	1 yr HL+Disch Igmny	Comm 6 mos Detn Curragh		WO/92/4/84	
23/09/19	Pannell A	Pte	5 Dragoon Gds	M	84 dys HL	Comm 42 dys DetnCurragh		WO/92/4/85	
23/09/19	Phillips F	Pte	5 Dragoon Gds	M	84 dys HL	Comm 42 dys DetnCurragh		WO/92/4/85	
23/09/19	Riddell TJ	Pte	5 Dragoon Gds	M	1 yr HL+Disch Igmny	Comm 6 mos Detn Curragh		WO/92/4/84	
23/09/19	Rutter S	Pte	5 Dragoon Gds	M	1 yr HL+Disch Igmny	Comm 6 mos Detn Curragh		WO/92/4/84	
23/09/19	Seddon TG	Pte	5 Dragoon Gds	M	1 yr HL+Disch Igmny	Comm 6 mos Detn Curragh		WO/92/4/85	
23/09/19	Smith EH	Pte	5 Dragoon Gds	M	84 dys HL	Comm 42 dys DetnCurragh		WO/92/4/85	
23/09/19	Smith HJ	Pte	5 Dragoon Gds	M	6 mos HL	Comm 84 dys DetnCurragh		WO/92/4/85	
23/09/19	Spence JD	Pte	5 Dragoon Gds	M	84 dys HL	Comm 42 dys DetnCurragh		WO/92/4/85	
23/09/19	Stanworth H	Pte	5 Dragoon Gds	M	1 yr HL+Disch Igmny	Comm 6 mos Detn Curragh		WO/92/4/85	
23/09/19	Stringer S	Pte	5 Dragoon Gds	M	1 yr HL+Disch Igmny	Comm 6 mos Detn Curragh		WO/92/4/85	
23/09/19	Sykes J	Pte	5 Dragoon Gds	M	1 yr HL+Disch Igmny	Comm 6 mos Detn Curragh		WO/92/4/85	
23/09/19	Whittaker T	Pte	5 Dragoon Gds	M	1 yr HL+Disch Igmny	Comm 6 mos Detn Curragh		WO/92/4/85	
23/09/19	Williams PH	Pte	5 Dragoon Gds	M	84 dys HL	Comm 42 dys DetnCurragh		WO/92/4/85	
23/09/19	Wright WS	Pte	5 Dragoon Gds	M	84 dys HL	Comm 42 dys DetnCurragh		WO/92/4/85	
24/09/19	Brown JW	Pte	5 Dragoon Gds	M	1 yr HL+Disch Igmny	Comm 6 mos Detn Curragh		WO/92/4/85	
24/09/19	Daley J	Pte	5 Dragoon Gds	M	1 yr HL+Disch Igmny	Comm 6 mos Detn Curragh		WO/92/4/85	
24/09/19	Evans SW	Pte	5 Dragoon Gds	M	1 yr HL+Disch Igmny	Comm 6 mos Detn Curragh		WO/92/4/85	

Date D/M/Y	Name	Rank	Unit	Offence	Finding/Punishment	Amendment	Location	PRO Reference File/Piece/Page	Note:
24/09/19	Heath LC	Pte	5 Dragoon Gds	M	Acquit		Curragh	WO/92/4/87	
24/09/19	Jones F	Pte	5 Dragoon Gds	M	1 yr HL+Disch Igmny	Comm 6 mos Detn	Curragh	WO/92/4/85	
24/09/19	Mackie GE	Pte	5 Dragoon Gds	M	84 dys HL	Comm 42 dys Detn	Curragh	WO/92/4/87	
24/09/19	Marsden J	Pte	5 Dragoon Gds	M	1 yr HL+Disch Igmny	Comm 6 mos Detn	Curragh	WO/92/4/86	
24/09/19	Molloy P	Pte	5 Dragoon Gds	M	1 yr HL+Disch Igmny	Comm 6 mos Detn	Curragh	WO/92/4/87	
24/09/19	Moore M	Pte	5 Dragoon Gds	M	Acquit		Curragh	WO/92/4/86	
24/09/19	Nicholson T	Pte	5 Dragoon Gds	M	1 yr HL+Disch Igmny	Comm 6 mos Detn	Curragh	WO/92/4/86	
24/09/19	Owens JW	Pte	5 Dragoon Gds	M	1 yr HL+Disch Igmny	Comm 6mos Detn	Curragh	WO/92/4/86	
24/09/19	Popham HH	Pte	5 Dragoon Gds	M	1 yr HL+Disch Igmny	Comm 6 mos Detn	Curragh	WO/92/4/86	
24/09/19	Prince J	Pte	5 Dragoon Gds	M	Acquit		Curragh	WO/92/4/87	
24/09/19	Ross A	Pte	King Edw Horse (att 5 Dragoon Gds)	M	56 dys Detn	Remit 21dys	Curragh	WO/92/4/86	
24/09/19	Smith RA	Pte	5 Dragoon Gds	M	1 yr HL+Igmny	Comm 6 mos Detn	Curragh	WO/92/4/86	
24/09/19	Smith RH	Boy	King Edward Horse	M	6 mos HL	Comm 84 dys Detn	Curragh	WO/92/4/87	
24/09/19	Smith W	Pte	5 Dragoon Gds	M	1 yr HL+Disch Igmny	Comm 6 mos Detn	Curragh	WO/92/4/87	
24/09/19	Steele FJ	Pte	5 Dragoon Gds	M	1 yr HL+Disch Igmny	Comm 6 mos Detn	Curragh	WO/92/4/86	
24/09/19	Stothard GW	Pte	5 Dragoon Gds	M	1 yr HL+Disch Igmny	Comm 6 mos Detn	Curragh	WO/92/4/86	
24/09/19	Swallow L	Pte	5 Dragoon Gds	M	1 yr HL+Disch Igmny	Comm 6 mos Detn	Curragh	WO/92/4/87	
24/09/19	Timms W	Pte	5 Dragoon Gds	M	1 yr HL+Disch Igmny	Comm 6 mos Detn	Curragh	WO/92/4/87	
24/09/19	Whitehead W	Pte	5 Dragoon Gds	M	1 yr HL+Disch Igmny	Comm 6 mos Detn	Curragh	WO/92/4/86	
24/09/19	Wragg GW	Pte	5 Dragoon Gds	M	1 yr HL+Disch Igmny	Comm 6 mos Detn	Curragh	WO/92/4/87	
24/09/19	Young A	Pte	5 Dragoon Gds	M	1 yr HL+Disch Igmny	Comm 6 mos Detn	Curragh	WO/92/4/86	
25/09/19	Blair D	Pte	5 Dragoon Gds	M	1 yr HL+Disch Igmny	Comm 6 mos Detn	Curragh	WO/92/4/86	
25/09/19	Burley H	Pte	2 Dragoon Gds	M	1 yr HL+Disch Igmny	Comm 6 mos Detn	Curragh	WO/92/4/86	
25/09/19	Dorans H	L/Cpl	5 Dragoon Gds	M	Acquit		Curragh	WO/92/4/86	
25/09/19	Hall W	L/Cpl	Derby Yeo (att 5 Dragoon Gds)	M	1 yr HL+Disch Igmny	6 mos Detn	Curragh	WO/92/4/86	
25/09/19	Hamilton F	Pte	5 Dragoon Gds	M	1 yr HL+Disch Igmny	Comm 6 mos Detn	Curragh	WO/92/4/87	
25/09/19	Harrison J	Pte	5 Dragoon Gds	M	1 yr HL+Disch Igmny	Comm 6 mos Detn	Curragh	WO/92/4/86	
25/09/19	Hartley H	L/Cpl	5 Dragoon Gds	M	6 mos HL	Comm 84 dys Detn	Curragh	WO/92/4/86	
25/09/19	Hayes P	Pte	King Edward Horse (att 5 DG)	M	1 yr HL+Disch Igmny	Comm 6 mos Detn	Curragh	WO/92/4/86	
25/09/19	Hudson FWA	Pte	5 Dragoon Gds	M	56 dys Detn	NC	Curragh	WO/92/4/86	
25/09/19	Jackson HB	Pte	5 Dragoon Gds	M	Acquit		Curragh	WO/92/4/86	
25/09/19	Johnston R	Pte	5 Dragoon Gds	M	56 dys Detn	NC	Curragh	WO/92/4/86	
25/09/19	Leah J	Pte	2 Dragoon Gds	M	1 yr HL+Disch Igmny	Comm 6 mos Detn	Curragh	WO/92/4/87	
25/09/19	Livingstone JF	Pte	5 Dragoon Gds	M	Acquit		Curragh	WO/92/4/86	
25/09/19	Moore F	Pte	5 Dragoon Gds	M	Acquit		Curragh	WO/92/4/87	
25/09/19	Mountford WH	L/Cpl	5 Dragoon Gds	M	Acquit		Curragh	WO/92/4/86	
25/09/19	Simmonds JF	Pte	5 Dragoon Gds	M	56 dys Detn	NC	Curragh	WO/92/4/86	
25/09/19	Stone HF	Pte	5 Dragoon Gds	M	1 yr HL+Disch Igmny	Comm 6 mos Detn	Curragh	WO/92/4/86	
26/09/19	Berry A	Pte	5 Dragoon Gds	M	1 yr HL+Disch Igmny	Comm 6 mos Detn	Curragh	WO/92/4/83	
26/09/19	Brownsdon S	Pte	5 Dragoon Gds	M	1 yr HL+Disch Igmny	Comm 6 mos Detn	Curragh	WO/92/4/83	
26/09/19	Bullen E	Pte	5 Dragoon Gds	M	1 yr HL+Disch Igmny	Comm 6 mos Detn	Curragh	WO/92/4/80	
26/09/19	Curran RN	Pte	5 Dragoon Gds	M	1 yr HL+Disch Igmny	Comm 6 mos Detn	Curragh	WO/92/4/80	
26/09/19	Curwen T	Pte	5 Dragoon Gds	M	1 yr HL+Disch Igmny	Comm 6 mos Detn	Curragh	WO/92/4/80	
26/09/19	Drury B	Pte	5 Dragoon Gds	M	1 yr HL+Disch Igmny	Comm 6 mos Detn	Curragh	WO/92/4/81	
26/09/19	Egglestone JW	Pte	5 Dragoon Gds	M	1 yr HL+Disch Igmny	Comm 6 mos Detn	Curragh	WO/92/4/81	
26/09/19	Greenfield A	Pte	5 Dragoon Gds	M	1 yr HL+Disch Igmny	Comm 6 mos Detn	Curragh	WO/92/4/81	
26/09/19	Henderson W	Pte	5 Dragoon Gds	M	1 yr HL+Disch Igmny	Comm 6 mos Detn	Curragh	WO/92/4/81	
26/09/19	Holding A	Pte	5 Dragoon Gds	M	1 yr HL+Disch Igmny	Comm 6 mos Detn	Curragh	WO/92/4/81	
26/09/19	King J	Pte	5 Dragoon Gds	M	1 yr HL+Disch Igmny	Comm 6 mos Detn	Curragh	WO/92/4/81	
26/09/19	Lambert A	Pte	5 Dragoon Gds	M	1 yr HL+Disch Igmny	Comm 6 mos Detn	Curragh	WO/92/4/83	
26/09/19	Livermore AW	Pte	5 Dragoon Gds	M	1 yr HL+Disch Igmny	Comm 6 mos Detn	Curragh	WO/92/4/81	
26/09/19	McClelland A	Pte	5 Dragoon Gds	M	1 yr HL+Disch Igmny	Comm 6 mos Detn	Curragh	WO/92/4/83	
26/09/19	Morris H	Pte	5 Dragoon Gds	M	1 yr HL+Disch Igmny	Comm 6 mos Dtn	Curragh	WO/92/4/83	
26/09/19	Nott WH	Pte	5 Dragoon Gds	M	1 yr HL+Disch Igmny	Comm 6 mos Detn	Curragh	WO/92/4/81	
26/09/19	O'Keeffe P	Pte	5 Dragoon Gds	M	1 yr HL+Disch Igmny	Comm 6 mos Detn	Curragh	WO/92/4/83	
26/09/19	O'Rourke J	Pte	5 Dragoon Gds	M	1 yr HL+Disch Igmny	Comm 6 mos Detn	Curragh	WO/92/4/83	
26/09/19	Pallister JF	Pte	5 Dragoon Gds	M	1 yr HL+Disch Igmny	Comm 6 mos Detn	Curragh	WO/92/4/81	
26/09/19	Ramsey JGS	Pte	5 Dragoon Gds	M	1 yr HL+Disch Igmny	Comm 6 mos Detn	Curragh	WO/92/4/83	
26/09/19	Roden GW	Pte	5 Dragoon Gds	M	1 yr HL+Disch Igmny	Comm 6 mos Detn	Curragh	WO/92/4/83	
26/09/19	Skipp WH	Pte	5 Dragoon Gds	M	1 yr HL+Disch Igmny	Comm 6 mos Detn	Curragh	WO/92/4/83	
26/09/19	Slater W	Pte	5 Dragoon Gds	M	1 yr HL+Disch Igmny	Comm 6 mos Detn	Curragh	WO/92/4/81	
26/09/19	Stevens DM	Pte	5 Dragoon Gds	M	1 yr HL+Disch Igmny	Comm 6 mos Detn	Curragh	WO/92/4/83	
26/09/19	Taylor ES	Pte	5 Dragoon Gds	M	1 yr HL+Disch Igmny	Comm 6 mos Detn	Curragh	WO/92/4/83	
26/09/19	Theirens RH	Pte	5 Dragoon Gds	M	5 yrs PS+Disch Igmny	Comm 2 yrs Detn	Curragh	WO/92/4/83	
26/09/19	Turks AJ	Pte	5 Dragoon Gds	M	2 yrs HL+Disch Igmny	Comm 1 yr Detn	Curragh	WO/92/4/81	
26/09/19	Williams B	Pte	5 Dragoon Gds	M	1 yr HL+Disch Igmny	Comm 6 mos Detn	Curragh	WO/92/4/83	
27/09/19	Brandall T	Dvr	RFA	M	18 mos HL	Comm to Detn	Deepcut	WO/86/88/138	67
27/09/19	Foulkes GJ	Dvr	RFA	M	2 yrs HL	Remit 6 mos +Comm to Detn	Deepcut	WO/86/88/138	

Date D/M/Y	Name	Rank	Unit	Offence	Finding/Punishment	Amendment	Location	PRO Reference File/Piece/Page	Note
27/09/19	Glover RJ	Dvr	RFA	M	1 yr HL	Comm to Detn	Deepcut	WO/86/88/138	
27/09/19	Gray A	Gnr	RFA	M	NG		Deepcut	WO/86/88/138	
27/09/19	Mills SC	Dvr	RFA	M	NG		Deepcut	WO/86/88/138	
29/09/19	Ainsworth C	L/Cpl	5 Dragoon Gds	M	18 mos HL +Disch Igmny	Comm 9 mos Detn Curragh		WO/92/4/83	68
29/09/19	Ambrose WJ	Pte	K Edw Horse	M	1 yr HL+Disch Igmny	Comm 6 mos Detn Curragh		WO/92/4/82	
29/09/19	Arthurs E	Pte	5 Dragoon Gds	M	1 yr HL+Disch Igmny	Comm 6 mos Detn Curragh		WO/92/4/82	
29/09/19	Atkinson T	Pte	5 Dragoon Gds	M	1 yr HL+Disch Igmny	Comm 6 mos Detn Curragh		WO/92/4/81	
29/09/19	Ayres J	Pte	5 Dragoon Gds	M	18 mos HL +Disch Igmny	Comm 9 mos Detn Curragh		WO/92/4/83	
29/09/19	Bartlett J	Pte	5 Dragoon Gds	M	1 yr HL+Disch Igmny	Comm 6 mos Detn Curragh		WO/92/4/81	
29/09/19	Bell D	Pte	5 Dragoon Gds	M	18 mos HL	Comm 9 mos Detn Curragh		WO/92/4/83	
9/09/19	Boyle J	Pte	5 Dragoon Gds	M	1 yr HL+Disch Igmny	Comm 6 mos Detn Curragh		WO/92/4/81	
29/09/19	Bradfield EE	Pte	5 Dragoon Gds	M	1 yr HL+Disch Igmny	Comm 6 mos Detn Curragh		WO/92/4/82	
29/09/19	Carroll W	Pte	5 Dragoon Gds	M	1 yr HL+Disch Igmny	Comm 6 mos Detn Curragh		WO/92/4/82	
29/09/19	Clarke F	Pte	5 Dragoon Gds	M	1 yr HL+Disch Igmny	Comm 6 mos Detn Curragh		WO/92/4/82	
29/09/19	Cossey A	Pte	5 Dragoon Gds	M	1 yr HL+Disch Igmny	Comm 6 mos Detn Curragh		WO/92/4/82	
29/09/19	Creedy WE	Pte	5 Dragoon Gds	M	1 yr HL+Disch Igmny	Comm 6 mos Detn Curragh		WO/92/4/81	
29/09/19	Davies HE	Pte	5 Dragoon Gds	M	1 yr HL+Disch Igmny	Comm 6 mos Detn Curragh		WO/92/4/82	
29/09/19	Dilworth WF	Pte	5 Dragoon Gds	M	1 yr HL+Disch Igmny	Comm 6 mos Detn Curragh		WO/92/4/82	
29/09/19	Ewington AH	Pte	5 Dragoon Gds	M	1 yr HL+Disch Igmny	Comm 6 mos Detn Curragh		WO/92/4/82	
29/09/19	Fisher GW	Pte	5 Dragoon Gds	M	1 yr HL+Disch Igmny	Comm 6 mos Detn Curragh		WO/92/4/82	
29/09/19	Gandy C	Pte	5 Dragoon Gds	M	1 yr HL+Disch Igmny	Comm 6 mos Detn Curragh		WO/92/4/82	
29/09/19	Gill J	Pte	5 Dragoon Gds	M	1 yr HL+Disch Igmny	Comm 6 mos Detn Curragh		WO/92/4/83	
29/09/19	Goodwin J	Pte	5 Dragoon Gds	M	1 yrs HL+Disch Igmny	Comm 9 mos Detn Curragh		WO/92/4/83	
29/09/19	Gough F	Pte	5 Dragoon Gds	M	1 yr HL+Disch Igmny	Comm 6 mos Detn Curragh		WO/92/4/82	
29/09/19	Greenhow WS	Pte	5 Dragoon Gds	M	1 yr HL+Disch Igmny	Comm 6 mos Detn Curragh		WO/92/4/81	
29/09/19	Heys H	Pte	5 Dragoon Gds	M	1 yr HL+Disch Igmny	Comm 6 mos Detn Curragh		WO/92/4/83	
29/09/19	Hoey G	Pte	5 Dragoon Gds	M	18 mos HL +Disch Igmny	Comm 9 mos Detn Curragh		WO/92/4/83	
29/09/19	Hogg E	Pte	5 Dragoon Gds	M	1 yr HL+Disch Igmny	Comm 6 mos Detn Curragh		WO/92/4/83	
29/09/19	Illingworth N	Pte	5 Dragoon Gds	M	1 yr HL+Disch Igmny	Comm 6 mos Detn Curragh		WO/92/4/82	
29/09/19	Jowett HW	Pte	5 Dragoon Gds	M	1 yr HL+Disch Igmny	Comm 6 mos Detn Curragh		WO/92/4/82	
29/09/19	Lord W	Pte	5 Dragoon Gds	M	1 yr HL+Disch Igmny	Comm 6 mos Detn Curragh		WO/92/4/83	
29/09/19	Matthews GF	Pte	5 Dragoon Gds	M	1 yr HL+Disch Igmny	Comm 6 mos Detn Curragh		WO/92/4/82	
29/09/19	Millward H	Pte	5 Dragoon Gds	M	1 yr HL+Disch Igmny	Comm 6 mos Detn Curragh		WO/92/4/82	
29/09/19	Moore GS	Pte	5 Dragoon Gds	M	1 yr HL+Disch Igmny	Comm 6 mos Detn Currragh		WO/92/4/81	
29/09/19	Pownall WD	Pte	5 Dragoon Gds	M	1 yr HL+Disch Igmny	Comm 6 mos Detn Curragh		WO/92/4/82	
29/09/19	Robinson H	Pte	5 Dragoon Gds	M	1 yr HL+Disch Igmny	Comm 6 mos Detn Curragh		WO/92/4/82	
29/09/19	Sibbald JS	Pte	5 Dragoon Gds	M	1 yr HL+Disch Igmny	Comm 6 mos Detn Curragh		WO/92/4/82	
29/09/19	Simpson J	Pte	5 Dragoon Gds	M	1 yr HL+Disch Igmny	Comm 6 mos Detn Curragh		WO/92/4/82	
29/09/19	Stones D	Pte	5 Dragoon Gds	M	1 yr HL+Disch Igmny	Comm 6 mos Detn Curragh		WO/92/4/82	
29/09/19	Wallace E	Pte	5 Dragoon Gds	M	1 yr HL+Disch Igmny	Comm 6 mos Detn Curragh		WO/92/4/82	
29/09/19	Watkinson W	Pte	5 Dragoon Gds	M	1 yr HL+Disch Igmny	Comm 6 mos Detn Curragh		WO/92/4/82	
29/09/19	White JH	L/Cpl	5 Dragoon Gds	M	1 yr HL+Disch Igmny	Comm 6 mos Detn Curragh		WO/92/4/81	
29/09/19	White JK	Pte	5 Dragoon Gds	M	1 yr HL+Disch Igmny	Comm 6 mos Detn Curragh		WO/92/4/82	
29/09/19	Wood H	Pte	5 Dragoon Gds	M	1 yr HL+Disch Igmny	Comm 6 mos Detn Curragh		WO/92/4/82	
29/09/19	Young CF	Pte	5 Dragoon Gds	M	1 yr HL+Disch Igmny	Comm 6 mos Detn Curragh		WO/92/4/82	
30/09/19	Ball S	Pte	5 Dragoon Gds	M	1 yr HL+Disch Igmny	Comm 6 mos Detn Curragh		WO/92/4/87	
30/09/19	Bentham J	Pte	5 Dragoon Gds	M	1 yr HL+Disch Igmny	Comm 6 mos Detn Curragh		WO/92/4/87	
30/09/19	Boyle C	Pte	5 Dragoon Gds	M	Acquit		Curragh	WO/92/4/87	
30/09/19	Gornall R	L/Cpl	5 Dragoon Gds	M	18 mos HL +Disch Igmny	Comm 9 mos Detn Curragh		WO/92/4/87	
30/09/19	Highley D	Pte	5 Dragoon Gds	M	1 yr HL+Disch Igmny	Comm 6 mos Detn Curragh		WO/92/4/87	
30/09/19	Kenyon TF	Pte	5 Dragoon Gds	M	1 yr HL+Disch Igmny	Comm 6 mos Detn Curragh		WO/92/4/87	
30/09/19	McKee W	Pte	6 Dragoon Gds (att 5 Dragoon Gds)	M	Acquit		Curragh	WO/92/4/87	
30/09/19	Norton E	Pte	5 Dragoon Gds	M	1 yr HL+Disch Igmny	Comm 6 mos Detn Curragh		WO/92/4/87	
30/09/19	Partington WE	Pte	2 Dragoon Gds	M	84 dys HL	Comm 42 dys DetnCurragh		WO/92/4/87	
30/09/19	Rimmer F	Pte	5 Dragoon Gds	M	1 yr HL+Disch Igmny	Comm 6 mos Detn Curragh		WO/92/4/87	
30/09/19	Sands WH	Pte	5 Dragoon Gds	M	1 yr HL+Disch Igmny	Comm 6 mos Detn Curragh		WO/92/4/87	
30/09/19	Smith W	Pte	5 Dragoon Gds	M	1 yr HL+Disch Igmny	Comm 6 mos Detn Curragh		WO/92/4/87	
30/09/19	Sutton WW	Pte	5 Dragoon Gds	M	1 yr HL+Disch Igmny	Comm 6 mos Detn Curragh		WO/92/4/87	
30/09/19	Taylor H	Pte	5 Dragoon Gds	M	1 yr HL+Disch Igmny	Comm 6 mos Detn Curragh		WO/92/4/87	
07/10/19	Crouch FE	Pte	2 Buffs	M	NG		Dover	WO/86/88/141	69
01/02/20	Hardy PT	Cpl	Ox & Bucks LI	M+Abs +Resisting+S9(1)	2 yrs HL+Rnks +DI	Remit 18 mos	Oxford/Depot	WO/92/4/95	
04/02/20	Carthy J	Gdsn	Irish Gds	M	5 yrs PS+Disch Igmny		Guildhall Wminster	WO/92/4/89	70

Date D/M/Y	Name	Rank	Unit	Offence	Finding/Punishment	Amendment	Location	PRO Reference File/Piece/Page	Note:
04/02/20	Flanagan J	Gdsn	Irish Gds	M	5 yrs PS + Disch Igmny		Guildhall Wminster	WO/92/4/89	
04/02/20	Moffatt P	Gdsn	Irish Gds	M	5 yrs PS + Disch Igmny		Guildhall Wminster	WO/92/4/89	
20/04/20	Matthews J	Pte	RASC	M	18 mos HL + Disch Igmny	18 mos Detn + Remit Disch	Avonmouth	WO/86/90/17	
04/05/20	Edmeads E	Cpl	1 Ox & Bucks LI	M+V(CSM)	Acquit		Cork	WO/92/4/90	71
01/09/20	Remfrey S	Pte	1 DCLI	M	2 yrs HL		Belfast	WO/86/90/140	
01/09/20	Podger HC	Pte	1 DCLI	M	1 yr HL		Belfast	WO/86/90/140	
29/10/20	Campbell M	Pte	2 KOSB	M+S40	NG		Devonport	WO/86/90/187	
25/01/21	Bade B	Pte	10 Hussars	Mx2+S9(1)x2	1 yr Detn		Curragh	WO/92/4/94	
25/01/21	Barker JA	Pte	10 Hussars	Mx2+S9(1)x2	1 yr Detn	Remit 3 mos	Curragh	WO/92/4/94	
25/01/21	Hill E	Pte	10 Hussars	Mx2+S9(1)x2	1 yr Detn		Curragh	WO/92/4/94	
25/01/21	Kent GA	Pte	10 Hussars	Mx2+S9(1)x2	1 yr Detn	Remit 3 mos	Curragh	WO/92/4/94	
25/01/21	Sullivan FG	Pte	10 Hussars	Mx2+S9(1)x2	1 yr Detn	Remit 3 mos	Curragh	WO/92/4/94	
25/01/21	Wild P	Pte	10 Hussars	Mx2+S9(1)	1 yr Detn	Remit 3 mos	Curragh	WO/92/4/94	
09/05/21	Burnett A	Gnr	RGA	M+S7(4)	2 yrs HL+DI	Comm to DI Not Conf	Field (Ireland)	WO/213/32/133	
09/05/21	Sheffield W	Gnr	RGA	M+S7(4)	2 yrs HL+DI	Comm to DI Not Conf	Field (Ireland)	WO/213/32/133	
09/05/21	Ward HC	Dvr	RGA	M+S7(2b)	2 yrs HL+DI	Comm to DI Not Conf	Field (Ireland)	WO/213/32/133	
18/05/21	Davies R	Dvr	RASC	M	12 mos HL+DI		Chelsea	WO/92/4/96	
18/05/21	Harrison R	Dvr	RASC	M	9 mos HL+DI		Chelsea	WO/92/4/96	
18/05/21	Newbold RF	Dvr	RASC	M	12 mos HL+DI		Chelsea	WO/92/4/96	
09/06/21	Agnew D	Pte	4 R Scots Greys	M+V(A/RSM)	18 mos HL		Edinburgh	WO/86/91/131	
09/06/21	Brealey JW	Pte	7 Dragoon Gds	M+V(A/RSM)	NG		Edinburgh	WO/86/91/131	
09/06/21	Campbell A	Pte	7 Dragoon Gds	M+V(A/RSM)	18 mos HL		Edinburgh	WO/86/91/131	
09/06/21	Crockett AE	Pte	4 Dragoon Gds	M+V(A/RSM)	2 yrs HL		Edinburgh	WO/86/91/131	
09/06/21	Dickson T	Pte	4 R Scots Greys	M+V(A/RSM)	18 mos HL		Edinburgh	WO/86/91/131	
09/06/21	Halpin R	Pte	7 Dragoon Gds	M+V(A/RSM)	2 yrs HL		Edinburgh	WO/86/91/131	
09/06/21	Hellard C	Pte	7 Dragoon Gds	M+V(A/RSM)	2 yrs HL		Edinburgh	WO/86/91/131	
09/06/21	Knight H	Pte	7 Dragoon Gds	M+V(A/RSM)	NG		Edinburgh	WO/86/91/131	
09/06/21	Massey C	Pte	7 Dragoon Gds	M+V(A/RSM)	NG		Edinburgh	WO/86/91/131	
09/06/21	Thomson F	Pte	7 Dragoon Gds	M+V(A/RSM)	2 yrs HL		Edinburgh	WO/86/91/131	
05/09/21	Booth A	Pte(L/Cpl)	1 Manchester	M+Disob(CQMS)+S7(3)	3 yrs PS	2yrs Detn	Field (Ireland)	WO/213/32/214	72
05/09/21	Carr J	Pte(L/Cpl)	1 Manchester	M+Disob(CQMS)+S7(3)	3 yrs PS	NG	Field (Ireland)	WO/213/32/214	
05/09/21	Downie A	Pte(L/Cpl)	1 Manchester	M+Disob(CQMS)+S7(3)	3 yrs PS	2yrs Detn	Field (Ireland)	WO/213/32/214	
05/09/21	Onslow R	Pte(L/Cpl)	1 Manchester	M+Disob(CQMS)+S7(3)	3 yrs PS	2yrs Detn	Field (Ireland)	WO/213/32/214	
28/04/22	Halford T	Pte	1 Leics	M+S40	1 yr HL	Comm to 56 dys	Field (Ireland)	WO/213/34/63	73

Notes

1. Bn. stationed in Leicester, 4.8.14
2. Reserve Bn. arrived Weymouth, August 1914. Upwey mutineers, see Narratives.
3. Unit with 124 Artillery Bde, 16(Irish) Div.
4. Locally raised in Dec 1914, taken over by WO on 23.6.15. August 1915 to Winchester as Pioneer Bn., 39 Div.
5. Bn. part of 49 Bde.,16 (Irish) Div.
6. Territorial Bns. at Newhaven providing drafts for overseas service. C.O.,Maj.Witten reprimanded on 23.7.15. *Horsham Times,* 1.5.15.
7. Bn. arrived at Bedford in July 1915, part of 203 Bde., 68 (2 Welsh) Div.
8. Bn. with 49 Bde., 16 (Irish) Div. WO33/779 shows detachment of Inniskilling Dragoons at Enniskillen.
9. Reserve Bn. with Thames and Medway garrison.
10. Posted from Aldershot to Witley, Nov. 1915. Bn with 117 Bde. , 49 Div.
11. War Diary commences Jan. 1916, no references.
12. At Tadworth during Dec. 1915.
13. Second Reserve formation.
14. Bn. posted to Ripon, Nov. 1915.
15. With 146 Bde., VIth A Reserve.
16. Bn. with 201 Bde., 67 Div., at Sevenoaks. Protest on parade over long hours of duty. *Times,* 16.3.16.
17. Accused with 2B Attached Coy., MG Training Centre, Belton Park Camp. Incident occurred 27.3.16. WO 83/24 pp 608/609; WO 84/12 JAG letter 8.4.16; *Grantham Journal* 6.5.16.
18. Ammunition column with 63 (2 Northumbrian) Div., accused refused to parade. WO 84/12 JAG letter 20/4/16.
19. Midland and Connaught District. Unit with 144 Bde., Vth A Reserve RFA.
20. At Warley Barracks on 8.5.16 attempts made to release detainees from guardroom. WO 84/12 JAG letter 23.5.16.
21. Unit with 69 (2 East Anglian) Div., Local Forces, Northern Command Div. HQ at Harrogate.
22. Bn. with 203 Bde., 68 (2 Welsh) Div.
23. Unit with Eastern Command (Northampton?). Established 17.3.16, the RDC was composed of men aged 41–60, unfit for service overseas. Linked with Lord French's inspection of Northants Volunteers, including 270 from Towcester, 21.11.16? *Northampton Herald,* 24.11.16.
24. Unit with 67 (2 Home Counties) Div.
25. 2/25 London, attached to 68 (2 Welsh) Div. from May 1917.
26. Transport Workers' Bn., formed Swindon, Dec 1916.
27. Originally 14(Reserve) Bn Royal Scots, part of 12 Reserve Bde.
28. Civilians and Canadian troops try to liberate soldier arrested by MPs in Folkstone, 12.8.17. CA: GCM: Pte. F. Cole.
29. See 28.
30. Horse transport drivers, refused to clean horse harness unnecessarily, 5.11.16. See CA:GCM: Pte W. Ackling et al.
31. Bn. with 1 Bde 1 (Canadian) Div., BEF, France.
32. Bn. with Tyne Garrison.
33. On train near Guildford, remanded deserters assault escort, 26.1.18. CA: DCM: Pte. J. Chambers.
34. Refusals to parade 29-30.1.18 at Pirbright Barracks. WO 84/17 JAG letter 7.2.18.
35. See 33.
36. RAF established 1.4.18. Blandford 21.3.18, Royal Flying Corps men refuse to parade for duty overseas. WO 84/17 JAG letter 20.4.18.
37. See 34 and 35.
38. 16, attached 3 Bn., stationed at Limerick. At Holyhead on 7.5.18 refused to parade. WO 84/17 JAG letter 25.5.18.
39. Bn. with 25 Bde., 8 Div., BEF, France.
40. All attached to 2 Canadian Command Depot. At night on 12-13 June tried to release Cpl. from custody. WO 84/17 JAG letter 26.6.18.
41. Bn. with 4 Bde., 2 (Canadian) Div., Northern France.
42. Bn. stationed at Maryhill, Glasgow.
43. Bn. with 193 Bde 64 (2 Highland) Div. in Norwich. Div Engineers at Taverham.
44. Part of Syren Force, while embarking for service with NREF fight for shore leave. Dundee Docks, 15.10.18. IWM DOCS: F. Hirst 15.10.18.
45. Bn. with West Lancashire Reserve Bde., Oswestry.
46. Bn. composed of soldiers too young for overseas service, with 14 Reserve Bde. at Kinmel Park in Nov 1918. WO 73/110.
47. In aftermath of racist attack on black troops of 2 Canadian Construction Coy., Pte. arrested 8.1.19, liberated from guardroom 10.1.19 by Connor and others, attached MD Wing 7. CA: DCM: Pte .Otto Connor. See also Morton, 'Kicking and Complaining'. Post-war demobilisation riots inthe Canadian Expeditionary Force, Canadian Historical Review, 61.3 Sept 1980; Putkowski, *Kinmel Park Camp Riots,* op. cit., pp 13–14.
48. Part of West Lancashire Reserve Bde.
49. Leet involved with attempt to liberate imprisoned soldier from Camp 10 guardroom, 10.1.19. WO 93/45 cites DCM 17/2/19. See Morton, op cit.; Putkowski, op. cit.
50. After MPs assault black soldier, circa 150 Canadian troops attack MPs at Goldalming police station, 9.2.19. Rioting in camp continues for two days. *Woking Observer*, 12.2.19.
51. On 11.2.19 at Renney Camp, violently confronted their CO. WO 84/19 JAG letter 18.2.19.
52. On 9.1.19 oncited soldiers to sieze lorries and "leave the Whitley camp area". WO 84/19 JAG letter 17.1.19.
53. Kinmel Park Camp rioters. See Putkowski, op.cit.
54. Possibly 20 Bde. RFA. See WO 73/110.
55. See 53.
56. Mutual hostility between civilians and Canadian troops in Guildford caused sustained rioting 11–13.3.19. *Woking Observer*, 14.5.19.
57. See 53 and 55.
58. Strike by 1,200 old and unfit soldiers 11–22.6.19 at Belmont Camp, Surrey. Demand demobilisation and object to being classed as fit for further military service. *Daily Herald* 14.6.19 – 11.7.19; *Sutton Advertiser*, 27.6.19, 18.7.19.
59. Stationed at Glencorse? WO 73/110. Possibly linked with other mutinies by Scottish Reserve troops objecting to being drafted for overseas service. For the latter, see *Daily Herald,* 13.6.19; *Aberdeen Daily Journal*, 18.6.19; *Edinburgh Evening Despatch,* 14.6.19.
60. 1Bde., RGA at Bordon, Hants strike 28.6.19. Aggrieved about pay, insufficient leave and terms of overseas service. *Daily Herald.* 3.7.19, 14.7.19; *Sutton Advertiser,* 18–25.7.19. Linked with RE who wewre court martialled at Bordon on 7–8 Sept 1919 (?).
61. Discontent over slow demobilisation leads to refusal to parade, burning down camp gymnasium and liberation of prisoners from guardroom by French Canadian 23 Resrve Bn. on 17.6.19. CA: DCM: Cpl. H. Bureau; *Ripon Observer*, 19.6.19; Morton, op.cit.
62. See 61.
63. War service men demanding demobilisation refuse to parade at Durrington Camp on 2.7.19. *Wiltshire Gazette,* 7.8.19; *Wiltshire Telegraph,* 2–9.8.19. See also *Daily Herald* 5.6.19.
64. See 61 and 62.
65. Unit at Portobello Barracks, attached to Dublin District HQ.
66. Troops demonstrate after GOC refuses to discuss their demobilisation. Unit with 3 Reserve Cavalry Bde. *Daily Herald*, 12.9.19.
67. Base Camp of 12 Bde., 3C Reserve. WO 73/110.
68. See 66.
69. At Dover since 19.4.19. Arrived Fermoy on 19.9.19.
70. After soldier was detained circa 100 others tried to release arrested man from guard room at Caterham Barracks. *Times* 17.1.20.
71. Bn. with 18 Bde., 6 Div.
72. Bn. at Kilworth with 16 Bde., 6 Div.
73. Bn. at Athlone since Jan 1920. WO 73/112.

Chronological list of men charged with mutiny – Abroad

Date D/M/Y	Name	Rank	Unit	Offence	Finding/Punishment	Amendment	Location	PRO Reference File/Piece/Page	Note:
11/10/14	Flynn G	Pte	R Munster Fus	M	5 yrs PS	Quashed	St Nazaire	WO/213/2/105	1
11/10/14	O'Neill M	Pte	R Munster Fus	M	3 yrs PS	Quashed	St Nazaire	WO/213/2/105	
11/10/14	Scannell G	Pte	R Munster Fus	M+Forcing Guard	4 yrs PS	Rem 1 yr/Quashed	St Nazaire	WO/213/2/105	
25/10/14	Collins A	Pte	RAMC	Incit M+St/V+S40	2 yrs HL	Rem 18 mos	Rouen	WO/213/2/133	
03/11/14	Dunn ET	A/Cpl	5 Dragoon Gds	Endeavg M	56 dys Detn	Comm 14	At Sea	WO213/1/74	2
03/11/14	Harrison [?]	A/Bdr	RHA	Endeavg M	56 dys Detn	Comm 14	At Sea	WO213/1/74	
11/03/15	Ahmad [?]	L/Naik	Malay SG Bty	M	3 yrs PS	Comm 2 yrs Imp	Singapore	WO/213/4/17	3
11/03/15	Ahmad Sultan	Gnr	Malay SG Bty	M	3 yrs PS	Comm 18 mos Imp	Singapore	WO/213/4/17	
11/03/15	Khan Mozhar	Gnr	Malay SG Bty	M	3 yrs PS	Comm 18 mos Imp	Singapore	WO/213/4/17	
11/03/15	Rahman Abdul	Gnr	Malay SG Bty	M	3 yrs PS	Comm 18 mos Imp	Singapore	WO/213/4/17	
05/04/15	Kay R	Pte	NZEF 3 Reinf	Incit M+Disob(Lt)	1 yr HL+DI		Zeitoun	WO/90/6/35	4
05/04/15	Kilpatrick R	Pte	NZEF 3 Reinf	Incit M+Disob(Lt)	2 yrs HL+DI		Zeitoun	WO/90/6/35	
05/04/15	McKendry A	Pte	NZEF 3 Reinf	Incit M+Disob(Lt)	2 yrs HL+DI		Zeitoun	WO/90/6/35	
05/04/15	O'Neill T	Pte	NZEF 3 Reinf	Incit M+Disob(Lt)	1 yr HL+DI		Zeitoun	WO/90/6/35	
05/04/15	Springer J	Cpl	NZEF 3 Reinf	Incit M+Disob(Lt)	3 yrs PS+DI		Zeitoun	WO/90/6/35	
13/09/15	Bailey J	Pte	6 KOR Lancs	M	Death	Comm to 2 yrs HL	Gallipoli	WO/213/5/79	5
23/09/15	Williams TR	Pte	RGA	M+S40	1 yr HL		Malta	WO/90/6/34	
23/09/15	Harris GH	Tpr	Aus Lt Horse	M+S40	3 yrs PS+DI		Malta	WO/90/6/34	
24/09/15	Rattigan F	Pte	10 Bn AIF	M+S40	NG		Malta	WO/90/6/35	
24/09/15	Gould GW	Spr	RE(TF)	M+S40	NG		Malta	WO/90/6/35	
20/12/15	Bonnana G	Pte	2 KO Malta (Militia)	M+AWOL +Loss property	112 dys Detn +Stoppages		Malta	WO/86/68/199	6
30/12/15	Bell WA	Tpr	4 Aust Lt Horse	M+Not Sup +Disob(APM)	1 yr HL	Remit 1 month	Malta	WO/90/6/40	7
30/12/15	Quinn D	Pte	1 KOSB	M+Not Sup +Disob(APM)	1 yr HL	Remit 1 month	Malta	WO/90/6/40	
30/12/15	Silva P	Pte	3 NZ Rifles	M+Not Sup +Disob(APM)	1 yr HL	Remit 1 month	Malta	WO/90/6/40	
30/12/15	Grainger L	Pte	11 Sherwood F'sters	M	28 dys FP1+Rnks		Steenbecque	WO/213/7/25	8
30/12/15	Dunn B	Pte (S/Smith)	ASC	Joining M	3 yrs PS	Comm to 2 yrs HL	Marseilles	WO/90/6/44	9
30/12/15	Gay G	Pte (S/Smith)	ASC	Joining M	3 yrs PS	Comm to 2 yrs HL	Marseilles	WO/90/6/44	
30/12/15	Harding B	Pte (S/Smith)	ASC	Joining M	3 yrs PS	Comm to 2 yrs HL	Marseilles	WO/90/6/44	
30/12/15	Harris F	Pte (S/Smith)	ASC	Joining M	3 yrs PS	Comm to 2 yrs HL	Marseilles	WO/90/6/44	
30/12/15	Miles FV	Pte (S/Smith)	ASC	Joining M	3 yrs PS	Comm to 2 yrs HL	Marseilles	WO/90/6/44	
30/12/15	Monteith GJ	Pte (S/Smith)	ASC	Joining M	3 yrs PS	Comm to 2 yrs HL	Marseilles	WO/90/6/44	
30/12/15	Popple JE	Pte (S/Smith)	ASC	Joining M	Acquit		Marseilles	WO/90/6/44	
30/12/15	Rooke GB	Pte (S/Smith)	ASC	Joining M	3 yrs PS	Comm to 2 yrs HL	Marseilles	WO/90/6/44	
30/12/15	Sims W	Pte (S/Smith)	ASC	Joining M	3 yrs PS	Comm to 2 yrs HL	Marseilles	WO/90/6/44	
30/12/15	Town GT	Pte (S/Smith)	ASC	Joining M	3 yrs PS	Comm to 2 yrs HL	Marseilles	WO/90/6/44	

Date D/M/Y	Name	Rank	Unit	Offence	Finding/Punishment	Amendment	Location	PRO Reference File/Piece/Page	Note:
30/12/15	Underwood CA (S/Smith)	Pte	ASC	Joining M	3 yrs PS	Comm to 2 yrs HL	Marseilles	WO/90/6/44	
30/12/15	Vizard J (S/Smith)	Pte	ASC	Joining M	3 yrs PS	Comm to 2 yrs HL	Marseilles	WO/90/6/44	
30/12/15	Williams W (S/Smith)	Pte	ASC	Joining M	3 yrs PS	Comm to 2 yrs HL	Marseilles	WO/90/6/44	
31/01/16	Africa Louis	Native Leader	S ASC	M	2 yr HL		Bissil BEA	WO/213/8/132	
31/01/16	Inyani Willie	Native Leader	S ASC	M	2 yr HL		Bissil BEA	WO/213/8/132	
31/01/16	Malefa W[illia]m	Native Leader	S ASC	M	NG		Bissil BEA	WO/213/8/132	
31/01/16	Malleysi Pohl	Native Leader	S ASC	M	NG		Bissil BEA	WO/213/8/132	
09/02/16	Smith JI	Pte	1 HLI	[M]S7(2b)	18 mos HL		Field (Mespot)	WO/90/7/70	10
15/02/16	Alcock MG	Pte	19 AIF	M+Disob	18 mos HL		Sinai Penin	WO/213/8/113	11
15/02/16	Anderson AG	Pte	19 AIF	M+Disob	18 mos HL		Sinai Penin	WO/213/8/113	
15/02/16	Fletcher WJ	Pte	19 AIF	M+Disob	12 mos HL		Sinai Penin	WO/213/8/113	
15/02/16	Hill P	Pte	19 AIF	M+Disob	18 mos HL		Sinai Penin	WO/213/8/113	
15/02/16	King EJ	Pte	19 AIF	M+Disob	18 mos HL		Sinai Penin	WO/213/8/113	
15/02/16	Rowlands TJ	Pte	19 AIF	M+Disob	12 mos HL		Sinai Penin	WO/213/8/113	
15/02/16	Walker JA	Cpl	19 AIF	M+Disob	3 yrs HL		Sinai Penin	WO/213/8/113	
15/02/16	Yeadon C[A/R?]	Pte	19 AIF	M+Disob	18 mos HL		Sinai Penin	WO/213/8/113	
05/05/16	Booker A	Pte	2 Ox & Bucks LI	M+Disob	5 yrs PS	Quashed	Field	WO/213/9/46	12
17/06/16	Langrish JG	Rfn	3 NZ Rifle Bde	M+S40	42 dys FP		Armentieres	WO/213/9/182	13
22/06/16	Groom W	Pte	1 Border	M+Insub+Disob	4 yrs PS	Susp	Louvencourt	WO/213/10/111	14
08/07/16	White HT	Pte	20 AIF	M+Drunk	18 mos HL		Field	WO/213/10/145	15
16/07/16	Ward JWH	Dvr	175 Bde RFA	M+Disob	28 dys FP1		Field	WO/213/11/24	16
19/07/16	Conway P	Pte	3(R) Munster Fus	Persuading M+Insub	Acquit		[Le] Havre	WO/90/6/67	17
19/07/16	Coffey J	Spr	Aust Mining Coy	Per M+Viol SO	5 yrs PS		[Le] Havre	WO/90/6/66	
19/07/16	Daly T	Pte	18 AIF	Per M+Viol SO	Acquit		[Le] Havre	WO/90/6/67	
19/07/16	Nearin J	Pte	2 CEF	Per M+Viol SO	Acquit		[Le] Havre	WO/90/6/67	
19/07/16	Magnusson GD	Gnr	11 Bty NZFA	Per M+Viol SO	Acquit		[Le] Havre	WO/90/6/67	
19/07/16	Moss EJ	Pte	18 AIF	Per M+Viol SO	5 yrs PS		[Le] Havre	WO/90/6/67	
19/07/16	Murphy R	Pte	18 AIF	Per M+Viol SO	5 yrs PS		[Le] Havre	WO/90/6/67	
19/07/16	Purcell W	Gnr	Aust Siege Bty	Per M+Viol SO	5 yrs PS		[Le] Havre	WO/90/6/67	
19/07/16	Sager WG	Pte	5 CEF	Per M +Insub	Acquit		[Le] Havre	WO/90/6/67	
19/07/16	Tepoorten JE	Pte	Can ASC	M+Insub	5 yrs PS		[Le] Havre	WO/90/6/67	
19/07/16	Williams SG	Pte	1 Wellington NZEF	Per M+Viol SO	Acquit		[Le] Havre	WO/90/6/67	
28/08/16	McKinley W	Pte	8/10 Gordons (att RE)	M x 2	5 yrs PS	Susp	Field	WO/213/11/9	18
28/08/16	Nelson T	Pte	8/10 Gordons (att RE)	M x 2	5 yrs PS	Susp	Field	WO/213/11/9	
28/08/16	O'Sullivan J	Pte	8/10 Gordons (att RE)	M x 2	Death	Comm 5 yrs PS	Field	WO/213/11/9	
28/08/16	Turner J	Pte	8/10 Gordons (att RE)	M x 2	2 yrs HL	Susp	Field	WO/213/11/9	
14/09/16	Ball A	Pte	2 KOYLI	M+Insub	3 yrs PS		Abancourt	WO/213/11/31	19
05/10/16	Delaney J	Pte	2 A&SH	M	Death	Comm 2 yrs PS	Rouen	WO/90/6/89	20
05/10/16	Garden J	Pte	1 HLI	M	Death	Comm 15 yrs PS	Rouen	WO/90/6/89	
05/10/16	Lewis WE	Gnr	124 Bde RFA	M	Death		Rouen	WO/90/6/89	
05/10/16	McCorkindale D	Pte	11 R Scots	M	Death	Comm 15 yrs PS	Rouen	WO/90/6/89	
05/10/16	Murphy MJ	Pte	6 Conn Rangers	M	Death	Comm 10 yrs PS	Rouen	WO/90/6/89	
05/10/16	Peden W	Dvr	ASC	M	Death	Comm 2 yrs HL	Rouen	WO/90/6/89	
05/10/16	Thom AG	Tpr	6 Dragoon (att RH Gds)	M	5 yrs PS	Comm 2 yrs HL	Rouen	WO/90/6/89	
11/10/16	Braithwaite J	Pte	2 Otago NZEF	M	Death		Rouen	WO/90/6/90	
11/10/16	Le Guier B	Pte	14 AIF	M	Death	Comm 2 yrs HL	Rouen	WO/90/6/90	
11/10/16	Little A	Pte	10 AIF	M+Striking(Sgt)	Death	Comm 2 yrs HL	Rouen	WO/90/6/89	
11/10/16	Mitchell FKW	Pte	5 AIF	M	Death	Comm 2 yrs HL	Rouen	WO/90/6/90	

Date D/M/Y	Name	Rank	Unit	Offence	Finding/Punishment	Amendment	Location	PRO Reference File/Piece/Page	Note:
11/10/16	Sheffield S	Pte	4 AIF	M	Death	Comm 2 yrs HL	Rouen	WO/90/6/90	
01/12/16	Claybrook AH	Pte	12 SWBdrs	M+Disob	18 mos HL	Comm 3 mos FP1	Field	WO/213/13/47	21
01/12/16	Cooke R	Pte	12 SWBdrs	M+Disob	18 mos HL	Comm 3 mos FP1	Field	WO/312/13/46	
01/12/16	French J	Pte	12 SWBdrs	M+Disob	18 mos HL	Comm 3 mos FP1	Field	WO/213/13/46	
01/12/16	Gummer E	Pte	12 SWBdrs	M+Disob	18 mos HL	Comm 3 mos FP1	Field	WO/213/13/47	
01/12/16	Hale TS	Pte	12 SWBdrs	M+Disob	18 mos HL	Comm 3 mos FP1	Field	WO/213/13/47	
01/12/16	Kelly SW	Pte	12 SWBdrs	M+Disob	18 mos HL	Comm 3 mos FP1	Field	WO/213/13/47	
01/12/16	Leather AW	Pte	12 SWBdrs	M(2)+Disob	7 yrs PS	Comm 2 yrs HL	Field	WO/213/13/46	
01/12/16	Marsden E	Pte	12 SWBdrs	M+Disob	18 mos HL	Comm 3 mos FP1	Field	WO/312/13/46	
01/12/16	Milne R	Pte	12 SWBdrs	M+Disob	2 yrs HL	Comm 3 mos FP1	Field	WO/213/13/46	
01/12/16	Price CR	Pte(L/Cpl)	12 SWBdrs	M+Disob	NG		Field	WO/213/13/46	
01/12/16	Rustage VA	Pte	12 SWBdrs	M+Disob	18 mos HL	Comm 3 mos FP1	Field	WO/213/13/47	
01/12/16	Samuel V	Pte	12 SWBdrs	M+Disob	18 mos HL	Comm 3 mos FP1	Field	WO/213/13/47	
01/12/16	Sutton W	Pte	12 SWBdrs	M+Disob	18 mos HL	Comm 3 mos FP1	Field	WO/213/13/47	
01/12/16	Thomas T	Pte	12 SWBdrs	M+Disob	18 mos HL	Comm 3 mos FP1	Field	WO/213/13/47	
01/12/16	Tough TF	Pte	12 SWBdrs	M+Disob	18 mos HL	Comm 3 mos FP1	Field	WO/213/13/47	
01/12/16	Turner E	Pte	12 SWBdrs	M+Disob	18 mos HL	Comm 3 mos FP1	Field	WO/312/13/46	
01/12/16	Walton R	Pte	12 SWBdrs	M+Disob	18 mos HL	Comm 3 mos FP1	Field	WO/312/13/46	
01/12/16	Watkins F	Pte	12 SWBdrs	M+Disob	18 mos HL	Comm 3 mos FP1	Field	WO/312/13/46	
05/12/16	Wood W	Pte	12 SWBdrs	M+Disob	NG		Field	WO/312/13/30	
23/12/16	Robson PL	Pte	8 SA Infy	M+S40	20 dys Detn+Ranks+Stop			W)/213/11/179	22
27/12/16	Gallagher P	Pte	60 AIF	M+Ins+Disob+Disch Igmny	2 yrs HL		At Sea	WO/213/13/97	23
10/01/17	Jenkins JH	Gnr	V/38 TMB	M+Disob	3 yrs PS		Esquelbecq	WO/213/13/138	24
10/01/17	Jones JM	Gnr	V/38 TMB	M+Disob	3 yrs PS		Esquelbecq	WO/213/13/138	
10/01/17	Loud FC	Gnr	V/38 TMB	M+Disob	3 yrs PS	Comm 1 yr HL	Esquelbecq	WO/213/13/138	
10/01/17	Morgan WE	Gnr	V/38 TMB	M+Disob	3 yrs PS		Esquelbecq	WO/213/13/138	
10/01/17	Thomas D	Gnr	V/38 TMB	M+Disob	3 yrs PS		Esquelbecq	WO/213/13/138	
11/01/17	Jones P	Gnr	V/38 TMB	M+S40	56 dys FP1		Esquelbecq	WO/213/13/138	
31/01/17	Sullivan RP	Pte	10 Royal Fus	M+Sleeping	Death	NC	Field	WO/213/13/172	25
04/04/17	Fellows R	Dvr	65 SAASC	M+Insub+S9(1)	10 yrs PS		Field SEF	WO/213/15/5	
13/04/17	Broom W	Pte(L/Cpl)	7 Suffolk	M+S40	9 mos HL	Rem 3 mos	Arras	WO/213/15/142	26
13/04/17	Brown A	Pte	5 Berks	M+S40	3 mos Stop	Rem 2 mos	Arras	WO/213/15/142	
13/04/17	Elsegood A	Pte	7 Norfolk	M+S40	9 mos HL	Rem 3 mos	Arras	WO/213/15/142	
13/04/17	Mullen T	Pte	R Marine Lab Corps	M	8 mos HL		Dunkirk	WO/213/14/138	27
13/04/17	Bullen RG	Pte	R Marine Lab Corps	M	1 yr HL		Dunkirk	WO/213/14/138	
13/04/17	Davidson L	Pte	R Marine Lab Corps	M	1 yr HL		Dunkirk	WO/213/14/138	
13/04/17	Gillies R	Pte	R Marine Lab Corps	M	1 yr HL		Dunkirk	WO/213/14/138	
13/04/17	McLaughlin G	Pte	R Marine Lab Corps	M	1 yr HL		Dunkirk	WO/213/14/138	
13/04/17	Murphy J	Pte	R Marine Lab Corps	M	1 yr HL		Dunkirk	WO/213/14/138	
13/04/17	Buckley M	Pte	13 R Berks	M	8 mos HL		Dunkirk	WO/213/14/138	28
13/04/17	Lewis HT	Pte	20 Lancs Fus	M	6 mos HL		Dunkirk	WO/213/14/138	
13/04/17	Veale W	Pte	7/8 R Irish Fus	M	8 mos HL		Dunkirk	WO/213/14/138	
13/04/17	McGuire P	Pte	7/8 R Irish Fus	M	8 mos HL		Dunkirk	WO/213/14/138	
13/04/17	Laverty J	Pte	1 B Watch	M	8 mos HL		Dunkirk	WO/213/14/138	
13/04/17	McNeal P	Pte	A & SH	M	1 yr HL		Dunkirk	WO/213/14/138	
13/04/17	Haw WE	Pte	2 Yorks att ASC	M	6 mos HL		Dunkirk	WO/213/14/138	
13/04/17	O'Neill J	Pte	ASC	M	1 yr HL		Dunkirk	WO/213/14/138	
13/04/17	Hoaldsworth C	Gnr	155 Bde RFA	M	8 mos HL		Dunkirk	WO/213/14/138	
05/06/17	Allcock A	Pte	1 Gn Sher Fstrs	M	2 yrs HL		Kantara Egypt	WO/213/15/176	29
05/06/17	Allmand E	Pte	1 Gn Sher Fstrs	M	2 yrs HL		Kantara Egypt	WO/213/15/176	
05/06/17	Arnold J	Pte	1 Gn Sher Fstrs	M	2 yrs HL		Kantara Egypt	WO/213/15/176	
05/06/17	Barker H	Pte	1 Gn Sher Fstrs	M	2 yrs HL		Kantara Egypt	WO/213/15/176	
05/06/17	Bennett J	Pte	1 Gn Sher Fstrs	M	2 yrs HL		Kantara Egypt	WO/213/15/176	
05/06/17	Bestwick TC	Pte	1 Gn Sher Fstrs	M	2 yrs HL		Kantara Egypt	WO/213/15/176	
05/06/17	Boolley WF	Pte	1 Gn Sher Fstrs	M	2 yrs HL		Kantara Egypt	WO/213/15/176	
05/06/17	Bowden WH	Pte	1 Gn Sher Fstrs	M	2 yrs HL		Kantara Egypt	WO/213/15/176	
05/06/17	Brookes TW	Pte	1 Gn Sher Fstrs	M	2 yrs HL		Kantara Egypt	WO/213/15/176	

Date D/M/Y	Name	Rank	Unit	Offence	Finding/Punishment	Amendment	Location	PRO Reference File/Piece/Page	Note:
05/06/17	Brown C	Pte	1 Gn Sher Fstrs	M	2 yrs HL		Kantara Egypt	WO/213/15/176	
05/06/17	Bullock H	Pte	1 Gn Sher Fstrs	M	2 yrs HL		Kantara Egypt	WO/213/15/176	
05/06/17	Burrows G	Pte	1 Gn Sher Fstrs	M	2 yrs HL		Kantara Egypt	WO/213/15/176	
05/06/17	Butler H	Pte	1 Gn Sher Fstrs	M	2 yrs HL		Kantara Egypt	WO/213/15/176	
05/06/17	Byrd J	Pte	1 Gn Sher Fstrs	M	2 yrs HL		Kantara Egypt	WO/213/15/176	
05/06/17	Cassidy J	Pte	1 Gn Sher Fstrs	M	2 yrs HL		Kantara Egypt	WO/213/15/176	
05/06/17	Chapman H	Pte	1 Gn Sher Fstrs	M	2 yrs HL		Kantara Egypt	WO/213/15/176	
05/06/17	Clay H	Pte	1 Gn Sher Fstrs	M	2 yrs HL		Kantara Egypt	WO/213/15/176	
05/06/17	Crisp C	Pte	1 Gn Sher Fstrs	M	2 yrs HL		Kantara Egypt	WO/213/15/176	
05/06/17	Ford J	Pte	1 Gn Sher Fstrs	M	2 yrs HL		Kantara Egypt	WO/213/15/176	
05/06/17	Freeman H	Pte	1 Gn Sher Fstrs	M	2 yrs HL		Kantara Egypt	WO/213/15/176	
05/06/17	Ganley H	Pte	1 Gn Sher Fstrs	M	2 yrs HL		Kantara Egypt	WO/213/15/176	
05/06/17	Hallam G	Pte	1 Gn Sher Fstrs	M	2 yrs HL		Kantara Egypt	WO/213/15/176	
05/06/17	Hammond H	Pte	1 Gn Sher Fstrs	M	2 yrs HL		Kantara Egypt	WO/213/15/176	
05/06/17	Hardy J	Pte	1 Gn Sher Fstrs	M	2 yrs HL		Kantara Egypt	WO/213/15/176	
05/06/17	Harrison GJ	Pte	1 Gn Sher Fstrs	M	2 yrs HL		Kantara Egypt	WO/213/15/176	
05/06/17	Harrison JW	Pte	1 Gn Sher Fstrs	M	2 yrs HL		Kantara Egypt	WO/213/15/176	
05/06/17	Harvey AE	Pte	1 Gn Sher Fstrs	M	2 yrs HL		Kantara Egypt	WO/213/15/177	
05/06/17	Haywood J	Pte	1 Gn Sher Fstrs	M	2 yrs HL		Kantara Egypt	WO/213/15/177	
05/06/17	Healy E	Pte	1 Gn Sher Fstrs	M	2 yrs HL		Kantara Egypt	WO/213/15/177	
05/06/17	Holmes S	Pte	1 Gn Sher Fstrs	M	2 yrs HL		Kantara Egypt	WO/213/15/177	
05/06/17	Horton E	Pte	1 Gn Sher Fstrs	M	2 yrs HL		Kantara Egypt	WO/213/15/177	
05/06/17	Howe J	Pte	1 Gn Sher Fstrs	M	2 yrs HL		Kantara Egypt	WO/213/15/177	
05/06/17	Lakin W	Pte	1 Gn Sher Fstrs	M	2 yrs HL		Kantara Egypt	WO/213/15/177	
05/06/17	Lamb W	Pte	1 Gn Sher Fstrs	M	2 yrs HL		Kantara Egypt	WO/213/15/177	
05/06/17	Leese G	Pte	1 Gn Sher Fstrs	M	2 yrs HL		Kantara Egypt	WO/213/15/177	
05/06/17	Lindsay F	Pte	1 Gn Sher Fstrs	M	2 yrs HL		Kantara Egypt	WO/213/15/177	
05/06/17	Loxley G	Pte	1 Gn Sher Fstrs	M	2 yrs HL		Kantara Egypt	WO/213/15/177	
05/06/17	Massey A	Pte	1 Gn Sher Fstrs	M	2 yrs HL		Kantara Egypt	WO/213/15/177	
05/06/17	McQuade F	Pte	1 Gn Sher Fstrs	M	2 yrs HL		Kantara Egypt	WO/213/15/177	
05/06/17	Mellors H	Pte	1 Gn Sher Fstrs	M	2 yrs HL		Kantara Egypt	WO/213/15/177	
05/06/17	Millward J	Pte	1 Gn Sher Fstrs	M	2 yrs HL		Kantara Egypt	WO/213/15/177	
05/06/17	Morris A	Pte	1 Gn Sher Fstrs	M	2 yrs HL		Kantara Egypt	WO/213/15/177	
05/06/17	Newton F	Pte	1 Gn Sher Fstrs	M	2 yrs HL		Kantara Egypt	WO/213/15/177	
05/06/17	Noble W	Pte	1 Gn Sher Fstrs	M	2 yrs HL		Kantara Egypt	WO/213/15/177	
05/06/17	Noton T	Pte	1 Gn Sher Fstrs	M	2 yrs HL		Kantara Egypt	WO/213/15/177	
05/06/17	Palfrey WR	Pte	1 Gn Sher Fstrs	M	2 yrs HL		Kantara Egypt	WO/213/15/177	
05/06/17	Parker G	Pte	1 Gn Sher Fstrs	M	2 yrs HL		Kantara Egypt	WO/213/15/177	
05/06/17	Pickles JR	Pte	1 Gn Sher Fstrs	M	2 yrs HL		Kantara Egypt	WO/213/15/177	
05/06/17	Ratcliffe H	Pte	1 Gn Sher Fstrs	M	2 yrs HL		Kantara Egypt	WO/213/15/177	
05/06/17	Rathbone H	Pte	1 Gn Sher Fstrs	M	2 yrs HL		Kantara Egypt	WO/213/15/177	
05/06/17	Riley W	Pte	1 Gn Sher Fstrs	M	2 yrs HL		Kantara Egypt	WO/213/15/177	
05/06/17	Robinson JEG	Pte	1 Gn Sher Fstrs	M	2 yrs HL		Kantara Egypt	WO/213/15/177	
05/06/17	Scoffham W	Pte	1 Gn Sher Fstrs	M	2 yrs HL		Kantara Egypt	WO/213/15/178	
05/06/17	Slater JE	Pte	1 Gn Sher Fstrs	M	2 yrs HL		Kantara Egypt	WO/213/15/178	
05/06/17	Smith J	Pte	1 Gn Sher Fstrs	M	2 yrs HL		Kantara Egypt	WO/213/15/178	
05/06/17	Stephenson L	Pte	1 Gn Sher Fstrs	M	2 yrs HL		Kantara Egypt	WO/213/15/178	
05/06/17	Street GS	Pte	1 Gn Sher Fstrs	M	2 yrs HL		Kantara Egypt	WO/213/15/178	
05/06/17	Taylor A	Pte	1 Gn Sher Fstrs	M	2 yrs HL		Kantara Egypt	WO/213/15/178	
05/06/17	Taylor S	Pte	1 Gn Sher Fstrs	M	2 yrs HL		Kantara Egypt	WO/213/15/178	
05/06/17	Ward W	Pte	1 Gn Sher Fstrs	M	2 yrs HL		Kantara Egypt	WO/213/15/178	
05/06/17	Wesman W	Pte	1 Gn Sher Fstrs	M	2 yrs HL		Kantara Egypt	WO/213/15/178	
05/06/17	Wilkinson J	Pte	1 Gn Sher Fstrs	M	2 yrs HL		Kantara Egypt	WO/213/15/178	
05/06/17	Yates J	Pte	1 Gn Sher Fstrs	M	2 yrs HL		Kantara Egypt	WO/213/15/178	
11/06/17	Daniels CH	Pte	1 Gn Sher Fstrs	M	2 yrs HL		Kantara Egypt	WO/213/15/175	
13/08/17	Kafope A bin	Pte	1/6 KAR	Mx2 + Striking	15 yrs PS + Disch Igmny		Tabora	WO/213/23/81	30
13/08/17	Mwanyivera A bin	Pte	1/6 KAR	Mx2 + Striking	15 yrs PS + Disch Igmny		Tabora	WO/213/23/81	
01/09/17	Banks JL	Pte	2 Otago NZEF	M	10 yrs PS		Field	WO/213/17/110	31
01/09/17	Duke T	Pte	2 Otago NZEF	M	10 yrs PS		Field	WO/213/17/110	
01/09/17	Frew G	Pte	2 Otago NZEF	M	10 yrs PS		Field	WO/213/17/110	
01/09/17	Leyden JF	Pte	2 Otago NZEF	M	10 yrs PS		Field	WO/213/17/110	
01/09/17	New[t/l?]on CW	Pte	2 Otago NZEF	M	10 yrs PS		Field	WO/213/17/110	
01/09/17	Plunkett J	Pte	2 Otago NZEF	M	10 yrs PS		Field	WO/213/17/110	
01/09/17	Reid S	Pte	2 Otago NZEF	M	10 yrs PS		Field	WO/213/17/110	
06/09/17	Abdalla Y	Labourer	Egyptian Lab Corps	M + S40	8 mos HL		Boulogne	WO/213/17/41	32
06/09/17	Acasha A	Labourer	Egyptian Lab Corps	M + S40	8 mos HL		Boulogne	WO/213/17/41	
06/09/17	Ahmed R	Labourer	Egyptian Lab Corps	M + S40	8 mos HL		Boulogne	WO/213/17/41	

Date D/M/Y	Name	Rank	Unit	Offence	Finding/Punishment	Amendment	Location	PRO Reference File/Piece/Page	Note:
06/09/17	Ali A	Labourer	Egyptian Lab Corps	M+S40	8 mos HL		Boulogne	WO/213/17/41	
06/09/17	Bahit AS	Labourer	Egyptian Lab Corps	M+S40	8 mos HL		Boulogne	WO/213/17/41	
06/09/17	Ibrahim S	Labourer	Egyptian Lab Corps	M+S40	8 mos HL		Boulogne	WO/213/17/41	
06/09/17	Mohamed A	Labourer	Egyptian Lab Corps	M+S40	8 mos HL		Boulogne	WO/213/17/41	
06/09/17	Sallam O	Labourer	Egyptian Lab Corps	M+S40	8 mos HL		Boulogne	WO/213/17/41	
06/09/17	Sarhan M	Labourer	Egyptian Lab Corps	M+S40	8 mos HL		Boulogne	WO/213/17/41	
06/09/17	Suleiman M	Labourer	Egyptian Lab Corps	M+S40	8 mos HL		Boulogne	WO/213/17/41	
12/09/17	Short JR	Cpl	24 North Fus	M	Death		Etaples	WO/213/17/119	33
18/09/17	Davi[e?]s JF	Pte	Aus MGC	M+Viol+Resist	10 yrs PS		Etaples	WO/213/17/151	
18/09/17	McIntosh R	Pte	R Sco Fus	M	10 yrs PS		Etaples	WO/213/17/151	
19/09/17	Flint GH	Tpr	Can Lt Horse	M	10 yrs PS	Comm 2 yrs HL	Etaples	WO/213/17/151	
04/11/17	Green W	Pte	6 LN Lancs	Drunk+Viol+M+S10(3)+Insol	5 yrs PS+DI		Mesopotamia	WO/90/7/143	34
12/11/17	Butlin A	Pte	10 Y & Lanc	M+Disob	6 mos HL	Comm 91 dys FP1	Field	WO/213/18/181	35
12/11/17	Firth J	Pte	10 Y & Lanc	M+Disob	6 mos HL	Comm 91 dys FP1	Field	WO/213/18/181	
12/11/17	Lievesley H	Pte	8 Lincs	M+Disob	9 mos HL		Field	WO/213/18/180	
12/11/17	Westmoreland G	Pte	8 Lincs	M+Disob	6 mos HL	Comm 91 dys FP1	Field	WO/213/18/180	
12/11/17	Covill G	Pte	4 Mddx	M+Disob	6 mos HL	Comm 91 dys FP1	Field	WO/213/18/181	
12/11/17	Filmar A	Pte	4 Mddx	M+Disob	6 mos HL	Comm 91 dys FP1	Field	WO/213/18/181	
12/11/17	Gunn F	Pte	4 Mddx	M+Disob	6 mos HL	Comm 91 dys FP1	Field	WO/213/18/181	
12/11/17	Hollings F	Pte	4 Mddx	M+Disob	6 mos HL	Comm 91 dys FP1	Field	WO/213/18/181	
12/11/17	Llewellin L	Pte	4 Mddx	M+Disob	6 mos HL	Comm 91 dys FP1	Field	WO/213/18/181	
12/11/17	Mitchell E	Pte	4 Mddx	M+Disob	6 mos HL	Comm 91 dys FP1	Field	WO/213/18/181	
12/11/17	New B	Pte	4 Mddx	M+Disob	6 mos HL	Comm 91 dys FP1	Field	WO/213/18/181	
12/11/17	Weatherley J	Pte	4 Mddx	M+Disob	6 mos HL	Comm 91 dys FP1	Field	WO/213/18/181	
21/11/17	April	Pte	SANLC	M+S40	3 yrs PS	Comm 2 yrs HL	Field	WO/213/31/109	36
21/11/17	Bethuel	Pte	SANLC	M+S40	3 yrs PS	Comm 2 yrs HL	Field	WO/213/31/109	
21/11/17	Elias	Pte	SANLC	M+S40	3 yrs PS	Comm 2 yrs HL	Field	WO/213/31/109	
21/11/17	Frans	Pte	SANLC	M+S40	3 yrs PS	Comm 2 yrs HL	Field	WO/213/31/109	
21/11/17	Hendrick	Pte	SANLC	M+S40	3 yrs PS	Comm 2 yrs HL	Field	WO/213/31/109	
21/11/17	Jack	Pte	SANLC	M+S40	3 yrs PS	Comm 2 yrs HL	Field	WO/213/31/109	
21/11/17	Jack	Pte	SANLC	M+S40	3 yrs PS	Comm 2 yrs HL	Field	WO/213/31/109	
21/11/17	Jacob	Pte	SANLC	M+S40	3 yrs PS	Comm 2 yrs HL	Field	WO/213/31/109	
21/11/17	Jacob	Pte	SANLC	M+S40	3 yrs PS	Comm 2 yrs HL	Field	WO/213/31/109	
21/11/17	Jacob	Pte	SANLC	M+S40	3 yrs PS	Comm 2 yrs HL	Field	WO/213/31/109	
21/11/17	Jim	Pte(L/Cpl)	SANLC	M+S40	3 yrs PS	Comm 2 yrs HL	Field	WO/213/31/109	
21/11/17	Johannes	Pte(L/Cpl)	SANLC	M+S40	3 yrs PS	Comm 2 yrs HL	Field	WO/213/31/109	
21/11/17	Klaas	Pte	SANLC	M+S40	3 yrs PS	Comm 2 yrs HL	Field	WO/213/31/109	
21/11/17	Mack	Pte	SANLC	M+S40	3 yrs PS	Comm 2 yrs HL	Field	WO/213/31/109	
21/11/17	Sam	Pte	SANLC	M+S40	3 yrs PS	Comm 2 yrs HL	Field	WO/213/31/109	
21/11/17	Simeon	Pte	SANLC	M+S40	3 yrs PS	Comm 2 yrs HL	Field	WO/213/31/109	
10/12/17	Peden W	Dvr	ASC	M	5 yrs PS		Field	WO/213/19/52	37
11/12/17	Clergy C	Pte	43 CEF	M+Disob	18 mos HL		Field	WO/213/19/116	38
11/12/17	Cuff SH	Pte	43 CEF	M+Disob	18 mos HL		Field	WO/213/19/116	
11/12/17	Graham WG	Pte	43 CEF	M+Disob	18 mos HL		Field	WO/213/19/116	
11/12/17	Primett H	Pte	43 CEF	M+Disob	18 mos HL		Field	WO/213/19/116	
23/12/17	Bonang AW	Pte	43 CEF	M+Disob	2 yrs HL		Field	WO/213/19/116	
17/12/17	Mademedsha J	Pte	SANLC	M	10 yrs PS		Capetown	WO/213/19/115	39
17/12/17	Makubedi K	Cpl	SANLC	M	12 yrs PS+Rnks		Capetown	WO/213/19/115	
17/12/17	Makuku J	Pte	SANLC	M	10 yrs PS		Capetown	WO/213/19/115	
17/12/17	Matume D	Pte	SANLC	M	10 yrs PS		Capetown	WO/213/19/115	
17/12/17	Rapatele A	L/Cpl	SANLC	M	10 yrs PS		Capetown	WO/213/19/115	
17/12/17	Rueben [?]	Pte	SANLC	M	10 yrs PS		Capetown	WO/213/19/115	
17/12/17	Sekgoba C	Pte	SANLC	M	10 yrs PS		Capetown	WO/213/19/115	
17/12/17	Wtsoane G	Pte	SANLC	M	10 yrs PS		Capetown	WO/213/19/115	
14/01/18	Bell J	Pte	1/4 R Sco Fus	M	10 yrs PS	Comm 2 yrs HL	Field	WO/213/21/34	40
14/01/18	Cunningham J	Pte	1/4 R Sco Fus	M	10 yrs PS	Comm 2 yrs HL	Field	WO/213/21/34	

Date D/M/Y	Name	Rank	Unit	Offence	Finding/Punishment	Amendment	Location	PRO Reference File/Piece/Page	Note:
14/01/18	Dunlop C	Pte	1/4 R Sco Fus	M	10 yrs PS	Comm 2 yrs HL	Field	WO/213/21/34	
14/01/18	Lennox J	Pte	1/4 R Sco Fus	M	10 yrs PS	Comm 2 yrs HL	Field	WO/213/21/34	
14/01/18	McMeecham M	Pte	1/4 R Sco Fus	M	10 yrs PS	Comm 2 yrs HL	Field	WO/213/21/34	
13/03/18	Baron JC	Gnr	RGA	M	1 yr HL	unexpired portion 30/4/18	Agra	WO/90/7/190	41
13/03/18	Bridge H	Gnr	RGA	M	1 yr HL	unexpired portion 30/4/18	Agra	WO/90/7/190	
13/03/18	Brown HW	Gnr	RGA	M	1 yr HL	unexpired portion 30/4/18	Agra	WO/90/7/190	
13/03/18	Carter W	Gnr	RGA	M	1 yr HL	unexpired portion 30/4/18	Agra	WO/90/7/190	
13/03/18	Collings EH	Gnr	RGA	M	1 yr HL	unexpired portion 30/4/18	Agra	WO/90/7/190	
13/03/18	Conway D	Gnr	RGA	M	1 yr HL	unexpired portion 30/4/18	Agra	WO/90/7/190	
13/03/18	Cranston HW	Gnr	RGA	M	1 yr HL	unexpired portion 30/4/18	Agra	WO/90/7/190	
13/03/18	Donnell J	Gnr	RGA	M	1 yr HL	unexpired portion 30/4/18	Agra	WO/90/7/190	
13/03/18	Fowler F	Gnr	RGA	M	1 yr HL	unexpired portion 30/4/18	Agra	WO/90/7/190	
13/03/18	Gager SE	Gnr	RGA	M	1 yr HL	unexpired portion 30/4/18	Agra	WO/90/7/190	
13/03/18	Gordon J	Gnr	RGA	M	1 yr HL	unexpired portion 30/4/18	Agra	WO/90/7/190	
13/03/18	Hotchkiss M	Gnr	RGA	M	1 yr HL	unexpired portion 30/4/18	Agra	WO/90/7/190	
13/03/18	Hounsell EA	Gnr	RGA	M	1 yr HL	unexpired portion 30/4/18	Agra	WO/90/7/190	
13/03/18	Martin S	Gnr	RGA	M	1 yr HL	unexpired portion 30/4/18	Agra	WO/90/7/190	
13/03/18	Niven A	Gnr	RGA	M	1 yr HL	unexpired portion 30/4/18	Agra	WO/90/7/190	
13/03/18	Noble A	Gnr	RGA	M	1 yr HL	unexpired portion 30/4/18	Agra	WO/90/7/190	
13/03/18	Palmer AE	Gnr	RGA	M	1 yr HL	unexpired portion 30/4/18	Agra	WO/90/7/190	
13/03/18	Plant F	Gnr	RGA	M	1 yr HL	unexpired portion 30/4/18	Agra	WO/90/7/190	
13/03/18	Preece W	Gnr	RGA	M	Acquit		Agra	WO/90/7/190	
13/03/18	Price E	Gnr	RGA	M	1 yr HL	unexpired portion 30/4/18	Agra	WO/90/7/190	
13/03/18	Proctor E	Gnr	RGA	M	1 yr HL	unexpired portion 30/4/18	Agra	WO/90/7/190	
13/03/18	Sampson F	Gnr	RGA	M	1 yr HL	unexpired portion 30/4/18	Agra	WO/90/7/190	
13/03/18	Sanders EW	Gnr	RGA	M	1 yr HL	unexpired portion 30/4/18	Agra	WO/90/7/190	
13/03/18	Smith J	Gnr	RGA	M	1 yr HL	unexpired portion 30/4/18	Agra	WO/90/7/190	
13/03/18	Smith L	Gnr	RGA	M	1 yr HL	unexpired portion 30/4/18	Agra	WO/90/7/190	
13/03/18	Stevens SH	Gnr	RGA	M	1 yr HL	unexpired portion 30/4/18	Agra	WO/90/7/190	
13/03/18	Taylor FH	Gnr	RGA	M	1 yr HL	unexpired portion 30/4/18	Agra	WO/90/7/190	
13/03/18	Thacker GH	Gnr	RGA	M	1 yr HL	unexpired portion 30/4/18	Agra	WO/90/7/190	
13/03/18	Warrener EG	Gnr	RGA	M	1 yr HL	unexpired portion 30/4/18	Agra	WO/90/7/191	
13/03/18	Winter C	Gnr	RGA	M	1 yr HL	unexpired portion 30/4/18	Agra	WO/90/7/191	
13/03/18	Wood A	Gnr	RGA	M	1 yr HL	unexpired portion 30/4/18	Agra	WO/90/7/190	
13/03/18	Wood LS	Gnr	RGA	M	1 yr HL	unexpired portion 30/4/18	Agra	WO/90/7/190	
13/03/18	Woodworth GW	Gnr	RGA	M	Acquit		Agra	WO/90/7/191	
13/03/18	Allen G	Gnr	RFA(att RGA)	M	1 yr HL	unexpired portion 30/4/18	Agra	WO/90/7/190	
13/03/18	Gurney P	Gnr	RFA(att RGA)	M	1 yr HL	unexpired portion 30/4/18	Agra	WO/90/7/190	
13/03/18	Longdon A	Dvr	RFA(att RGA)	M	1 yr HL	unexpired portion 30/4/18	Agra	WO/90/7/190	

Date D/M/Y	Name	Rank	Unit	Offence	Finding/Punishment	Amendment	Location	PRO Reference File/Piece/Page	Note:
13/03/18	Skene H	Gnr	RFA(att RGA)	M	1 yr HL	unexpired portion 30/4/18	Agra	WO/90/7/190	
13/03/18	Williamson H	Gnr	RFA(att RGA)	M	1 yr HL	unexpired portion 30/4/18	Agra	WO/90/7/191	
13/03/18	Mitchell BA	Gnr	RHA(att RGA)	M	1 yr HL	unexpired portion 30/4/18	Agra	WO/90/7/190	
04/04/18	Barber SH	Pte	2 Gn/Beds	M+S7(3)	Acquit		Karachi	WO/90/7/191	42
04/04/18	Bushell WJ	Pte	2 Gn/Beds	M+S7(3)	1 yr Detn	Remit 6 mos	Karachi	WO/90/7/191	
04/04/18	Ives GK	Pte	2 Gn/Beds	M+S7(3)	3 yrs PS	Comm 2 yrs HL	Karachi	WO/90/7/191	
04/04/18	Jones SH	Pte	2 Gn/Beds	M+S7(3)	5 yrs PS	Remit 2 yrs HL	Karachi	WO/90/7/191	
04/04/18	Perring G	Pte	2 Gn/Beds	M+S7(3)	5 yrs PS	Remit 1yr	Karachi	WO/90/7/191	
04/04/18	Topley TC	Pte	2 Gn/Beds	M+S7(3)	3 yrs PS	Comm 2 yrs HL	Karachi	WO/90/7/191	
04/04/18	Wadman W	Pte	2 Gn/Beds	M+S7(3)	5 yrs PS	Remit 2 yrs HL	Karachi	WO/90/7/191	
04/04/18	Williams A	Pte	2 Gn/Beds	M+S7(3)	2 yrs HL	Comm 12 mos Detn	Karachi	WO/90/7/191	
15/04/18	Gillespie W	Pte	49 MG Coy	M	NG		Field	WO/213/21/99	43
15/04/18	Arthur H	Pte	2 R Irish	M	5 yrs PS	Susp	Field	WO/213/21/98	
15/04/18	Bolger J	Pte	2 R Irish	M	5 yrs PS	Susp	Field	WO/213/21/98	
15/04/18	Bragnell J	Pte	2 R Irish	M	5 yrs PS	Susp	Field	WO/213/21/98	
15/04/18	Byrne J	Pte	2 R Irish	M	5 yrs PS	Susp	Field	WO/213/21/98	
15/04/18	Carey J	Pte	2 R Irish	M	5 yrs PS	Susp	Field	WO/213/21/99	
15/04/18	Clarke E	Pte	2 R Irish	M	5 yrs PS	Susp	Field	WO/213/21/98	
15/04/18	Connelly J	Pte	2 R Irish	M	5 yrs PS	Susp	Field	WO/213/21/98	
15/04/18	Connor L	Pte	2 R Irish	M	5 yrs PS	Susp	Field	WO/213/21/98	
15/04/18	Gregory W	Pte	2 R Irish	M	5 yrs PS	Susp	Field	WO/213/21/98	
15/04/18	Heggarty W	Pte	2 R Irish	M	5 yrs PS	Susp	Field	WO/213/21/98	
15/04/18	Histed T	Pte	2 R Irish	M	5 yrs PS	Susp	Field	WO/213/21/99	
15/04/18	Huggins H	Pte	2 R Irish	M	5 yrs PS	Susp	Field	WO/213/21/99	
15/04/18	McDonald L	Pte	2 R Irish	M	5 yrs PS	Susp	Field	WO/213/21/98	
15/04/18	Purcell J	Pte	2 R Irish	M	5 yrs PS	Susp	Field	WO/213/21/98	
15/04/18	Reed E	Pte	2 R Irish	M	5 yrs PS	Susp	Field	WO/213/21/99	
15/04/18	Tugby P	Pte	2 R Irish	M	5 yrs PS	Susp	Field	WO/213/21/98	
15/04/18	Wells J	Pte	2 R Irish	M	5 yrs PS	Susp	Field	WO/213/21/98	
15/04/18	Welsh T	Pte	2 R Irish	M	5 yrs PS	Susp	Field	WO/213/21/98	
15/04/18	Arwin A	Pte	7 R Irish	M	5 yrs PS	Susp	Field	WO/213/21/97	
15/04/18	Byrne J	Pte	7 R Irish	M	NG		Field	WO/213/21/98	
15/04/18	Byrne S	Pte	7 R Irish	M	NG		Field	WO/213/21/97	
15/04/18	Clarey T	Pte	7 R Irish	M	5 yrs PS	Susp	Field	WO/213/21/98	
15/04/18	Collins J	Pte	7 R Irish	M	NG		Field	WO/213/21/98	
15/04/18	Commins P	Pte	7 R Irish	M	5 yrs PS	Susp	Field	WO/213/21/97	
15/04/18	Connors J	Pte	7 R Irish	M	5 yrs PS	Susp	Field	WO/213/21/98	
15/04/18	Cotter F	Pte	7 R Irish	M	5 yrs PS	Susp	Field	WO/213/21/97	
15/04/18	Donigan B	Pte	7 R Irish	M	5 yrs PS	Susp	Field	WO/213/21/98	
15/04/18	Donovan J	Pte	7 R Irish	M	5 yrs PS	Susp	Field	WO/213/21/97	
15/04/18	Howell E	Pte	7 R Irish	M	5 yrs PS	Susp	Field	WO/213/21/97	
15/04/18	Hussey A	Pte	7 R Irish	M	5 yrs PS	Susp	Field	WO/213/21/98	
15/04/18	Justice C	Pte	7 R Irish	M	5 yrs PS	Susp	Field	WO/213/21/97	
15/04/18	Kane T	Pte	7 R Irish	M	5 yrs PS	Susp	Field	WO/213/21/97	
15/04/18	Kelleher J	Pte	7 R Irish	M	5 yrs PS	Susp	Field	WO/213/21/97	
15/04/18	Kenny J	Pte	7 R Irish	M	5 yrs PS	Susp	Field	WO/213/21/97	
15/04/18	Lavery F	Pte	7 R Irish	M	5 yrs PS	Susp	Field	WO/213/21/98	
15/04/18	Magee M	Pte	7 R Irish	M	5 yrs PS	Susp	Field	WO/213/21/97	
15/04/18	Mallon W	Pte	7 R Irish	M	5 yrs PS	Susp	Field	WO/213/21/97	
15/04/18	Maloney P	Pte	7 R Irish	M	5 yrs PS	Susp	Field	WO/213/21/98	
15/04/18	McCafferty R	Pte	7 R Irish	M	5 yrs PS	Susp	Field	WO/213/21/97	
15/04/18	McCauley W	Pte	7 R Irish	M	5 yrs PS	Susp	Field	WO/213/21/98	
15/04/18	Murphy M	Pte	7 R Irish	M	NG		Field	WO/213/21/97	
15/04/18	O'Malley M	Pte	7 R Irish	M	5 yrs PS	Susp	Field	WO/213/21/97	
15/04/18	Slattery M	Pte	7 R Irish	M	5 yrs PS	Susp	Field	WO/213/21/97	
15/04/18	Sweeney T	Pte	7 R Irish	M	5 yrs PS	Susp	Field	WO/213/21/97	
15/04/18	Tudor F	Pte	7 R Irish	M	5 yrs PS	Susp	Field	WO/213/21/97	
15/04/18	Tulley M	Pte	7 R Irish	M	5 yrs PS	Susp	Field	WO/213/21/97	
15/04/18	Wickham J	Pte	7 R Irish	M	5 yrs PS	Susp	Field	WO/213/21/98	
15/04/18	Willis F	Pte	7 R Irish	M	5 yrs PS	Susp	Field	WO/213/21/97	
15/04/18	Wilson W	Pte	7 R Irish	M	5 yrs PS	Susp	Field	WO/213/21/98	
15/04/18	Kealley S	Pte	7 R Irish Fus	M	NG		Field	WO/213/21/98	
15/04/18	Austin GW	Pte	7/8 R Innis Fus	M	5 yrs PS	Susp	Field	WO/213/21/96	
15/04/18	Barham R	Pte	7/8 R Innis Fus	M	5 yrs PS	Susp	Field	WO/213/21/96	
15/04/18	Baxter J	Pte(L/Cpl)	7/8 R Innis Fus	M	7 yrs PS	Susp	Field	WO/213/21/95	
15/04/18	Bell M	Pte(L/Cpl)	7/8 R Innis Fus	M	7 yrs PS	Susp	Field	WO/213/21/96	
15/04/18	Blair E	Pte	7/8 R Innis Fus	M	5 yrs PS	Susp	Field	WO/213/21/96	
15/04/18	Bothwell W	Pte	7/8 R Innis Fus	M	5 yrs PS	Susp	Field	WO/213/21/94	

Date D/M/Y	Name	Rank	Unit	Offence	Finding/Punishment	Amendment	Location	PRO Reference File/Piece/Page	Note:
15/04/18	Boulton GH	Pte	7/8 R Innis Fus	M	5 yrs PS	Susp	Field	WO/213/21/96	
15/04/18	Bridge H	Pte	7/8 R Innis Fus	M	5 yrs PS	Susp	Field	WO/213/21/96	
15/04/18	Casey P	Pte	7/8 R Innis Fus	M	5 yrs PS	Susp	Field	WO/213/21/97	
15/04/18	Colbert F	Pte	7/8 R Innis Fus	M	5 yrs PS	Susp	Field	WO/213/21/96	
15/04/18	Donaughey J	Pte	7/8 R Innis Fus	M	5 yrs PS	Susp	Field	WO/213/21/95	
15/04/18	Eades G	Pte	7/8 R Innis Fus	M	5 yrs PS	Susp	Field	WO/213/21/95	
15/04/18	Elliot F	Pte	7/8 R Innis Fus	M	5 yrs PS	Susp	Field	WO/213/21/96	
15/04/18	Fitzpatrick T	Pte	7/8 R Innis Fus	M	5 yrs PS	Susp	Field	WO/213/21/95	
15/04/18	Flannigan J	Pte(L/Cpl)	7/8 R Innis Fus	M	7 yrs PS	Susp	Field	WO/213/21/95	
15/04/18	Froom EH	Pte	7/8 R Innis Fus	M	5 yrs PS	Susp	Field	WO/213/21/96	
15/04/18	Fullerton J	Pte	7/8 R Innis Fus	M	5 yrs PS	Susp	Field	WO/213/21/95	
15/04/18	Goden E	Pte(L/Cpl)	7/8 R Innis Fus	M	7 yrs PS	Susp	Field	WO/213/21/96	
15/04/18	Hanrattey B	Pte	7/8 R Innis Fus	M	5 yrs PS	Susp	Field	WO/213/21/95	
15/04/18	Harrigan C	Pte	7/8 R Innis Fus	M	5 yrs PS	Susp	Field	WO/213/21/96	
15/04/18	Hewett J	Pte	7/8 R Innis Fus	M	5 yrs PS	Susp	Field	WO/213/21/95	
15/04/18	Howard C	Pte	7/8 R Innis Fus	M	5 yrs PS	Susp	Field	WO/213/21/96	
15/04/18	Johnson GL	Pte	7/8 R Innis Fus	M	5 yrs PS	Susp	Field	WO/213/21/95	
15/04/18	Kemble F	Pte(L/Cpl)	7/8 R Innis Fus	M	7 yrs PS	Susp	Field	WO/213/21/96	
15/04/18	Kemp S	Pte	7/8 R Innis Fus	M	5 yrs PS	Susp	Field	WO/213/21/96	
15/04/18	Kerwain E	Pte	7/8 R Innis Fus	M	5 yrs PS	Susp	Field	WO/213/21/95	
15/04/18	King J	Pte	7/8 R Innis Fus	M	5 yrs PS	Susp	Field	WO/213/21/96	
15/04/18	Kinney F	Pte	7/8 R Innis Fus	M	5 yrs PS	Susp	Field	WO/213/21/96	
15/04/18	Lock G	Pte	7/8 R Innis Fus	M	5 yrs PS	Susp	Field	WO/213/21/96	
15/04/18	Lyttle L	Pte	7/8 R Innis Fus	M	5 yrs PS	Susp	Field	WO/213/21/95	
15/04/18	Macintyre P	Pte	7/8 R Innis Fus	M	5 yrs PS	Susp	Field	WO/213/21/95	
15/04/18	Mackay W	Pte	7/8 R Innis Fus	M	5 yrs PS	Susp	Field	WO/213/21/94	
15/04/18	Marriott A	Pte	7/8 R Innis Fus	M	5 yrs PS	Susp	Field	WO/213/21/94	
15/04/18	McNamee G	Pte	7/8 R Innis Fus	M	5 yrs PS	Susp	Field	WO/213/21/95	
15/04/18	Moir J	Pte	7/8 R Innis Fus	M	5 yrs PS	Susp	Field	WO/213/21/96	
15/04/18	Mooney H	Pte	7/8 R Innis Fus	M	5 yrs PS	Susp	Field	WO/213/21/96	
15/04/18	Morphet T	Pte	7/8 R Innis Fus	M	5 yrs PS	Susp	Field	WO/213/21/95	
15/04/18	Moxon T	Pte	7/8 R Innis Fus	M	5 yrs PS	Susp	Field	WO/213/21/95	
15/04/18	Mullen R	Pte	7/8 R Innis Fus	M	NG		Field	WO/213/21/97	
15/04/18	O'Dea B	Pte	7/8 R Innis Fus	M	5 yrs PS	Susp	Field	WO/213/21/95	
15/04/18	O'Donoghue D	Pte	7/8 R Innis Fus	M	5 yrs PS	Susp	Field	WO/213/21/95	
15/04/18	O'Neall W	Pte	7/8 R Innis Fus	M	5 yrs PS	Susp	Field	WO/213/21/96	
15/04/18	Powell CT	Pte	7/8 R Innis Fus	M	NG		Field	WO/213/21/97	
15/04/18	Pratt O	Pte	7/8 R Innis Fus	M	5 yrs PS	Susp	Field	WO/213/21/96	
15/04/18	Prentice W	Pte	7/8 R Innis Fus	M	5 yrs PS	Susp	Field	WO/213/21/96	
15/04/18	Price J	Pte	7/8 R Innis Fus	M	5 yrs PS	Susp	Field	WO/213/21/96	
15/04/18	Priest FC	Pte	7/8 R Innis Fus	M	5 yrs PS	Susp	Field	WO/213/21/97	
15/04/18	Raddock NG	Pte	7/8 R Innis Fus	M	5 yrs PS	Susp	Field	WO/213/21/95	
15/04/18	Reynolds P	Pte	7/8 R Innis Fus	M	5 yrs PS	Susp	Field	WO/213/21/97	
15/04/18	Rowan T	Pte	7/8 R Innis Fus	M	5 yrs PS	Susp	Field	WO/213/21/97	
15/04/18	Rush EW	Pte	7/8 R Innis Fus	M	5 yrs PS	Susp	Field	WO/213/21/96	
15/04/18	Rush P	Pte	7/8 R Innis Fus	M	5 yrs PS	Susp	Field	WO/213/21/96	
15/04/18	Sargeant A	Pte	7/8 R Innis Fus	M	5 yrs PS	Susp	Field	WO/213/21/95	
15/04/18	Searson S	Pte	7/8 R Innis Fus	M	5 yrs PS	Susp	Field	WO/213/21/95	
15/04/18	Simm J	Pte	7/8 R Innis Fus	M	5 yrs PS	Susp	Field	WO/213/21/94	
15/04/18	Staples G	Pte	7/8 R Innis Fus	M	5 yrs PS	Susp	Field	WO/213/21/94	
15/04/18	Stevenson J	Pte	7/8 R Innis Fus	M	5 yrs PS	Susp	Field	WO/213/21/95	
15/04/18	Thompson R	Pte	7/8 R Innis Fus	M	5 yrs PS	Susp	Field	WO/213/21/95	
15/04/18	Turner A	Pte	7/8 R Innis Fus	M	NG		Field	WO/213/21/95	
15/04/18	Wain J	Pte	7/8 R Innis Fus	M	5 yrs PS	Susp	Field	WO/213/21/94	
15/04/18	Waller GH	Pte(L/Cpl))	7/8 R Innis Fus	M	7 yrs PS	Susp	Field	WO/213/21/95	
15/04/18	Wilson W	Cpl	7/8 R Innis Fus	M	10 yrs PS	Susp	Field	WO/213/21/95	
15/04/18	Woods J	Pte(L/Cpl)	7/8 R Innis Fus	M	7 yrs PS	Susp	Field	WO/213/21/95	
15/04/18	Yard F	Pte	7/8 R Innis Fus	M	5 yrs PS	Susp	Field	WO/213/21/94	
15/04/18	Young FG	Pte	7/8 R Innis Fus	M	NG		Field	WO/213/21/96	
15/04/18	Yoxall T	Pte	7/8 R Innis Fus	M	5 yrs PS	Susp	Field	WO/213/21/94	
24/04/18	Smith E	Pte	RGA	Mx2	10 yrs PS	2 yrs HL	Field Italy	WO/213/22/30	
27/04/18	Jelly J	Pnr (A/LCpl)	RE	M+Disob	Death	Comm 5 yrs PS	Field Italy	WO/213/22/28	
02/05/18	Edwards T	Pte	8 SWB	M+Disob	10 yrs PS	Comm 2 yrs HL	Field SEF	WO/213/22/30	44
02/05/18	Roddy S	Pte	1 KOYLI	M+Disob	10 yrs PS	Comm 2 yrs HL	Field SEF	WO/213/22/30	
02/05/18	Mansfield E	Pte	1 Suffolk	M+Disob	10 yrs PS	Comm 2 yrs HL	Field SEF	WO/213/22/30	
02/05/18	Samuel J	Pte	10 B Watch	M+Disob	10 yrs PS	Comm 2 yrs HL	Field SEF	WO/213/22/30	
02/05/18	Fulford A	Pte	11 Worc	M+Disob	10 yrs PS	Comm 2 yrs HL	Field SEF	WO/213/22/30	
02/05/18	Purchase W	Pte	11 Worc	M+Disob	10 yrs PS	Comm 2 yrs HL	Field SEF	WO/213/22/30	
02/05/18	Roper C	Pte	11 Worc	M+Disob	10 yrs PS	Comm 2 yrs HL	Field SEF	WO/213/22/30	
02/05/18	Fields W	Pte	12 Lancs Fus	M+Disob	10 yrs PS	Comm 2 yrs HL	Field SEF	WO/213/22/30	

Date D/M/Y	Name	Rank	Unit	Offence	Finding/Punishment	Amendment	Location	PRO Reference File/Piece/Page	Note:
02/05/18	Jones J	Pte	12 Lancs Fus	M+Disob	10 yrs PS	Comm 2 yrs HL	Field SEF	WO/213/22/30	
02/05/18	Whalley H	Pte	7 Wilts	M+Disob	10 yrs PS	Comm 2 yrs HL	Field SEF	WO/213/22/30	
06/05/18	Brodie JN	2/Lt	Welsh H (att 21 Rifle Bde)	M+Drunk	Dism+Repr	NC	Alexandria	WO/90/8/18	45
09/05/18	1968	Coolie	Chinese Lab Corps	M+Striking	2 yrs HL		Field	WO/213/22/50	
09/05/18	40749	Coolie	Chinese Lab Corps	M+Striking	1 yr HL		Field	WO/213/22/50	
10/05/18	Vieillese W	Pte	Maur Lab Bn	M(S7-2B)	2 yrs HL		Mespot	WO/90/7/151	46
10/05/18	Samanne R	Pte	Maur Lab Bn	M(S7-2B)	18 mos HL		Mespot	WO/90/7/151	
10/05/18	Bousset J	Pte	Maur Lab Bn	M(S7-2B)	6 mos HL		Mespot	WO/90/7/151	
10/05/18	Auguste A	Pte	Maur Lab Bn	M(S7-2B)	3 mos FP1		Mespot	WO/90/7/151	
10/05/18	Lafleur G	Pte	Maur Lab Bn	M(S7-2B)	6 mos HL		Mespot	WO/90/7/151	
12/05/18	25348	Coolie	Chinese Lab Corps	M+Insub+Disob	6 mos HL	Quashed	Field	WO/213/22/111	
12/05/18	Allen JG	Dvr/L/Bdr	RFA	M	1 yr HL	Susp	Field	WO/213/22/153	
12/05/18	Bergendorff O	Gnr/L/Bdr	RFA	M	1 yr HL	Susp	Field	WO/213/22/153	
12/05/18	Hawkins A [DCM]	Cpl	RFA	M	1 yr HL	Susp	Field	WO/213/22/153	
12/05/18	Hawkins FT	Dvr/L/Bdr	RFA	M	1 yr HL	Susp	Field	WO/213/22/153	
12/05/18	Peters H	Gnr/L/Bdr	RFA	M	1yr HL	Susp	Field	WO/213/22/153	
12/05/18	Pickstone G	Bdr	RFA	M	1 yr HL	Susp	Field	WO/213/22/153	
12/05/18	Roffey R	Bdr	RFA	M	1 yr HL	Susp	Field	WO/213/22/153	
12/05/18	Wright J	Gnr/L/Bdr	RFA	M	1 yr HL	Susp	Field	WO/213/22/153	
29/05/18	Brown H	Pte	9(S) E Lancs	M	1 yr HL		SEF	WO/213/23/179	47
29/05/18	Brown J	Pte	9(S) E Lancs	M	1 yr HL		SEF	WO/213/23/179	
29/05/18	Carter J	Pte	9(S) E Lancs	M	1 yr HL		SEF	WO/213/23/179	
29/05/18	Crabtree EJ	Pte	9(S) E Lancs	M	1 yr HL		SEF	WO/213/23/179	
29/05/18	Devine TH	Pte	9(S) E Lancs	M	1 yr HL		SEF	WO/213/23/179	
29/05/18	Dewhurst G	Pte	9(S) E Lancs	M	1 yr HL		SEF	WO/213/23/179	
29/05/18	Entwistle E	Pte	9(S) E Lancs	M	1 yr HL		SEF	WO/213/23/179	
29/05/18	Fullalove JP	Pte	9(S) E Lancs	M	1 yr HL		SEF	WO/213/23/179	
29/05/18	Greaves H	Pte	9(S) E Lancs	M	1 yr HL		SEF	WO/213/23/179	
29/05/18	Henry R	Pte	9(S) E Lancs	M	1 yr HL		SEF	WO/213/23/179	
29/05/18	Higgins J	Pte	9(S) E Lancs	M	1 yr HL		SEF	WO/213/23/179	
29/05/18	Hirst JL	Pte	9(S) E Lancs	M	1 yr HL		SEF	WO/213/23/179	
29/05/18	Kay W	Pte	9(S) E Lancs	M	1 yr HL		SEF	WO/213/23/179	
29/05/18	Knowles J	Pte	9(S) E Lancs	M	1 yr HL		SEF	WO/213/23/179	
29/05/18	Lee HE	Pte	9(S) E Lancs	M	1 yr HL		SEF	WO/213/23/179	
29/05/18	Livesey J	Pte	9(S) E Lancs	M	1 yr HL		SEF	WO/213/23/179	
29/05/18	Miller W	Pte	9(S) E Lancs	M	1 yr HL		SEF	WO/213/23/179	
29/05/18	Mulligan J	Pte	9(S) E Lancs	M	1 yr HL		SEF	WO/213/23/179	
29/05/18	Murphy A	Pte	9(S) E Lancs	M	1 yr HL		SEF	WO/213/23/179	
29/05/18	Prangley W	Pte	9(S) E Lancs	M	1 yr HL		SEF	WO/213/23/179	
29/05/18	Sterrett W	Pte	9(S) E Lancs	M	1 yr HL		SEF	WO/213/23/179	
29/05/18	Townend R	Pte	9(S) E Lancs	M	1 yr HL		SEF	WO/213/23/179	
29/05/18	Walmsley J	Pte	9(S) E Lancs	M	1 yr HL		SEF	WO/213/23/179	
29/05/18	Whelan D	Pte	9(S) E Lancs	M	1 yr HL		SEF	WO/213/23/179	
30/05/18	Edwards T	Gnr	RFA	M+Striking	Death	Comm 3 yrs PS	Field Italy	WO/213/22/126	
04/06/18	Levitt A	Pte	2 KSLI	M+Disob	10 yrs PS	Comm 2 yrs HL	Field SEF	WO/213/23/40	48
28/06/18	Cameron A	Tpr(L/Cpl)	1 Aus MG Sqdn	M	NG		Field EEF	WO/213/28/138	49
28/06/18	Graham M	Cpl	17 Coy ICC	M	NG		Field EEF	WO/213/28/138	
28/06/18	Chancellor HKT	Cpl	4 Aus Lt Horse	M	NG		Field EEF	WO/213/28/138	
28/06/18	Ashenden HE	Tpr(L/Cpl)	5 Aus Lt Horse	M	NG		Field EEF	WO/213/28/138	
28/06/18	Buchan GM	Tpr(L/Cpl)	8 Aus Lt Horse	M	NG		Field EEF	WO/213/28/138	
28/06/18	Doueal A	Cpl	9 Aus Lt Horse	M	NG		Field EEF	WO/213/28/138	
29/06/18	Morris AR	Cpl	1 Aus Lt Horse	M	NG		Field EEF	WO/213/26/112	
29/06/18	Kerr SJ	Cpl	8 Aus Lt Horse	M	NG		Field EEF	WO/213/26/112	
29/06/18	Hastie CE	Cpl	Aus Engrs	M	NG		Field EEF	WO/213/26/112	
29/06/18	Jenkinson CE	Tpr(L/Cpl)	Aus Prov Corps	M	NG		Field EEF	WO/213/26/112	
29/06/18	Keogh TE	Cpl(A/Sgt)	Aus Prov Corps	M	NG		Field	WO/213/26/112	
01/07/18	Thomson C	Cpl	3 Aus Sig Troop	M	NG		Field EEF	WO/213/28/138	
01/07/18	Rowe FB	Cpl	Aus ASC	M	NG		Field EEF	WO/213/28/138	
01/07/18	Rowling K	Cpl	Aus ASC	M	NG		Field EEF	WO/213/28/138	
01/07/18	Boswell W	Tpr(L/Cpl)	NZEF	M	NG		Field EEF	WO/213/28/138	

Date D/M/Y	Name	Rank	Unit	Offence	Finding/Punishment	Amendment	Location	PRO Reference File/Piece/Page	Note:
01/07/18	Impey A	Tpr/(L/Cpl)	NZEF	M	NG		Field EEF	WO/213/28/138	
23/07/18	Cain G	Dvr	ASC (SA)	M	2 yrs HL		Field	WO/213/24/168	
23/07/18	Jacobs CP	Dvr	ASC (SA)	M+Ins+Threat	Death	Comm 10 yrs PS	Field	WO/213/24/168	
23/07/18	Jeremiah W	Dvr	ASC (SA)	M	5 yrs PS		Field	WO/213/24/168	
23/07/18	Koert J	Dvr	ASC (SA)	M	2 yrs HL		Field	WO/213/24/168	
23/07/18	Lewis W	Dvr	ASC (SA)	M	5 yrs PS	Comm 2 yrs HL	Field	WO/213/24/168	
23/07/18	Lorenzo FS	Dvr Whlr	ASC (SA)	M	Life PS	Comm 5 yrs	Field	WO/213/24/168	
23/07/18	May M	Dvr	ASC (SA)	M	1 yr HL		Field	WO/213/24/168	
23/07/18	Mennik N	Dvr	ASC (SA)	M	5 yrs PS	Comm 2 yrs HL	Field	WO/213/24/168	
23/07/18	Minto P	Dvr	ASC (SA)	M	5 yrs PS	Comm 2 yrs PS	Field	WO/213/24/168	
23/07/18	Nisagie J	Dvr	ASC (SA)	M	2 yrs HL		Field	WO/213/24/168	
23/07/18	Peterson A	Dvr	ASC (SA)	M	6 mos HL		Field	WO/213/24/168	
23/07/18	Phillips K	Dvr L/Cpl	ASC (SA)	M	6 mos HL		Field	WO/213/24/168	
23/07/18	Scholtz J	Dvr L/Cpl	ASC (SA)	M	2 yrs HL		Field	WO/213/24/168	
23/07/18	Smith RW	Dvr	ASC (SA)	M	Life PS	Comm 5 yrs	Field	WO/213/24/168	
23/07/18	Williams H	Dvr	ASC (SA)	M	Life PS	Comm 5 yrs PS	Field	WO/213/24/168	
05/08/18	Adams A	Dvr	ASC (SA)	M+S40	18 mos HL		Field	WO/213/24/129	
05/08/18	Adendorf M	Dvr	ASC (SA)	M+S40	9 mos HL		Field	WO/213/24/129	
05/08/18	Barends K	Dvr	ASC (SA)	M+S40	9 mos HL		Field	WO/213/24/129	
05/08/18	Danster D	Dvr	ASC (SA)	M+S40	1 yr HL		Field	WO/213/24/129	
05/08/18	Du Plessie A	Dvr	ASC (SA)	M+S40	9 mos HL		Field	WO/213/24/129	
05/08/18	Jaantyes M	Dvr	ASC (SA)	M+S40	1 yr HL		Field	WO/213/24/129	
05/08/18	Jacobs J	Dvr	ASC (SA)	M+S40	9 mos HL		Field	WO/213/24/129	
05/08/18	Jonkers J	Dvr	ASC (SA)	M+S40	1 yr HL		Field	WO/213/24/129	
05/08/18	Maton J	Dvr	ASC (SA)	M+S40	9 mos HL		Field	WO/213/24/129	
05/08/18	Meadows J	Dvr	ASC (SA)	M+S40	9 mos HL		Field	WO/213/24/129	
05/08/18	Mettlekamp J	Dvr	ASC (SA)	M+S40	9 mos HL		Field	WO/213/24/129	
05/08/18	Mullens C	Dvr	ASC (SA)	M+S40	9 mos HL		Field	WO/213/24/129	
05/08/18	Peterson J	Dvr	ASC (SA)	M+S40	9 mos HL		Field	WO/213/24/129	
05/08/18	Thomas W	Dvr	ASC (SA)	M+S40	18 mos HL		Field	WO/213/24/129	
05/08/18	Uys E	Dvr	ASC (SA)	M+S40	1 yr HL		Field	WO/213/24/129	
12/09/18	Coleman J	Pte	Scot Rifles	M(x2)	10 yrs PS	One charge quashed	Field	WO/213/25/177	50
12/09/18	Mackey M	Pte	B Watch	M(x2)	10 yrs PS	One charge quashed	Field	WO/213/25/177	
12/09/18	McCormack C	Pte	KOSB	M(x2)	10 yrs PS	Rem 2 yrs/ one charge NC	Field	WO/213/25/177	
12/09/18	Porter T	Pte	A&S Hdrs	M(x2)	10 yrs PS	One charge quashed	Field	WO/213/25/177	
12/09/18	Urquhart S	Pte	Gordon Hdrs	M(x2)	10 yrs PS	One charge quashed	Field	WO/213/25/177	
08/10/18	Stringer T	Dvr	RFA	M+Disob	5 yrs PS	Susp	Field	WO/213/25/158	
13/10/18	Bell WH	Spr	3 Aus Tun Coy	M+Disob	1 yr HL	NC	Field	WO/213/30/136	51
13/10/18	Brownhill FH	Spr	3 Aus Tun Coy	M+Disob	1 yr HL	NC	Field	WO/213/30/136	
13/10/18	Buck O	Spt	3 Aus Tun Coy	M+Disob	1 yr HL	NC	Field	WO/213/30/136	
13/10/18	Edmonds FW	Spr	3 Aus Tun Coy	M+Disob	1 yr HL	NC	Field	WO/213/30/136	
13/10/18	Hancock ER	Spr	3 Aus Tun Coy	M+Disob	1 yr HL	NC	Field	WO/213/30/136	
13/10/18	Martin J	Spr	3 Aus Tun Coy	M+Disob	1 yr HL	NC	Field	WO/213/30/136	
13/10/18	McLean TD	Spr	3 Aus Tun Coy	M+Disob	1 yr HL	NC	Field	WO/213/30/136	
13/10/18	Moore AW	Spr	3 Aus Tun Coy	M+Disob	1 yr HL	NC	Field	WO/213/30/137	
13/10/18	Sandercourt W	Spr	3 Aus Tun Coy	M+Disob	1 yr HL	NC	Field	WO/213/30/136	
13/10/18	Terrell SJ	Spr	3 Aus Tun Coy	M+Disob	1 yr HL	NC	Field	WO/213/30/136	
13/10/18	Thomas RG [DCM]	Spr	3 Aus Tun Coy	M+Disob	1 yr HL	NC	Field	WO/213/30/136	
13/10/18	Ulph RW	Spr	3 Aus Tun Coy	M+Disob	1 yr HL	NC	Field	WO/213/30/136	
14/10/18	Bennett H	Pte	7 Leic	M	Death	Comm 15 yrs PS	Field	WO/213/26/45	52
14/10/18	Knight F	Pte	7 Leic	M	Death	Comm 15 yrs PS	Field	WO/213/26/45	
15/10/18	Alyward AE	Cpl	1 Inf Bn AIF	M+Des	10 yrs PS+Rnks	Guilty of Des	Field	WO/213/28/180	53
15/10/18	Anderson EH	Pte	1 Inf Bn AIF	M+Des	3 yrs PS	Guilty of Des	Field	WO/213/28/200	
15/10/18	Atoff M	Pte	1 Inf Bn AIF	M+Des	3 yrs PS	Guilty of Des	Field	WO/213/28/199	
15/10/18	Austin HC	Pte	1 Inf Bn AIF	M+Des	3 yrs PS	Guilty of Des	Field	WO/213/28/199	
15/10/18	Baker B	Pte	1 Inf Bn AIF	M+Des	3 yrs PS	Guilty of Des	Field	WO/213/28/197	
15/10/18	Barclay AS	Pte	1 Inf Bn AIF	M+Des	3 yrs PS	Guilty of Des	Field	WO/213/28/197	
15/10/18	Bardney R	Pte (L/Cpl)	1 Inf Bn AIF	M+Des	8 yrs PS	Guilty of Des	Field	WO/213/28/199	
15/10/18	Barnes WH	Pte	1 Inf Bn AIF	M+Des	3 yrs PS	Guilty of Des	Field	WO/213/28/196	
15/10/18	Barnett A	Pte	1 Inf Bn AIF	M+Des	3 yrs PS	Guilty of Des	Field	WO/213/30/44	
15/10/18	Beckman EG	Pte	1 Inf Bn AIF	M+Des	3 yrs PS	Guilty of Des	Field	WO/213/28/200	

Date D/M/Y	Name	Rank	Unit	Offence	Finding/Punishment	Amendment	Location	PRO Reference File/Piece/Page	Note:
15/10/18	Beggs R	Pte (L/Cpl)	1 Inf Bn AIF	M+Des	5 yrs PS	Guilty of Des	Field	WO/213/28/199	
15/10/18	Bennett C	Pte	1 Inf Bn AIF	M+Des	3 yrs PS	Guilty of Des	Field	WO/213/28/107	
15/10/18	Besley EA	Pte (L/Cpl)	1 Inf Bn AIF	M+Des	10 yrs PS	Guilty of Des	Field	WO/213/28/200	
15/10/18	Blackwood TJ	L/Cpl (T/Cpl)	1 Inf Bn AIF	M+Des	8 yrs PS+Rnks	Guilty of Des	Field	WO/213/28/199	
15/10/18	Boland E	Pte	1 Inf Bn AIF	M+Des	3 yrs PS	Guilty of Des	Field	WO/213/28/200	
15/10/18	Bootle WJ	Pte	1 Inf Bn AIF	M+Des	3 yrs PS	Guilty of Des	Field	WO/213/28/197	
15/10/18	Brisset J	Cpl	1 Inf Bn AIF	M+Des+Abs	Rnks	G of Abs	Field	WO/213/30/56	
15/10/18	Brandon CS	Pte	1 Inf Bn AIF	M+Des	3 yrs PS	Guilty of Des	Field	WO/213/28/196	
15/10/18	Brown PG	Pte (L/Cpl)	1 Inf Bn AIF	M+Des	NG		Field	WO/213/28/200	
15/10/18	Bruce DG	Pte	1 Inf Bn AIF	M+Des	3 yrs PS	Guilty of Des	Field	WO/213/28/197	
15/10/18	Burgess A	Pte	1 Inf Bn AIF	M+Des	3 yrs PS	Guilty of Des	Field	WO/213/28/197	
15/10/18	Carmody O	Pte	1 Inf Bn AIF	M+Des	3 yrs PS	Guilty of Des	Field	WO/213/28/197	
15/10/18	Carr SF	Pte (L/Cpl)	1 Inf Bn AIF	M+Des	5 yrs PS	Guilty of Des	Field	WO/213/28/198	
15/10/18	Carroll F	Pte	1 Inf Bn AIF	M+Des	3 yrs PS	Guilty of Des	Field	WO/213/28/198	
15/10/18	Case W	Pte	1 Inf Bn AIF	M+Des	3 yrs PS	Guilty of Des	Field	WO/213/28/198	
15/10/18	Casey AB	Pte	1 Inf Bn AIF	M+Des	3 yrs PS	Guilty of Des	Field	WO/213/28/199	
15/10/18	Cheeseman CH	Pte	1 Inf Bn AIF	M+Des	3 yrs PS	Guilty of Des	Field	WO/213/28/197	
15/10/18	Clark HS	Pte	1 Inf Bn AIF	M+Des	NG		Field	WO/213/28/198	
15/10/18	Clift A	Pte	1 Inf Bn AIF	M+Des	3 yrs PS	Guilty of Des	Field	WO/213/28/198	
15/10/18	Cook GM	Pte	1 Inf Bn AIF	M+Des	3 yrs PS	Guilty of Des	Field	WO/213/28/200	
15/10/18	Cooney R	Cpl	1 Inf Bn AIF	M+Des	8 yrs PS+Rnks	Guilty of Des	Field	WO/213/28/180	
15/10/18	Cooper AH	Pte	1 Inf Bn AIF	M+Des	3 yrs PS	Guilty of Des	Field	WO/213/28/197	
15/10/18	Coughlin HB	Pte	1 Inf Bn AIF	M+Des	3 yrs PS	Guilty of Des	Field	WO/213/28/197	
15/10/18	Couley JJ [MM]	Pte	1 Inf Bn AIF	M+Des	3 yrs PS	Guilty of Des	Field	WO/213/28/196	
15/10/18	Creith BW	Pte	1 Inf Bn AIF	M+Des	3 yrs PS	Guilty of Des	Field	WO/213/28/198	
15/10/18	Davis EB	Pte (L/Cpl)	1 Inf Bn AIF	M+Des	3 yrs PS	Guilty of Des	Field	WO/213/28/198	
15/10/18	Dawson JR	Pte(L/Cpl)	1 Inf Bn AIF	M+Des	5 yrs PS	Guilty of Des	Field	WO/213/28/180	
15/10/18	Delaney AF	Pte	1 Inf Bn AIF	M+Des	3 yrs PS	Guilty of Des	Field	WO/213/28/180	
15/10/18	Dick CE	Pte	1 Inf Bn AIF	M+Des	3 yrs PS	Guilty of Des	Field	WO/213/28/197	
15/10/18	Dobbie RR	Pte	1 Inf Bn AIF	M+Des	3 yrs PS	Guilty of Des	Field	WO/213/28/197	
15/10/18	Downton NJ	Pte	1 Inf Bn AIF	M+Des	3 yrs PS	Guilty of Des	Field	WO/213/28/197	
15/10/18	Doyle NA	Pte	1 Inf Bn AIF	M+Des	3 yrs PS	Guilty of Des	Field	WO/213/28/199	
15/10/18	Dunne AW	Pte	1 Inf Bn AIF	M+Des	3 yrs PS	Guilty of Des	Field	WO/213/28/196	
15/10/18	Earle J	Pte	1 Inf Bn AIF	Mx2+Des	3 yrs PS	Guilty of Des	Field	WO/213/28/197	
15/10/18	Ellen J	Pte	1 Inf Bn AIF	M+Des	3 yrs PS	Guilty of Des	Field	WO/213/28/198	
15/10/18	Ellis AJ	Pte	1 Inf Bn AIF	M+Des	NG		Field	WO/213/28/197	
15/10/18	Faulkner WH	Pte	1 Inf Bn AIF	M+Des	3 yrs PS	Guilty of Des	Field	WO/213/28/196	
15/10/18	Fish EW	Pte	1 Inf Bn AIF	M+Des	3 yrs PS	Guilty of Des	Field	WO/213/28/199	
15/10/18	Flynn M	Pte	1 Inf Bn AIF	M+Des	3 yrs PS	Guilty of Des	Field	WO/213/28/196	
15/10/18	Garrett JC	Pte	1 Inf Bn AIF	M+Des	3 yrs PS	Guilty of Des	Field	WO/213/28/200	
15/10/18	Gavin AR	Pte (L/Cpl)	1 Inf Bn AIF	M+Des	NG		Field	WO/213/28/200	
15/10/18	Glover JH	Pte	1 Inf Bn AIF	M+Des	3 yrs PS	Guilty of Des	Field	WO/213/28/199	
15/10/18	Goggins DH	Pte	1 Inf Bn AIF	M+Des	3 yrs PS	Guilty of Des	Field	WO/213/28/199	
15/10/18	Grubb J	Pte (L/Cpl)	1 Inf Bn AIF	M+Des	NG		Field	WO/213/28/200	
15/10/18	Guilfoyle H	Pte	1 Inf Bn AIF	M+Des	5 yrs PS	Guilty of Des	Field	WO/213/28/199	
15/10/18	Ham EH	Pte	1 Inf Bn AIF	M+Des	3 yrs PS	Guilty of Des	Field	WO/213/28/196	
15/10/18	Hancock HT	Pte	1 Inf Bn AIF	M+Des	3 yrs PS	Guilty of Des	Field	WO/213/28/196	
15/10/18	Harragon WL	Cpl (L/Sgt)	1 Inf Bn AIF	M+Des	10 yrs PS+Rnks	Guilty of Des	Field	WO/213/28/180	
15/10/18	Hasthorpe M	Pte	1 Inf Bn AIF	M+Des	3 yrs PS	Guilty of Des	Field	WO/213/28/180	
15/10/18	Hiscock C	Pte	1 Inf Bn AIF	M+Des	NG		Field	WO/213/28/198	
15/10/18	Holmes WJ	Pte	1 Inf Bn AIF	M+Des	3 yrs PS	Guilty of Des	Field	WO/213/28/198	
15/10/18	Horden TC	Pte (L/Cpl)	1 Inf Bn AIF	M+Des	5 yrs PS	Guilty of Des	Field	WO/213/28/197	
15/10/18	Humphreys DW	Pte	1 Inf Bn AIF	M+Des	3 yrs PS	Guilty of Des	Field	WO/213/28/199	
15/10/18	Hunt SJ	Pte	1 Inf Bn AIF	M+Des	3 yrs PS	Guilty of Des	Field	WO/213/28/199	
15/10/18	James W	Pte	1 Inf Bn AIF	M+Des	3 yrs PS	Guilty of Des	Field	WO/213/28/197	
15/10/18	Jeffries H	Pte	1 Inf Bn AIF	M+Des	3 yrs PS	Guilty of Des	Field	WO/213/28/199	
15/10/18	Johnstone CJ	Pte	1 Inf Bn AIF	M+Des	3 yrs PS	Guilty of Des	Field	WO/213/28/196	
15/10/18	Lang PTB	Pte	1 Inf Bn AIF	M+Des	3 yrs PS	Guilty of Des	Field	WO/213/28/200	
15/10/18	Laughrey GA	Pte (L/Cpl)	1 Inf Bn AIF	M+Des	NG		Field	WO/213/28/200	
15/10/18	Lavender TW	Pte	1 Inf Bn AIF	M+Des	3 yrs PS	Guilty of Des	Field	WO/213/28/196	
15/10/18	Lawrence A	Pte	1 Inf Bn AIF	M+Des	3 yrs PS	Guilty of Des	Field	WO/213/28/196	
15/10/18	Lawrence J	Pte	1 Inf Bn AIF	M+Des	3 yrs PS	Guilty of Des	Field	WO/213/28/197	
15/10/18	Lindsay GS	Pte	1 Inf Bn AIF	M+Des	3 yrs PS	Guilty of Des	Field	WO/213/28/196	
15/10/18	Mackey M	Pte	1 Inf Bn AIF	M+Des	3 yrs PS	Guilty of Des	Field	WO/213/28/196	
15/10/18	Marshall ACO	Pte	1 Inf Bn AIF	M+Des	3 yrs PS	Guilty of Des	Field	WO/213/28/198	
15/10/18	Martin W	Pte	1 Inf Bn AIF	M+Des	10 yrs PS+Rnks	Guilty of Des	Field	WO/213/28/199	
15/10/18	McKay RHC	Cpl	1 Inf Bn AIF	M+Des	3 yrs PS	Guilty of Des	Field	WO/213/28/199	
15/10/18	McNamee JB	Pte	1 Inf Bn AIF	M+Des	3 yrs PS	Guilty of Des	Field	WO/213/28/198	
15/10/18	Miller DM	Pte	1 Inf Bn AIF	M+Des	3 yrs PS	Guilty of Des	Field	WO/213/28/198	
15/10/18	Moran JA	Pte	1 Inf Bn AIF	M+Des	5 yrs PS	Guilty of Des	Field	WO/213/28/197	
15/10/18	Muir CW	Pte (L/Cpl)	1 Inf Bn AIF	M+Des	3 yrs PS	Guilty of Des	Field	WO/213/28/195	
15/10/18	Mullins A	Pte	1 Inf Bn AIF	M+Des	3 yrs PS	Guilty of Des	Field	WO/213/28/195	
15/10/18	Murphy T	Pte	1 Inf Bn AIF	M+Des	3 yrs PS	Guilty of Des	Field	WO/213/28/195	

Date D/M/Y	Name	Rank	Unit	Offence	Finding/Punishment	Amendment	Location	PRO Reference File/Piece/Page	Note:
15/10/18	Noon J	Pte	1 Inf Bn AIF	M+Des	3 yrs PS	Guilty of Des	Field	WO/213/28/197	
15/10/18	O'Connell WL	Pte	1 Inf Bn AIF	M+Des	NG		Field	WO/213/28/198	
15/10/18	Orr E	Pte	1 Inf Bn AIF	M+Des	3 yrs PS	Guilty of Des	Field	WO/213/28/200	
15/10/18	Page G	Pte	1 Inf Bn AIF	M+Des	3 yrs PS	Guilty of Des	Field	WO/213/28/198	
15/10/18	Palmer TG	Pte	1 Inf Bn AIF	M+Des	3 yrs PS	Guilty of Des	Field	WO/213/28/199	
15/10/18	Parish EC	Pte	1 Inf Bn AIF	M+Des	3 yrs PS	Guilty of Des	Field	WO/213/28/198	
15/10/18	Paton PP	Pte	1 Inf Bn AIF	M+Des	NG		Field	WO/213/28/198	
15/10/18	Patten JC	Pte	1 Inf Bn AIF	M+Des	3 yrs PS	Guilty of Des	Field	WO/213/28/196	
15/10/18	Pettit LW	Pte (L/Cpl)	1 Inf Bn AIF	M+Des	5 yrs PS	Guilty of Des	Field	WO/213/28/199	
15/10/18	Phillips H	Pte	1 Inf Bn AIF	M+Des	3 yrs PS	Guilty of Des	Field	WO/213/28/198	
15/10/18	Pittock WH	Cpl	1 Inf Bn AIF	M+Des	8 yrs PS+Rnks	Guilty of Des	Field	WO/213/28/197	
15/10/18	Porter EM	Pte (L/Cpl)	1 Inf Bn AIF	M+Des	3 yrs PS	Guilty of Des	Field	WO/213/28/199	
15/10/18	Preston EC	Pte (L/Cpl)	1 Inf Bn AIF	M+Des	5 yrs PS	Guilty of Des	Field	WO/213/28/196	
15/10/18	Roberts WR	Pte	1 Inf Bn AIF	M+Des	3 yrs PS	Guilty of Des	Field	WO/213/28/198	
15/10/18	Robinson AW	Pte	1 Inf Bn AIF	M+Des	3 yrs PS	Guilty of Des	Field	WO/213/28/199	
15/10/18	Robson WJ	Pte	1 Inf Bn AIF	M+Des	3 yrs PS	Guilty of Des	Field	WO/213/28/199	
15/10/18	Rogers RS	Pte	1 Inf Bn AIF	M+Des	3 yrs PS	Guilty of Des	Field	WO/213/28/199	
15/10/18	Ronson C	Pte	1 Inf Bn AIF	M+Des	3 yrs PS	Guilty of Des	Field	WO/213/28/196	
15/10/18	Rook AJ	Pte	1 Inf Bn AIF	M+Des	3 yrs PS	Guilty of Des	Field	WO/213/28/198	
15/10/18	Ross AS	Pte	1 Inf Bn AIF	M+Des	NG		Field	WO/213/28/198	
15/10/18	Selmes LJ	Pte	1 Inf Bn AIF	M+Des	3 yrs PS	Guilty of Des	Field	WO/213/28/196	
15/10/18	Settle J	Pte	1 Inf Bn AIF	M+Des	3 yrs PS	Guilty of Des	Field	WO/213/28/198	
15/10/18	Shirvington C	Pte	1 Inf Bn AIF	M+Des	3 yrs PS	Guilty of Des	Field	WO/213/28/197	
15/10/18	Sidebotham WE	Pte	1 Inf Bn AIF	M+Des	NG		Field	WO/213/28/198	
15/10/18	Slater H	L/Cpl (T/Cpl)	1 Inf Bn AIF	M+Des	7 yrs PS+Rnks	Guilty of Des	Field	WO/213/28/198	
15/10/18	Smith FR	Cpl	1 Inf Bn AIF	M+Des	8 yrs PS+Rnks	Guilty of Des	Field	WO/213/28/199	
15/10/18	Smith TR	Pte	1 Inf Bn AIF	M+Des	3 yrs PS	Guilty of Des	Field	WO/213/28/196	
15/10/18	Stafford R	Pte	1 Inf Bn AIF	M+Des	3 yrs PS	Guilty of Des	Field	WO/213/28/198	
15/10/18	Steele DN	Pte (L/Cpl)	1 Inf Bn AIF	M+Des	5 yrs PS	Guilty of Des	Field	WO/213/28/196	
15/10/18	Stokes EF	Pte	1 Inf Bn AIF	M+Des	3 yrs PS	Guilty of Des	Field	WO/213/28/198	
15/10/18	Taplin RC	Cpl	1 Inf Bn AIF	M+Des	10 yrs PS+Rnks	Guilty of Des	Field	WO/213/28/199	
15/10/18	Tickner HH	Pte	1 Inf Bn AIF	M+Des	3 yrs PS	Guilty of Des	Field	WO/213/28/195	
15/10/18	Travers WF	Pte	1 Inf Bn AIF	M+Des	3 yrs PS	Guilty of Des	Field	WO/213/28/196	
15/10/18	Vaught R	Pte	1 Inf Bn AIF	M+Des	3 yrs PS	Guilty of Des	Field	WO/213/28/200	
15/10/18	Vidler WT	Pte	1 Inf Bn AIF	M+Des	3 yrs PS	Guilty of Des	Field	WO/213/28/196	
15/10/18	Voysey E	Pte	1 Inf Bn AIF	M+Des	3 yrs PS	Guilty of Des	Field	WO/213/28/199	
15/10/18	Walker E	Pte (L/Cpl)	1 Inf Bn AIF	M+Des	5 yrs PS	Guilty of Des	Field	WO/213/28/199	
15/10/18	Wethered GF	Cpl	1 Inf Bn AIF	M+Des	8 yrs PS+Rnks	Guilty of Des	Field	WO/213/28/195	
15/10/18	Whatmore T	Pte	1 Inf Bn AIF	M+Des	3 yrs PS	Guilty of Des	Field	WO/213/28/197	
15/10/18	White GE	Pte	1 Inf Bn AIF	M+Des	3 yrs PS	Guilty of Des	Field	WO/213/28/197	
15/10/18	Winchester R	Pte	1 Inf Bn AIF	M+Des	3 yrs PS	Guilty of Des	Field	WO/213/28/197	
15/10/18	Woodford A	Pte	1 Inf Bn AIF	M+Des	3 yrs PS	Guilty of Des	Field	WO/213/28/196	
15/10/18	Young LS	Pte	1 Inf Bn AIF	M+Des	3 yrs PS	Guilty of Des	Field	WO/213/28/195	
16/10/18	Brad G	Pte	1 NZ Div Employ M Coy		6 mos HL	Susp	Field	WO/213/25/165	54
16/10/18	Dinneen G	Pte	1 NZ Div Employ M Coy		6 mos HL	Susp	Field	WO/213/25/165	
16/10/18	Doyle A	Pte	1 NZ Div Employ M Coy		6 mos HL	Susp	Field	WO/213/25/165	
16/10/18	Findlay RC	Pte	1 NZ Div Employ M Coy		6 mos HL	Susp	Field	WO/213/25/165	
16/10/18	Finlayson R	Pte	1 NZ Div Employ M Coy		6 mos HL	Susp	Field	WO/213/25/165	
16/10/18	Gilkenson J	Pte	1 NZ Div Employ M Coy		6 mos HL	Susp	Field	WO/213/25/165	
16/10/18	Grimwood H	Pte	1 NZ Div Emp B M		6 mos HL	Susp	Field	WO/213/25/165	
16/10/18	Hincks W	Pte	1 NZ Div Emp B M		6 mos HL	Susp	Field	WO/213/25/165	
16/10/18	Kelly JJ	Pte	1 NZ Div Emp B M		6 mos HL	Susp	Field	WO/213/25/165	
16/10/18	McGregor J	Pte	1 NZ Div Emp B M		6 mos HL	Susp	Field	WO/213/25/165	
16/10/18	Narbey A	Pte	1 NZ Employ Coy	M	6 mos HL	Susp	Field	WO/213/25/165	
16/10/18	Schrader PF	Pte	1 NZ Div Employ M Coy		6 mos HL	Susp	Field	WO/213/25/165	
16/10/18	Sinclair C	Pte	1 NZ Div Emp B M		6 mos HL	Susp	Field	WO/213/25/165	
16/10/18	Williams EJ	Pte	1 NZ Div Emp B M		NG		Field	WO/213/25/165	
18/10/18	Bell WH	Spr	3 Aus Tun Coy	M+Disob	2 yrs HL	Susp	Field	WO/213/26/66	55
18/10/18	Brownhill FH	Spr	3 Aus Tun Coy	M+Disob	2 yrs HL	Susp	Field	WO/213/26/66	
18/10/18	Buck O	Spr	3 Aus Tun Coy	M+Disob	2 yrs HL	Susp	Field	WO/213/26/65	
18/10/18	Edmonds FW	Spr	3 Aus Tun Coy	M+Disob	2 yrs HL	Susp	Field	WO/213/26/65	
18/10/18	Hancock ER	Spr	3 Aus Tun Coy	M+Disob	2 yrs HL	Susp	Field	WO/213/26/66	
18/10/18	Harvey G	Spr	3 Aus Tun Coy	M+Disob	2 yrs HL	Susp	Field	WO/213/26/66	

Date D/M/Y	Name	Rank	Unit	Offence	Finding/Punishment	Amendment	Location	PRO Reference File/Piece/Page	Note:
18/10/18	Martin J	Spr	3 Aus Tun Coy	M+Disob	2 yrs HL	Susp	Field	WO/213/26/66	
18/10/18	McLean TD	Spr	3 Aus Tun Coy	M+Disob	2 yrs HL	Susp	Field	WO/213/26/65	
18/10/18	Moore AW	Spr	3 Aus Tun Coy	M+Disob	2 yrs HL	Susp	Field	WO/213/26/65	
18/10/18	Sandercott W	Spr	3 Aus Tun Coy	M+Disob	2 yrs HL	Susp	Field	WO/213/26/66	
18/10/18	Terrell SJ	Spr	3 Aus Tun Coy	M+Disob	2 yrs HL	Susp	Field	WO/213/26/66	
18/10/18	Thomas RG [DCM]	Spr	3 Aus Tun Coy	M+Disob	2 yrs HL	Susp	Field	WO/213/26/66	
18/10/18	Ulph RW	Spr	3 Aus Tun Coy	M+Disob	2 yrs HL	Susp	Field	WO/213/26/65	
07/11/18	Moorcroft AA	Dvr	Aust FA	M+Esc	35 dys FP2		Field	WO/213/26/94	
19/11/18	Wrigley L	Rfn	12(S) Rifle Bde	M+Abs+S40	28 dys FP1		Field	WO/213/26/49	56
05/12/18	Thomas EL	Pte	1/7 RW Fus	M+S40(6e)	NG		Field	WO/213/27/171	57
09/12/18	Sadler LC	Cpl	11 KRRC	M+S40	6 mos HL+Rnks	Comm 90 dys FP2	Field	WO/213/27/42	58
22/12/18	Aspinall HL	Pte	AASC	M	NG		Field	WO/213/27/184	59
22/12/18	McNeill HS	Pte	24 AIF	M	NG		Field	WO/213/27/184	
22/12/18	Hansen AJ	Pte (L/Cpl)	28 AIF	M	4 yrs PS		Field	WO/213/27/184	
22/12/18	Colsell H	Pte	41 AIF	M	2 yrs HL		Field	WO/213/27/184	
22/12/18	Doxford TR	Pte(L/Cpl)	5 AIF	M	NG		Field	WO/213/27/184	
22/12/18	Tonk DE	Pte	56 AIF	M	4 yrs PS		Field	WO/213/27/184	
22/12/18	Heggart TH	Pte	8 AIF	M	5 yrs PS		Field	WO/213/27/184	
22/12/18	Farr WH	Rfn	18 KRRC	M	5 yrs PS		Field	WO/213/27/184	
23/12/18	Brickwood HE	Cpl	8 Lincs	M	4 mos HL+Rnks	Imp	Field	WO/213/28/8	60
23/12/18	Ledicott CF	Sgt	8 Lincs	M+S40	6 mos HL+Rnks	Imp	Field	WO/213/28/8	
23/12/18	Church H	L/Cpl	11 R Fus	M	5 yrs PS		Field	WO/213/28/141	61
23/12/18	Jobe C	Pte	11 R Fus	M	5 yrs PS		Field	WO/213/28/141	
23/12/18	McDonald J	Pte	11 R Fus	M	5 yrs PS		Field	WO/213/28/141	
24/12/18	Archer E	Pte	6 (S) BWI	M+Disob	3 yrs 6 mos PS		Field Italy	WO/213/27/24	62
24/12/18	Brown E	Pte	6 (S) BWI	M+Disob	3 yrs 6 mos PS		Field Italy	WO/213/27/24	
24/12/18	Campbell S	Pte	6 (S) BWI	M+Disob	3 yrs 6 mos PS		Field Italy	WO/213/27/24	
24/12/18	Donaldson M	Pte	9 (S) BWI	M+Disob+Esc	5 yrs PS		Field Italy	WO/213/27/25	
24/12/18	Douglas B	Pte	6 (S) BWI	M+Disob	3 yrs 6 mos PS		Field Italy	WO/213/27/24	
24/12/18	Edwards E	Pte	9 (S) BWI	M+Disob+Esc	8 yrs PS		Field Italy	WO/213/27/25	
24/12/18	Fender S	Pte	6 (S) BWI	M+Disob	3 yrs 6 mos PS		Field Italy	WO/213/27/24	
24/12/18	Francis R	Pte	6 (S) BWI	M+Disob	3 yrs 6 mos PS		Field Italy	WO/213/27/24	
24/12/18	Golding D	Pte	6 (S) BWI	M+Disob	3 yrs 6 mos PS		Field Italy	WO/213/27/24	
24/12/18	Harvey L	Pte	6 (S) BWI	M+Disob	3 yrs 6 mos PS		Field Italy	WO/213/27/24	
24/12/18	Hinds R	Pte	6 (S) BWI	M+Disob	3 yrs 6 mos PS		Field Italy	WO/213/27/24	
24/12/18	Howard E	Pte	9 (S) BWI	M+Disob+Esc	5 yrs PS		Field Italy	WO/213/27/25	
24/12/18	James B	Pte	6 (S) BWI	M+Disob	3 yrs 6 mos PS		Field Italy	WO/213/27/24	
24/12/18	Jepp C	Pte	6 (S) BWI	M+Disob	3 yrs 6 mos PS		Field Italy	WO/213/27/24	
24/12/18	Junior W	Pte	9 (S) BWI	M+Disob+Esc	5 yrs PS		Field Italy	WO/213/27/25	
24/12/18	Knight A	Pte	9 (S) BWI	M+Disob+Esc	5 yrs PS		Field Italy	WO/213/27/25	
24/12/18	Laurence D	Pte	6 (S) BWI	M+Disob	3 yrs 6 mos PS		Field Italy	WO/213/27/24	
24/12/18	Loious T	Pte	6 (S) BWI	M+Disob	3 yrs 6 mos PS		Field Italy	WO/213/27/24	
24/12/18	Lorde G	Pte	9 (S) BWI	M+Disob+Esc	5 yrs PS		Field Italy	WO/213/27/25	
24/12/18	Mannings M	Pte	6 (S) BWI	M+Disob	3 yrs 6 mos PS		Field Italy	WO/213/27/24	
24/12/18	Marshall A	Pte	9 (S) BWI	M+Disob+Esc	8 yrs PS		Field Italy	WO/213/27/25	
24/12/18	Martin S	Pte	6 (S) BWI	M+Disob	3 yrs 6 mos PS		Field Italy	WO/213/27/24	
24/12/18	McCallum S	Pte	6 (S) BWI	M+Disob	3 yrs 6 mos PS		Field Italy	WO/213/27/24	
24/12/18	McLeod B	Pte	9 (S) BWI	M+Disob+Esc	5 yrs PS		Field Italy	WO/213/27/25	
24/12/18	Morgan W	Pte	6 (S) BWI	M+Disob	3 yrs 6 mos PS		Field Italy	WO/213/27/24	
24/12/18	Myers D	Pte	9 (S) BWI	M+Disob+Esc	10 yrs PS		Field Italy	WO/213/27/25	
24/12/18	Oxley W	Pte	9 (S) BWI	M+Disob+Esc	5 yrs PS		Field Italy	WO/213/27/25	
24/12/18	Palmer C	Pte	6 (S) BWI	M+Disob	3 yrs 6 mos PS		Field Italy	WO/213/27/24	
24/12/18	Peers F	Pte	6 (S) BWI	M+Disob	3 yrs 6 mos PS		Field Italy	WO/213/27/24	
24/12/18	Powell L	Pte	6 (S) BWI	M+Disob	3 yrs 6 mos PS		Field Italy	WO/213/27/24	
24/12/18	Shaw C	Pte	9 (S) BWI	M+Disob+Esc	5 yrs PS		Field Italy	WO/213/27/25	
24/12/18	Smith D	Pte	6 (S) BWI	M+Disob	3 yrs 6 mos PS		Field Italy	WO/213/27/24	
24/12/18	Tyrrell A	Pte	6 (S) BWI	M+Disob	3 yrs 6 mos PS		Field Italy	WO/213/27/24	
24/12/18	Watley J	Pte	6 (S) BWI	M+Disob	3 yrs 6 mos PS		Field Italy	WO/213/27/24	
24/12/18	Yard B	Pte	9 (S) BWI	M+Disob+Esc	5 yrs PS		Field Italy	WO/213/27/25	
27/12/18	Allen N	Pte	4 BWI	M+Disob	3 yrs PS	Comm 2 yrs HL	Field Italy	WO/213/27/23	
27/12/18	Beckford R	Pte	4 BWI	M+Disob	3 yrs PS	Comm 2 yrs HL	Field Italy	WO/213/27/23	
27/12/18	Blake J	Pte	4 BWI	M+Disob	3 yrs PS	Comm 2 yrs HL	Field Italy	WO/213/27/23	
27/12/18	Carey W	Pte	4 BWI	M+Disob	3 yrs PS	Comm 2 yrs HL	Field Italy	WO/213/27/23	
27/12/18	Davis A	Pte	4 BWI	M+Disob	3 yrs PS	Comm 2 yrs HL	Field Italy	WO/213/27/23	
27/12/18	Dickenson H	Pte	4 BWI	M+Disob	3 yrs PS	Comm 2 yrs HL	Field Italy	WO/213/27/23	

Date D/M/Y	Name	Rank	Unit	Offence	Finding/Punishment	Amendment	Location	PRO Reference File/Piece/Page	Note:
27/12/18	Evans W	Pte	4 BWI	M+Disob	3 yrs PS	Comm 2 yrs HL	Field Italy	WO/213/27/23	
27/12/18	Griffiths A	Pte	4 BWI	M+Disob	3 yrs PS	Comm 2 yrs HL	Field Italy	WO/213/27/23	
27/12/18	Hamilton J	Pte	4 BWI	M+Disob	3 yrs PS	Comm 2 yrs HL	Field Italy	WO/213/27/23	
27/12/18	Hutchinson H	Pte	4 BWI	M+Disob	3 yrs PS	Comm 2 yrs HL	Field Italy	WO/213/27/23	
27/12/18	Sanches A	Pte	9 BWI	M	Death	Comm 20 yrs PS	Field Italy	WO/213/27/81	
27/12/18	Spence A	Pte	4 BWI	M+Disob	3 yrs PS	Comm 2 yrs HL	Field Italy	WO/213/27/23	
27/12/18	Williams A	Pte	4 BWI	M+Disob	3 yrs PS	Comm 2 yrs HL	Field Italy	WO/213/27/23	
28/12/18	Munroe J	Pte	9 BWI	M+Striking	20 yrs PS	Remit 6 yrs	Field Italy	WO/213/27/25	
28/12/18	Davidson T	Cpl	1/6 HLI	M+Insub+Disob	6 mos HL		Field	WO/213/28/25	63
28/12/18	Penman WTC	Cpl	1/6 HLI	M+Disob	6 mos HL		Field	WO/213/28/25	
28/12/18	Reddin H	Cpl	1/6 HLI	M+Insub+Disob	6 mos HL		Field	WO/213/28/62	
28/12/18	Russell J	Pte(L/Cpl)	1/6 HLI	M+Disob	6 mos HL		Field	WO/213/28/25	
28/12/18	Taylor J	Pte(L/Cpl)	1/6 HLI	M+Disob	42 dys FP1		Field	WO/213/28/25	
01/01/19	Orr R	Pte	1/10 Manch	M+Abs+S40(2)	5 yrs PS	Comm 3 yrs HL	Field	WO/213/28/106	64
04/01/19	Brown I	Pte	BWI	[M]7(3a)	18 mos HL	Remit 1 yr	Mesopotamia	WO/90/7/169	65
04/01/19	Flores E	Pte	BWI	[M]7(2)	3 yrs PS	Comm 1 yr HL	Mesopotamia	WO/90/7/169	
04/01/19	Lightfoot WJ	Pte	BWI	[M]7(3a)x2	5 yrs PS	Comm 2 yrs HL	Mesopotamia	WO/90/7/169	
04/01/19	Lowe J	Pte	BWI	[M]7(3a)x2	10 yrs PS	R[emit?] 7 yrs	Mesopotamia	WO/90/7/169	
04/01/19	Anderson W	Pte (AL/Cpl)	2/7 R Wars	M	5 yrs PS		Field	WO/213/28/72	66
04/01/19	Friar R	Pte(L/Cpl)	2/7 R Wars	M	5 yrs PS		Field	WO/213/28/72	
04/01/19	Greenway H	Pte(L/Cpl)	2/7 R Wars	M	5 yrs PS		Field	WO/213/28/72	
04/01/19	Keighley J	Cpl	2/7 R Wars	M	5 yrs PS		Field	WO/213/28/72	
04/01/19	Lodge SJ	Pte (AL/Cpl)	2/7 R Wars	M	5 yrs PS		Field	WO/213/28/72	
04/01/19	Robinson J	Pte (AL/Cpl)	2/7 R Wars	M	5 yrs PS		Field	WO/213/28/72	
04/01/19	Watson H	Cpl	2/7 R Wars	M	5 yrs PS		Field	WO/213/28/72	
05/01/19	Fellasters G	Pte	2/7 R Wars	M	NG		Field	WO/213/27/71	
05/01/19	Harrison D	Pte	2/7 R Wars	M	3 yrs PS		Field	WO/213/27/122	
06/01/19	Capock H	Pte	Lab Cps	M+S40	NG		Field	WO/213/27/37	
06/01/19	Cross R	Pte	Lab Cps	M+S40	NG		Field	WO/213/27/37	
06/01/19	Dean A	Pte	Lab Cps	M+S40	NG		Field	WO/213/27/37	
06/01/19	Gillingham P	Pte	Lab Cps	M+S40	NG		Field	WO/213/27/37	
06/01/19	Henson CE	Pte	Lab Cps	M+S40	NG		Field	WO/213/27/37	
06/01/19	Morrison J	Pte	Lab Cps	M+S40	NG		Field	WO/213/27/37	
07/01/19	McGrane G	Pte	2 Gor Hdrs	M+S40	1 yr HL		Field	WO/213/27/154	67
09/01/19	Armitage E	Pte	9 MGC	M+S40	28 dys x 2	Comm to 2 [dys?]	Field	WO/213/27/200	68
10/01/19	Mundle J	Pte	6 BWI	M	3 yrs PS		Field Italy	WO/213/27/81	69
13/01/19	Davies B	Pte	5/6 R Welsh Fus	M+S40	90 dys FP2		Field EEF	WO/213/29/42	70
13/01/19	Dowse RJ	Pte	5/6 R Welsh Fus	M+S40	90 dys FP2		Field EEF	WO/213/29/42	
13/01/19	Ferrington F	Pte	5/6 R Welsh Fus	M+S40	90 dys FP2		Field EEF	WO/213/29/42	
13/01/19	Ellis T	Pte	4/5 Welsh Regt	M+S40	90 dys FP2		Field EEF	WO/213/29/42	
16/01/19	Arcanthe L	Pte	Labour Bn	M	84 dys Detn		Mesopotamia	WO/90/7/169	71
16/01/19	Fox J	Pte	Labour Bn	M	84 dys Detn		Mesopotamia	WO/90/7/169	
16/01/19	Green H	Pte	Labour Bn	M	1 yr HL		Mesopotamia	WO/90/7/169	
16/01/19	Maniquois M	Pte	Labour Bn	M	84 dys Detn		Mesopotamia	WO/90/7/169	
16/01/19	Renelle E	Pte	Labour Bn	M	84 dys Detn		Mesopotamia	WO/90/7/169	
16/01/19	Renelle J	Pte	Labour Bn	M	84 dys Detn		Mesopotamia	WO/90/7/169	
16/01/19	Sophie E	Pte(A/Cpl)	Labour Bn	M	2 yrs HL		Mesopotamia	WO/90/7/169	
17/01/19	Beal A	Pte	35 MGC	Mx2	2 yrs HL	Remit 6 mos	Field	WO/213/28/121	72
17/01/19	Brighton LC	Pte	34 MGC	Mx2	2 yrs HL	Remit 18 mos	Field	WO/213/28/120	
17/01/19	Budden F	Pte	35 MGC	Mx2	2 yrs HL	Remit 18 mos	Field	WO/213/28/121	
17/01/19	Bundy AE	Pte	35 MGC	Mx2	2 yrs HL	Remit 18 mos	Field	WO/213/28/121	
17/01/19	Cattanach M	Pte	35 MGC	Mx2	2 yrs HL	Remit 18 mos	Field	WO/213/28/120	
17/01/19	Cavanagh W	Pte	35 MGC	Mx2	1 yr HL	Remit 6 mos	Field	WO/213/28/121	
17/01/19	Craydon FH	Pte	35 MGC	Mx2	2 yrs HL	Remit 18 mos	Field	WO/213/28/121	
17/01/19	Freeman W	L/Cpl	35 MGC	M	2 yrs HL	Remit 6 mos	Field	WO/213/28/120	
17/01/19	Hart T	L/Cpl	35 MGC	M	2 yrs HL	Remit 18 mos	Field	WO/213/28/120	
17/01/19	Hayle HV	Pte	35 MGC	Mx2	2 yrs HL	Remit 18 mos	Field	WO/213/28/120	
17/01/19	Jones JR	Pte	35 MGC	Mx2	2 yrs HL	Remit 18 mos	Field	WO/213/28/120	
17/01/19	Kirkham ST	Pte	35 MGC	Mx2	2 yrs HL	Remit 18 mos	Field	WO/213/28/120	
17/01/19	Mackessy T	Pte	35 MGC	Mx2	2 yrs HL	Remit 6 mos	Field	WO/213/28/120	

Date D/M/Y	Name	Rank	Unit	Offence	Finding/Punishment	Amendment	Location	PRO Reference File/Piece/Page	Note:
17/01/19	May W	Pte	35 MGC	Mx2	2 yrs HL	Remit 18 mos	Field	WO/213/28/121	
17/01/19	Meek J	Pte	35 MGC	Mx2	2 yrs HL	Remit 18 mos	Field	WO/213/28/120	
17/01/19	Peacock H	Pte	35 MGC	Mx2	2 yrs HL	Remit 18 mos	Field	WO/213/28/120	
17/01/19	Pocock E	Pte	35 MGC	Mx2	2 yrs HL	Remit 18 mos	Field	WO/213/28/121	
17/01/19	Porter GE	Pte	35 MGC	M	NG		Field	WO/213/28/121	
17/01/19	Ringrose R	Pte	35 MGC	Mx2	2 yrs HL	Remit 18 mos	Field	WO/213/28/120	
17/01/19	Sankey J	L/Cpl	35 MGC	M	2 yrs HL	Remit 18 mos	Field	WO/213/28/120	
17/01/19	Smith R	Pte	35 MGC	Mx2	2 yrs HL	Remit 18 mos	Field	WO/213/28/121	
17/01/19	Snow W	Pte	35 MGC	Mx2	2 yrs HL	Remit 18 mos	Field	WO/213/28/121	
17/01/19	Truby JT	Pte	35 MGC	Mx2	1 yr HL	Remit 6 mos	Field	WO/213/28/120	
17/01/19	Wakefield W	Pte	35 MGC	Mx2	2 yrs HL	Remit 6 mos	Field	WO/213/28/121	
18/01/19	Carolus F	Pte	1 Cape Corps	M+Disob	28 dys FP1	Quashed	Mustapha	WO/90/8/61	73
18/01/19	Williams J	Pte	1 Cape Corps	M+Disob	10 yrs PS	Comm 3 mos FP1/Quashed	Mustapha	WO/90/8/61	
20/01/19	Baatjes M	Pte	1 Cape Corps	M+Disob	5 yrs PS	Quashed	Mustapha	WO/90/8/61	
21/01/19	McDonell C	Pte	3 Can MGC	Mx2	5 yrs PS		Field	WO/213/28/189	74
21/01/19	Taylor CM	L/Cpl	Can Engrs	M+S7(3b)	2 yrs HL+Rnks		Field	WO/213/28/108	
23/01/19	Butler PW	Pte	PPCLI	M+Abs	2 yrs HL	Remit/Quashed	Field	WO/213/28/107	
23/01/19	Roberts W	Pte	3 Can MGC	M+Abs+S40	2 yrs HL		Field	WO/213/28/108	
23/01/19	Baker HW	Pte	2/6 R Wars	M+Abs+Br	14 dys FP1		Field	WO/213/27/167	75
25/01/19	Bray E	Spr	Can Engrs	M+Disob	28 dys FP2		Field	WO/213/29/55	76
25/01/19	Hutchins VG	Spr	Can Engrs	M+Disob	28 dys FP2		Field	WO/213/29/55	
25/01/19	Keenan G	Spr	Can Engrs	M+Disob	NG		Field	WO/213/29/55	
25/01/19	McKenna JF	Spr	Can Engrs	M+Disob	NG		Field	WO/213/29/55	
25/01/19	Muir WJC	Spr	Can Engrs	M+Disob	NG		Field	WO/213/29/55	
25/01/19	Mullis WW	Spr	Can Engrs	M+Disob	NG		Field	WO/213/29/55	
25/01/19	O'Riley J	Spr	Can Engrs	M+Disob	NG		Field	WO/213/29/55	
25/01/19	Orr A	Spr	Can Engrs	M+Disob	NG		Field	WO/213/29/55	
25/01/19	Rozell H	Spr	Can Engrs	M+Disob	NG		Field	WO/213/29/55	
25/01/19	Savchok A	Spr	Can Engrs	M+Disob	NG		Field	WO/213/29/55	
25/01/19	Way R	Spr	Can Engrs	M+Disob	28 dys FP2		Field	WO/213/29/55	
25/01/19	White JE	Spr	Can Engrs	M+Disob	NG		Field	WO/213/29/55	
25/01/19	Wilson RH	Spr	Can Engrs	M+Disob	NG		Field	WO/213/29/55	
27/01/19	Nunan P	Pte	3 Can MGC	M	5 yrs PS		Field	WO/213/28/189	
01/02/19	Cattell S	Pte (A/LCpl)	1/7 RW Fus	M+S40	21 dys FP2		Field	WO/213/29/27	77
01/02/19	Day G	Pte	9 E Surrey	M+S40	NG		Field	WO/213/28/60	78
01/02/19	Samarzich L	Spr	Can Engrs	M+Disob	28 dys FP2		Field	WO/213/28/71	79
01/02/19	Smith C	Spr	Can Engrs	M+Disob	28 dys FP2		Field	WO/213/28/71	
01/02/19	Sweeney E	Spr	Can Engrs	M+Disob	28 dys FP2		Field	WO/213/28/71	
01/02/19	Turner J	Pte	29 MGC	M+S40	1 yr HL	Remit 6 mos	Field	WO/213/28/73	80
04/02/19	Dowson W	Cpl	RE	M	10 yrs PS+Rnks	Remit 5 yrs PS	Field	WO/213/28/46	
04/02/19	Green W	L/Cpl	RE	M+S40	9 mos HL		Field	WO/213/28/46	
04/02/19	Poole WD	Pte	RE	M+S40	9 mos HL+Rnks		Field	WO/213/28/46	
04/02/19	Shuttleworth G	L/Cpl	RE	M	10 yrs PS+Rnks	Remit 5 yrs PS	Field	WO/213/28/46	
04/02/19	Wilson A	L/Cpl	RE	M+S40	15 mos HL		Field	WO/213/28/46	
03/02/19	Miller TC	Cpl	43 R Fus	M+S40+S7(2)	5 yrs PS+Rnks		Field	WO/213/28/165	81
03/02/19	Slater H	Gnr	RFA	M+Insub+S7(2)	90 dys FP1		Field	WO/213/28/165	
03/02/19	Walters W	Sgt	18 Bn Scot Rifs	M+Insub+S7(2)	12 mos HL+Rnks		Field	WO/213/28/165	
04/02/19	Arnold G	Pte	71 Lab Coy	M	Acquit		Rouen	WO/90/8/58	82
04/02/19	Barnes AG	Pte	26 R Fus	M	90 dys FP1		Rouen	WO/90/8/58	
04/02/19	Butters RE	Pte	23 AIF	M	90 dys FP1		Rouen	WO/90/8/58	
04/02/19	Casey W	Pte	26 R Fus	M	90 dys FP1		Rouen	WO/90/8/58	
04/02/19	Chiverrell WH	Pte	28 CEF	M	56 dys FP1		Rouen	WO/90/8/58	
04/02/19	Cope HE	Dvr	RE	M	90 dys FP1		Rouen	WO/90/8/58	
04/02/19	Coster J	Pte	2 Hants	M	90 dys FP1		Rouen	WO/90/8/58	
04/02/19	Cryer W	Dvr	RFA	M	56 dys FP1		Rouen	WO/90/8/58	
04/02/19	Donkin RB	Pte	21 AIF	M	56 dys FP1		Rouen	WO/90/8/58	
04/02/19	Dyer S	Pte	1 Som LI	M	90 dys FP1		Rouen	WO/90/8/58	
04/02/19	Eglinton TR	Pte	1/13 Lond	M	90 dys FP1		Rouen	WO/90/8/58	
04/02/19	France W	Pte	11 North Fus	M	90 dys FP1		Rouen	WO/90/8/58	
04/02/19	Gilmartin J	Spr	RE	M	90 dys FP1		Rouen	WO/90/8/58	
04/02/19	Green P	Pte	13 E Lancs	M	90 dys FP1		Rouen	WO/90/8/58	

Date D/M/Y	Name	Rank	Unit	Offence	Finding/Punishment	Amendment	Location	PRO Reference File/Piece/Page	Note:
04/02/19	Guthrie M	Pte	8 AIF	M	90 dys FP1		Rouen	WO/90/8/58	
04/02/19	Jeffrey EAV	Pte	155 Lab Coy	M	90 dys FP1		Rouen	WO/90/8/58	
04/02/19	Lavendar G	Pte	4 AIF	M	90 dys FP1		Rouen	WO/90/8/58	
04/02/19	Lewis AJ	Pte	19 RW Fus	M	5 yrs + 3 mos PS		Rouen	WO/90/8/58	
04/02/19	Nicholas FF	Pte	1/6 L'pool	M	56 dys FP1		Rouen	WO/90/8/58	
04/02/19	Quarton H	Pte	10 Hussars	M	3 yrs PS		Rouen	WO/90/8/58	
04/02/19	Puckeridge J	Pte	55 AIF	M	90 dys FP1		Rouen	WO/90/8/58	
04/02/19	Robinson MH	Pte	1 R Berks	M	Acquit		Rouen	WO/90/8/58	
04/02/19	Sheppard H	Pte	23 AIF	M	90 dys FP1		Rouen	WO/90/8/58	
04/02/19	Smalley J	Pte	2 Manch	M	3 yrs + 9 mos PS		Rouen	WO/90/8/58	
04/02/19	White W	Pte	4 Mddx	M	Acquit		Rouen	WO/90/8/58	
04/02/19	Biddle LH	Pte	26 AIF	M	56 dys FP1		Rouen	WO/90/8/59	
04/02/19	Bozeat WJ	Pte	34 AIF	M	90 dys FP1		Rouen	WO/90/8/59	
04/02/19	Bradley FW	Pte	5 Aus Pnrs	M	3 yrs 6 mos PS		Rouen	WO/90/8/59	
04/02/19	Cawthan JC	Pte	37 AIF	M	90 dys FP1		Rouen	WO/90/8/59	
04/02/19	Ferguson WJ	Pte	1 Aus MGB	M	90 dys FP1		Rouen	WO/90/8/59	
04/02/19	Grasso G	Pte	51 AIF	M	Acquit		Rouen	WO/90/8/59	
04/02/19	Hutchinson G	Pte	22 AIF	M	3 yrs 3 mos PS		Rouen	WO/90/8/59	
04/02/19	Kembrey A	Pte	13 AIF	M	3 yrs 9 mos PS		Rouen	WO/90/8/59	
04/02/19	Leech E	Pte	46 AIF	M	90 dys FP1		Rouen	WO/90/8/59	
04/02/19	Lyons P	Pte	18 AIF	M	3 yrs 9 mos PS		Rouen	WO/90/8/59	
04/02/19	McDonald A	Pte	NZ Pnr	M	Acquit		Rouen	WO/90/8/59	
04/02/19	McNally J	Pte	14 AIF	M	90 dys FP1		Rouen	WO/90/8/59	
04/02/19	Millin GL	Pte	60 AIF	M	90 dys FP1		Rouen	WO/90/8/59	
04/02/19	Meres S	Pte	1 Aus MGB	M	3 yrs + 3 mos PS		Rouen	WO/90/8/59	
04/02/19	Murphy JC	Pte	49 AIF	M	90 dys FP1		Rouen	WO/90/8/59	
04/02/19	Nassau H	Pte	15 AIF	M	28 dys FP1		Rouen	WO/90/8/59	
04/02/19	Newell A	Pte	57 AIF	M	90 dys FP1		Rouen	WO/90/8/59	
04/02/19	O'Sullivan C	Pte	2 AIF	M	3 yrs 6 mos PS		Rouen	WO/90/8/59	
08/02/19	Bate R	Pte	21 Manch	M+Abs	6 mos HL		Field	WO/213/28/58	83
08/02/19	Burton R	Pte	21 Manch	M+Abs	6 mos HL		Field	WO/213/28/58	
08/02/19	Byrne H	Pte	21 Manch	M+Abs	6 mos HL		Field	WO/213/28/58	
08/02/19	Carson R	Pte	21 Manch	M+Abs	6 mos HL		Field	WO/213/28/58	
08/02/19	Durham W	Pte	21 Manch	M+Abs	6 mos HL		Field	WO/213/28/58	
08/02/19	Fryers W	Pte	21 Manch	M+Abs	6 mos HL		Field	WO/213/28/58	
08/02/19	Grimshaw H	Pte	21 Manch	M+Abs	6 mos HL		Field	WO/213/28/58	
08/02/19	Hall J	Pte	21 Manch	M+Abs	6 mos HL		Field	WO/213/28/58	
08/02/19	Hunt J	Pte	21 Manch	M+Abs	6 mos HL		Field	WO/213/28/58	
08/02/19	Lovell W	Pte	21 Manch	M+Abs	6 mos HL		Field	WO/213/28/58	
08/02/19	Moores TH	Pte	21 Manch	M+Abs	6 mos HL		Field	WO/213/28/58	
08/02/19	Morgan J	Pte	21 Manch	M+Abs	6 mos HL		Field	WO/213/28/58	
08/02/19	Park JR	Pte	21 Manch	M+Abs	6 mos HL		Field	WO/213/28/58	
08/02/19	Pedley J	Pte	21 Manch	M+Abs	6 mos HL		Field	WO/213/28/58	
08/02/19	Rawlinson F	Pte	21 Manch	M+Abs	6 mos HL		Field	WO/213/28/58	
08/02/19	Reynolds W	Pte	21 Manch	M+Abs	NG		Field	WO/213/28/58	
08/02/19	Roberts C	Pte	21 Manch	M+Abs	6 mos HL		Field	WO/213/28/58	
08/02/19	Roberts F	Pte	21 Manch	M+Abs	6 mos HL		Field	WO/213/28/58	
08/02/19	Robson H	Pte	21 Manch	M+Abs	6 mos HL		Field	WO/213/28/58	
08/02/19	Rodgers P	Pte	21 Manch	M+Abs	9 mos HL		Field	WO/213/28/58	
08/02/19	Rush JA	Pte	21 Manch	M+Abs	6 mos HL		Field	WO/213/28/58	
08/02/19	Smith J	Pte	21 Manch	M+Abs	6 mos HL		Field	WO/213/28/58	
08/02/19	Stubbs W	Pte	21 Manch	M+Abs	6 mos HL		Field	WO/213/28/58	
08/02/19	Taylor B	Pte	21 Manch	M+Abs	6 mos HL		Field	WO/213/28/58	
08/02/19	Thompson AS	Pte	21 Manch	M+Abs	6 mos HL		Field	WO/213/28/58	
08/02/19	Whittle J	Pte	21 Manch	M+Abs	6 mos HL		Field	WO/213/28/59	
08/02/19	Williamson T	Pte	21 Manch	M+Abs	NG		Field	WO/213/28/59	
08/02/19	Wilmot E	Pte	21 Manch	M+Abs	6 mos HL		Field	WO/213/28/58	
10/02/19	Balmbro T	Pte	8 KOYLI	M+Disob+S40	10 yrs PS	Quashed	Field	WO/90/8/55	84
10/02/19	Butterick J	L/Cpl	8 KOYLI	M+Disob+S40	Acquit		Field	WO/90/8/55	
10/02/19	Chamberlain F	Pte	8 KOYLI	M+Disob+S40	5 yrs PS	Quashed	Field	WO/90/8/55	
10/02/19	Dodds HS	L/Cpl	8 KOYLI	M+Disob+S7(4)	Acquit		Field	WO/90/8/54	
10/02/19	Field R	L/Cpl	8 KOYLI	M+Disob+S40	Acquit		Field	WO/90/8/54	
10/02/19	Harrison J	L/Cpl	8 KOYLI	M+Disob+S7(4)	Acquit		Field	WO/90/8/54	
10/02/19	Hyland T	Pte	8 KOYLI	M+Disob+S40	5 yrs PS	Quashed	Field	WO/90/8/55	
10/02/19	Jarrod CH	Pte	8 KOYLI	M+Disob+S40	5 yrs PS	Quashed +Rem 2 yrs	Field	WO/90/8/55	
10/02/19	Knapp JJ	Pte	8 KOYLI	M+Disob+S40	5 yrs PS	Quashed +Rem 2 yrs	Field	WO/213/28/54	
10/02/19	Lewis J	Pte	8 KOYLI	M+Disob+S40	Acquit		Field	WO/90/8/55	
10/02/19	Whitton R	Pte	8 KOYLI	M+Disob+S40	6 mos Imp	Quashed	Field	WO/90/8/55	
10/02/19	Williamson T	Pte	8 KOYLI	M+Disob+S40	5 yrs PS	Quashed	Field	WO/90/8/55	

Date D/M/Y	Name	Rank	Unit	Offence	Finding/Punishment	Amendment	Location	PRO Reference File/Piece/Page	Note:
20/02/19	Barlow JH	Pte	RASC	Mx2+S40	5 yrs PS		Field	WO/213/28/169	85
20/02/19	Collins D	Pte	RASC	Mx2+S40	1 yr HL		Field	WO/213/28/169	
20/02/19	Forrest A	Pte	RASC	Mx2+S40	NG		Field	WO/213/28/169	
20/02/19	Halstead EA	Pte	RASC	Mx2+S40	1 yr HL	Remit 6 mos	Field	WO/213/28/169	
20/02/19	Helliker WC	Pte	RASC	Mx2+S40	NG		Field	WO/213/28/169	
20/02/19	Lawrence JF	Pte	RASC	Mx2+S40	1 yr HL	Remit 3 mos	Field	WO/213/28/169	
20/02/19	Thomasson WP	Pte	RASC	Mx2+S40	3 yrs PS		Field	WO/213/28/169	
27/02/19	Barlow J	Pte	Manch Regt	M+Des	56 dys FP2	Remit 21 dys	Field	WO/213/28/134	
28/02/19	Woiters FC	Pte	2 R Sussex Regt	M+Esc	1 yr HL		Field	WO/213/28/157	86
05/03/19	Coons L	Pte	21 CEF	M+S40	70 dys FP2	Comm	Field	WO/213/28/202	87
07/03/19	Barker FW	Dvr	RFA	Mx2	1 yr HL	Remit 3 mos	Field	WO/213/29/12	
07/03/19	Chapman HRH	Bdr	RFA	Mx2	1 yr HL+Rnks	Remit 3 mos	Field	WO/213/29/12	
07/03/19	McCarthy P	Dvr	RFA	M	90 dys FP2		Field	WO/213/29/12	
07/03/19	Scarborough J	Dvr	RFA	M	90 dys FP2		Field	WO/213/29/12	
07/03/19	Turner JW	Dvr	RFA	M+Des+Drunk+Losing Prop	2 yrs HL		Field	WO/213/29/169	
12/03/19	Clements R	Pte	3 Gn Beds	M+Disob	2 yrs Detn	Comm 1 yr Detn	Meiktila	WO/90/8/199	88
12/03/19	Parrish D	Pte	3 Gn Beds	M+Disob	2 yrs Detn	Comm 1 yr Detn	Meiktila	WO/90/8/199	
17/03/19	Hanson AE	L/Cpl	13 Yorks	M	2 yrs HL		Field/NREF	WO/213/29/35	89
17/03/19	Griffiths PH	L/Cpl	13 Yorks	M	2 yrs HL		Field/NREF	WO/213/29/35	
24/03/19	Abrahams R	Gnr	RFA	M	11 yrs PS	Quashed	Field	WO/213/29/91	90
24/03/19	Anderson TG	Pte	25 AIF	M	8 yrs PS		Field	WO/213/29/89	
24/03/19	Andrews R	Gnr	Can FA[arty]	M	10 yrs PS		Field	WO/213/29/89	
24/03/19	Baines CD	Pte	22 AIF	M	10 yrs PS		Field	WO/213/29/91	
24/03/19	Baldwin GE	Pte	17 AIF	M	8 yrs PS		Field	WO/213/29/91	
24/03/19	Bell CG	Pte	30 AIF	M	8 yrs PS		Field	WO/213/29/91	
24/03/19	Blackwood PE	Pte	3 AIF	M	11 yrs PS		Field	WO/213/29/91	
24/03/19	Bradshaw J	Dvr	RFA	M	15 yrs PS		Field	WO/213/29/89	
24/03/19	Brissenden CL	Pte	18 AIF	M	10 yrs PS		Field	WO/213/29/90	
24/03/19	Broadhead AS	Pte	50 AIF	M	13 yrs PS		Field	WO/213/29/88	
24/03/19	Brock JJ	Pte	8 AIF	M	12 yrs PS		Field	WO/213/29/90	
24/03/19	Brown R	Pte	17 AIF	M	11 yrs PS		Field	WO/213/29/90	
24/03/19	Bunting C	Pte	23 AIF	M	13 yrs PS		Field	WO/213/29/89	
24/03/19	Burn AE	Pte	25 AIF	M	12 yrs PS		Field	WO/213/29/89	
24/03/19	Cadigan CJ	Pte	33 AIF	M	23 yrs PS		Field	WO/213/29/89	
24/03/19	Cambridge JG	Pte	2 AIF	M	10 yrs PS		Field	WO/213/29/91	
24/03/19	Clark HL	Pte	28 CEF	M	20 yrs PS		Field	WO/213/29/91	
24/03/19	Clarke H	Pte	19 AIF	M	11 yrs PS		Field	WO/213/29/89	
24/03/19	Cranes CA	Pte	17 AIF	M	11 yrs PS		Field	WO/213/29/90	
24/03/19	Crawford A	Dvr	RFA	M	10 yrs PS		Field	WO/213/29/89	
24/03/19	Cregg CD	Pte	10 AIF	M	10 yrs PS		Field	WO/213/29/88	
24/03/19	Crooks R	Pte	2 AIF	M	10 yrs PS		Field	WO/213/29/91	
24/03/19	Curnew JB	Pte	3 Can MGC	M	Death	Comm PS/Life	Field	WO/213/29/89	
24/03/19	Devenish JE	Pte	20 AIF	M	11 yrs PS		Field	WO/213/29/90	
24/03/19	Devine J	Pte	6 R Innis Fus	M	11 yrs PS		Field	WO/213/29/89	
24/03/19	Doyle D	Pte	14 AIF	M	9 yrs PS		Field	WO/213/29/90	
24/03/19	Fagan A	Pte	1/7 Ches	M	18 yrs PS		Field	WO/213/29/88	
24/03/19	Fallon A	Pte	2/4 KOYLI	M	10 yrs PS		Field	WO/213/29/88	
24/03/19	Floyd W	Pte	33 AIF	M	9 yrs PS		Field	WO/213/29/88	
24/03/19	Ford J	Pte	58 AIF	M	10 yrs PS		Field	WO/213/29/90	
24/03/19	Fortis SL	Pte	Lab Corps	M	11 yrs PS		Field	WO/213/29/89	
24/03/19	Foster WA	Pte	17 AIF	M	10 yrs PS		Field	WO/213/29/90	
24/03/19	Fraser HA	Pte	14 AIF	M	11 yrs PS		Field	WO/213/29/90	
24/03/19	Gale G	Pte	2 Aus Pnr AIF	M	11 yrs PS		Field	WO/213/29/91	
24/03/19	Gallagher P	Pte	12 AIF	M	10 yrs PS		Field	WO/213/29/90	
24/03/19	Gay EH	Pte	27 AIF	M	10 yrs PS		Field	WO/213/29/88	
24/03/19	Goodwin LR	Pte	19 AIF	M	10 yrs PS		Field	WO/213/29/91	
24/03/19	Grant CC	Pte	8 AIF	M	9 yrs PS		Field	WO/213/29/89	
24/03/19	Hall HW	Pte	45 AIF	M	11 yrs PS		Field	WO/213/29/90	
24/03/19	Hancock GC	Pte	20 AIF	M	11 yrs PS		Field	WO/213/29/88	
24/03/19	Harris S	Pte	1 W Yorks	M	PS/Life		Field	WO/213/29/90	
24/03/19	Harrison LR	Pte	7 AIF	M	10 yrs PS		Field	WO/213/29/89	
24/03/19	Harvey WA	Pte	46 AIF	M	9 yrs PS		Field	WO/213/29/90	
24/03/19	Hawkins G	Pte	10 E Yorks	M	18 yrs PS		Field	WO/213/29/88	
24/03/19	Hayes L	Pte	4 AIF	M	10 yrs PS		Field	WO/213/29/89	
24/03/19	Heffernan PJ	Pte	15 AIF	M	11 yrs PS		Field	WO/213/29/88	
24/03/19	Henderson JJ	Pte	49 AIF	M	11 yrs PS		Field	WO/213/29/88	

Date D/M/Y	Name	Rank	Unit	Offence	Finding/Punishment	Amendment	Location	PRO Reference File/Piece/Page	Note:
24/03/19	Higgins F	Pte	22 AIF	M	No Finding/Sentence		Field	WO/213/29/89	
24/03/19	Hodges HM	Gnr	4 Aus DAC	M	9 yrs PS		Field	WO/213/29/90	
24/03/19	Hutchinson TJ	Pte	58 AIF	M	15 yrs PS		Field	WO/213/29/89	
24/03/19	Jansen O	Spr	3 Aust Lt Ry For Coy	M	9 yrs PS		Field	WO/213/29/88	
24/03/19	Jones W	Pte	2 Can Mtd Rif	M	7 yrs PS		Field	WO/213/29/91	
24/03/19	Kelly DW	Pte	46 AIF	M	11 yrs PS		Field	WO/213/29/90	
24/03/19	King AE	Pte	45 AIF	M	9 yrs PS		Field	WO/213/29/90	
24/03/19	Kirkby JK	Pte	8 AIF	M	10 yrs PS		Field	WO/213/29/90	
24/03/19	Lawry W	Pte	2 Aus Pnr	M	12 yrs PS		Field	WO/213/29/91	
24/03/19	Maltby GE	Pte	49 AIF	M	11 yrs PS		Field	WO/213/29/91	
24/03/19	Malthouse SHJ	Pte	10 AIF	M	10 yrs PS		Field	WO/213/29/88	
24/03/19	McArthur T	Pte	1/4 R Scots	M	12 yrs PS		Field	WO/213/29/88	
24/03/19	McCallan GH	Pte	9 AIF	M	11 yrs PS		Field	WO/213/29/89	
24/03/19	McConaghy D	Pte	R Can	M	10 yrs PS		Field	WO/213/29/88	
24/03/19	McDonnell C	Pte	3 Can MGC	M	Death	Comm PS/Life	Field	WO/213/29/90	
24/03/19	McDonnell C	Pte	25 AIF	M	11 yrs PS		Field	WO/213/29/91	
24/03/19	McGregor A	Pte	46 AIF	M	19 yrs PS		Field	WO/213/29/88	
24/03/19	McPherson J	Pte	2 R Scots	M	11 yrs PS		Field	WO/213/29/88	
24/03/19	Mead S	Pte	19 AIF	M	11 yrs PS		Field	WO/213/29/90	
24/03/19	Moran R	Pte	25 CEF	M	11 yrs PS		Field	WO/213/29/90	
24/03/19	Nicholls AW	Pte	23 AIF	M	11 yrs PS		Field	WO/213/29/88	
24/03/19	Noakes H	Pte	Lab Corps	M	10 yrs PS		Field	WO/213/29/89	
24/03/19	O'Donohue WM	Pte	46 AIF	M	10 yrs PS		Field	WO/213/29/89	
24/03/19	O'Neill P	Pte	18 AIF	M	9 yrs PS		Field	WO/213/29/91	
24/03/19	Pascoe EJ	Pte	4 AIF	M	9 yrs PS		Field	WO/213/29/91	
24/03/19	Pierce HE	Pte	4 AIF	M	12 yrs PS		Field	WO/213/29/89	
24/03/19	Powardy HR	Pte	50 AIF	M	12 yrs PS		Field	WO/213/29/89	
24/03/19	Preston S	Pte	50 AIF	M	10 yrs PS		Field	WO/213/29/88	
24/03/19	Primm J	Rfn	3 Rif Bde	M	11 yrs PS		Field	WO/213/29/88	
24/03/19	Pritchard SP	Pte	6 KSLI	M	Death	Comm PS/Life	Field	WO/213/29/90	
24/03/19	Reid WHV	Pte	32 AIF	M	11 yrs PS		Field	WO/213/29/88	
24/03/19	Roche GR	Pte	45 AIF	M	11 yrs PS		Field	WO/213/29/90	
24/03/19	Rogers E	Pte	18 AIF	M	11 yrs PS		Field	WO/213/29/89	
24/03/19	Rollason HH	Pte	15 AIF	M	9 yrs PS		Field	WO/213/29/91	
24/03/19	Ryan JH	Pte	59 AIF	M	9 yrs PS		Field	WO/213/29/88	
24/03/19	Stephenson WA	Pte	13 AIF	M	11 yrs PS		Field	WO/213/29/89	
24/03/19	Stirling H	Pte	9 AIF	M	10 yrs PS		Field	WO/213/29/90	
24/03/19	Taylor JA	Pte	Lab Corps	M	10 yrs PS		Field	WO/213/29/88	
24/03/19	Taylor CM	Pte	Can Engrs	M	PS/Life		Field	WO/213/29/88	
24/03/19	Twaits R	Pte	50 AIF	M	11 yrs PS		Field	WO/213/29/90	
24/03/19	Villalard C	Pte	6 York & Lanc	M	10 yrs PS		Field	WO/213/29/89	
24/03/19	Wallace J	Pte	14 AIF	M	11 yrs PS		Field	WO/213/29/90	
24/03/19	Wallis P	Pte	10 AIF	M	11 yrs PS		Field	WO/213/29/91	
24/03/19	Watkins JB	Pte	23 AIF	M	11 yrs PS		Field	WO/213/29/90	
24/03/19	Webb WH	Dvr	Aus[t] FA[rty]	M	10 yrs PS		Field	WO/213/29/88	
24/03/19	West NF	Spr	Aus[t] Engrs	M	12 yrs PS		Field	WO/213/29/88	
24/03/19	White JW	Pte	1 R Dub Fus	M	10 yrs PS		Field	WO/213/29/88	
24/03/19	Wilson JHC	Pte	4 AIF	M	11 yrs PS		Field	WO/213/29/90	
24/03/19	Woodbury PA	Pte	1 Aus Pnr Bn	M	9 yrs PS		Field	WO/213/29/89	
24/03/19	Yates F	Pte	Lab Corps	M	10 yrs PS		Field	WO/213/29/91	
27/03/19	Baron A	Spr	101 Field Coy RE	M+Disob	5 yrs PS	Remit 2 yrs	Field Italy	WO/213/28/191	91
27/03/19	Elder J	Spr	101 Field Coy RE	M+Disob	5 yrs PS		Field Italy	WO/213/28/191	
27/03/19	Oliver AE	Spr (L/Cpl)	101 Field Coy RE	M+Disob	5 yrs PS		Field Italy	WO/213/28/191	
27/03/19	Read H	Spr	101 Field Coy RE	M+Disob	5 yrs PS		Field Italy	WO/213/28/191	
27/03/19	Syring A	Spr	101 Field Coy RE	M+Disob	5 yrs PS	Remit 2 yrs	Field Italy	WO/213/28/191	
29/03/19	Strasburg J	Pte	39 R Fus	M+Insub	1 yr HL	Remit 6 mos	Field EEF	WO/213/29/86	92
13/04/19	Davies W	Pte	26 RW Fus	M+Striking	15 yrs PS	Remit 10 yrs	Field	WO/213/29/177	93
24/04/19	Bickerton W	Gnr	RFA	M+Disob	5 mos HL		Field	WO/213/29/160	94
24/04/19	Bishop C	Gnr	RFA	M+Disob	5 mos HL		Field	WO/213/29/160	
24/04/19	Blair J	Dvr	RFA	M+Disob	5 mos HL		Field	WO/213/29/160	
24/04/19	Cartwright A	Dvr	RFA	M+Disob	NG		Field	WO/213/29/160	
24/04/19	Gardener R	Gnr	RFA	M+Disob	5 mos HL		Field	WO/213/29/160	
24/04/19	Grimstone H	Dvr	RFA	M+Disob	5 mos HL		Field	WO/213/29/160	
24/04/19	Hague A	Dvr	RFA	M+Disob	5 mos HL		Field	WO/213/29/160	

Date D/M/Y	Name	Rank	Unit	Offence	Finding/Punishment	Amendment	Location	PRO Reference File/Piece/Page	Note:
24/04/19	Harvey A	Gnr	RFA	M+Disob	5 mos HL		Field	WO/213/29/160	
24/04/19	Hayden J	Gnr	RFA	M+Disob	5 mos HL		Field	WO/213/29/160	
24/04/19	Herbert A	Dvr	RFA	M+Disob	NG		Field	WO/213/29/160	
24/04/19	Jackman H	Gnr (AL/Bdr)	RFA	M+Disob	5 mos HL		Field	WO/213/29/160	
24/04/19	Kelly E	Dvr	RFA	M+Disob	NG		Field	WO/213/29/160	
24/04/19	Murray W	Dvr	RFA	M+Disob	5 mos HL		Field	WO/213/29/160	
24/04/19	Nelson J	Dvr	RFA	M+Disob	NG		Field	WO/213/29/160	
24/04/19	Snell A	Dvr	RFA	M+Disob	5 mos HL		Field	WO/213/29/160	
24/04/19	Southwick S	Gnr	RFA	M+Disob	NG		Field	WO/213/29/160	
02/05/19	Antoine B	Pte	1 BWI	Mx2+Disob	18 mos HL	Remit 12 mos	Field Italy	WO/213/29/37	95
02/05/19	Gonzales BAE	Pte	1 BWI	Mx2+Disob	18 mos HL	Remit 12 mos	Field Italy	WO/213/29/37	
02/05/19	Laguerre E	Pte	1 BWI	Mx2+Disob	18 mos HL	Remit 12 mos	Field Italy	WO/213/29/37	
04/05/19	Alexander A	Pte	1 BWI	M	6 mos HL		Field Italy	WO/213/29/37	
04/05/19	Cuffy A	Pte	1 BWI	M	6 mos HL		Field Italy	WO/213/29/37	
04/05/19	Sealey C	Pte	1 BWI	M	6 mos HL		Field Italy	WO/213/29/37	
09/05/19	Alsey A	Pte	3 Essex	M	3 yrs PS	Comm 4 mos HL	Field Italy	WO/213/29/73	96
09/05/19	Brockbank S	Pte	3 Essex	M	3 yrs PS	Comm 4 mos HL	Field Italy	WO/213/29/73	
09/05/19	Harris F	Pte	3 Essex	M	3 yrs PS	Comm 4 mos HL	Field Italy	WO/213/29/73	
09/05/19	Smith E	Pte	3 Essex	M	3 yrs PS	Comm 4 mos HL	Field Italy	WO/213/29/72	
09/05/19	Wright F	Pte	3 Essex	M	3 yrs PS	Comm 4 mos HL	Field Italy	WO/213/29/73	
09/05/19	Aggette F	Spr	RE	M	2 yrs HL	Remit 20 mos/ Quashed	Field Italy	WO/213/29/73	
09/05/19	Cummings C	Spr	RE	M	2 yrs HL	Remit 20 mos/ Quashed	Field Italy	WO/213/29/73	
09/05/19	Hall A	Spr	RE	M	2 yrs HL	Remit 20 mos/ Quashed	Field Italy	WO/213/29/73	
09/05/19	Howlett H	Spr	RE	M	2 yrs HL	Remit 20 mos /Quashed	Field Italy	WO/213/29/73	
09/05/19	May AE	Spr	RE	M	2 yrs HL	Remit 20 mos/ Quashed	Field Italy	WO/213/29/73	
09/05/19	McNicol N	Spr	RE	M	2 yrs HL	Remit 20 mos/ Quashed	Field Italy	WO/213/29/73	
09/05/19	Sutherland AG	Spr	RE	M	2 yrs HL	Remit 20 mos/ Quashed	Field Italy	WO/213/29/73	
09/05/19	Thomas R	Spr	RE	M	2 yrs HL	Remit 20 mos/ Quashed	Field Italy	WO/213/29/73	
09/05/19	Wilson D	Spr	RE	M	2 yrs HL	Remit 20 mos/ Quashed	Field Italy	WO/213/29/73	
09/05/19	Wright W	Pnr	RE	M	2 yrs HL	Remit 20 mos/ Quashed	Field Italy	WO/213/29/73	
10/05/19	Berry W	Pte (AL/Cpl)	RAMC	M+S40	6 mos HL	Comm 28 dys FP2	Field	WO/213/30/17	97
10/05/19	Bridle G	Pte	RAMC	M	6 mos HL	Comm 28 dys FP2	Field	WO/213/30/17	
10/05/19	Casey C	Pte (AL/Cpl)	RAMC	M+S40	6 mos HL	Comm 28 dys FP2	Field	WO/213/30/17	
10/05/19	Coxon G	Pte	RAMC	M	6 mos HL	Comm 28 dys FP2	Field	WO/213/30/17	
10/05/19	Hilton WG	Pte	RAMC	M	6 mos HL	Comm 28 dys FP2	Field	WO/213/30/17	
10/05/19	Hope AH	Pte	RAMC	M	6 mos HL	Comm 28 dys FP2	Field	WO/213/30/17	
10/05/19	Jackson GA	Pte	RAMC	M	6 mos HL	Comm 28 dys FP2	Field	WO/213/30/17	
10/05/19	Jeffries F	Pte	RAMC	M	6 mos HL	Comm 28 dys FP2	Field	WO/213/30/17	
10/05/19	Kennedy B	Pte	RAMC	M	6 mos HL	Comm 28 dys FP2	Field	WO/213/30/17	
10/05/19	Moore R	Pte	RAMC	M	6 mos HL	Comm 28 dys FP2	Field	WO/213/30/17	
10/05/19	Paul HJ	Pte	RAMC	M	6 mos HL	Comm 28 dys FP2	Field	WO/213/30/17	
10/05/19	Potts C	Pte	RAMC	M	6 mos HL	Comm 28 dys FP2	Field	WO/213/30/17	
10/05/19	Stafford J	Pte	RAMC	M	6 mos HL	Comm 28 dys FP2	Field	WO/213/30/17	
10/05/19	Williams JA	Pte	RAMC	M	6 mos HL	Comm 28 dys FP2	Field	WO/213/30/17	
10/05/19	Parris HN	Cpl	1 BWI	M+S40	90 dys FP2+Rnks	Remit 62 dys	Field	WO/213/29/49	98
11/05/19	Allen J	Pte	2 W India	M	7 yrs PS	Comm 2 yrs HL	Field EEF	WO/213/30/28	99
11/05/19	Allen W	Pte	2 W India	M	7 yrs PS	Comm 2 yrs HL	Field EEF	WO/213/30/28	
11/05/19	Anderson H	Pte	2 W India	M	5 yrs PS	Comm 1 yr HL	Field EEF	WO/213/30/27	
11/05/19	Bernard S	Pte	2 W India	M	7 yrs PS	Ammend 2 yrs HL	Field EEF	WO/213/30/28	
11/05/19	Brown J	Pte	2 W India	M	7 yrs PS	Comm 2 yrs HL	Field EEF	WO/213/30/28	
11/05/19	Brown S	Pte	2 W India	M	7 yrs PS	Comm 2 yr HL	Field EEF	WO/213/30/28	
11/05/19	Cole H	Pte	2 W India	M	7 yrs PS	Comm 2 yrs HL	Field EEF	WO/213/30/27	
11/05/19	Collins R	Pte	2 W India	M	5 yrs PS	Comm 1 yr HL	Field EEF	WO/213/30/28	
11/05/19	Gibbs JE	Pte	2 W India	M	7 yrs PS	Comm 2 yrs HL	Field EEF	WO/213/30/28	
11/05/19	Gordon J	Pte	2 W India	M	5 yrs PS	Comm 1 yr HL	Field EEF	WO/213/30/28	

Date D/M/Y	Name	Rank	Unit	Offence	Finding/Punishment	Amendment	Location	PRO Reference File/Piece/Page	Note:
11/05/19	Hemmings T	Pte	2 W India	M	7 yrs PS	Comm 2 yrs HL	Field EEF	WO/213/30/28	
11/05/19	Kelly D	Pte	2 W India	M	5 yrs PS	Comm 1 yr HL	Field EEF	WO/213/30/28	
11/05/19	Lewis S	Pte	2 W India	M	5 yrs PS	Comm 1 yr HL	Field EEF	WO/213/30/28	
11/05/19	Marlow E	Pte	2 W India	M	7 yrs PS	Comm 2 yrs HL	Field EEF	WO/213/30/28	
11/05/19	May C	Pte	2 W India	M	5 yrs PS	Comm 1 yr HL	Field EEF	WO/213/30/28	
11/05/19	McKenzie C	Pte	2 W India	M	5 yrs PS	Comm 1 yr HL	Field EEF	WO/213/30/28	
11/05/19	Miller G	Pte	2 W India	M	5 yrs PS	Comm 1 yr HL	Field EEF	WO/213/30/28	
11/05/19	Millings G	Pte	2 W India	M	5 yrs PS	Comm 1 yr HL	Field EEF	WO/213/30/28	
11/05/19	Nelson J	Pte	2 W India	M	5 yrs PS	Comm 1 yr HL	Field EEF	WO/213/30/28	
11/05/19	Reid C	Pte	2 W India	M	7 yrs PS	Comm 2 yrs HL	Field EEF	WO/213/30/28	
11/05/19	Ricketts R	Pte	2 W India	M	5 yrs PS	Comm 1 yr HL	Field EEF	WO/213/30/27	
11/05/19	Roberts G	Pte	2 W India	M	7 yrs PS	Comm 2 yrs HL	Field EEF	WO/213/30/28	
11/05/19	Robinson E	Pte	2 W India	M	5 yrs PS	Comm 1 yr HL	Field EEF	WO/213/30/28	
11/05/19	Salmon W	Pte	2 W India	M	7 yrs PS	Comm 2 yrs HL	Field EEF	WO/213/30/28	
11/05/19	Shaw A	Pte	2 W India	M	7 yrs PS	Comm 2 yrs HL	Field EEF	WO/213/30/27	
11/05/19	Taylor E	Pte	2 W India	M	5 yrs PS	Comm 1 yr HL	Field EEF	WO/213/30/28	
11/05/19	Taylor N	Pte	2 W India	M	7 yrs PS	Comm 2 yrs HL	Field EEF	WO/213/30/28	
11/05/19	Wallcutt H	Pte	2 W India	M	5 yrs PS	Comm 1 yr HL	Field EEF	WO/213/30/27	
11/05/19	Watson J	Pte	2 W India	M	7 yrs PS	Comm 2 yrs HL	Field EEF	WO/213/30/28	
11/05/19	White J	Pte	2 W India	M	7 yrs PS	Comm 2 yrs HL	Field EEF	WO/213/30/28	
11/05/19	Wiles C	Pte	2 W India	M	7 yrs PS	Comm 2 yrs HL	Field EEF	WO/213/30/27	
11/05/19	Wilson G	Pte	2 W India	M	7 yrs PS	Comm 1 yr HL	Field EEF	WO/213/30/28	
13/05/19	Foster A	Pte	257 P of W Coy	M+S40(2)	6 mos Imp	Comm 90 dys FP2	Field	WO/213/30/31	100
13/05/19	Hudson S	Pte	257 P of W Coy	M+S40(2)	92 dys HL		Field	WO/213/30/31	
13/05/19	Milson W	Pte	257 P of W Coy	M+S40(2)	112 dys HL	Comm 90 dys FP2	Field	WO/213/30/31	
13/05/19	Thomson J	Pte	257 P of W Coy	M+S40(2)	6 mos HL	56 dys FP1	Field	WO/213/30/31	
13/05/19	Webster A	Pte	257 P of W Coy	M+S40(2)	6 mos Imp	Comm 90 dys FP2	Field	WO/213/30/31	
13/05/19	Woodhead E	Cpl	257 P of W Coy	M+S40(2)	9 mos HL+Rnks		Field	WO/213/30/31	
14/05/19	Allan D	Dvr	372 Coy CAHT	M	5 yrs PS	Comm 1 yr HL	Field	WO/213/30/12	101
14/05/19	Binneker C	Dvr	372 Coy CAHT	M	5 yrs PS		Field	WO/213/30/12	
14/05/19	Brandt P	Dvr	372 Coy CAHT	M	5 yrs PS	Remit 2 yrs	Field	WO/213/30/12	
14/05/19	Charles J	Dvr	372 Coy CAHT	M	5 yrs PS	Comm 1 yr HL	Field	WO/213/30/12	
14/05/19	Christian C	Dvr	372 Coy CAHT	M	5 yrs PS		Field	WO/213/30/12	
14/05/19	Davids J	Cpl	372 Coy CAHT	M	5 yrs PS		Field	WO/213/30/12	
14/05/19	de Vries J	Dvr	372 Coy CAHT	M	5 yrs PS		Field	WO/213/30/12	
14/05/19	Ferlander S	Dvr	372 Coy CAHT	M	5 yrs PS	Remit 2 yrs	Field	WO/213/30/12	
14/05/19	Fredericks A	Dvr	372 Coy CAHT	M	5 yrs PS		Field	WO/213/30/12	
14/05/19	Free H	Dvr	372 Coy CAHT	M	5 yrs PS	Comm 2 yrs HL	Field	WO/213/30/12	
14/05/19	Garadies J	Dvr	372 Coy CAHT	M	5 yrs PS	Comm 2 yrs HL	Field	WO/213/30/12	
14/05/19	Gelant F	Dvr	372 Coy CAHT	M	5 yrs PS	Remit 2 yrs	Field	WO/213/30/12	
14/05/19	Grove J	Dvr	372 Coy CAHT	M	5 yrs PS		Field	WO/213/30/12	
14/05/19	Hendricks J	Dvr	372 Coy CAHT	M	5 yrs PS	Comm 2 yrs HL	Field	WO/213/30/12	
14/05/19	Hendricks F	Dvr	372 Coy CAHT	M	5 yrs PS	Remit 2 yrs	Field	WO/213/30/12	
14/05/19	Jacobs C	Dvr	372 Coy CAHT	M	5 yrs PS	Remit 2 yrs	Field	WO/213/30/11	
14/05/19	Jacobs W	Dvr	372 Coy CAHT	M	5 yrs PS	Remit 2 yrs	Field	WO/213/30/12	
14/05/19	January N	Dvr	372 Coy CAHT	M	5 yrs PS	Remit 2 yrs	Field	WO/213/30/12	
14/05/19	Johnson P	Dvr	372 Coy CAHT	M	5 yrs PS	Remit 2 yrs	Field	WO/213/30/12	
14/05/19	Julius A	Dvr	372 Coy CAHT	M	5 yrs PS	Comm 1 yr HL	Field	WO/213/30/12	
14/05/19	King G	Dvr	372 Coy CAHT	M	5 yrs PS	Remit 2 yrs	Field	WO/213/30/12	
14/05/19	Le Roux G	Dvr	372 Coy CAHT	M	5 yrs PS		Field	WO/213/30/12	
14/05/19	Louw J	Dvr	372 Coy CAHT	M	5 yrs PS	Remit 2 yrs	Field	WO/213/30/12	
14/05/19	Martin H	Dvr	372 Coy CAHT	M	5 yrs PS		Field	WO/213/30/12	
14/05/19	Nicholson J	Dvr	372 Coy CAHT	M	5 yrs PS	Remit 2 yrs	Field	WO/213/30/12	
14/05/19	Petersen J	Dvr	372 Coy CAHT	M	5 yrs PS	Remit 2 yrs	Field	WO/213/30/12	
14/05/19	Rispel A	Dvr	372 Coy CAHT	M	5 yrs PS		Field	WO/213/30/11	
14/05/19	Sababies J	Dvr	372 Coy CAHT	M	5 yrs PS		Field	WO/213/30/11	
14/05/19	Schmidt J	Dvr	372 Coy CAHT	M	5 yrs PS	Remit 2 yrs	Field	WO/213/30/11	
14/05/19	Slinger J	Dvr	372 Coy CAHT	M	5 yrs PS	Remit 2 yrs	Field	WO/213/30/11	
14/05/19	Van Diemen F	Dvr	372 Coy CAHT	M	5 yrs PS	Comm 2 yrs HL	Field	WO/213/30/11	
14/05/19	Wilmot E	Dvr	372 Coy CAHT	M	5 yrs PS	Remit 2 yrs	Field	WO/213/30/11	
15/05/19	Buddle P	Spr	RE	M+Disob	1 yr IHL		Field	WO/213/29/137	
15/05/19	Carpenter A	Cpl	RE	M+Disob	1 yr IHL+Rnks		Field	WO/213/29/137	
15/05/19	Carson W	Spr	RE	M+Disob	1 yr IHL		Field	WO/213/29/137	
15/05/19	Edmunds A	Spr	RE	M+Disob	1 yr IHL		Field	WO/213/29/137	
15/05/19	Grier A	Spr	RE	M+Disob	1 yr IHL		Field	WO/213/29/137	
15/05/19	Henry J	Spr	RE	M+Disob	1 yr IHL		Field	WO/213/29/137	
15/05/19	Kellet A	Spr	RE	M+Disob	1 yr IHL		Field	WO/213/29/137	
15/05/19	Leech H	Spr	RE	M+Disob	1 yr IHL		Field	WO/213/29/137	
15/05/19	Lindon JS	Spr	RE	M+Disob	1 yr IHL		Field	WO/213/29/137	
15/05/19	Mecklenburgh C	Spr	RE	M+Disob	1 yr IHL		Field	WO/213/29/137	

Date D/M/Y	Name	Rank	Unit	Offence	Finding/Punishment	Amendment	Location	PRO Reference File/Piece/Page	Note:
15/05/19	Mills A	Spr	RE	M+Disob	1 yr IHL		Field	WO/213/29/137	
15/05/19	Mitchell D	Spr	RE	M+Disob	1 yr IHL		Field	WO/213/29/137	
15/05/19	Rawlinson E	Spr	RE	M+Disob	1 yr IHL		Field	WO/213/29/137	
15/05/19	Robertshaw G	Spr	RE	M+Disob	1 yr IHL		Field	WO/213/29/137	
15/05/19	Smith GWP	Spr	RE	M+Disob	1 yr IHL		Field	WO/213/29/137	
15/05/19	Summersby W	Spr	RE	M+Disob	1 yr IHL		Field	WO/213/29/137	
15/05/19	Wellington FA	Spr	RE	M+Disob	1 yr IHL		Field	WO/213/29/137	
16/05/19	Bestwick C	Pte	17 L'pool	M	2 yrs HL	Remit 18 mos	NREF	WO/213/29/181	102
16/05/19	Collier FD	Pte(L/Cpl)	17 L'pool	M	2 yrs HL	Remit 18 mos	NREF	WO/213/29/181	
16/05/19	Lewis WO	Pte	17 L'pool	M	2 yrs HL	Remit 18 mos	NREF	WO/213/29/181	
16/05/19	Cole HA	Pte(L/Cpl)	13 Yorks	M	2 yrs HL	Remit 18 mos	NREF	WO/213/29/181	
16/05/19	Metcalfe JE	Cpl (AL/Sgt)	13 Yorks	M	2 yrs HL+Rnks		NREF	WO/213/29/181	
16/05/19	Holt S	A/Bdr	RGA	M	NG		Field	WO/213/29/148	
16/05/19	Robinson J	AL/Bdr	RGA	M	NG		Field	WO/213/29/148	
16/05/19	Kite FJ	Signlr	RGA	M	6 mos HL	Comm 84 dys FP1 Quashed	Field	WO/213/29/148	
16/05/19	Lucas EC	Dvr	RGA	M	6 mos HL	Comm 84 dys FP1 Quashed	Field	WO/213/29/148	
16/05/19	Page FT	AL/Bdr	RGA	M	9 mos HL	Remit 3 mos	Field	WO/213/29/148	
16/05/19	Smith LE	AL/Bdr	RGA	M	9 mos HL	Remit 3 mos/ Quashed	Field	WO/213/29/148	
16/05/19	Treadwell HW	Dvr	RGA	M	6 mos HL	Comm 84 dys FP1 Quashed	Field	WO/213/29/148	
16/05/19	Livesey HH	AL/Bdr	RGA	M	[No further details recorded]		Field	WO/213/29/148	
17/05/19	Louden FH	Pte	4 Tank Bn	M	6 mos HL		Field	WO/213/29/127	103
19/05/19	Lester WH	Pte	2/23 London	M+Insub+S40	6 mos HL		Field	WO/213/30/27	104
27/05/19	Cooksey H	Pte	2/6 R Wars	M+S40	2 yrs HL	Remit 1 yr	Field	WO/213/30/64	105
27/05/19	Crisp WA	Pte	2/6 R Wars	M+S40	2 yrs HL	Remit 1 yr	Field	WO/213/30/64	
27/05/19	Davies W	Pte	2/6 R Wars	M+S40	2 yrs HL	Remit 1 yr	Field	WO/213/30/64	
27/05/19	Dixon T	Pte	2/6 R Wars	M+S40	2 yrs HL	Remit 1 yr	Field	WO/213/30/64	
27/05/19	Eden W	Pte	2/6 R Wars	M+S40	2 yrs HL	Remit 1 yr	Field	WO/213/30/64	
27/05/19	Found L	Pte	2/6 R Wars	M+S40	2 yrs HL	Remit 1 yr	Field	WO/213/30/64	
27/05/19	Howells A	Pte	2/6 R Wars	M+S40	2 yrs HL	Remit 1 yr	Field	WO/213/30/64	
27/05/19	Ingram GE	Pte	2/6 R Wars	M+S40	2 yrs HL	Remit 1 yr	Field	WO/213/30/64	
27/05/19	Lyons SB	Pte	2/6 R Wars	M+S40	2 yrs HL	Remit 1 yr	Field	WO/213/30/64	
27/05/19	Pearman A	Pte	2/6 R Wars	M+S40	2 yrs HL	Remit 1 yr	Field	WO/213/30/64	
27/05/19	Plumbley AM	Pte	2/6 R Wars	M+S40	2 yrs HL	Remit 1 yr	Field	WO/213/30/64	
27/05/19	Reynolds JH	Pte	2/6 R Wars	M+S40	2 yrs HL	Remit 1 yr	Field	WO/213/30/64	
27/05/19	Sidwell W	Pte	2/6 R Wars	M+S40	2 yrs HL	Remit 1 yr	Field	WO/213/30/64	
27/05/19	Wood GW	Pte	2/6 R Wars	M+S40	2 yrs HL	Remit 1 yr	Field	WO/213/30/64	
05/06/19	Herbert JJ	Gnr	RFA	M+S40	5 yrs HL		Field	WO/213/30/64	
09/06/19	Coulden A	Pte	2 R I Fus	M+XOS+S40	9 mos HL		Field EEF	WO/213/30/126	106
09/06/19	Fitzgerald P	Pte	2 R I Fus	M+S40	21 dys FP2	Quashed	Field EEF	WO/213/30/126	
09/06/19	Kirk D	Pte	2 R I Fus	M+S40	42 dys FP2		Field EEF	WO/213/30/126	
09/06/19	McElroy J	Pte	2 R I Fus	M+XOS+S40	1 yr HL		Field EEF	WO/213/30/126	
09/06/19	McQuillan D	Pte	2 R I Fus	M+S40	NG		Field EEF	WO/213/30/126	
09/06/19	Ward J	Pte	2 R I Fus	M+XOS+S40	6 mos HL		Field EEF	WO/213/30/126	
09/06/19	Harris F	Pte	Lab Corps	M+S40	1 yr HL		Field	WO/213/30/120	
12/06/19	Anderson C	Pte	2 MGC	M+Disob(2)+S40	5 yrs PS	Comm 2 yrs HL	Field	WO/213/29/122	107
12/06/19	Barker H	Pte	2 MGC	M+Disob(2)+S40	5 yrs PS	Comm 2 yrs HL	Field	WO/213/29/122	
12/06/19	Barr WJ	Pte	2 MGC	M+Disob(2)+S40	5 yrs PS		Field	WO/213/29/122	
12/06/19	Battersby HM	Pte	2 MGC	M+Disob(2)+S40	5 yrs PS		Field	WO/213/29/122	
12/06/19	Brennan M	Pte	2 MGC	M+Disob(2)+S40	5 yrs PS	Comm 2 yrs HL	Field	WO/213/29/122	
12/06/19	Bryson H	Pte	2 MGC	M+Disob(2)+S40	5 yrs PS	Remit 2 yrs	Field	WO/213/29/122	
12/06/19	Collins WG	Pte	2 MGC	M+Disob(2)+S40	5 yrs PS	Remit 2 yrs	Field	WO/213/29/122	
12/06/19	Grapes C	Pte	2 MGC	M+Disob(2)+S40	5 yrs PS	Remit 2 yrs	Field	WO/213/29/122	
12/06/19	Green FC	Pte	2 MGC	M+Disob(2)+S40	5 yrs PS	Remit 2 yrs	Field	WO/213/29/122	
12/06/19	Harrison W	Pte	2 MGC	M+Disob(2)+S40	5 yrs PS	Remit 1 yr	Field	WO/213/29/122	
12/06/19	Hodgson P	Pte	2 MGC	M+Disob(2)+S40	5 yrs PS	Remit 2 yrs	Field	WO/213/29/122	
12/06/19	Howe L	Pte	2 MGC	M+Disob(2)+S40	5 yrs PS	Comm 2 yrs HL	Field	WO/213/29/122	
12/06/19	Jones JW	Pte	2 MGC	M+Disob(2)+S40	5 yrs PS	Comm 2 yrs HL	Field	WO/213/29/122	
12/06/19	Lever TG	Pte	2 MGC	M+Disob(2)+S40	5 yrs PS	Comm 2 yrs HL	Field	WO/213/29/122	
12/06/19	Milne RW	Pte	2 MGC	M+Disob(2)+S40	5 yrs PS	Remit 2 yrs	Field	WO/213/29/122	

Date D/M/Y	Name	Rank	Unit	Offence	Finding/Punishment	Amendment	Location	PRO Reference File/Piece/Page	Note:
12/06/19	Randall H	Pte	2 MGC	M+Disob(2)+S40	5 yrs PS		Field	WO/213/29/122	
12/06/19	Redgrave J	Pte	51 Rif Bde (att 2 MGC)	M+Disob(2)+S40	5 yrs PS	Comm 2 yrs HL	Field	WO/213/29/122	
12/06/19	Ross G	Pte	2 MGC	M+Disob(2)+S40	5 yrs PS	Remit 2 yrs	Field	WO/213/29/122	
12/06/19	Saunders HP	Pte	2 MGC	M+Disob(2)+S40	5 yrs PS	Comm 2 yrs HL	Field	WO/213/29/122	
12/06/19	Sherring J	Pte	2 MGC	M+Disob(2)+S40	5 yrs PS	Comm 2 yrs HL	Field	WO/213/29/122	
12/06/19	Stephens E	Pte	2 MGC	M+Disob(2)+S40	5 yrs PS	Comm 2 yrs HL	Field	WO/213/29/122	
12/06/19	Stocks WA	Rfn	51 Rif Bde (att 2 MGC)	M+Disob(2)+S40	5 yrs PS	Comm 2 yrs HL	Field	WO/213/29/122	
12/06/19	Threlfell E	Pte	2 MGC	M+Disob(2)+S40	5 yrs PS		Field	WO/213/29/122	
12/06/19	Weinberg S	Pte	2 MGC	M+Disob(2)+S40	5 yrs PS	Remit 2 yrs	Field	WO/213/29/122	
12/06/19	Wormald S	Pte	2 MGC	M+Disob(2)+S40	5 yrs PS	Remit 2 yrs	Field	WO/213/29/122	
17/06/19	Bean HG	Pte	1/1 C of Lon Yeo	M+S40	NG		Field EEF	WO/213/30/104	108
7/06/19	Gale H	Pte	1/1 C of Lon Yeo	M+S40	NG		Field EEF	WO/213/30/104	
18/06/19	Gray FW	S/Smith	1/1 C of Lon Yeo	M+S40	75 dys Stop	Remit 53 dys	Field	WO/213/30/96	
18/06/19	Griffin AJ	Pte	1/1 C of Lon Yeo	M+S40	NG		Field	WO/213/30/96	
18/06/19	Smallbone GW	Pte	1/1 C of Lon Yeo	M+S40	NG		Field	WO/213/30/96	
18/06/19	Hambrook E	L/Cpl	1/1 C of Lon Yeo	M+S40	NG		Field EEF	WO/213/30/97	
18/06/19	Fitzgerald NJ	Pte	2 AIF	M+Disob	14 mos HL		Field	WO/213/30/131	
18/06/19	Travis R	Pte	2 AIF	M+Disob	2 yrs HL		Field	WO/213/30/131	
18/06/19	Richards AA	Pte	5 AIF	M+Disob	5 mos HL		Field	WO/213/30/131	
18/06/19	McLeod R	Dvr	10 AIF	M+Disob	19 mos HL		Field	WO/213/30/131	
24/06/19	Baker NG	Sig	RFA	M+Disob	1 yr HL		Field	WO/213/29/137	
24/06/19	Cole RW	Gnr	RFA	M+Abs	NG		Field	WO/213/29/137	
24/06/19	Davies GH	Gnr	RFA	M+Abs	1 yr HL		Field	WO/213/29/137	
24/06/19	Dyer GH	Gnr	RFA	M	18 mos HL		Field	WO/213/29/137	
24/06/19	Grocutt E	Gnr	RFA	M	NG		Field	WO/213/29/137	
24/06/19	Jackson F	Gnr	RFA	M+Disob	1 yr HL		Field	WO/213/29/137	
24/06/19	Murray T	Gnr	RFA	M+Disob	2 yrs HL		Field	WO/213/29/137	
30/06/19	Coldwell FH	Gnr	RFA	M	10 yrs PS		Field EEF	WO/213/30/104	
05/07/19	Sykes H	Pte	9 Northumberland Fus	M+S40	3 yrs PS	Comm 1 yr HL	Field	WO/213/30/109	109
07/07/19	Guthrie A	Bdr	RFA	M+S5+S40(x2)	90 dys FP2		Field	WO/213/30/84	
14/07/19	Wright GCM	Bdr (A/Cpl)	RFA	M+7(2)	6 mos HL + Rnks		Field	WO/213/30/81	
13/07/19	Deriagin I	Pte	1 Slav-Brit Legion	M	Death		Field	WO213/32/58	110
13/07/19	Kanieff A	Pte	1 Slav-Brit Legion	M	NG		Field	WO213/32/58	
13/07/19	Lasheff T	Pte	1 Slav-Brit Legion	M	NG		Field	WO213/32/58	
13/07/19	Pesochnikoff J	Sgt	1 Slav-Brit Legion	M	Death		Field NREF	WO/213/32/59	
13/07/19	Sakharoff F	Pte	1 Slav-Brit Legion	M	Death		Field	WO/213/32/58	
13/07/19	Shouliatieff T	Pte	1 Slav-Brit X Legion	M	Death	Comm 10 yrs PS	Field	WO/213/32/58	
13/07/19	Tenentieff H	Pte	1 Slav-Brit Legion	M	NG		Field	WO213/32/58	
14/07/19	Artemenko G	Pte	1 Slav-Brit Legion	M	NG		Field NREF	WO/213/32/59	
14/07/19	Bitel S	Pte	1 Slav-Brit Legion	M	Death		Field NREF	WO/213/32/59	
14/07/19	Cherbukin F	Pte	1 Slav-Brit Legion	M	Death		Field NREF	WO/213/32/	
14/07/19	Elisaieff I	Pte	1 Slav-Brit Legion	M	Death		Field NREF	WO/213/32/59	
14/07/19	Kanieff P	Cpl	1 Slav-Brit Legion	M	Death		Field NREF	WO/213/32/59	
14/07/19	Lashkoff V	Pte	1 Slav-Brit Legion	M	Death		Field NREF	WO/213/32/59	
14/07/19	Petonhoff M	Pte	1 Slav-Brit Legion	M	Death	Comm 10 yrs PS	Field NREF	WO/213/32/59	
14/07/19	Posdjeef N	Pte	1 Slav-Brit Legion	M	Death		Field NREF	WO/213/32/59	

Date D/M/Y	Name	Rank	Unit	Offence	Finding/Punishment	Amendment	Location	PRO Reference File/Piece/Page	Note:
14/07/19	Taratin P	Pte	1 Slav-Brit Legion	M	Death		Field NREF	WO/213/32/59	
14/07/19	Volkoff P	Pte	1 Slav-Brit Legion	M	Death		Field NREF	WO/213/32/59	
15/07/19	Zouev AM	2 Lt	1 Slav-Brit Legion	M	Acquit	No evidence	Field	WO/90/8/85	
17/07/19	Bykoff V	Pte	1 Slav-Brit Legion	M	Death	Comm 10 yrs PS	Field NREF	WO/213/32/59	
17/07/19	Evstraloff P	Pte	1 Slav-Brit Legion	M	Death	Comm 10 yrs PS	Field NREF	WO/213/32/59	
17/07/19	Kozhin V	Pte	1 Slav-Brit Legion	M	NG		Field NREF	WO/213/32/59	
17/07/19	Miarid G	Pte	1 Slav-Brit Legion	M	Death	Comm 10 yrs PS	Field NREF	WO/213/32/59	
17/07/19	Piasosky A	Pte	1 Slav-Brit Legion	M	NG		Field NREF	WO/213/32/59	
17/07/19	Roond I	Pte	1 Slav-Brit Legion	M	NG		Field NREF	WO/213/31/59	
17/07/19	Sharoff V	Pte	1 Slav-Brit Legion	M	Death	Comm 10 yrs PS	Field NREF	WO/213/32/59	
17/07/19	Tonkikh V	Pte	1 Slav-Brit Legion	M	Death	Comm 10 yrs PS	Field NREF	WO/213/32/59	
17/07/19	Coffey W	Cpl	1 MGC	M	5 mos Imp+Rnks		Field	WO/213/30/82	111
17/07/19	Hill N	Cpl	1 MGC	M	5 mos Imp+Rnks		Field	WO/213/30/82	
17/07/19	Owen EL	Pte (A/Cpl)	1 MGC	M	5 mos Imp		Field	WO/213/30/82	
17/07/19	Snell FJ	Pte (A/Cpl)	1 MGC	M	5 mos Imp		Field	WO/213/30/82	
23/07/19	Sova S	Pte	17 Worc	M+S40	1 yr HL		Field	WO/213/30/135	112
26/07/19	Waters F	Sgt	R Berks (att 1/OBLI)	M+S40	6 mos HL+Rnks	Comm 91 dys Imp	Field NREF	WO/213/30/106	113
29/07/19	Arundale L	Pte	30 MGC	M+Disob	1 yr HL		Field	WO/213/30/119	114
29/07/19	Barnes F	Pte	30 MGC	M+Disob	1 yr HL		Field	WO/213/30/119	
29/07/19	Brooks RR	Pte	30 MGC	M+Disob	1 yr HL		Field	WO/213/30/119	
29/07/19	Chapman W	Pte	30 MGC	M+Disob	1 yr HL		Field	WO/213/30/119	
29/07/19	Cogger AN	Pte	30 MGC	M+Disob	1 yr HL		Field	WO/213/30/119	
29/07/19	Dunn R	Pte	30 MGC	M+Disob	1 yr HL		Field	WO/213/30/119	
29/07/19	Ellis EJ	Pte	30 MGC	M+Disob	1 yr HL		Field	WO/213/30/119	
29/07/19	Fowler A	Pte	30 MGC	M+Disob	1 yr HL		Field	WO/213/30/119	
29/07/19	Humpreys B	Pte	30 MGC	M+Disob	1 yr HL		Field	WO/213/30/119	
29/07/19	Marsh B	Pte	30 MGC	M+Disob	1 yr HL		Field	WO/213/30/119	
29/07/19	McCall TM	Pte	30 MGC	M+Disob	1 yr HL		Field	WO/213/30/119	
29/07/19	Page EE	Pte	30 MGC	M+Disob	1 yr HL		Field	WO/213/30/119	
29/07/19	Stevenson W	Pte	30 MGC	M+Disob	1 yr HL		Field	WO/213/30/119	
29/07/19	Whitehouse AJ	Pte	30 MGC	M+Disob	1 yr HL		Field	WO/213/30/119	
29/07/19	Wolfe WG	Pte	30 MGC	M+Disob	1 yr HL		Field	WO/213/30/119	
31/07/19	Chappell LR	Pte	9 MGC	M+Abs/Br	6 mos HL		Field	WO/213/30/141	115
31/07/19	Dabell W	Pte	9 MGC	M+Abs/Br	6 mos HL	Quashed	Field	WO/213/30/141	
31/07/19	Fox LF	Pte	9 MGC	M+Abs/Br	6 mos HL		Field	WO/213/30/141	
31/07/19	Gamble F	Pte	9 MGC	M+Abs/Br	6 mos HL		Field	WO/213/30/141	
31/07/19	Johnston T	Cpl	9 MGC	Mx2	12 mos HL+Rnks		Field	WO/213/30/76	
31/07/19	Lucas AF	Pte	9 MGC	M+Abs/Br	6 mos HL		Field	WO/213/30/141	
31/07/19	Radcliffe G	Pte	9 MGC	M+Abs/Br	6 mos HL		Field	WO/213/30/141	
31/07/19	Shepherd AE	Pte	9 MGC	M+Abs/Br	6 mos HL	Quashed	Field	WO/213/30/141	
31/07/19	Whiteman A	Pte	9 MGC	M+Abs/Br	6 mos HL	Quashed	Field	WO/213/30/141	
02/08/19	Thompson H	Pte	11 R Fus	M+Viol+Thr+Insol	10 yrs PS		Field	WO/213/30/160	116
11/08/19	Harris F	Pte	Lab Corps	M+S40	42 dys FP2		Field	WO/213/30/120	
21/08/19	Enright W	Pte	45 Royal Fus	No offence/Mutiny?	Death	2 yrs HL	NREF	WO/213/31/27	
21/08/19	Crisp	Pte	45 Royal Fus	No offence/Mutiny?	Death	2 yrs HL	NREF	WO/213/31/27	
23/08/19	Aberman P	Pte	39 R Fus	M	5 yrs PS	Comm 1 yr HL	Field EEF	WO/213/31/24	117
23/08/19	Barkin H	Pte	39 R Fus	M	5 yrs PS	Comm 1 yr HL	Field EEF	WO/213/31/24	
23/08/19	Bass G	Pte	39 R Fus	M	5 yrs PS	Comm 1 yr HL	Field EEF	WO/213/31/24	
23/08/19	Blumenthal B	Pte	39 R Fus	M	NG		Field EEF	WO/213/31/23	
23/08/19	Chaitman B	Pte	39 R Fus	M	5 yrs PS	Comm 1 yr HL	Field EEF	WO/213/31/24	
23/08/19	Davidson A	Pte	39 R Fus	M	NG		Field EEF	WO/213/31/25	
23/08/19	Ehrlick L	Pte	39 R Fus	M	NG		Field EEF	WO/213/31/23	
23/08/19	Eisenstat H	Pte	39 R Fus	M	5 yrs PS	Comm 1 yr HL	Field EEF	WO/213/31/24	

Date D/M/Y	Name	Rank	Unit	Offence	Finding/Punishment	Amendment	Location	PRO Reference File/Piece/Page	Note:
23/08/19	Elden E	Pte	39 R Fus	M	5 yrs PS	Remit	Field EEF	WO/213/31/25	
23/08/19	Feldman B	Pte	39 R Fus	M	5 yrs PS		Field EEF	WO/213/31/23	
23/08/19	Feldman J	Pte	39 R Fus	M	5 yrs PS	Comm 1 yr HL	Field EEF	WO/213/31/25	
23/08/19	Finkelstein F	Pte	39 R Fus	M	5 yrs PS	Comm 1 yr HL	Field EEF	WO/213/31/24	
23/08/19	Foreman I	Pte	39 R Fus	M	5 yrs PS		Field EEF	WO/213/31/23	
23/08/19	Frankel A	Pte	39 R Fus	M	5 yrs PS	Comm 1 yr HL	Field EEF	WO/213/31/24	
23/08/19	Goldman B	Pte	39 R Fus	M	NG		Field EEF	WO/213/31/23	
23/08/19	Goldman M	Pte	39 R Fus	M	5 yrs PS	Comm 1 yr HL	Field EEF	WO/213/31/24	
23/08/19	Gunchar I	Pte	39 R Fus	M	5 yrs PS	Comm 1 yr HL	Field EEF	WO/213/31/24	
23/08/19	Horowitz J	Pte	39 R Fus	M	5 yrs PS	Comm 1 yr HL	Field EEF	WO/213/31/25	
23/08/19	Hurvutz J	Pte	39 R Fus	M	5 yrs PS	Comm 1 yr HL	Field EEF	WO/213/31/25	
23/08/19	Kalis I	Pte	39 R Fus	M	6 yrs PS	Comm 1 yr HL	Field EEF	WO/213/31/25	
23/08/19	Klein M	Pte	39 R Fus	M	5 yrs PS	Comm 1 yr HL	Field EEF	WO/213/31/24	
23/08/19	Krantz A	Pte	39 R Fus	M	NG		Field EEF	WO/213/31/24	
23/08/19	Lasry SH	Pte	39 R Fus	M	5 yrs PS	Comm 1 yr HL	Field EEF	WO/213/31/24	
23/08/19	Levitan B	Pte	39 R Fus	M	5 yrs PS	Comm 1 yr HL	Field EEF	WO/213/31/25	
23/08/19	Lichenstein I	Pte	39 R Fus	M	5 yrs PS	Comm 1 yr HL	Field EEF	WO/213/31/24	
23/08/19	Lifschitz M	Pte	39 R Fus	M	NG		Field EEF	WO/213/31/24	
23/08/19	Mintz N	Pte	39 R Fus	M	NG		Field EEF	WO/213/31/24	
23/08/19	Murman I	Pte	39 R Fus	M	NG		Field EEF	WO/213/31/23	
23/08/19	Nemcheck M	Pte	39 R Fus	M	5 yrs PS	Comm 1 yr HL	Field EEF	WO/213/31/25	
23/08/19	Nordockovitch B	Pte	39 R Fus	M	5 yrs PS	Comm 1 yr HL	Field EEF	WO/213/31/24	
23/08/19	Petrofsky P	Pte	39 R Fus	M	NG		Field EEF	WO/213/31/25	
23/08/19	Prince N	Pte	39 R Fus	M	NG		Field EEF	WO/213/31/24	
23/08/19	Resnik S	Pte	39 R Fus	M	5 yrs PS	Comm 1 yr HL	Field EEF	WO/213/31/25	
23/08/19	Sauber A	Pte	39 R Fus	M	NG		Field EEF	WO/213/31/24	
23/08/19	Schorr H	Pte	39 R Fus	M	NG		Field EEF	WO/213/31/24	
23/08/19	Sherenitz D	Pte	39 R Fus	M	5 yrs PS	Comm 1 yr HL	Field EEF	WO/213/31/24	
23/08/19	Singer A	Pte	39 R Fus	M	5 ys PS	Comm 1 yr HL	Field EEF	WO/213/31/24	
23/08/19	Smith N	Pte	39 R Fus	M	NG		Field EEF	WO/213/31/24	
23/08/19	Strauss H	Pte	39 R Fus	M	NG		Field EEF	WO/213/31/24	
23/08/19	Tandet J	Pte	39 R Fus	M	6 yrs PS	Comm 1 yr HL	Field EEF	WO/213/31/24	
23/08/19	Tobin D	Pte	39 R Fus	M	6 yrs PS	Rem 3 yrs/ Comm 1 yr HL	Field EEF	WO/213/31/24	
23/08/19	Wein H	Pte	39 R Fus	M	5 yrs PS	Comm 1 yr HL	Field EEF	WO/213/31/24	
23/08/19	Zamasthansky N	Pte	39 R Fus	M	5 yrs PS		Field EEF	WO/213/31/23	
23/08/19	Zorowski N	Pte	39 R Fus	M	5 yrs PS		Field EEF	WO/213/31/23	
08/09/19	McLaren R	Pte	24 CEF	M+Des+Esc +S40/S41	2 yrs HL		Field	WO/213/30/141	118
16/09/19	Barrett E	Pte	1/4 KOYLI (att 365 POW Coy)	M+Abs+Disob	3 yrs PS	Comm 1 yr HL	Field	WO/213/31/69	119
16/09/19	Bibb J	Pte	1/4 KOYLI (att 365 POW Coy)	M+Abs+Disob	3 yrs PS	Comm 1 yr HL	Field	WO/213/31/69	
16/09/19	Bowen M	Pte	1/4 KOYLI (att 365 POW Coy)	M+Abs+Disob	5 yrs PS	Comm 2 yrs HL	Field	WO/213/31/68	
16/09/19	Burton FA	Pte	1/4 KOYLI (att 365 POW Coy]	M+Abs+Disob	3 yrs PS	Comm 1 yr HL	Field	WO/213/31/69	
16/09/19	Coley TH	Pte	1/4 KOYLI (att 365 POW Coy)	M+Abs+Disob	3 yrs PS	Comm 1 yr HL	Field	WO/213/31/69	
16/09/19	Graham R	Pte	1/4 KOYLI (att 365 POW Coy)	M+Abs+Disob	3 yrs PS	Comm 1 yr HL	Field	WO/213/31/69	
16/09/19	Jennings A	Pte	1/4 KOYLI (att 265 POW Coy)	M+Abs+Disob	3 yrs PS	Comm 1 yr HL	Field	WO/213/31/69	
16/09/19	Kent T	Pte	1/4 KOYLI (att 365 POW Coy)	M+Abs+Disob	3 yrs PS	Comm 1 yr HL	Field	WO/213/31/69	
16/09/19	Miller R	Pte	1/4 KOYLI (att 365 POW Coy)	M+Abs+Disob	3 yrs PS	Comm 1 yr HL	Field	WO/213/31/69	
16/09/19	Peregrine JB	Pte	1/4 KOYLI (att 365 POW Coy)	M+Abs+Disob	3 yrs PS	Comm 1 yr HL	Field	WO/213/31/69	
16/09/19	Robinson W	Pte	1/4 KOYLI (att 365 POW Coy)	M+Abs+Disob	3 yrs PS	Comm 1 yr HL	Field	WO/213/31/69	
16/09/19	Spriggs A	Pte	1/4 KOYLI (att 365 POW Coy)	M+Abs+Disob	3 yrs PS	Comm 1 yr HL	Field	WO/213/31/69	
16/09/19	Thorton W	Pte	1/4 KOYLI (att 365 POW Coy)	M+Abs+Disob	3 yrs PS	Comm 1 yr HL	Field	WO/213/31/69	
16/09/19	Turner G	Pte	1/4 KOYLI (att 365 POW Coy)	M+Abs+Disob	3 yrs PS	Comm 1 yr HL	Field	WO/213/31/69	
07/10/19	Cooper WJ	Cpl(A/Sgt)	6 R Marines	M(2)+S40	NG		Field NREF	WO/213/30/179	120

Date D/M/Y	Name	Rank	Unit	Offence	Finding/Punishment	Amendment	Location	PRO Reference File/Piece/Page	Note:
08/10/19	Biddle C	Pte(A/Cpl)	RAOC	M+S40	NG		Field	WO/213/31/4	121
08/10/19	Cook A	Pte (A/LSgt)	RAOC	M+S40	NG		Field	WO/213/31/4	
08/10/19	Curtis A	Pte(A/Cpl)	1/4 KOYLI (att RAOC)	M+S40	NG		Field	WO/213/31/4	
08/10/19	Hooley A	Pte(A/Cpl)	7 S Staffs (att RAOC)	M+S40	NG		Field	WO/213/31/4	
08/10/19	Miller AF	Pte	LN Lancs (att RAOC)	M	NG		Field	WO/213/31/6	
08/10/19	Webster T	Pte(A/Cpl)	RAOC	M+S40	NG		Field	WO/213/31/4	
28/10/19	Lee CEW	L/Cpl	76 Lab Coy	M+Disob+S40	3 yrs PS	Comm 2 yrs HL	Field	WO/213/31/80	
04/11/19	Green AP	Pte	2 Y[orks] & Lancs	M+Disob +Insub Lang	4 yrs PS	Comm 2 yrs HL	Basrah	WO/90/7/205	122
04/11/19	Tarren F	L/Cpl	2 Y[orks] & Lancs	M+Drunk	60 dys FP2		Basrah	WO/90/7/205	
05/11/19	Ingram T	Pte	2 Y[orks] & Lancs	M+Disob	Acquit		Basrah	WO/90/7/205	
05/11/19	Melson J	Pte	2 Y[orks] & Lancs	M	4 yrs PS	Comm 2 yrs HL	Basrah	WO/90/7/205	
05/11/19	Richards JH	Pte	2 Y[orks] & Lancs	M+Disob	5 yrs PS	Comm 2 yrs HL	Basrah	WO/90/7/205	
05/11/19	Wake N	Pte	2 Y[orks] & Lancs	M+S9(1)	4 yrs PS	Comm 2 yrs HL	Basrah	WO/90/7/205	
06/11/19	Hartley S	Pte	2 Y[orks] & Lancs	M+Disob	5 yrs PS	Comm 2 yrs HL	Basrah	WO/90/7/205	
06/11/19	Holland JHB	Pte	2 Y[orks] & Lancs	M+XSO*	5 yrs PS	Comm 2 yrs +*Quashed	Basrah	WO/90/7/205	
06/11/19	Stacey EW	Pte	2 Y[orks] & Lancs	M	4 yrs PS	Comm 2 yrs HL	Basrah	WO/90/7/205	
07/11/19	Beck T	Pte	2 Y[orks] & Lancs	M+S40	6 mos HL		Basrah	WO/90/7/205	
07/11/19	Lax J	Pte	2 Y[orks] & Lancs	M	4 yrs PS	Comm 2 yrs HL	Basrah	WO/90/7/205	
07/11/19	Milner G	Pte	2 Y[orks] & Lancs	M+S7(3B)	5 yrs PS	Comm 2 yrs HL	Basrah	WO/90/7/205	
07/11/19	Portman HE	Pte	2 Y[orks] & Lancs	M+S9(1)	4 yrs PS	Comm 2 yrs HL	Basrah	WO/90/7/205	
05/03/20	Codd A	Pte	2 Ches	M+Disob	2 yrs HL	Rem 18 mos	Field ABS	WO/213/31/168	123
05/03/20	Draper A	Pte	2 Ches	M+Disob	2 yrs HL	Rem 18 mos	Field ABS	WO/213/31/168	
05/03/20	Jackson J	Pte	2 Ches	M+Disob	2 yrs HL	Rem 18 mos	Field ABS	WO/213/31/168	
05/03/20	King G	Pte	2 Ches	M+Disob	9 mos HL	Rem 3 mos	Field ABS	WO/213/31/168	
05/03/20	McGuire EM	Pte	2 Ches	M+Disob	2 yrs HL	Rem 18 mos	Field ABS	WO/213/31/168	
05/03/20	Monks L	Pte	2 Ches	M+Disob	2 yrs HL	Rem 18 mos	Field ABS	WO/213/31/168	
05/03/20	Pearson H	Pte	2 Ches	M+Disob	2 yrs HL	Rem 18 mos	Field ABS	WO/213/31/168	
05/03/20	Roberts A	Pte	2 Ches	M+Disob	18 mos HL	Rem 1 yr	Field ABS	WO/213/31/168	
05/03/20	Shelly F	Pte	2 Ches	M+7(2b)	2 yrs HL		Field ABS	WO/213/31/168	
05/03/20	Smith D	Pte	2 Ches	M+Disob	2 yrs HL	Rem 18 mos	Field ABS	WO/213/31/168	
24/03/20	McCarthy D	Pte	2 R Mun Fus	M+XO+S2+7(2b)	9 mos HL		Field EEF	WO/213/31/142	
24/03/20	McCarthy M	Pte	2 R Mun Fus	M+XO+S2+7(2b)	9 mos HL		Field EEF	WO/213/31/142	
24/03/20	Oakley F	Pte	2 R Mun Fus	M(2)+XO+S2	2 yrs HL		Field EEF	WO/213/31/142	
14/04/20	Vincent W	Pte	47 R Fus (att 29 Liverpool)	M+S40	6 mos HL		Field	WO/213/31/142	124
14/04/20	Vizer HC	Pte	47 R Fus (att 29 Liverpool)	M+S40	6 mos HL		Field	WO/213/31/142	
14/04/20	Walsh T	Pte	47 R Fus (att 29 Liverpool)	M+S40	6 mos HL		Field	WO/213/31/142	
14/04/20	Watts SC	Pte	47 R Fus (att 29 Liverpool)	M+S40	6 mos HL		Field	WO/213/31/142	
14/04/20	Williams T	Pte	47 R Fus (att 29 Liverpool)	M+S40	6 mos HL		Field	WO/213/31/142	
20/04/20	Bailey J	Pte	RASC	M+Disob	3 mos FP2		Field ABS	WO/213/31/171	
20/04/20	Chappell J	Pte	RASC	M+Disob	3 mos FP2		Field ABS	WO/213/31/171	
20/04/20	Colwell A	Pte	RASC	M+Disob	3 mos FP2		Field ABS	WO/213/31/171	
20/04/20	Forbes J	Pte	RASC	M+Disob	3 mos FP2		Field ABS	WO/213/31/171	
20/04/20	Little T	Pte	RASC	M+Disob	3 mos FP2		Field ABS	WO/213/31/171	
20/04/20	Warbrick J	Pte	RASC	M+Disob	3 mos FP2		Field ABS	WO/213/31/171	
20/04/20	Warsdale H	Pte	RASC	M+Disob	3 mos FP2		Field ABS	WO/213/31/171	

Date D/M/Y	Name	Rank	Unit	Offence	Finding/Punishment	Amendment	Location	PRO Reference File/Piece/Page	Note:
26/04/20	Craig J	Pte	2 Liverpool	M+S40/S7(3b)	Acquit		Khartoum	WO/90/8/83	
26/04/20	Dandy W	Pte	2 Liverpool	M+Disob+S40/S7(3b)	6 mos Detn+Stop 122 dys Detn+Stop	Remit 122 dys	Khartoum	WO/90/8/83	
26/04/20	Gordon JH	Pte	2 Liverpool	M+S40/S7(3b)	Acquit		Khartoum	WO/90/8/83	
26/04/20	May J	Pte	2 Liverpool	M+Disob+S40/S7(3b)	6 mos Detn+Stop; 122 dys Detn+Stop	Remit 122 dys Detn + Stop	Khartoum	WO/90/8/83	
26/04/20	Troy J	Pte	2 Liverpool	M+Resist+Esc+S40+S7(3b)	14 dys Detn	Remit Sentence	Khartoum	WO/90/8/83	
05/07/20	Cannon W	Pte	2 R Dublin Fusiliers	M+Disob(Capt)	5 yrs PS	Comm 1 yr Detn	Constantinople	WO/90/8/84	125
05/07/20	Daniels C	Pte	2 DLI	M+Disob(Capt)	12 yrs PS	Comm 2 yrs Detn	Constantinople	WO/90/8/84	
05/07/20	Doyle H	Pte	2 R DLI	M+Disob(Capt)	12 yrs PS	Comm 2 yrs Detn	Constantinople	WO/90/8/84	
05/07/20	Failes NC	Pte	2 DLI	M+Disob(Capt)	12 yrs PS	Comm 2 yrs Detn	Constantinople	WO/90/8/84	
05/07/20	Lamb J	Gnr	RFA	M+Disob(Capt)+S7(3b)	12 yrs PS	Comm 2 yrs Detn	Constantinople	WO/90/8/84	
05/07/20	McFarlane J	Pte	2 R Scots Fus	M+Disob(Capt)+S7(3b	5 yrs PS	Comm 1 yr Detn	Constantinople	WO/90/8/84	
05/07/20	Thompson T	Pte	2 East Yorks	M + Disob(Capt)	5 yrs PS	Comm 1 yr Detn	Constantinople	WO/90/8/84	
16/07/20	Garner J	Pte	2 York & Lanc	M	1 yr HL		Kasvin	WO/90/7/208	126
16/07/20	Hoult A	Pte	2 York & Lanc	M	1 yr HL		Kasvin	WO/90/7/208	
16/07/20	Robinson E	Pte	2 York & Lanc	M	1 yr HL		Kasvin	WO/90/7/208	
16/07/20	Wraith E	Pte	2 York & Lanc	M	1 yr HL		Kasvin	WO/90/7/208	
24/07/20	Mason W	Pte	1 Royal Welsh Fus	M+Insol(L/Cpl)+S40	Death	5yrs PS	Ranikhet	WO/90/8/194	127
26/07/20	Morris W	Pte	1 Royal Welsh Fus	M+Insol(Sgt)+S40	Death	5yrs PS	Ranikhet	WO/90/8/194	
29/07/20	Craig A	Pte	RAOC	M+S7(3b)	4 yrs PS		Field	WO/213/32/22	
29/07/20	Jones CH	Civilian	att RAOC	M+Disob+S7(3b)	5 yrs PS		Field	WO/213/32/22	
29/07/20	Kershaw J	Pte	2 Dragoon Gds (att RAOC)	M+S7(3b)	4 yrs PS		Field	WO/213/32/22	
29/07/20	White JJ	Pte	RAOC	M+S7(3b)	4 yrs PS		Field	WO/213/32/22	
23/08/20	Coleman P	Cpl	1 Connaught Rangers	M+S7(3)	Acquit		Dagshai	WO/90/8/189	128
23/08/20	Davis J	Cpl	1 Connaught Rangers	M+S7(3)	2 yrs HL + RANKS+DI		Dagshai	WO/90/8/189	
23/08/20	Donohue P	Pte(L/Cpl)	1 Connaught Rangers	M+S7(3)	2 yrs HL+DI		Dagshai	WO/90/8/189	
23/08/20	Hughes J	Pte(L/Cpl)	1 Connaught Rangers	M+S7(3)	1 yr HL+DI		Dagshai	WO/90/8/189	
23/08/20	Lloyd J	Sgt	1 Connaught Rangers	M	Acquit		Dagshai	WO/90/8/189	
23/08/20	O'Donnell C	Pte(L/Cpl)	1 Connaught Rangers	M+S7(3)	Acquit		Dagshai	WO/90/8/189	
23/08/20	O'Donoghue J	Cpl	1 Connaught Rangers	M+S7(3)	1 yr HL+Ranks+DI		Dagshai	WO/90/8/189	
25/08/20	Coote WJ	Pte	1 Connaught Rangers	M	1 yr HL+DI		Dagshai	WO/90/8/188	
25/08/20	Cox P	Pte(L/Cpl)	1 Connaught Rangers	M	Acquit		Dagshai	WO/90/8/188	
25/08/20	Dyer P	Cpl	1 Connaught Rangers	M	3 yrs PS+Rnks+DI		Dagshai	WO/90/8/188	
25/08/20	Fallon J	Pte(L/Cpl)	1 Connaught Rangers	M	2 yrs HL+DI		Dagshai	WO/90/8/188	
25/08/20	Gallagher J	Pte(L/Cpl)	1 Connaught Rangers	M	Acquit		Dagshai	WO/90/8/188	
25/08/20	Lopeman PJ	Pte(L/Cpl)	1 Connaught Rangers	M	2 yrs HL+DI		Dagshai	WO/90/8/188	
25/08/20	Lynott J	Pte(L/Cpl)	1 Connaught Rangers	M	2 yrs HL+DI		Dagshai	WO/90/8/188	
25/08/20	Madigan D	Pte	1 Connaught Rangers	M	Acquit		Dagshai	WO/90/8/188	
25/08/20	McGrath J	Pte(L/Cpl)	1 Connaught Rangers	M	1 yr HL+DI		Dagshai	WO/90/8/188	
25/08/20	Miranda J	Pte	1 Connaught Rangers	M	2 yrs HL+DI		Dagshai	WO/90/8/188	

Date D/M/Y	Name	Rank	Unit	Offence	Finding/Punishment	Amendment	Location	PRO Reference File/Piece/Page	Note:
25/08/20	Murray TJ	Cpl	1 Connaught Rangers	M	5 yrs PS+Rnks+	Remit 2 yrs	Dagshai	WO/90/8/188	
25/08/20	Regan D	Pte	1 Connaught Rangers	M	5 yrs PS+DI	Remit 1 yr	Dagshai	WO/90/8/188	
25/08/20	Walsh J	Pte	1 Connaught Rangers	M	5 yrs PS+DI		Dagshai	WO/90/8/188	
25/08/20	Willis P	Pte(L/Cpl)	1 Connaught Rangers	M	3 yrs PS+DI		Dagshai	WO/90/8/188	
25/08/20	Woods J	Sgt	1 Connaught Rangers	M	10 yrs PS+Rnks+DI+Forfeits MM	Remit 2 yrs	Dagshai	WO/90/8/188	
30/08/20	Coman W	Pte	1 Connaught Rangers	M	15 yrs PS+DI		Dagshai	WO/90/8/188	
30/08/20	Delaney V	Pte	1 Connaught Rangers	M+S7(2)	Death	Life PS	Dagshai	WO/90/8/188	
30/08/20	Flannery J	L/Cpl	1 Connaught Rangers	M	Death	Life PS	Dagshai	WO/90/8/188	
30/08/20	Gogarty PJ	Pte	1 Connaught Rangers	M	Death	Life PS	Dagshai	WO/90/8/189	
30/08/20	Hawes J	Pte	1 Connaught Rangers	M	Death	Life PS	Dagshai	WO/90/8/189	
30/08/20	Hayes A	Pte	1 Connaught Rangers	M	10 yrs PS+DI		Dagshai	WO/90/8/188	
30/08/20	Keenan W	Pte	1 Connaught Rangers	M+S7(2)+S7(1)	10 yrs PS+DI		Dagshai	WO/90/8/188	
30/08/20	Kelly P	Pte	1 Connaught Rangers	M+S7(2)+S7(1)	10 yrs PS+DI		Dagshai	WO/90/8/188	
30/08/20	Lally S	Pte	1 Connaught Rangers	M	20 yrs PS+DI	Remit 5 yrs	Dagshai	WO/90/8/189	
30/08/20	Lynch J	Pte	1 Connaught Rangers	M	10 yrs PS+DI	Remit 5 yrs	Dagshai	WO/90/8/189	
30/08/20	Maher P	Pte	1 Connaught Rangers	M	10 yrs PS+DI	Remit 5 yrs	Dagshai	WO/90/8/189	
30/08/20	McGowan J	Pte	1 Connaught Rangers	M	Life PS+DI		Dagshai	WO/90/8/188	
30/08/20	Moran T	Pte	1 Connaught Rangers	M	Death	Life PS	Dagshai	WO/90/8/189	
30/08/20	O'Connell J	Pte	1 Connaught Rangers	M	10 yrs PS+DI		Dagshai	WO/90/8/188	
30/08/20	Scanlon J	Pte	1 Connaught Rangers	M	20 yrs PS+DI	Remit 5 yrs	Dagshai	WO/90/8/189	
30/08/20	Sweeney P	Pte	1 Connaught Rangers	M	Life PS+DI	20 yrs PS	Dagshai	WO/90/8/189	
31/08/20	Carmichael J	Gnr	Bermuda Royal Artillery	M	Acquit		Bermuda	WO/90/8/84	
31/08/20	Ford B	Gnr	Bermuda Royal Artillery	M	Acquit		Bermuda	WO/90/8/84	
31/08/20	Galloway JA	Gnr	Bermuda Royal Artillery	M	Acquit		Bermuda	WO/90/8/84	
01/09/20	Gardiner J	Gnr	Bermuda Royal Artillery	M+Esc+S6(1d)	2 yrs HL+DI		Bermuda	WO/90/8/84	
04/09/20	Buckley JJ	Pte	1 Connaught Rangers	M+S7(3b)	Life PS+DI		Dagshai	WO/90/8/187	129
04/09/20	Burland W	Pte	1 Connaught Rangers	M+S7(3b)	5 yrs PS+DI	Remit 2 yrs	Dagshai	WO/90/8/187	
04/09/20	Cherry P	Pte	1 Connaught Rangers	M+S7(3b)	15 yrs PS+DI	Remit 2 yrs	Dagshai	WO/90/8/187	
04/09/20	Conlon M	Boy	1 Connaught Rangers	M+S7(3b)	10 yrs PS+DI		Dagshai	WO/90/8/188	
04/09/20	Daly J	Pte	1 Connaught Rangers	M+S7(3b)	3 yrs PS+DI	2 yrs HL	Dagshai	WO/90/8/187	
04/09/20	Daly JJ	Pte	1 Connaught Rangers	M+S7(3b)	Death		Dagshai	WO/90/8/187	
04/09/20	Devers JJ	Pte	1 Connaught Rangers	M+S7(3b)	Life PS+DI	20 yrs PS+DI	Dagshai	WO/90/8/187	
04/09/20	Devine T	Pte	1 Connaught Rangers	M+S7(3b)	Death	Life PS	Dagshai	WO/90/8/187	
04/09/20	Egan E	Pte	1 Connaught Rangers	M+S7(3b)	Death	Life PS	Dagshai	WO/90/8/187	
04/09/20	Fitzgerald M	Pte	1 Connaught Rangers	M+S7(3b)	Death	Life PS	Dagshai	WO/90/8/187	
04/09/20	Gleeson JJ	Pte	1 Connaught Rangers	M+S7(3b)	Death	Life PS	Dagshai	WO/90/8/187	

Date D/M/Y	Name	Rank	Unit	Offence	Finding/Punishment	Amendment	Location	PRO Reference File/Piece/Page	Note
04/09/20	Gorman J	Pte	1 Connaught Rangers	M+S7(3b)	7 yrs PS+DI		Dagshai	WO/90/8/187	
04/09/20	Hewson J	L/Cpl	1 Connaught Rangers	M+S7(3b)	7 yrs PS+DI		Dagshai	WO/90/8/187	
04/09/20	Hynes P	Pte	1 Connaught Rangers	M+S7(3b)	Death	Life PS	Dagshai	WO/90/8/187	
04/09/20	Kearney M	Pte	1 Connaught Rangers	M+S7(3b)	15 yrs PS+DI		Dagshai	WO/90/8/187	
04/09/20	Kearns M	Pte	1 Connaught Rangers	M+S7(3b)	3 yrs PS+DI		Dagshai	WO/90/8/187	
04/09/20	Kelly J	Pte	1 Connaught Rangers	M+S7(3b)	Death	Life PS	Dagshai	WO/90/8/187	
04/09/20	Kelly P	Cpl	1 Connaught Rangers	M+S7(3b)	10 yrs PS+Rnks+DI	Remit 3 yrs PS	Dagshai	WO/90/8/187	
04/09/20	Kerrigan C	Pte	1 Connaught Rangers	M+S7(3b)	Death	20 yrs PS	Dagshai	WO/90/8/188	
04/09/20	Loftus JJ	Pte	1 Connaught Rangers	M+S7(3b)	Acquit		Dagshai	WO/90/8/187	
04/09/20	Mangan PJ	Pte	1 Connaught Rangers	M+S7(3b)	3 yrs PS+DI	2 yrs HL+DI	Dagshai	WO/90/8/187	
04/09/20	McConnell P	Pte	1 Connaught Rangers	M+S7(3b)	Acquit		Dagshai	WO/90/8/187	
04/09/20	McGrath J	Pte	1 Connaught Rangers	M+S7(3b)	5 yrs PS+DI		Dagshai	WO/90/8/187	
04/09/20	Moorehouse JJ	Pte	1 Connaught Rangers	M+S7(3b)	Life PS+DI	20 yrs PS	Dagshai	WO/90/8/187	
04/09/20	Oliver J	Pte	1 Connaught Rangers	M+S7(3b)	Death	Life PS	Dagshai	WO/90/8/187	
04/09/20	Prendergast F	Pte	1 Connaught Rangers	M+S7(3b)	3 yrs PS+DI		Dagshai	WO/90/8/187	
04/09/20	Scally P	Pte	1 Connaught Rangers	M+S7(3b)	10 yrs PS+DI	Remit 3 yrs	Dagshai	WO/90/8/187	
04/09/20	Shallow W	Pte	1 Connaught Rangers	M+S7(3b)	10 yrs PS+DI	Remit 3 yrs	Dagshai	WO/90/8/187	
10/09/20	Mannion P	Pte(L/Cpl)	1 Connaught Rangers	M+S7(3b)	15 yrs PS+DI		Dagshai	WO/90/8/189	
10/09/20	Moran FJ	Pte(L/Cpl)	1 Connaught Rangers	M+S7(3b)	10 yrs PS+DI		Dagshai	WO/90/8/189	
07/01/21	McCombie A	Pte	Tank Corps	M	1 yr HL	Comm to Detn	Ramadi	WO/213/33/2	130
29/04/21	Bedford W	Pte	West India Regt	M+Abs+Striking(Maj)+S9(1)	5 yrs PS+DI	Remit 2 yrs	Jamaica	WO/90/8/87	
29/04/21	Bradley S	Pte	West India Regt	M+Abs+S9(1)	6 mos Detn		Jamaica	WO/90/8/87	
29/04/21	Campbell S	Pte	West India Regt	M+Abs+Disob	112 dys Detn	Remit 56 dys	Jamaica	WO/90/8/87	
29/04/21	Foreman OG	Pte	West India Regt	M+Abs+S9(1)	5 yrs PS+DI	Remit 2 yrs	Jamaica	WO/90/8/87	
29/04/21	Norman J	Pte	West India Regt	M+Abs+S10(3)+S9(1)	5 yrs PS+DI	Remit 2 yrs	Jamaica	WO/90/8/87	
23/05/21	Harris T	Dvr	RFA	M+S9(1)	3 mos FP2		Hinaidi	WO/213/33/16	131
23/05/21	James D	Dvr	RFA	M+S9(1)	3 mos FP2		Hinaidi	WO/213/33/16	
23/05/21	Jones E	Dvr	RFA	M+S9(1)	6 mos Detn		Hinaidi	WO/213/33/15	
23/05/21	Palmer W	Dvr	RFA	M+S9(1)	3 mos FP2		Hinaidi	WO/213/33/15	
23/05/21	Williams D	Dvr	RFA	M+S9(1)	3 mos FP2		Hinaidi	WO/213/33/16	
23/05/21	Wright A	Dvr	RFA	M+S9(1)	3 mos FP2		Hinaidi	WO/213/33/15	
05/07/21	Geary T	Pte/LCpl	2 Royal Irish	M+S7(3b)	3 yrs PS	NC	Chakrata	WO/90/8/170	132
05/07/21	O'Brien T	Pte/LCpl	2 Royal Irish	Mx2+Disob(Lt)+S7(3b)x2	4 yrs PS	Remit 1 yr	Chakrata	WO/90/8/170	
05/07/21	O'Keefe D	Pte/LCpl	2 Royal Irish	Mx2+S7(3b)	Acquit		Chakrata	WO/90/8/170	
18/07/21	Maulson J	Pte	2 Essex	M+Theft+S18(4b)	1 yr HL+DI		Malta	WO/90/8/87	133
26/07/21	Charman J	Cpl	RASC	M+S41+S40	1 yr HL+Rnks+DI		Malta	WO/90/8/87	
23/08/22	Kennedy T	Pte	1 Cheshire	M+Disob(Sgt Maj)+S40	1 yr Detn		Ranikhet	WO/90/8/172	134
27/09/22	Cowan J	Pte	1 Black Watch	M+Des+Theft+S18(4)	2 yrs HL+DI		Allahabad	WO/90/8/172	135
27/09/22	Morey J	Pte	1 Black Watch	M+Des+Theft+S18(4)	2 yrs HL+DI		Allahabad	WO/90/8/172	

Notes

1. After heavy casualties, 2 Royal Munster Fus. during October 1914 were being re-formed with drafts from Ireland. St. Nazaire was a vital base port for the BEF between August and December 1914.
2. 5 Dragoon Guards with 1 Cavalry Div.
3. Four of eleven MSG soldiers jailed for involvement in the 5 Light Infantry mutiny, Singapore, 15.2.15.IORL: L/MIL/17/19/48; L/MIL/7/17261.
4. Cairo, 2.4.15, thousands of British and ANZAC troops burned, looted and attacked Egyptians in Cairo. Zeitoun was NZEF base camp. Boyack, op. cit., pp 25–31.
5. Bn. in bivouacs at 'A' Beach, Suvla, carrying out shore fatigues under enemy fire 3–21.9.15. R. Westlake, *British Battalions at Gallipoli* (Leo Cooper, London, 1996), p. 15.
6. Locally raised unit. Mutiny occurs in the aftermath of confrontation at Sliema with convalescents on 30.11.15.
7. Sliema, Malta, on 30.11.15, after an incident involving convalescents and Maltese Militia, a crowd of mostly Australian troops surround and stone militia men. AWM: GCM, Tpr. W.A. Bell et al.
8. Bn. with 70 Bde., 8 Div.. Steenbecque is near St.Julien in the Ypres Salient,Belgium.
9. The accused were all farriers.
10. The Bn. was attached to 8 Bde., 3 (Lahore) Div., suffering great privations after the British military debacle at Hanna (21.1.16). See A.J. Barker, *The Neglected War* (Faber, London, 1967), p. 217–225.
11. Bn. with 5 Bde., 2 (Australian) Div., training in Egypt.
12. Bn. with 5 Bde., 2 Div. in billets at Bully Grenay.
13. Bn. with NZ Div., arrived in France April 1916.
14. Bn. with 87 Bde., 29 Div. at Acheux, preparing for the attack on Beaumont Hamel (1.7.16).
15. Bn. with 5 Bde., 2 (Australian) Div. near Pozieres. Bn. was badly mauled by an enemy raid on 6.5.16. P. Charlton, *Pozieres* (Methuen Haynes, North Ryde, 1986), pp. 82–4.
16. 175 (Staffordshire) Artillery Bde., 34 Div., supporting the assault on Bazentin 14-17.7.16.
17. On 22.6.17 at No.9 Stationery Hospital, 500 convalescents stone MPs and release patients undergoing FP1. AWM: FGCM Spr JH Coffey, 1 Tunnelling Coy; WO 95/4032.
18. Bn. (amalgamation of Nos. 8 and 10 Bns., 11.5.16) with 44 Bde., 15 (Scottish) Div. near Contalmaison.
19. Bn. part of 97 Bde., 32 Div. en route from Bouzincourt (16.7.16) to Hem-Hardinal (18.10.16). Accused may have been an inmate at one of Abancourt's two military prisons.
20. Blargies (Abancourt) Prison mutiny, see Narratives..
21. Bn. with 119 Bde., 40 Div. at Pont Remy. On 1.12.16 men of D Coy. refuse to fall in on defaulters parade. WO 95/2606.
22. Bn. with 3 South African Infantry Bde., 2 East African Div.
23. Bn with 15 Bde., 5 (Australian) Div. in France.
24. This trench mortar battery was part of 38 (Welsh) Division.
25. Bn. with 111 Bde., 37 Div. in North East France
26. All Bns. with 35 Bde., 12 (Eastern) Div. Engaged in battle of Arras 9.4.17–12.5.17.
27. RMLC were employed as dockworkers.
28. Units with various Divs.; convalescents, reinforcements or prisoners?
29. Formed Lichfield, July 1915. To Malta then Egypt 1915. Prisoners sent to Alexandria, 12.6.17.
30. Stationed in German East Africa.
31. Bn. with 2 Bde., NZ Div., soldiers under close arrest refuse to leave guardroom. C. Pugsley, *On the Fringe of Hell* (Hodder & Stoughton, London,1991), p. 146.
32. Upset over weather, air raids and contracts, 1400 ELC men at Boulogne strike on 5.9.17. Over 20 killed when garrison troops open fire. WO 95/83.
33. Etaples Mutiny, see Narratives.
34. Bn. with 38 Bde.,13 Div., 3 Tigris Corps, Mesopotamia.
35. All Bns. with 63 Bde.,37 Div., withdrawn from battle of Passchendaele on 16.10.17.
36. 18 Coy. SANLC, Rouen. Circa 2,000 SANLC men strike over contracts, 18.10.17. WO 95/83; WO 256/23; WO 95/83.
37. See 20. Pte. William Peden was released from jail on 4.11.20. PRO, Kew, PCOM 6/39, line 9906.
38. Bn. with 9 Bde.,3 (Canadian) Division.
39. Mutiny aboard ship en route to South Africa. Makubedi v. Gutsche (1917), South African Supreme Court Reports 632.
40. Bn. with 156 Bde., 52 Div. in rain sodden trenches at Ramleh, Palestine. Raided by Germans 12.1.18. WO 95/4607.
41. 74 Coy. RGA, Meerut Division, India.
42. Bn. with Meerut Division, India. Arrived Delhi from Dehra Dun, March 1918.
43. All with 16 (Irish) Div. After 21.3.18 German attack on Ronnsoy, 7/8 Inniskilling Fus., 2 and 7 Royal Irish Regt., 16 (Irish) Div. formed into 49 Bde. Composite Bn. 15.4.18. On 20.4.18, 2 Royal Irish Regt. reconstituted from 49 Composite Bn.War Diaries: 7/8 Inniskilling Fus., 10–22.4.18, WO 95/1977; 2 Royal Irish Regt, 20/4/18, WO 95/1979.
44. These mutineers may all have been 1915 non-combatants with RAMC in Salonika who objected to being drafted into infantry units. WO329: Ptes. Fulford, Purchase, Roper. See also WO 95/4759, 11–26.1.18.
45. Welsh Horse Yeomanry (dismounted), with 231 Bde.,74 Div. to France early May 1918. 21 Rifle Bde. arrived Egypt 1916. Brodie had twice previously been court martialled for drunkeness. WO 90/8 pp. 4, 42.
46. See 71.
47. Bn. with 65 Bde., 22 Div. in Macedonia, British Salonika Force.
48. Bn. with 80 Bde., 27 Div. in Macedonia, British Salonika Force.
49. Most units with Imperial Mounted Div. in Palestine.
50. Protest by 5000 under aged soldiers about poor rations at Etaples Base, France. *Daily Herald*, 8.2.19.
51. Unit attached to Heavy Artillery, 1 Corps. On 25.9.18 accused refused to go into trenches without their paybooks. The trial took place on 13.10.18. AWM: FGCM Spr. F.W. Edmonds et al.
52. Bn. with 110 Bde.,37 Div., south of Le Quesnoy.
53. Exhausted after attacking enemy lines, at midnight 20–21.9.18 accused all went absent from the trenches after being detailed for a further assault. AWM: Diary: CEW Bean AWM 606/198/2.
54. Accused refused to work in the NZ Div. laundry. Pugsley, *On the Fringe of Hell*, op. cit., p. 146.
55. See 51. Because the original findings were not confirmed, accused were re-tried at Braguemont on 17.10.18. Sentences were confirmed on 18.10.19 and suspended on 3.11.18. AWM: FGCM Spr. W.H. Bell, 3 Tunnelling Coy.
56. Bn with 60 Bde., 20 Div. near Maubeuge.
57. Bn. with 102 Bde., 34 Div. near Dendre.
58. Bn. with 59 Bde, 20 (Light) Div. in Toutencourt-Mariuex area.
59. On 14.11.18 at No.39 Military Hospital, Le Havre, 1000 AIF troops, including patients from No.39 Military Hospital, liberate prisoners from No.1 FP compound. AWM: FGCM Pte .(L/Cpl.) James Hansen, 28 Bn., AIF.
60. Bn. with 63 Bde., 37 Div. at Walincourt. WO 95/2595.
61. Bn. with 54 Bde.,18 (Eastern) Div.. WO 95/ 2045.
62. Mutiny at Taranto Base, Italy after Sgt. of 7 BWIR shot a private on 8.12.18. 9 Bn. was disbanded 24.1.19. J.E. Edmonds & H.R. Davies, *History of the Great War: Military Operations, Italy 1915-1919* (HMSO, London,1949), pp. 386–7; WO 95/4256; WO 95/4255..
63. Bn. with 157 Bde., 52 Div. after 11.11.1918 engaged in clearing up the area around Mons.
64. Bn. with 126 Bde., 42 (East Lancashire) Div. near Charleroi, Belgium.
65. British Honduras Contingent, Inland Water Transport, Basra/lines of Communication, Mesopotamia.
66. Bn. with 182 Bde., 61 (2 South Midland) Div. near Doullens.
67. Bn. with 20 Bde., 7 Div. near Vicenza, Italy.
68. Unit with 9 (Scottish) Div., Cologne area, Rhine bridgehead.
69. Bn. at Taranto Base, Italy.
70. Bns. with 53 (Welsh) Div. at Alexandria, Egypt.
71. Mauritius Labour Company at Magil, Mesopotamia struck work on 6.1.19, demanding to return home. WO 95/5279. See 46. Nominal roll of Bn. in R-H. Hart, *Les Volontaires Mauriciens Aux Armees (1914-1918)* (GPSO, Port Louis, Mauritius,1919).
72. Coy. with 12 Bn., MGC, with 12 (Eastern) Div. engaged in training and salvage work at Auberchicourt, near Douai.
73. 1 Cape Corps, Egypt. For the Bn., see L.D. Difford *The Cape Corps* (Hortors, Cape Town 1921).
74. Units with 3 (Canadian) Div. at Nivelles. On 14.12.18 circa 400 men of 7 Bde. and 9 Field Coy., Canadian Engineers protest about food, billets and carrying packs. McDonell (or MacDonell) was later sentenced to death (commuted) while in No.7 Military Prison. WO 95/3857, WO 95/3858. CA: FGCM Ptes. C. MacDonell; P. Nunan 3 Canadian MGC.
75. Bn. with 182 Bde., 61 (2 South Midland) Div. near Doullens.
76. See 74.
77. Bn. with 160 Bde., 53 (Welsh) Div. at Alexandria, Egypt.
78. Bn. with 72 Bde., 24 Div. at Tournai.
79. See 74 and 76.
80. Coy. part of 10 Bn., MGC with 10 (Irish) Div. in Cairo.
81. Men returning from leave to units refuse to entrain at Calais Base on 28.1.19. Circa 5000 demand to be sent back to Britain and demobilised. Suppressed by 35 Div. on 30.1.19. Haig Papers, Acc 3155/135–6; G. Dallas & D. Gill, op. cit., pp. 115–120.
82. GCM 22.1.19–4.2.19. Protest by inmates on 19.11.18 after guards assaulted prisoner, No.2 Military Prison, Rouen. AWM: GCM Pte. R.B. Donkin, 21 Bn., AIF.
83. Bn. with 7 Bde., 25 Div. engaged in salvage work at Poix du Nord, Valenciennes. HM King presents new colours 3.2.19. Routine Orders for 8.2.19 missing from 7 Bde. War Diary, WO95/2242.
84. Bn with 70 Bde., 23 Div. On 10.2.19 Bn. sent from Montecchia di Crosara to Arzignano and reduced to cadre strength. WO 95/4240.
85. PCOM 6/39, lines 7770–1 record Ptes. John Kenny Barlow and Peter Thomasson released from Winchester Jail 25.11.19.
86. Bn. with 2 Bde., 1 Div. at Bonn, Rhine bridgehead.
87. Bn. with 4 Bde., 2 Canadian Div., Rhine bridgehead. Div. in process of demobilisation.
88. Formed Dec. 1915. To India Feb. 1916, stationed in Burma.
89. 26.2.19 refused to relieve US troops on Dvina Front. M. Kettle *Churchill and the Archangel Fiasco* (Routledge, London, 1992), pp. 177.
90. Protest by 400 inmates about ill-treatment at No.7 Military Prison, Calais. Guards' machine guns wound one prisoner. Postal report on Discipline 3–17.3.19, Haig Papers, Acc 3155/H22OE.

91 Unit with (reduced to cadre strength) 23 Div., Arzignano–Vicenza area.
92 Bn. in Ramleh-Ludd area, Palestine. After trouble between 40 Bn. and local Arabs, 39 Bn. ordered to Surafend for fatigue duties. FO 371/4238.
93 Bn. (formerly 4 Garrison Bn., Royal Welsh Fus.) with 176 Bde., 29 (North Midland) Div. at Calais.
94 Medal Roll entry for Dvr. Henry Grimstone, RFA suggests this mutiny occurredin Egypt. PRO, WO 329.
95 1 BWI from Egypt at Taranto, Italy. WO 95/4373.
96 Bn. with 148 Bde., 49 Div. in Nov. 1918. Escorting POWs engaged in clearing up battlefields in Belgium(?)
97 For RAMC grievances generally, see *Daily Herald*, 28.4.19, 10.6.19.
98 1 BWI from Egypt at Taranto, Italy.
99 At Ludd, 2 Bn., West India Regt., 3 (Lahore) Div. protested about not being granted pay increase awarded to white troops. Palestine Lines of Communication.WO 95/4732. See War Diary, 18.5.19, WO 95/4732; GHQ EEF to WO, 3.4.19, WO 33/960.
100 POW escorts.
101 Unit located in Boulogne-Outreau with detachment at Etaples. See also 24.6.18, 11.11.18, WO 95/3992.
102 Dvina Front, North Russia. Accused refused to engage in offensive operations against the Bolsheviks on 18.4.19. *Daily Herald*, 28.8.19.
103 Unit stationed at Arras.
104 Bn. with 21 Bde., 30 Div. in Boulogne-Etaples area.
105 Bn. with 182 Bde., 61 (2 South Midland) Div. at Base Ports, Northern France. On 18.5.19 Div. sends force to suppress trouble between BWIR and Chinese Labourers at Abancourt. Demobilisation commences 27.5.19.
106 Bn. with 31 Bde., 10 (Irish) Div.
107 At Evinghoven, Germany , 2 Bn., MGC (2 Div.) refused to parade on 10.6.19 in protest over long hours of work. WO 95/1334.
108 Originally the 'Rough Riders', 19.8.18 became 103 MGC, 1 Army, Northern France.
109 Bn. with 183 Bde., 61 (2 South Midland) Div. in Abancourt area. Drafts being sent to Egypt and South Russia.
110 At Troitsa 7.7.19 Slavo-British Legion mutineers killed their officers and defected to the Bolsheviks. Operations Report: Allied Forces, Archangel, Appendix V, IWM: Ironside Papers . *Times,* 25.7.19.
111 MG Bn. with 1 Div., Bonn, British Army of the Rhine.
112 Pioneer Bn. with 40 Div., Northern France. Objections by other ranks about being drafted for service in Egypt reported by *Daily Herald* , 25.8.19.
113 1 OBLI with Grogan's Bde. (formerly Dvina Force), WO 95/5422.
114 30 MG Bn. with 30 Division in Boulogne-Etaples area. First unit to be demobilised did not leave for UK until mid-May, 1919.
115 Unit with 3 Div., British Army of the Rhine.
116 Bn. with 18 Div. which ceased to exist in March,1919.
117 Jewish troops, 38 Bn. (Bir Salem, 2.7.19) and 39 Bn. (Ludd, 3.7.19) protest over antisemitism and non-demobilisation. 40 Bn. also refuse posting to Cyprus. FO 371/4238; J.H. Patterson *With the Judeans in the Palestine Campaign* (Hutchinson, London, 1922), ch. xxxi.
118 Bn. with 5 Bde., 2 Canadian Div., all units returned to Canada by May, 1919.
119 Bn. with 148 Bde. , 49 Div. in France and Belgium. Div. reduced to cadres, March 1919.
120 At Koikori 7–9.9.19, two companies, 6 Royal Marines refused to attack Bolsheviks. Over 90 marines were court martialled by the Royal Navy, 13 sentenced to death (commuted) for cowardice. IWM DOCS: Drage Papers, pp. 30–1; *Daily Herald,* 28.11.19.
121 See 119. S. Staffs Bn. War Diary ends May 1919, WO 95/1816.
122 Bn. War Diary ends Feb. 1919, WO 95/1610.
123 2 Ches Bn. with 83 Bde., 28 Div., Dardanelles Defences, Turkey.
124 47 Royal Fus., formed for special service in Russia 18.4.19, was disbanded on 24.12.19. 29 Liverpool, formed 10.5.19, went to France 22.7.19 and was disbanded 7.8.20. WO 380/12.
125 Bn. with 84 Bde., 28 Div., Dardanelles Defences, Haidar Pasha, Turkey.
126 With Norperforce, North West Persia.
127 Bn. with Meerut Division, Northern Command in Kumaun district, India.
128 Coys. at Jullundur (27.6.20) and Solon (31.6.20–1.7.20), North India protest about British military atrocities in Ireland. Pte. James Daley, executed Dagshai, 2.11.20. A. Babington *The Devil to Pay* (Leo Cooper, London,1991).
129 See 128.
130 Adjacent to the Euphrates River, East of Baghdad, Mesopotamia.
131 Mesopotamia.
132 Bn. with Meerut Division, Northern Command, India.
133 WO 329 indicates Pte. Jack Maulson, 2 Leicestershire.
134 Bn.with Meerut Division, Northern Command in Kumaun district, India.
135 Bn. with Allahabad Bde., Lucknow Division, North-East India.

Bibliography

Primary sources
Australia: National Archives, Canberra
   Unit histories
   Courts martial proceedings
Australian War Memorial, Canberra
   Diaries of CEW Bean
   Courts martial proceedings
Imperial War Museum Department of Documents Unpublished Mss.:
   D. Doe
   M. Hardie
   A.E. Henderson
   C.C. Miller
   W.J. Kendall
   C.J. Lane
   M.I. Leared
   W.B. St. Leger
   R.W. Thomas
   P. Tweed
India Office Records and Library, British Library
   Chelmsford Collection, MSS Eur. E. 264
   Military Department Papers, series: L/MIL/3 ; L/MIL/5; L/MIL/17
Labour Party Archives
   Records of War Emergency: Workers National Committee
Liddell Hart Centre for Military Archives, King's College, London
   Papers of:
   Major A. Stuart
   Field Marshal Sir William Robertson
National Archives of Canada
   Courts martial proceedings
New Zealand: National Archives
   Courts martial proceedings
Private collection: W. Turner
   Ms Diary of Fred Sayer
Public Record Office, Kew: Official Records
   Air Ministry, series: AIR/1
   Colonial Office, series: CO 318
   Foreign Office, series: FO 371
   War Office, series: WO 95; WO 32; WO 33; WO 71; WO 84; WO 73; WO 107; WO 213; WO 256
Royal Military Police Archives, Chichester
   FWW File: Stragglers
Scottish Public Record Office, Edinburgh
   Papers of Field Marshal Sir Douglas Haig

Secondary sources
Reports:
   Statistical Abstract Relating to British India from 1910–11 to 1919–20 (HMSO, London, 1922)
   Statistics of the Military effort of the British Empire during the Great War 1914–1920 (HMSO, London, 1922)
Newspapers:
   Bombay Chronicle
   Bristol Gazette
   Christchurch Star (NZ)
   Daily Express
   Daily Herald
   Daily News
   Dartmouth & South Hams Chronicle
   Dorchester Mail
   Dreadnought
   John Bull
   Manchester Guardian
   Le Monde
   Nottingham Journal
   Poole, Parkstone & East Dorset Herald
   Streatham News
   Tribunal
   The Times
   Wellington Evening Post (NZ)
   Weymouth Telegram
Journals and periodicals:
   Administrative Science Quarterly
   British Journal of Sociology
   Canadian Historical Review
   Gunfire, Journal of First World War History
   Historical Journal
   History Today
   Journal of African History
   Journal of Contemporary History
   Journal of Legal History
   Listener (NZ)
   Lobster
   Mohlomi, Journal of South African Historical Studies
   Past & Present
   Science & Society
   Solidarity
   Stand To! Journal of the Western Front Association
   Western Front Association Bulletin
Books:
   W. Allison & J. Fairley, *The Monocled Mutineer* (Quartet Books, London, 1978).
   T. Ashworth, *Trench Warfare 1914–1918* (Macmillan, London, 1980)
   A. Babington, *For the Sake of Example: Capital Courts Martial 1914–18* (Leo Cooper, London, 1983)
   A. Babington, *The Devil to Pay* (Leo Cooper, London, 1991).
   AJ Barker, *The Neglected War* (Faber, London, 1967)
   A. Baxter, *We will not cease* (Victor Gollancz, London 1939)
   J. Baynes, *Morale* (Cassell, London, 1967
   I.F.W. Beckett & K. Simpson, *A Nation at Arms: A social history of the British Army in the First World War* (MUP, 1985)
   I.F.W. Beckett (ed.), *The Army and the Curragh Incident* (Army Historical Society, London, 1986)
   W.R. Bion, *The Long Weekend 1879-1919* (Free Association Books, London, 1986)
   J.M. Bourne, *Britain and the Great War 1914-1918* (Edward Bond, London, 1989)
   N. Boyack, *Behind the Lines* (Allen & Unwin, Wellington NZ, 1989)
   M. Bragg, *Speak for England* (Alfred Knopf, New York, 1977)
   C. Braithwaite, *Conscientious Objections to Compulsions under the Law* (William Sessions, York, 1995)

M. Brown, *Tommy Goes to War* (J.M. Dent, London, 1980 edn.),
M. Brown & S. Seaton, *The Christmas Truce* (Leo Cooper, London, 1984)
B. Carman & J. McPherson, *Bimbashi MacPherson* (BBC Publications, London, 1983)
P. Charlton, *Pozieres* (Methuen Haynes, North Ryde, 1986)
B.E.W. Childs, *Episodes & Reflections* (Cassell, London, 1930)
J.H. Cockfield, *With Snow on their Boots* (Macmillan, London, 1998).
F.P. Crozier, *The Men I Killed* (Michael Joseph, London, 1937)
G. Dallas & D. Gill, *The Unknown Army: Mutinies in the British Army in World War 1* (Verso, London, 1985)
P. Dennis, *The Territorial Army 1906–1940* (Royal Historical Society, London, 1987)
J.C. Dunn, *The War the Infantry knew* (King, London, 1938)
J.E. Edmonds & H.R. Davies *History of the Great War: Operations, Italy 1915–1919* (HMSO, London, 1949)
R. Furneaux, *Massacre at Amritsar* (Allen & Unwin, London, 1963).
J.G. Fuller, *Troop Morale and Popular Culture in the British and Dominion Armies 1914–1918* (Clarendon Press, Oxford, 1990
D. Gill & J.J. Putkowski, *The British Base Camp at Etaples 1914–1918* (Musee Quentovic, Etaples-sur-Mer, 1997)
D. Gordon, *Quartered in Hell* (Doughboy Historical Society, Missoula, 1982)
L. Grafftey-Smith, *Bright Levant* (J Murray, London, 1970)
A. Grundlingh, *Fighting their own War* (Ravan Press, Johannesburg, 1987),
J.W. Graham, *Conscription and Conscience* (Allen & Unwin, London, 1922)
A.J. Guy et al (eds.), *Military Miscellany 1* (Army Records Society, London, 1977)
R.W.E. Harper & H. Miller, *Singapore Mutiny* (O.U.P., Singapore, 1984).
R-H Hart, *Les Volontaires Mauriciens Aux Armées (1914–1918)* (GPSO, Port Louis, Mauritius, 1919)

A.M. Henniker, *Transportation on the Western Front* (HMSO, London, 1937)
G. Hodges, *The Carrier Corps: Military Labour in the East African Campaign 1914–1918* (Greenwood, Connecticut, 1986)
Institute of Royal Engineers, Chatham, *Work under the Director of Works (France)*, (Mackay & Co., Chatham, 1924)
Christoph Jahr, *Gewöhnliche Soldaten–Desertion und Deserteuer im deutschen und britischer heer 1914–1918* (Vandenhoeck & Ruprecht, Göttingen, 1998)
L. James, *Mutiny in the British and Commonwealth Forces 1797–1956* (Buchan & Enright, London, 1987)
N.D.G. James, *Plain Soldiering* (Hobnob Press, Salisbury, 1987)
M. Kettle, *Churchill and the Archangel Fiasco* (Routledge, London, 1992)
A. Killick, *Mutiny!* (Militant, London, 1976)
B.C. Lake, *Knowledge for War* (Harrison & Sons, London, n.d.)
D. Lamb, *Mutinies 1917–1919* (Solidarity, London 1975)
W. Moore, *The Thin Yellow Line* (Leo Cooper, London, 1974)
Manual of Military Law (War Office, London, 1914)
T.J. Mitchell & G.M. Smith, *History of the Great War: Medical Services – Casualties and Medical Statistics* (HMSO, London, 1931)
E.M. Muenger, *The British Military dilemma in Ireland: Occupation Politics 1886–1914* (Gill & Macmillan, Dublin, 1991)
B.R. Nanda, *Gandhi, Pan-Islamism, Imperialism and Nationalism in India* (OUP, Oxford, 1989)
M. O'Dwyer, *India as I knew It* (Constable, London, 1925)
G. Oram, *Death Sentences passed by military courts of the British Army 1914–1924* (Francis Boutle, London, 1998)
J.H. Patterson, *With the Judeans in the Palestine Campaign* (Hutchinson, London, 1922)
G. Pedroncini, *Les Mutineries de 1917* (Presses Universitaires, Paris, 1967)
R.J. Popplewell, *Intelligence and Imperial Defence* (Cass, London, 1995)

C. Pugsley, *On the Fringe of Hell* (Hodder & Stoughton, Auckland 1991)
J.J. Putkowski, *The Kinmel Park Camp Riots 1919* (Flintshire Historical Society, Hawarden 1989)
A. Rothstein, *The Soldiers' Strikes of 1919* (Macmillan, London, 1980)
A. Rumbold, *Watershed in India* (Athlone Press, London, 1979)
A.P. Ryan, *Mutiny at the Curragh* (Macmillan, London, 1956)
G.D. Sheffield *The Redcaps* (Brassey's, London, 1994)
P. Simkins, *Kitchener's Army: Raising the New Armies 1914–1916* (MUP, 1988)
G.R. Singleton-Gates, *Bolos & Barishnyas* (Gale & Polden, Aldershot, 1920)
L.V. Smith, *Between Mutiny and Obedience* (Princeton University Press, New Jersey, 1994)
M. Summerskill, *China on the Western Front* (Summerskill, London, 1982)
B. Thomson, *Queer People* (Hodder & Stoughton, London, 1922)
R. Westlake, *British Battalions at Gallipoli* (Leo Cooper, London, 1996)
N. Woodyatt, *Under Ten Viceroys* (London, 1922)
'Warden', *'His Majesty's Guests' – Secrets of the Cells* (London, Jarrolds, n.d.)